Exploring
Macroeconomics

PATHWAYS TO PROBLEM SOLVING

WITHDRAWN

Robert L. Sexton
PEPPERDINE UNIVERSITY

THE DRYDEN PRESS
HARCOURT BRACE COLLEGE PUBLISHERS
FORT WORTH   PHILADELPHIA   SAN DIEGO   NEW YORK
AUSTIN   ORLANDO   SAN ANTONIO
TORONTO   MONTREAL   LONDON   SYDNEY   TOKYO

Publisher
George Provol
Acquisitions Editor
Gary Nelson
Product Manager
Debbie K. Anderson
Developmental Editor
Amy Porubsky
Project Editor
Rebecca Dodson
Art Director
Linda Beaupré
Production Manager
Lois West
Photo/Permissions Editor
Linda Blundell

ISBN: 0-03-022924-3
Library of Congress Catalog Card Number: 98-73562

Address for editorial correspondence:
The Dryden Press
301 Commerce Street, Suite 3700
Fort Worth, TX 76102

Address for domestic orders:
The Dryden Press
6277 Sea Harbor Drive
Orlando, FL 32887-6777
1-800-782-4479

Address for international orders:
International Customer Service
The Dryden Press
6277 Sea Harbor Drive
Orlando, FL 32887-6777

Web site address: http://www.hbcollege.com

Printed in the United States of America
7 8 9 0 1 2 3 4 5 6   048   9 8 7 6 5 4 3 2 1

The Dryden Press
Harcourt Brace College Publishers

About the Author

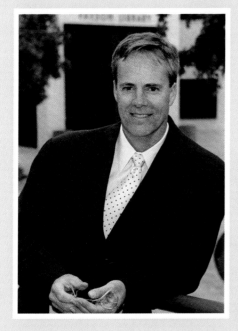

Robert L. Sexton is currently Professor of Economics at Seaver College, Pepperdine University, and the Pepperdine School of Public Policy. Professor Sexton has also been a Visiting Professor at the University of California at Los Angeles in the Anderson Graduate School of Management and the Department of Economics.

Professor Sexton's research ranges across many fields of economics: labor economics, environmental economics, law and economics, economic education, and economic history. He has written several books and has published more than 35 research papers, many in top economic journals such as *The American Economic Review, Southern Economic Journal, Economics Letters, Journal of Urban Economics,* and *The Journal of Economic Education.* Professor Sexton has also written more than 100 other articles that have appeared in books, magazines, and newspapers.

Professor Sexton received the Pepperdine Professor of the Year Award in 1991 and 1997, and the Howard A. White Memorial Teaching Award in 1994; he was named a Harriet and Charles Luckman Teaching Fellow in 1994.

Professor Sexton resides in Agoura Hills, California, with his wife, Julie, and their three children, Elizabeth, Katherine, and Tommy.

In memory of my father
1913–1996

Thanks Dad,
I love you.

A MODULAR APPROACH TO PROBLEM SOLVING (MAPS)

As you can see from a cursory flip, this book is different. I designed it to be different. This book differs from traditional economics texts in two important ways: (1) its modular presentation, and (2) its *focus* on economics as a problem-solving science.

The two goals of *Exploring Macroeconomics* are encapsulated in one mnemonic, MAPS: a **M**odular **A**pproach to **P**roblem **S**olving. As you will see, these ideas are not mere constructs; rather, they are complements that work together to create a unique learning experience for your students.

THE MODULAR APPROACH: WHAT AND WHY?

Exploring Macroeconomics uses a modular approach in its presentation of economic ideas and concepts. Information is presented in small, self-contained sections rather than in large blocks of text. My enthusiasm for and dedication to this approach stems from a study of learning theory research, which indicates that students retain information much better when it is broken down into short, "digestible" sections. Students *will* be more successful in mastering and retaining economic principles through this approach.

Unlike standard textbook construction, the modular approach is distinctly more compatible with the modern communication style with which most students are familiar and comfortable: short, intense, and exciting bursts of information. Rather than being distracted and discouraged by the seeming enormity of the task before them, students are more likely to work through a short, self-contained concept before getting up from their desks. The student is more likely to read and process the material before he or she proceeds to the next concept, a point that is particularly important in economics, where one idea is often a building block that serves as the foundation for the next.

In executing the modular approach in *Exploring Macroeconomics*, every effort has been made to take the intimidation out of economics. The idea of sticking to the basics and reinforcing student mastery, concept by concept, coupled with the careful display of pictures, charts, and graphs, has been done with the student in mind. But students aren't the only ones to benefit from this approach. The modular presentation allows instructors greater flexibility in planning their courses. More importantly, instructors benefit from having a student population that has actually read the textbook and prepared for class!

THE MODULAR APPROACH: HOW?

The philosophy of the modular approach takes form in the basic structure and organization of *Exploring Macroeconomics* and is also embodied in the accompanying Student Workbook.

The Text Organization

Exploring Macroeconomics is presented in 17 Modules, each of which is comprised of approximately 6–8 short Concepts. These Concepts are self-contained learning units, typically presented in 2–4 page, bite-size sections that include all of the relevant graphs and tables as well as numerous colorful photos for the topic at hand. Each Concept begins with a number of key questions designed to introduce the important ideas to be presented. These questions serve as landmarks for students: If they can answer these questions after reading the material, they have prepared well. This tool is reinforced by the Concept Check points and questions that appear at the end of each Concept. Key points summarize concisely the major ideas that the student should have retained, and short questions, the answers to which can be found in the back of the book, give students an opportunity to check their mastery before proceeding.

The Student Workbook

At the end of each Concept, students are encouraged to turn to the related section in the Student Workbook. The Student Workbook for use with *Exploring Macroeconomics* is an extension of the text, both in philosophy and in execution. Like the text, the workbook is designed on a Concept-by-Concept basis. After reading each Concept in the text, the student can turn to the Workbook and test his or her mastery of the material with true-false, multiple-choice, and discussion and application questions that cover only the topics covered in that Concept. If students can answer these questions, they can be confident that they have mastered the topic. In addition to these Concept-based questions, additional exercises are provided at the end of each Module that draw on and integrate all of the material in the Module. In short, the Workbook, like the text, is designed at every step to instill your students with confidence in their own abilities to master the tools of economics.

THE PROBLEM-SOLVING APPROACH: WHAT AND WHY?

Economics is a collection of problem-solving tools that can be applied to many social, political, and business issues. Even everyday issues can be more easily understood when one has a good handle on the "economic way of thinking." However, in the words of a Lake Wobegon philosopher Garrison Keillor, "Just because you sleep in a garage doesn't make you a car." In other words, picking up the terminology of economics is not enough; students have to learn when and how to use their new tools. Economic principles aren't just definitions to memorize; they are valuable tools that can help students analyze a whole host of issues and problems in the world around them. It is this philosophy that serves as the focus for the problem-solving approach in *Exploring Macroeconomics,* which is designed to serve two key purposes: (1) to facilitate student mastery of concepts both theoretically and in application, and (2) to communicate a sense of relevancy to students.

THE PROBLEM-SOLVING APPROACH: HOW?

The problem-solving approach is evident throughout *Exploring Macroeconomics*—in the basic organization of the text and in the supporting pedagogical elements. This approach is also embodied in the well-integrated student ancillary materials that are packaged with the text, collectively known as the Integrated Learning System.

The Text Organization

By presenting material in a Concept-by-Concept, building-block format that encourages and reinforces students at every step, the modular approach directly supports the problem-solving focus of the text. The modular approach breaks difficult concepts into digestible parts and then offers students opportunities to evaluate their level of understanding before proceeding. In this way, students are provided with an optimal format in which to master the economic tools that they will need and to develop confidence in their own abilities and understanding of these ideas.

Learning Tools

Key Questions. Each Concept begins with a list of questions that highlight the primary ideas that the student should learn from the material. These questions are intended to serve as a preview and to pique students' interest in the material to come.

Text Heads. Many paragraphs in the text have headings that are structured as questions. The philosophy be-

hind this approach is that if students develop the habit of asking themselves such questions, they will become much more effective learners; that is, they will begin to learn to ask the right questions themselves.

Tune Up. Tune Up boxes are scattered throughout the text as a way of reinforcing and checking student comprehension of important or more difficult concepts. These elements provide students with an opportunity to test their mastery of new tools through short applications. Students can then check their work immediately against the answer given at the bottom of the box, providing them immediate feedback and encouragement in the learning process.

Applications. There are numerous applications to everyday life situations scattered throughout the text. These applications were chosen specifically with students in mind, and they are designed to help students find the connection between economics and their lives. With that, economic principles are applied to everyday problems and issues, such as classroom cheating, sexually transmitted diseases, teenage drug use, juvenile crime, on-line betting, road kill, and the cost of raising children.

In addition to the large number of in-text examples, one integrative application is presented in the last Concept of each Module as a platform for tying together some of the primary ideas presented in the Module. Also, there are two special boxed applications, "In the News" and "Global Watch," scattered throughout each Module.

In the News. "In the News" applications focus primarily on current news stories that are relevant and thought-provoking. These articles are placed strategically throughout the text to solidify particular concepts. In an effort to emphasize the breadth and diversity of the situations to which economic principles can be applied, these articles have been chosen from sources that range from *National Geographic* to *Wired* magazine.

Global Watch. Whether we are concerned with understanding yesterday, today, or tomorrow, and whether we are looking at a small, far-away country or a large next-door neighbor, economic principles can strengthen our grasp on many global issues. "Global Watch" articles were chosen to help students understand the magnitude and character of the change occurring around the world today and to introduce them to some of the economic causes and implications of this change. To gain a greater perspective on a particular economy or the planet as a whole, it is helpful to compare important economic indicators around the world. For this reason, "Global Watch" applications will sometimes be used to present relevant comparative statistics.

Concept Checks. Each Concept in a Module ends with a Concept Check box. This element contains 4–6 short sentences emphasizing the important points in each section. It also includes 4–6 questions designed to test students' comprehension of the basic points of the Concept just covered. If students can answer these questions, they can feel confident about proceeding to the next topic.

Memory Devices. Mnemonic devices are used where appropriate as an extra aid to help students remember certain important ideas. For example, "PYNTE," the old-English spelling of *pint,* is used to help students remember the major demand shifters: *P,* price of related goods; *Y,* income; *N,* number of buyers; *T,* tastes; and *E,* expectations.

Photos. The text contains hundreds of colorful pictures. They are not, however, mere decoration; rather, these photos are an integral part of the book, for both learning and motivation purposes. The photos are carefully placed where they reinforce important concepts, and they are accompanied with inquisitive captions designed to encourage students to extend their understanding of particular ideas.

Exhibits. Graphs, tables, and charts are important economic tools. These tools are used throughout *Exploring Macroeconomics* to illustrate, clarify, and reinforce economic principles. Text exhibits are designed to be as clear and simple as possible, and they are carefully coordinated with the text material.

THE INTEGRATED LEARNING SYSTEM

The Integrated Learning System is more than an extension of the problem-solving approach to student success that characterizes *Exploring Macroeconomics;* it is, in fact, an integral part of that approach. Individually, the elements of this system—the Student Workbook, EconActive CD-ROM, and Student Web Site—can help your students take the small steps toward a mastery of microeconomics. Collectively, these elements serve as a key to your students' ultimate goal: their mastery of the economic way of thinking and the development of a confidence in their abilities to use those tools elsewhere. This, I believe, is the ultimate success, but it is a success that must come gradually, one step at a time. The Integrated Learning System helps students take those steps by reinforcing basic concepts and ensuring student mastery at every point, using the same basic student-friendly and interactive style that characterizes the text.

Student Workbook

The Student Workbook for use with *Exploring Macroeconomics* reinforces the basic problem-solving approach of the text. On a Concept-by-Concept basis, the Student Workbook guides the student through various exercises designed to test their comprehension and mastery, including true-false, multiple-choice, and application-type questions. These exercises proceed from the relatively easy to the more difficult, thus allowing students to experience success and generate feelings of confidence as they proceed. Then, at the end of each Module, students can enjoy

and learn from "The Lowells," a cartoon strip that illustrates a key concept from the Module and then tests student understanding of that idea. The answers to all Student Workbook activities are included in the Workbook, so that students can get immediate feedback on their work.

EconActive CD-ROM

The EconActive CD-ROM is designed to allow your students to get even more interactive and involved in their own learning process. In addition to guided tutorials with new examples and graphs, the EconActive CD-ROM also includes Java-powered, interactive graphs. The power of Java allows students to manipulate a variable or variables on a graph and immediately see the effects of those changes on the graph. The hands-on interaction that these Java-powered graphs provide illustrates and reinforces economic relationships in a way that a static graph and explanation cannot. As with the Student Workbook, the interactive graphs and the other materials on the EconActive CD-ROM are designed to reinforce student mastery and success at each point.

Student Web Site

A Student Web Site has been developed to accompany *Exploring Macroeconomics.* In addition to providing students with a secondary access to many of the learning tools that appear on their EconActive CD-ROM (including the Java-powered interactive graphs), the Student Web Site gives students access to other resources they can use to test their understanding of key economic concepts. These tools include online, interactive quizzes (multiple-choice, matching, and true-false) that provide students with immediate feedback, cyberproblems with links to relevant data or Web sites, and additional applications.

SUPPLEMENTS FOR THE INSTRUCTOR

The following ancillaries are available to instructors:

Test Bank
Computerized Test Bank
Instructor's Resource Manual
Electronic Resource Manual
Power Point Presentation
Instructor Web Site
Video Lecture Starters

WALL STREET JOURNAL EDITION

One goal in teaching the principles of economics is to provide students a better understanding of the world around them. Many instructors, therefore, encourage students to read about economic issues in the newspaper as they take the course. Those instructors may want to consider the special *Wall Street Journal Edition* of this text. The edition is the same as the standard edition but includes a ten-week subscription to *The Wall Street Journal*. Students can activate their subscriptions simply by completing and mailing the business reply card found in the back of the book. Talk to your Dryden Press sales representative for more information, or call 1-800-237-2665.

The Wall Street Journal is a registered trademark of Dow Jones & Company, Inc.

ACKNOWLEDGMENTS

I would like to extend special thanks to the following colleagues for their valuable insight during the manuscript phase of this project. I owe a debt of gratitude to Philip Graves, University of Colorado; Gary Galles, Pepperdine University; Richard Vedder, Ohio University; Dwight Lee, University of Georgia; Robert M. Escudero, Pepperdine University; Ron Batchelder, Pepperdine University; Steve Jackstadt, University of Alaska, Anchorage; Lee Huskey, University of Alaska, Anchorage; Robert Clower, University of South Carolina and Gary M. Walton, University of California, Davis.

Without the devotion and creativity of several people at The Dryden Press, this book would not have been possible. My appreciation goes to Gary Nelson, without whom this project would never have materialized and Amy Winston, whose detail and motivation improved the book tremendously. Also thanks to George Provol, Becky Dodson, Linda Beaupré, Linda Blundell, Lois West, Rosemarie Console, Brad Balaban, Debbie K. Anderson, Amy Porubsky, Barrett Lackey, and Kimberly Powell.

In addition, my family deserves special gratitude—my wife Julie, daughters Elizabeth and Katherine, and my son Tommy. They are an inspiration to my work. Also, special thanks to my mother Willa and my brother Bill.

Thanks to all of my colleagues who reviewed the project. From very early on in the writing phase all the way up to publication, your comments were very important to me.

Jack Adams, University of Arkansas, Little Rock

James Q. Aylsworth, Lakeland Community College

G.E. Breger, University of South Carolina

Gilbert L. Christopher, Jr., Wingate University

Andrew J. Dane, Angelo State University

John W. Dorsey, University of Maryland

David Eaton, Murray State University

Mary E. Edwards, St. Cloud State University

Robert M. Escudero, Pepperdine University

Gary Galles, Pepperdine University

Phil Graves, University of Colorado

Stanley Keil, Ball State University

Ronald Kessler, British Columbia Institute of Technology

Saleem Khan, Bloomsburg University

Philip King, San Francisco State University

Thomas Maloy, Muskegon Community College

Pete Mavrokordatas, Tarrant County Junior College

Thomas Porebski, Trinton College

Tom Potiowsky, Portland State University

Sue Lynn Sasser, William Woods University

Mark Strazicich, University of Central Florida

Howard Whitney, Franklin University

The Dryden Press conducted a national survey of professors who offered tremendous feedback on the ideas and teaching style presented with this text. A special thanks to all participants, including the following:

Steve Abid, Grand Rapids Community College

Fatma Wahdan Antar, Manchester Community College

Donald C. Balch, University of South Carolina

Randall Barnes, San Diego Miramar College

Cihan Bilginsoy, University of Utah

Barbara L. Brogan, Northern Virginia Community College

George W.M. Bullion, Indiana University–Purdue

Dennis Byrne, University of Akron

James E. Clark, Wichita State University

Joe B. Copeland, University of North Alabama

Kenneth M. Cross, Southwest Virginia Community College

John P. Dahlquist, College of Alameda

David E. Davis, University of Oregon, USDA

Richard Deitz, Rochester Institute of Technology

Mike Dunton, Delmar College

David H. Eaton, Murray State University

Dipak Ghosh, Emporia State University

Spencer R. Graf, University of Virginia

Paul F. Haas, Bowling Green State University

Peter W. Harman, Rhode Island College

Barry Haworth, University of Louisville

Wei-Chiao Huang, Western Michigan University

Paul A. Joray, Indiana University–South Bend

Patrick Joyce, Michigan Technological University

Saleem M. Khan, Bloomsburg University of Pennsylvania

Ghebre Y. Keleta, Grambling State University

Syrous Kooros, Nicholls State University

Rose M. LaMont, Modesto Junior College

Michael B. Lehmann, University of San Francisco

Stephen E. Lile, Western Kentucky University

Vernon Lynch, Fort Lewis College

Dayle Mandelson, University of Wisconsin–Stout

James M. McQuiston, University of Southern Mississippi

Green R. Miller, Morehead State University

Masoud Moghaddam, St. Cloud State University

Marie T. Mora, New Mexico State University

Amlan Mitra, Purdue University–Calumet

William R. Pedersen, Southeastern Louisiana University

Chris Phillips, Somerset Community College

Etienne E. Pracht, Louisiana State University

Rarahmand Rezvani, Montclair State University

Mark Strazicich, University of Central Florida

Thomas A. Swanke, West Virginia State College

Robert E. Tansky, St. Clair County Community College

Neil Terry, West Texas A&M University

Jesus M Valencia, Slippery Rock University

John R. Wagner, Westfield State College

Karen T. Wilson, Delta College

Willard E. Witte, Indiana University–Bloomington

Lewis Woodruff, Sinclair Community College

Douglas Woolley, Radford University

Edward G. Young, University of Wisconsin–Eau Claire

Contents

MODULE 1 ECONOMICS: TEN POWERFUL IDEAS 2

Ⓐ **Economics: A Definition 4**
What is economics?

Ⓑ **Wants and Desires 7**
Can all of our wants and desires be satisfied?

IN THE NEWS: CLINTON MOURNS THE LOSS OF
TWO REMARKABLE WOMEN 9

Ⓒ **Scarcity 10**
Did nature provide enough for all of our wants?

Ⓓ **Choices 12**
Can we have our cake and eat it too?

Ⓔ **Marginal Thinking 15**
What is the rule of rational choice?

TUNE UP: DO INCENTIVES
MATTER? 18

Ⓕ **Incentives Matter 17**
Do people respond to incentives?

IN THE NEWS: SURVEY FINDS
CHEATING NOT UNCOMMON AMONG TOP U.S.
HIGH SCHOOL STUDENTS 19

GLOBAL WATCH: DRUNK DRIVING
DRAWS GLOBAL WRATH 20

Ⓖ **Specialization and Trade 21**
How can specialization and trade lead to greater economic growth?

TUNE UP: COMPARATIVE ADVANTAGE 21

Ⓗ **Markets and the Price System 24**
Can markets and the price system make consumers and producers better off?

IN THE NEWS: MICHAEL
JORDAN SIGNS NEW CONTRACT 23

Ⓘ **Government Policies 27**
Can appropriate government policies improve our economic well-being?

Ⓙ **Economic Growth 30**
Can economic growth improve overall standards of living?

GLOBAL WATCH: CORRELATION OF
INVESTMENT AND GROWTH 31

Ⓚ **Price Stability 32**
Will price stability enable producers and consumers to make better plans and
decisions?

Ⓛ **Application: Laws and Enforcement Costs 34**
How can strict laws function as incentives to influence behavior?

ONE STEP BEYOND 36

MODULE 2   THE ROLE AND METHOD OF ECONOMICS   38

Ⓐ   **Economics as a Science   40**
Why is economics useful?

Ⓑ   **Economic Behavior   43**
Can economists predict human behavior?

Ⓒ   **Economic Theory   45**
Why do we need a theory?

IN THE NEWS: HEAVY METAL MUSIC AND TEEN SUICIDE   51

Ⓓ   **Problems with Scientific Thinking   48**
What are the key problems in scientific thinking?

Ⓔ   **Positive and Normative Analysis   52**
Why is it important that we distinguish between positive and normative analysis?

Ⓕ   **Application: Scientists and Global Warming   56**
Why must we be so careful about association and correlation?

ONE STEP BEYOND   57

APPENDIX: WORKING WITH GRAPHS   58

MODULE 3   SCARCITY AND THE ECONOMIZING PROBLEM   64

IN THE NEWS: BILL GATES, THE ENTREPRENEUR   68

Ⓐ   **The Factors of Production   66**
What are the factors of production?

TUNE UP: THE PRODUCTION POSSIBILITIES CURVE   71

Ⓑ   **The Production Possibilities Curve   69**
Why is the production possibilities curve useful?

GLOBAL WATCH: GOVERNMENT SPENDING AS A PERCENTAGE OF GDP, 1920 AND 1996   74

Ⓒ   **Production Decisions   73**
What and how much should we produce?

TUNE UP: DID THE MARKET FAIL?   75

Ⓓ   **Production Methods   76**
How will we produce those goods and services?

IN THE NEWS: LABOR-SAVING ANTI-THEFT DEVICES   77

Ⓔ   **Distribution of Output   78**
Who will get the goods and services we produce?

Ⓕ   **Efficiency in Production   79**
How can we use our scarce resources efficiently?

GLOBAL WATCH: FIVE RICHEST AND FIVE POOREST NATIONS IN OUTPUT PER PERSON   81

Ⓖ   **Production and Growth   81**
What do we have to sacrifice today to achieve greater economic growth?

TUNE UP: PRODUCTION POSSIBILITIES CURVE   83

Ⓗ   **Application: Tourism versus Ecosystems   84**
Can we have more tourism and a better environment at the same time?

ONE STEP BEYOND   85

MODULE 4 SUPPLY AND DEMAND 86

Ⓐ **Markets 88**
What is a market?

Ⓑ **Money and Relative Prices 90**
Why are relative prices so important?

Ⓒ **The Law of Demand 92**
What is the difference between needs and wants?

Ⓓ **The Demand Curve 96**
Why is the demand curve negatively sloped?

Ⓔ **Shifts in the Demand Curve 99**
What are the major variables that determine the position of the demand curve?

Ⓕ **The Law of Supply 108**
Why is the supply curve positively sloped?

Ⓖ **Shifts in the Supply Curve 110**
What are the major variables that determine the position of the supply curve?

Ⓗ **Application: A Shift in the Demand for Cuban Cigars 116**
Which variables have impacted the demand curve for Cuban cigars?

ONE STEP BEYOND 117

MODULE 5 MARKETS IN MOTION 118

Ⓐ **Market Equilibrium Price and Quantity 120**
Why is the concept of market equilibrium such a valuable tool?

Ⓑ **Changes in Equilibrium Price and Quantity 124**
What happens to equilibrium price and quantity when we shift the supply or
demand curve?

Ⓒ **Shifting Supply and Demand Together 128**
What happens when supply and demand both shift?

Ⓓ **Temporary Disequilibrium 133**
What happens when companies do not correctly anticipate the demand for their
products?

Ⓔ **Price Controls 136**
What are price ceilings and price floors?

Ⓕ **Application: Supply and Demand in the Market for Super
Bowl Tickets 140**
How does the market for Super Bowl tickets work?

ONE STEP BEYOND 141

IN THE NEWS: LUNDBERG SURVEY SAYS
GASOLINE PRICES HIT HISTORIC
LOW IN 1998 90

TUNE UP: TOOLING UP: RELATIVE PRICES 91

IN THE NEWS: GOODYEAR BEGINS SEARCH
FOR HIGHWAY HEROES 94

IN THE NEWS: IS THERE A DEMAND CURVE
FOR ROADKILL 97

IN THE NEWS: CAN A WIENER BECOME A
POORER SUBSTITUTE FOR
HAMBURGER 100

TUNE UP: SUBSTITUTE GOODS 101

TUNE UP: COMPLEMENTARY GOODS 102

TUNE UP: NORMAL AND INFERIOR
GOODS 103

TUNE UP: EXPECTATIONS OF
HIGHER PRICES 104

IN THE NEWS: WHAT IS A
TAMAGOTCHI? 106

TUNE UP: CHANGES IN DEMAND VERSUS
CHANGES IN QUANTITY DEMANDED 106

TUNE UP: SUPPLIERS' INPUT PRICES 111

TUNE UP: EXPECTATIONS CAN SHIFT
SUPPLY 112

TUNE UP: TAXES AND
REGULATION AS SUPPLY SHIFTERS 112

IN THE NEWS: SUPPLY SHIFTERS IN THE OIL
INDUSTRY 113

TUNE UP: CHANGE IN SUPPLY VERSUS
CHANGE IN QUANTITY SUPPLIED 115

TUNE UP: SHORTAGES 121

TUNE UP: SHORTAGES AND SURPLUSES 122

GLOBAL WATCH: COFFEE, COCOA PRICES RISE
ON EL NIÑO CONCERNS 126

TUNE UP: THE IMPACT OF A CHANGE IN
DEMAND ON EQUILIBRIUM PRICE AND
QUANTITY 126

TUNE UP: THE IMPACT OF A CHANGE IN
SUPPLY ON EQUILIBRIUM PRICE AND
QUANTITY 127

TUNE UP: SHIFTS IN BOTH SUPPLY AND
DEMAND 130

IN THE NEWS: KIDNEYS FOR SALE? 131

MODULE 6 GOVERNMENT AND THE ECONOMY 142

Ⓐ **Government and Property Rights 144**
Should government protect property rights?

Ⓑ **Government and Externalities 146**
Should government intervene to correct externalities?

Ⓒ **Government and Public Goods 150**
Should government provide public goods and services?

IN THE NEWS: RUDOLPH THE RED-TAPED
REINDEER 155

Ⓓ **Government and Information Costs 153**
Should government provide information to consumers?

Ⓔ **Other Government Functions 157**
How does government try to prevent insufficient competition and achieve its macroeconomic goals?

Ⓕ **Government and Income Distribution 159**
Should government work to create more equality in income distribution?

TUNE UP: RATIONAL IGNORANCE 164

Ⓖ **Public Choice 162**
Is politics influenced by self-interest?

IN THE NEWS: WILD PITCH 166

IN THE NEWS: CONTROVERSIAL TRANSIT BILL
PASSES IN HOUSE 171

Ⓗ **Spending and Taxation 168**
How do we pay for government?

GLOBAL WATCH: A GLOBAL COMPARISON OF
TAXATION 172

Ⓘ **Application: Revving Up the Helmet Law Debate 174**
Can a balance of the freedom of the rider and the freedom of the taxpayer be found?

ONE STEP BEYOND 176

MODULE 7 INTRODUCTION TO THE MACROECONOMY 178

Ⓐ **Macroeconomic Goals 180**
What are the three major macroeconomic goals?

TUNE UP: CYCLICAL UNEMPLOYMENT 189

Ⓑ **Employment and Unemployment 182**
What is the unemployment rate?

GLOBAL WATCH: UNEMPLOYMENT AROUND
THE GLOBE, 1996 191

IN THE NEWS: A LIGHT THAT NEVER
GOES OUT 192

Ⓒ **Different Types of Unemployment 188**
What are the different types of unemployment?

TUNE UP: INFLATION 194

Ⓓ **Inflation 193**
Why is price level stability important?

TUNE UP: ANTICIPATED INFLATION AND
INTEREST RATES 196

GLOBAL WATCH: AVERAGE ANNUAL INFLATION
RATES, SELECTED COUNTRIES, 1996 197

Ⓔ **Economic Growth 198**
What are the benefits of economic growth?

IN THE NEWS: IS THE BUSINESS
CYCLE GONE? 202

Ⓕ **Economic Fluctuations 200**
What are economic fluctuations?

IN THE NEWS: JAPANESE GOVERNMENT
EXPECTS SLOW RECOVERY 203

Ⓖ **Application: Economic Freedom and Economic Growth 204**
Does economic freedom guarantee economic growth?

ONE STEP BEYOND 206

MODULE 8 ECONOMIC GROWTH 208

Ⓐ **Economic Growth 210**
What is economic growth?

Ⓑ **The Impact of Economic Growth 212**
How does economic growth impact other variables?

Ⓒ **Determinants of Economic Growth 217**
What changes lead to economic growth?

Ⓓ **Population Growth and Economic Growth 221**
How can an increasing population affect economic growth?

Ⓔ **Desirability of Economic Growth 223**
Why wouldn't economic growth be desirable?

Ⓕ **Application: Economic Growth and Relative Happiness 225**
Is economic growth the key to greater happiness?

ONE STEP BEYOND 227

MODULE 9 MEASURING ECONOMIC PERFORMANCE 228

Ⓐ **The Circular Flow Model 230**
Why does total spending equal total income?

Ⓑ **National Income Accounting: Measuring Economic Performance 232**
How can we measure our nation's economic performance?

Ⓒ **The Expenditure Approach to Measuring GDP 234**
What are the four categories of purchases in the expenditure approach?

Ⓓ **The Income Approach to Measuring GDP 238**
How do we compute GDP using the income approach?

Ⓔ **Problems in Calculating an Accurate GDP 241**
What factors make it difficult to accurately calculate GDP?

Ⓕ **Problems with GDP as a Measure of Economic Welfare 246**
How does GDP fail to accurately measure economic welfare?

Ⓖ **Application: The Declining *Real* Cost of Living in America 250**
What are the shortcomings of using money prices to calculate the cost of living?

ONE STEP BEYOND 252

IN THE NEWS: THE NEW ECONOMY? 219

TUNE UP: DEFINING GDP 233

IN THE NEWS: THE BOX-OFFICE LEADERS 242

IN THE NEWS: HOW ACCURATE IS THE CPI INDEX? 244

IN THE NEWS: AN INVALUABLE ENVIRONMENT 248

TUNE UP: PROBLEMS WITH MEASURING GDP 249

MODULE 10   AGGREGATE DEMAND   254

Ⓐ **Consumption: The Primary Determinant of Aggregate Demand   256**
What happens to consumption as income rises?

Ⓑ **Investment, Government Spending, and Net Exports   258**
How do investment, government spending, and net exports impact aggregate demand?

Ⓒ **The Aggregate Demand Curve   261**
What is the aggregate demand curve?

TUNE UP: CHANGES IN AGGREGATE DEMAND   265

Ⓓ **Shifts in the Aggregate Demand Curve   264**
What causes the aggregate demand curve to shift?

Ⓔ **Application: The Consumer Confidence Index   267**
How are changes in consumer confidence reflected in aggregate demand?

ONE STEP BEYOND   268

MODULE 11   AGGREGATE SUPPLY AND MACROECONOMIC EQUILIBRIUM   270

TUNE UP: THE SHORT-RUN AGGREGATE SUPPLY CURVE   273

Ⓐ **The Aggregate Supply Curve   272**
What do the short-run and long-run aggregate supply curves represent?

TUNE UP: SHIFTS IN THE SHORT-RUN AGGREGATE SUPPLY CURVE   278

Ⓑ **Shifts in the Aggregate Supply Curve   275**
What causes the aggregate supply curves to shift?

Ⓒ **Macroeconomic Equilibrium   279**
What are demand-pull and cost-push inflation?

Ⓓ **Application: El Niño and the AD/AS Model   282**
How did El Niño impact aggregate supply?

ONE STEP BEYOND   284

MODULE 12   FISCAL POLICY   286

GLOBAL WATCH: GOVERNMENT SPENDING AS A PERCENT OF GDP   289

Ⓐ **Fiscal Policy   288**
What is fiscal policy?

IN THE NEWS: STEALTH BOMBERS AND MULTIPLIERS   293

Ⓑ **The Multiplier Effect   291**
How can the total impact of an initial increase in purchases be calculated?

IN THE NEWS: JAPAN'S LEADER FAVORS PERMANENT TAX CUTS   297

Ⓒ **Fiscal Policy and the AD/AS Model   295**
How can government stimulus or contraction of aggregate demand change inflation or unemployment?

IN THE NEWS: TAXATION, GOVERNMENT ACTIVITY, AND ECONOMIC GROWTH   302

Ⓓ **Possible Obstacles to Effective Fiscal Policy   299**
What factors can reduce the effectiveness of a fiscal policy?

IN THE NEWS: ENTITLEMENT FRAUD GIVES "PRISON SECURITY" NEW MEANING   304

Ⓔ **Automatic Stabilizers   303**
How do automatic stabilizers affect the economy?

Ⓕ **Supply-Side Fiscal Policy 305**
Does fiscal policy have a supply side?

Ⓖ **Fiscal Policy in Its Prime—The 1960s 308**
Why were the early 1960s a model for effective fiscal policy?

Ⓗ **Financing the Deficit 310**
How does the government finance its budget deficit?

Ⓘ **Application: The Balanced Budget Amendment 312**
Do we want a balanced budget amendment?

ONE STEP BEYOND 314

MODULE 13   MONEY AND THE BANKING SYSTEM   316

Ⓐ **What Is Money? 318**
What are the different forms of money?

Ⓑ **The Functions of Money 324**
What is the purpose of money?

Ⓒ **The Demand for Money 327**
Why do people choose to hold money?

Ⓓ **How Banks Create Money 330**
What is the process for increasing the supply of money?

Ⓔ **The Money Multiplier 335**
How does a new loan lead to multiple expansions in the money supply?

Ⓕ **The Collapse of America's Banking System, 1920–1933 339**
What led to the collapse of the banking system between 1920 and 1933?

Ⓖ **Application: Internet Banking 341**
Are internet banks the banks of the future?

ONE STEP BEYOND 343

MODULE 14   THE FEDERAL RESERVE SYSTEM AND
MONETARY POLICY   344

Ⓐ **The Federal Reserve System 346**
What is the role of a central bank?

Ⓑ **The Equation of Exchange 349**
How does the equation of exchange help our understanding of the role of money in the economy?

Ⓒ **Implementing Monetary Policy: Tools of the Fed 351**
What are the three major tools of the Fed?

Ⓓ **Money, Interest Rates, and Aggregate Demand 358**
How do changes in money supply and money demand affect interest rates in the money market?

IN THE NEWS: SHOULD WE GET RID OF THE PENNY? 319

TUNE UP: DEMAND DEPOSITS 320

IN THE NEWS: USING CREDIT CARDS ON THE INTERNET 321

TUNE UP: THE BARTER SYSTEM 325

TUNE UP: THE MULTIPLE EXPANSION PROCESS 336

IN THE NEWS: CHANGES IN THE BANKING INDUSTRY 337

TUNE UP: OPEN MARKET OPERATIONS 352

TUNE UP: TOOLS OF THE FED 354

TUNE UP: THE DISCOUNT RATE 355

TUNE UP: TOOLS OF THE FED 355

IN THE NEWS: THE FED AND THE MEDIA 356

TUNE UP: MONEY AND THE AD/AS MODEL 360

IN THE NEWS: FED LEAVES INTEREST RATES ALONE 361

(E) **Problems in Implementing Monetary Policy** 363
What factors can limit the effectiveness of monetary policy?

(F) **Application: The Independence of the Fed** 366
Should the Fed be independent from the administration and Congress?

ONE STEP BEYOND 367

MODULE 15   INFLATION, UNEMPLOYMENT, AND EXPECTATIONS   368

IN THE NEWS: TIGHT LABOR MARKET MAKING
IT HARD FOR FAIR TO FIND TEMPORARY
WORKERS 372

(A) **The Phillips Curve** 370
Is there a relationship between unemployment and inflation?

(B) **The Phillips Curve Over Time** 373
Why does the Phillips curve shift?

(C) **Rational Expectations** 376
What is the rational expectations theory?

(D) **Wage and Price Controls and Indexing** 379
What purpose do wage and price controls and indexing serve?

(E) **Application: The Role of Expectations in Macroeconomics** 383
Are rational expectations the same as perfect information?

ONE STEP BEYOND   384

MODULE 16   INTERNATIONAL TRADE   386

IN THE NEWS: *BAYWATCH* IS WORLD
WATCHED 389

(A) **The Growth in World Trade** 388
How important is international trade?

TUNE UP: COMPARATIVE ADVANTAGE 393

IN THE NEWS: THE MIRACLE OF TRADE 394

(B) **Comparative Advantage and Gains from Trade** 391
What is the difference between comparative advantage and absolute advantage?

(C) **Supply and Demand in International Trade** 396
Who gains and who loses from exports and imports?

(D) **Tariffs, Import Quotas, and Subsidies** 399
How do tariffs, import quotas, and subsidies impact the domestic economy?

(E) **Application: Common Misperceptions on Trade** 403
Are the welfare gains associated with trade overstated?

ONE STEP BEYOND   405

MODULE 17   INTERNATIONAL FINANCE   406

TUNE UP: TRADE GAPS 411

(A) **The Balance of Payments** 408
What is the difference between the balance of payments and the balance of trade?

Ⓑ **Exchange Rates 412**
How do exchange rates affect the demand for foreign goods?

Ⓒ **Equilibrium Changes in the Foreign Exchange Market 415**
What forces cause the supply and demand for currencies to shift?

Ⓓ **Flexible Exchange Rates 421**
How are exchange rate changes different with flexible rates than with a fixed-rate system?

Ⓔ **Application: The United States Intervenes to Boost the Yen 426**
Why did the United States buy yen in the currency market?

ONE STEP BEYOND 428

Answers to Concept Check Questions 431

Glossary 465

Index 471

TUNE UP: EXCHANGE RATES 414

IN THE NEWS: BIG MAC CURRENCIES 418

IN THE NEWS: BIG MAC CURRENCIES 419

TUNE UP: DETERMINANTS OF EXCHANGE RATES 420

Economics: Ten Powerful Ideas

A. Economics: A Definition
What is economics?

B. Wants and Desires
Can all of our wants and desires
be satisfied?

C. Scarcity
Did nature provide enough
for all of our wants?

D. Choices
Can we have our cake and eat it too?

E. Marginal Thinking
What is the rule of rational choice?

F. Incentives Matter
Do people respond to incentives?

G. Specialization and Trade
How can specialization and trade lead to greater economic growth?

H. Markets and the Price System
Can markets and the price system make consumers
and producers better off?

I. Government Policies
Can appropriate government policies improve our economic well-being?

J. Economic Growth
Can economic growth improve overall standards of living?

K. Price Stability
Will price stability enable producers and consumers
to make better plans and decisions?

L. Application: Laws and Enforcement Costs
How can strict laws function as incentives to influence behavior?

Economics: A Definition

- What is economics?
- Do our wants and desires grow over time?

ECONOMICS—A WORD WITH MANY DIFFERENT MEANINGS

The term "economics" means different things to different people. Even the pronunciation of the word varies; some pronounce it with a long *e*, while others combine the *e* with the *c* into *ec* (as in *tech* or *wreck*). As to the meaning of the word, some individuals think economics involves the study of the stock market and corporate finance, and it does—in part. Others think that economics is concerned with the wise use of money and other matters of personal finance, and it is—in part. Still others think that economics involves forecasting or predicting what business conditions will be in the future, and again, it does—in part. The word economics is, after all, derived from the Greek word *oeconomicus*, which refers to the management of household affairs.

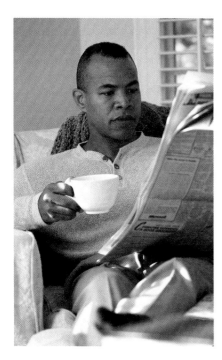

The front page of a newspaper is usually filled with articles that are related to economics either directly or indirectly.

A Unique Way of Looking at Human Behavior

Economics is a unique way of analyzing many areas of human behavior. Indeed, the range of topics to which economic analysis is applied is quite broad! As a result, many researchers have discovered that the economic approach to human behavior sheds light on social problems that have been with us for a long time: discrimination, education, crime, divorce, political favoritism, and many more. In fact, economics is front-page news almost every day, whether it involves politicians talking about balancing budgets, business executives talking about restructuring to cut costs, or the average citizen trying to figure out how much it will cost taxpayers to reduce crime. Economics is all of this and more.

Growing Wants and Scarce Resources

Precisely defined, **economics** is the study of the allocation of our scarce resources to satisfy our unlimited wants for goods and services. **Resources** are those things, such as tools, machinery, and factories, that are used to make goods and services. Water, land, and trees are **natural resources.** The problem is that our wants exceed what our resources can produce, a fact that we call **scarcity.** Scarcity forces us to make choices on how to best use our limited resources. We want more things; we want different things. We want materialistic things that we can touch and hold. We also want intangible things like friendship, love, spirituality, knowledge, and so on. Because resources are scarce, however, no one can have all of the goods and services he or she desires. Scarcity forces us all to make choices. And whenever we have to choose, we must do without something else that we also desire. This want that we choose not to satisfy cannot be recovered—it is a lost opportunity. This lost opportunity is the cost of the choice we actually make. This is the economic problem: *Scarcity forces us to choose, and choices are costly because we must give up other opportunities.* This economizing problem is evident in every aspect of our lives, even those things that appear decidedly non-economic in nature.

"O.K., who can put a price on love? Jim?"

Drawing by Ziegler: Copyright 1991 *The New Yorker* Magazine, Inc.

ECONOMICS IS ALL AROUND US

Although many things that we desire in life are considered to be "non-economic," economics concerns anything that is considered worthwhile to some human being. For instance, love, sexual activity, and religion have value for most people. However, even these have an economic dimension. Consider religion, for example. Concern for spiritual matters has led to the development of institutions such as churches and temples that provide religious and spiritual services. These services are goods that many people desire. Love and sex likewise have received economists' scrutiny. One product of love, the institution of the family, is an important economic decision-making unit. Also, sexual activity results in the birth of children, one of the most important "goods" that humans desire.

Even time has an economic dimension. In fact, perhaps the most valuable single good we possess is time. We all have the same limited amount of time per day, and how we divide our time between work and leisure (including perhaps study, sleep, exercise, etc.) is a distinctly economic matter. Virtually everything we decide to do, then, has an economic dimension.

THE 10 POWERFUL IDEAS OF ECONOMICS

Most of economics is really knowing certain principles well and knowing when and how to apply them. We think that there are 10 powerful ideas that serve as the

Economics can make us look at everything—even the value of our time—differently.

foundation of economics. These few basic ideas will repeatedly occur throughout the text and are presented in this Module as a preview of what is to come. If you develop a good understanding of these principles and master the problem-solving skills inherent in them, they will serve you well for the rest of your life. As Bill Gates, CEO of Microsoft, has said, just being intelligent is not enough for success: "To succeed, you also have to know how to make choices and how to think more broadly." As you will see, Mr. Gates's tools for success are the cornerstones of the economic way of thinking!

1. Economics is a problem-solving science.
2. Economics is the study of the allocation of scarce resources to satisfy unlimited wants.
3. Our wants exceed our resources, so we must make choices.

---

1. What is the definition of economics?
2. Why does scarcity force us to make choices?
3. Why are choices costly?
4. Why do even "non-economic" issues have an economic dimension?
5. If a genie gave you three wishes, would that solve the problem of scarcity for you?

B Wants and Desires

- What are resources?
- What are goods and services?
- What are tangible and intangible goods?
- What are economic goods?

WHAT ARE RESOURCES?

As you already know, economics is concerned primarily with how we satisfy our unlimited wants and desires in a world of limited resources. As we noted earlier, resources are the scarce inputs that are used to produce the goods and services that we want. Resources, both "man"-made and natural, can include such things as machinery, tools, time, air, water, trees, land, and the knowledge of how to productively employ them (technology). These resources, however, are finite. Only so much knowledge, so many trees, so much water, and so many tools are available for our use at any given time. It follows, then, that because these resources are limited, the things that can be produced from them—goods and services—are also limited.

WHAT ARE GOODS AND SERVICES?

"Goods" and "services" are those things that we value or desire. **Goods** tend to be tangible things—objects that can be seen, held, heard, tasted, or smelled. But there are also goods that we cannot reach out and touch, called **intangible goods.** Intangible goods include such things as fairness for all, friendship, knowledge, security, intelligence, and health. While some intangible goods have no price tags, a *USA Today* poll showed that the wealthy would be willing to pay top dollar, if they could, for a place in heaven ($640,000), true love ($487,000), and a great intellect ($407,000). **Services** are intangible because they are less

An airplane is a good, but taking a trip on an airplane involves a service.

overtly visible, but they are no less valuable than goods. An airplane is a good, but taking a trip on an airplane involves the provision of a service.

All goods and services, whether they are tangible or intangible, are scarce and can be subjected to economic analysis. In fact, these scarce goods that are created from scarce resources are called **economic goods.**

WHAT ARE BADS?

In contrast to goods, **bads** are those items that we do not desire or want. For most people, garbage, pollution, weeds, and crime are bads. People tend to want to eliminate or minimize bads, so they will often pay to have bads, like garbage, removed. Then, the elimination of the bad—garbage removal, for example—becomes a good.

ARE THOSE WHO WANT MORE GREEDY?

We all want more tangible and intangible goods and services. In economics, we assume that more goods lead to greater satisfaction, or **utility,** and that bads lead to dissatisfaction, or **disutility.** However, because we assume that people want more goods and wish to eliminate or minimize bads does not mean that economics presumes that people are selfish and greedy. For example, Mother Teresa spent much of her time helping others because that is what she wanted to do with her time. Many people give much of their income and time to charitable or religious organizations. That is, they commit their time, and other scarce resources, to achieving the "good" of charitable giving. Clearly, then, many desires, like building new friendships

or helping charities, can hardly be defined as selfish, yet these are desires that many people share. In other words, "self-interest" is not the same as "selfishness."

"Christmas shopping is going to be easy for this year, Mom. There's hardly anything I don't want!"

CLINTON MOURNS THE LOSS OF TWO REMARKABLE WOMEN

Last year, when President Clinton was mourning the passing of two remarkable women, he made the following observations. "While both Mother Teresa and Princess Diana had vastly different backgrounds and lived in very different worlds, both were committed to providing compassion to those who needed it most—the desperately poor, the abandoned, the sick, and the dying. Each woman in her own way demonstrated what it is to live a life of meaning, with concern for others. They both will be remembered for the gifts they left for others."

CONSIDER THIS:
Providing charity is a desire or want to some.

CONCEPT CHECK

1. Resources are the scarce inputs used to produce goods and services.
2. Goods and services are things that we value.
3. Goods can be tangible (physical) or intangible (love, compassion, and intelligence).
4. Economic goods are goods created from limited resources.

1. What are resources?
2. How do finite resources impact our ability to produce goods and services?
3. What must be true for something to be an economic good?
4. Does wanting more tangible and intangible goods and services make us selfish?
5. Why might sunshine be scarce in Seattle but not in Tucson?

Scarcity

■ Do we all face scarcity?

■ Do our wants and desires change over time?

DOES EVERYONE FACE SCARCITY?

We all face scarcity, because no one can have all of the goods and services that he or she desires. However, because we all have different wants and desires, scarcity affects everyone differently. For example, a child in an underdeveloped country may face a scarcity of food and clean drinking water, while a rich person might face a scarcity of garage space for his growing antique car collection. Likewise, a harried middle-class working mother may find time for exercise particularly scarce, while a pharmaceutical company may be concerned with the scarcity of the natural resources it uses in its production process. Clearly, then, while its effects vary, no one can escape scarcity.

CAN PEOPLE BECOME SO RICH THAT THEY DON'T HAVE TO CHOOSE?

We often hear it said of rich people that "He has everything" or "She can buy anything she wants." Actually, even the richest person must live with scarcity and must, at some point, choose one want or desire over another, and, of course, we all have only 24 hours in a day! The problem is that as we get more affluent, we learn of new luxuries to provide us with satisfaction. Wealth, then, creates a new set of wants to be satisfied. There is no evidence that people would not find a valuable use for additional income, no matter how rich they become. Even the wealthy individual who decides to donate all of her money to charity faces the constraints of scarcity. If she had greater resources, she could do still more for others.

Clearly, though, the concepts of scarcity and choice are relative in nature. For example, in the extreme case of a person with very limited resources, the cost that he might pay for, say, a nice shirt or sweater might be starvation. That is, his limited resources can support nothing beyond the basic necessities of life. For a multimillionaire, on the other hand, the cost of a shirt or sweater would be imperceptibly small. Scarcity for that individual might mean

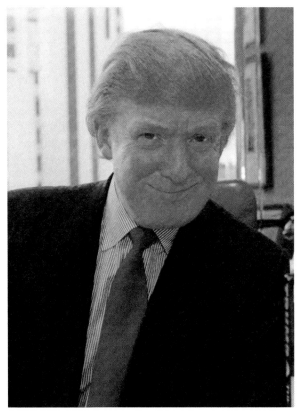

Does Donald Trump face the problem of scarcity?

choosing between a plane and a yacht. The point here is that even though the choices that the wealthy are forced to make may seem less crucial than those made by a relatively poor person, they are still choices and they still reflect a scarcity of resources.

ARE SCARCITY AND GROWING EXPECTATIONS HERE TO STAY?

It is probably clear by now that scarcity never has and never will be eradicated. The same creativity that permits new methods to produce goods and services in greater quantities also reveals new wants. Thus, the small black-and-white television set that provided so much enjoyment for viewers raised on radio would now be considered an inadequate form of entertainment by most. Two generations ago, only the well-to-do had telephones; today telephones are provided to some welfare recipients on the grounds that they are a "necessity." It is also possible that while people seem to be happier at a point in time the more goods and services they can buy, over a period of time, a rising quantity of goods and services may not increase human happiness. Why? There are several possibilities, but it is very possible that our wants grow as fast, if not faster, than our ability to meet those wants, so we still feel scarcity as much or more than we did before.

New wants quickly replace old ones.

CONCEPT CHECK

1. Scarcity will always be with us.
2. Our wants grow over time, so scarcity will never be eliminated.

3. Scarcity is a fact for everyone.

---

1. Does everyone face scarcity?
2. Why does scarcity affect each of us differently?
3. Why can't a country become so technologically advanced that its citizens won't have to choose?

4. If Penny Pincher became a billionaire after winning the largest lottery ever, would she still face scarcity?

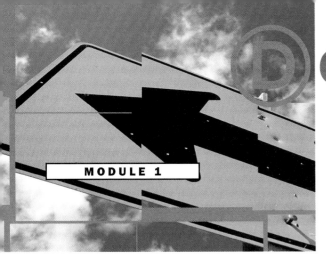

D Choices

- Why do we have to make choices?
- What do we give up when we have to choose?
- Why are "free" lunches not free?
- Are prices and costs the same thing?

MODULE 1

DOES SCARCITY FORCE US TO MAKE COSTLY CHOICES?

We may want two luxury cars in every garage, nice homes, good tasting and wholesome food, all enjoyed in a pristine environment with zero pollution. If we had unlimited resources, and thus an ability to produce all of the goods and services anyone wanted, we would not have to choose among those desires. If we did not have to make meaningful economic choices, the study of economics would not be necessary. The essence of economics is to fully understand the implications that scarcity has for wise decision making. This suggests another way to define economics: Economics is the study of the choices we make among our many wants and desires.

WHAT WOULD YOU HAVE TO GIVE UP TO TRAIN FOR A MARATHON?

We all have to make important choices with our time every day. Suppose you were a marathon runner. Would your training be a scarce good? Of course it would, because you would have to give up other things to run. The time you spend working out has a cost, because it comes at the expense of that same time spent at other valued activities like studying, socializing, watching TV, or sleeping.

WHENEVER WE CHOOSE, DO WE LOSE?

We are all faced with the fact of scarcity, and as a consequence, we must make choices. Because none of us can "afford" to buy everything we want, each time we do decide to buy one good or service, we reduce our ability to buy other things we would also like to have. If you buy a new car this year, you may not be able to afford your next best choice—the vacation you've been planning. You must choose. The cost of the car to you is the value of the vaca-

Time spent running costs time spent doing something else.

tion that must be foregone. The highest or best foregone opportunity resulting from a decision is called the **opportunity cost.** Another way to put this is that "to choose is to lose." To get more of anything that is desirable, you must accept less of something else that you also value.

WHAT IS THE OPPORTUNITY COST OF GOING TO COLLEGE OR HAVING A CHILD?

The average person often does not correctly consider opportunity costs when thinking about costs. For example, the cost of going to college is not just the direct costs of tuition and books. It also includes the opportunity cost of your time, which for many people is the greatest part of their costs. Specifically, the time spent going to school is time that could have been spent on a job earning, say, $25,000 a year. What is the cost of rearing a child to the age of 18? There are the obvious costs: clothes, piano lessons, time spent at soccer practices, food, visits to the doctor, and so on. But there are also other substantial opportunity costs incurred in rearing a child. For example, consider the opportunity cost if one of the parents chooses to give up his or her job to stay at home. Then, the time spent in child rearing is time that could be used making money and pursuing a career. These opportunity costs must be included in the total costs of raising a child.

EXHIBIT 1	WOMEN'S SHAVING OVER A LIFETIME

Women's shaving over a lifetime

Number of times	6,336
Minutes	32,000
Hours	533
Days	22

SOURCE: Schick

Time spent shaving is time that could have been used for something else, but you must value "hair-free surfaces" more than other uses of that time, or you would not shave.

IS THAT REALLY A FREE LUNCH, A FREEWAY, OR A FREE BEACH?

The expression *"there's no such thing as a free lunch"* clarifies the relationship between scarcity and opportunity cost. Suppose the school cafeteria is offering "free" lunches today. While the lunch is free to you, is it really free from society's perspective? The answer is no, because some of society's scarce resources will have been used in the preparation of the lunch. The issue is whether the resources that went into creating that lunch could have been used to produce something else of value. Clearly, the labor and materials (food-service workers, lettuce, meat, plows, tractors, fertilizer, and so forth) that went into the production of the lunch could have been used in other ways. They had an opportunity cost, and thus were not free. Whenever you hear the word "free"—freeways, free beaches, free libraries, free admission, and so on—an alarm should go off in your head. Very few things are free, in the sense that they use none of society's scarce resources. So what does a free lunch really mean? It is, technically speaking, a "subsidized" lunch—a lunch using society's scarce resources, but one for which you personally do not have to pay.

ARE PRICES AND COSTS DIFFERENT?

Prices and costs are not the same thing. A **price** reflects the monetary value of a good or service; it is an objective fact. However, costs are personal and subjective. Costs reflect the relative value of foregone goods or services to individuals. For example, would a $100,000 BMW cost more to a richer rather than a poorer person? The price is the same—both would have to give up $100,000 of other goods and services to buy the car—but the costs are likely to be different. Even if the poorer person, by selling everything he had, could buy it, he still might view a BMW as frivolous because he would likely place a higher value on the things he would have to give up for the BMW—like food, clothing, and shelter. That is, although the price of

I DON'T KNOW ABOUT YOU, BUT THIS ISN'T DOING A <u>THING</u> FOR MY SELF-ESTEEM!

FREE KITTENS

© 1987 Thaves/Reprinted with permission. Newspaper dist. by NEA, Inc.

Are kittens free? Raising a kitten certainly isn't free; it requires lots of scarce resources, including vaccinations, food, and time.

the car does not change, the cost may be greater to the poorer person because of the value he places on the sacrificed goods. Because costs are personal and subjective, we cannot objectively compare the values individuals place on goods and services. However, we can say that different people are likely to place different values on the same goods and services, even if they have the same price tag.

Luxury Is Habit Forming

Is the price of a BMW the same to different buyers? How about the cost?

CONCEPT CHECK

1. Because of scarcity we have to make choices.
2. When we are forced to choose, we give up the highest valued alternative.
3. Opportunity cost is what you give up when you make a choice.

1. Would we have to make choices if we had unlimited resources?
2. What is given up when we make a choice?
3. What do we mean by opportunity cost?
4. Why is there no such thing as a free lunch?
5. How are prices and costs different?

6. Why was the opportunity cost of staying in college higher for Tiger Woods than for most undergraduates?
7. Why is the opportunity cost of the time spent getting an MBA typically lower for a 22-year-old straight out of college than for a 45-year-old experienced manager?

Marginal Thinking

- What do we mean by marginal changes?
- What is the rule of rational choice?
- Why do we use the word "expected" with marginal benefits and costs?

CHOICES ARE PRIMARILY MARGINAL—NOT ALL OR NOTHING

Most choices involve how much of something to do, rather than whether or not to do something. It is not whether you eat, but how much you eat. Hopefully, the question is not whether to study but instead how much to study this semester. For example, "If I studied a *little* more, I might be able to improve my grade," or "If I had a *little* better concentration when I was studying, I could improve my grade." This is what economists call marginal thinking because the focus is on the additional, or marginal, choices. Marginal choices involve the effects of adding or subtracting from the current situation. In trying to make themselves better off, people alter their behavior if the expected marginal benefits to them from doing so outweigh the expected marginal costs they will bear. This is what economists call **the rule of rational choice.** The term *expected* is used with marginal benefits and costs because the world is uncertain in many important respects, so the actual result of changing behavior may not always make people better off—but on average it will. However, as a matter of rationality, people are assumed to engage only in behavior that they think ahead of time will make them better off. That is, they will only pursue an activity if expected marginal benefits are greater than the expected marginal costs, or $E(MB) > E(MC)$. This fairly unrestrictive and realistic view of individuals seeking self-betterment can be used to analyze a variety of social phenomena.

DO JAYWALKERS USE RATIONAL DECISION MAKING?

Imagine that a friend of yours crosses a busy street without using the designated crosswalk at the traffic signal. Is her decision to jaywalk a rational one?

Weighing the expected marginal benefits and costs, your friend might recognize that it is prohibitively costly

EXHIBIT 1   SCALES OF ECONOMICS

Is this decision to jaywalk a rational one?

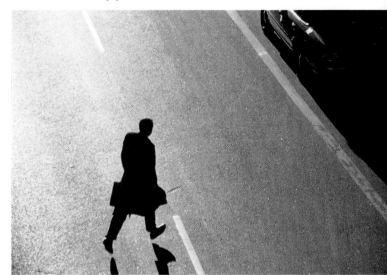

for the police and the legal system to monitor the behavior of the thousands of pedestrians that live in her city. As a result, the chance of her being caught is small. She also probably knows that, even if she did get caught, the penalty for jaywalking for a first offense is likely to be a warning. The costs, then, don't look too high. Also, your friend recognizes that the value of her time is a limited resource. The time she saves by jaywalking rather than waiting for the light can be spent pursuing other activities. After weighing the expected costs and benefits of waiting for a long light versus jaywalking, she decides to take a chance. While it is important to note that her decision might ultimately be a bad one—she might receive a citation or, worse, she could get hit by a car—people make decisions based on what they *expect* to happen, not on what actually happens. Clearly, then, your friend's decision to jaywalk was rational from her perspective. Similarly, because both benefits and costs are subjective (individual specific), a more cautious person with a lower value of time might rationally have chosen not to jaywalk.

IS THE GOAL OF ZERO POLLUTION RATIONAL?

What would we have to give up—that is, what costs would we have to incur—in order to achieve *zero* pollution? A lot! You could not drive a car, fly in a plane, or even ride bikes, especially if everybody else is riding bikes too (because congestion is a form of pollution). How would you get to school, go out on a date, or go to the grocery store? Everyone would have to grow his or her own food, because foods are transported, stored, and produced

using machinery and equipment that pollute. And even growing your own food would be a problem because many plants emit natural pollutants. We could go on and on. The point is not that we shouldn't be concerned about the environment; rather, it is that we have to weigh the expected marginal benefits of a cleaner environment against the expected marginal costs of a cleaner environment. It is the net, or difference, that is important. In this case, given the large expected marginal costs, a decision to pursue a state of zero pollution would not be rational.

What would you be willing to give up to eliminate the rush-hour congestion you face?

CONCEPT CHECK

1. Economists are usually interested in the effects of additional, or marginal, changes in a given situation.
2. People try to make themselves better off.
3. People make decisions based on what they *expect* to happen.

4. The rule of rational choice states that individuals will pursue an activity if they expect the marginal benefits to be greater than the marginal costs, or $E(MB) > E(MC)$.

1. What are marginal choices? Why does economics focus on them?
2. What is the rule of rational choice?
3. Why does rational choice involve expectations?
4. Why do students often stop taking lecture notes when a professor announces that the next few minutes of material will not be on any future test or assignment?

5. If you decide to speed to get to a doctor's appointment and then get into an accident as a result, does your decision to speed invalidate the rule of rational choice?

Incentives Matter

- Can we predict how people will respond to changes in incentives?
- What are positive incentives?
- What are negative incentives?

DO PEOPLE RESPOND TO INCENTIVES?

In acting rationally, people are responding to incentives. That is, they are reacting to fluctuations—both positive and negative—in the relevant cost–benefit structure. In fact, much of human behavior can be explained and predicted as a response to incentives. Consider the economic view of crime. Why do criminals engage in their "occupation"? Presumably because the "job," even with its risks, is considered to be preferable to alternative forms of employment. For criminals, the benefits of their actions are higher and/or the opportunity costs of them are lower than is the case for non-criminals. In some cases, the criminal cannot get a legitimate job at a wage he or she would find acceptable, so the cost of engaging in crime in terms of other income foregone may be quite low. At other times, the likelihood of being caught is small, so the expected cost is negligible. Also, for some, the moral cost of a crime is low, while for others it is high. The benefits, in terms of wealth gained, are clear. If the expected gains or benefits from committing a crime outweigh the expected costs, the activity is pursued.

If the unemployment rate rose significantly, what would you expect to happen to crime rates?

For most policy purposes, the primary concern is not what causes the level of crime to be what it is but, rather, what causes the level of crime to change. The changes in the crime rate in recent decades can be largely explained in terms of such a benefit–cost framework. If the benefits of crime rise, say, in the form of larger real "hauls," and/or if the costs fall due to a reduced likelihood of being caught or of being imprisoned if caught, then economists would expect the amount of crime to rise. Likewise, economists would expect the crime rate to fall in response to increased police enforcement, stiffer punishments, or an increase in the employment rate. Whether this analysis tells the complete story is debatable, but the use of the economic framework in thinking about the problem provides a plausible explanation.

WHAT ARE POSITIVE AND NEGATIVE INCENTIVES?

Almost all of economics can be reduced to incentive [$E(MB)$ versus $E(MC)$] stories, where consumers and producers are driven by incentives that affect expected costs or benefits. Prices, wages, profits, taxes, and subsidies are all examples of economic incentives. Incentives can be classified into two types: positive and negative. **Positive incentives** are those that either increase benefits or reduce costs and thus result in an increase in the level of the related activity or behavior. **Negative incentives,** on the other hand, either reduce benefits or increase costs, resulting in a decrease in the level of the related activity or behavior. For example, a tax on cars that emit lots of pollution (an increase in costs) would be a negative incentive that would lead to a reduction in the amount of pollution emitted. On the other hand, a subsidy to electric cars (an increase in benefits) would be a positive incentive that would encourage greater consumption and production of electric cars. Human behavior is shaped and influenced in predictable ways by such changes in economic incentives, and economists use this information to predict what will happen when the benefits and costs of any choice are changed.

WILL BIRTH RATES FALL IF THE TAX DEDUCTION FOR DEPENDENTS IS REMOVED?

Although it would not change everyone's behavior, overall we would expect birth rates to fall if the tax deduction for dependents was eliminated, because it would then be more expensive for couples to raise children. We would also predict that couples would choose to have fewer children if the government imposed a birth tax on couples. Clearly, both of these policy changes would serve as negative incentives to having children, because both increase the costs of having kids. In essence, what either of these policies would do is change the benefit–cost equation, and altering this equation typically leads to predictable results.

A subsidy on electric cars would be a positive incentive that would encourage greater consumption and production of these vehicles.

T U N E   U P

DO INCENTIVES MATTER?

Q: Do you think there are fewer drug traffickers in Singapore than there would be if the mandatory sentence was five years with parole for good behavior?

A: Singapore's tough drug-trafficking penalty—death—would clearly impact the cost–benefit ratios of would-be smugglers. Lighter sentences would probably result in more drug smuggling, because the overall cost of breaking the law would be reduced.

IMPORTANT NOTICE

Please DO NOT remove this portion of the form from your passport/ travel document. You are required to surrender this portion of the form to the Immigration Officer at the check point at the time of your departure.

WARNING
DEATH FOR DRUG TRAFFICKERS
UNDER SINGAPORE LAW

(1)

SURVEY FINDS CHEATING NOT UNCOMMON AMONG TOP U.S. HIGH SCHOOL STUDENTS

WASHINGTON (CNN)—Cheating, risky sexual behavior, and drug and alcohol use are activities found among high achievers in the nation's high schools, according to the 26th annual survey of students listed in "Who's Who among American High School Students."

However, students who took part in the survey named the "decline of moral and social values" as the greatest crisis confronting the nation and the number one problem facing teenagers.

Cheating: 89 percent of the students said cheating is common at their schools, and 76 percent admitted they had cheated on schoolwork themselves. Of those who cheated, 94 percent said they never got caught, and only 5 percent of those caught said they were punished. "In theory, we all want this to be a better world," said Jackie Knoll, 17, a senior in Montrose, Michigan. "In reality, we have to get this test done and we have to get an A. I think the bright kids are honest, but there is a lot of pressure to excel."

Drugs and alcohol: About half of students surveyed said drugs and alcohol are "easy or not very difficult" to obtain at

school, while 8 out of 10 students said there is a lot of alcohol use among students in their schools. About 1 in 10 of the students surveyed admitted driving after drinking and about one in four said they have been in cars with drivers who had too much to drink.

Guns: About 28 percent knew someone who had brought a weapon to school, and 45 percent said they own or have access to some kind of gun.

Note: The Who's Who annual survey was conducted among 3,351 16- to 18-year-old students around the country who have an "A" or "B" average. Of those surveyed, 98 percent plan to attend college after high school graduation.

SOURCE: http://cnn.com/US/9601/student_survey/

CONSIDER THIS:
Can we predictably alter human behavior by changing the incentive structure—the expected marginal benefits and/or the expected marginal costs? For example, what do you think would happen to the amount of cheating if more effective ways of catching cheating were implemented or if the penalties were increased? What if drugs, alcohol, and guns all became more difficult to obtain? In each of these situations, we have changed the cost–benefit ratio and would expect behavior to change in predictable directions.

DRUNK DRIVING DRAWS GLOBAL WRATH

PETER GRIER

Alcohol and automobiles are a combustible combination all over the world. Cultural attitudes towards drinking and driving do differ from nation to nation. Penalties vary widely, too: In Bulgaria and El Salvador, driving under the influence can bring the death penalty. In Turkey, offenders may be simply driven 10 miles from town, dumped, and forced to walk home under police escort. . . .

Americans may think that Europe has a more relaxed attitude towards drinking and driving than does the United States. In general, that is not the case. . . . Most U.S. states set the level at which a driver is declared legally drunk at 0.10 percent alcohol in his or her bloodstream. Fifteen have a lower limit of 0.08. . . . European nations tend to have lower blood-alcohol limits. Countries that set the bar at 0.08 include Austria, Canada, Denmark, Great Britain, Ireland, and Spain. France's legal limit is 0.05 (0.08 percent risks time in jail). Other nations with this relatively low limit include Belgium, Finland, Greece, the Netherlands, and Norway.

And while research is sketchy, it appears fewer drivers get behind the wheel drunk in Europe than do in the United States. One study conducted in the late 1980s indicated that about 8 percent of U.S. drivers on the road at night had blood-alcohol levels of 0.05 or higher. The comparable number from France was 5 percent; for Britain, 3 percent; and for the Nordic countries, a remarkably low 1 percent.

SOURCE: http://plweb.csmonitor.com/plweb-turbo/cg

EXHIBIT 1	WHEN YOU'RE LEGALLY DRUNK

When you're legally drunk
(by blood–alcohol level)

.10%

.08%

.05%

Norway   Canada   34 U.S.States

CONSIDER THIS:
The Nordic countries (Finland, Norway, and Sweden) all have lower legal blood-alcohol limits than the United States, and at least one study shows that lower blood-alcohol rates and tougher punishments are deterring many from drinking and driving. How many drunk drivers do you think are on the road in Bulgaria and El Salvador?

CONCEPT CHECK

1. People respond to incentives in predictable ways.
2. A negative incentive increases costs or reduces benefits, thus discouraging consumption or production.
3. A positive incentive decreases costs or increases benefits, thus encouraging consumption or production.

---

1. What is the difference between positive incentives and negative incentives?
2. According to the rule of rational choice, would you do more or less of something if its expected marginal benefits increased?
3. According to the rule of rational choice, would you do more or less of something if its expected marginal costs increased?
4. How does the rule of rational choice imply that young children are typically more likely to misbehave at a supermarket checkout counter than at home?
5. Why do many parents refuse to let their children have dessert before they eat the rest of their dinner?

Specialization and Trade

MODULE 1

- What is the relationship between opportunity cost and specialization?
- What are the advantages of specialization in production?

WHY DO PEOPLE SPECIALIZE?

As you look around you, you can see that people specialize in what they produce. They tend to dedicate their resources to one primary activity, whether it be child-rearing, driving a cab, or making bagels. Why is this? The answer, short and simple, is opportunity costs. By concentrating their energies on the activity to which they are best suited, individuals incur lower opportunity costs. This allows them to make the best use of (and thus gain the most benefit from) their limited resources. If a person, a region, or a country can produce a good or service at a lower opportunity cost than others, we say that they have a **comparative advantage** in the production of that good or service.

DO WE ALL SPECIALIZE?

We all specialize to some extent and rely on others to produce most of the goods and services we want. The work that we choose to do reflects our specialization. For example, we may specialize in selling or fixing automobiles. The wages for that work can then be used to buy goods from a farmer who has chosen to specialize in the production of food. Likewise, the farmer can use the money earned from selling his produce to get his tractor fixed by someone who specializes in that activity.

Specialization is evident not only among individuals but among regions and countries as well. In fact, the story of the economic development of the United States and

TUNE UP

COMPARATIVE ADVANTAGE

Q: Should an attorney who types 100 words per minute hire a secretary to type her legal documents, even though he can only type 50 words per minute? If the attorney does the job, she can do it in 5 hours; if the secretary does the job, it takes him 10 hours. The attorney makes $100 an hour, and the secretary earns $10 an hour. Which one has the comparative advantage (the lowest opportunity cost) in typing documents?

A: If the attorney types her own documents, it will cost $500 ($100 per hour x 5 hours). If she has the secretary type her documents, it will cost $100 ($10 per hour x 10 hours). Clearly, then, the lawyer should hire the secretary to type her documents, because the secretary has the comparative advantage (lowest opportunity cost) in this case, despite being half as good in absolute terms.

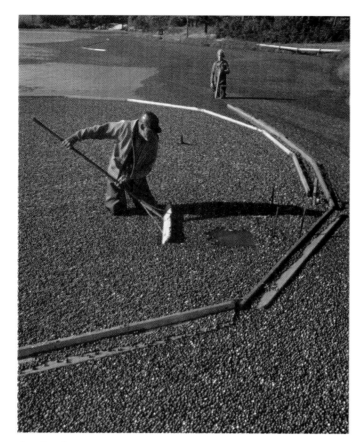

Cranberries are cultivated in bogs found primarily in the northeastern United States. Is this an example of regional specialization?

the rest of the world involves specialization. Within the United States, the Midwest with its wheat, the coastal waters of the Northeast with their fishing fleets, and the tall timbers of the Northwest are each examples of regional specialization.

WHAT ARE THE ADVANTAGES OF SPECIALIZATION?

In a small business, employees may perform a wide variety of tasks—from hiring to marketing. As the size of the company increases, each employee can now be used in a

more specialized job, with a consequent increase in output per worker. The primary advantages of specialization are that employees acquire greater skill from repetition, they avoid wasted time in shifting from one task to another, and they do the types of work for which they are best suited.

The advantages of specialization are seen throughout the workplace. For example, in larger firms, personnel relations can be conducted by specialists; accounting is put in the hands of full-time accounting experts instead of someone with half a dozen other tasks. The owner of a small retail store selects the location for the store primarily through guesswork, placing it where she believes sales would be high or where an empty, low-rent building is available. In contrast, larger chains have store sites selected by experts who have experience in analyzing the factors that make different locations relatively more desirable like traffic patterns, income levels, demographics, and so on.

Specialization is also possible with capital equipment. As a firm increases its scale of operations, it can replace nonspecialized equipment capable of performing a wide number of tasks with specialized equipment designed for various specific operations. This also increases a firm's productivity.

CAN SPECIALIZATION AND TRADE LEAD TO GREATER WEALTH AND PROSPERITY?

Voluntary exchange directly increases wealth by making both parties better off (or they wouldn't trade). It is the prospect of wealth-increasing exchange that leads to productive specialization. That is, trade increases wealth by allowing a person, a region, or a nation to specialize in those products that it produces better and to trade for those products that others produce better. For example, say the United States is better at producing wheat than Brazil, and Brazil is better at producing coffee than the United States. So the United States and Brazil would benefit if the United States produces wheat and trades some of it to Brazil for coffee. Coffee growers in the United States could grow coffee in expensive greenhouses, but it would result in higher coffee costs and prices, while leaving fewer resources available for employment in more productive jobs, such as wheat production.

MICHAEL JORDAN SIGNS NEW CONTRACT

In late August of 1997, the Chicago Bulls basketball organization signed superstar Michael Jordan to a one-year contract. The agreement was apparently reached after a quick meeting in Las Vegas between Jordan and Bulls owner Jerry Reinsdorf.

The *Chicago Tribune* reported that Jordan was seeking a one-year deal worth at least $36 million. Jordan has led the Bulls to their fifth NBA crown in seven years. In addition, he is reported to make millions more in commercial endorsements.

CONSIDER THIS:
Michael Jordan is a decent golfer and a good baseball player, and he may even enjoy these sports better than basketball. In fact, Michael did quit basketball to play baseball for the Chicago White Sox organization. What did it cost Michael to play baseball?

CONCEPT CHECK

1. We all specialize.
2. Specialization is important for individuals, businesses, regions, and nations.
3. Specialization and trade increase wealth.
4. The person, region, or country that can produce a good or service at a lower opportunity cost than other producers has a comparative advantage in the production of that good or service.

1. Why do people specialize?
2. What do we mean by comparative advantage?
3. Why does the combination of specialization and trade make us better off?
4. If you can mow your lawn in half the time it takes your younger brother to do it, do you have a comparative advantage in mowing the lawn?
5. If you became far more productive than before in completing yard chores, could that eliminate your current comparative advantage in doing the dishes?
6. Could a student who gets a C in one class but a D or worse in everything else have a comparative advantage in that class over someone who gets a B in that class but an A in everything else?
7. How can Michael Jordan help feed more poor people by playing basketball than by serving meals in a homeless shelter?

Markets and the Price System

- How does a market system allocate scarce resources?
- What are the important signals that market prices communicate?
- What are the effects of price controls and price supports?
- What causes miscommunication in the market system?

HOW DO WE DETERMINE WHO GETS WHAT?

Our collective wants far outweigh what the scarce resources nature has provided can produce. So how should we allocate those scarce resources? Some methods of resource allocation might be perceived as bad and counterproductive, like the "survival of the fittest" competition that exists on the floor of the jungle. Physical violence has been used since the beginning of time, as people, regions, and countries attack one another to gain control over resources. One might argue that government should allocate scarce resources on the basis of equal shares or according to need. However, this approach poses problems because of diverse individual preferences, the problem of ascertaining needs, and the negative work and investment incentives involved. In reality, society is made up of many approaches to resource allocation. However, for now, let us take a closer look at the predominant form of allocating goods in most countries—the market system.

HOW DOES THE MARKET SYSTEM WORK TO ALLOCATE RESOURCES?

The market system provides a way for producers and consumers to communicate about the allocation of scarce resources. Individuals indicate their wants and desires through their actions and inactions in the marketplace, and it is this collective "voice" that determines how resources are allocated. But how is this information communicated? Market prices serve as the language of the market system. By understanding what these market prices mean, you can get a better understanding of the vital function that the market system performs.

HOW DO MARKET PRICES PROVIDE IMPORTANT INFORMATION?

Market prices communicate important information to both consumers and producers. These prices communicate in-

In countries that do not use a free market system, there is no clear communication between consumers and suppliers. Bottlenecks, inefficiency, low-quality goods, and shortages often result.

formation about the relative availability of products to consumers, and they provide producers with critical information about the relative value that consumers place on those products. In effect, market prices provide a way for both consumers and producers to communicate about the relative value of resources. This communication results in a shifting of resources from those uses that are less valued to those that are more valued. We will see how this works beginning in Module 4.

WHAT EFFECT DO PRICE CONTROLS HAVE ON THE MARKET SYSTEM?

Government policies sometimes force prices above or below what they would be in a market economy. These are called **price controls.** Unfortunately, these controls often impose harm on the same people they are trying to help, in large part by short-circuiting the market's information transmission function. That is, price controls effectively strip the market price of its meaning for both consumers and suppliers. Consider the following examples: agricultural price supports and the minimum wage.

Agricultural Price Supports

Consider the effects of agricultural price supports on those whose low incomes make proper nutrition a genuine problem. Is a dairy farmer allowed to supply milk to a poor family (or any other family) at prices lower than the government allows? No! That action is currently illegal in the United States because of government restrictions on the prices of dairy products. These government price supports can destroy the communication between farmers and consumers that is provided by the market system, and can lead to the creation of huge stockpiles of some food products.

Minimum Wage

Consider how minimum-wage legislation censors effective communication from teenagers to employers. Many teenagers would like to tell prospective employers, "I have few skills and college is not possible for me. But I am willing to work hard for a low wage now, while I have only a few financial responsibilities, in order to acquire the experience and training necessary for a better paying job later." It is true that in the absence of minimum-wage legislation, some teenagers will express their willingness to work for wages many might consider "obscenely" low.

But an increase in the minimum wage has two effects on teenage employment: (1) The higher minimum wage increases the number of teenagers who want jobs, sometimes even causing them to drop out of school; and (2) the higher minimum wage for low-skilled workers discourages hir-

ing. Together these effects can lead to a large surplus of teenage workers that are actively seeking jobs. That is, the price control can prevent thousands of unemployed youths from preparing productively for their future. Journalists and broadcasters could fill the news with stories of jobless teenagers and the need to expand employment opportunities for our nation's youth. But the effectiveness of this information would be very small in comparison with the information conveyed by lower wages, which would serve to tell employers that teenagers are willing and able to work for less.

CAN THE MARKET FAIL?

The market mechanism is a simple but effective and efficient general means of allocating resources among alternative uses. However, those same markets can sometimes lead to problems as well. For example, a steel firm, as a byproduct of making steel, might put soot and other forms of "crud" into the air. When it does this, it imposes costs on others not connected with using or producing steel from the steel mill. For example, the soot may require homeowners to paint their homes more often, entailing a cost. And studies show that respiratory diseases are greater in areas with more severe air pollution, imposing costs and often shortening life itself. In addition, the steel mill might discharge chemicals into a stream, thus killing wildlife and spoiling recreational activities for the local population. Economists call this type of situation, where the economy fails to allocate resources efficiently on its own, a **market failure.** The case of market failure will be taken up in more detail in Module 6.

In addition, we cannot depend on the market economy to always communicate honestly and accurately. Some firms may have **market power** to distort prices in their favor. For example, the only regional cement company in the area has the ability to charge a higher price and provide lower-quality services than if the company was in a highly competitive market. In this case, the lack of competition can lead to higher prices and reduced product quality. And without adequate information, unscrupulous producers may be able to misrepresent their products to the disadvantage of unwary consumers. This, too, is considered in more depth in Module 6.

If the government subsidizes farmers, they may produce more than consumers want at that price, leading to inefficiency.

The government may be able to correct some market failures through regulation and the dissemination of information. The function of government in the marketplace will be discussed in greater detail in the next Concept.

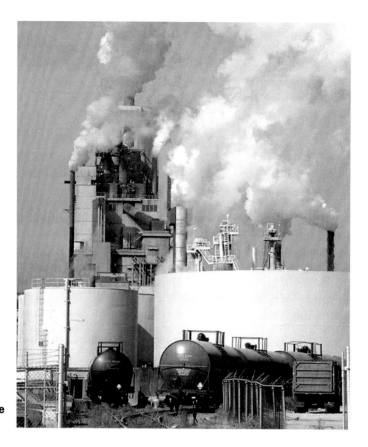

Sometimes markets fail because producers have too little incentive to clean up their wastes.

CONCEPT CHECK

1. Scarcity forces us to allocate our limited resources.
2. Market prices provide important information to buyers and sellers.

3. Price controls distort market signals.
4. Markets do not always communicate all information accurately.

---

1. Why must every society choose some manner by which to allocate its scarce resources?
2. How does a market system allocate resources?
3. What do market prices communicate to others in society?

4. How do price controls undermine the market as a communication device?
5. Why can markets sometimes fail to allocate resources efficiently?

Government Policies

- Why do we need government at all?
- Why can't we rely exclusively on the "invisible hand" of the market to determine economic decisions?
- Why is it so important that the government protect our property rights?

CAN APPROPRIATE GOVERNMENT POLICIES IMPROVE OUR WELL-BEING?

Political scientists, economists, and philosophers have theorized for centuries about the role of the government in society. Governments are institutions devised by humans to serve the collective or group will. According to Nobel laureate Douglass North, the rise in government's role since the Middle Ages reflects changes in perceptions as to the benefits or rewards from such activity relative to the costs of carrying out the activity. At least seven reasons have been used to justify government involvement into the economic decision-making process: (1) government provides a legal framework that enforces and protects property rights; (2) some goods and services are inherently "public"

One of the key functions of government is to provide a legal framework that protects and enforces property rights and contracts.

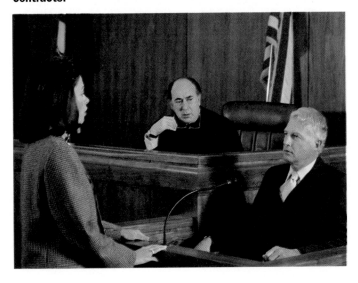

in character, like national defense; (3) a lack of competition in some cases has led markets to operate inefficiently; (4) by providing information, government can help participants in market activity make better decisions; (5) the existence of externalities—like pollution—can cause inappropriate market signals; (6) the market-determined income distribution may be considered unfair or inequitable; or (7) the overall level of output, employment, or prices may be viewed as being inappropriate if determined by the market mechanism alone.

WHY ARE PROPERTY RIGHTS SO IMPORTANT?

When consumers buy a house, a car, or a pizza, they have purchased the right to use these goods in a way they, not someone else, sees fit. (Of course, the use must also be within the existing legal system; that is, just because you own a car does not give you the right to drive it recklessly.) These rights are called property rights.

Property rights give individuals broad powers to use, sell, rent, dispose of, or enhance the value of goods. If property rights are well defined and respected, then the owner of a resource has confidence that he or she will, by maintaining ownership, benefit from any increase in the future value of the resource. Property rights, then, serve as a powerful incentive for individuals to maintain and conserve their resources.

Why does graffiti cover the walls of public rest rooms but is seldom seen on the walls of bathrooms in private homes? Probably because people are more concerned with the future value of property they own than of property they do not own. In the same sense, if you own your car, you have an incentive to keep the car in good condition with regular oil changes. Do you think this incentive might be less strong if you lease your car rather than buy it?

Why don't we see graffiti in our bathrooms at home?

WHAT IS THE LAW OF UNINTENDED CONSEQUENCES?

When considering the role of government in economic affairs and decisions, it is wise to remember that the actual results of actions are not always as initially intended. This is called the **law of unintended consequences.** As economists, we must always look for the secondary effects of an action that may occur along with the initial effects. In the area of public policy, the government is often well intentioned when it adopts policies to help unskilled workers, poor farmers, or tenants in search of affordable housing; however, such policies can also cause unintended consequences, which may completely undermine the intended effects. For example, rent controls may have an immediate effect of lowering rents, but secondary effects may well include very low vacancy rates, discrimination against low-income and large families, and deterioration of the quality of rental units. Similarly, minimum-wage increases may help many unskilled workers or apprentices, but will result in higher unemployment and a reduction in fringe benefits, such as vacations and discounts to employees. And agricultural price supports may initially help stabilize farmers' incomes, but may eventually lead to unused surpluses of foodstuffs for which the taxpayers will have to pay. As we will learn in the following modules, society has to make tough decisions, and if the government subsidizes some program or groups of people in one area, then something must always be given up somewhere else. The "law of scarcity" can not be repealed!

1. Government can improve our well-being.
2. Property rights provide important incentives.
3. Government policies can correct (and prevent) problems in the market system.

4. The law of unintended consequences states that the results of certain actions may not always be as clear as they initially appear.

---

1. What justifications are there for government involvement in the economic decision-making process?
2. What are property rights?
3. How do different property rights alter incentives?

4. What is the law of unintended consequences?
5. Why is the law of unintended consequences so important in making public policy?
6. Why is the shared, common area of a dormitory often messier than the students' individual rooms?

Economic Growth

■ Why is economic growth desirable?
■ Can there be negative side effects of economic growth?
■ How can a nation improve its economic growth rate?

ECONOMIC GROWTH CAN IMPROVE STANDARDS OF LIVING

The desire to bring about a long-term increase in the output of goods and services has been expressed with varying degrees of intensity in nearly every economy. The richest nations today have perhaps 50 to 100 times the output levels per person of the poorest countries.

IS ECONOMIC GROWTH GOOD OR BAD?

To be sure, there is not unanimous agreement that economic growth is desirable; some have been outspoken about negative impacts that often accompany economic growth, such as increased environmental problems, growing inequalities, higher crime, a decline in moral standards, and so on. Still, economic growth is proclaimed as a "good" thing by most people, and in many countries it has been the primary concern with respect to public policy. Economic growth, of course, enhances the potential amount of individual consumption; the greater the economic growth, the more goods we and our descendants will have to consume in the future. Economic growth also increases a nation's potential military and political power and enhances prestige.

WHAT CAN A COUNTRY DO TO INCREASE ITS ECONOMIC GROWTH?

Nations engage in a variety of policies designed to increase output over time. Some of these policies are designed to increase capital formation—the construction of tools and machinery today, which increases output in future time periods. In addition, new technology and the adoption of more efficient methods of doing things will lead to higher economic growth rates. Nations with high investment and capital formation have higher average annual economic growth rates (measured in gross domestic product, or GDP), while nations devoting smaller amounts of their output to capital formation have lower growth rates.

Investment in factories and equipment can lead to greater economic growth in the future.

EXHIBIT 1 — CORRELATION OF INVESTMENT AND GROWTH

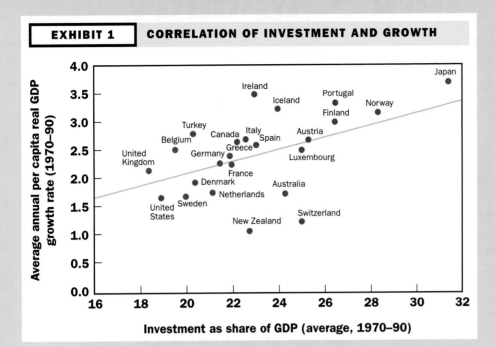

Investment as share of GDP (average, 1970–90)

Average annual per capita real GDP growth rate (1970–90) — y-axis: 0.0, 0.5, 1.0, 1.5, 2.0, 2.5, 3.0, 3.5, 4.0

x-axis: 16, 18, 20, 22, 24, 26, 28, 30, 32

Labeled points: Japan, Ireland, Iceland, Portugal, Norway, Finland, Turkey, Belgium, Canada, Italy, Spain, Austria, Germany, Greece, United Kingdom, France, Luxembourg, Denmark, Australia, Netherlands, Sweden, United States, New Zealand, Switzerland

CONSIDER THIS:
Exhibit 1 shows that there is a close correlation between investment and economic growth. Most economists agree that investment (like new machinery and technology) is an important component of economic growth.

CONCEPT CHECK

1. Economic growth can improve living standards.
2. There can also be negative effects from economic growth, including higher crime and increased environmental problems.
3. A country can increase its economic growth through technology and investing in physical capital (machines and tools) and human capital (education and training).

1. Why do we want economic growth to take place?
2. Can economic growth have negative side effects?
3. What sorts of policies can encourage economic growth?
4. Is it possible for economic growth to increase the quality of the environment?
5. If a country is building a bridge or road that nobody uses, will that kind of investment contribute to economic growth?

Price Stability

- What is inflation?
- What is deflation?
- What are the problems associated with inflation?
- How does inflation distort market signals?

WHAT IS INFLATION? WHAT IS DEFLATION?

When overall prices are rising (even though some prices may be falling), we have **inflation.** When overall prices are falling (even though some prices may be rising), we have **deflation.** In either case, the purchasing power of money is changing. With inflation, the purchasing power of money is falling; with deflation, it is rising. Ideally, an economy would have a stable monetary environment—a situation in which the economy is experiencing neither inflation nor deflation.

DOES A STABLE MONETARY ENVIRONMENT LEAD TO BETTER DECISION MAKING?

A stable monetary environment leads to price stability and enables producers and consumers to better coordinate their plans and decisions through the market. Inflation brings about changes in incomes of persons, and these changes may be undesirable. The redistributional impact of inflation need not be the result of conscious public policy; it just happens. Moreover, inflation can raise one nation's prices relative to prices in other countries, which will either lead to difficulties in financing purchases of foreign goods or to a decline in the value of the national currency relative to that of other countries. In its extreme form, inflation can lead to a complete erosion of faith in the value of money. After both World Wars, prices in Germany rose so fast that, in some cases, people finally refused to take paper money, insisting instead on payment in goods or metals.

DOES INFLATION DISTORT PRICE SIGNALS?

In periods of high and variable inflation, households and firms have a difficult time distinguishing changes in the relative prices of individual goods and services from changes in the general price level of all goods and services. Inflation distorts the information that flows from price signals. Does the good have a higher price because it has become relatively more scarce, and therefore more valuable relative to

other goods, or did the price rise along with all other prices because of inflation? This muddying of the information reflected in prices undermines good decision making.

WATCHING OUT FOR INFLATION CAN WASTE TIME AND OTHER RESOURCES

Households nervous about higher inflation rates in the future that may never materialize may decide to reduce their current saving and increase their current consumption instead. In an inflationary climate, investors nervous about hikes in wages and interest rates might pass up investments, particularly long-term investments that might have been pursued if prices were stable. In addition, households, producers, and investors will spend costly resources looking for ways to guard their assets and wealth from inflation. If it were not for unpredictable prices, these resources could be used more productively from society's perspective.

Unanticipated changes in overall prices increase uncertainty for decision makers.

1. When overall prices are rising, we have inflation.

2. When overall prices are falling, we have deflation.

3. A stable monetary environment allows consumers and producers to do a better job coordinating their plans and decisions.

4. Consumers, producers, and investors spend costly resources guarding their assets against inflation.

---

1. What is inflation?

2. What is deflation?

3. Why is price stability useful?

4. How can inflation distort price signals?

5. Why is the mere *possibility* of inflation costly to society?

6. Why does writing a five-year supply agreement for coal become more difficult when the future price level becom33es more uncertain?

Application: Laws and Enforcement Costs

Most of economics comes down to the fifth powerful idea—incentives matter. Can you see how the concepts of (1) incentives matter and (2) scarcity are demonstrated in this article?

MONTANA RAISES FINES FOR VIOLATORS

JOHN HOLT

Violators of Montana fish and game laws will pay at least twice as much in fines under a bill signed into law by Governor Marc Raciot. Senate Bill 210 increases the minimum fine for violations from $50 to $100 and the maximum fine from $1,000 to $2,000.

Other increases include the following:

1. The fine for illegally killing a black bear has been doubled to $2,000.

2. The fine for illegally catching a bull trout has increased from $10 to $500.

3. The fine for illegally killing an arctic grayling has increased from $10 to $300.

SOURCE: *Outdoor Life,* August 1995.

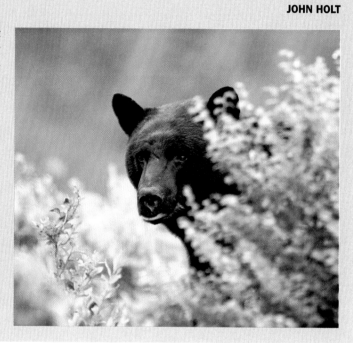

Sometimes it is less expensive to substitute tougher statutes and fines for increasing state or federal budgets to enforce laws more vigorously. In this case, an alternative to charging higher fines would be to add additional rangers, game wardens, and the like. However, this might prove to be prohibitively expensive because costly scarce resources would have to be used to comb the vast wilderness, which is not easily patrolled. Because the probability of being detected is lower, the higher fine should deter some from illegal hunting and fishing activities without adding additional and costly wildlife personnel. That is, substituting fines for monitoring is a relatively inexpensive method for deterring illegal behavior. For example, if the fine for illegally killing a black bear was raised to $100,000 and a five-year mandatory prison sentence, we would expect that the Department of Fish and Game would only have to enforce the laws casually; that is, because incentives matter, most hunters would be deterred by the stringent fine. This line of reasoning can be used in other areas of public policy. For example, a lower blood-alcohol level requirement on drinking and driving can be substituted for more costly choices like sobriety checkpoints and increasing the number of police officers.

IN THE BLEACHERS   By Steve Moore

"It's a Fed! ... Act natural."

Are laws against fishing without a license tough to enforce?

SOURCE: Moore, Universal Press Syndicate, May 19, 1998. Also see http://www.uexpress.com

ONE STEP BEYOND

Do incentives matter? You bet! Need an incentive to check out your Workbook? The problems and questions you will find in the Workbook and on your EconActive CD-ROM will help to reinforce your understanding of key concepts and ideas for each Module. Check them out!

1. Which of the following is an example of a positive incentive?

   A. Your dad says he will ground you if you flunk your high school physics class.

   B. The police in your town give a speeding ticket to anyone who drives over 25 miles per hour.

   C. Your math teacher says she will give a free laptop computer to each student who scores over 90 percent on the midterm exam.

   D. Your piano teacher raps you on the knuckles every time you hit a wrong note.

2. Which of the following is an example of a negative incentive?

   A. The Seattle Mariners give Ken Griffey, Jr. $10,000 for every home run he hits.

   B. The Chicago Bulls fine Dennis Rodman $10,000 every time he is late for practice.

   C. The New York Liberty give Rebecca Lobo $10,000 each time she scores over 30 points in a game.

   D. Mercury Records give Hanson an extra $300,000 for each week any of their songs is number one on the Billboard charts.

The Role and Method of Economics

A. Economics as a Science
Why is economics useful?

B. Economic Behavior
Can economists predict human behavior?

C. Economic Theory
Why do we need a theory?

D. Problems with Scientific Thinking
What are the key problems in scientific thinking?

E. Positive and Normative Analysis
Why is it important that we distinguish between
positive and normative analysis?

F. Application: Scientists and Global Warming
Why must we be so careful about association and correlation?

Appendix: Working with Graphs

Economics as a Science

MODULE 2

■ How is economics similar to other social sciences?
■ What are macroeconomics and microeconomics?
■ Are microeconomic tools important to macroeconomists?
■ Why study economics?

WHY IS ECONOMICS A SOCIAL SCIENCE?

Like psychology, sociology, anthropology, and political science—the social sciences—economics is concerned with reaching generalizations about human behavior. Because the social sciences all have the same primary focus, it should not come as a surprise that the investigations in these spheres often overlap and can complement one another. For example, an economist might analyze the impact of a given tax policy, while a political scientist might examine the process that led to the adoption of the policy. Or an economist might study the change in the crime rate, while a psychologist may try to figure out what makes the criminal mind work. Social scientists, then, may be studying the same issue but from different perspectives.

MACROECONOMICS AND MICROECONOMICS

Conventionally, we distinguish two main branches of economics, macroeconomics and microeconomics. **Macroeconomics** deals with the total economy; it looks at economic problems as they influence the whole of society. For example, topics covered in macroeconomics include discussions of inflation, unemployment, business cycles, and economic growth. **Microeconomics,** by contrast, deals with the smaller units within the economy, attempting to understand the decision-making behavior of firms and households and their interaction in markets for particular goods or services. Microeconomic topics include discussions of health care, agricultural subsidies, the price of energy or running shoes, the distribution of income, and the impact of unions on wages.

We Look at the Small to Understand the Large

While macroeconomics and microeconomics might emphasize different topics, they are both ultimately striving to understand people's behavior. Microeconomics analyzes smaller pieces of the economy, in part to better understand the large. The study of microeconomics has

Microeconomics helps us understand why ice cream costs what it does, while macroeconomics increases our understanding of inflation, unemployment, and economic growth.

helped economists gain a greater understanding about many macroeconomic topics, including interest rates, economic growth, unemployment, and the price level. However, both are concerned with social coordination—how humans interact with each other in a dynamic world.

WHY STUDY ECONOMICS?

While there are many good reasons to study economics, perhaps the best reason is that so many of the things of concern in the world around us are at least partly economic in character. A quick look at newspaper headlines reveals the vast range of problems that are related to economics—global warming, welfare reform, health care, education, and Social Security. The study of economics improves your understanding of these concerns. A student of economics becomes aware that, at a basic level, much of economic life involves choosing among alternative possible courses of action—making choices between our conflicting wants and desires in a world of scarcity. Economics provides some clues as to how to intelligently evaluate these options and determine the most appropriate choices in given situations. But economists learn quickly that there are seldom easy, clear-cut solutions to the problems we face—the easy problems were solved long ago!

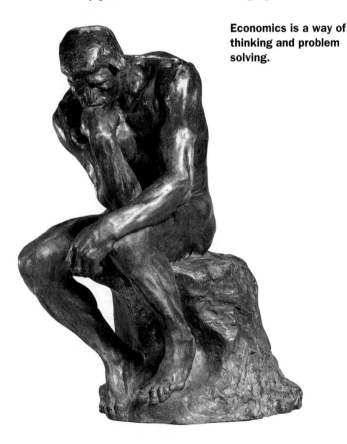

Economics is a way of thinking and problem solving.

Of course, there are other reasons to study economics. Many students take introductory college-level economics courses because they are required to as part of a general education curriculum or breadth requirements. But why do the committees that establish these requirements include economics? In part, because economics helps develop a disciplined method of thinking about problems. You see, while economics may not always give you clear-cut answers, it will give you something very useful: the economic way of thinking. The problem-solving tools you will develop by studying economics will prove valuable to you both in your personal and professional life, regardless of your career choice.

Will You Ever Really Use This Stuff?

The basic tools of economics are valuable to people in all walks of life and in all career paths. Newspaper reporters benefit from economics, because the problem-solving perspective it teaches trains them to ask intelligent questions whose answers will better inform their readers. Engineers, architects, and contractors usually have alternative ways to build. Architects learn to combine technical expertise and artistry with the limitations imposed by finite resources. That is, they learn how to evaluate their options from an economic perspective. Clothing designers face similar problems, because costs are a constraint in both creating and marketing new apparel. Will the added cost of a more expensive fabric be outweighed by the added sales revenues that are expected to result? Economists cannot answer such questions in a general sense because the answers depend on the circumstances. Economists can, however, pose these questions and provide criteria that clothing designers can use in evaluating the appropriateness of one fabric as compared to another. The point is that the economic way of thinking causes those in many types of fields to ask the right kinds of questions. As John Maynard Keynes once remarked:

> The object of our analysis is not to provide a machine or method of blind manipulation, which will furnish an infallible answer, but to provide ourselves with an organized and orderly method of thinking out particular problems; and, after we have reached a provisional conclusion by isolating the complicating factors one by one, we then have to go back on ourselves and allow, as well as we can, for the probable interactions of the factors amongst themselves. This is the nature of economic thinking."[1]

Will an Understanding of Economics Make You a Financial Wizard?

Some people think that economics may be a useful course of study, hoping that it will tell them how to become successful in a financial sense. If this is your goal in studying economics, you may be disappointed. While most economists make a good living, few have gotten very rich from their knowledge of economics. In fact, if economists had some secret for making money in, for example, the stock market, they would likely be using those secrets to their own financial advantage rather than making less money doing things such as teaching. Moreover, if economists did have some secret for making money, they would not be

[1] See J. M. Keynes, *General Theory of Employment Interest and Money* (New York: Harcourt Brace, 1936), p. 297.

likely to let non-economists in on it, because economic theory suggests (as will be clear later) that disclosure of the secret would reduce or eliminate the possibility of the economists' earning further income from this knowledge. Still, having some knowledge of the workings of market forces is likely to help individuals make more informed and appropriate decisions, including financial decisions. In short, economics won't necessarily make you rich, but it may keep you from making some decisions that would make you poorer.

While economics is a problem-solving science, it probably won't make you a stock market genius.

CONCEPT CHECK

1. Economics is concerned with reaching generalizations about human behavior.
2. Economics provides tools to intelligently evaluate and decide on choices.
3. Macroeconomics deals with the aggregate, or total, economy.
4. Microeconomics focuses on smaller units within the economy—firms and households.

1. What makes economics a social science?
2. What distinguishes macroeconomics from microeconomics?
3. Why is it worth studying economics?
4. Why is the market for running shoes considered a microeconomic topic?
5. Why is inflation considered a macroeconomic topic?

Economic Behavior

- What is self-interest?
- What is rational behavior?
- Why is observation more difficult in the social sciences?
- Can economists predict human behavior?

SELF-INTEREST AND RATIONAL BEHAVIOR

Is it rational for people to try to improve their own situation? Economists think so. We call this **self-interest.** Economists assume that self-interest is the motivation behind economic behavior. To economists, individuals are acting "rationally" if they are striving to do their best to achieve their goals with their limited income, time, and knowledge. That is, economists believe that when individuals act to advance their own self-interest, it is rational behavior.

ACTION AND INACTIONS HAVE CONSEQUENCES

Most economists also believe that rational behavior includes *trying* to anticipate the likely future consequences of one's behavior. For example, if someone with a suspended driver's license chooses to illegally drive an automobile, we presume that the individual considered the consequences of this action before he made that decision. That does not necessarily mean that he will not drive illegally, merely that he will consider the consequences of that action—perhaps a serious jail sentence or an impounded car—before he makes his choice. Or if someone decides to take up smoking, she is presumed by economists to have thought about the consequences of that action. An individual may still decide to smoke, but he or she will have at least considered the potential results of that action. Actions (even inactions, which are choices to not make changes) have consequences!

WHY ARE OBSERVATION AND PREDICTION HARDER IN THE SOCIAL SCIENCES?

Working from observations, scientists try to make generalizations that will enable them to predict certain events. However, observation and prediction are more difficult in the social sciences than in physical sciences such as physics, chemistry, and astronomy. Why? The major reason for the difference is that the social scientists, including economists, are concerned with *human* behavior. And human behavior is more variable and often less readily predictable than the behavior of experiments observed in a laboratory. However, by looking at the actions of a large group of people, economists can still make many reliable predictions about human behavior.

WHY DO ECONOMISTS PREDICT ON A GROUP LEVEL?

Economists' predictions usually refer to the collective behavior of large groups rather than to that of specific individuals. Why is this? Looking at the behaviors of a large group allows economists to discern general patterns of actions. For example, consider what would happen if the price of air travel from the United States to Europe was reduced drastically, say from $500 to $200, because of the invention of a more fuel-efficient jet. What type of predictions could we make about the effect of this price reduction on the buying habits of typical consumers?

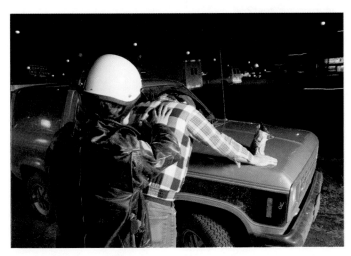

Actions have consequences!

What Does Individual Behavior Tell Us?

Let's look first at the responses of individuals. As a result of the price drop, some people will greatly increase their intercontinental travel, taking theater weekends in London or week-long trips to France to indulge in French food. Some people, however, are terribly afraid to fly, and the price reduction will not influence their behavior in the slightest. Others might detest Europe and, despite the lowered airfares, prefer to spend a few days in Aspen, Colorado, instead. A few people might respond to the airfare reduction in precisely the opposite way from ours: At the lower fare, they might make fewer trips to Europe, because they might believe (rightly or wrongly) that the price drop would be accompanied by a reduction in the quality of service, greater crowding, or reduced safety. In short, we cannot predict with any level of certainty how a given individual will respond to this airfare reduction.

What Does Group Behavior Tell Us?

While we cannot say what each individual will do, within a group of persons, we can predict with great accuracy that more flights to Europe will be sold at lower prices than at higher prices, holding other things such as income and preferences constant. We cannot predict exactly how many more tickets will be sold at $200 than at $500, but we can

Flug Flight		nach to	über via	planm. scheduled	verspätet delayed	Schalter Counter
LG	302	LUXEMBURG		930		113-33
AZ	419	TURIN		935		339-34
LH	1122	NEAPEL		935		113-33
LH	1906	MADRID		935		113-33
LH	1022	STUTTGART HBF.		935		-
AF	1701	LYON		940		683-68
AY	822	HELSINKI		940		113-33
AA	071	SFRANCISCO-DALLAS		945		731-73
AF	743	PARIS		945		683-68
LH	1116	VENEDIG		945		113-33
DL	023	DALLAS		950		478-48
GA	892	AMSTERDAM		950		721-72

Abflug

If airfares to Europe rise, what would you expect to happen to the number of people traveling to Europe by plane?

predict the direction of the impact and approximate the extent of the impact. By observing the relationship between the price of goods and services and the quantities people purchase in different places and during different time periods, it is possible to make some reliable generalizations about how much people will react to changes in the prices of goods and services. Economists use this larger picture of the group for most of their theoretical analysis.

CONCEPT CHECK

1. It is rational for people to act in their own self-interest and try to improve their situation.
2. People try to anticipate the likely consequences of their actions.
3. Economists generally predict group behavior rather than individual behavior.

1. What do economists mean by self-interest?
2. What does rational behavior involve?
3. Why are observation and prediction more difficult in the social sciences?
4. Why do economic predictions refer to the behavior of groups of people rather than individuals?
5. Why is it typically rational for students to make some mistakes (get less than 100 percent) on a test?
6. Can you sometimes get a high grade on a test without studying? Does that mean that additional studying does not lead to higher grades?

MODULE 2

Economic Theory

- What are economic theories?
- What can we expect out of our theories?
- Why do we need to abstract?
- What is a hypothesis?
- What is empirical analysis?

WHAT ARE ECONOMIC THEORIES?

A theory is an established explanation that accounts for known facts or phenomena. Specifically, **economic theories** are statements or propositions about patterns of human behavior that are expected to take place under certain circumstances. These theories help us to sort out and understand the complexities of economic behavior. People ask many things of theories. But most of all, we expect a good theory to explain and predict well. A good economic theory, then, should help us to better understand and, ideally, predict human economic behavior.

WHY IS ABSTRACTION NECESSARY?

Economic theories cannot realistically include every event that has ever occurred. This is true for the same reason that

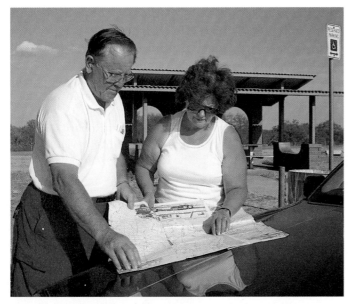

How is economic theory like a map?

a newspaper or history book does not include every world event that has ever happened. We must abstract. A road map of the United States may not include every creek, ridge, and gully from Los Angeles to Chicago—indeed, such a map would be too large to be of value—but it will provide enough information for a traveler to reach Chicago if traveling by car from Los Angeles. Likewise, an economic theory provides a broad view, not a detailed examination, of human economic behavior.

HOW DO ECONOMISTS DEVELOP THEIR THEORIES?

The beginning of any theory is a hypothesis, a testable proposition that makes some type of prediction about behavior in response to certain changed conditions. A hypothesis in economic theory is a testable prediction about how people will behave or react to a change in economic circumstances. For example, if the prices charged for compact discs (CDs) increase, we might hypothesize that fewer CDs would be sold or if the price of CDs fell we might hypothesize that more CDs would be sold. Once a hypothesis is stated, it is tested by comparing what it predicts to what actually happens.

Why Do We Use Empirical Analysis?

To see if our hypothesis is valid, we must engage in an empirical analysis. That is, we must examine the data to see if our hypothesis fits well with the facts. If the hypothesis is consistent with real-world observations, it is accepted; if it does not fit well with the facts, it is "back to the drawing board."

Determining whether an economic hypothesis is acceptable is more difficult than is the case in the natural or physical sciences. A chemist, for example, can observe chemical reactions under laboratory conditions. He or she can alter the environment to meet the assumptions of the hypothesis and can readily manipulate the variables (chemicals,

Economists are not so fortunate to have controlled experiments like this.

temperatures, and so on) crucial to the proposed relationship. Such controlled experimentation is seldom possible in economics. The laboratory of economists is usually the real world. And unlike a chemistry lab, economists cannot easily control all the other variables that might influence human behavior.

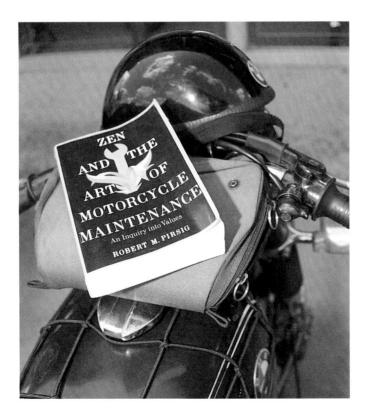

FROM HYPOTHESIS TO THEORY

After gathering his or her data, an economic researcher must then evaluate the results to determine whether the hypothesis is supported or refuted. If it is supported, the hypothesis can then be tentatively accepted as an economic theory.

Zen and the Art of Scientific Thinking

Economists, like motorcycle mechanics, interweave theory and observations to solve problems. For example, an economist might hypothesize that people tend to buy more oranges at lower prices than higher prices. He then might test that hypothesis; and if he then observed in one region after another that when the price of oranges increased, people bought fewer oranges and that when the price of oranges fell, people bought more oranges, he would conclude that people tend to buy more oranges at lower prices than at higher prices. This is the pathway to scientific thinking that leads to problem solving. Robert Pirsig, in his classic book, *Zen and the Art of Motorcycle Maintenance*, maps out this pathway in the following excerpt.

Part Three, [is] that part of formal scientific method called experimentation . . . A motorcycle mechanic, . . . who honks the horn to see if the battery works is informally conducting a true scientific experiment. He is testing a hypothesis by putting the question to nature . . . An experiment is never a failure solely because it fails to achieve predicted results. An experiment is a failure only when it also fails adequately to test the hypothesis in question, when the data it produces don't prove anything one way or another. Skill at this point consists of using experiments that test only the hypothesis in question, nothing less, nothing more. If the horn honks, and the mechanic concludes that the whole electrical system is working, he is in deep trouble. He has reached an illogical conclusion. The honking horn only tells him that the battery and horn are working. To design an experiment properly he has to think very rigidly in terms of what directly causes what . . . The horn doesn't make the cycle go. Neither does the battery, except in a very indirect way. The point at which the electrical system *directly* causes the engine to fire is at the spark plugs, and if you don't test here, at the output of the electrical system, you will never really know whether the failure is electrical or not.

To test properly the mechanic removes the plug and lays it against the engine so that the base around the plug is electrically grounded, kicks the starter lever and watches the spark-plug gap for a blue spark. If there isn't any he can conclude one of two things: (a) there is an electrical failure or (b) his experiment is sloppy. If he is experienced he will try it a few more times, checking connections, trying every way he can think of to get that plug to fire. Then, if he can't get it to fire, he finally concludes that (a) is correct, there's an electrical failure, and the experiment is over . . .

. . . skill comes in stating no more than the experiment has proved. It hasn't proved that when he fixes the electrical system the motorcycle will start. There may be other things wrong. But he does know that the motorcycle isn't going to run until the electrical system is working . . ."[1]

---

[1] Robert Pirsig, *Zen and the Art of Motorcycle Maintenance* (New York: William Morrow and Company, Inc.), pp. 93–96.

Was Dinkins' hypothesis tested empirically?

THE FAR SIDE   By GARY LARSON

"Oh, and *that* makes me feel even worse! ... I laughed at Dinkins when he said his new lenses were indestructible."

CONCEPT CHECK

1. Economic theories are statements about patterns of human behavior.
2. We must abstract.
3. A hypothesis makes a prediction about human behavior.

4. We use empirical analysis to examine the data and see if our hypothesis fits well with the facts.

---

1. What are economic theories?
2. What is the purpose of a theory?
3. Why must economic theories be abstract?

4. What is a hypothesis? How do we determine if it is tentatively accepted?

MODULE 2

Problems with Scientific Thinking

- What is the *ceteris paribus* assumption?
- If events are associated with each other, does that mean one event caused the other to happen?
- What is the fallacy of composition?

In our discussion of economic theory and model building, we have not yet mentioned that there are certain problems that may hinder scientific and logical thinking. We will discuss several problems of concern in this Concept.

WHAT IS THE *CETERIS PARIBUS* ASSUMPTION?

One condition common to virtually all theories in economics is usually expressed by use of the Latin expression *ceteris paribus.* This roughly means "let everything else be equal" or "holding everything else constant." In trying to assess the effect of one variable on another, we must isolate their relationship from other events that might also influence the situation that the theory tries to explain or predict. To make this clearer, we will illustrate this concept with a couple of examples.

Suppose you develop your own theory describing the relationship between studying and exam performance: If I study harder, I will perform better on the test. That sounds logical, right? Holding other things constant *(ceteris paribus),* this is likely to be true. However, what if you studied harder but inadvertently overslept the day of the exam, or were so sleepy during the test that you could not "think straight," failing it? Or what if you studied the wrong material? While it may look like additional studying did not improve your performance, the real problem may lie in the impact of other variables such as sleep deficiency or how you studied.

Researchers must be careful to hold other things constant *(ceteris paribus).* For example, in 1936, cars were inexpensive by modern standards, yet few were purchased; in 1949, cars were much more expensive, but more were bought. This

It Needs No Breaking-In

You can take a Ford V-8 right out of the dealer's showrooms and drive it across the country. For it needs no breaking-in. You can drive it 60 miles an hour the day you buy it. . . . This means more efficient, useful service for every one—more enjoyable motoring because you do not have to drag along for 500 or 1000 miles. . . . The reason for this fine-car feature is as important as the result. . . . The Ford V-8 needs no breaking-in because of unusual accuracy in the manufacture of moving parts and the smoothness of bearing surfaces. Clearances are correct when you buy the car. You do not have to depend on a long wearing-in period to eliminate tightness and insure smooth running. . . . Formerly, only the most expensive cars could be driven at normal speed from the beginning. That still holds true today—except in the case of the Ford V-8. . . . Fine-car construction means fine-car performance.

NEW FORD V·8 FOR 1936

$25 A MONTH, WITH USUAL DOWN-PAYMENT, BUYS ANY NEW FORD V-8 CAR ON UCC ½ PER CENT PER MONTH FINANCE PLANS

Between 1936 and 1949, car prices increased and sales increased. Does this mean that people are willing to buy more at higher prices than at lower prices?

statement appears to imply that people prefer to buy more when prices are higher. However, we know from ample empirical observations that this is not the case—buyers are only willing to buy more at lower prices, *ceteris paribus.* Several other important variables, particularly the purchasing power of dollars, the income of potential car buyers, and the quality of cars, were not constant over this period.

IS ASSOCIATION ALWAYS CAUSATION?

Without a theory of causation, no scientist could sort out and understand the enormous complexity that occurs in the real world. But one must always be careful not to confuse **association** with **causation.** In other words, the fact that two sets of phenomena are related does not necessarily mean that one caused the other to occur. For example, say a ground hog awakes after a long winter of hibernation, climbs out of his hole, sees his shadow—and then six weeks of bad weather ensue. Did the groundhog cause the bad weather? Similarly, Cal Ripkin's consecutive game streak in baseball started at the same time that the Weather Channel was introduced on television. Does that mean that the two events are systematically related? It is highly unlikely.

Confusing association and causation can lead to three different types of misinterpretations. First, there may be no causation between the two variables. Second, there may be a third variable that is responsible for causing both events.

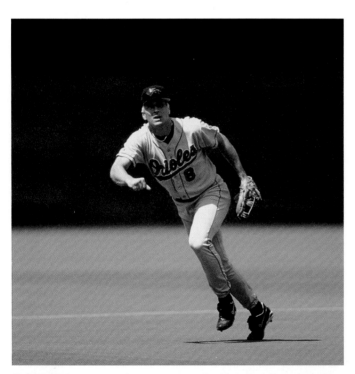

Cal Ripkin's consecutive game streak started at the same time the Weather Channel went on the air. Did one cause the other to happen?

Third, the causality may run in the opposite direction. Let us look at each of these problems separately.

No Causation between the Two Variables

Although two variables may appear to be interrelated, they may not be related at all. For example, if students sitting in the back of the classroom get lower grades on a particular test, does that mean that sitting in the back of the classroom causes lower grades? Clearly, the answer is no.

It is also important to remember that the reoccurrence of a certain relationship between two variables does not necessarily strengthen the argument for causation. That is, because two things happen together more than once does not necessarily make it more likely that one causes the other. Similar events, or clusters, often happen by chance. For example, the pockets of cancer that occur around power lines may not be related to the power lines at all—they may just be clusters.

"I have some good news. While your cholesterol level has remained the same, the research findings have changed."

Additional Variable Causing the Relationship

Although two variables may appear to be causally related, it may be that a third, unidentified factor is in fact responsible for the relationship. For example, the Food and Drug Administration proposed banning the artificial sweetener saccharin for human use in 1978 because studies indicated that the substance caused bladder cancer in rats. However, in 1992, researchers discovered that it was saccharin's interaction with the rat urine, a third variable, rather than saccharin itself, that made rats susceptible to bladder cancer.

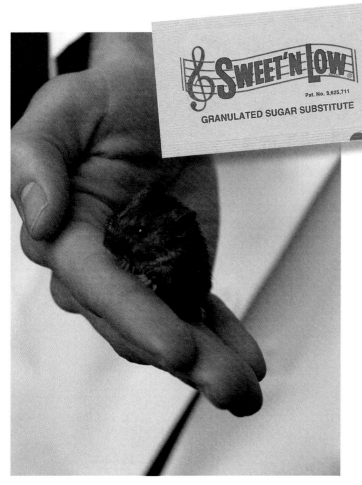

Sometimes a third variable is responsible.

Causality May Run in the Opposite Direction

Sometimes it may appear that one variable causes another, when, in fact, just the opposite is true. For example, the fact that overweight individuals drink diet soda does not mean that diet soda causes obesity. It is much more likely that the opposite is true: Overweight individuals drink diet soda to help them control their weight. Likewise, although a rooster always crows before the sun comes up, it does not cause the sun to rise; rather, the light from the sunrise causes the rooster to crow.

WHAT IS THE FALLACY OF COMPOSITION?

One must also be careful with problems associated with aggregation, particularly the **fallacy of composition.** That is, even if something is true for an individual, it is not necessarily true for many individuals as a group. For example, say you are at a Green Bay Packer game and you decide to stand up to get a better view of the playing field. This works as long as no one else stands up. But what would happen if everyone stood up at the same time? Then, standing up would not let fans see better. Hence, what may be true for an individual does not always hold true in the aggregate. The same can be said of arriving to class early to get a better parking place—what if everyone arrived early? Or studying harder to get a better grade in a class that is graded on a curve—what if everyone studied harder? All of these are examples of the fallacy of composition.

Why Is There an Association between Ice Cream Sales and Crime? Did you know that when ice cream sales rise, so do crime rates? What do you think causes the two events to occur together? Some might think that the higher crime rate might be caused by the sugar "high" in the ice cream. Excess sugar in a snack was actually used in court testimony in a murder case—the so called "twinkie defense." However, it is more likely that crime peaks in the summer because of weather, more people on vacations (leaving their homes vacant), teenagers out of school, and so on. It just happens that ice cream sales also peak in those months because of weather. The lesson: One must always be careful not to confuse *association* with *causation*.

Can you get a better view by standing up?

HEAVY METAL MUSIC AND TEEN SUICIDE

KAREN R. SCHEEL

Many parents and mental health professionals have watched the rising rate of adolescent suicide and the growing popularity of heavy metal music among teenagers and wondered, with some concern, if there is any connection between the two phenomena. A new study . . . offers the first direct assessment of the suicidal risk of American adolescent heavy metal fans compared to that of peers who do not like heavy metal music.

For the study, 121 midwestern public high school students (mean age 17.2) were given two psychological assessments, the Reasons for Living Inventory (RFL) and the Suicide Risk Questionnaire (SRQ) (both measures of risk for suicide), and their musical preferences were assessed.

Compared with fans of country, pop/mainstream, rock, and rap music, heavy metal fans had lower scores on the RFL (indicating greater risk of suicide) and they were more likely to say they occasionally or seriously thought about killing themselves (74 percent versus 35 percent for females; 42 percent versus 15 percent for males).

But the author cautions that while these findings "do suggest that a teenager's liking of heavy metal music may be a useful 'red flag' for suicidal vulnerability for psychologists and other professionals who work with adolescents," she adds that these findings should not be thought of as indicative of imminent suicidal risk and that they "are not suggestive of any important causal effects of heavy metal listening on suicidality."

Does heavy metal music cause increases in teen suicide rates?

CONSIDER THIS:
Note how the researcher cautions against any determination of causality. Perhaps the causality runs in the other direction: Kids that are at greater risk for suicide may like heavy metal music. Perhaps some other variables are causing the association, like genetic predisposition, peer pressure, environment, or a host of other things.

SOURCE: http://cybertowers.com/selfhelp/boards/teen/boardl.shtml. December 12, 1997.

CONCEPT CHECK

1. In order to isolate the effects of one variable on another, we use the *ceteris paribus* assumption.
2. The fact that two events are related does not mean that one caused the other to occur.
3. What is true for the individual is not necessarily true for the group.

1. Why do economists hold other things constant *(ceteris paribus)*?
2. What is the relationship between association and causation?
3. To what types of misinterpretations does confusing association and causation lead?
4. What is the fallacy of composition?

5. If U.S. consumers bought more gasoline in 1998, when prices averaged $1.20 per gallon, than they did in 1970, when prices averaged $0.30 per gallon, does that mean that people buy more gas at higher prices? Why or why not?
6. If rain dancing is correlated with rain, does that mean that rain dancing causes rain? Why or why not?
7. Why could getting up earlier to beat the other fishermen to the fish lead anglers to catch the same number of fish at 5 A.M. as they would at noon?

Positive and Normative Analysis

■ What is positive analysis?
■ What is normative analysis?
■ Why do economists disagree?

WHAT IS POSITIVE ANALYSIS?

Most economists view themselves as scientists seeking the truth about the way people behave. They make speculations about economic behavior, and then (ideally) they try to assess the validity of these predictions based on human experience. Their work emphasizes how people behave, rather than how they should behave. In the role of scientist, an economist tries to objectively observe patterns of behavior without reference to the appropriateness or inappropriateness of that behavior. This objective, value-free approach, utilizing the scientific method, is called **positive analysis.** In positive analysis, we want to know the impact of variable A on variable B. We want to be able to test a hypothesis. For example, the following is a positive statement: If rent controls are imposed, vacancy rates will fall. This statement is testable. A positive statement does not have to be a true statement, but it does have to be a testable statement.

However, keep in mind that it is doubtful that even the most objective scientist can be totally value-free in his or her analysis. An economist may well emphasize data or evidence that supports his hypothesis, putting less weight on other evidence that might be contradictory. This, alas, is human nature. But a good economist/scientist strives to be as fair and objective as possible in evaluating evidence and in stating conclusions based on the evidence.

WHAT IS NORMATIVE ANALYSIS?

Economists, of course, have opinions and make value judgments. When economists, or anyone else for that matter, express opinions about some economic policy or happening, they are stating in part how they believe things should be, not just facts as to the way things are. Opinions expressed about the desirability of various actions are called **normative statements.** Normative statements in-

Because of normative analysis, it is not unusual, as in 1996, for two presidential candidates with different policy beliefs to each receive the support of Nobel Prize winners in economics.

volve judgments about what should be or what ought to happen. For example, one could judge that incomes should be more equally distributed. If there is a change in tax policy that makes incomes more equal, there will be positive economics questions that can be investigated, such as how work behavior will change. But we cannot say, as scientists, that such a policy is good or bad; rather, we can point to what will likely happen if the policy is adopted.

WHY DO I NEED TO KNOW THE DIFFERENCE?

The distinction between positive and normative analysis is important. It is one thing to say that everyone should have universal health care, a normative statement, and quite another to say that universal health care would lead to greater worker productivity, a testable positive statement. It is important to distinguish between positive and normative analysis because many controversies in economics revolve around policy considerations that contain both. When economists start talking about how the economy *should* work rather that how it does work, they have entered the normative world of the policymaker.

IS DISAGREEMENT IN ECONOMICS UNIQUE?

While professional economists differ frequently on economic policy questions, there is probably less disagreement than the media would have you believe. Disagreement is common in most disciplines—seismologists trying to predict earthquakes or the eruption of volcanoes differ; historians can be at odds over the interpretation of historical events; psychologists differ on proper ways to rear children; nutritionists debate the merits of large doses of vitamin C; and so on.

The majority of disagreements in economics stem from normative issues, as differences in values or policy beliefs result in conflict. As we discussed earlier in this Module, an economist inevitably emphasizes specific facts over others when trying to develop support for his or her own hypothesis. As a result, disagreements can result when one economist gives weight to facts that have been minimized by another, and vice versa.

Is Freedom More Important Than Fairness?

Some economists are very concerned about individual freedom and liberty, thinking that any encroachment on individual decision making is, other things equal, bad. Persons with this philosophic bent are inclined to be skeptical of any increased government involvement in the economy, unless the objective evidence is overwhelming that the intervention will have profound beneficial economic consequences.

On the other hand, some economists are very concerned with what they consider an unequal, "unfair," or unfortunate distribution of income, wealth, or power, and view governmental intervention as desirable in righting injustices that they believe exist in a market economy. To these persons, the threat to individual liberty alone is not sufficiently great to reject governmental intervention in the face of perceived economic injustice.

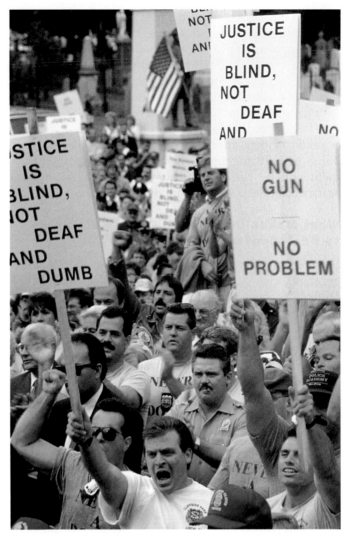

Just as there are differences in opinions among individuals, so too are there differences of opinion among scientists.

Which Economic Theory Is Valid?

Aside from philosophic differences, there is a second reason why economists may differ on any given policy question. Specifically, they may disagree as to the validity of a given economic theory for the policy in question. Suppose two economists have identical philosophical views, and that those views have led them to the identical conclusion that unemployment should be reduced to end injustice and hardship. The first economist believes that the government should lower taxes and increase spending to reach the objective, while the second economist believes that the lower unemployment goal can be reached with fewer undesirable consequences by increasing the amount of money in public hands by a variety of banking policies.

The two economists differ because the empirical evidence relating to economic theories dealing with the cause of unemployment appears somewhat conflicting. Some evidence suggests government taxation and spending policies are effective in reducing unemployment, while other evidence would suggest that the prime cause of unnecessary unemployment lies with faulty monetary policy. Still other evidence is consistent with the view that, over long periods, neither approach mentioned here is of much value in reducing unemployment, and that unemployment will be part of our existence regardless of what macroeconomic policies we follow.

What Makes One Theory Come to Be Accepted over Others?

Some economists do a recognizably better job of holding constant other appropriate variables. Also, information tends to become better over time, either because we have longer time periods to analyze or because databases can be assembled to answer a specific question. And statistical techniques for analyzing the available data are improving as well, and certain of those techniques are becoming more accepted than others. Finally, it may sometimes be the case that human behavior actually changes over time, so that a theory that explained behavior fairly well in the past comes to be replaced by another theory that is more relevant to current behavior.

DO ECONOMISTS EVER AGREE WITH EACH OTHER?

Although you may not believe it after reading the previous discussion, economists don't always disagree. In fact, according to a survey among members of the American Economic Association, most economists agree on a wide range of issues, including rent control, import tariffs, export restrictions, the use of wage and price controls to curb inflation, and the minimum wage (Exhibit 1). Often, economists argue that if market forces are allowed to work freely, economic analysis can predict certain phenomena with a high degree of success. For example, if Florida suf-

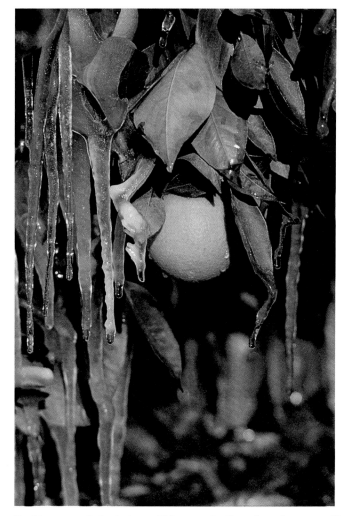

Could you predict what would happen to the price of oranges if a frost ruined much of the orange crop?

fers a severe winter and the frost ruins much of the state's orange crop, there will be fewer oranges. Consumers who place a higher value on the remaining supply of oranges will outbid those who place lower values on it, and the price of oranges will rise.

| EXHIBIT 1 | ECONOMISTS DO AGREE |

Over 70 percent of economists agree that these statements are correct:

1. A ceiling on rents (rent control) reduces the quantity and quality of housing available (92.9% agree).

2. Tariffs and import quotas usually reduce general economic welfare (92.6% agree).

3. A minimum wage increases unemployment among the young and unskilled (78.9% agree).

4. Inflation is primarily a monetary phenomenon (70.1% agree).

Approximately 70 percent of economists agree that these statements are not accurate:

5. The cause of the rise in gasoline prices that occurred in the wake of the Iraqi invasion of Kuwait is the monopoly power of the large oil companies (69.3% agree).

6. Wage–price controls are a useful policy option in the control of inflation (73.9% agree).

SOURCE: Adapted from Richard M. Alston, J. R. Kearl, and Michael B. Vaughn, "Is There Consensus among Economists in the 1990s?" *American Economic Review,* May 1992, 203–209.

CONCEPT CHECK

1. Positive analysis is objective and value-free.
2. Normative analysis involves value judgments and opinions about the desirability of various actions.
3. Disagreement is common in most disciplines.
4. Most disagreement among economists stems from normative issues.

---

1. What is positive analysis? Must positive analysis be testable?
2. What is normative analysis? Is normative analysis testable?
3. Why is the positive–normative distinction important?
4. Why are there policy disagreements among economists?

5. Is the statement, "UFOs land in my back yard at least twice a week," a positive statement? Why or why not?
6. Is there any way to scientifically determine if the "rich" pay their "fair share" of taxes? Why or why not?

Application: Scientists and Global Warming

How might disagreements in the scientific community affect the cost–benefit analysis of pollution regulation and subsequent governmental policy discussions?

Is global warming an inevitable catastrophe just waiting to happen? No one knows for sure. A 1989 *Time* magazine article stated, "The possible consequences [of global warming] are so scary that it is only prudent for governments to slow the build up of carbon dioxide through preventive measures." On the other hand, a 1994 *Time* magazine article titled "The Ice Man Cometh?" dismissed warnings of global warming as "apocalyptic" and readers were told to "start worrying about the next ice age instead."

Scientists have to sell their stories. So are we cooling down or warming up? The answer is that we have been warming up in this century. But there is ambiguity as to why we are warming up. Is it due to the build-up of greenhouse gases? And to what extent are humans responsible for global warming versus poorly understood natural processes? No one knows for sure. Surface temperature readings in the 1990s are the hottest on record. However, highly accurate satellite-based atmospheric temperature measurements report that the earth's atmosphere actually cooled by .13 degrees Celsius from 1979 to 1993. While the amount of global warming from 1881 to 1993 was 0.54 degrees Celsius, almost 70 percent of that increase occurred during the first half of this period, before the biggest build-up of greenhouse gases.

And we must consider the cost of choosing to control greenhouse gases now. Professor William Nordhaus of Yale University writes, "Given the high costs of controls [on greenhouse gases] . . . and the modest estimated impact of climate change along with other urgent concerns (nuclear proliferation, poverty, drug use, violence and civil wars), we might conclude that global warming should be demoted to a second-tier issue."

There are two important points here. First, while we should be concerned about the environment, we should also be equally concerned that every effort is made to produce objective science based on positive analysis rather than "political" science based on normative analysis. Second, as Professor Nordhaus states, life is about very tough choices, and good, positive analysis can help us make those choices better.

A final observation is that there are many different ways to achieve a given reduction in greenhouse gases by, say, the year 2050: We can clean up a lot now and a little later, or a lot later and a little now. Because the global circulation models will be far more accurate in a mere decade, some argue that it would be prudent to postpone very expensive controls until the seriousness of the problem can be better assessed.

Steve Sack, *Minneapolis Star Tribune*, 1997.

Do incentives matter? You bet! Need an incentive to check out your Workbook? Come on in and meet the Lowell family! You'll learn some important economic concepts—including incentives matter—simply by following them through their adventures and mishaps!

1. In the recent congressional debate about agricultural price supports, senators, congressmen, and experts made the following four statements. Which of these statements is a normative statement?

   A. Price supports are important because America should preserve the small family farm.

   B. Without price supports the price of wheat and corn will fall by over 20 percent.

   C. The decline in commodity prices caused by the removal of price supports will result in fewer, larger farms.

   D. The decline in commodity prices caused by the removal of price supports will reduce the number of tractors sold in the United States.

"If you use your Workbook and EconActive CD-ROM, you will get a better grade in economics." Is that a positive or a normative statement? To be sure, check out the exercises in your Workbook and then work the sample quizzes on the EconActive CD-ROM!

Appendix: Working with Graphs

MODULE 2

WHY ARE GRAPHS SO IMPORTANT?

Sometimes the use of visual aids, such as graphs, greatly enhances our understanding of a theory. It is much the same as finding your way to a friend's house with the aid of a map rather than with detailed verbal or written instructions. Graphs are important tools for economists. They allow us to better understand the workings of the economy. To economists, a graph can be worth a thousand words. Graphs will be used throughout this text to enhance the understanding of important economic relationships. This appendix provides a guide on how to read and create your own graphs.

The most useful graph for our purposes is one that merely connects a vertical line (the Y-axis) with a horizontal line (the X-axis), as seen in Exhibit 1. The intersection of the two lines occurs at the origin, which is where both variables are equal to zero. In Exhibit 1, we see that the graph has four quadrants or "boxes." In this textbook we will be primarily concerned with the shaded box in the upper right-hand corner. You can see that this portion of the graph deals exclusively with positive numbers. Always keep in mind that moving to the right on the horizontal axis and up along the vertical axis each lead to higher values.

What Are Dependent and Independent Variables?

A **variable** is a quantity that can take on different numeric values. A **dependent variable** is one that *depends* on the independent variables. That is, the dependent variable value changes according to the values of the independent variables, while an **independent variable** is truly independent—on its own. An independent variable is not influenced by any other variable. The independent variable is determined outside the relationship in question—no matter what happens to the other variables in the equation. For example, imagine a two-variable world. The two variables are weight and food consumption. As food

| EXHIBIT 1 | PLOTTING A GRAPH |

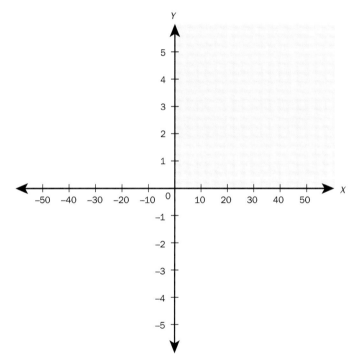

In the upper right-hand corner, we see that the graph includes a positive figure for the Y-axis and the X-axis. As we move to the right along the horizontal axis, the numerical values increase. As we move up along the vertical axis, the numerical values increase.

consumption (the independent variable) changes, weight (the dependent variable) changes, holding all other variables constant. In this example, we see that weight depends on how much food we eat. Theoretical relationships involving one dependent variable and one independent variable can be expressed in a simple two-dimensional graph.

USING GRAPHS AND CHARTS TO SHOW A SINGLE VARIABLE

Exhibit 2 presents three common types of graphs. The **pie chart** in Exhibit 2(a) shows where takeout food is taken. For example, we see that 53 percent of takeout food is taken home, 19 percent is eaten in the car, and 14 percent is taken to work. That is, each slice in the pie chart represents where the food is taken.

Exhibit 2(b) is a bar graph that shows the most popular tourist attractions in the United States. The height of the line represents the annual attendance at these popular tourist attractions. According to this graph, Disneyland was the most popular amusement/theme park in 1996.

EXHIBIT 2   PIE CHART, BAR GRAPH, AND TIME-SERIES GRAPH

---

a. Pie Chart

Where is take-out food taken?

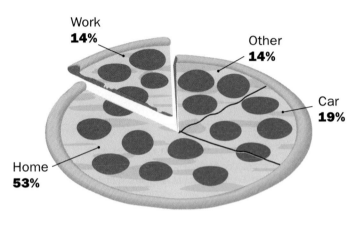

SOURCE: Beef Industry Council.

c. Time Series Graph

Prices and Inflation Ease, 1986–1997

SOURCE: U.S. Department of Labor.

b. Bar Graph

Most popular Amusement/Theme Parks, by number of visitors, 1996

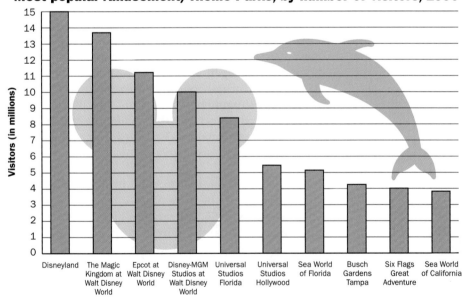

SOURCE: Amusement Business.

Exhibit 2(c) is a **time-series graph.** This type of graph shows changes over time. This is a visual tool that allows us to observe important trends over a certain period of time. In Exhibit 2(c) we see a graph that shows the percentage changes in inflation rates over time. The horizontal axis shows us the passage of time, and the vertical axis shows us the inflation growth, in percentage terms. From the graph we can see the trends in inflation from 1986 to 1997.

USING GRAPHS TO SHOW THE RELATIONSHIP BETWEEN TWO VARIABLES

While the graphs and chart in Exhibit 2 are important, they do not allow us to show the relationship between two variables. To more closely examine the structure of and functions of graphs, let us consider the story of Wanda Blade. Wanda is an avid inline skater who has aspirations of strutting her freestyle stuff at the Z Games next year. To get there, however, Wanda knows she will have to put in many hours of practice. But how many hours? In search of information about the practice habits of other skaters, Wanda logged onto the Internet at inline@rad.com, where she pulled up the results of a study conducted by ESPM 3 that indicated the score of each Z Games competitor and the amount of practice time per week spent by each skater. The results of this study (see Exhibit 3) indicated that skaters had to practice 10 hours per week to receive a score of 4.0, 20 hours per week to receive a score of 6.0, 30 hours per week to get a score of 8.0, and 40 hours per week to get a perfect score of 10. What does this information tell Wanda? By using a graph, Wanda can more clearly determine the relationships between practice time and overall score.

What Is a Positive Relationship?

The study that Wanda found on scores and practice times revealed what is called a **direct relationship,** often also called a **positive relationship.** A direct relationship means that the variables move in the same direction. That is, an increase in one variable (practice time) is accompanied by an increase in another variable (overall score), or a decrease in one variable (practice time) is accompanied by a decrease in another variable (overall score). In short, the variables move in the same direction.

What Is a Negative Relationship?

When two variables move in opposite directions, we say that there is an **inverse,** or **negative, relationship** between the two variables. That is, when one variable rises, the other variable falls, or when one variable decreases, the other variable increases.

EXHIBIT 3	A POSITIVE RELATIONSHIP	

Skater	Z Games Score	Practice Time per Week
A	4	10
B	6	20
C	8	30
D	10	40

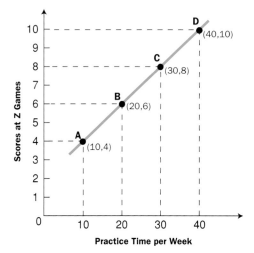

The inline skaters' practice times and scores in the competition are plotted on the graph. Each participant is represented by a point. The graph shows that those skaters who practiced the most scored the highest. This is called a positive, or direct, relationship.

THE GRAPH OF A DEMAND CURVE

Let us now examine the most important graphs in all of economics—the graph of a demand curve. In Exhibit 4, we see the demand curve for compact discs (CDs) for Roland Rocks. It shows the price of CDs on the vertical axis and the quantity of CDs purchased per month on the horizontal axis. Every point in the space shown represents a price and quantity combination. The downward-sloping line, labeled Demand Curve, shows the different combinations of price and quantity purchased. Note that the higher you go up on the vertical (price) axis, the smaller the quantity purchased on the horizontal axis and the lower you go down on the vertical (price axis) the greater the quantity purchased.

In Exhibit 4, we see that moving up the vertical price axis from the origin, the price of CDs increases from $5 to $25 in increments of $5. Moving out along the horizontal quantity axis, the quantity purchased increases from zero to five CDs per month. Point A represents a price of $25 and a quantity of one CD, point B represents a price of $20 and a quantity of two CDs, point C, $15 and a quantity of three CDs, and so on. When we connect all of these points we have what economists call a **curve**. As you can see, curves are sometimes drawn as straight lines for ease of illustration. Moving down along the curve, we see that as the price falls, the quantity that is purchased is greater; moving up the curve to higher prices, the quantity purchased is smaller. That is, when CDs become less expensive, Roland buys more CDs. When CDs become more expensive, Roland buys fewer CDs, perhaps choosing to go to the movies or buy a pizza instead.

EXHIBIT 4 | A NEGATIVE RELATIONSHIP

Combination	Price of CDs	Quantity of CDs Purchased
A	$25	1
B	20	2
C	15	3
D	10	4
E	5	5

The downward slope of the curve means that price and quantity purchased are inversely, or negatively, related: When one increases, the other decreases. That is, moving down along the demand curve from point A to point E, we see that as price falls, the quantity purchased increases. Moving up along the demand curve from point E to point A, we see that as the price increases, the quantity purchased falls.

USING GRAPHS TO SHOW THE RELATIONSHIP BETWEEN THREE VARIABLES

Although only two variables are shown on the axes, graphs can be used to show the relationship between *three* variables. For example, say we add a third variable—income—to our earlier example. Our three variables are now income, price, and quantity purchased. If Roland's income

rises, say he gets a raise at work, he is now able to buy more CDs than before at each possible price. As a result, the whole demand curve shifts outward to a new position that lies to the right of the old curve. That is, with the new income, Roland uses some of it to buy more CDs. This is seen in the graph in Exhibit 5(a). On the other hand, if Roland's income falls, say he quits his job to go back to school, he now has less income to buy CDs. This causes the whole demand curve to shift inward to a new position to the left of the old curve. This is seen in the graph in Exhibit 5(b).

EXHIBIT 5 | SHIFTING A CURVE

a. Demand Curve with Higher Income

b. Demand Curve with Lower Income

What Is the Difference between a Movement and a Shift in the Curve?

It is important to remember the difference between a movement up and down along a curve and a shift in the whole curve. A change in one of the variables on the graph, like price or quantity purchased will cause a movement along the curve, say, from point A to point B as shown in Exhibit 6. A change in one of the variables not shown, like income in our example, will cause the whole curve to shift, like the change from D_0 to D_1 in Exhibit 6.

EXHIBIT 6   SHIFTS VERSUS MOVEMENTS

Quantity of CDs Purchased

WHAT IS A SLOPE?

In economics, we sometimes refer to the steepness of the lines or curves on graphs as the slope. A slope can be either positive (upward sloping) or negative (downward sloping). A curve that is **downward sloping** represents an inverse, or negative, relationship between the two variables

and slants downward from left to right, as seen in Exhibit 7(a). A curve that is **upward sloping** represents a direct, or positive relationship, between the two variables and slants upward from right to left, as seen in Exhibit 7(b).

How Do We Measure the Slope of a Linear Curve?

A straight line curve is called a linear curve. The slope of a linear curve between two points measures the relative rates of change of two variables. Specifically, the slope of a linear curve can be defined as the ratio of the change in the Y value to the change in the X value. The slope can also be expressed as the ratio of the rise to the run, where the rise is the change in the Y variable (along the vertical axis) and the run is the change in the X variable (along the horizontal axis).

$$\text{Slope} = \frac{\text{RISE}}{\text{RUN}} = \frac{\text{Change in the } Y \text{ variable (vertical axis)}}{\text{Change in the } X \text{ variable (horizontal axis)}}$$

In Exhibit 8, we show two linear curves, one with a positive slope and one with a negative slope. In Exhibit 8(a), the slope of the positively sloped linear curve from point A to B is 1/2, because the rise is 1 (from 2 to 3) and the run is 2 (from 1 to 3). In Exhibit 8(b), the negatively sloped linear curve has a slope of –4—the "rise" is –8 (a fall of 8 from 10 to 2) and a run of 2 (from 7 to 9), which gives us a slope of –4 (–8 ÷ 2). Note the appropriate signs on the slopes: There is a minus sign on the negatively sloped line and a plus sign on the positively sloped line.

EXHIBIT 7   DOWNWARD- AND UPWARD-SLOPING LINEAR CURVES

a. Downward-Sloping Linear Curve

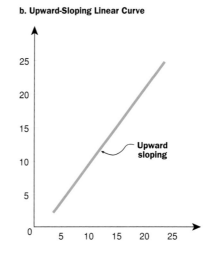

b. Upward-Sloping Linear Curve

| EXHIBIT 8 | SLOPES OF POSITIVE AND NEGATIVE LINEAR CURVES |

a. Positive Slope

b. Negative Slope

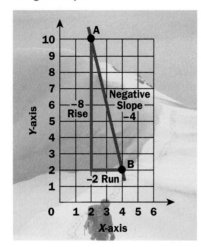

How Do We Find the Slope of a Nonlinear Curve?

In Exhibit 9, we show the slope of a nonlinear curve. A nonlinear curve is a line that actually curves. Here the slope varies from point to point along the curve. However, we can find the slope of this curve at any given point by drawing a straight line tangent to that point on the curve. A tangency is when a straight line just touches the curve without actually crossing it. At point A, we see that the slope of the positively sloped line that is tangent to the curve has a +1 slope—the line rises one unit and runs one unit. At point B, the line is horizontal, so it has zero slope. At point C, we see a slope of –2, because the negatively sloped line has a rise of –2 units (a fall of two units) for every one unit run.

Remember that failure to understand graphs are the reason that many students have problems with economics, so make sure that you understand this material before going on to Module 3.

| EXHIBIT 9 | THE SLOPE OF A NONLINEAR CURVE |

Scarcity and the Economizing Problem

A. The Factors of Production
What are the factors of production?

B. The Production Possibilities Curve
Why is the production possibilities curve useful?

C. Production Decisions
What and how much should we produce?

D. Production Methods
How will we produce those goods and services?

E. Distribution of Output
Who will get the goods and services we produce?

F. Efficiency in Production
How can we use our scarce resources efficiently?

G. Production and Growth
What do we have to sacrifice today to achieve
greater economic growth?

H. Application: Tourism versus Ecosystems
Can we have more tourism and a better environment at the same time?

The Factors of Production

- What are the four factors of production?
- What is labor?
- What is land?
- What is capital?
- What is entrepreneurship?

WHAT ARE THE FOUR FACTORS OF PRODUCTION?

The three kinds of **resources**—**land, labor,** and **capital**—are each in limited supply and must be used in any productive activity. They are the "inputs" that result in "outputs" of final goods and services in the economy. The fourth factor of production, **entrepreneurship,** is the decision-making input that is concerned with the application of these resources and with identifying new possibilities, new products, and new methods of production.

You might want to use the word *CELL* to help you remember the four factors of production: *C*, capital; *E*, entrepreneurship; *L*, land; and *L*, labor.

What Is Labor?

The resource called **labor** includes the total of both physical and mental effort expended by people in the economy. In economics, we are concerned with both the quantity and the quality of labor. Increases in the quantity of labor, relative to the population, means more workers and fewer dependents. Increases in the quality of labor increases workers' productivity. Both factors can lead to greater economic growth.

What Is Land?

Economists stretch the term land to include all natural resources coming from the earth. Trees, animals, water, minerals and so on are all considered to be "land" for our purposes, along with the physical space normally thought

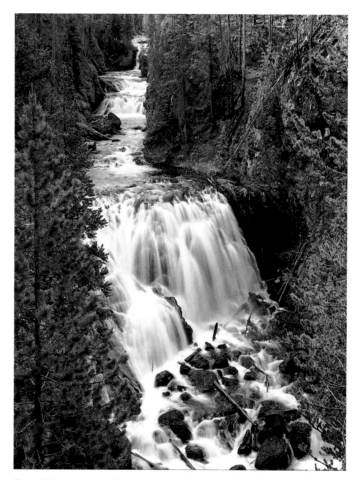

Everything you see here—water, trees, rocks, air, and, of course, land—is land to an economist.

of as land. Suppose you are making a table. You will need wood, metal, glass, plastic, stone, fiberglass, or some combination of these and possibly other materials. As a producer, you must choose which specific materials to use. In a market economy, you will see that it is largely prices (which reflect relative scarcity) that influence this decision, but under any system, the relative scarcity or availability of various materials will have a bearing on making production decisions.

What Is Capital?

Human-made resources that are used to produce final goods are called **capital goods.** Office buildings, tools, machines, and factories are all considered capital goods. Fishing nets are also capital goods, because they are made for the purpose of "producing" the final good—fish. When we invest in factories, machines, research and development, or education, we increase the potential to create more goods and services in the future.

When thinking about capital, most of us tend to think first of money. However, when considering capital in economics, it is important not to confuse capital goods with money capital. **Money capital** is not regarded as a distinct factor of production or as a good to be consumed. Rather, it is regarded as an instrument of exchange—a means by which other commodities are acquired. Money is essential for the efficient exchange of goods among households, business firms, and other economic decision-making units, but it may be best thought of as the "oil" that allows production and consumption to run smoothly.

What Is an Entrepreneur?

Someone has to make tough and risky decisions about how to combine land, labor, and capital together, which goods or services to produce, how many to produce, and so on. This decision maker is often called an **entrepreneur.** The management skills and innovative talents of entrepreneurs are crucial in expanding an economy's ability to produce goods over time.

Entrepreneurs are always looking for new ways to improve production techniques or to create new products. They are driven by the lure of a positive incentive—profits. It is this opportunity to make a profit that leads entrepreneurs to take risks. However, entrepreneurs do not have to be a Bill Gates (Microsoft) or a Henry Ford (Ford Motor Company). In some sense, we are all entrepreneurs when we try new products or when we find better ways to manage our households or our study time. Rather than money, then, our profits might take the form of greater enjoyment, additional time for recreation, or better grades.

Because a factory is built to produce other goods, it is considered to be a capital good.

BILL GATES, THE ENTREPRENEUR

When Bill Gates was in the sixth grade, his parents decided he needed counseling. He was at war with his mother, Mary, an outgoing woman who harbored the belief that he should do what she told him. She would call him to dinner from his basement bedroom, which she had given up trying to make him clean, and he wouldn't respond. "What are you doing?" she once demanded over the intercom. "I'm thinking," he shouted back. "You're thinking?" "Yes, Mom, I'm thinking," he said fiercely. "Have you ever tried thinking?"

The psychologist they sent him to "was a really cool guy," Gates recalls. "He gave me books to read after each session, Freud stuff, and I really got into psychology theory." After a year of sessions and a battery of tests, the counselor reached his conclusion. "You're going to lose," he told Mary. "You had better just adjust to it because there's no use trying to beat him." Mary was strong-willed and intelligent herself, her husband recalls, "but she came around to accepting that it was futile trying to compete with him."

A lot of computer companies have concluded the same. In the 21 years since he dropped out of Harvard to start Microsoft, William Henry Gates, III, 41, has thrashed competitors in the world of desktop operating systems and application software. Now he is attempting the audacious feat of expanding Microsoft from a software company into a media and content company.

In the process he has amassed a fortune . . . . The 88 percent rise in Microsoft stock in 1996 meant he made on paper more than $10.9 billion, or about $30 million a day. That makes him the world's richest person, by far. But he's more than that. He has become the Edison and Ford of our age. A technologist turned entrepreneur, he embodies the digital era.

His success stems from his personality: an awesome and at times frightening blend of brilliance, drive, competitiveness, and personal intensity . . . he has "incredible processing power" and "unlimited bandwidth," an agility at "parallel processing" and "multitasking." Watch him at his desk, and you see what they mean. He works on two computers, one with four frames that sequence data streaming in from the Internet, the other handling the hundreds of e-mail messages and memos that extend his mind into a network. He can be so rigorous as he processes data that one can imagine his mind may indeed be digital: no sloppy emotions or analog fuzziness, just trillions of binary impulses coolly converting input into correct answers.

Bill Gates receives profits for his entrepreneurial efforts.

SOURCE: "In Search of the Real Bill Gates," *Time*, 149, no. 2, January 13, 1997.

CONCEPT CHECK

1. Capital, entrepreneurship, land, and labor (CELL) are the four factors of production.
2. Labor is the physical and mental effort expended in production.
3. Land includes all of our natural resources.
4. Capital consists of all the human-made resources that are used to produce final goods.
5. An entrepreneur is the decision maker that combines the capital, land, and labor into production.

1. What are factors of production?
2. What do economists mean by land? Labor? Capital? Entrepreneurship?
3. What is the difference between capital goods and money capital?
4. Why do you think economists often refer to training that increases the quality of workers' skills as "adding to human capital"?
5. What are some of the ways that students act as entrepreneurs as they seek higher grades?

The Production Possibilities Curve

- What is a production possibilities curve?
- What are consumption goods?
- What are investment goods?
- What is the law of increasing opportunity costs?

WHAT IS A PRODUCTION POSSIBILITIES CURVE?

The problem of deciding what to produce and in what quantities is sometimes illustrated visually by the use of a simple graph called a **production possibilities curve** (Exhibit 1). The production possibilities curve represents the potential total output combinations of any two goods for an economy. That is, it illustrates an economy's potential for allocating its limited resources to producing various combinations of goods. If an economy is operating on the production possibilities curve, then that economy is oper-

ating at full capacity, given the inputs and technology available to the economy.

How Do We Show Inefficiency on the Production Possibilities Curve?

If it is not operating at full capacity, the economy is operating inefficiently. As a result, actual output is less than potential output. If this occurs, the economy is operating inside the production possibilities curve. And operating inside the production possibilities curve reflects inefficiency in the economy. The concept of inefficiency will be covered in greater detail in Concept F of this Module.

EXHIBIT 1	A PRODUCTION POSSIBILITIES CURVE

Combination	Fishing Nets	Fish
A	50	0
B	40	350
C	30	600
D	20	800
E	10	900
F	0	950

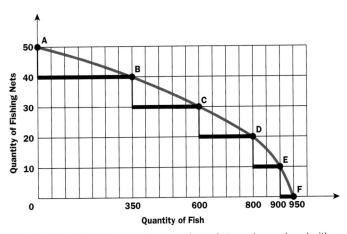

The production possibilities curve represents the potential amounts of two products that can be produced with given resources. It also illustrates the opportunity cost of producing more of a product. For example, if we increase fishing net output from 10 to 20 units (moving from point E to point D), we must produce 100 fewer units of fish (800 instead of 900). The opportunity cost of the 10 additional nets is therefore 100 units of fish. We can see that, moving up the curve from F, an additional 10 units of fishing nets costs society more and more fish—the law of increasing opportunity cost. The increasing opportunity cost is illustrated by the bold horizontal lines.

WHAT ARE CONSUMPTION GOODS AND INVESTMENT GOODS?

To more clearly illustrate the production possibilities curve, we will use an example involving an island economy that produces just two goods, fish and fishing nets. The fact that we have many goods in the real world makes actual decision making more complicated, but it does not alter the basic principles being illustrated. In this example, you can think of the fish as being symbolic of all the goods we consume that bring us immediate satisfaction. These goods are called **consumption goods.** Similarly, think of the fishing nets as being symbolic of all of the goods that give little immediate pleasure but that help increase the output of goods and services in future time periods, thus providing us with satisfaction at a later date. We call these **investment goods.**

Fish are a consumption good; fishing nets are investment goods.

Each point on the production possibilities curve shown in Exhibit 1 represents the potential amounts of fish and fishing nets that can be produced in a given time period, given the quantity and quality of resources available in the economy to use for production.

Note in Exhibit 1 that if we devoted all of our resources to making fishing nets, we could produce 50 new nets, but no fish (point A). If, on the other hand, we chose to devote all of our resources to catching fish, we could catch 950 fish, but produce no new nets (point F).

In reality, we would probably not choose either of these extreme production possibilities. Why? A nation that produced only nets (investment goods) would quickly starve to death (ignoring, for the time being, trade possibilities with other countries). On the other hand, if a nation devoted all of its resources to making consumption goods, such as fish, it would soon find its ability to produce deteriorating, as older resources (such as machines or, in this case, fishing nets) wear out. Thus, even economies that just want to maintain their current output must use some of their resources to replace some of their stock of output-creating investment goods, like fishing nets.

Therefore, nations would rarely opt for production possibility A or production possibility F, preferring instead to produce a mixture of goods. For example, the economy in question might produce 40 nets and 350 fish (point B), or perhaps 30 nets and 600 fish (point C). Still other combinations, such as point D, are possible, as long as all of the economy's resources are being used efficiently in production.

WHAT IS THE COST OF A FISHING NET?

The true cost of a fishing net in this economy is revealed by the production possibilities curve. By moving along the curve, the cost (really opportunity cost) of an additional fishing net is the number of fish that must be foregone as the limited resources are shifted from producing fish to producing fishing nets. For example, suppose the economy has been operating at point C, making 20 nets and catching 800 fish annually. Suppose now that people decide they want to produce 10 more fishing nets. To do this, they must reduce fish output to 600, a decrease of 200. Thus, the opportunity cost of those 10 additional fishing nets is the 200 fish that have to be given up as workers, raw materials, and so on are diverted from fishing to the production of 10 additional nets. In making the decision about whether to shift its resources, this society must somehow decide if the benefits of the 10 added fishing nets exceed the opportunity cost (200 fish) of having those fishing nets.

WHAT DOES A BOWED PRODUCTION POSSIBILITY CURVE MEAN?

Note that the production possibility curve in Exhibit 1 is not a straight line. It is concave from below (that is, bowed outward from the origin). Looking at the figure, you can see that at very low net output, a small increase in the number of nets produced will lead to only a small reduction in fish output. For example, increasing fishing net output from 0 to 10, or 10 units (moving from point F to point E on the curve), requires the use of resources capable of producing 50 fish. This means that for each net added between 0 and 10, an average of 5 fish are given up (50 divided by 10). When many nets are already being made, however, many more fish must be given up when switching additional resources from fish to fishing net production. Moving from point B to point A, for example, a reduction in fish output of 350 (from 350 to 0) releases resources to produce 10 more nets (the output of nets rises from 40 to 50). At this point, then, the average cost of each additional fishing net obtained, then, is 35 units of fish (350 divided by 10), considerably more than the 5 fish required in the earlier scenario. This difference shows us that opportunity costs have not remained constant, but have risen, as more fishing nets are produced. It is this increasing opportunity cost, then, that results in the bowed production possibilities curve.

Why Is There an Increasing Opportunity Cost?

A basic reason for the **increasing opportunity cost** of additional fishing net output as more nets are produced is that some resources cannot be easily adapted from their current uses to alternative uses. For example, some resources used in catching fish are difficult or impossible to use in the manufacture of fishing nets (e.g., fishing boats). At low levels of current fishing net output, rather large increases in output are obtained by switching easily adaptable resources, such as poor fishermen, from fishing to making nets. Soon these resources are exhausted and resources and workers that are less well suited or appropriate for net manufacture (or are better adapted to fishing) must be released from fishing in order to increase fishing net output. For example, a skilled fisherman may be an expert at catching fish but a very bad net maker, because he lacks the training and skills necessary in that occupation. So, using the skilled fisherman to make nets results in a relatively greater opportunity cost (that is, more fish lost) than using the poor fisherman to make nets. Hence, the production of additional fishing nets becomes increasingly costly as more nets are produced.

T U N E   U P

THE PRODUCTION POSSIBILITIES CURVE

Q: Imagine that you are the overseer on a small island that only produces two goods, cattle and wheat. About a quarter of the land is not fertile enough for growing wheat, so cattle graze on it. What would happen if you tried to produce more and more wheat, extending your planting even to the less-fertile soil?

Will the costs of growing wheat increase as you continue to grow more and more wheat on this island?

A: This is the law of increasing opportunity costs in action. As we planted more and more of our acreage in wheat, we would move into some of the rocky, less-fertile land and, consequently, wheat yields on the additional acreage would fall. If we tried to plant the entire island with wheat, we would find that some of the rocky less-fertile acreage would yield virtually no extra wheat. It would, however, have been great for cattle grazing—a large loss. Thus, the opportunity cost of using that marginal land for wheat rather than cattle grazing would be very high. The law of increasing opportunity cost occurs because resources are not homogeneous (identical) and are not equally adaptable for producing cattle and wheat; some acres are more suitable for cattle grazing, while others are more suitable for wheat growing. This is seen in Exhibit 2, where the horizontal lines represent the opportunity cost of growing more wheat in terms of cattle production sacrificed. You can see that as wheat production increases, the opportunity costs in terms of lost cattle production rises.

EXHIBIT 2 | **OPPORTUNITY COSTS FOR CATTLE AND WHEAT**

1. The production possibilities curve represents the potential total output combinations of two goods available to a society.
2. If the economy is operating within the production possibilities curve, the economy is operating inefficiently; this means that actual output is less than potential output.
3. Goods that we consume and give us immediate satisfaction are called consumption goods; goods that give us little immediate pleasure but help increase output in future time periods are called investment goods.

4. A bowed production possibility curve means that the opportunity costs of producing additional units of a good rise as society produces more of that good (the law of increasing opportunity costs).

---

1. What does a production possibilities curve illustrate?
2. What distinguishes consumption goods and investment goods?
3. How are opportunity costs shown by the production possibilities curve?
4. Why do the opportunity costs of added production increase with output?
5. How does the production possibilities curve illustrate increasing opportunity costs?

6. If people reduced their saving (thus reducing the funds available for investment), what would that do to society's production possibilities curve over time?
7. If Robin's son, Crusoe, could produce 20 fishing nets in a day or catch 60 fish in a day, while Robin could produce only 10 fishing nets a day or catch 20 fish a day, who would you pick to begin making fishing nets first? Why?

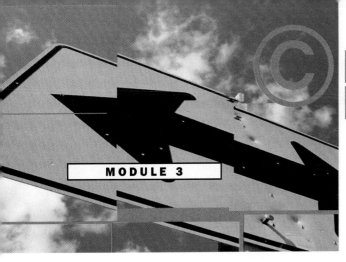

Production Decisions

MODULE 3

■ What goods and services will be produced?
■ What is a command economy?
■ What is decentralized decision making?
■ What is consumer sovereignty?

WHAT ECONOMIC QUESTIONS DO ALL SOCIETIES FACE?

Because of scarcity, certain economic questions must be answered regardless of the level of affluence of the society or its political structure. In the remainder of this Module, we will consider five fundamental questions that inevitably must be faced: (1) What and how much to produce? (2) How will we produce these goods and services? (3) Who will get the goods and services we produce? (4) How can we use our scarce resources efficiently? and (5) Will current sacrifices necessary for more rapid economic growth be worth the gains that growth will offer future generations? These questions are unavoidable in a world of scarcity.

What and How Much Should We Produce?

Because our wants exceed the amount of goods and services that can be produced from our limited resources, a decision must be made about which wants should have

How do we decide which colors and options to include with these cars?

priority over others. Should we produce lots of cars and few school buildings, or relatively few cars and more school buildings? Once we have decided how many cars to produce, we must also decide how many of them should be equipped with automatic rather than manual transmissions. How many should be painted red? Black? Forest green? How many should be sports cars, and how many should be four-wheel-drive sport utility vehicles? Because we have so many wants, answering these questions is not at all simple.

HOW DO DIFFERENT TYPES OF ECONOMIC SYSTEMS ANSWER THESE QUESTIONS?

Economies are organized in different ways to answer the question of what and how much to produce. The dispute over the best way to answer the what and how much to produce question has inflamed passions for centuries. Should decisions be made centrally by a planning board, as in North Korea, Cuba, or China? Sometimes these highly centralized economic systems are referred to as **command economies.** Under this type of regime, decisions about how many tractors or automobiles to produce are largely determined by a government official or committee associated with the central planning organization. That same group decides on the number and size of school buildings, refrigerators, shoes, and so on. Note that decisions are not made by "organizations" but rather by individuals within them, and the incentives those individuals face will impact their decisions regardless of the economic system.

Other countries, including the United States, much of Europe, and, increasingly, Asia and elsewhere, have largely adopted a decentralized decision-making process, with literally millions of individual producers and consumers of goods and services determining what goods, and how many of them, will be produced. A country that uses such a decentralized decision-making process to determine what is to be produced is often referred to as a **market economy.** Actually, no nation has a pure market economy. Most countries, including the United States, can

The degree of government involvement in the economy varies widely in different countries, but over the past 75 years in nearly all industrial countries, government involvement (shown here as the level of government spending) has expanded.

Entire courses in economics are devoted to the alternative methods of organizing economies to deal with scarcity (called *comparative economic systems*). The bulk of this book is taken up with the analysis of how such decisions are made in the mixed market economy. However, you should remember that the decision of what to produce inevitably must be made because of scarcity, regardless of whether that decision is centralized or decentralized, or whether the means of production is privately or publicly owned.

SOURCE: *The Economist*, September 20, 1997.

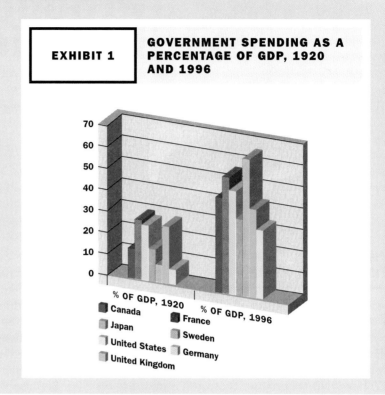

| EXHIBIT 1 | GOVERNMENT SPENDING AS A PERCENTAGE OF GDP, 1920 AND 1996 |

% OF GDP, 1920
% OF GDP, 1996

■ Canada
■ France
■ Japan
■ Sweden
■ United States
■ Germany
■ United Kingdom

be said to have **mixed economies.** In such economies, some production decisions are made centrally by the government, while other decisions are made in a decentralized fashion through the interaction of individual producers and purchasers who are sometimes combined, for reasons which will become clear later, into groups of individuals such as corporations, unions, foundations, and the like.

HOW ARE PRODUCTION DECISIONS MADE IN MARKET ECONOMIES?

You already know that individuals play a major role in the decision-making processes of market economies. But how do individuals control the production decisions in these economies? The answer is that people "vote" in economic affairs with their dollars (or pounds or francs). This concept is called **consumer sovereignty** (the consumer is "king"). Television, VCRs, cellular telephones, pagers, camcorders, and computers, for example, became part of our lives because consumers "voted" hundreds of dollars apiece on these goods. As they bought more color TVs, consumers "voted" fewer dollars on black-and-white TVs. Similarly, record albums gave way to tapes and CDs as consumers voted for these items with their dollars. Consumer sovereignty, then, explains how individual consumers in market economies determine what and how much is to be produced.

Who decided that consumers would use CDs rather than record players?

TUNE UP

DID THE MARKET FAIL?

Q: Adam was a college graduate with a double major in economics and art. A few years ago, Adam decided that he wanted to pursue a vocation that utilized both of his talents. In response, he shut himself up in his studio and created a watercolor collection, "Graphs of Famous Recessions." With high hopes, Adam put his collection on display for buyers. After several years of displaying his econ-art, however, the only one interested in the collection was his eight-year-old sister, who wanted the picture frames for her room. Recognizing that Adam was having trouble pursuing his chosen occupation, Adam's friend Karl told him that the market had failed. What do you think? Is Karl right?

A: No. Markets provide important signals, and the signal being sent in this situation is that Adam should look for some other means of support—something that society values. Remember the function of consumer sovereignty in the marketplace. Clearly, consumers were not voting for Adam's art.

"We feel he's either going to be an artist or an economist."

CONCEPT CHECK

1. Every economy has to decide what and how much to produce.
2. In a command economy the what and how much decision is largely determined by the government.
3. In a decentralized market economy millions of buyers and sellers determine what and how much to produce.

---

1. Why does scarcity force us to decide what to produce?
2. How is a command economy different from a market economy?
3. How does consumer sovereignty determine production decisions in a market economy?
4. Do you think that what and how much an economy produces depends on who will get the goods and services produced in that economy? Why or why not?
5. Why do consumers have to "vote" for a product with their dollars for it to be a success?

Production Methods

- How do we produce the goods and services we want?
- What is a capital-intensive production method?
- What is a labor-intensive production method?

HOW DO WE PRODUCE GOODS AND SERVICES?

All economies, regardless of their political structure, must decide how to produce the goods and services that they want—because of scarcity. Goods and services can generally be produced in several ways. For example, a ditch can be dug by many workers using their hands, by a few workers with shovels, or by one person with a backhoe. A decision must be made as to which method is most appropriate. The larger the quantity of the good and the more elaborate the form of capital (remember, goods like shov-

"LEROY HAS FOUND A GREAT LABOR-SAVING DEVICE... IT'S CALLED 'TOMORROW.'"

els or large earthmoving machines that enhance the production of other goods and services are called capital), the more labor that is saved and is thus made available for other uses. From the example, you might be tempted to conclude that it is desirable to use the biggest, most elaborate form of capital. But would you really want to plant your spring flowers with huge earthmoving machinery? The most capital-intensive method of production (that is, the method with a high capital-to-labor input ratio) may not always be the best. The best method is the least-cost method.

WHAT IS THE "BEST" FORM OF PRODUCTION?

The best or "optimal" form of production will usually vary from one economy to the next. For example, earthmoving machinery is used in digging large ditches in the United States and Europe, while in less-developed countries, such as India, China, or Pakistan, shovels are often used. Similarly, when a person in the United States cuts the grass, he or she may use his or her own labor and a power lawn mower, whereas in a poorer country, a hand mower would probably be used. In a still poorer country, grass might well be cut with an even simpler tool, such as a scythe, or it might not be cut at all. Why do these "optimal" forms of production vary so drastically? Compared to capital, labor is relatively cheap and plentiful in India but relatively scarce and expensive in the United States. In contrast, capital (machines and tools, mainly) is comparatively plentiful and cheap in the United States but scarcer and more costly in India. That is, in India, production would tend to be more **labor intensive,** or labor driven. In the United States, production would tend to be more **capital intensive,** or capital driven. Each nation tends to use the production processes that conserve its relatively scarce (and thus relatively more expensive) resources and use more of its relatively abundant resources.

LABOR-SAVING ANTI-THEFT DEVICES

LONDON, ENGLAND: Sainsbury's, one of the UK's big three supermarket chains, has started installing Checkpoint Systems' RF (radio frequency) anti-theft system on its high-value products. . . . Checkpoint's source tagging involves the insertion of a paper-thin RF label into products or packaging at the time of manufacture. This provides the retailer with items that require no further anti-theft tagging on the shop floor—so saving time and money, the company claims. It [the RF system] also, officials claim, offers an even greater deterrent to theft, as no one, not even staff, is aware of which products are tagged, or where the tag is hidden.

SOURCE: Newsbytes News Network: http://www.newsbytes.com. September 8, 1997. Copyright 1997, Newsbytes News Network

> **CONSIDER THIS:**
> This is an example of substituting labor-saving technology for expensive human monitoring. If the price is right, capital will be substituted for labor.

CONCEPT CHECK

1. The best form of production is the one that conserves the relative scarce resources and uses more of the abundant resource.
2. When capital is relatively scarce and labor plentiful, production tends to be labor intensive.
3. When capital is relatively abundant and labor relatively scarce, production tends to be capital intensive.

---

1. Why must we choose among multiple ways of producing the goods and services we want?
2. Why might production be labor intensive in one economy, but be capital intensive in another?
3. If a tourist from the United States notices on an overseas trip that other countries don't produce crops "like they do back home," would he be right to conclude that farmers in the other country produce crops less efficiently than U.S. farmers?
4. Why are the golf tee areas on driving ranges in Japan often multileveled, while they are usually on a single level in the United States?

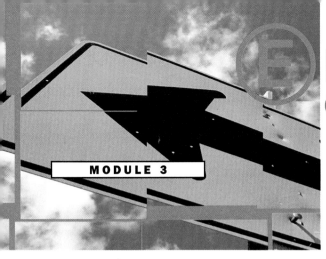

Distribution of Output

- Who gets the final goods and services?
- What is the relationship between scarce resources and income?

HOW ARE GOODS AND SERVICES DISTRIBUTED?

In every society, some mechanism must exist to determine how goods and services are to be distributed among the population. Who gets what? Why do some people get to consume or use far more goods and services than others? This question of distribution is so important that wars and revolutions have been fought over it. Both the French and Russian Revolutions were concerned fundamentally with the distribution of goods and services. Even in societies where political questions are usually settled peacefully, the question of the distribution of income is an issue that always arouses strong emotional responses. As we shall see, in a market economy, with private ownership and control of the means of production, the amount of output one is able to obtain depends on one's income, which depends on the quantity and quality of the scarce resources that the individual controls. For example, Tiger Woods makes a lot of money because he has unique and marketable skills as a golfer. This may or may not be viewed as "fair," an issue we shall look at in detail later in the book.

WHY DO BIG-NAME STARS MAKE $15–20 MILLION A FILM?

Some actors and actresses reap incredibly high salaries for their appearances in movies. Why? The reason that these actors and actresses are being paid such a large amount of money is because they control scarce resources—their talent and name recognition. In essence, what the studios are betting on is that the contribution of these stars to sales will more than offset the costs of their services. That is, they expect that by employing one of these actors or actresses, rather than a less-well-known actor or actress, they will reap greater profits. In addition, if others were not competing for their unique talents, stars would not be stars.

Why do Hollywood stars get paid so much for a film?

CONCEPT CHECK

1. In a market economy, the amount of output one is able to obtain depends on one's income.

2. The amount of one's income depends on the quantity and the quality of the scarce resources that the individual controls.

1. In a market economy, what determines "who gets what"?

2. In what way does scarcity determine income?

Efficiency in Production

MODULE 3

- What are unemployed resources?
- What are underemployed resources?
- What is efficiency?

ARE WE USING OUR RESOURCES EFFICIENTLY?

While the questions of deciding what, how, and for whom to produce are vital, they are not the only concerns that societies have. Most modern economies have resources that are idle, at least for some period of time. If those resources were *not* idle, people would have more scarce goods and services available for their use.

If those who, for whatever reason, are unable to employ their resources in the manner they wish, we have a serious problem. For example, consider the unemployed coal miner who is unable to find work at a "reasonable" wage, or those unemployed in depressed times when plants are

If this coal miner loses his job, will he be able to find work?

already operating below capacity. Clearly, the resources of these individuals are not being used efficiently.

WHAT ARE UNEMPLOYED AND UNDEREMPLOYED RESOURCES?

The fact that plants can operate below capacity suggests that it is not just labor resources that should be most effectively used. Rather, all resources entering into production must be used effectively. However, for several reasons, social concern focuses on labor. First, labor costs are the largest share of production costs. Also, **unemployed** or **underemployed laborers** (whose resources are not being used to their full potential) may have mouths to feed at home, while an unemployed machine does not (although the owner of the unemployed machine may). Finally, in terms of equity, most owners of nonlabor inputs, like capital and land, tend to be richer than those owning only their own labor. For all of these reasons, attention has focused on the unemployment of labor.

MATCHING RESOURCES TO BEST USE IS NOT ALWAYS EASY

The problem of matching resources, especially labor, with the many potentially valuable uses for them is a real problem in every society. Simplistic solutions to this problem abound. For example, a simple way to reduce unemployment would be to make it a criminal offense to be unemployed! Such a solution, however, would not relieve the underlying problem of attempting to match the resources available to the uses best suited to them. The problem of underutilized resources can be illustrated by the production possibilities curve introduced earlier. Consider Exhibit 1, which reproduces the production possibilities curve used earlier (p. 69). With resources fully employed, this economy could produce a variety of combinations of fishing nets and fish, including points C (30 fishing nets, 600 fish) and D (20 fishing nets, 800 fish).

EXHIBIT 1 | PRODUCTION POSSIBILITIES WITH UNEMPLOYED RESOURCES

WHY IS AN EFFICIENT USE OF RESOURCES IMPORTANT TO ME?

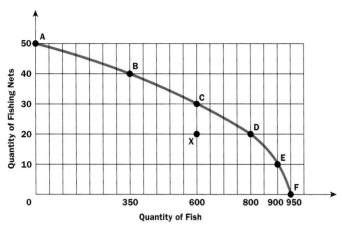

At point X, resources are unemployed or underemployed, so it is possible to increase both fish and fishing net production without incurring any opportunity costs.

Suppose some resources are unemployed or are not being put to their best uses. The economy would then be operating at a point, such as X, inside the production possibilities curve. At point X, 20 fishing nets and 600 fish are being produced. By putting unemployed resources to work or by putting already employed resources to better uses, we could expand the output of fishing nets by 10 (moving to point C) without giving up any fish. Alternatively, we could boost fish output by 200 fish (moving to point D) without reducing fishing net output. We could even get more of both fish and fishing nets moving to a point on the curve between C and D. Increasing or improving the utilization of resources, then, can lead to greater output of all goods. That is why economists, and you too, have an interest in the efficient use of all of society's resources: There can be more of everything we care about for all of us as a result. Thus, **efficiency** requires society to use its resources to the fullest extent—getting the most from our scarce resources.

CONCEPT CHECK

1. Unemployed and underemployed resources mean that the economy is not working to its full potential.
2. Operating inside the production possibilities curve is an inefficient use of society's resources.
3. Efficiency requires society to use its resources to the fullest extent.

1. Why are we concerned with unemployed or underemployed resources in a society?
2. What do we mean by efficiency, and how is it related to underemployment of resources?
3. How are efficiency and inefficiency illustrated with a production possibilities curve?
4. Will a country that makes being unemployed illegal be more productive than one that does not? Why or why not?
5. If a 68-year-old worker in the United States chooses not to work at all, does that mean that the United States is functioning inside its production possibilities curve? Why or why not?

Production and Growth

- How much should we sacrifice today to get more in the future?
- How do we show economic growth on the production possibilities curve?

HOW MUCH ARE WE WILLING TO GIVE UP TODAY TO GET MORE TOMORROW?

Another question facing all economies is the extent to which the current sacrifices necessary for more rapid economic growth will pay dividends in the future. Are the sacrifices you are making really worth it? These growth questions can be crucial to a country's well-being. How have some nations, such as Hong Kong, been able to rapidly expand their output of goods and services over time, while others, such as many African nations, have apparently been unable to increase their standards of living at all? What are the costs and benefits to society of more rapid, as opposed to slower, growth in output? What is the best, or "optimal," rate of growth?

GLOBAL WATCH

FIVE RICHEST AND FIVE POOREST NATIONS IN OUTPUT PER PERSON

The rate of economic growth differs among economies. If they could fast forward past the process of growth to the final result, most people would find faster growth to their liking. Few would prefer the real per-person output of $450 per year in Ethiopia to the $20,000 to $25,000 per person, per year available in countries as diverse as Switzerland and the United States.

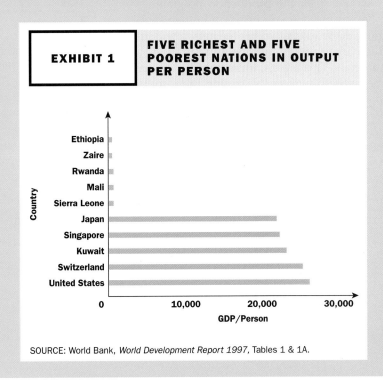

| EXHIBIT 1 | FIVE RICHEST AND FIVE POOREST NATIONS IN OUTPUT PER PERSON |

SOURCE: World Bank, *World Development Report 1997*, Tables 1 & 1A.

Clearly, the optimal rate of growth will vary depending on the resources available in the economy. The primary point is that, regardless of the rate, sacrifices must be made for growth to occur.

HOW DO SACRIFICES LEAD TO GROWTH?

Specifically, to generate economic growth, a society must produce fewer consumer goods—like video games, stereos, cars, and so on—in the present and produce more capital goods. They must, then, sacrifice some consumption of consumer goods in the present in order to experience growth in the future. Why? Investing in capital goods like computers, and other new technological equipment, as well as investing in **human capital** by upgrading skills and knowledge, will shift out the economy's production possibilities over time. This will increase the future production capacity of the economy. That is, the economy that invests more now (consumes less now) will be able to produce, and therefore consume, more in the future.

This idea can be clearly illustrated by using the production possibilities curve (Exhibit 2). In terms of the production possibilities curve, economic growth means an outward shift in the "menu" of possible bundles of output. With growth comes the possibility to have more of both goods than were previously available. Suppose we were producing at point C (30 nets, 600 fish) on our original production possibilities curve. Additional resources and new methods of using them (technological progress) can lead to new production possibilities creating the potential for more of all goods (or more of some with no less of others). These increases would push the production possibilities curve outward. For example, if you invest in human capital, such as training the workers making the nets, it will increase the productivity of those workers. As a result, they will produce more nets. This means, ultimately, that fewer resources will be used to make nets, freeing them to be used for catching fish—resulting in a greater number of fish. Notice that, at point Z on the new curve, it is possible to produce 35 fishing nets and 750 fish, more of both goods than were previously produced, at point C.

GROWTH DOESN'T ELIMINATE SCARCITY

With all of this discussion of growth, it is important to remember that growth, or increases in a society's output, does not make scarcity disappear. Even when output has grown more rapidly than population so that people are made better off, they still face trade-offs: At any point along the production possibilities curve, in order to get more of one thing, you must give up something else. There are no free lunches *on* the production possibilities curve.

EXHIBIT 2	ECONOMIC GROWTH AND PRODUCTION POSSIBILITIES

Economic growth shifts the production possibilities curve outward, allowing increased output of both fish and fishing nets (compare point Z with point C).

PRODUCTION POSSIBILITIES CURVE

Q: The production possibilities curve shown in Exhibit 3 illustrates the choices faced by an economy that makes military goods and consumer goods. How are the economic concepts of scarcity, choice, opportunity costs, efficiency, and economic growth illustrated in this production possibilities curve framework?

A: In Exhibit 3 we can show scarcity, because resource combinations outside the production possibilities curve, like point D, are unattainable without economic growth. If the economy is operating efficiently, we are somewhere on the production possibilities curve, like point B or point C. However, if the economy is operating inefficiently, we are operating inside the production possibilities curve, like point A. We can also see in this graph that to get more military goods you must give up consumer goods—that is, there is an opportunity cost. Finally, we see that over time, with economic growth, the whole production possibilities curve can shift outward.

| EXHIBIT 3 | PRODUCTION POSSIBILITIES CURVE |

CONCEPT CHECK

1. Economies must decide how much current consumption they are willing to sacrifice for greater growth in the future.
2. Economic growth is represented by an outward shift of the production possibilities curve.
3. Economic growth increases the possibility of producing more of all goods.
4. Despite economic growth, scarcity inevitably remains a fact of life.

---

1. What is the essential question behind issues of economic growth?
2. What is the connection between sacrifices and economic growth?
3. How is economic growth shown in terms of production possibilities curves?
4. Why doesn't economic growth eliminate scarcity?
5. What would happen to the production possibilities curve in an economy where a new innovation greatly increased its ability to catch fish but did not change its ability to make fishing nets?

Application: Tourism versus Ecosystems

Is it possible to have more goods and services and a cleaner environment? Consider that question as you read the article below.

Canada's main transcontinental railway and transcontinental highway roll side-by-side down the length of Banff's main valley. On the busiest weekends, the road is clotted with cars, RVs, and tour buses, and a brown haze of exhaust fumes veils the celebrated vistas. Within the park lie three ski resorts and the town of Banff—home to 7,000 permanent residents. On the typical summer day, the townies may see 25,000 tourists streaming through their streets.

One local businessman and town council member remarked, "Environmentalists love to talk gloom and doom—but all you have to do is drive five miles out of town and you're in the middle of miles and miles of nothing but nature. You get tired of looking at all these big bare mountains; what's wrong with putting a restaurant or a little chalet up there to make it nicer for the people who come here?"

One thing that is wrong with it, according to a biologist who has studied wildlife throughout the Rocky Mountains, is that the human presence in Banff is wreaking havoc on the area's fragile makeup. "I'd say the park is in very, very poor condition compared with what is was 10 years ago, 20 years ago, 30 years ago," declared the biologist. "There's been a major decline in most of our large predators—black bears, grizzlies, wolverines, lynx, cougars. Such species are one of our best indicators of overall ecological health, and the way things are going, most of these animals will not survive here."

SOURCE: Adapted from "Rocky Times in Banff," *National Geographic*, July 1995.

Can Banff have more tourism *and* a better environment?

The principal point of this article is that choices have costs. In order to totally preserve the ecosystem of Banff, it would mean fewer tourists and commercial ventures. In this case, society must make a value judgment. If Banff is overdeveloped what will be the cost to future generations who will not be able to appreciate the visual splendors of this special "hamlet" nestled in the Canadian Rockies? On the other hand, how can you possibly accommodate the growing numbers of daily visitors without building additional restaurants, motels, and so on? Society must choose. This is demonstrated in the production possibilities curve in Exhibit 1. Society can choose point A (high

EXHIBIT 1 | PRODUCTION POSSIBILITIES CURVE

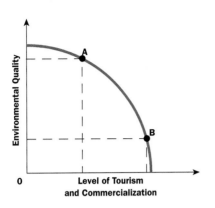

environmental quality but lower tourism *or* point B (more tourism and commercialization at the expense of the ecosystem), but society must choose. It involves a trade-off, and in this case Canada must choose between tourism and ecosystems.

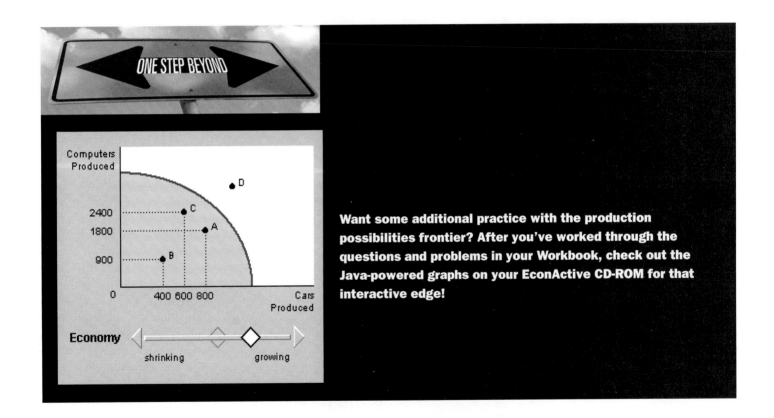

ONE STEP BEYOND

Want some additional practice with the production possibilities frontier? After you've worked through the questions and problems in your Workbook, check out the Java-powered graphs on your EconActive CD-ROM for that interactive edge!

Supply and Demand

A. Markets
What is a market?

B. Money and Relative Prices
Why are relative prices so important?

C. The Law of Demand
What is the difference between needs and wants?

D. The Demand Curve
Why is the demand curve negatively sloped?

E. Shifts in the Demand Curve
What are the major variables that determine the position
of the demand curve?

F. The Law of Supply
Why is the supply curve positively sloped?

G. Shifts in the Supply Curve
What are the major variables that determine the position
of the supply curve?

H. Application: A Shift in the Demand for Cuban Cigars
Which variables have impacted the demand curve for Cuban cigars?

Ⓐ Markets

- Is a market just a geographic location?
- What are transaction costs?
- Why is it so difficult to define a market?

Is this a market?

Is this a market?

WHAT IS A MARKET?

Although we usually think of a **market** as a place where some sort of exchange occurs, a market is not really a place at all. A market is "a set of rules or an arrangement for the negotiation of exchange between buyers and sellers." You can think of a market as any situation where buyers, sellers, and middlepersons are in sufficiently close contact with one another to carry on exchange under a set of rules or customs. This means that supermarkets, the New York Stock Exchange, drug stores, roadside stands, garage sales, and restaurants are all markets.

The roles of buyers and sellers are undoubtedly familiar to you, but what is a middleperson? A middleperson is an individual who brings buyers and sellers together. For example, a realtor is a middleperson who exchanges information between buyers and sellers in the real estate market. Middlepersons help to reduce the **transaction costs**—the costs of making exchanges or transactions in a market.

WHY IS IT SO HARD TO *PRECISELY* DEFINE A MARKET?

Every market is different. That is, the conditions under which the exchange between buyers and sellers takes place can vary. These differences make it hard to precisely

Is this a market?

Is this a market?

define a market. After all, an incredible variety of exchange arrangements exists in the real world—organized securities markets, wholesale auction markets, foreign exchange markets, real estate markets, labor markets, and so forth.

The problem of defining a market is further compounded by goods being priced and traded in various ways at various locations by various kinds of buyers and sellers. For some goods, such as concrete, markets are numerous and more or less geographically isolated. Because transportation costs are so high relative to selling prices that the good will not be shipped any substantial distance, buyers are usually in contact only with local producers. Price and output are thus determined in a number of small

markets. In other industries, markets are national or even global. Automobile manufacturers, for example, sell to dealers throughout the world and determine prices and output largely on the basis of considerations relating to the domestic and global economies. Despite their differences, however, all of these situations are illustrations of markets in action.

Markets are not even defined by any moment in time: Goods can trade across space and time. For example, there are futures markets where buyers and sellers can trade bales of cotton that do not even exist yet. The important point is not what a market looks like, but what it does—it facilitates trade.

CONCEPT CHECK

1. Markets consist of buyers, sellers, and middle-persons making exchanges with one another.
2. Transaction costs are the costs of making exchanges in a market.

3. Markets can be regional, national, or global.

1. What are transaction costs?
2. Why is it hard to precisely define a market?
3. Why do you get your produce at a supermarket rather than directly from farmers?

4. Why do the prices people pay for similar items at garage sales vary more than the prices they pay for similar items in a department store?

Money and Relative Prices

■ What is a money price?
■ What is a relative price?

WHAT IS A MONEY PRICE?

Over the past 50 years, few goods have fallen in **money price**—that is, the price that you or I would pay in dollars and cents. The money price is sometimes called the absolute or nominal price, expressed in dollars of current purchasing power. There have been a few well-known examples of falling money prices—personal calculators, cellular telephones, video recorders, home computers, and so on—but the evidence indicates that *most* prices have risen in money terms.

Does the money price of most goods fall?

LUNDBERG SURVEY SAYS GASOLINE PRICES HIT HISTORIC LOW IN 1998

According to a March 1998 survey, the average annual cost of gasoline to consumers in 1998 (in inflation-adjusted 1998 dollars) was the lowest since 1920, the beginning of recorded pump prices.

Prices have fallen despite rising taxes and more money spent to make environmentally cleaner gasoline by the oil industry. The reasons for the lower gasoline prices are: lower crude oil prices, improved technology in refining, distribution, and marketing, and most recently, the price wars among refiners and distributors.

The average retail price for all grades of gasoline was $1.09 per gallon in March of 1998. That's $1.18 less than it was in 1981, when pump prices reached an all-time high of $2.27 per gallon.

SOURCE: Cable News Network, Inc. (http://cnn.com/US/9803/08/briefs.pm/gas.prices/index.html), March 1998.

CONSIDER THIS:
Gasoline prices, when measured against the average price of all goods and services (that is, relative to the price of other goods and services), reached an all-time low in 1998, even though the money price of gasoline in the 1960s was far lower, at only 30 to 40 cents per gallon.

WHAT IS THE DIFFERENCE BETWEEN MONEY PRICES AND RELATIVE PRICES?

Money prices themselves are of little importance to most economic decisions in a world where virtually all prices are changing. It is **relative price,** the price of one good relative to others, that is crucial. If the price of movies rises relative to all other goods, we would predict that fewer people would go to the movies, *ceteris paribus.* They would look for alternative forms of entertainment, such as bowling, the video arcade, or watching television, or they might just go to the movies less frequently.

If the price of movies rises relative to other types of entertainment, will fewer people go to the movies?

T U N E   U P

TOOLING UP: RELATIVE PRICES

Q: Mary Witt-Chilldren, a former economics major, has a theory about couples who eat out at restaurants. Her theory is as follows: When compared with childless couples, couples with young children, when dining *without* their kids, are more likely to eat out at an expensive restaurant than at an inexpensive restaurant, *ceteris paribus.* Do you think Mary is on to something?

A: The key to this question is relative prices. Add a $20 babysitting charge to the cost of an inexpensive meal and to an expensive meal:

	Inexpensive Meal	Expensive Meal
Babysitting	$20	$ 20
Meal for two	20	80
Total	$40	$100

When couples with children go out to eat without their kids, will they be more likely to go to an expensive or inexpensive restaurant, *ceteris paribus?*

As you can see from the table, the babysitter's cost doubles the price of the inexpensive meal from $20 to $40, a 100 percent increase ($20/$20 = 100 percent). By comparison, the cost of a babysitter only increases the total price of the expensive meal from $80 to $100, a 25 percent increase ($20/$80 = 25 percent). Thus, for couples with children, the relative price of an expensive meal as compared to that of an inexpensive meal is lower. So for those couples with small children, we would predict a greater proportion of dinners out to be at expensive restaurants, *ceteris paribus.*

CONCEPT CHECK

1. The money price is what one pays in terms of dollars and cents.
2. The relative price is the price of one good relative to another.
3. Over time, money prices have risen for most goods.

---

1. How are money prices and relative prices different?
2. Why are economists so concerned about relative prices?
3. The money price of most goods has risen over time. What does that mean?
4. If Motel 6 began by charging $6 per night for a room but now charges $36 per night, what would have to be true for the relative price of its motel rooms to have fallen in that period?

The Law of Demand

- What is the law of demand?
- Why do we say demand reflects willingness to pay?
- What is the difference between *needs* and *wants?*

WHAT IS THE LAW OF DEMAND?

Some laws are made to protect us, like "no speeding" or "no driving after drinking," while other laws are "natural" laws that are observed as behavior in various physical and social settings. One such natural law is the **law of demand,** which relates the price of a good to the quantity of that good demanded. According to the law of demand, the quantity of a good or service demanded varies inversely with its price, *ceteris paribus.* More directly, the law of demand says that, other things being equal, when the price (P) of a good or service falls, the quantity demanded (Q_d) increases, and conversely, if the price of a good or service rises, the quantity demanded decreases.

$$P \uparrow \Rightarrow Q_d \downarrow \quad \text{and} \quad P \downarrow \Rightarrow Q_d \uparrow$$

In the law of demand, price represents the sacrifice that a buyer must make in order to obtain a good. If obtaining a good required greater sacrifice than before, would you want as much of it? The relationship described by the law of demand is an **inverse,** or **negative, relationship,** because the variables move in opposite directions.

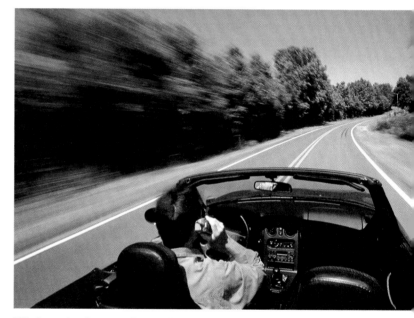

What can be done to alter reckless driving behavior?

DOES THE LAW OF DEMAND MAKE SENSE?

Stop reading for a second and try to think of a contradiction to the law of demand. Can you think of an item for which you would rather pay more than less? Have you ever heard anyone on a television or radio advertisement boasting that they have the highest prices in town? Just imagine the owner of a car dealership saying: "If you can find prices higher anywhere, bring in the receipt and we will match it. We won't be beat!"

If you had any product for sale and could not sell it, would you raise the price or lower it? You get the point. If you raise the price, you will sell less, *ceteris paribus* (that is, holding other variables such as income and taste constant). If you lower the price, you will sell more, holding everything else constant. Or if the opportunity cost of robbing a bank rises for any reason—say, because of a greater probability of being caught, of being convicted, or of receiving a stiffer sentence—we would expect fewer robberies. This is the law of demand, too, because we expect less of certain activities if the costs or prices of those activities rise.

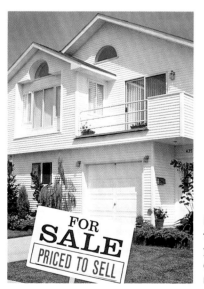

If your house had been on the market for a year and you could not sell it at the current price, would you raise the price or lower it?

WILL A CHANGE IN THE PRICE (OR COST) CHANGE DRIVING BEHAVIOR?

Malibu Canyon is a winding, two-lane road, where one driver can legally pass another in only a few places. What would we expect most drivers to do if the local judge declared that anyone crossing the solid, double-yellow lines would have to pay a $10,000 fine? Or what if the fatality statistics for the year were posted at the entrance of the canyon? Would this alter some drivers' "desire" to speed?

At some price, even the thrill-seekers would slow down, and each of the above circumstances should reduce the demand for speed (so, incidentally, would bad brakes, bald tires, and poor visibility). On the other hand, compulsory seat belts and airbags (side, front, and back) might cause drivers to drive faster. That is, making the car safer (or less safe) changes the ultimate cost to the driver and may alter his or her risk behavior.

IS DEMAND A WILLINGNESS TO PAY?

Demand is more than an imaginary desirability notion. For example, if you were to say, "I really would like a new Porsche," this statement, to be a true demand, must imply a willingness to pay for the Porsche. In every instance, one must be willing to give up other goods or services in order to get a desired good. For example, say you go to Tower Records and state that, at $15, you want one Smashing Pumpkins compact disc. The money measure here is merely a convenience. What you are really saying is that you are willing to give up $15 of anything else you might have purchased to get the CD. The concept of demand, then, really involves comparing goods with goods, not goods with money. It represents a willingness to pay (give up other goods) to get additional amounts of the good under consideration.

WHY IS THERE A NEGATIVE RELATIONSHIP BETWEEN PRICE AND QUANTITY DEMANDED?

As we mentioned earlier, the law of demand describes a negative relationship between price and quantity demanded. When price goes up, the quantity demanded goes down, and vice versa. But why is this so? The primary reason for this inverse relationship is the **substitution effect**. At higher prices, buyers increasingly substitute other goods for the good that now has a higher relative price. For example, if the price of orange juice increases, some consumers may substitute out of orange juice into other juices, such as apple or tomato juice, or perhaps water, milk, or coffee. This is what economists call the substitution effect of a price change. Of course, if the relative price of orange juice fell, then consumers would substitute out of other products and increase their quantity of orange juice demanded, because the lower relative price now makes it a more attractive purchase. The

primary reason for the inverse relationship between price and quantity demanded is the substitution effect.

WHAT IS THE DIFFERENCE BETWEEN *NEEDS* AND *WANTS?*

The law of demand puts the concept of basic human "needs," at least as an analytical tool, to rest. **Needs** are those things that you must have at any price. That is, there are no substitutes. There are usually plenty of substitutes for any good available, some better than others. The law of demand, with its inverse relationship between price and quantity demanded, implies that even so-called needs are more or less urgent, depending on the circumstances (opportunity costs). Whenever you hear somebody say, "I need a new car," "I need a new stereo," or "I need new clothes," always be sure to ask: What does the person really mean? At what price does that person "need" the good?

Do you *need* a new stereo or do you *want* a new stereo at the current price? Would you still "need" a new stereo if a new one cost $15,000?

For example, the person who claims that he or she needs a new car must sacrifice the items that could have been purchased if he or she did not purchase the car—perhaps jet skis, a stereo, clothes, and so on. In addition, there are many substitutes for cars, including motorcycles, buses, car pools, hitchhiking, or moving closer to work. In Module 1, we discussed the rule of rational choice, which must be applied here: Do the expected marginal benefits from purchasing a new car exceed the expected marginal costs? That is the relevant question. To answer that question wisely, we must realize that there are substitutes for just about everything and that decisions require choices, which always imply costs. Hence, we must weigh the benefits against the costs even for so-called needs.

GOODYEAR BEGINS SEARCH FOR HIGHWAY HEROES

Akron, OH—Each year, nominations for the Goodyear National Highway Hero roll in from motorists, fellow truck drivers, law enforcement officials, and trucking company representatives across the country. Previous years' nominees have demonstrated a wide range of heroics— from a driver who snatched a child out of a swirling tornado's path to a driver who posts pictures of missing children on the sides of his rig.

SOURCE: PR Newswire and The Goodyear Tire & Rubber Company, September 8, 1997.

CONSIDER THIS:
Some people will help others even when the costs are high. The truck driver who pulled the child out of the way of the swirling tornado wanted to save a stranger's life even when the cost to him, the possibility that he might lose his own life, was high. Since most people wouldn't risk their own life to save a stranger's, it demonstrates that benefits and costs are subjective.

Why would a truck driver risk his own life to pull an endangered child from the path of a tornado? Given the alternative, the death of a child, he was willing to risk his own life.

DO WE *NEED* MORE FREEWAYS?

Commuters are constantly complaining about how long it takes to drive to work. Do we *need* more freeways?

Perhaps many commuters would like to see more taxpayer dollars going toward freeways instead of museums, schools, or parks. Remember, the concept of need implies some type of urgency and conveys the message: "I will give up anything to get it." The real question is: At what price do we want more freeways? Would we need more freeways if the price of downtown parking was $1,000 a day? Probably not. Try to train yourself to think that we want different amounts of goods and services at different opportunity costs, and that costs are more than just dollars and cents. For example, a person who normally does not speed while driving may do so if the relevant benefit of speed rises—for example, if he is late for his final exam or wedding, or if she is on her way to the hospital to deliver her baby.

SHOULD THERE BE EXPRESS LANES FOR URGENT NEEDS AT THE SUPERMARKET?

Occasionally, we encounter huge lines at all the open check-out counters in our local supermarkets. Perhaps we should have an express lane for people who have urgent needs. What do you think of this idea?

This idea would probably fail because a lot of people would develop what they felt were urgent needs if the "urgent need" line was much shorter than the other lines. It would be inevitable that the system would fall apart. In fact, it would be fun to guess what might be defined as an urgent need. It might include: "I am really in a hurry because I have to get home to clean up my apartment" or "I need to get back to the dorm to type my overdue term paper." Many people would perceive their needs as more urgent than other people's urgent needs. This is a reason that the concept of needs falls apart as a means of explaining behavior. It is impossible to make the concept of need useful when it is so hard to define or compare among people.

Would we "need" new freeways if parking was $1,000 a day?

WHAT DO WE NEED? DOES IT DEPEND ON WHAT WE HAVE TO GIVE UP?

Water, air, and food are all items necessary to keep us alive. However, in the extreme, we may not even need these items. Imagine a hypothetical situation in which your car breaks down in the middle of the desert and there is no one within 100 miles. No one knows where you are. You and your eight-year-old daughter have no food or water, and you don't own a cellular telephone. Your only option is walking to find help. After 50 miles, you come across one bottle of water—enough for one of you to survive. You need water, but do you need water at the cost of your daughter's life? Perhaps you do not even "need" your life if you have to give up something more valuable to you— your daughter's life. While this is an extreme example, it emphasizes the point that a need implies *at any cost* and also illustrates that costs and benefits vary with different individuals and situations.

Similarly, most would not consider taking the life of another, but under certain circumstances—self-defense in a life or death situation, war, or even disconnecting the life-support system of a terminally ill loved one—some might. While any of these circumstances may alter the decisions of some individuals, they may not have impact on others. Costs and benefits are subjective.

Need water?

CONCEPT CHECK

1. The law of demand states that when the price of a good falls (rises), the quantity demanded rises (falls), *ceteris paribus*.
2. Demand is a willingness to pay for what you want.
3. The term *needs* implies that there are no substitutes.
4. Because there are substitutes for most goods, economists use the term *wants* rather than *needs*.

---

1. What is an inverse, or negative, relationship?
2. How do lower prices change buyers' incentives?
3. How do higher prices change buyers' incentives?
4. How does demand represent willingness to pay?
5. Why do economists prefer talking about wants and desires rather than needs?
6. If even a minor cheating infraction was punished by expulsion, what would happen to the extent of cheating on campus?
7. Assume that we "need" water, food, clothing, and shelter to survive. Why is talking about these as needs not very helpful in analyzing choices that must be made among them?

The Demand Curve

- What is an individual demand schedule?
- What is an individual demand curve?
- What is a market demand schedule?
- What is a market demand curve?

WHAT IS AN INDIVIDUAL DEMAND SCHEDULE?

The **individual demand schedule** of an individual buyer for a product reveals the different amounts of that product the person would be willing to buy at various possible prices in a particular time interval. For example, Bob, a college student, enjoys drinking coffee. How many pounds of coffee will Bob be willing to buy at various prices during the year? At a price of $3 a pound, Bob buys 15 pounds of coffee over the course of a year. If the price is higher, at $4 per pound, he might only buy 10 pounds; if it is lower, say $1 per pound, he might buy 25 pounds of coffee during the year. Bob's demand for coffee for the year is summarized in the demand schedule in Exhibit 1. Bob might not be consciously aware of the amounts that he would purchase at prices other than the prevailing one. But that does not alter the fact that he has a schedule, in the sense that he would have bought various other amounts had other prices prevailed. It must be emphasized that the schedule is a list of alternative possibilities. At any one time, only one of the prices will prevail, and thus a certain quantity will be purchased.

WHAT IS AN INDIVIDUAL DEMAND CURVE?

By plotting the different prices and corresponding quantities demanded from Bob's demand schedule in Exhibit 1 and then connecting them, we can create an **individual demand curve** for Bob (Exhibit 2). From the curve, we can see that when the price is higher, Bob demands fewer pounds of coffee, and when the price is lower, he demands more pounds of coffee. The curve is merely an aid for understanding, summarizing compactly the information in the demand schedule. For any price, the curve reveals the quantity of coffee Bob would purchase.

EXHIBIT 2	BOB'S DEMAND CURVE FOR COFFEE

The dots represent various quantities of coffee that Bob would be willing to buy at different prices in a given time period. The demand curve is formed by connecting the dots representing these price–quantity demanded pairs.

EXHIBIT 1	BOB'S DEMAND SCHEDULE FOR COFFEE

Price (per pound)	Quantity Demanded (pounds per year)
$5	5
4	10
3	15
2	20
1	25

IS THERE A DEMAND CURVE FOR ROADKILL?

SARA CORBETT

"**Y**ou can pan-fry it, grill it, or put it in chili," reports Elizabeth Hatch of West Danville, Vermont. "And it makes the best lasagne you ever ate." At the Elks Lodge in Montpelier, chef Norm Champagne prepares it *au poivre*, deglazing the pan with brandy. "Folks who think it's weird don't bother to come around," he says.

Clear your plate for a helping of roadkill. Partly in response to a shorter moose-hunting season, Vermonters have found a way to get their fill of the knob-kneed beast: Follow the squealing tires. Under a program sanctioned by the state, a game warden will be dispatched any time a moose is reported killed

by a passing vehicle. The carcass is winched onto a truck, driven to a butcher, and packaged into five-pound parcels. The meat then makes its way to dining room tables, according to a lengthy waiting list. The price per pound: $1.25. "It's the only way to get the stuff anymore," says game warden Evan Eastman. Regarding splattered moose's effect on the palate, opinions vary. "A leaner rendering of beef," says one fan. "A less stringy version of horse meat," claims another. A more reluctant connoisseur puts it this way: "Needs garlic."

SOURCE: *Outside*, June 1995, p. 32.

WHAT IS A MARKET DEMAND CURVE?

Although we introduced this concept in terms of the individual, economists usually speak of the demand curve in terms of large groups of people—a whole nation, a community, or a trading area. As you know, every single individual has his or her demand curve for every product. The horizontal summing of the demand curves of many individuals is called the **market demand curve.**

Suppose the consumer group is comprised of Homer, Marge, and the rest of their small community, Springfield,

and that the product is still coffee. The effect of price on the quantity of coffee demanded by Marge, Homer, and the rest of Springfield is given in the demand schedule and demand curves shown in Exhibit 3. Homer would be willing to buy 20 pounds of coffee per year at a price of $4 per pound, and 25 pounds per year at $3 per pound. Marge would be willing to buy 10 pounds per year at $4, and 15 pounds per year at $3. The rest of Springfield would be willing to buy 2,970 pounds at $4, and 4,960 pounds at $3. The market demand curve is simply the (horizontal) sum of the quantities Homer, Marge, and the rest of Springfield

---

EXHIBIT 3	**CHEATING A MARKET DEMAND CURVE**

a. Creating a Market Demand Schedule for Coffee

Quantity Demanded (pounds per year)

Price (per pound)	Homer	+	Marge	+	Rest of Springfield	=	Market Demand
$4	20	+	10	+	2,970	=	3,000
$3	25	+	15	+	4,960	=	5,000

b. Creating a Market Demand Curve for Coffee

demand at each price. That is, at $4, the quantity demanded in the market would be 3,000 pounds of coffee (20 + 10 + 2,970 = 3,000), and at $3, the quantity demanded in the market would be 5,000 pounds of coffee (25 + 15 + 4,960 = 5,000).

In Exhibit 4, we offer a more complete set of prices and quantities from the market demand for coffee during the year. Remember, the market demand curve shows the amounts that all the buyers in the market would be willing to buy at various prices. For example, if the price of coffee is $2 per pound, consumers in the market would collectively be willing to buy 8,000 pounds per week. At $1 per pound, the amount demanded would be 12,000 pounds per week.

DON'T FORGET ABOUT RELATIVE PRICES!

Suppose you were exploring the inflation that prevailed in the United States during the 1960s and 1970s. You found that from 1960 to 1973, the price of gasoline at the pump rose markedly, but the quantities of gasoline demanded did not fall. Is this a flaw in the law of demand?

No. While it is true that gasoline prices in dollars rose significantly over this period, so did just about everything else—including wages. As it turns out, the relative price of gasoline, the price of gasoline as compared to that of other goods, did not change much over this period. Thus, we would not expect this to cause a fall in the quantity demanded (holding other things constant, especially income). That is, because the *relative* price did not rise, we would not expect a fall in gasoline consumption as a result.

EXHIBIT 4 — A MARKET DEMAND CURVE

a. Market Demand Schedule for Coffee

Price (per pound)	Total Quantity Demanded (pounds per year)
$5	1,000
4	3,000
3	5,000
2	8,000
1	12,000

b. Market Demand Curve for Coffee

CONCEPT CHECK

1. An individual demand curve is a graphical representation of the different amounts of a good a person would be willing to buy at various prices.

2. The market demand curve shows the amount of a good that all the buyers in the market would be willing to buy at various prices.

1. What is an individual demand schedule?
2. What difference is there between an individual demand curve and a market demand curve?

3. Why does the amount of dating on campus tend to decline just before and during final exams?

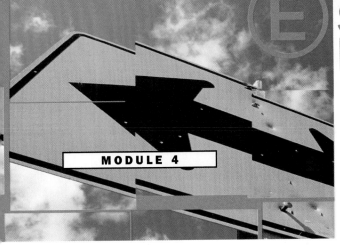

Shifts in the Demand Curve

- What is the difference between a change in demand and a change in quantity demanded?
- What are substitutes and complements?
- What are normal and inferior goods?
- How does the number of buyers affect the demand curve?
- How do changes in taste affect the demand curve?
- How do changing expectations affect the demand curve?

WHAT IS THE DIFFERENCE BETWEEN A CHANGE IN DEMAND AND A CHANGE IN QUANTITY DEMANDED?

Economists think consumers are influenced by the prices of goods when they make their purchasing decisions. At lower prices, people prefer to buy more of a good than at higher prices, holding other factors constant. Why? Primarily, it is because goods are substitutes in various degrees for one another. A rise in the price of one good results in less of it, and more of other now relatively more attractive alternative goods, being bought. For example, an increase in the price of coffee might tempt some buyers to switch from buying coffee to buying tea or soft drinks. Understanding this relationship between price and how much consumers are willing to purchase is so important that economists make a clear distinction between it and the various other factors that can influence consumer behavior. A change in a good's own-price is said to lead to a **change in quantity demanded.** That is, it "moves you along" a given demand curve. In contrast, a change in one of the other five factors that can influence consumer behavior—the prices of closely related goods, the incomes of demanders, number of demanders, tastes of demanders, and expectations of demanders—is said to lead to a **change in demand.** That is, a change in one of these factors shifts the entire demand curve. An increase in demand shifts the demand curve to the right; a decrease in demand shifts the demand curve to the left, as seen in Exhibit 1.

Remember that the law of demand expresses a relationship that is expected to hold when the *ceteris paribus* assumptions are met. If all these other factors are held constant, quantity demanded varies inversely with price (that is, if the price rises, the quantity demanded falls, and if the price falls, the quantity demanded rises). The *ceteris paribus* assumption allows us to isolate the effect of the price of a good on the quantity of that good that is demanded from other possible determinants. While this distinction may seem confusing to you at first, it will become clearer as we discuss in greater detail the five variables that lead to a change in demand.

EXHIBIT 1   DEMAND SHIFTS

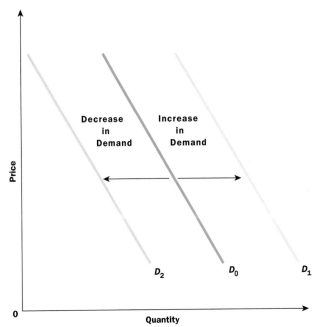

An increase in demand shifts the demand curve to the right. A decrease in demand shifts the demand curve to the left.

WHAT IS PYNTE?

The variables that shift the demand curve can be recalled using a memory device: PYNTE (the Old English spelling of *pint*). PYNTE stands for: P, prices of closely related goods; Y, incomes of demanders; N, number of demanders; T, tastes of demanders; and E, expectations of demanders. All of these variables are capable of shifting the demand curve to the right or left. We will now look more closely at each of these variables.

THE PRICES OF OTHER CLOSELY RELATED GOODS (*P*)

Each good and service has its own-price. But what does **own-price** mean? If Coca Cola sells a two-liter plastic bottle for $1, then $1 is said to be the own-price. Own-price,

The price of the item in question is its own-price.

then, is just the price of the item or service in question. Consumers are influenced by the own-price of a good or service in deciding how much of that good or service they want to buy. That relationship is summarized in the law of demand. However, consumers are also influenced by the prices of other goods and services—substitute goods and complementary goods.

Substitute Goods

Suppose you go into a store to buy RC Cola and you observe that Pepsi is on sale for half its usual price. Is it possible that you might decide to buy Pepsi instead of RC Cola? Economists argue that this is the case, and empirical tests have confirmed that persons are responsive to both own-prices and the prices of other goods. Note that, in this example, Pepsi is said to be a substitute for RC Cola. We can call it a **substitute good.** Generally speaking, the closer one good is as a substitute for a second good, the greater the impact that a change in the price of the first good will have on the willingness of consumers to buy the second. Thus, if the price of paper towels goes up, the impact on my decision to purchase RC Cola is likely to be negligible because my demand for cola is probably not closely related to how many paper towels I use. A fall in the price of a substitute good will, other things being equal, reduce demand for the good in question (a leftward shift); conversely, an increase in the price of a substitute will increase demand for the good in question (a rightward shift). If the price of apples rises, you are more likely to demand more oranges at the prevailing price for oranges, assuming you view these goods as substitutes. You should remember, however, that what are substitute goods for one person may not be so for another person, because personal tastes differ.

Good and Poor Substitutes

There are good substitutes and poor substitutes. For most people, good substitutes include butter and margarine, and Coca-Cola and Pepsi. Poor substitutes might include

CAN A WIENER BECOME A POORER SUBSTITUTE FOR HAMBURGER?

Ashland, OR—The Oscar Mayer "Wienermobile" has been dogged along its cross-country tour this summer by a protesting pig—or rather a protester in a pig get-up—courtesy of the animal rights group People for the Ethical Treatment of Animals (PETA).

"Kids would lose their lunch if they knew what actually went into a wiener," says PETA President Ingrid Newkirk.

SOURCE: "Animal Activists Get Violent," *The Christian Science Monitor*, August 29, 1997.

CONSIDER THIS:
If many parents and their kids were influenced dramatically by this message from PETA, hot dogs would no longer be considered a close substitute for hamburgers by those families. As a result, we would predict that many would no longer increase their demand for hot dogs in response to an increase in the price of hamburgers.

If hot dogs and hamburgers are substitutes, what would happen to the demand for hot dogs if the price of hamburgers increased?

SUBSTITUTE GOODS

Q: Suppose that you and your roommate are each partial to your own brand of soft drink. However, when the price of your brand, Sprite, increases, you decide to give your roommate's brand, 7-Up, a try. What would we call these two goods? Can you describe the change you would expect to see in the demand curve for 7-Up as the price for your soda, Sprite, increases?

A: If the price of one good increases and, as a result, an individual buys more of another good, the two related goods are substitutes. That is, buying more of one reduces purchases of the other. In Exhibit 2(a), we see that as the price of Sprite increased—a movement up along your demand curve for it—you increased your demand for 7-Up, resulting in a shift in the demand for 7-Up (Exhibit 2(b)). However, if you hated your roommate's brand of soft drink, then it might not matter if she were giving it away, but that is highly unlikely. The substitution effect varies among individuals, but in the aggregate, we can recognize substitutes fairly well. For example, if the price of gasoline increased significantly relative to other goods, we would predict that more people would car pool, buy cars that were more fuel efficient, use mass transit more often, shop less frequently, and so on, because each of these is a substitute for gasoline for some people.

EXHIBIT 2

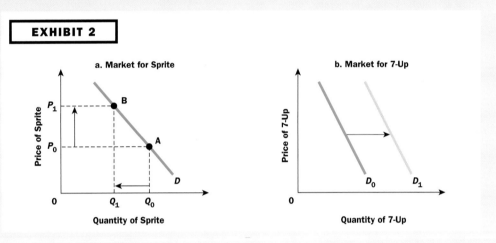

a. Market for Sprite

b. Market for 7-Up

economic textbooks and T-shirts, or hammers and shoes. Between these extremes, the quality of substitutes may be less clear. Consider, for example, children and pets. If the cost of raising children rises relative to other things, what will happen to the demand for pets? For some people—those who see a pet as an adequate substitute for a child—it would increase (shift to the right). These are a few examples of good and bad substitutes, keeping in mind that the degree of substitutability varies with different individuals.

Complementary Goods

Economists recognize that individuals are influenced not only by the prices of substitute goods but also by the prices of **complementary goods.** Complementary goods are things that "go together," often consumed and used simultaneously, such as skis and bindings, or hot dogs and mustard. For example, if the price of motorcycles rises sharply, other things equal, the demand for the complementary motorcycle helmets will fall. Why is this? As the price of motorcycles rises, *ceteris paribus,* fewer motorcycles are sold (a change in the quantity of motorcycles demanded, not in motorcycle demand!). Thus, people will also demand fewer motorcycle helmets at prevailing prices (a

change in demand for motorcycle helmets, not in quantity demanded!). Likewise, a decrease in the price of stereo equipment probably will lead to an increase in the demand (a rightward shift) for compact discs and tapes, because falling stereo prices should, other things equal, lead to greater sales of stereo equipment (an increase in quantity demanded) and an increase in demand for

"Come on. If you sell beer, you must sell peanuts."

COMPLEMENTARY GOODS

Q: As he looked over the rackets hanging on the wall of the local sports shop, Clay Kort, an aspiring young tennis player, noticed that the price of the rackets was much higher (due to cost increases) than last month. Clay predicted that this increase in the relative price of tennis rackets would probably lead to a reduced demand for tennis balls. Do you agree with Clay?

A: Clay realized that there would be fewer tennis players on the courts if tennis rackets increased in price. In Exhibit 3(a) we see that as the price of tennis rackets increases, the quantity of tennis rackets demanded falls. And with fewer tennis rackets being purchased, we would also expect people to decrease their demand (a leftward shift) for tennis balls (Exhibit 3(b)). There are many other athletic equipment examples of complements: skis and bindings, golf clubs and golf balls, bows and arrows, and so on.

EXHIBIT 3

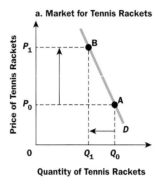

a. Market for Tennis Rackets

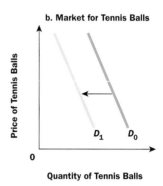

b. Market for Tennis Balls

complements like compact discs and tapes that are played on the stereo equipment. To summarize: An increase in the price of a complementary good will reduce demand for the product in question; a decrease in the price of a complementary good will increase demand for the product in question.

If the price of motorcycles rises, what do you think will happen to motorcycle helmet demand, *ceteris paribus?*

THE INCOME OF THE CONSUMER (*Y*)

Economists have observed that the consumption of goods and services is generally positively related to the income available to consumers. (Note: Economists often use the symbol Y to denote *income* because, in the discussion of macroeconomics, the letter I is used to denote *investment*.) Empirical studies support the notion that as individuals receive more income they tend to increase their purchases of most goods and services. For example, at your present level of income, the quantity of Porsche or Mercedes-Benz cars you demand at prevailing prices is probably zero. You tell yourself that you cannot afford such a luxury car. The opportunity cost is too great. If you were to buy a new Porsche, you simply could not live in the quality of housing that you deem appropriate, you could not obtain the amount of other consumer goods that you would like, and you would be forced to drastically curtail your travel below your usual levels.

On the other hand, if your income were to suddenly increase substantially (say, for instance, you won your state Lotto), then the opportunity cost of that new Porsche might not seem that prohibitive any longer. Remember, the price of the Porsche is still equal to the goods that you have to give up to buy it. However, you are now richer and you can buy more of all goods and services than before the

NORMAL AND INFERIOR GOODS

Q: Chester Drawer owns a furniture shop. With the recent boom in the economy (higher average income per person and fewer people unemployed), can Chester expect to sell more furniture?

A: Yes. In general, furniture is considered a normal good, so a rise in income will increase the demand for furniture (Exhibit 4(a)). However, if Chester sells unfinished, used, or lower-quality furniture, the demand for his products may fall, as higher incomes allow customers to buy furniture that is finished, new, or is of higher quality. Chester's furniture would then be an inferior good (Exhibit 4(b)).

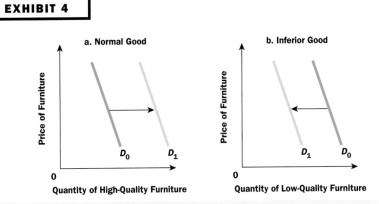

EXHIBIT 4

a. Normal Good

Price of Furniture

D_0 D_1

0

Quantity of High-Quality Furniture

b. Inferior Good

Price of Furniture

D_1 D_0

0

Quantity of Low-Quality Furniture

Lotto drawing. Thus, the cost of the car to you, in terms of the value to you of other items foregone, is now less than before, increasing the likelihood that you will buy it. Other things held equal, rising income usually leads to an increase in the demand for goods (a shift of the demand curve to the right), and decreasing income usually leads to a decrease in the demand for goods (a shift of the demand curve to the left).

Normal and Inferior Goods

Where higher incomes lead to a greater demand for the good, the good is called a **normal good.** However, there are some goods for which rising income leads to reduced demand. These are called **inferior goods.** For example, inferior goods for most people might include do-it-yourself haircuts, used cars, clothes from thrift shops, mail-order dentures, mini-mart burritos, store-brand products, and so on. Suppose most individuals prefer steak to hamburger, but usually buy hamburger because it is cheaper. Hamburger, then, is considered to be inferior to steak. As incomes rise, many persons may switch from buying hamburger to buying steak. Thus, the demand for hamburger may actually fall as incomes rise over this range. However, the concept of inferior versus normal goods differs among groups. Hamburger may be an inferior good in some countries, but not in others. In poorer countries where hamburger is still something of a luxury food, increased incomes may lead to greater demand for ham-

If people consume fewer fast-food meals when they become wealthier, what kind of good is a fast-food meal?

burger (and perhaps less demand for beans or rice). Whether goods are normal or inferior, the point here is that increasing income influences demand—usually positively, but sometimes negatively.

NUMBER OF BUYERS (N)

The demand for a good or service will vary with the size of the potential consumer population. The demand for wheat, for example, rises as population increases, because the added population wants to consume some wheat-derived products, like bread or cereal. Marketing experts, who closely follow the patterns of consumer behavior with regards to a particular good or service, are usually vitally concerned with the "demographics" of the product—the vital statistics of the potential consumer population, including size, income, and age characteristics. For example, market researchers for baby food companies keep a close watch on the birth rate.

TASTE CHANGES (T)

The demand for a good or service may increase or decrease suddenly with changes in fashions or fads. These non-price, non-income-related causes of changes in demand are said to be due to "taste changes." These taste changes may be triggered by advertising or promotion, by a news story, by the behavior of some popular public figure, and so on. One area in which taste changes are noticeable is in apparel. Shirt lapels, coat lapels, and ties change frequently. Recently, we have seen a resurgence in miniskirts as "the thing" to wear. But overall, in the last 10 years, skirts of all types suffered a decline in demand, as women began wearing pants in unprecedented numbers. Casual clothes in general have grown in popularity for both men and women.

Changes in preferences naturally lead to shifts in demand. Much of the predictive power of economic theory, however, stems from the assumption that tastes are relatively stable, at least over a substantial period of time. Tastes *do* change, though. A person may grow tired of one type of recreation or peanut butter and try another type. Changes in occupation, number of dependents, state of health, and age also tend to alter preferences. The birth of a baby may cause a family to spend less on recreation and more on food and clothing. Illness increases the demand for medicine and lessens purchases of other goods. A cold winter increases the demand for fuel. Changes in customs and traditions also affect preferences, and the development of new products draws consumer preferences away from other goods. Compact discs have replaced record albums, just as inline skates have replaced traditional roller skates.

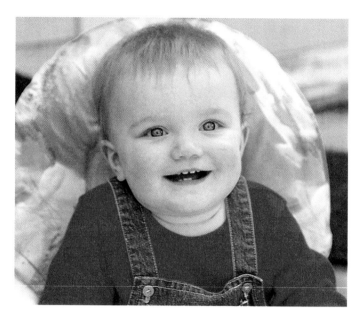

What happens to the demand for baby products when birth rates increase?

EXPECTATIONS ABOUT THE FUTURE (E)

Sometimes the demand for a good or service in a given time period will dramatically increase or decrease because consumers expect the good to change in price or availability at some future date. When the Korean War broke out in the summer of 1950, car sales boomed because consumers were fearful that automobile production would be stopped, just as it had a few years earlier at the beginning of World War II. Individuals moved up the date of their new car purchases to avoid not being able to get one for several years.

TUNE UP

EXPECTATIONS OF HIGHER PRICES

Q: Say it was just announced that next year there will be a 15 percent luxury tax charged on all purchases of new recreational vehicles (RVs). How would this impact current demand?

A: If potential buyers expect the future price of recreational vehicles to rise, you can bet that current sales will rise, holding gasoline prices and other important variables constant. In Exhibit 5, we see that the current demand curve for recreational vehicles will shift to the right as a result of the higher anticipated prices of new recreational vehicles.

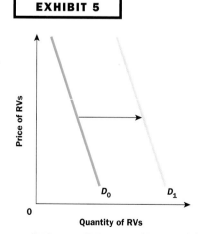

EXHIBIT 5

As it turned out, automobile production was not discontinued during the Korean War—but what was important in terms of demand was what people *expected* to happen, rather than what actually happened.

Fairly often, prospective changes in tax laws lead to changes in consumer behavior. For example, if people expect the relative price of automobiles to rise in three months because of a new tax on cars or the addition of newly mandated expensive anti-pollution equipment (which may, from the individual's perspective, have high costs relative to benefits), the demand for cars during the next three months will be enhanced, and car dealers will advertise, "Buy your car now before the price increase." Other examples, such as waiting to buy a home computer (because price reductions on electronic goods now may lead to expectations of further price reductions), are also common.

CHANGES IN DEMAND VERSUS CHANGES IN QUANTITY DEMANDED—REVISITED

Economists put particular emphasis on the impact of a change in the price of the good in question (own-price) on consumer behavior. We are interested in distinguishing between consumer behavior related to the price of a good itself (movement *along* a demand curve) from such behavior related to other things (shifts *of* the demand curve).

As indicated earlier, the expression we use to describe the effect of price changes of a good on its own sales is different from the expression we use to describe the impact any of the other factors (PYNTE) on a consumer's willingness to purchase that good. If the own-price of a good changes, we say that this leads to a "*change in quantity demanded*." If one of the five other factors influencing consumer behavior changes, we say that this leads to a "*change in demand*." Use the expression, "There was an increase in the quantity demanded," when the price of the good itself fell, or "There was a decrease in the quantity demanded" when the price of the good itself increased. Use the expression, "The demand for the good changes," when the factor influencing behavior was something (PYNTE) other than a change in own-price. The effects of some of the determinants that cause a change in demand (shifters) are reviewed in Exhibit 6.

| EXHIBIT 6 | POSSIBLE DEMAND SHIFTERS |

WHAT IS A TAMAGOTCHI?

Appealing virtual reality creatures, Tamagotchi ("tom-ah-got-chee") were first discovered in Japan. Tamagotchi hatch from tiny eggs after traveling millions of light years through cyberspace. With proper care and feeding (accomplished by pushing buttons on the egg), Tamagotchi quickly grow into adorable virtual reality pets in a wide variety of shapes and personalities.

Enormously popular in Japan, Tamagotchi have been adopted by children, teens, and adults of both sexes. Although there have been unsubstantiated reports of Tamagotchi sightings over Hawaii, the main flock is not expected to arrive in the United States until this summer.

SOURCE: www.bandai.com. September 15, 1997.

CONSIDER THIS:
The Tamagotchi did hit the United States in the summer of 1997, and as predicted, the demand was strong. The subsequent popularity of the toy pushed the demand curve for Tamagotchi to the right.

TUNE UP

CHANGES IN DEMAND VERSUS CHANGES IN QUANTITY DEMANDED

Q: Roxanne Rolls has a vast collection of compact discs. Demonstrate graphically the two following scenarios: (1) Roxanne buys more CDs because the price of CDs has fallen; and (2) Roxanne buys more CDs because her grandparents just told her that they are going to give her an extra $500 a month while she is going to college.

A: In the first scenario there is an own-price change, so there is a change in the quantity demanded (i.e., a movement along the demand curve). Movement along a demand curve shows a change in the quantity demanded due to a good's own-price changing. In the second scenario, when the grandparents provide the gift, there is an increase in demand. Anytime there is a change in one of the PYNTE variables, there is a change in demand (not quantity demanded). In this case, the whole demand curve shifts as a result of the increase in income.

In Exhibit 7, the movement from A to B is called an *increase in quantity demanded,* and the movement from B to A is called a *decrease in quantity de-*manded. Economists use the phrase "increase or decrease in quantity demanded" to describe movements along a given demand curve. However, the change from A to C is called an *increase in demand,* and the change from C to A is called a *decrease in demand*. The phrase "increase or decrease in demand" is reserved for a shift in the whole curve. So if Roxanne buys more CDs because the price fell, we say there was an increase in quantity demanded. However, if she buys more CDs even at the current price, say $15, we say there is an increase in demand. In this case, the increase in income was responsible for the increase in demand, as Roxanne chose to spend some of her new income on CDs.

EXHIBIT 7

1. A change in the quantity demanded describes a movement along a given demand curve.
2. A change in demand shifts the entire demand curve. An increase in demand shifts the demand curve to the right; a decrease shifts it to the left.
3. A change in the price of a substitute or complement shifts the demand curve for the good in question.
4. Changes in income cause demand curve shifts.
5. The position of the demand curve will vary according to the number of consumers in the market.
6. Taste changes will shift the demand curve.
7. Changes in expected relative prices can shift the current demand curve.

---

1. What is the difference between a change in demand and a change in quantity demanded?
2. If the price of zucchini increases and it causes the demand for yellow squash to rise, what do we call the relationship between zucchini and yellow squash?
3. If incomes rise and, as a result, demand for jet skis increases, how do we describe that good?
4. How do expectations about the future influence the demand curve?
5. Would a change in the price of ice cream cause a change in the demand for ice cream? Why or why not?
6. Would a change in the price of ice cream likely cause a change in the demand for frozen yogurt, a substitute?
7. If plane travel is a normal good and bus travel is an inferior good, what will happen to the demand curves for plane and bus travel if people's incomes increase?

The Law of Supply

- What is the law of supply?
- What is an individual supply curve?
- What is a market supply curve?

WHAT IS THE LAW OF SUPPLY?

The market's answer to the fundamental question, "What do we produce, and in what quantities?" depends on the interaction of buyers and sellers. Demand is only half the story. The willingness and ability of suppliers to provide the good are equally important factors that must be weighed by decision makers in all societies. As in the case of demand, several factors are important to suppliers. One important factor, again, is the own-price of the good. While behavior will vary among individual suppliers, economists expect that other things being equal, the quantity supplied will vary directly with the price of the good. This relationship is called the **law of supply.** Following the law of supply, the higher the price of the good (P), the greater the quantity supplied (Q_s), and the lower the price of the good, the smaller the quantity supplied.

$$P\uparrow \Rightarrow Q_s\uparrow \quad \text{and} \quad P\downarrow \Rightarrow Q_s\downarrow$$

The relationship described by the law of supply is a direct, or positive, relationship, because the variables move in the same direction.

WHY IS THERE A POSITIVE RELATIONSHIP BETWEEN PRICE AND QUANTITY SUPPLIED?

Firms supplying goods and services want to increase their profits, and the higher the price per unit, the greater the profitability generated by supplying more of that good. For example, if you were a coffee grower, wouldn't you much rather be paid $5 a pound than $1 a pound?

There is another reason that supply curves are upward sloping. The law of increasing opportunity costs demonstrated that when we hold technology and input prices constant, increased opportunity costs will be required to produce additional units of a good. That is, when we produce more of anything, we use the most-efficient resources (those with the lowest opportunity cost) first and then draw on less-efficient resources (those with higher opportunity cost) only if still more of the good in question is to

If it costs more to increase oil production from a field, then oil prices would have to rise in order for producers to increase their output.

be produced. So, if costs are rising for producers as they produce more units, they must receive a higher price to compensate them for their higher costs. In short, increasing production costs means that suppliers will require higher prices to induce them to increase their output.

WHAT IS AN INDIVIDUAL SUPPLY CURVE?

To illustrate the concept of an individual supply curve, let's return to our coffee example, but this time we are referring to the amount of coffee that an individual supplier, John Valdez, is willing to supply in one year. The law of supply can be illustrated, like the law of demand, by a table or graph. John's supply schedule for coffee is shown in Exhibit 1(a). The price–quantity supplied combinations

EXHIBIT 1 | AN INDIVIDUAL SUPPLY CURVE

a. John's Supply Schedule for Coffee

Price (per pound)	Quantity Supplied (pounds per year)
$5	80
4	70
3	50
2	30
1	10

b. John's Supply Curve for Coffee

EXHIBIT 2 | A MARKET SUPPLY CURVE

a. Market Supply Schedule for Coffee

	Quantity Supplied (pounds per year)				
Price	John	x	Other Producers	=	Market Supply
$5	80	×	100	=	8,000
4	70	×	100	=	7,000
3	50	×	100	=	5,000
2	30	×	100	=	3,000
1	10	×	100	=	1,000

b. Market Supply Curve for Coffee

The dots on this graph indicate different quantities of coffee that producers would be willing to supply at various prices. The line connecting those combinations is the market supply curve.

were then plotted and joined to create the individual supply curve shown in Exhibit 1(b). Note that the **individual supply curve** is upward sloping as you move from left to right. At higher prices, it will be more attractive to increase production. Existing firms, or growers, will produce more at higher prices than at lower prices.

WHAT IS A MARKET SUPPLY CURVE?

The **market supply curve** may be thought of as the horizontal summation of the supply curves for individual forms. For simplicity, let's assume that there are 100 coffee producers (including John) and that all of them have the same supply curves as John. The market supply schedule, which reflects the total quantity supplied at each price by the 100 coffee producers, is shown in Exhibit 2(a). Exhibit 2(b) illustrates the resulting market supply curve for this group of coffee producers.

CONCEPT CHECK

1. The law of supply states that the higher (lower) the price of the good, the greater (smaller) the quantity supplied.
2. There is a positive relationship between price and quantity supplied because profit opportunities are greater at higher prices and because the higher production costs of increased output means that suppliers will require higher prices.
3. The market supply curve is a graphical representation of the amount of goods and services that suppliers are willing to supply at various prices.

1. What is a direct, or positive, relationship?
2. What are the two reasons why a supply curve is positively sloped?
3. What is the difference between an individual supply curve and a market supply curve?

4. When we say that the supply curve for economics tutoring services is upward sloping, what relationship does that statement represent?

Shifts in the Supply Curve

MODULE 4

- What is the difference between a change in supply and a change in quantity supplied?
- What are the major supply shifters?

WHAT IS THE DIFFERENCE BETWEEN A CHANGE IN QUANTITY SUPPLIED VERSUS A CHANGE IN SUPPLY?

Changes in the price of a good lead to **changes in quantity supplied** by suppliers, just as changes in the price of a good lead to changes in quantity demanded by buyers. Similarly, a **change in supply,** whether an increase or a decrease, will occur for reasons other than changes in the price of the product itself, just as changes in demand are due to factors (PYNTE) other than the price of the good. In other words, a change in the own-price of a good, leading to a change in quantity supplied, is shown as a movement along a given supply curve. A change in any other factor that can affect supplier behavior (supplier input prices; prices of related goods; expectations; number of suppliers; and technology, taxes, tampering, and temperature), leading to a change in supply, results in a shift in the entire supply curve. An increase in supply shifts the supply curve to the right; a decrease in supply shifts the supply curve to the left, as seen in Exhibit 1.

WHAT IS SPENT?

We now have another memory device, SPENT, to aid in our understanding of the supply shifters. SPENT stands for: S, supplier input prices; P, prices of related goods; E, expectations; N, number of suppliers; and T, technology, taxes, tampering, and temperature. We will now look at each of these determinants of supply—factors that determine the position of the supply curve—in greater depth.

SUPPLIER INPUT PRICES (S)

Suppliers are strongly influenced by the costs of inputs used in the production process. Other things equal, the supply of a good at any given price will decline if labor or other input costs increase. This will cause the supply curve to shift to the left. Higher labor, materials, energy, or other

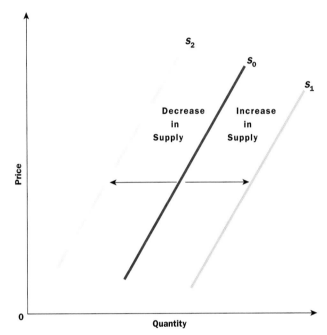

| EXHIBIT 1 | SUPPLY SHIFTS |

An increase in supply shifts the supply curve to the right. A decrease in supply shifts the supply curve to the left.

costs increase the cost of production, reducing the per-unit profit potential at existing prices. If input prices fall, the supply curve will shift to the right—more will be supplied at each and every price.

PRICE OF CLOSELY RELATED GOODS (P)

Let's say you own your own farm, on which you plant cotton and barley. Then, the price of barley falls and farmers reduce the quantity supplied of barley, as seen in Exhibit 3(a). What effect would the lower price of barley have on your cotton production? Easy—it would increase the

TUNE UP

SUPPLIERS' INPUT PRICES

Q: The price of fertilizer has doubled in the last year. Do you think the rising price of fertilizer will have any effect on the supply of food at the market?

A: This is an example of an increase in suppliers' input prices, which will cause the supply curve for farmers to shift to the left. While there may be no immediate effect on the price of food already on store shelves (the change in fertilizer costs does not affect that), this new higher price of fertilizer increases the costs of farm production. At the original price, less will be supplied. In Exhibit 2, we can see that the higher fertilizer prices have caused the supply curve for food to shift to the left.

EXHIBIT 2

What will happen to the farmers' costs of production if fertilizer prices rise?

supply of cotton. You would want to produce relatively less of the crop that had fallen in price (barley) and relatively more of the now more attractive other crop (cotton). This example demonstrates why the price of related goods is important as a supply shifter as well as a demand shifter. Producers tend to substitute the production of more-profitable goods for that of less-profitable goods. This is desirable from society's perspective as well, because more-profitable goods tend to be those considered more valuable by society, while less-profitable goods are usually considered less valuable. Hence, the lower price in the

barley market has caused an increase in supply (a rightward shift) in the cotton market, as seen in Exhibit 3(b). We call these two goods **substitutes in production.**

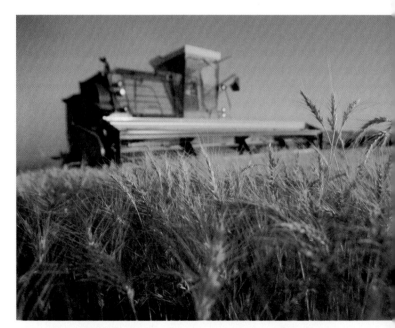

If a farmer is growing both corn and wheat on his field and the price of wheat falls, will the farmer increase his supply of corn, *ceteris paribus?*

| **EXHIBIT 3** | **SUBSTITUTES IN PRODUCTION** |

EXPECTATIONS CAN SHIFT SUPPLY

Q: Jed just moved from Tennessee to Beverly Hills. He was shooting at a possum in his backyard, when he discovered a black liquid oozing out of the ground—oil. If Jed expects the future relative price of oil to be much higher next year because of tensions in the Middle East, will he put his oil on the market this year?

A: No. People aren't always right, but they do respond to their expectations—their guesses of what the future will bring. If Jed expects the price to be much higher next year, he will attempt to keep his supply of new-found oil until next year. If, on the other hand, Jed expects prices to be lower next year, he will supply the oil now.

EXPECTATIONS (*E*)

A third factor shifting supply is the suppliers' expectations. If producers expect a higher price in the future, they will supply less now than they otherwise would have, preferring to wait and sell when their goods will be more valuable. Similarly, if they expect prices to fall in the future, they will supply more now rather than wait until their goods are expected to be worth less. By moving goods to the time periods when they are most highly valued, this activity, sometimes called speculation, tends to reduce sharp price fluctuations that would otherwise occur and to smooth the consumption of goods over time (reducing "feast or famine" situations).

A major disaster like a flood or a hurricane can reduce the supply of crops.

NUMBER OF SUPPLIERS (*N*)

We are normally interested in market demands and supplies (because they together determine prices and quantities) rather than in the behavior of individual consumers and firms. As we discussed earlier, the supply curves of individual suppliers can be summed horizontally to create a market supply curve. An increase in the number of suppliers leads to an increase in supply, denoted by a rightward shift in the supply curve. An exodus of suppliers has the opposite impact, a decrease in supply, which is indicated by a leftward shift in the supply curve.

THE FOUR Ts (TECHNOLOGY, TAXES, TAMPERING, AND TEMPERATURE) (*T*)

Most of us think of prices as constantly rising, given the existence of inflation, but in fact, decreases in costs often occur because of technological progress, and such advances can lower prices. Human creativity works to find

TAXES AND REGULATION AS SUPPLY SHIFTERS

Q: How do taxes and regulations deter producers from supplying larger quantities of certain goods?

A: Taxes and regulations both shift the supply curve to the left, as seen in Exhibit 4. These variables increase the costs of production, *ceteris paribus*, although the degree to which producers are deterred will vary with the regulatory rule and/or the tax selected.

EXHIBIT 4

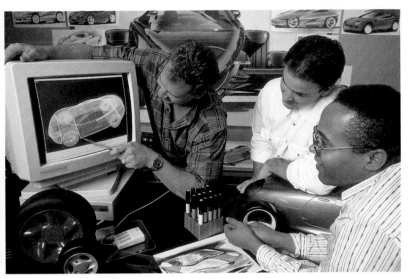

new ways to produce goods and services using fewer or less-costly inputs of labor, natural resources, or capital. In recent years, despite generally rising prices, the prices of electronic equipment such as computers, cellular telephones, and VCRs have fallen dramatically. At any given price in the 1990s, suppliers were willing to provide many more (of a given quality of) computers than in the 1970s, simply because technology had dramatically reduced the cost of providing them. Graphically, the increase in supply is indicated by a shift to the right in the supply curve.

Supply may also change because of changes in the legal and regulatory environment in which firms operate. Government regulations can influence the costs of production to the firm, leading to cost-induced supply changes similar to those just discussed. For example, if new safety or anti-pollution requirements increase labor and capital costs, the increased cost will result, other things equal, in a decrease in supply, shifting the supply curve to the left, or up. An increase in a government-imposed minimum wage may

Technological advances can lower the costs of production, *ceteris paribus.*

SUPPLY SHIFTERS IN THE OIL INDUSTRY

CRUDE OIL SAVINGS PASSED ON TO CONSUMERS: While crude oil prices go up and down over the short term, the long-term trend since the early 1980s has been toward more abundant, less-expensive supplies. Crude oil costs have declined from $1.41 per gallon in 1981 to 41 cents per gallon in 1995 (in inflation-adjusted 1995 dollars). These savings are reflected in the pump price of gasoline.

NEW TECHNOLOGIES CUT COSTS: By utilizing improved new technologies, the oil industry's downstream sector—which handles the manufacturing, marketing, and distribution of gasoline—has been able to cut costs significantly, and pass savings on to consumers at the pump. In 1981, downstream costs contributed 58.4 cents to the price of a gallon of gasoline. In 1995, these costs amounted to less than 37.1 cents per gallon.

A number of new technologies contributed to these savings, including: Long-haul pipelines, which have increasingly replaced less-efficient truck and barge transport of crude oil and petroleum products; newer, more efficient tankers with high-speed loading and unloading capabilities; pay-at-the-pump equipment and other labor-saving devices at service stations; new

computer-based inventory management techniques which allow companies to track their supplies more efficiently, assuring that most inventory is en route to users in tankers and in pipelines, rather than sitting idle in costly storage facilities; computerized processing that allows refiners to tailor their operations to obtain the optimum mix of products. Refiners are also now able to produce gasoline and other light fuels from grades of crude oil that, with older technology, were generally useful only for production of heavy boiler fuels and asphalt—products that aren't in high demand like unleaded gasoline.

TAXES: A GROWING PORTION OF PURCHASE PRICE: Gasoline prices declined in 1995 even though gasoline taxes were increasing. In that year, gasoline taxes became the single largest component in the cost of gasoline, more than either crude oil or marketing, refining, and distribution. They comprised 42.4 cents of the pump price of every gallon of gasoline, including 18.4 cents a gallon in federal taxes, 22 cents a gallon in weighted average state taxes, and an estimated 2 cents per gallon in average local taxes. In 1981, when prices reached an all-time high, taxes were just 27.7 cents per gallon in 1995 inflation-adjusted terms.

CLEAN AIR PROGRESS WITH LOWER PUMP PRICES: The falling costs of producing gasoline have occurred despite the requirements to make new, cleaner-burning fuels. In all, several billions of dollars have been spent on such new products and processes.

CONSIDER THIS:
Here we see some important shifters of the supply curve. Crude oil prices are supplier input prices (S); if they fall, we know the supply curve shifts to the right, *ceteris paribus.* Technology, taxes, and tampering are part of the four Ts. Remember, technology lowers costs of production and would tend to shift the supply curve to the right, *ceteris paribus.* On the other hand, tampering and taxes would tend to raise the costs of production, shifting the supply curve to the left, *ceteris paribus.*

Note: The study was prepared by API's Policy Analysis and Strategic Planning Department.
SOURCE: http://www.api.org/news/prices95.htm. September 15, 1997.

have a similar effect by raising labor costs and decreasing supply in markets where many low-wage workers are employed. Certain types of taxes can also alter the costs of production borne by the supplier, causing the supply curve to shift to the left at each price.

Government regulations (tampering) sometimes result in drastic supply curve shifts, such as when the production of a product is essentially prohibited for reasons of safety or environmental concerns. For example, the regulations placed on the production of some pesticides led some producers to stop making the product, shifting the supply curve far to the left.

In addition, temperature (more generally speaking, weather) can certainly affect the supply of certain commodities, particularly agricultural products and transportation services. A drought or freezing temperatures will almost certainly cause the supply curves for many crops to shift to the left.

CHANGE IN SUPPLY VERSUS CHANGE IN QUANTITY SUPPLIED—REVISITED

The SPENT mnemonic describes the five major reasons, other than own-price, why sellers might be willing to supply different amounts of goods and services. If the own-price of a good changes, we say this leads to a *change in the quantity supplied*. If one of the SPENT factors influences the seller's behavior, we say this leads to a *change in supply*. For example, if production costs rise because of a wage increase or higher fuel costs, then other things remaining constant, we would expect a decrease in supply—that is, a leftward shift in the supply curve. Alternatively, if some variable, like lower input prices, causes the costs of production to fall, the supply curve will shift to the right. Exhibit 5 illustrates the effect of some of the determinants that cause shifts in the supply curve.

| EXHIBIT 5 | POSSIBLE SUPPLY SHIFTERS |

TUNE UP

CHANGE IN SUPPLY VERSUS CHANGE IN QUANTITY SUPPLIED

Q: Terry Cloth is a cotton farmer. Demonstrate graphically the two following scenarios: (1) the price of cotton has risen; and (2) good weather has caused an unusually abundant cotton harvest.

A: In the first scenario, there is an own-price change, so there is a change in quantity supplied (i.e., a movement along the supply curve). In the second scenario, the good weather causes the supply curve for cotton to shift to the right. This is called a change in supply (not quantity supplied). A shift in the whole supply curve is caused by one of the SPENT variables, not by a change in the good's own-price.

As shown in Exhibit 6, the movement from A to B is called an increase in quantity supplied, and the movement from B to A is called a decrease in quantity supplied. However, the change from B to C is called an increase in supply and the movement from C to B is called a decrease in supply.

EXHIBIT 6

A ⟷ B   Change in quantity supplied

B ⟷ C   Change in supply

---

1. What is the difference between a change in supply and a change in quantity supplied?
2. What causes a movement along a supply curve?
3. What causes a shift in the entire supply curve?
4. If a seller expects the price of a good to rise in the near future, how will that affect his current supply curve?
5. Would a change in the price of wheat change the supply of wheat? Would it change the supply of corn, if wheat and corn can be grown on the same type of land?
6. If a guitar manufacturer had to increase its wages in order to keep its workers, what would happen to the supply of guitars as a result?
7. What happens to the supply of baby-sitting services in an area when many teenagers get their driver's licenses at about the same time?

Application: A Shift in the Demand for Cuban Cigars

What demand factors (PYNTE) have led to an increase in the demand for cigars? Do you think the "forbidden fruit" factor has shifted the demand curve?

WHERE THERE'S SMOKE: DEMAND FOR CIGARS FUELS SMUGGLING OF CUBAN CONTRABAND

ANNE-MARIE O'CONNOR

SAN DIEGO—The sweetest forbidden fruit at the border nowadays is not white, powdery, or from Colombia.

And it may not seem like the biggest threat to the Western world. But U.S. Customs Service officials are all fired up about a recent surge of the smuggling of Cuban cigars into San Diego.

In recent weeks, there have been back-to-back record seizures at the San Diego border, netting a cache of nearly 5,000 cigars with an estimated value of $283,500 on the black market, San Diego customs spokeswoman Bobbie Cassidy said.

The August seizures put San Diego squarely on the map of the Cuban contraband cigar trail, an exploding black market fueled by the yuppie cigar craze and a worldwide dictate that Cuba makes the champagne of *puros.*

"It's big money," said Rudy Camacho, top U.S. Customs administrator in San Diego. "It's a new smuggling trend, and it's indicative of the demand the American consumer has out there."

Nationwide, seizures of Cuban cigars have increased sixfold in the past three years, to more than $1.1 million worth in fiscal 1996, according to the Customs Service.

That's a leap from $318,401 in 1995 and a mere $142,014 in 1994, according to the service, which officials say reflects an increase in black market prices for the cigars as well as in seizures.

"It's the forbidden fruit factor," said Mike Sheehan, spokesman for customs in Miami, where Cuban cigars have become a status symbol for the terminally hip of South Beach.

"The fact that it's illegal and difficult to obtain makes it all the more desirable." . . . At the heart of Cuban cigar fever is the trendiness of cigars. In the past few years, cigars have become favored accessories for the likes of Demi Moore and Arnold Schwarzenegger. They have inspired the glossy specialty magazine *Cigar Aficionado,* whose cover has featured everyone from supermodel Claudia Schiffer to Castro, the man who made Cuban cigars emblematic.

Los Angeles Times, September 7, 1997, p. A30.

The popularity of cigars has increased nationwide over the past few years. With that, the demand for cigars, including the prized Cuban-made brands, has increased dramatically. This article identifies two possible reasons for this increase in demand for Cuban cigars: (1) trendiness, and (2) the forbidden fruit factor.

The first reason, trendiness, points to one of the PYNTE shifters, changes in taste (T). As we discussed in this Module, changes in preferences naturally lead to shifts in demand. Such is the case with Cuban cigars, which have become a popular status symbol in high-society circles.

The second reason, the forbidden fruit factor, provides a less satisfactory explanation of this change in demand. It has been illegal to import Cuban cigars since the 1960s, so why would the forbidden fruit factor suddenly become a significant factor? In short, then, the major cause for the increase in the demand for Cuban cigars is a change in tastes, which has pushed the demand curve for this contraband good to the right.

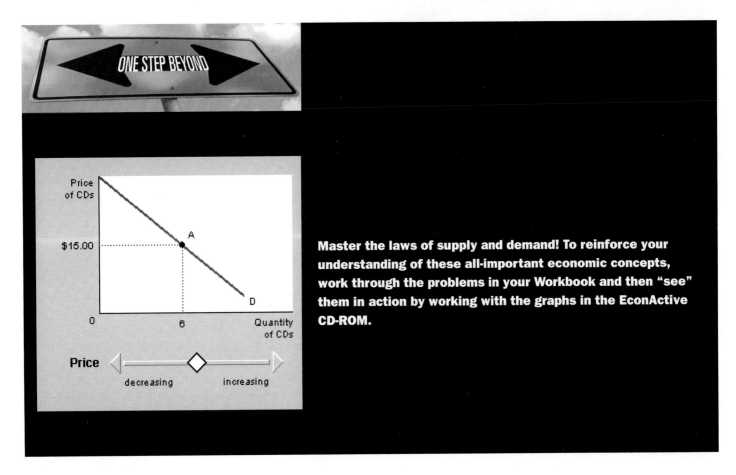

Master the laws of supply and demand! To reinforce your understanding of these all-important economic concepts, work through the problems in your Workbook and then "see" them in action by working with the graphs in the EconActive CD-ROM.

Markets in Motion

A. Market Equilibrium Price and Quantity
Why is the concept of market equilibrium such a valuable tool?

B. Changes in Equilibrium Price and Quantity
What happens to equilibrium price and quantity when we shift the supply or demand curve?

C. Shifting Supply and Demand Together
What happens when supply and demand both shift?

D. Temporary Disequilibrium
What happens when companies do not correctly anticipate the demand for their products?

E. Price Controls
What are price ceilings and price floors?

F. Application: Supply and Demand in the Market for Super Bowl Tickets
How does the market for Super Bowl tickets work?

Market Equilibrium Price and Quantity

- What is the equilibrium price?
- What is the equilibrium quantity?
- What is a shortage?
- What is a surplus?

BRINGING SUPPLY AND DEMAND TOGETHER

Enough has been said for now about demand and supply separately. Bearing in mind our discussion of the "fuzzy" nature of many real-world markets, we now bring supply and demand together. How do supply and demand operate together to answer the first fundamental question facing all societies: What will be produced and in what quantities?

WHAT IS THE EQUILIBRIUM PRICE AND QUANTITY?

The market solution to this basic question is quite simple: Production and exchange will be determined by the price at which the quantity demanded equals the quantity supplied. This price is said to be an **equilibrium price,** and the quantity associated with this price is said to be an **equilibrium quantity,** because they are a price and a quantity that tend not to change. The result is stable if there are no unsettling forces at work to change either the quantity sold in the

market or the price at which it is sold. Only a change in one of the **determinants of demand** (PYNTE) or supply (SPENT) will alter the situation and lead to a change in quantity or price, or both. As long as these determinants remain unchanged, price and quantity will tend to remain at their equilibrium levels.

WHAT ARE SHORTAGES AND SURPLUSES?

The equilibrium market solution is best understood with the help of a simple graph. Let's return to the coffee example we used in our earlier discussions of supply and demand. Exhibit 1 combines the market demand curve for coffee with the market supply curve. At $3 per pound, buyers are willing to buy 5,000 pounds of coffee and sellers are willing to supply 5,000 pounds of coffee. Neither may be "happy" about the price, because the buyer would like a lower price and the seller would like a higher price. But both buyers and sellers are able to carry out their purchase and sales plans at that $3 price. However, at any

---

EXHIBIT 1	**A HYPOTHETICAL MARKET SUPPLY AND DEMAND SCHEDULE FOR COFFEE**

Price	Quantity Supplied	Quantity Demanded	Difference	State of Market
$5	8,000	1,000	7,000	Surplus
4	7,000	3,000	4,000	Surplus
3	5,000	5,000	0	Equilibrium
2	3,000	8,000	−5,000	Shortage
1	1,000	12,000	−11,000	Shortage

The equilibrium is $3 per pound and 5,000 pounds of coffee, where quantity demanded and quantity supplied are equal. At higher prices, quantity supplied exceeds quantity demanded, resulting in a surplus. Below $3, quantity demanded exceeds quantity supplied, leading to a shortage.

---

other price, either suppliers or demanders would be unable to trade as much as they would like at that price. As you can see on the graph, at $4 per pound, the quantity of coffee demanded would be 3,000 pounds but the quantity supplied would be 7,000 pounds. At that price, a **surplus** or excess quantity supplied would exist. That is, growers would be willing to sell more coffee than demanders would be willing to buy. To cut growing inventories, frustrated suppliers would cut their price and cut back on production. And as prices fall, consumers will buy more, ultimately eliminating the unsold surplus, at the equilibrium.

What would happen if the price of coffee was cut to $1 per pound? The yearly quantity demanded of 12,000 pounds would be greater than the 1,000 pounds that pro-

ducers would be willing to supply at that low price. So, at $1 per pound, a **shortage** or excess quantity demanded would exist. Because of the coffee shortage, frustrated buyers would be forced to compete for the existing supply, bidding up the price. The rising price would have two effects: (1) producers would be willing to increase the quantity supplied; and (2) the higher price would decrease the quantity demanded. Together, these two effects would ultimately eliminate the shortage, at the equilibrium.

Again, only at $3 does neither a shortage nor a surplus exist. Thus, $3 is an equilibrium price, a steady price that will remain until the good's demand or supply curve is shifted by some consideration other than the price of coffee.

TUNE UP

SHORTAGES

Q: Imagine that you own a butcher shop. Recently, you have noticed that at about noon, you run out of your daily supply of chicken. Puzzling over your predicament, you hypothesize that you are charging less than the equilibrium price for your chicken. Should you raise the price of your chicken? Explain using a simple graph.

A: If the price you are charging is below the equilibrium price (P_E), then you can draw a horizontal line from that price straight across Exhibit 2 and see where it intersects the supply and demand curves. The point where this horizontal line intersects the demand curve indicates how much chicken consumers are willing to buy at that below-equilibrium price (P_{BE}). Likewise, the intersection of this horizontal line with the supply curve indicates how much chicken producers are willing to supply at P_{BE}. From this, it is clear that a shortage (or excess quantity demanded) exists, because consumers want more chicken (Q_D) than producers are willing to supply (Q_S) at this relatively low price. This excess quantity demanded will result in competition among buyers that will push prices up and eliminate the shortage. That is, it would make sense to raise your price on the chicken. As price moves towards the equilibrium price, consumers are willing to purchase less (some will substitute fish, steak, and ground round), and producers will have an incentive to supply more chicken. Excess quantity demanded, or a shortage, results from a price below the equilibrium price.

EXHIBIT 2

Price of Chicken (vertical axis), Quantity of Chicken (horizontal axis). Curves S and D intersect at P_E. At P_{BE}, a Shortage exists between Q_S and Q_D.

What is truly amazing is the fact that producers respond to the rather complex wants of the population without having tremendous shortages or surpluses, and the fact that in a "free market" we cannot point to any single individual or agency that makes the decision of what to produce. We often say the decision is made by "the market" or "market forces," but this is of little help in pinpointing the name and place of the decision maker. In fact, no single person makes decisions about the quantity and quality of televisions, cars, beds, or any other goods or services consumed in the American economy. Literally millions of people, both producers and consumers, participate in the decision-making process. To paraphrase a statement made popular by the first great modern economist, Adam Smith, it is as if an *invisible hand* works to coordinate the efforts of millions of diverse participants in the complex process of producing and distributing goods and services.

HOW ARE MARKETS LIKE NON–RUSH-HOUR TRAFFIC?

Consumers and drivers are both motivated by self-interest. Just as there are many different consumers in the marketplace, there are many different types of drivers, with different preferences and attitudes towards risk. Despite these differences, we see that the social interaction on highways is quite amazing. No one is there to direct the actions of drivers, yet when drivers see that one lane is moving faster than others, a few drivers will switch lanes until the flow of traffic is approximately equal in all lanes. Such marginal adjustments are critical to the unregulated coordination process in the marketplace as well as on the highway.

How are markets and uncongested freeways similar?

TUNE UP

SHORTAGES AND SURPLUSES

Q: Plans are being made for the Concert of the Millennium. It is going to be a three-hour, one-time-only concert with no taping and no satellite feeds. All of the performers will make a brief appearance before returning to their point of origin. The artists will be playing some of their all time favorite hits: Kurt Cobain ("Smells like Teen Spirit"), Bob Marley ("I Shot the Sheriff"), Richie Valens ("La Bamba"), Jim Morrison ("Light My Fire"), Jimi Hendrix ("Purple Haze"), John Lennon ("Imagine"), Tupac Shakur ("Dear Mama"), Elvis ("Hound Dog"), Janis Joplin ("Just a Little Piece of my Heart"), Jerry Garcia ("Keep On Truckin"), Buddy Holly ("Everyday"), John Denver ("Rocky Mountain High"), and Frank Sinatra ("My Way"). The site is still undecided, but the promoters are considering Angel Stadium in California or Sun Devil Stadium in Arizona.

Hints: What will the supply curve look like if the stadium has a total capacity of 70,000 seats? Will changing the price alter the supply curve for this event? What would demand for the concert relative to the supply likely be at $1? at $100,000? at $1 million?

A: Of course, we can only speculate on consumer response to this bizarre hypothetical concert scenario. However, we can still make conjectures and have a little fun. Exhibit 3 shows the demand and supply curves for this scenario. At $1 per ticket, we would expect millions to show up for the concert, far more than the 70,000 available seats. Clearly, a serious shortage would appear at that price. At $1 million, the concert promoters might only fill a few hundred seats—a surplus. We could only guess what the equilibrium price might be for this rather unique concert.

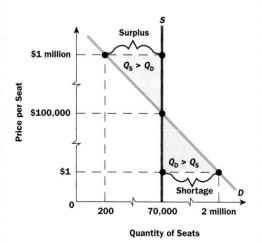

EXHIBIT 3

Quantity of Seats

1. The intersection of the supply and demand curve determines the equilibrium price and quantity exchanged in a market.
2. If the price is set above the equilibrium price, there will be a surplus or excess quantity supplied.
3. If the price is set below equilibrium price, there will be a shortage or excess quantity demanded.
4. Shortages and surpluses set in motion forces that tend to move the market toward the equilibrium price and quantity unless otherwise prevented.

---

1. How does the intersection of supply and demand indicate the equilibrium price and quantity in a market?
2. What can cause a change in the supply and demand equilibrium?
3. What must be true about the price charged for there to be a shortage?
4. What must be true about the price charged for there to be a surplus?
5. Why do market forces tend to eliminate both shortages and surpluses?
6. Why do economists refer to the "invisible hand" of the market?
7. If tea prices were above their equilibrium level, what force would tend to push tea prices down? If tea prices were below their equilibrium level, what force would tend to push tea prices up?
8. Why does the time you spend in supermarket checkout lines tend to be about the same, regardless of which line you are in?

Changes in Equilibrium Price and Quantity

- What happens to equilibrium price and quantity when we shift the demand curve?
- What happens to equilibrium price and quantity when we shift the supply curve?

As we discussed in Module 4, demand curves can shift when any of the PYNTE (but not the price of the good itself) factors change, and supply curves can shift when any of the SPENT factors change (but not the price of the good itself). These changes (shifts) in the demand and supply curves will lead to changes in the equilibrium price and equilibrium quantity.

HOW DOES A CHANGE IN DEMAND AFFECT EQUILIBRIUM PRICE AND QUANTITY?

A shift in the demand curve—caused by a change in (P) the price of a related good, (Y) income, (N) the number of buyers, (T) tastes, or (E) expectations—results in a change in both equilibrium price and equilibrium quantity. But how and why does this happen? This intersection can be most clearly explained through the use of an example.

The demand for restaurant meals in the little town of Diner is clearly affected by changes in consumer incomes. The willingness of consumers to pay for restaurant meals is illustrated in Exhibit 1, where line D_0 reflects current demand. Suppose, then, that incomes rise and that

Will higher incomes increase the demand for restaurant meals?

| EXHIBIT 1 | AN INCREASE IN DEMAND |

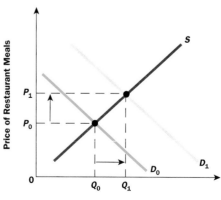

An increase in demand shifts the demand curve to the right, resulting in a new higher equilibrium price (P_1) and equilibrium quantity (Q_1).

consumers, now more affluent, increase their demand for restaurant meals. This means that, at any given price, the demand for these meals will be greater than before. The demand curve shifts to the right to represent this change in consumers' willingness to pay for restaurant meals. The new demand curve, D_1, in Exhibit 1 illustrates the resulting demand curve after this increase in income. Assume, for the moment, that the supply curve remains unchanged in this scenario; that is, assume that a rise in general income levels does not directly influence the ability or desire to produce and supply additional restaurant meals. As you can see, this increase in demand results in a higher equilibrium price (from P_0 to P_1) and an increase in the equilibrium quantity (from Q_0 to Q_1). If, in this same scenario, incomes were to fall rather than rise, both the equilibrium quantity and the equilibrium price would decrease as a result.

HOW DOES A CHANGE IN SUPPLY AFFECT EQUILIBRIUM PRICE AND QUANTITY?

Like a shift in demand, a shift in the supply curve will also influence both equilibrium price and equilibrium quantity, assuming that demand for the product has not changed. Recall from Module 4, each of the factors in SPENT—(S) suppliers' input prices, (P) the price of related goods, (E) expectations, (N) the number of sellers, and (T) technology, taxes, temperature, and tampering—can shift the supply curve. Consider the market for calculators, for example. In the late 1970s, technological breakthroughs led to lower input prices and an increase in the number of suppliers in the calculator market as established firms increased production and new firms entered the industry. These developments subsequently led to an increase in supply. In Exhibit 2, this increase in supply is indicated in the rightward shift from S_0 to S_1. At P_0, consumers would not buy Q_1 calculators. Only at a lower price will consumers be willing to buy this larger supply of calculators. As you can see, the increase in the supply of calculators resulted in a lower equilibrium price (from P_0 to P_1) and a higher equilibrium quantity (from Q_0 to Q_1).

Again, in the same scenario, if the supply of calculators decreased rather than increased, perhaps because of an expensive labor settlement, the reverse would be true. An expensive labor settlement would effectively increase the input costs in the calculator market, shifting the supply curve to the left. This decrease in supply would then drive the equilibrium price up and force the equilibrium quantity down.

| EXHIBIT 2 | AN INCREASE IN SUPPLY |

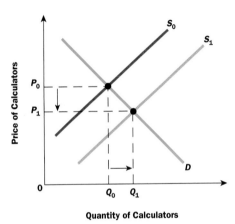

An increase in the supply curve, *ceteris paribus*, causes the equilibrium price to fall (from P_0 to P_1) and the equilibrium quantity to rise (from Q_0 to Q_1).

COFFEE, COCOA PRICES RISE ON EL NIÑO CONCERNS

LONDON (Reuters)—Coffee and cocoa prices have risen sharply in the past few weeks, as concern that a developing El Niño weather pattern could hit harvests has lured buyers to the market.

CONSIDER THIS:
In the summer of 1997 many buyers expected coffee and cocoa harvests to be lower in 1998 as a result of El Niño. As a result, they increased their current demand for coffee and cocoa. As shown in Exhibit 3, this change in consumers' expectations has resulted in an increase in demand—a shift in the demand curve from D_0 to D_1. This shift has resulted in a higher equilibrium price for coffee (from P_0 to P_1) and a higher equilibrium quantity (from Q_0 to Q_1).

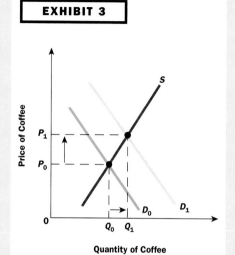

EXHIBIT 3

SOURCE: August 28, 1997, Reuters America Inc. http://www.newspage.com/NEWSPAGE/info/d18. . . ic.pre/public/B.d0828140.400.drt77100.htm.

If, due to changing expectations, consumers buy more coffee this year, what would you expect to happen to the price?

TUNE UP

THE IMPACT OF A CHANGE IN DEMAND ON EQUILIBRIUM PRICE AND QUANTITY

Q: Why are gasoline prices higher in the summer than in the winter?

A: More people travel during the summer months than during the winter months. Therefore, the demand for gasoline increases during the summer. The greater demand for gasoline during the summer sends prices upward, *ceteris paribus*. As shown in Exhibit 4, the rightward shift of the demand curve results in an increase in both equilibrium price and quantity.

EXHIBIT 4

TUNE UP

THE IMPACT OF A CHANGE IN SUPPLY ON EQUILIBRIUM PRICE AND QUANTITY

EXHIBIT 5

Q: Why are strawberries more expensive in winter than in summer?

A: Assuming that consumers' tastes and income are fairly constant throughout the year, the answer lies on the supply side of the market. The supply of strawberries is lower during the winter, because strawberries are out of season. As shown in Exhibit 5, this decrease in supply shifts the supply curve to the left, resulting in a higher equilibrium price (from P_0 to P_1) and a lower equilibrium quantity (from Q_0 to Q_1).

CONCEPT CHECK

1. Changes in demand and supply will cause a change in the equilibrium price and/or quantity.

2. Changes in supply will cause a change in the equilibrium price and/or quantity.

1. When demand increases, does that create a shortage or a surplus at the original price?

2. What happens to equilibrium price and quantity as a result of a demand increase?

3. When supply increases, does that create a shortage or a surplus at the original price?

4. What happens to equilibrium price and quantity as a result of a supply increase?

5. Why do heating-oil prices tend to be higher in the winter?

6. Why are evening and weekend long-distance calls cheaper than weekday long-distance calls?

Shifting Supply and Demand Together

■ What happens when both supply and demand shift in the same time period?

■ What is an indeterminate solution?

WHAT HAPPENS IF BOTH SUPPLY AND DEMAND SHIFT IN THE SAME TIME PERIOD?

We have discussed that as part of the continual adjustment process that occurs in the marketplace, supply and demand can each shift in response to many different factors, with the market then adjusting toward the new equilibrium. We have, so far, only considered what happens when just one such change occurs at a time. In these cases, we learned that the results of these adjustments in supply and demand on the equilibrium price and quantity are predictable. However, very often, supply and demand will both shift *in the same time period.* That is, supply and demand will shift simultaneously in response to both PYNTE and SPENT factors. Can we predict what will happen to equilibrium prices and equilibrium quantities in these situations?

As you will see, when supply and demand move at the same time, we can predict the change in one variable (price or quantity), but we are unable to predict the direction of

effect on the other variable with any certainty. This change in the second variable, then, is said to be **indeterminate,** because it cannot be determined without additional information about the size of the relative shifts in supply and demand. This concept will become more clear to you as we work through the following example.

Simultaneous Supply Increase with Demand Decrease

When considering this scenario, it might help you to break it down into its individual parts. As you learned in the last Concept, an increase in supply (a rightward shift in the supply curve) results in a decrease in the equilibrium price and an increase in the equilibrium quantity. A decrease in demand (a leftward movement of the demand curve), on the other hand, results in a decrease in both the equilibrium price and the equilibrium quantity. These shifts are shown in Exhibit 1(a). Taken together, then, these changes

---

| **EXHIBIT 1** | **SHIFTS IN SUPPLY AND DEMAND** |

a. A Little Increase in Supply and a Big Decrease in Demand

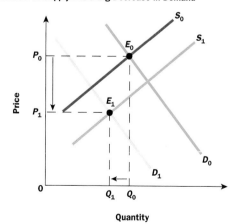

If the decrease in demand (leftward shift) is greater than the increase in supply (rightward shift), the equilibrium quantity will fall.

b. A Big Increase in Supply and a Little Decrease in Demand

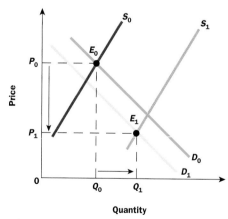

If the increase in supply (rightward shift) is greater than the decrease in supply (leftward shift), the equilibrium quantity will rise.

---

will clearly result in a decrease in the equilibrium price, because both the increase in supply and the decrease in demand work to push this price down. This drop in equilibrium price is shown in the movement from E_0 to E_1.

The effect of these changes on equilibrium price is clear, but how does the equilibrium quantity change? The impact on equilibrium quantity is indeterminate, because the increase in supply increases the equilibrium quantity and the decrease in demand decreases it. In this scenario, the change in the equilibrium quantity will vary depending on the relative changes in supply and demand. If, as shown in Exhibit 1(a), the decrease in demand is greater than the increase in supply, the equilibrium quantity will decrease. If, however, as shown in Exhibit 1(b), the increase in supply is greater than the decrease in demand, the equilibrium quantity will increase.

Demand and Supply Simultaneously Increase or Decrease

It is also possible that both demand and supply will increase (or decrease). This has, for example, been the case with VCRs. As a result of technological breakthroughs and lower input costs, the supply curve for VCRs shifted to the right. That is, at any given price, more VCRs were offered than before. But with rising income and an increasing number of buyers in the market, the demand for VCRs increased as well. As shown in Exhibit 2, both the increased demand and increased supply functioned to increase the equilibrium quantity—more VCRs were sold. The equilibrium price could have either gone up (because of increased demand) or down (because of increased supply), depending on the relative sizes of the demand and supply shifts. Price is, in this case, the indeterminate variable. However, in the case of the VCRs, we know that the supply curve shifted more than the demand curve, so that the effect of increased supply pushing prices down outweighed the effect of increased demand pushing prices up. As a result, the equilibrium price of VCRs has dropped (from P_0 to P_1) over time.

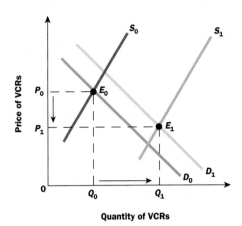

EXHIBIT 2	AN INCREASE IN THE DEMAND AND SUPPLY OF VCRS

The increase in supply and demand caused in increase in the equilibrium quantity. Price is the indeterminate variable. Because the supply curve shifted more than the demand curve, the price fell.

THE COMBINATIONS OF SUPPLY AND DEMAND SHIFTS

The eight possible changes in demand and/or supply are presented in Exhibit 3, along with the resulting changes in equilibrium quantity and equilibrium price. While memorizing such a table is one way of "learning" the impact of the various possible changes in demand and supply, you will find it more profitable to draw a little graph, such as shown in Exhibit 4, whenever a situation of changing demand and/or supply arises, remembering that an increase in either demand or supply means a rightward shift in the curve, while a decrease in either means a leftward shift. Remember that where both demand and supply change, one of the two equilibrium values, price or quantity, will change in an indeterminate manner (can increase or decrease).

EXHIBIT 3	THE EFFECT OF CHANGING DEMAND AND/OR SUPPLY

If Demand	and Supply	then Equilibrium Quantity	and Equilibrium Price
1. Increases	Stays unchanged	Increases	Increases
2. Decreases	Stays unchanged	Decreases	Decreases
3. Stays unchanged	Increases	Increases	Decreases
4. Stays unchanged	Decreases	Decreases	Increases
5. Increases	Increases	Increases	Indeterminate*
6. Decreases	Decreases	Decreases	Indeterminate*
7. Increases	Decreases	Indeterminate*	Increases
8. Decreases	Increases	Indeterminate*	Decreases

*May increase, decrease, or remain the same, depending on the size of the change in demand relative to the change in supply.

EXHIBIT 4   THE COMBINATIONS OF SUPPLY AND DEMAND SHIFTS

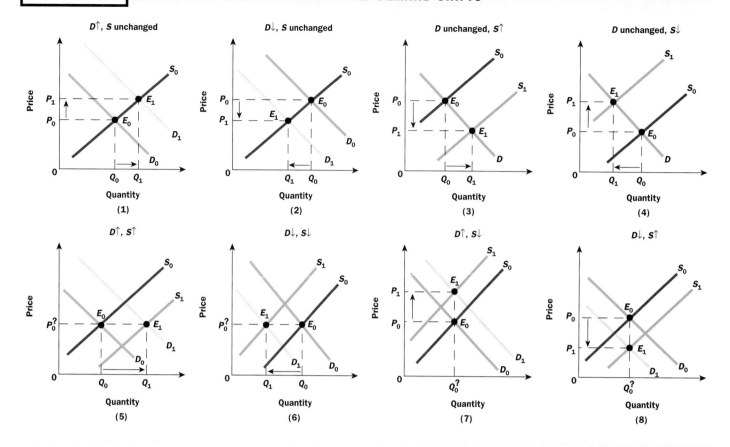

(1) $D\uparrow$, S unchanged

(2) $D\downarrow$, S unchanged

(3) D unchanged, $S\uparrow$

(4) D unchanged, $S\downarrow$

(5) $D\uparrow$, $S\uparrow$

(6) $D\downarrow$, $S\downarrow$

(7) $D\uparrow$, $S\downarrow$

(8) $D\downarrow$, $S\uparrow$

TUNE UP

SHIFTS IN BOTH SUPPLY AND DEMAND

Q: As a result of fiber optic technology, the production costs for long-distance calls have fallen. Graph this phenomenon, assuming for the moment that demand remains stable. What happened to the equilibrium price and quantity? What happens if there is a simultaneous increase in demand because of a rise in income?

A: Lower costs of production shift the supply curve to the right. With this increase in supply, the price of long-distance phone calls falls and the quantity demanded (and exchanged, in equilibrium) rises. This change is shown in Exhibit 5(a), with the movement from E_0 to E_1. If there is a simultaneous increase in demand, equilibrium quantity rises further, but the impact on equilibrium price now becomes indeterminate—that is, we need to know the magnitude of the increase in demand compared to the magnitude of the increase in supply to determine whether the price will rise or fall. This situation is shown in Exhibit 5(b).

EXHIBIT 5

a. Increase in Supply

b. Simultaneous Increase in Supply and Demand

KIDNEYS FOR SALE?

A Chinese newspaper published in New York advertises "kidney transplant in mainland China. Don't miss the opportunity."

House lawmakers have demanded an investigation into an *ABCNEWS Prime Time Live* report that organs from executed Chinese prisoners are being sold on the international black market. Rep. Frank Wolf, R-Va., said there is "strong evidence that federal and state laws have been broken." "We're talking about real men and women being killed for someone who can pay for parts of their bodies," said Rep. Linda Smith, R-Wash.

Chinese Embassy spokesman Yu Shuning said the allegations of organ sales were "sheer fabrication," noting that the sale of human organs is prohibited in China.

Working undercover, ABC News correspondent Brian Ross responded to an advertisement in a New York-based Chinese language newspaper offering a kidney transplant in China and visited the doctor who told him about the grisly process.

"The doctor told us he had hospitals for transplants using prisoners' kidneys," said Ross. "Dr. Zhou Wei Zhang, who worked at one of the hospitals, told us the kidneys are actually removed in the field, moments after prisoners are shot. The total price—$30,000." But on a hidden ABC News camera, the doctor asks for part of the $30,000 payment in advance.

Apple Yoonuch, a woman from Bangkok, Thailand, said she underwent a transplant at the Nanfung Military Hospital in China, Ross reported. "Third of January, the doctor called me that there will be an execution," Yoonuch said. "It means that prisoners, some prisoners, are going to be shot dead. So I have to come over and prepare myself to get the operation, kidney operation." An embassy statement said the organs of executed criminals are used in transplants rarely and only with the consent of the prisoners or their families.

An official with the International Transplantation Society said the practice is barbaric and "makes me cringe." "The consent issue as far as I'm concerned is a bogus issue," said Dr. Ronald Guttman. "It's a justification for what they're doing." *Prime Time Live* also aired videotape made by the Chinese military showing guards making sure an executioner's gun is placed at the back of a condemned person's head. This is done to protect the organs from damage during the execution, and to ensure the organs are as fresh as possible when extracted.

http://abcnews.com/sections/world/china1015/index.html (October 22, 1997).

Do markets always lead to ethical outcomes?

> **CONSIDER THIS:**
> If, in fact, this report is accurate (the Chinese deny the allegations), then we might ask these questions: Do supply and demand work better when markets are tempered by shared moral beliefs? Does unconstrained self-interest sometimes result in behavior that most would find unacceptable?

Frank and Ernest

© 1997 Thaves/Reprinted with permission. Newspaper dist. by NEA, Inc.

Why is the market price higher for a wise man than for wise guys?

CONCEPT CHECK

1. Supply and demand curves can each shift simultaneously in response to changes in both SPENT and PYNTE factors.

2. When there are simultaneous shifts in both supply and demand curves, we will be able to determine one, but not both, of the variables. Either the equilibrium price or the equilibrium quantity will be indeterminate, without more information.

---

1. What would have to be true for both supply and demand to shift in the same time period?
2. How do we "add up" the effects of simultaneous changes in both supply and demand on equilibrium prices and quantities?
3. When both supply and demand shift, what added information do we need to know in order to determine in which direction the indeterminate variable changes?

4. If both buyers and sellers of coffee expect coffee prices to rise in the near future, what will happen to coffee prices and sales today?
5. If demand for peanut butter increases and supply decreases, what will happen to equilibrium price and quantity?

Temporary Disequilibrium

- What is anticipated demand?
- Can anticipated demand be less than the actual demand?

REACHING EQUILIBRIUM: DO YOU REMEMBER CABBAGE PATCH DOLLS?

In 1983, Coleco, a major American toy company, started importing from China a handmade creation called "Cabbage Patch Dolls." The dolls took America by storm, and as the fad grew, newspapers were filled with accounts of otherwise dignified grandmothers fighting with one another, trying to get a store's last Cabbage Patch doll for their grandchildren.

WHY WERE SHOPPERS FIGHTING IN THE AISLES?

While Coleco showed great perceptiveness in coming up with the Cabbage Patch idea, it also initially goofed. It significantly underpriced the dolls, given their popularity, thereby reducing their revenues and profits compared to what they could have been, and causing all sorts of frustration among Cabbage Patch fans. Coleco, in short, inaccurately guessed the location of the demand curve. A firm selling a product typically sells it to a store and suggests a retail price. That initial price represents the firm's best guess as to where the demand and supply curves will intersect, if the good has many close competitors. Typically, the firm knows the supply curve pretty well, because it is determined by what the firm must pay to acquire various quantities of inputs, particularly wages. But businesses have to guess at the public reaction to the product; often that guessing is aided by market research, which provides information on consumer tastes and preferences.

Consider Exhibit 1. In a given period in late 1983, Coleco might have guessed that the demand curve for Cabbage Patch Dolls looked like the lower of the two demand curves ($D_{ANTICIPATED}$), suggesting that a price of $20 would have "cleared the market"—that is, would result in neither a shortage nor a surplus.

In fact, as the dolls caught on, demand was much greater than anticipated, say, that represented by the top demand curve (D_{ACTUAL}) in Exhibit 1. By pricing the product at $20, enormous shortages were created (shown as AB in Exhibit 1), and the firm was losing lots of potential revenue. Coleco could have charged $35 and even sold a few more dolls (upward sloping supply curve), making far greater profits.

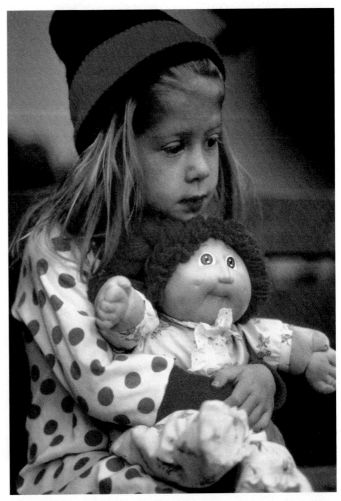

What happens when you don't accurately anticipate consumer demand?

HOW DID THE MARKET RESOLVE THE DISEQUILIBRIUM?

Clearly, the initial Cabbage Patch situation, shown in Exhibit 1, was a disequilibrium condition. As we have learned, however, disequilibrium is a temporary condition, because market forces will intervene and move the market back towards equilibrium. In this case, the excess quantity demanded at $20 was a signal to the marketplace; the participants, acting in their own self-interest, responded to bring the market back to equilibrium.

In the case of the Cabbage Patch Dolls, an alerted Coleco quickly raised its price to reduce the disequilibrium. Following the law of supply, it makes sense for the company to want to increase output, and Coleco did, in this case, by having its Chinese suppliers increase deliveries (at increased costs, reflecting the greater costs of more hurried production rates). The combination of a higher price for the Coleco dolls, plus the increase in the supply of Cabbage Patch-like substitutes, largely eliminated the market shortage within months.

In time, the Cabbage Patch fad wore down, causing the demand curve to shift to the left (that is, at any price, de-

EXHIBIT 1 — **THE CABBAGE PATCH DOLL SHORTAGE**

mand was less than before). This caused both prices and sales to fall. The Cabbage Patch story had come full circle—market adjustments had reallocated resources successfully to deal with even such a fickle fad.

Sometimes anticipated demand may not be the same as actual demand.

1. Sometimes anticipated demand is different than actual demand.

2. While disequilibrium is possible, the period spent in disequilibrium tends to be very short for most goods and services, because a disequilibrium sets up profit incentives to move the market toward equilibrium prices.

1. What happens in a market when demand is greater than anticipated?

2. How do market adjustments resolve the temporary disequilibrium that results when demand is incorrectly estimated?

3. If the maker of Beanie Babies found that its inventories were plummeting, what kind of temporary disequilibrium would that indicate?

Price Controls

- What are price controls?
- What are price ceilings?
- What are price floors?

WHAT ARE PRICE CONTROLS?

While nonequilibrium prices can crop up in the private sector, reflecting uncertainty, they seldom last for long. Governments, however, often impose nonequilibrium prices for significant time periods. **Price controls** involve the use of the power of the state to establish prices different from the equilibrium prices that would otherwise prevail. The motivations for price controls vary with the market under consideration: a maximum, or **ceiling,** price is often set for goods deemed "important," like housing, or a minimum, or **floor,** may be set on wages because wages are the primary source of income for most people.

Price controls are not always implemented by the federal government. Local governments (and, more rarely, private companies) can and do impose local price controls. One fairly well-known example is rent controls. The inflation of the late 1970s meant rapidly rising rents, and some communities, such as Santa Monica, California, decided to do something about it. In response, they limited how much landlords could charge for rental housing.

PRICE CEILINGS: RENT CONTROL

Rent control experiences can be found in many cities across the country. San Francisco, Berkeley, and New York City all have had some form of rent control. While the rules may vary from city to city and over time, generally the price (or rent) of an apartment remains fixed over the tenure of an occupant, except for allowable annual increases tied to the cost of living or some other price index. When an occupant moves out, the owner can usually, but not always, raise the rent to a near-market level for the next occupant. The controlled rents for existing occupants, however, are generally well below-market rental rates.

Results of Rent Controls

First, persons living in rent controlled apartments have a good deal, one that they would lose by moving as their family circumstances or income change. Tenants thus are reluctant to give up their governmentally granted right to a below-market rent apartment. Second, because the rents received by landlords are constrained and below market levels, the rate of return (roughly, the profit) on housing investments falls compared to that on other forms of real estate not subject to rent controls, like office rents or mortgage payments on condominiums. Hence, the incentive to construct new housing is reduced. Where rent controls are truly effective, there is generally little new construction going on and a shortage of apartments that persists and grows over time.

Third, since landlords are limited in what rent they can charge, there is little incentive to improve or upgrade

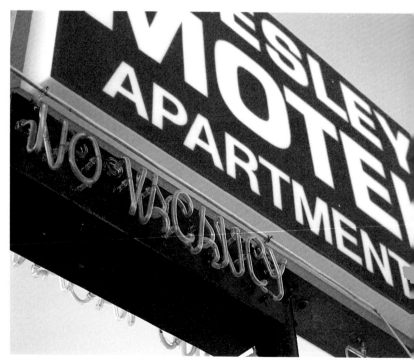

The effect of rent controls is shortages.

apartments, say, by putting in new kitchen appliances or new carpeting, in order to get more rent. In fact, there is some incentive to avoid routine maintenance, thereby lowering the cost of apartment ownership to a figure approximating the controlled rental price, although the quality of the housing stock will deteriorate over time.

A fourth impact of rent controls is that they promote housing discrimination. Where rent controls do not exist, a prejudiced landlord might willingly rent to someone he believes is undesirable, simply because the undesirable family is the only one willing to pay the requested rent (and the landlord is not willing to lower the rent substantially to get a desirable family, since this could translate into the loss of thousands of dollars in income). With rent controls, there are likely to be many families wanting to rent the controlled apartment, some desirable and some undesirable, as seen by the landlord, simply because the rent is at a below-equilibrium price. The landlord can indulge in his "taste" for discrimination without any additional financial loss beyond that required by the controls.

Consequently, he or she will be more likely to choose to rent to a desirable family, perhaps a family without children or pets, rather than an undesirable one, perhaps one with lower income and so a greater risk of non-payment.

Exhibit 1 shows the impact of rent control. If the price ceiling is set below the market price, the quantity demanded will increase to Q_D from Q^* and the quantity supplied will fall to Q_S from Q^*. The rent control policy will therefore create a shortage, the difference between Q_S and Q_D.

PRICE FLOORS: THE MINIMUM WAGE

Suppose the government decided to increase the **minimum wage rate** for workers. The argument for doing so is simple: Existing minimum wages do not allow for a very high standard of living, and a higher minimum wage will allow workers (those continuing to work, and maintaining their hours worked, anyway!) to live better than before. Ever since 1938, when the first minimum wage was established (at 25 cents per hour), the federal government has, by legislation, made it illegal to pay most workers an amount below the current legislated minimum wage.

The quantity of labor demanded, as for other goods, varies inversely with its price, because at a lower price or wage, employers find it more profitable to hire more workers. Likewise, the supply of labor varies directly with price; at higher wages, more persons have an incentive to work (and the existing workers have an incentive to work longer hours).

If the government raises the minimum wage, the quantity of labor supplied to the market grows, because more are willing to work at a higher wage rate. However, the quantity of labor demanded falls because some employers would find it unprofitable to hire low-skilled workers at the higher wage rate. Examine Exhibit 2. At $5.15 an hour, there may be a gap between the quantity of labor demanded and the quantity supplied, AB; this represents willing workers who will be unable to find jobs. However, if the wage were increased by government mandate to $10, the gap between quantity demanded and quantity

EXHIBIT 1	RENT CONTROLS

EXHIBIT 2	THE UNEMPLOYMENT EFFECTS OF MINIMUM WAGE

What do you think would happen to the number of unskilled workers getting jobs if we raised the minimum wage to $50 an hour? How many more people would be sitting here?

supplied, CD, would be much larger. An increase in the minimum wage would, therefore, create additional unemployment.

The additional unemployment created by higher minimum wages is not evenly distributed among various racial, demographic, and educational groups in our population. An increase in the minimum wage will not have any important impact, for example, on the unemployment rate for physicians, all of whom earn far more than $10 an hour. Rather, the impact falls mainly on the least-experienced, least-skilled persons, holding the lowest-paying jobs. A large proportion of these jobs are held by teenagers. Those who continue to hold jobs after the minimum wage is increased gain substantially, and thereby are vociferous supporters of efforts to increase the minimum. Yet another group of persons suffers tremendously more from the higher minimum wage—they lose their jobs or are unable to get them in the first place (for new labor market entrants) and suffer a decline in earnings, not a gain. Others would be frustrated when they unsuccessfully attempted to get a job at $10 an hour. Although studies disagree somewhat on the precise magnitudes, they largely agree that minimum wage laws do create some unemployment, and that the unemployment is concentrated among teenagers, blacks, and other minorities. Minimum wage laws are one reason that black and teenage unemployment rates are at least twice as high as unemployment for white adults.

The above analysis does not "prove" minimum wage laws are "bad" and should be abolished. To begin with, there is the empirical question of how much unemployment is caused by increases in minimum wages. Secondly, the cost of higher unemployment might be viewed by some as a reasonable price to pay for assuring that those with jobs get a "decent" wage. The analysis does point out, however, that there is a cost to having minimum wages, and the burden of increases in the minimum wages falls not only on employers and purchasers of products made more costly by the minimum wage but also on poor, low-income Americans who become unemployed when such increases occur.

1. Price controls involve government mandates to keep prices above or below the market-determined equilibrium price.
2. Price ceilings are government-imposed maximum prices.
3. If price ceilings are set below the equilibrium price, shortages will result.
4. Price floors are government-imposed minimum prices.
5. If price floors are set above the equilibrium price, surpluses will result.

---

1. How is rent control an example of a price ceiling?
2. What predictable effects result from price ceilings like rent control?
3. How is the minimum wage law an example of a price floor?
4. What predictable effects result from price floors like the minimum wage?
5. What may happen to the amount of discrimination against groups such as families with children, pet owners, smokers, or students when rent control is imposed?
6. Why does rent control often lead to condominium conversions?

Application: Supply and Demand in the Market for Super Bowl Tickets

Why does ticket scalping occur? What role do ticket scalpers play in the market for Super Bowl tickets?

JUST THE TICKET FOR SUPER BOWL FANS

STEPHEN HAPPEL AND MARIANNE M. JENNINGS

TEMPE, Ariz.—You can't help but admire the power and influence of the Super Bowl. What else can close down Miami's freeways for hours on a Sunday afternoon for a parade of VIP limos? What else can cause a sacred Indian burial ground to be plowed up, without resistance, for a glitzy football theme park lasting just one week? Stronger than a sovereign nation, the National Football League rules in most situations. But the free market is the one force that eludes the NFL offense, despite its determined efforts.

The Super Bowl is a high-demand, limited-supply event. This year, in Tempe, there are some 80,000 seats for the 30th playing of football's crowning moment. The NFL has done such a good marketing job that half of the United States wants to attend. Yet, the league has no intention of allowing them in. Market control is the NFL goal.

For the first 29 Super Bowls, ticket prices for all stadium seats were the same regardless of location. So much for the market! This year's game has differential prices ($200, $250, and $350), "to more adequately reflect differences in seat quality," a league spokesman says. But with present market prices ranging from $1,000 to $3,000, the NFL has not priced to what the market will bear.

Even with the NFL in charge, scalping is inevitable. So many want seats, and some who receive official tickets are willing to sell them. Each year hundreds of ticket scalpers from across the United States descend on the host city a week before the game to trade from temporary command posts in motel rooms. Scalpers always appear at the stadium even when the probability of arrest is high.

Rather than ramming ahead into the force of the market, the NFL should try a reverse. Scalpers should be allowed to operate license-free at one location on game day. Phoenix pioneered such an ordinance for the 1995 NBA All-Star Game, and as we outlined on this page last year, the results have overwhelmingly benefited the customers. Search costs are minimized. Prices are lower. The nuisance effects of congested street corners, aggressive sellers and fights are gone. Counterfeit tickets are almost nonexistent. The common area will simply make shopping easier for those rabid fans who are willing to pay what it takes to achieve a once-in-a-lifetime dream.

The NFL, alas, has no plans for a reverse. League rules prohibit anyone affiliated with the NFL from scalping Super Bowl tickets. Also, the host city is required to have an antiscalping ordinance enforced at the event.

The Super Bowl's status as the top sporting event in the United States means that the vast majority of tickets never reach the open market. Yet the human spirit coupled with market forces still emerges as fans and scalpers search for each other. Just outside the stadium, within the shadow of the mighty NFL, they will meet. Neither ordinances nor screening can stop them. Even the NFL can't sack the laws of supply and demand.

> Mr. Happel is a professor of economics and associate dean at the College of Business at Arizona State University, where Ms. Jennings is a professor of legal and ethical studies. George Alper, a Tempe ticket trader, contributed to this article.

SOURCE: Stephen Happel and Marianne Jennings, "Just the Ticket for Super Bowl Fans," *The Wall Street Journal*, January 25, 1996.

According to Happel and Jennings, for the first 29 years of the Super Bowl, the NFL did not differentiate their prices on the basis of seating—all seats regardless of location fetched the same price. Finally, in 1996, the NFL decided they should set their prices to reflect seat quality, so they did: $200, $250 and $350. Even at these new higher prices the NFL faced a situation of excess quantity demanded, or a shortage. As a result of the shortage, the ticket scalpers were getting anywhere from $1,000 to $3,000 per ticket—5 to 10 times the ticket price.

Would there be ticket scalping if the tickets were selling for $3,000 to $4,000 a piece? Maybe for the very best seats but, at that price, there would certainly be less work for scalpers. But when tickets are priced well below equilibrium, there is an important function for scalpers. Their objective is profit, no doubt, but they also provide an important function for society—they try to get tickets in the hands of people who value the tickets the most. The profits of buying from someone who values the tickets less and selling to those who value it more brings scalpers in from all over the United States—"even when the probability of arrest is high." As Happel and Jennings so aptly state, "Even the NFL can't sack the laws of supply and demand."

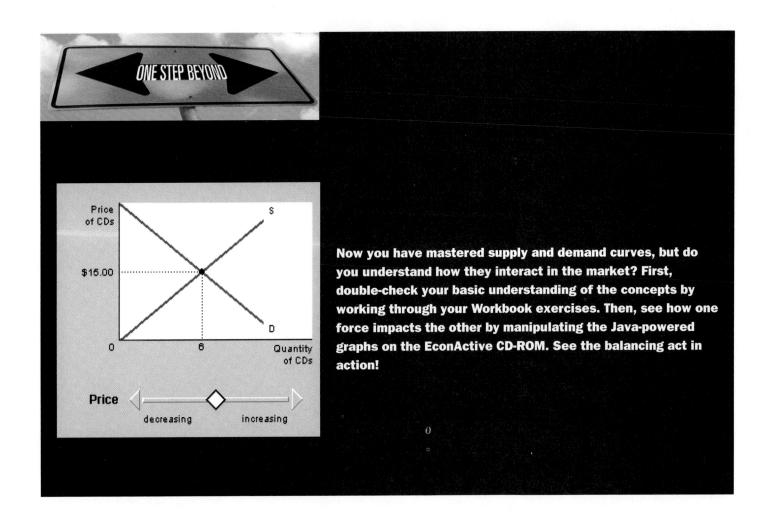

Now you have mastered supply and demand curves, but do you understand how they interact in the market? First, double-check your basic understanding of the concepts by working through your Workbook exercises. Then, see how one force impacts the other by manipulating the Java-powered graphs on the EconActive CD-ROM. See the balancing act in action!

Government and the Economy

A. Government and Property Rights
Should government protect
property rights?

B. Government and Externalities
Should government intervene to correct externalities?

C. Government and Public Goods
Should government provide public goods and services?

D. Government and Information Costs
Should government provide information to consumers?

E. Other Government Functions
How does government try to prevent insufficient competition
and achieve its macroeconomic goals?

F. Government and Income Distribution
Should government work to create more equality in income distribution?

G. Public Choice
Is politics influenced by self-interest?

H. Spending and Taxation
How do we pay for government?

I. Application: Revving Up the Helmet Law Debate
Can a balance of the freedom of the rider and the freedom
of the taxpayer be found?

Government and Property Rights

MODULE 6

- What are property rights?
- How does government protect rights?
- What is the right of eminent domain?

GOVERNMENT INTERVENTION: HOW MUCH IS TOO MUCH?

For centuries, political scientists and economists have argued about the role of government in society. When is government intervention good or bad? Is there too much government involvement or too little? In Module 1, we touched on two primary justifications given for government intervention in the market system—market failure and externalities.

In this Module, we will address seven arguments for government intervention: (1) enforcement of property rights, (2) externalities, (3) provision of public goods, (4) information costs, (5) imperfect competition in markets, (6) macroeconomic goals, and (7) income distribution. In these discussions, we provide arguments both for and against this intervention in an attempt to help you understand the appropriate role of government in a market economy. The first point of contention, property rights, is discussed below.

WHY ARE PROPERTY RIGHTS SO IMPORTANT?

As we discussed in Module 1, property rights give individuals the power to use, sell, rent, dispose of, or enhance the value of the resources they own. The government defines and protects property rights through the legal system and police protection. By defining and enforcing these rights, the government actually provides incentives or disincentives for certain economic activities. On a basic level, if use of your own resources is protected, then it is clearly in your best interest to put those resources to their highest valued use. Otherwise, the value of those resources will be diminished to some degree and you will be less well off than you could have been. In this way, then, property rights are vital to the proper functioning of the market system, because they act as incentives that encourage all participants to use their resources efficiently.

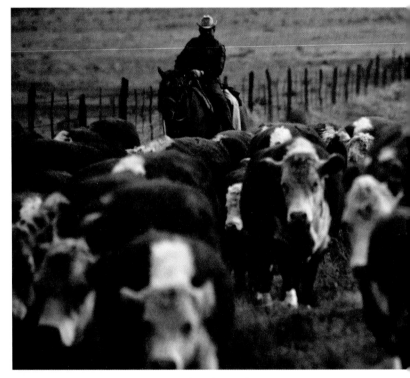

When cattle ranchers are responsible for their cattle damage, they will act to reduce that damage. This might mean fencing their property.

CAN GOVERNMENT ASSUME OWNERSHIP OF PRIVATE PROPERTY?

However, while few would argue against the enforcement of property rights in general, some do point out that the government may wish to reduce the rights of private individuals to utilize their own resources in some instances. Thus, we have zoning laws that prohibit a person from building a factory or erecting a big billboard in predominantly residential areas. Owners of stores in some states are prohibited from operating on Sunday because of "blue" laws, and utility companies and local governments often have easement rights that allow them to construct water and sewer lines across private property. Indeed, through the ancient right of **eminent domain,** governments can assume ownership of private property if compensation is made to the original owners. If the government did not have this right, an individual property owner could block the construction of a new highway or hold out for a very high price. We often face such property rights issues.

1. Property rights give individuals the power to use, sell, rent, dispose of, or enhance the value of their resources.
2. By defining and enforcing property rights, government provides incentives and disincentives for certain economic activities.
3. The right of eminent domain allows government to assume ownership of private property if it compensates the owner.

1. What are the arguments for government intervention in the economy?
2. How is government enforcement of property rights necessary to a market economy?
3. How does the government right of eminent domain affect property rights?
4. Would many bicycles be produced in a country where a person maintained his ownership of a bicycle only as long as he was sitting on it? Why?
5. How do laws against selling stolen property make private property rights more secure?

Government and Externalities

- What is a negative externality?
- How are negative externalities internalized?
- What is a positive externality?
- How are positive externalities internalized?

The forces represented by supply and demand perform an extremely complicated and valuable function. However, these market forces do not always produce the "right" amount of all goods and services. That is, sometimes the market system fails to produce efficient outcomes because of side effects economists call externalities. An **externality** is said to occur whenever there are physical impacts (benefits or costs) of an activity on individuals not directly involved in the activity. If the impact on the outside party is negative, it is called a **negative externality;** if the impact is positive, it is called a **positive externality.**

WHAT ARE NEGATIVE EXTERNALITIES?

The classic example of a negative externality is pollution from an air-polluting factory. If the firm uses clean air in production and returns dirty air to the atmosphere, it has created a negative externality. The polluted air has "spilled over" to outside parties. Now people in the neighboring communities may experience higher incidences of disease, dirtier houses, and other property damage. Such damages are real costs, but because no one owns the air, the firm does not have to pay for its use. This is unlike the other resources the firm uses in production. A steel mill has to pay for its other inputs, like labor, capital, energy, and raw materials, because it must compensate the owners of those inputs for their use. If a firm can avoid paying the cost it imposes on others—the external costs—it has lowered its own costs of production, but not the true cost to society.

Examples of negative externalities are numerous: the roommate that plays his stereo too loud at 2:00 in the morning, the neighbor's dog that barks all night long or leaves "messages" on your front lawn, the gardener that runs his leaf blower on full power at 7:00 A.M. on a Saturday.

Graphing External Costs

In Exhibit 1, we see the market for steel. We also notice that at each level of output, the first supply curve, S_0, is lower

The government can intervene and help eliminate or minimize negative externalities such as pollution.

than the second, S_1. The reason for this is simple: S_0 only includes the private costs to the firm—the capital, entrepreneurship, land, and labor for which it must pay. However, S_1 includes all of those costs plus the external costs that production imposes on others. That is, if the firm could somehow be required to compensate those damaged, it would increase the cost of production for the firm and cause a leftward shift in the supply curve. In Exhibit 1, we see that if the government stepped in and made the firm pay for the external costs, then the output of steel would fall to Q_1, and the price would rise to P_1. However, if the government does not step in, the real price from society's standpoint is higher than P_1, at P_2. While the buyers of steel may only be paying P_0, there are also the implicit costs incurred by the bystanders who are suffering from the ill effects of the pollution. These costs are measured by the difference between P_0 and P_2. If the suppliers of steel are not aware of or not responsible for the external costs, they will tend to produce too much from society's standpoint. The efficiency loss from this overproduction is represented by the shaded area in Exhibit 1.

The supply curve S_1 includes the costs of production reflected by the private supply curve S_0, plus the external costs (such as pollution). Market production is greater and market price is lower than is socially desirable when externalities are not internalized. The shaded area designates the efficiency loss from overproduction.

WHAT CAN THE GOVERNMENT DO TO CORRECT FOR A NEGATIVE EXTERNALITY?

The government can intervene in market decisions in an attempt to take account of these negative externalities. It may do this by estimating the amount of those external costs and then taxing the manufacturer by that amount, forcing the manufacturer to internalize (bear) the costs.

Pollution Taxes

Pollution taxes are designed to internalize negative externalities. If government could impose a pollution tax or an effluent fee equal to the exact size of the external cost, then the firm would produce at the socially desired level of output, Q_1. That is, the tax would shift the supply curve for steel up to S_1 and would provide an incentive for the firm to produce at the efficient level of output. An additional feature of this approach is that tax revenues would be generated that could be used to compensate those that had suffered damages from the pollution, or that could be used (or returned to taxpayers) in some other productive way.

Regulation

Alternatively, the government might simply prohibit certain types of activities causing pollution, or might force firms to clean up their emissions. The purchase and use of new pollution-control devices can also increase the cost of production and shift the supply curve to the left, from S_0 to S_1.

RUBES

How to tell when water pollution
has reached unacceptably high levels

WHAT ARE POSITIVE EXTERNALITIES?

For some goods, the individual consumer does not receive all of the benefits. This is not the case for, say, a hamburger; if you buy it, you get all of its benefits. However, consider education, well-kept home exteriors, beautiful art, or even praying mantises and ladybugs as alternatives to pesticides. Certainly, when you "buy" an education, you receive many of its benefits: greater future income, more choice of future occupations, and the consumption value of knowing more about life as a result of classroom (and extracurricular) learning. These benefits, however, great as they may be, are not all of the benefits associated with your education. You may be less likely to be unemployed or commit crimes, or you may end up curing cancer or solving some other social problem of importance. These nontrivial benefits are the *positive* external consumption benefits of education.

Why does the government subsidize and produce so much education? Presumably because the private market

Governments provide some services because of the positive externalities.

does not provide enough. It is argued that the education of a person benefits not only that person, but all of society, because a more informed citizenry can make more intelligent collective decisions that benefit everyone. Another example: Why do public health departments sometimes offer "free" inoculations against certain communicable diseases, such as influenza? Partly because, by protecting one group of citizens, everyone gets some protection; if the first citizen does not get the disease, it prevents that person from passing it on to others. Many governmental efforts in the field of health and education are justified on the basis of perceived positive externalities. Of course, because positive externalities are often difficult to measure, it is hard to empirically demonstrate whether many governmental health and educational programs achieve their intended purpose.

Graphing External Benefits

Let's take the case of a new vaccine against the common cold. The market for the vaccine is shown in Exhibit 2. The demand curve D_0 represents the prices and quantities that buyers would be willing to pay to reduce their probability of catching the common cold. The supply curve shows the amounts that suppliers would offer for sale at different prices. However, at the equilibrium output, we are far

| EXHIBIT 2 | POSITIVE EXTERNALITIES |

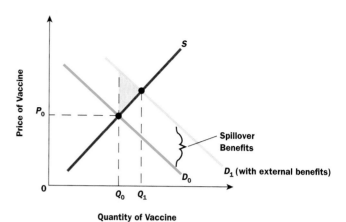

The private demand curve plus external benefits constitutes the social demand curve, D_1. The market output falls short of the socially optimal output, Q_1, and the market underproduces the good. The shaded area indicates the associated efficiency loss.

short of the desirable level of output for these vaccination shots. Why? The reason is that many people benefit from the vaccines. Those who do not have to pay for the vaccines are now less likely to be infected because others took the vaccine. If we could add the benefits that are derived by nonpaying consumers, the demand curve would shift to the right, from D_0 to D_1. The greater level of output, Q_1, that would result if D_1 were the observed demand reflects the total benefits and the desirable output level. However, because producers are unable to collect payments from all of those who are benefiting from the good or service, the market has a tendency to underproduce. In this case, the market is not producing enough vaccinations from society's standpoint. The efficiency loss associated with underproduction is represented by the shaded area in Exhibit 2.

WHAT CAN THE GOVERNMENT DO TO CORRECT FOR POSITIVE EXTERNALITIES?

How could society correct for this market failure? Two particular methods of achieving the higher preferred output are subsidies and regulations.

Subsidies

Government could either give refunds to individuals who receive an inoculation or they could provide an incentive for businesses to give their employees "free" inoculations at the office. Public schools receive huge subsidies from the government—of course, you pay for some of it as a taxpayer. If the subsidy was exactly equal to external benefits of inoculation, the demand curve would shift from D_0 to D_1, resulting in an efficient level of output, Q_1.

Regulation

The government could also pass a regulation requiring each person to get an inoculation shot. This would also shift the demand curve to the right toward the efficient level of output.

In summary, when there are positive externalities, the private market supplies too little of the good in question (such as education or inoculations for communicable diseases). When there are negative externalities, the market supplies too much. In either case, buyers and sellers are receiving the wrong signals. The producers and consumers are not doing what they do because they are evil; rather, both the well-intentioned and the ill-intentioned behave according to the incentives they face. The free market, then, works fine in providing most goods, but it functions less well without regulations, taxes, and subsidies in providing others.

NON-GOVERNMENT SOLUTIONS TO EXTERNALITIES

Sometimes the externality problems can be handled by individuals without the intervention of government. For example, moral and social codes may prevent some people from littering, driving gas-guzzling cars, or using gas-powered mowers and log burning fireplaces. In short, people may decide to take steps on their own to minimize negative externalities. For example, many environmental groups receive money from private sources to handle problems associated with negative externalities. These benefactors are acting on their own to reduce negative externalities. The same self-regulation also applies to positive externalities. For example, philanthropists frequently donate money to public and private schools. In part, this must be because they view the positive externalities from education as a good buy for their charitable dollars.

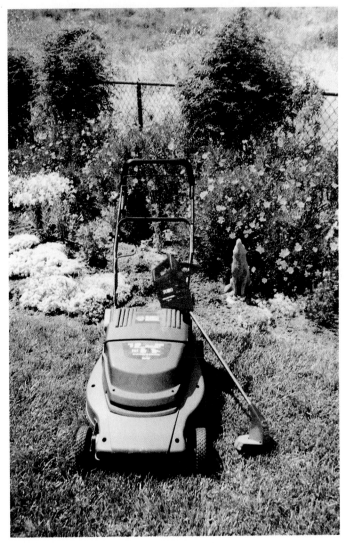

Some may switch from gas mowers and trimmers to battery-powered equipment to minimize negative externalities.

CONCEPT CHECK

1. If a market activity has a negative physical impact on an outside party, that side effect is called a negative externality.
2. The government can use pollution taxes or other forms of regulation to correct the overallocation problem associated with negative externalities.
3. If a market activity has a positive physical impact on an outside party, that side effect is called a positive externality.
4. The government can provide subsidies or other forms of regulation to correct the underallocation problem associated with positive externalities.

---

1. Why are externalities also called spillover effects?
2. How are externalities related to property rights?
3. How do external costs affect the price and output of a polluting activity?
4. How can the government intervene to force producers to internalize external costs?
5. How does internalizing the external costs improve efficiency?

6. How do external benefits affect the output of an activity that causes them?
7. How can the government intervene to force external benefits to be internalized?
8. Why do most cities have more stringent noise laws for the early morning and late evening hours than for during the day?

Government and Public Goods

■ What are public goods?
■ What is the free rider problem?
■ Why does the government provide public goods?

WHAT IS A PUBLIC GOOD?

Externalities are not the only culprit behind resource misallocations. Another source of market failure is what economists call **public goods.** As used by economists, this term refers not to how particular goods are purchased—by a government agency rather than some private economic agent—but to the properties that characterize them. A private good such as a hamburger has two critical properties in the present context. First, if you buy it, it is yours—nobody else can have it (unless you let them, in which case you no longer have it). This property is referred to as **excludability.** Second, the user of a private good receives *all* the benefits of its consumption. Consumption of a private good is therefore **rivalrous.**

Unlike private goods, the consumption of public goods is both nonexcludable and nonrivalrous. One example of a public good is national defense. Whatever the level of national defense, we all benefit from it (consumption is nonrivalrous). That is, once the military has its defense in place, everyone is protected simultaneously. In addition, it is prohibitively costly to exclude anyone from consuming

national defense. For example, if you lived at 16 Main Street and you weren't willing to pay to be protected, it would be too costly to exclude you. That is, it is too difficult to exclude anyone from consuming a public good (consumption is nonexcludable).

WHAT IS A FREE RIDER?

Public goods are closely related to externalities and to something called the **free rider problem.** Suppose the quality of the air where you live is undesirable, so you clean it up. Perhaps you reduce your own pollution by substituting a cleaner wood-burning stove for a highly polluting one, or even by placing a huge filter upwind of your home. Because air quality is largely a public good, you know that others will benefit. It might well be advantageous from society's perspective for the air to be cleaned up in this way, but what incentive do your neighbors have to pay for the benefits they will receive?

The answer, of course, is very little. They know that if you choose to clean up the air, they cannot be prevented from receiving the benefits. They also know, individually, that not one of them would honestly be willing to pay enough to affect your decision. In other words, they may attempt to become what are known as "free riders." Because you do not receive compensation for the benefits accruing to them, you will not clean up and will pollute more than you would otherwise.

Now suppose a "Save the Whales" group came to your neighborhood collecting funds with which to lobby for protection of the blue whales (whose existence is a public good according to the definition). You may have a genuine interest in the whale's continued existence, but what incentives to contribute do you face? Suppose the whale's survival is actually worth $100 to you. If the 100 million households in the United States each made a similar contribution, this would add up to about $10 billion. You might write a check for $100. Or you might reason as follows: "If I give $100, there is no guarantee that the whale gets saved, because my contribution is negligible relative to the

Government provides important public goods, such as national defense.

No one has property rights over blue whales, so who has an incentive to protect this valuable asset?

amount required to convene conferences, pass legislation, buy up existing boats, and so on. Furthermore, if I don't give $100, the whale may get saved anyhow, and I'll continue to receive the benefits of its existence plus the benefits of the $100." Taking the latter course represents a rational attempt to become a free rider. The rub is that if everyone attempts to take a free ride, the ride will not exist.

PROPERTY RIGHTS AND FREE RIDES

It is easy to see how property rights figure into this discussion of the free rider problem by pursuing the previous examples. If air quality were like land quality, where rights of ownership and use were easy to prescribe and enforce, each "owner" of air would have an incentive to protect the value of his or her asset just as people paint their homes, rotate their crops, and take similar actions to maintain the value of other assets. The nature of air, however, precludes this—it is difficult to own.

For example, why are blue whales, condors, and bighorn sheep endangered when cows, chickens, and ordinary sheep are not? The property rights associated with cows and similar animals give their owners the incentive to care for them. Nobody owns whales (or acts as if they did); hence, whale users are not charged a price to reflect the scarcity of whales, as they would be if cows were scarce. An ironic conclusion emerges: It is often believed that the price system of capitalist economies is responsible for our environmental woes, when in fact the opposite is true. The problem is a lack of prices (charging a zero price for the use of socially scarce air or wildlife). Where prices work properly, we do not have environmental problems.

There is, however, a qualification to this assertion that there would be no environmental problems if the price system worked properly. The assertion takes, as seems appropriate to economists, negative externalities to be synonymous with environmental problems. This means that it

is human values that matter and that some environmental degradation may be optimal: When the benefits of producing a polluting good are greater than the full social costs, there are no "environmental problems," in the sense that efforts to improve the environment further would make us worse off.

On both the supply and the demand side, it is clear that we are likely to get too little of public goods without some intervention—indeed, we generally get zero! On the supply side, nonexcludability precludes charging consumers for benefits received. As a result, producers are not able to cover their costs of producing public goods from revenues. On the demand side, individual consumers have an incentive to be free riders, further reducing the likelihood that goods having benefits greater than costs will be produced. Public goods, then, are not profitable to produce.

As a result of the nonexclusion provision of public goods, the free rider problem prevents the private market from supplying the efficient amount of the public goods. The government may be able to step in to overcome the free rider problem. For example, if national defense has total benefits that are greater than total costs, the government can provide defense and have all taxpayers pay for it. Without the government supplying national defense, some households may choose not to pay for it knowing that it is too difficult to keep them from receiving the benefits of protection.

WHEN ARE PUBLIC GOODS NOT GOOD?

Arguments surrounding the government provision of public goods often involve the contention that production of many public goods represent an inefficient use of resources. But how? When evaluating the desire for a public good, the government cannot accurately assess the desires of market participants. In its assessment of the desire for a public good, the government must, just like other suppliers of goods, complete a benefit–cost analysis that weighs the benefits of providing the good against the cost that must be incurred to provide that good.

Consider the case of a new highway. Before it builds the highway, the appropriate government agency will undertake a benefit–cost analysis of the situation. In this case, it must evaluate consumers' willingness to pay for the highway against the costs that will be incurred for construction and maintenance. However, those individuals that want the highway have an incentive to exaggerate their desire for it. At the same time, individuals who will be displaced or otherwise harmed by the highway have an incentive to exaggerate the harm that will be done to them. Together, these elements make it difficult for the government to accurately assess need. Ultimately, their evaluations are reduced to educated guesses about the net impact, weighing both positive and negative effects, of the highway on all parties concerned.

1. A public good is both nonrival in consumption (one person's usage of it does not diminish another's ability to use it) and nonexclusive (no one can be excluded from using it).

2. A free rider is someone who attempts to enjoy the benefits of a good without paying for it.

3. The government provides public goods because the free rider problem results in underproduction of these goods in the marketplace.

1. How are public goods different from private goods?
2. Why does the free rider problem arise in the case of public goods?
3. How does the free rider problem relate to property rights?
4. In what way can government provision of public goods solve the free rider problem?

5. Why is it difficult for the government to determine the proper amount of a public good to produce?
6. How does a TV broadcast have characteristics of a public good?
7. Can lighthouse services be privately provided if all of the boats using the services of a lighthouse are heading for the port nearest that lighthouse? Why or why not?

Government and Information Costs

- What are information costs?
- How does the government disseminate information?
- Should the government be in the information business?

WHAT ARE INFORMATION COSTS?

It is assumed that persons buying or selling goods in the marketplace are acting in a manner that maximizes their satisfaction, or utility. For consumers to do this, however, they must have accurate information about the quality and characteristics of the goods and services in question.

Information can be treated like most other scarce goods: It is desirable and limited, and people are willing to pay a positive price to obtain it. In short, people are willing to pay a certain cost to obtain information. Just as in any other cost-benefit evaluation, however, individuals will stop searching for information when the cost of obtaining that additional information outweighs the benefit they expect to gain from it. This is why consumers are willing to spend more time researching before a car purchase than before buying toothpaste. Unlike the toothpaste purchase, the consequence of making a mistake when buying a car is significant, so the cost of gathering information is relatively small compared to the benefit that can be gained.

However, when information costs to consumers are greater than the perceived benefits, consumers will make less-informed decisions. As the late Nobel Laureate George Stigler pointed out years ago, "It is perfectly rational for people to make 'poor' decisions if the cost of information necessary to make good decisions exceeds the benefits." For example, consider the case of Pete Moss, an average consumer who desires to buy a lawn edger. Pete finds two virtually identical edgers, each costing $250. Because (as far as he knows) the cost to him ($250) is identical regardless of his purchase choice, Pete buys the first edger. Unbeknown to Pete, however, the blade on that edger is made of lower-quality materials, increasing the likelihood of accidents and product failure. Because he lacked the appropriate information, Pete made a poorer decision than he might have.

HOW DOES THE GOVERNMENT DISSEMINATE INFORMATION?

Much legislation passed at the federal as well as the state and local levels in the past 50 years seems directed towards reducing information costs and keeping consumers from making dangerous or worthless purchases. The U.S. Department of Agriculture inspects meat and rates its quality, giving consumers some information about meat quality. The inspection of scales used in markets is carried out by state and local governments to protect customers from misinformation. The Securities and Exchange Commission attempts to protect investors from unwitting losses by requiring sellers of securities to provide certain forms of information, to have training, and so forth. Another well-established form of consumer protection is **occupational licensing** laws for professions. Occupational licenses are now required to practice medicine, law, plumbing, marriage counseling, and so on.

Proponents of these laws argue that they assure consumers that certain minimal quality standards will be met, thus reducing private information costs. If a doctor has a license, which can be obtained by passing a licensing exam, presumably he or she has had reasonably good training in medicine. In recent years, consumer groups have pushed for new forms of protection in the form of information, such as warning labels on products that contain possible cancer-causing agents, "truth in lending" laws requiring interest rates and other loan terms to be stated clearly and honestly, laws forcing tire manufacturers to grade their tires according to uniform federal standards, and so on.

Sometimes the government provides warning labels on products to inform consumers.

Sometimes, rather than providing consumers with information about potentially injurious products and letting them make their own purchase decisions, the government simply bans the product. Examples include bans on the sale of certain insecticides and, more recently, the decision to take certain diet drugs off the market.

Sometimes governments ban certain products.

Governmental information services are not limited to purchasers of goods and services, but also extend to suppliers. For decades, the federal government has provided information to farmers on how to produce various types of agricultural products, via a system of county extension agents. Government has also mandated that producers reveal information like miles per gallon in city and highway driving on new cars or energy usage on electric appliances. Likewise it provides added information on weather conditions, prices, projected supplies, and so on. Also, suppliers of labor services—workers—are provided labor market information through state employment bureaus.

WHAT ARE THE OBJECTIONS TO GOVERNMENT INFORMATION SERVICES?

Few will quarrel with the objective of reducing information costs to consumers and suppliers, permitting more intelligent market decisions and leading to greater satisfaction. However, one can still oppose certain types of governmental action in this area on the grounds that the costs of providing the information are too high, that the government is disseminating inaccurate or misleading information, or that special-interest groups have managed to manipulate the regulation to their own advantage, which may not be in the public interest.

For example, occupational licensing laws supposedly protect misinformed consumers from getting shoddy services, but these laws may also restrict competition, reducing the supply of workers providing these services and leading to higher prices. For example, each plumber can gain thousands of dollars in income by sharply limiting the number of competing plumbers, so some plumbers are willing to pay money and use their time to insure that occupational licensing of plumbers serves to restrict the supply of plumbers and thus competition. As a consequence of the restrictive licensing, hundreds of thousands of customers may pay $40 or $50 more a year for plumbing services, but these consumers either do not know about the effects of these restrictions or do not regard that potential cost to be big enough to make a fuss, so a small pressure group of plumbers could continue to control the licensing board. While it does not always work this way, it is possible that occupational licensing may do as much harm as good.

Likewise, Sam Peltzman has argued that the Food and Drug Administration, in its attempts to prevent drugs from going on sale when we are not certain as to their safety, has saddled pharmaceutical firms with so much higher information costs in the form of testing of new drugs that the companies have markedly reduced the amount of new life-saving drugs coming on the market. In its attempt to be sure that drugs are 100 percent safe, the FDA forces companies to spend millions of dollars on extremely elaborate testing, even where the drug has clear medical benefits and only a remote possibility of harm. On balance, the FDA *may* actually be raising the death and illness rate, not lowering it, because in its effort to keep bad drugs off the market, it also keeps good drugs off the market that may save thousands of lives.

Also, there can be much disagreement as to the methods the government uses to change consumer behavior for the

What do you think would happen to taxi fares if licenses were not required?

good. For example, years ago, the government decided to warn people of the dangers of cigarette smoking by requiring labeling information on cigarettes. Some would argue, however, that if cigarette smoking is truly as dangerous as alleged, the use of cigarettes should be banned. Taking another philosophical approach, some would condemn the prohibition of, say, cigarettes, arguing "Let adults decide for themselves if they wish to incur the health risks associated with tobacco consumption, as long as they do not impose harm on others." The "do at your own risk" group believes that government activity should be confined, at most, to providing individuals information and allowing them to make their own decisions.

Government-provided information, then, can be a good and efficient mechanism for reducing market failure from information costs. On the other hand, excessive governmental information policies can actually worsen the allocation of resources when the information provided is costly, relatively useless, and/or creates other market imperfections, such as a monopoly due to licensing.

"But the government won't let me market it until I figure out a way to attach a warning label."

IN THE NEWS

RUDOLPH THE RED-TAPED REINDEER

It's a good thing Santa Claus lives and works at the North Pole rather than in the United States. If he had his shop in this country, Santa would have to function under so many laws and regulations that the federal government would likely close him down, leaving millions of boys and girls disappointed on Christmas morning.

Just consider some of the government agencies that could threaten Santa's work:

1. *The Fish and Wildlife Service.* Santa's sleigh is pulled by reindeer. But while reindeer are not an endangered species, flying reindeer are quite rare, and there is only one red-nosed reindeer known to exist. So under the Endangered Species Act, Dancer and Prancer might be allowed to continue working, but Rudolph would have to be placed in a safe habitat.

2. *The Occupational Safety and Health Administration.* It is not at all clear that Santa's workshop would pass federal OSHA standards for workplace safety. Does Santa have too many elves packed into a small room? Are there an adequate number of fire extinguishers and fire escapes?

3. *The Equal Employment Opportunity Commission.* It is clear that Santa hires a large number of vertically challenged people—elves. But all of these elves appear to be white males, which leaves the suspicion that Santa is in violation of the Civil Rights Act.

4. *The Federal Aviation Administration.* Santa's flying sleigh would need to be equipped with seat belts to be used on take-offs and landings. Since he flies over water, his sleigh would need a life preserver. The sleigh would also need the proper lighting—a real problem since Rudolph's nose is red, which would normally indicate the rear of the flying object rather than the front.

5. *The Commerce Department.* Santa is involved in the transport of consumable goods, which means he would be subject to certain weight restrictions and proper placarding of his sleigh if any hazardous materials were on board. Furthermore, regulations limit the number of hours a person can operate a vehicle transporting goods. After 10 hours behind the reins, Santa would probably have to take an 8-hour break, impeding his ability to finish his worldwide job on Christmas Eve.

6. *The National Labor Relations Board.* Is Santa using cheap elf labor, or is he paying his elves at least minimum wage? Is he giving them a lunch break? Paying overtime? Providing elf health insurance? A retirement plan?

All of these issues are important, yet Santa is avoiding them by doing business at the North Pole. Which raises another vital concern: By "dumping" toys in the United States at below-market prices (to wit, free), Santa is subjecting U.S. toy manufacturers and dealers to unfair competition and putting countless Americans out of work.

There's only one solution: Washington should impose stiff tariffs on goods imported from the North Pole, lifting them only when Santa ends his unfair trade practices and brings his operation up to American health and safety standards.

SOURCE: Merrill Matthews, Jr., *The Wall Street Journal*, December 24, 1997, Section A10.

CONSIDER THIS:
Sometimes too much regulation can be burdensome to any economy.

1. Individuals will search for additional information as long as the marginal benefit gained from that information is greater than the marginal cost of obtaining it.

2. The government can reduce information costs to consumers and producers, permitting them to make better decisions.

3. Government information policies can be costly if the information provided is inaccurate, misleading, or relatively useless, or results in other market imperfections.

---

1. How long should you continue to seek more information before making a decision?

2. What is the rationale for government provision of information?

3. What are the objections to government provision of information?

4. Why do consumers spend more time researching a home purchase than an electric can opener purchase?

5. If someone argues that we need occupational licensing of gardeners to guarantee that misinformed consumers don't get shoddy service, is that person more likely to be a (highly trained) gardener or a homeowner who uses a gardening service? Why?

Other Government Functions

■ How does government discourage insufficient competition?
■ What are the primary macroeconomic goals of government?
■ How does government attempt to reach these goals?

INSUFFICIENT COMPETITION IN MARKETS

Another justification given for government intervention is to correct cases of insufficient competition that arise in the marketplace. As we discussed in Module 1, **monopoly,** or one-supplier, situations result in higher prices and lower quantities traded than might otherwise be supported by the market. When such conditions of restricted competition arise, the communication system of the marketplace is disrupted, causing the market to function inefficiently, to the detriment of consumers. For this reason, since the 1880s, the federal government has engaged in antitrust activities designed to encourage competition and discourage monopoly conditions. Specifically, the Antitrust Division of the Department of Justice and the Federal Trade Commission attempt to increase competition by attacking monopolistic practices.

MACROECONOMIC GOALS: FULL EMPLOYMENT, PRICE STABILITY, AND ECONOMIC GROWTH

The market mechanism does not assure fulfillment of some economic goals, most notably full employment but also stable prices and a high rate of economic growth. In the past 50 years, many have come to feel that governments can intervene in the economy to increase employment, stabilize prices, and/or bring about a greater growth in output over time. In particular, the objective of full employment has been used to justify government interventions. The apparent failure of the "self-correcting" market economy during the Great Depression led to a call for governmental involvement through spending and taxation programs designed to increase output and reduce unemployment.

Unemployment

During the 1930s, the unemployment rate rose to more than 20 percent of the labor force, and among some groups, notably female and minority workers, unemployment rates were even higher. For example, 75 percent of the black women of Detroit in early 1931 who wanted to work were unable to find a job. The concern over unemployment manifested itself in the passage of legislation committing the nation to a goal of full employment consistent with price stability, the Employment Act of 1946. Government policies, like taxes, and government spending can stimulate the economy when we are at less than full employment.

Massive unemployment in the Great Depression prompted passage of the Employment Act of 1946.

Other Government Functions

Inflation

An increase in the overall price level increases burdens on people with fixed incomes, particularly when the inflation is not anticipated. As we discussed in Module 1, inflation leads to market uncertainties and inefficiencies. In addition, incomes may be redistributed by changing prices, leading to a distribution that may conflict with national policy objectives. Again, policies of altering tax levels, government spending, and bank behavior have been used to deal with the problem of rising prices.

Economic Growth

Other goals, such as increasing the rate of economic growth over time, also sometimes command governmental attention, not only in the United States but also in many other countries of the world. In the United States, the question of the long-term performance of the economy has figured in most presidential campaigns and has influenced many public policy decisions.

There is much debate as to how successful economic intervention by the government has been in achieving these goals. Some economists believe that intervention is counterproductive. There is even greater disagreement among economists and policymakers over which goal to emphasize: What is the greater evil, unemployment or inflation?

CONCEPT CHECK

1. Government encourages competition and discourages monopoly, or one-supplier conditions, through its antitrust activities.
2. Many economists believe that lower taxes and government spending can promote employment when the economy is not operating close to full capacity.
3. With appropriate levels of taxation and government spending, coupled with sound banking policies, the government can help to keep inflation in check.

1. Why would the government want to prevent market conditions of insufficient competition?
2. What are the macroeconomic goals of government intervention in the economy?
3. What government policy changes might be effective in increasing employment in recessions?
4. What government policy changes might be effective in controlling inflation?

Government and Income Distribution

MODULE 6

- What tools does government use to redistribute income?
- What are subsidies?
- What are transfer payments?

DOES THE MARKET DISTRIBUTE INCOME FAIRLY?

Not only does the market determine what goods are going to be produced, and in what quantities, but it also determines, through the interaction of demand and supply for productive resources, the distribution of output among members of society. It is the opinion of some that the market distribution of income produces disparities that violate a common sense of equity or fairness. For example, in the 1920s, the wealthiest 1 percent of income recipients received some 15 percent of the nation's income, and the top 5 percent received 30 percent, while the poorest 20 percent received only about 5 percent. Given these conditions, it is not surprising that many believed that community welfare could be increased by taking some income from the very rich and distributing it to the poor or even to the middle class.

There are three major ways that government redistributes income: taxes, subsidies, and transfer payments. We will now examine each of these methods in turn.

Taxes

In addition to being one of the primary ways that the government finances its activities, taxes are an important tool for redistributing income. Specifically, one type of tax, a progressive tax, is designed to take a larger percentage of higher incomes as compared to lower incomes. In this way, progressive taxes help to reduce income disparities. The federal income tax is an example of a progressive tax. The progressive tax and other types of taxes will be discussed in greater detail later in this Module.

Taxes are one way to attempt to change the distribution of income.

Government Subsidies

A second way that governments can help the less affluent is by the use of governmental revenues to provide low-cost public services. Inexpensive public housing, subsidized public transport, and even public parks are services that probably serve the poor to a greater extent than the rich. "Free" public education is viewed by many as an equalizing force in that it opens opportunities for children of less prosperous members of society to obtain the skills necessary for employment that could improve their economic status.

Transfer Payments

A third means by which income redistribution can be carried out by government is through direct transfer payments. Transfer payments are income payments made by the government to the poor and aged for which no goods or services are exchanged. Transfer payments to individuals are a very rapidly growing form of governmental activity, now involving more public expenditure than for such traditional government programs as national defense or education. Between 1965 and 1995, federally funded transfer payments to individuals went from less than 6 percent of total output to roughly 15 percent of total output.

Public assistance programs, such as food stamps, Medicaid, and welfare payments, for example, are designed to raise the living standards of the poor. Social Security programs provide incomes to older persons who have little ability, or perhaps desire, to obtain work-related income. Social Security accounts for nearly half of all transfer payments. This includes retirement pensions, as well as survivor and disability benefits. Benefits for the unemployed in the form of unemployment compensation are also an important form of transfer payments. A rapidly growing form of transfer payment is in the area of health care, mostly as a consequence of the Medicare program for the elderly and the Medicaid program for the poor.

In a sense, many transfer payments are simply deferred compensation to employees, where certain job-related payments are not made until the individual retires, resigns, or is laid off. Social Security, other retirement programs for government workers, veteran's benefits, and unemployment compensation are examples. Recipients "earned" these payments by work done and taxes paid in an earlier period. Still, some economists, particularly those with a conservative bent, worry about the impact on work incentives of transferring a growing proportion of income from the working to the nonworking population. Whether there is any validity to these concerns is an empirical question, one that has received increasing attention as transfer payments have grown. Many would support such payments, of course, even if they had some negative impact on the willingness of productive persons to work, as serving useful social purposes.

WHAT IS THE IMPACT OF GOVERNMENT ON THE DISTRIBUTION OF INCOME?

This is not an easy question to answer authoritatively, but it would appear to be in the direction of equalizing the distribution somewhat. While the tax system may be roughly "neutral," government expenditures go to lower- and middle-income classes far more than to upper-income groups (as measured as a proportion of income of those groups). During the first great expansion in government activity in the 1930s and 1940s, when progressive income taxation was first vigorously used and Social Security was inaugurated, income distribution in the United States moved sharply in the direction of equality. By one measure, the share of total income received by the top 5 percent of income recipients fell from 26 percent in 1929 to 17 percent in 1947. Since 1947, there is some dispute as to how much income inequality has been reduced; some argue that it has changed "very little," while others say it has increased. This issue will be explored in more detail later in this book. It is highly likely, however, that the impact of the expansion of government activity has been to reduce inequality at least somewhat from what it otherwise would have been.

Have government programs designed to reduce inequality worked?

ARE THERE OBJECTIONS TO THIS GOVERNMENT INTERVENTION?

As with other aspects of government intervention, the equity argument can generate some sharp disagreements. What is "fair" for one person may seem highly "unfair" to someone else. While one person may find it terribly unfair for some individuals to earn many times the amount that other individuals who work equally hard earn, another person may find it highly unfair to ask one group, the relatively rich, to pay a much higher proportion of their income in taxes than another group. Disputes over governmental income distribution policies have been important in domestic political campaigns in recent years; income distribution, indeed, has been the major economic issue in most of the great political upheavals of the past few centuries. Thus, politicians are constantly debating the fairness of the tax system, calling for reform of the welfare system, debating the merits of food stamps and public housing, and so on.

CONCEPT CHECK

1. The government redistributes income through taxes, subsidies, and transfer payments.
2. Government subsidizes some public services, such as housing and transportation, to help the less fortunate.
3. Transfer payments, such as food stamps and Medicaid, are income payments made by the government to the poor and aged for which no goods or services are exchanged.

---

1. What is the basic argument in favor of government redistribution of income?
2. What are the objections to government intervention intended to redistribute income?
3. How does the government use taxes, subsidies, and transfer payments to redistribute income toward lower-income groups?
4. If a government wanted to make the distribution of income more equal, would it be more effective to impose a tax on luxury cars or on food?

G Public Choice

MODULE 6

- What is public choice theory?
- What is rational ignorance?
- Why do special-interest groups arise?

As we have discussed in this Module, when the market fails, as in the externality or the public good case, it may be necessary for government to intervene and make public choices. However, according to Buchanan and Tullock, government actions in response to externalities may make matters worse.[1] That is, just because markets have failed to generate efficient results doesn't necessarily mean that government can do a better job. One explanation for this is presented in *public choice theory*.

WHAT IS PUBLIC CHOICE THEORY?

Public choice theory is the application of economic principles to politics. Public choice economists believe that government actions are an outgrowth of individual behavior. Specifically, they assume that the behavior of individuals in politics, like those in the marketplace, will be influenced by self-interest. Bureaucrats, politicians, and voters make choices that they believe will yield them expected marginal benefits that are greater than their expected marginal costs. There are, of course, differences between the private sector and the public sector in the "rules of the game." But the self-interest assumption is central to the analysis of behavior in both arenas.

IS SCARCITY ALIVE AND WELL IN THE PUBLIC SECTOR?

The self-interest assumption is not the only similarity between the market and public sectors. For example, scarcity is present in the public sector as well as the private sector. Public schools and public libraries come at the expense of something else. Competition is also present in the public sector, as different government agencies compete for government funds, and lobbyists compete with each other to get through favored legislation.

Are politicians' actions driven by self-interest?

IS INFORMATION MORE COSTLY IN THE POLITICAL ARENA?

While there are similarities between market choice and political choice, there are also differences. For instance, the amount of information that is necessary to make an

[1] See James M. Buchanan and Gordon Tullock, *The Calculus of Consent* (Chicago: The University of Chicago Press, 1962).

efficient decision is much greater in political markets than private markets. In a private market, about the only information that a potential buyer needs to know is how much he or she is willing to pay for the good and how much the seller is willing to accept for the good. The market price informs the buyer how much is necessary to entice the seller to supply the good. Only one question remains: Is the good worth more to the consumer than he or she is willing to pay? If so, the consumer will purchase the good; if not, the consumer will not purchase the good.

Information is much more difficult to obtain when a political good is being considered. The problem is that political decisions usually affect a lot of people. For example, if voters decide to increase national defense, everyone will receive more and pay higher taxes for the additional national defense. However, for such a political decision to result in an efficient result, it will require that we have information on *everyone's preferences*, not just those of an individual buyer and an individual seller.

WHAT IS AN INDIVIDUAL-CONSUMPTION-PAYMENT LINK?

In private markets, when a shopper goes to the supermarket to purchase groceries, the shopping cart is filled with many different goods that the consumer presumably wants and is willing to pay for; this reflects the **individual-consumption-payment link.** The link breaks down when there is an assortment of political goods that have been decided on by majority rule. These political goods might include such items as additional national defense, additional money for the space program, new museums, new public schools, increased foreign aid, and so on. While an individual might be willing to pay for some of those goods, it is unlikely that he or she will want to consume or pay for all of them that have been placed in the political shopping cart. However, if the majority has decided that these political goods are important, the individual will have to purchase the goods through higher taxes, whether he or she values the goods or not.

VOTER APATHY AND SPECIAL-INTEREST GROUPS

Representative democracy has been a successful mechanism for making social choices in many countries. But there are some important differences in the way it is ideally supposed to work and how it actually does work.

One of the keys to an efficiently working democracy is a concerned and informed electorate. Everyone is supposed to take time to study the issues and candidates and then carefully weigh the relevant information before deciding how to vote. Although an informed citizenry is desirable from a social point of view, it is not clear that individuals will find it personally desirable to become politically informed.

Is this person picking the items she wants? Do taxpayers always pay for what they want?

What Are the Costs of Being Politically Informed?

Obtaining detailed information about issues and candidates is costly. Many issues are very complicated, and a great deal of technical knowledge and information is necessary to make an informed judgment on them. To find out what candidates are really going to do requires a lot more than listening to their campaign slogans. It requires studying their past voting records, reading a great deal that has been written either by or about them, and asking them questions at public meetings. Taking the time and trouble to do these things—and more—is the cost that each eligible voter has to pay personally for the benefits of being politically informed.

What Are the Benefits of Being Politically Informed?

Basically, there are two benefits of being politically informed. Some people simply enjoy being informed. These people will be willing to make an effort to acquire some information on public issues just for the sake of knowledge. The other benefit from being informed has nothing to do with satisfying intellectual curiosity. By being politically informed, individuals may be knowledgeable to influence social decisions in directions that will yield them greater benefits. Unfortunately, this does little to motivate most people to become informed, because it isn't much of a benefit. The probability of one person's vote having any effect on an election is practically zero. With many thousands often voting in local elections and millions voting in state and national elections, each citizen is safe in assuming that his or her vote really won't change the outcome.

What Is Rational Ignorance?

So, for most people, the costs of becoming politically informed are substantial, while the benefits are negligible. As a result, most people limit their quest for political information to listening to the radio on the way to work, conversations with friends, casual reading, and other things they normally do anyway. Even though most people in society might be better off if everyone became more informed, it isn't worth the cost for most individuals to make an effort to become informed themselves. As a result, these individuals assume a state of **rational ignorance.**

There are obvious advantages to be realized if the public became more politically aware. Unfortunately, there doesn't seem to be any easy or desirable way of overcoming the problem of rational ignorance. Perhaps the government could require everyone to become politically well informed. However, if the government did that, how would they determine when an individual is adequately informed? Unfortunately, most of us find a close correlation between how much others agree with us and how well informed we think they are. Hence, pushing very far in the direction of having the government require and test political awareness might lead to abuses that could more than offset the benefits of having a more informed society. According to public choice economists, political apathy is not the result of moral decay or lack of patriotism in our society. It's simply the result of individuals acting rationally ignorant.

What Are Special-Interest Groups?

This does not mean that public choice economists think that everyone is politically apathetic or rationally ignorant. This obviously is not the case. Many have a large stake in being politically informed on particular issues. For example,

T U N E   U P

RATIONAL IGNORANCE

Q: With only two out of three eligible voters registered, the "motor voter" bill has recently been passed, which will use the Department of Motor Vehicles to increase voter registration. If voter registration is done in conjunction with drivers' licenses, it is estimated that 91 percent of the eligible voters will then be registered to vote. Will this resolve the problem of rational ignorance?

A: Not according to public choice economists. They believe reasons for "voter apathy" have little to do with the number of voters registered and everything to do with individual incentives. That is, no matter how many voters are registered, individuals will still weigh the benefits and costs of acquiring additional information before voting.

"I think voter apathy is terrible...everybody should turn out and vote for either what's-his-name or you-know-who."

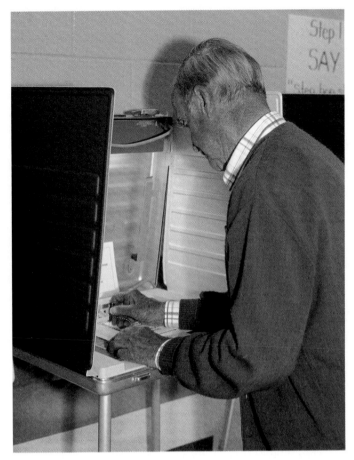

Why is voter turnout frequently so low?

individuals may have a strong motivation to organize a political pressure group. As a group, these individuals are more likely to influence decision makers and have a far greater impact on the outcome of a social decision than they would with just their one vote. Also, members of these **special-interest groups** will find it easier to organize because of the commonality of their goals and purpose. And the smaller the group and the more specific their interest, the less costly it will become to organize and get everyone to contribute his or her share. Hence, it is not surprising that special-interest groups are often able to bring a great deal of political pressure to bear on certain public decisions.

What About Those Not in the Special-Interest Group?

Individuals who are not in the special-interest group will pay the bill if the special-interest group is successful. Why can't the majority of citizens effectively counter the political power of a minority group? The answer to this question lies in the fact that the majority makes up such a large group. If the special-interest group is successful in getting everyone else to pay for a project that benefits them, the cost will be spread over such a large number of taxpayers that the amount any one person will have to pay is negligible. There isn't much motivation for an individual citizen to spend time and effort to resist an interest group, even if it were guaranteed that this resistance would be effective.

With Special-Interest, A Few Gain at the Expense of Many

When a special-interest issue comes up that benefits the few at the expense of the many, it is likely that elected representatives will be solicited by special-interest groups. Because the special-interest activity will likely impose only small costs on each individual taxpayer, those paying the bill may know little or nothing about it. That is, if each representative believes that a favorable vote will be recognized and appreciated by those in favor of it and will go virtually unnoticed by those paying the bill, then he or she might be willing to support the special-interest group. Because getting reelected and receiving financial support are obviously important to elected representatives, special-interest groups will be effective at influencing their voting behavior. The other side of the coin is that it is difficult to reduce the size of government programs once they are in place. Government programs that arise because of the influence of special interests will generally be perpetuated by the influence of those same special interests. The elimination of such a program will deny a few significant benefits, while saving each general taxpayer but a few dollars in taxes. This might explain why it is so difficult politically to reduce government spending, even if the majority of the voters favored such a reduction in general. When people argue for cutting government spending, they invariably have in mind government programs other than the ones that benefit them. So any attempt to reduce government spending by isolating one program at a time generally meets strong resistance from those benefiting from the program under review and receives little support from the millions of taxpayers who will save but a few dollars each if the program were eliminated.

WHAT IS THE BEST WAY TO CONTROL GOVERNMENT?

According to public choice economists, the best hope for controlling government is by presenting a political package that calls for a simultaneous reduction in many programs. No special interest will be willing to sacrifice its program if it expects to be required to continue paying for the program of others. But if government has grown to the point where people feel that they are not getting their money's worth for the taxes they pay, then many groups will be willing to see their program reduced—if it means some savings on the taxes paid to support everyone else's programs.

WILD PITCH

ROGER G. NOLL

WASHINGTON—Even at a time when major league sports have become a cartoon of financial excess, the proposed new home for the Yankees is breathtaking in its audacity. Excluding land value, a multipurpose mausoleum on Manhattan's West Side would cost a billion dollars.

Independent studies of sports facilities invariably conclude that they provide no significant economic benefits. A sports team does increase overall income in a community slightly, but the increase never offsets the stadium's financing and operating costs. And because a team has relatively few (but very highly paid) employees, it usually causes overall employment in a city to fall because it can drive other entertainment businesses to cut back or close.

Stadiums are bad investments, which is why the teams themselves are never willing to pay for them. New York City would generate more cash by putting the money in a savings account.

Why do cities pour hundreds of millions into new stadiums? With intense competition for sports franchises, not even New York can keep a team without subsidizing it. New Jersey and New York have at various times fought over the Giants, Jets, Yankees, and Mets. The sad thing is that the states need not be competitors: Fans could easily support a third team in both football and baseball. But each league is a monopoly, doing what monopolists do best: making the product scarce to hike up the price.

There is a far cheaper way to keep the Yankees. Bribe them. A new stadium could give the Yankees an additional $10 million in profits each year. So instead of spending $80 million annually to finance and operate a new stadium, New York could just hand the Yankees $10 million. Or, even better, the city could pay $100,000 for each game

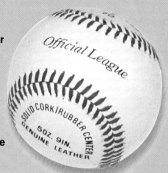

won, with a million-dollar bonus for winning the pennant.

This plan would save the city money, improve the Yankee's bottom line and benefit fans, who would be less likely to have a team that collapsed in the stretch.

Roger G. Noll is a visiting fellow at the Brookings Institution.

SOURCE: *New York Times*, 4/11/96, p. A17.

CONSIDER THIS:
Many big cities have either built or are planning on building large sports arenas, largely at the taxpayers' expense. According to proponents, the new sports arenas will bring recognition and fame to the city, and this will benefit everyone who lives in the city because they will be living in a more prestigious community. Hence, everyone in the city should contribute to the sports arena, whether they go to the games or not.

This is a weak argument. The people who receive the primary benefits from a better sports arena are first, the owners, second, the players, and third, those who frequent it to watch ball games. Further, it's easy to prevent a fan from receiving this benefit if he or she doesn't pay at the gate. The assertion that everyone would benefit from the arena whether they go to the games or not has to be questioned. A sports arena will generate growth and congestion that many will find undesirable. To these people, being forced to pay for a big sports center makes no sense.

Perhaps some people who never go to a sporting event may feel a little bit better just knowing they can. This is what economists call *option demand*. But does this justify commandeering funds from everyone in the city to build a sports arena? What about fine restaurants? Certainly fine restaurants enhance the reputation of the city. Many people are happy to know that one is nearby, waiting to serve them, whether they visit it or not. But most people would find a proposal to publicly finance restaurants very farfetched. If desirable side effects justified government subsidies, well-kept yards, car washes, toothpaste, deodorants, and smiles would all qualify for a handout.

Regardless of the desirability of requiring the public to pay for certain things, it should be noted that special-interest groups expend a lot of effort to get subsidies for those things from which they receive enjoyment and profit. Many of these efforts have been successful; the sports arena example is only one of many. The more "cultured," and usually wealthier, members of many cities have managed to obtain government support for symphonies, operas, ballet, and the performing arts in general. The stated justification for requiring everyone to pay for entertainment that caters primarily to the tastes of the rich is similar to that given for subsidizing sports arenas. Supposedly, everyone in a community will benefit, even those who prefer to sit home with a can of beer and watch all-star wrestling on television.

CAN LESS BE MORE?

Public choice economists are convinced that we can get more from government only by having less government. They recognize that the advantage of government is found in its ability to establish a legal and economic environment that provides general opportunity for people to benefit from their own efforts through productive cooperation with others. But they also see the threat of government if its power is captured by organized special interests and used to advance narrow objectives by imposing costs on the general public. And if the government becomes a vehicle for promoting special interests, it fails in its primary responsibility of expanding opportunities for all. That is, instead of creating opportunities for people to benefit through productive cooperation with each other, government will have created the illusion that people can benefit at the expense of each other. Public choice economists are not callously indifferent to the social benefits that government can provide. In fact, the difference between public choice economists and those who see every social ill as justification for expanding government is not a difference in moral vision. Instead, it is a difference in their understanding of how government actually works. Public choice economists lean toward less government not because they want less from government, but because they believe that it is important to get more opportunities from its actions.

CONCEPT CHECK

1. Public choice theory is the theory that the behavior of individuals in politics, like that in the marketplace, is influenced by self-interest.
2. Rational ignorance is the condition in which voters tend to be relatively uninformed about political issues because of high information costs and low benefits of being politically informed.
3. A special-interest group is a political pressure group formed by individuals with a common political objective.
4. Special-interest groups are more likely to have an impact on the outcome of a social decision than their members would if they voted individually.

1. What principles does the public choice analysis of government behavior share with the economic analysis of market behavior?
2. Why is it rational to be relatively less informed about most political choices than about your own market choices?
3. Why can't the majority of citizens effectively counter the political power of special-interest groups?
4. According to public choice theorists, what is the primary advantage of government? What is the biggest threat from government?
5. Why are college students better informed about their own teachers' and schools' policies than about national education issues?
6. How can you be forced to pay for something you do not want to "buy" in the political sector? Is this sometimes good?
7. Why do you think news reporters are more informed than average citizens about public policy issues?

Spending and Taxation

MODULE 6

- What has happened to the growth of government spending?
- How does government finance its spending?
- What are progressive and regressive taxes?

THE CHANGING ROLE OF GOVERNMENT

It is impossible to precisely measure the degree of governmental involvement in the economy with any single number. Nonetheless, patterns in the ratio of government spending to total output over time should tell us something about the changing governmental role, even if the figures for any specific point in time cannot indicate accurately the precise level of involvement.

Exhibit 1 shows the growth in total government spending in the United States as a percentage of output over time. The graph suggests that the growth of the government sector has indeed been substantial. Total government spending has grown from about 11 percent of output in 1929 to almost 35 percent today. A large part of the growth in the relative importance of government occurred between 1965 and 1980.

However, there has been a slower relative growth in government purchases, and indeed no growth in government purchases as a percentage of output since 1975. Then why has *total* government spending increased from 25 per-

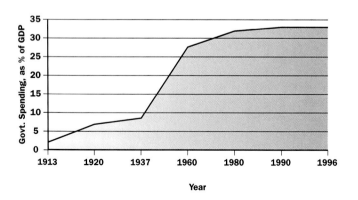

| EXHIBIT 1 | GROWTH IN GOVERNMENT, 1913–1996 |

SOURCE: *The Economist*, September 20, 1997.

cent of total output to almost 35 percent of total output? The answer is the increase in transfer payments for programs such as Social Security and welfare. Income transfer payments have risen from roughly 5 percent of total output in 1965 to 14 percent in 1997.

WHAT AREAS OF GOVERNMENTAL INVOLVEMENT IN THE ECONOMY HAVE GROWN?

Areas of government growth can be determined partly by looking at statistics of the types of government spending, although we would remind you again that the statistics fail to accurately reflect the growing impact of government regulation of the private sector's decision-making process. Exhibit 2 shows categories of government spending as a proportion of total spending.

During the 1920s, most government spending was for such traditional activities as highways, police and fire protection, and sanitation. Approximately one-fourth of governmental spending was for such social concerns as education, health, and public assistance. At that time, national defense accounted for a very small proportion of total spending. During the Great Depression of the 1930s, the welfare function became somewhat more important and other activities less important. During the 1940s, defense spending grew incredibly, accounting for more than three-quarters of the total spending by government in some years of World War II. While defense spending declined in relative importance after 1945, it grew again during the Korean War (1950–1953) and remained high during the Cold War of the 1950s. The share of government spending going for military purposes declined sharply after the mid-1950s, even with the Vietnam War of the 1960s. By the mid-1970s, less than 20 percent of total federal government spending was for defense. The big relative gainer in terms of spending has been for non-defense social concerns. The biggest single area of growth has come in social insurance, such as social security and other government pension programs. Spending in 1974 for social insurance was more than 10 times as great as in 1950. Other areas had rapid

| EXHIBIT 2 | GOVERNMENT EXPENDITURES |

a. Federal Expenditures, 1996

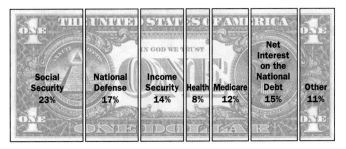

| Social Security 23% | National Defense 17% | Income Security 14% | Health 8% | Medicare 12% | Net Interest on the National Debt 15% | Other 11% |

b. State and Local Expenditures, 1993

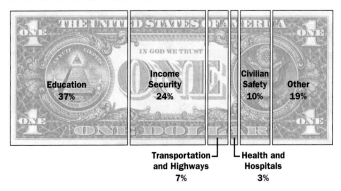

| Education 37% | Income Security 24% | Civilian Safety 10% | Other 19% |

Transportation and Highways 7%

Health and Hospitals 3%

spending growth as well. Educational expenditures, for example, tripled in the 1960s alone. By the mid-1970s, roughly half of government spending was for social concerns such as education, health, and public housing, for the first time in the nation's history. In the 1980s and 1990s, we have seen a continued increase in income transfer payments including Social Security, welfare, and unemployment compensation.

Exhibit 2(a) shows that 37 percent of federal government spending went to Social Security and **income security programs.** Another 20 percent was spent on **health care** and **Medicare** for the elderly. The rest of federal expenditures include national defense (17 percent), interest on the national debt (15 percent) and miscellaneous items such as foreign aid, education, agriculture, transportation and housing (11 percent).

Exhibit 2(b) shows that state and local spending is very different than federal spending. Education and public welfare account for roughly 60 percent of the state and local expenditures. Other areas of state and local spending include highways, housing, and police and fire protection.

HOW DOES GOVERNMENT GENERATE ITS REVENUE?

Governments have to pay their bills like any person or institution that spends money. But how do they obtain revenue? Two major avenues are open: taxation and borrowing. A third possibility, printing money for governmental use, is of lesser importance in most Western nations in recent decades. At this point, we will discuss the use of taxation as a revenue-generating mechanism.

TYPES OF TAXATION

In most years, a large majority of government activity is financed by taxation. What kinds of taxes are levied on the American population?

At the federal level, most taxes or levies are on income. Exhibit 3 shows that about 60 percent of tax revenues come in the form of income taxes on individuals and corporations, called **personal income taxes** and **corporate income taxes,** respectively. Most of the remaining revenues come from **payroll taxes,** which are levied on work related income—payrolls. These taxes are used to pay for Social Security and compulsory insurance plans like Medicare. This tax is split between employees and the employers. The Social Security share of federal taxes has steadily risen as the proportion of the population over 65 has grown and as Social Security benefits have been increased. Consequently, payroll taxes have risen significantly in recent years. In 1997, the employee and the employer were each required to pay 7.65 percent of the employee's income up to $65,400. In addition, employees and employers each must pay a 1.45 percent tax on all employee wages to pay for Medicare. Other taxes on items like gasoline, liquor, and tobacco products provide for a small proportion of government revenues, as do custom duties, estate and gift taxes, and some minor miscellaneous taxes and user charges. The United States federal government relies more heavily on income-based taxes than nearly any other government in the world. Most other governments rely more heavily on sales taxes, excise taxes, and custom duties.

Is an Excise Tax Fair?

Some consider an excise tax, a sales tax on individual products such as alcohol, tobacco, and gasoline, to be the least fair type of tax. This type of tax on specific items will impose a far greater burden, as a percentage of income, on the poor and middle class than on the wealthy, because low-income families pay a greater proportion of their income on these taxes than do high-income families.

In addition, excise taxes may lead to economic inefficiencies. By isolating a few products and subjecting them to discriminatory taxation, consumption taxes subject economic choices to political manipulation and lead to inefficiency.

EXHIBIT 3 | TAX REVENUES

a. Tax Revenues, Federal Government, 1997

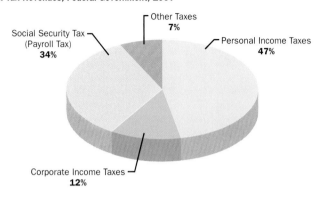

SOURCE: *Economic Report of the President, 1998.*

b. Tax Revenues, State and Local Governments, 1993

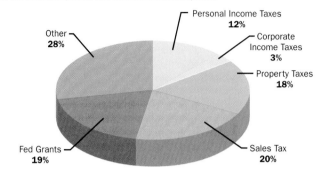

SOURCE: *Economic Report of the President, 1997, p. 397.*

What Is a Progressive Tax?

One impact of substantial taxes on income is that the effective "take home" income of Americans is significantly altered by the tax system. **Progressive taxes,** of which the federal income tax is one example, are designed so that those with higher incomes pay a greater proportion of their income in taxes. As we noted earlier in the Module, a progressive tax is one tool that the government can use to redistribute income. It should be noted, however, that certain types of income are excluded from income for taxation purposes. Much of this income is earned primarily by wealthy persons, such as interest on municipal bonds, although some of the excluded income is income in kind, such as foods stamps or other transfer income, that goes primarily to the poor.

What Is a Regressive Tax?

Payroll taxes, the second most important income source for the federal government, are actually **regressive;** that is, they take a greater proportion of the income of lower-income groups than higher-income groups. The reasons for this are simple. For example, Social Security and Medicare taxes are imposed as a fixed proportion (now 7.65 on employees and an equal amount on employers) of wage and salary income up to $62,700; beyond that income level, wages and salaries are only subject to the 1.45% Medicare tax. Also, wealthy persons have relatively more property income that is not subject to Social Security or Medicare taxes. Adding together individual income and Social Security taxes, the Federal tax system is probably only slightly progressive. The same would hold if other taxes are included.

HOW DO STATE AND LOCAL GOVERNMENT FINANCE ACTIVITIES?

Historically, the major source of state and local revenue has been property taxes. In recent decades, state and local governments have relied increasingly on sales and income taxes for revenues (see Exhibit 3b). Today, sales taxes account for roughly 20 percent of revenues, while personal and corporate income taxes account for 15 percent of revenues. Another 19 percent of state and local revenues come from the federal government in grants. The remaining share of revenues comes from license fees and user charges (e.g., payment for sewers, occupational license fees, tuition fees) and other taxes.

SHOULD WE HAVE A FLAT TAX?

Some politicians and individuals believe that we should scrap the current progressive income tax and replace it with a **flat tax.** A flat tax is designed so that everybody would be charged the same percentage of their income above some certain stipulated income level. How would a flat tax work? What do you think would be the advantages and disadvantages of a flat tax?

Actually, if the flat tax plan allowed individuals to deduct a standard allowance of, say, $20,000 from their wages, the tax would still be progressive. This is how it would work. If you were earning less than $20,000 a year, you would not have to pay any income taxes. However, if you earned $50,000 a year, and the flat tax rate was 15 percent, after subtracting your $20,000 allowance you would be paying taxes on $30,000. In this system, you would have

Used by permission of Chip Bok and Creators Syndicate.

CONTROVERSIAL TRANSIT BILL PASSES IN HOUSE

Ignoring objections from the White House and fiscal conservatives, the House voted 337 to 80 to pass a massive $217 billion transportation bill Wednesday evening.

The spending bill has been blasted by the Clinton administration as well as fiscal conservatives who call it a budget buster and "pork-barrel legislation" run amok. The Senate already has passed its own six-year, $214 billion plan. Both chambers are racing to finish legislation before supplemental money runs out May 1. The bill covers a virtual smorgasbord of programs that give nearly every congressional district a piece of federal largess to call its own. Besides the traditional funds for bridges and roads, the bill would build bike paths, buy clean-fuel buses, and study road congestion relief.

Fiscal conservatives criticized the bill for setting aside 5 percent of the money, more than $9 billion, for 1,463 projects that indi-vidual lawmakers requested for their districts. Republicans were given 55 percent of the money and Democrats 45 percent, and the complaint, strongly denied by the bill's backers, was that pork barrel politicking decided who got what. "I think it's doubtful that well over 1,400 projects are deserving of federal attention," said Rep. Porter Goss, R-Fla., noting that the last six-year program enacted in 1991 had only 539 such projects.

The proposed projects include a $100,000 rail-highway feasibility study in Muncie, Indiana, a $4.5 million pedestrian and bicycle path in New London, Connecti-cut, and a $97 million widening of the I-40 cross-town bridge in Oklahoma City. Watch-dog groups, like Citizens Against Government Waste, pointed to a $12 million allocation for an Appalachian Transportation Institute and $3 million for a television documentary on highways as prime examples of the bill's excesses.

SOURCE: ABCNEWS.com. The Associated Press and Reuters contributed to this report. Also see:

http://www.abcnews.com/sections/us/congresswatchindex/congresswatchindex.html

---

CONSIDER THIS:
Is Congress slipping back to its old spending habits? The President has blasted the legislation because it is full of pork. According to John Kasich, the House Budget Chairman, "Pigs get fat and hogs get slaughtered. This bill is a hog." While the house bill will probably not be approved in this form, it does demonstrate that pork is still alive and well in America.

A GLOBAL COMPARISON OF TAXATION

CONSIDER THIS:
Taxpayers in other parts of the developed world have a heavier per capita tax burden than those in the United States.

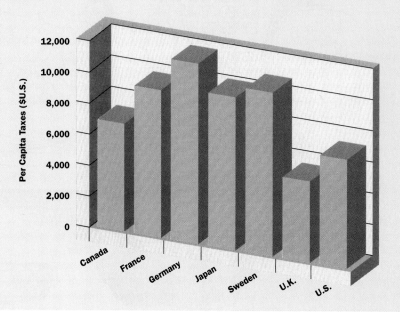

to pay $4,500 in taxes (.15 X $30,000) and your average tax rate would be 6 percent ($3,000/$50,000 = .09). Now, say you made a $100,000 a year. After taking your $20,000 allowance, you would have to pay a 15 percent tax on $80,000, and you would owe the government $12,000. Notice, however, that your average tax rate would be higher: 12 percent ($12,000/$100,000 = 12%) as opposed to 9 percent. So if the flat tax system allows individual taxpayers to take a standard allowance, like most flat tax proposals, then the tax is actually progressive. That is, lower- and middle-income families will pay, on average, a smaller average tax rate, even though everyone has the same tax rate over the stipulated allowance.

The advantages of the flat tax are that all of the traditional exemptions, like entertainment deductions, mortgage interest deductions, business travel expenses, and charitable contribution deductions, would be out the door, along with the possibilities of abuses and misrepresentations that go with tax deductions. Taxpayers could fill out tax returns like they did in the old days, in a space about the size of a postcard. Advocates argue that the government could collect the same amount of tax revenues, but

the tax would be much more efficient, as many productive resources would be released from looking for tax loopholes to doing something productive from society's standpoint. In fact, according to the Internal Revenue Service, the federal government has long collected roughly the same revenues, despite changing top marginal tax rates, which have gone from a high of 91 percent in 1960–1965 to a low of 28 percent in 1988–1990.

Of course, some versions of the flat tax will hurt certain groups. Not surprisingly, realtors and homeowners, who like the mortgage interest deductions, and tax accountants, who make billions every year preparing tax returns, will not be supportive of a flat tax with no deductions. And, of course, many legitimate questions would inevitably arise, such as: What would happen to the size of charitable contributions if the charitable contribution deductions was eliminated? And how much will the housing sector be hurt if the mortgage interest deduction was eliminated or phased out? In addition, the critics of the flat tax believe that the tax is not progressive enough to eliminate the inequities in income and are skeptical of the tax-revenue-raising capabilities of a flat tax.

1. Income transfer payments have risen sharply since 1965.
2. Over a third of federal spending goes towards pensions and income security programs.
3. A progressive tax takes a greater proportion of the income of higher-income groups than of lower-income groups.
4. A regressive tax takes a greater proportion of the income of lower-income groups than of higher-income groups.

1. What accounts for most of the growth of government spending as a share of total output since 1965?
2. What options are available for a government to finance its spending?
3. What is the difference between a progressive tax and a regressive tax?
4. What are some advantages and disadvantages of a flat tax? Would it be progressive?

APPLICATION: Revving up the Helmet Law Debate

Should the government intervene and require motorcycle helmets? How does the debate illustrate the effects of a negative externality? Why are taxpayers concerned? Can you think of a compromise that would make motorcyclists and taxpayers who pay for uninsured motorcycle drivers happy? In other words, how might the externality be internalized to the satisfaction of all parties?

NOTES AND QUOTES FROM THE PREZ, MAY 1997

By the time you read this the Colorado Legislature will have concluded another session. No helmet law bill was introduced in Colorado, Utah, or Wyoming this year. It may be because we have won in these states so many times people are starting to get the message, or it could be that we have worked hard to get those pro-helmet law jerks out of office . . .

Due to at least some of the above listed reasons Arkansas, Guam, and Texas have repealed their helmet laws for adults. Arkansas has a helmet law for those under 21, Guam has a helmet law for those under 18, and Texas apparently has a helmet law for those under 18.

Texas had a problem in their House. It seems someone wanted the law to be for those under 21 and mandatory rider education, with the funds to come out of the general fund. Fortunately, the House sponsor adopted the Senate version in its entirety. The trend by some people to try for an under 21 repeal does not set well with many Legislators, not because they are for helmet laws, but because 18 year olds are adults. It is unfortunate that many so called rights groups are too willing to compromise someone else's freedom, health, and lives.

SOURCE: http://usff.com/RFJ/RFJhome.html.

Many states have now passed mandatory motorcycle helmet laws. And proponents have lauded them as huge successes. But despite this seemingly convincing "proof" of the law's success, opponents remain unconvinced. They have argued that requiring state-approved helmets would have only a minor effect in reducing head injuries and the resulting fatalities, largely because they do little good in most accidents, which occur at more than 20 m.p.h., and may even cause accidents by impairing peripheral vision and hearing.

However, the biggest unresolved objection of the helmet law opponents has never been the issue of safety, but rather the loss of personal freedom involved. They believe that they have the right to choose not to wear a helmet, even given higher risks. After all, each of us sacrifices some safety for thrills, convenience, and savings. For example, heavier cars are generally safer than compact cars, but many people find the savings from driving a small car worth the safety sacrificed. And don't we sacrifice some safety for thrills when we ski, snowboard, hang glide, or skateboard?

Even if one concedes that wearing a helmet does decrease the chance of head injuries, why do some motorcyclists choose not to wear them? Motorcyclists revel in the thrill and sense of freedom they experience. Wearing a bulky motorcycle helmet greatly reduces the quality of this experience for many, and they claim to be willing to pay the price, in terms of reduced safety, for the enjoyment of riding without a helmet.

Helmet law supporters argue that requiring all motorcycle riders to wear helmets would save taxpayers millions of dollars a year, primarily in health care costs.

Ironically, beneath the rhetoric, both opponents and proponents of mandatory helmet laws are seeking freedom. Opponents want the freedom to ride as they wish, even though costs are currently imposed on others in the process. Proponents are arguing for freedom from having to pay the bills for those injured because they chose not to wear a helmet.

Given that under our present health care system, taxpayers assume responsibility for medical care beyond that paid for by insurance, the central problem is really that the freedom to ride without a helmet violates the freedom of taxpayers from footing others' bills. Mandating helmets appears to many as a reasonable compromise, if states are to continue to pick up this tab. However, why must there be such a compromise? Let the riders absorb that cost through mandatory liability insurance. Then riders would not have to sacrifice their freedom, but neither would taxpayers.

Mandatory personal injury insurance, with sufficient coverage, could easily be included as part of motorcycle registration or licensing. Assuming such a law was actually enforced, unlike so many mandatory automobile insurance laws, motorcyclists would finally be required to bear the true costs of not wearing helmets (although insurance companies would have to be allowed to differentiate between helmeted and helmet-less riders in setting their rates). The outcome of such an approach would be far superior to the current compromise. As opposed to mandating helmets, which restricts one type of freedom to enhance another, requiring insurance would allow motorcyclists to maintain their freedom of choice, while giving taxpayers freedom from paying injured motorcyclists' health care tab.

Whether you think its involvement is too much, too little, or just about right, government clearly has a significant impact on the market system. Through the cyberproblems on your EconActive CD-ROM, you can access current information sources on the World Wide Web that will help you to examine specific areas of government intervention, such as transfer payments like Social Security.

Introduction to the Macroeconomy

A. Macroeconomic Goals
What are the three major macroeconomic goals?

B. Employment and Unemployment
What is the unemployment rate?

C. Different Types of Unemployment
What are the different types of unemployment?

D. Inflation
Why is price level stability important?

E. Economic Growth
What are the benefits of economic growth?

F. Economic Fluctuations
What are economic fluctuations?

G. Application: Economic Freedom and Economic Growth
Does economic freedom guarantee economic growth?

Macroeconomic Goals

- What are the most important macroeconomic goals in the United States?
- Are these goals universal?
- How has the United States pursued these goals?

THREE MAJOR MACROECONOMIC GOALS

Nearly every society has been interested in three major macroeconomic goals: (1) maintaining employment of human resources at relatively high levels, meaning that jobs are relatively plentiful and financial suffering from lack of work and income is relatively uncommon; (2) maintaining prices at a relatively stable level so that consumers and producers can make better decisions; and (3) achieving a high rate of economic growth, meaning a growth in real per capita total output over time.

WHAT OTHER GOALS ARE IMPORTANT?

In addition to these primary goals, concern has been expressed at various times and places about other economic issues, some of which are essentially microeconomic in character. For example, concern about the "quality of life" has prompted some societies to try to reduce "bads" such as pollution and crime, and increase goods and services such as education and health services. Another goal has been "fairness" in the distribution of income or wealth. Still another goal present in many nations at one time or another has been becoming self-sufficient in the production of certain goods or services. For example, in the 1970s, the United States implemented policies that reduced U.S. reliance on other nations for supplies of oil, partly for reasons of national security.

HOW DO VALUE JUDGMENTS AFFECT ECONOMIC GOALS?

In stating that nations have economic goals, we must acknowledge that nations are made up of individuals. Individuals within a society may differ considerably in their evaluation of the relative importance of certain issues, or even whether certain "problems" are really problems after all. For example, economic growth, viewed positively by most persons, is not considered so favorably by others.

What are the major macroeconomic policy goals? Why are they important?

While some citizens may think the income distribution is just about right, others might think it provides insufficient incomes to the poorer members of society, while still others think it involves taking too much income from the relatively well-to-do and thereby reduces incentives to carry out productive income-producing activities.

ACKNOWLEDGING OUR GOALS: THE EMPLOYMENT ACT OF 1946

Many economic problems—particularly those involving unemployment, price instability, and economic stagnation—are pressing concerns for the U.S. government. In fact, it was the concern over both unemployment and price instability that led to the passage of the **Employment Act of 1946,** in which the United States committed itself to policies designed to reduce unemployment in a manner consistent with price stability. This was the first formal acknowledgment of these primary macroeconomic goals. Likewise, many forms of legislation have been adopted that are designed to increase the rate of economic growth.

CONCEPT CHECK

1. The most important macroeconomic goals are full employment, price stability, and economic growth.
2. Individuals each have their own reasons for valuing certain goals rather than others.
3. The United States showed its commitment to the major macroeconomic goals with the Employment Act of 1946.

---

1. What are the three major economic goals of most societies?

2. What is the Employment Act of 1946? Why was it significant?

Employment and Unemployment

MODULE 7

- What are the consequences of unemployment?
- What is the unemployment rate?
- Does unemployment affect everyone equally?
- What causes unemployment?
- Is full employment desirable?

WHAT ARE THE CONSEQUENCES OF HIGH UNEMPLOYMENT?

Nearly everyone agrees that it is unfortunate when a person who wants a job cannot find one. A loss of a job can mean financial insecurity and a great deal of anxiety. High rates of unemployment in a society can lead to increased tensions and despair. A family without income from work undergoes great suffering, as its savings fade and it wonders where it is going to obtain the means to survive. Society loses some potential output of goods when some of its productive resources—human or non-human—remain idle, and potential consumption is also reduced. Clearly, then, there is a loss in efficiency when people willing to work and productive equipment remain idle. That is, other things equal, relatively high rates of unemployment are almost universally viewed as undesirable.

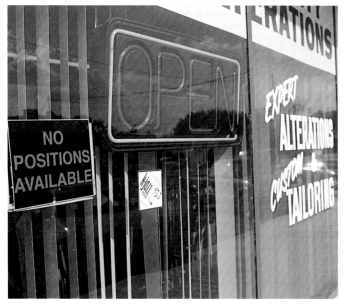

What are the costs to society of high unemployment?

WHAT IS THE UNEMPLOYMENT RATE?

When discussing unemployment, economists and politicians refer to the **unemployment rate.** In order to calculate the unemployment rate, you must first understand another important concept—the **labor force.** The labor force is the number of people over the age of 16 who are available for employment, regardless of whether or not they are currently employed, as seen in Exhibit 1. The civilian labor force figure excludes all those in the armed services and those in prison or mental hospitals. Those outside of the labor force also include homemakers, retirees, and full-time students. These groups are excluded from the labor force because they are not considered currently available for employment.

When we say that the unemployment rate is 5 percent, we mean that 5 percent of the population over the age of 16 who are willing and able to work are unable to obtain a job. The 5 percent means that 5 out of 100 people in the total labor force are unemployed. To calculate the unemployment rate, we simply divide the number of unemployed by the number in the labor force.

Unemployment rate = Number of unemployed / Labor force

In June 1998, the number of civilians unemployed in the United States was 6.2 million and the civilian labor force totalled 137.5 million. Using this data, we can calculate that the unemployment rate in June 1998 was 4.5 percent.

Unemployment rate = 6.2 million / 137.5 million = .045 = 4.5 percent

WHAT WAS THE WORST CASE OF UNEMPLOYMENT IN THE UNITED STATES?

By far the worst employment downturn in U.S. history was the Great Depression, which began in late 1929 and continued until 1941. Unemployment fell from only 3.2 percent of the labor force in 1929 to more than 20 percent in the early 1930s, and double-digit unemployment

EXHIBIT 1   THE U.S. LABOR FORCE, 1997

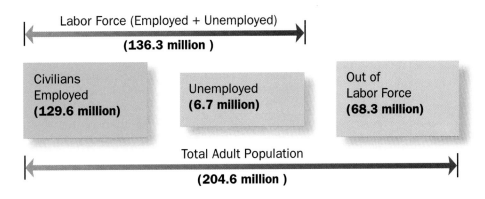

Labor Force (Employed + Unemployed)
(136.3 million)

Civilians Employed (129.6 million)

Unemployed (6.7 million)

Out of Labor Force (68.3 million)

Total Adult Population
(204.6 million)

SOURCE: U.S. Department of Labor

persisted through 1941. The debilitating impact of having millions of productive persons out of work led Americans (and persons in other countries too) to say "Never again." Some economists would argue that modern macroeconomics, with its emphasis on the determinants of unemployment and its elimination, truly began in the 1930s.

ARE THERE SIGNIFICANT VARIATIONS IN THE UNEMPLOYMENT RATE?

Exhibit 2 shows the unemployment rates over the last 37 years. Unemployment since 1960 has ranged from a low of

3.5 percent in 1969 to a high of 9.7 percent in 1982, with the average rate over the entire period slightly exceeding 5.5 percent. Unemployment in the worst years is twice or more than what it is in good years. Before 1960, variations tended to be even more pronounced.

ARE UNEMPLOYMENT STATISTICS ACCURATE REFLECTIONS OF THE LABOR MARKET?

In periods of prolonged recession, some individuals think that the chances of landing a job are so bleak that they quit looking. These people are called "discouraged workers."

EXHIBIT 2   UNEMPLOYMENT RATES, 1960–1997

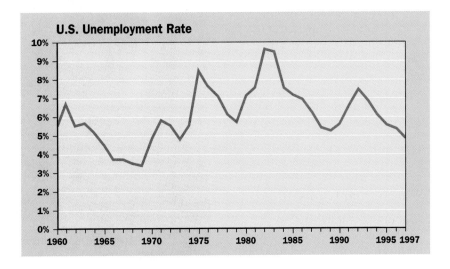

U.S. Unemployment Rate

SOURCE: U.S. Bureau of Labor Statistics.

Are these jobs included in the official labor statistics?

Individuals who have not actively sought work for four weeks are not counted as unemployed; instead, they fall out of the labor force. Also, people looking for full-time work who grudgingly settle for a part-time job are counted as "fully" employed, yet they are only "partly" employed. However, at least partially balancing these two biases in government employment statistics is the number of people that are overemployed—that is, working overtime or extra jobs. Also, there are a number of jobs in the underground economy (drugs, prostitution, gambling, and so on) that are not reported at all. In addition, there may be many people that claim they are actually seeking work when, in fact, they may just be going through the motions so that they can continue to collect unemployment compensation or receive other government benefits.

WHO ARE THE UNEMPLOYED?

Unemployment usually varies greatly between different segments of the population and over time.

Education as a Factor in Unemployment

According to the Bureau of Labor Statistics, the unemployment rate among college graduates is significantly lower than for those without a high school diploma across sex and race. In January 1998, unemployment rates for individuals without a high school diploma was 8.4 percent, versus 2.0 percent for college graduates. Also, college graduates have lower unemployment rates than those with some college education, but who have not completed a bachelor's degree (3.5 percent).

Age, Sex, and Race as Factors in Unemployment

The incidence of unemployment varies widely among the population. Unemployment tends to be greater among the very young, among blacks and other minorities, and among less-skilled workers. Adult female unemployment tends to be higher than adult male unemployment.

Considering the great variations in unemployment for different groups in the population, we calculate separate unemployment rates for groups classified by sex, age, race, family status, and type of occupation. Exhibit 3 shows unemployment rates for various groups for the year 1996. Note that the variation around the average unemployment rate for the total population of 5.4 percent was considerable. The unemployment rate for blacks and Hispanics averaged nearly twice the rate for whites, a phenomenon that has persisted throughout the post–World War II period. Unemployment among teenagers was much higher than even among blacks, at 16.7 percent. Some would regard teenage unemployment a lesser evil than unemployment among adults, because most teenagers have parents or guardians on whom they can rely for subsistence. On the other hand, some social scientists have observed a relationship between teenage unemployment, criminal activity, and social tensions.

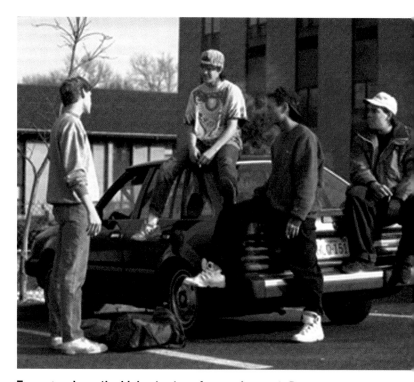

Teenagers have the highest rates of unemployment. Do you think it would be easier for them to find jobs if they had more experience and higher skill levels?

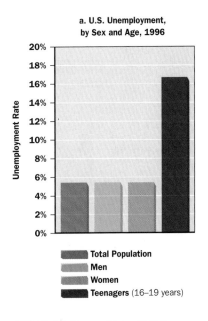

a. U.S. Unemployment,
by Sex and Age, 1996

- Total Population
- Men
- Women
- Teenagers (16–19 years)

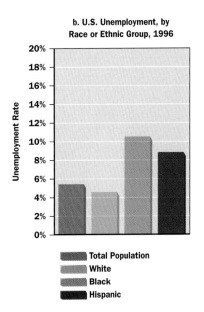

b. U.S. Unemployment, by
Race or Ethnic Group, 1996

- Total Population
- White
- Black
- Hispanic

SOURCE: U.S. Bureau of Labor Statistics.

REASONS FOR UNEMPLOYMENT

According to the Bureau of Labor Statistics, there are four main categories of unemployed workers: job losers (temporarily laid off or fired), job leavers (quit), re-entrants (worked before and now reentering labor force), and new entrants (entering the labor force for first time—primarily teenagers). It is a common misconception that most workers are unemployed because they have lost their jobs. While job losers may typically account for 50 to 60 percent of the unemployed, a sizeable fraction is due to job leavers, new entrants, and re-entrants, as seen in Exhibit 4.

| EXHIBIT 4 | REASONS FOR UNEMPLOYMENT |

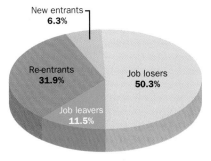

New entrants
6.3%

Re-entrants
31.9%

Job losers
50.3%

Job leavers
11.5%

Approximately 6.4 million people in the United States were unemployed in January 1998. Here is why they were unemployed, by reasons given.

SOURCE: U.S. Bureau of Labor Statistics, January 1998.

SHOULD THE GOVERNMENT ATTEMPT TO ACHIEVE FULL EMPLOYMENT?

Full employment is not necessarily a desirable goal. While unemployment is painful to those who have no source of income, reducing unemployment is not costless. In the short run, a reduction in unemployment may come at the expense of a higher rate of inflation, especially if the economy is close to full capacity, where resources are almost fully employed. Also, trying to match employees with jobs quickly may lead to significant inefficiencies because of mismatches between the worker's skill level and the level of skill required for a job. For example, the economy would be wasting a lot of resources subsidizing education if people with Ph.D.s in biochemistry were driving taxis or tending bar. That is, the skills of the employee may be higher than that necessary for the job, resulting in what economists call **underemployment.** Alternatively, employees may be placed in jobs beyond their abilities, which would also lead to inefficiencies.

HOW IMPORTANT IS THE AVERAGE DURATION OF UNEMPLOYMENT?

The *duration* of unemployment is equally as important as the amount of unemployment. The financial consequences of a head of household being unemployed four or five weeks are usually not extremely serious, particularly if the individual is covered by an unemployment compensation system. The impact becomes much more serious if a person

If he gets the job, will he be underemployed?

is unemployed for several months. Therefore, it is useful to look at the average duration of unemployment to discover what percent of the labor force is unemployed for more than a certain time period, say 15 weeks. Exhibit 5 presents data on the duration of unemployment in 1998. As you can see in this table, almost 45 percent of the unemployed were out of work less than five weeks, and only 15.2 percent of the total unemployed were out of work for more than six months. The duration of unemployment tends to be greater when the amount of unemployment is high, and smaller when the amount of unemployment is low. Unemployment of any duration, of course, means a potential loss of output. This loss of current output is permanent; it is not made up when unemployment starts falling again.

EXHIBIT 5	DURATION OF UNEMPLOYMENT, JANUARY 1998

Duration	Percent Unemployed
Less than 5 weeks	44.3%
5 to 14 weeks	28.8
15 to 26 weeks	11.7
27 weeks and over	15.2

SOURCE: U.S. Bureau of Labor Statistics.

1. The consequences of unemployment to society include a reduction in potential output and consumption—a decrease in efficiency.
2. The unemployment rate is found by dividing the number of people officially unemployed by the number in the labor force.
3. Unemployment rates are the highest for minorities, the young, and less-skilled workers.
4. There are four main categories of unemployed workers: job losers, job leavers, re-entrants, and new entrants.
5. The duration of unemployment tends to be greater (smaller) when the amount of unemployment is high (low).

---

1. What happens to the unemployment rate when the number of unemployed people increases, *ceteris paribus?* When the labor force grows, *ceteris paribus?*
2. How might the official unemployment rate understate the "true" degree of unemployment? How might it overstate it?
3. Why might the fraction of the unemployed who are job leavers be higher in a period of strong labor demand?
4. Suppose you live in a community of 100 people where no one was unwilling or unable to work. If 80 people are over 16 years old and 72 people are employed, what is the employment rate in that community?
5. What would happen to the unemployment rate if a substantial group of unemployed people started going to school full time? What would happen to the size of the labor force?
6. What happens to the unemployment rate when people become discouraged workers? Does anything happen to employment in this case?

Different Types of Unemployment

- What is frictional unemployment?
- What is structural unemployment?
- What is cyclical unemployment?
- What is seasonal unemployment?
- What is the natural rate of unemployment?

In examining the status of and changes in the unemployment rate, it is important to recognize that there are numerous types of unemployment. In this Concept, we will examine these different types of unemployment and evaluate the relative impact of each on the overall unemployment rate.

WHAT IS FRICTIONAL UNEMPLOYMENT?

Some unemployment results from persons being temporarily between jobs. For example, consider Bill Board, an advertising executive who was fired in Chicago on March 1 and is now actively looking for similar work in San Francisco. This is an example of **frictional unemployment.** Of course, all workers do not get fired from their jobs; some may voluntarily quit their jobs. In either case, frictional unemployment is short term and results from the normal turnover in the labor market, such as when people change from one job to another.

SHOULD WE WORRY ABOUT FRICTIONAL UNEMPLOYMENT?

Geographic and occupational mobility are considered to be good for the economy because they generally lead human resources to go from activities of relatively low productivity or value to areas of higher productivity, increasing output in society as well as the wage income of the mover. Hence, frictional unemployment, while not good in itself, is a by-product of a healthy phenomenon, and because it is often short-lived, it is therefore not generally viewed as a serious problem. While the amount of frictional unemployment varies somewhat over time, it is unusual for it to be much less than 2 percent of the labor force. Actually, frictional unemployment tends to be somewhat greater in periods of low unemployment, when job opportunities are plentiful. This high level of job opportunities stimulates mobility, which, in turn, creates some frictional unemployment.

Would there be less frictional unemployment if potential employers and prospective employees had better information about each other?

WHAT IS STRUCTURAL UNEMPLOYMENT?

A second type of unemployment is **structural unemployment.** Like frictional unemployment, structural unemployment is related to occupational movement or mobility, or, in this case, to a lack of mobility. Structural unemployment reflects the existence of persons who lack the necessary skills for jobs that are available. For example, if a machine operator in a manufacturing plant loses his job, he could still remain unemployed despite the existence of several openings for computer programmers in his community. The quantity of unemployed workers conceivably could equal the number of job vacancies, but the unemployment persists because of the unemployed's lack of skills. Given the existence of structural unemployment, it is wise to look at both unemployment and job vacancy statistics in assessing labor market conditions. Structural unemployment, like frictional unemployment, reflects the dynamic dimension of a changing economy. Over time, new jobs open up that require new skills, while old jobs that required different skills disappear. It is not surprising, then, that many persons advocate government-subsidized retraining programs as a means of reducing structural unemployment.

The dimensions of structural unemployment are debatable, in part because of the difficulty in precisely defining the term in an operational sense. Structural unemployment varies considerably—sometimes it is very low and at other times, like the 1970s and early 1980s, it is high. To some extent, in this latter period, jobs in the traditional sectors like autos and oil gave way to jobs in the computer and biotechnology sectors. Consequently, structural unemployment was higher.

What type of unemployment would occur if these coal miners lost their jobs as a result of a reduction in demand for coal and needed retraining to find other employment?

IMPERFECTIONS AND UNEMPLOYMENT

To a considerable extent, one can view both frictional and structural unemployment as phenomena resulting from imperfections in the labor market. For example, if individuals seeking jobs and employers seeking workers had better information about each other, the amount of frictional unemployment would be considerably lower. It takes time for suppliers of laborers to find the demanders of labor services, and it takes time and money for labor resources to acquire the necessary skills. But because information is not costless, and because job search also is costly, the bringing of demanders and suppliers of labor services together does not occur instantaneously.

WHAT IS CYCLICAL UNEMPLOYMENT?

In well over half of the years between 1960 and 1996, the unemployment rate exceeded 5.5 percent. Clearly, then, unemployment in many years is composed of more than just frictional and structural unemployment. In years of relatively high unemployment, some joblessness may result from an insufficient level of demand for goods and services. The demand for labor is derived from the demand for goods and services, so when the level of demand decreases, the demand for labor drops as well. We call this **cyclical unemployment.**

Most economists believe cyclical unemployment is the most volatile form of unemployment. Furthermore, many economists believe that insufficiency in aggregate demand explains most pronounced variations in the rate of unemployment over time.

CAN CYCLICAL UNEMPLOYMENT BE REDUCED?

Given its volatility and dimensions, governments, rightly or wrongly, have viewed unemployment resulting from inadequate demand to be especially correctable through government policies. Most of the attempts to solve the unemployment problem have placed an emphasis on increasing aggregate demand. Attempts to reduce frictional unemployment by providing better labor market information and to reduce structural unemployment through job retraining have also been made, but these efforts have received fewer resources and much less attention from policymakers.

TUNE UP

CYCLICAL UNEMPLOYMENT

Q: Are layoffs more prevalent during a recession than a recovery? Do most resignations occur during a recovery?

A: Layoffs are more likely to occur during a recession. When times are bad, employers are often forced to let workers go. Resignations are relatively more prevalent during good economic times, because there are more job opportunities for those seeking new jobs.

WHAT IS SEASONAL UNEMPLOYMENT?

Some unemployment occurs because certain types of jobs are seasonal in nature. This type of unemployment is called **seasonal unemployment.** For example, a ski instructor in Aspen might become seasonally unemployed at the end of April when ski season is over. Or a roofer in Minnesota may become seasonally unemployed during the harsh winter months. Even a forest firefighter in a National Park might only be employed during the summer and fall, when forest fires peak. Occupations that experience either sharp seasonal shifts in demand or are subject to changing weather conditions may lead to seasonal unemployment.

What type of unemployment would occur if these firefighters lost their jobs at the end of the fire season?

WHAT ELSE CAN AFFECT THE UNEMPLOYMENT RATE?

It is likely that some unemployment reflects certain institutional aspects of the economy. For example, some unemployed persons may show little drive in seeking new employment, given the existence of unemployment com-

pensation. Unemployment compensation lowers the opportunity cost of being unemployed. Say a worker making $400 a week when employed receives $220 in compensation when unemployed; as a result, the cost of losing his job is not $400 a week in foregone income, but only $180. It has been estimated that the existence of unemployment compensation programs may raise overall unemployment rates by as much as 1 percent. Other studies have shown that in some cases, minimum-wage laws create an above-equilibrium price (wage) for labor, where the quantity of labor supplied exceeds the quantity demanded, meaning unemployment exists. Racial and sex discrimination may also cause some unemployment. Restrictive practices of labor unions (such as limiting membership into the union) may also contribute to some unemployment, as do laws restricting job entry (e.g., laws requiring a license to sell real estate or repair your toilet).

If unemployment compensation benefits increased, would this line be even longer?

DOES NEW TECHNOLOGY LEAD TO GREATER UNEMPLOYMENT?

Although many believe that technological advances inevitably result in the displacement of workers, this is not necessarily the case. If the new equipment is a substitute for labor, then it might displace workers. For example, many fast-food restaurants have substituted self-service beverage bars for workers. However, new capital equipment means that new workers will be needed to manufacture and repair the new equipment. The most famous example of this is the computer, which was supposed to displace thousands of workers. Instead, the computer generated a whole new growth industry that created jobs. The key point is that new inventions are generally cost saving, and these cost savings will generally generate higher incomes for producers and lower prices and better products for consumers, benefits that will ultimately result in the

Will new technology in one industry displace workers in the whole economy?

growth of other industries. The problem is that it is easy to just see the initial effect (displaced workers) of technological advances, without recognizing the implications of that invention throughout the whole economy over time.

WHAT IS THE NATURAL RATE OF UNEMPLOYMENT?

It is interesting to observe that over the period during which annual unemployment data are available, the median, or "typical," annual unemployment rate has been at or slightly above 5 percent. Some economists call this typical unemployment rate the **natural rate of unemploy-**

ment. When unemployment rises well above 5 percent, we have abnormally high unemployment; when it falls below 5 percent, we have abnormally low unemployment. The natural rate of unemployment of approximately 5 percent roughly equals the sum of frictional and structural unemployment when they are at a maximum. Thus, one can view unemployment rates below the natural rate as reflecting the existence of a below-average level of frictional and structural unemployment. When unemployment rises above the natural rate, however, it reflects the existence of cyclical unemployment.

WHAT EXACTLY IS FULL EMPLOYMENT?

There is some dispute over what constitutes full employment. Literal full employment (everyone who wants a job can have one without any need to spend time searching) is virtually impossible, given the existence of frictional and structural unemployment. During the 1960s, government economists and politicians generally suggested that full employment existed whenever the unemployment rate was 4 percent or less. In the early 1970s, economists generally accepted the notion that full employment should meaningfully be defined as being present when the unemployment rate was 5 percent or less. Because the actual rate of unemployment during the late 1970s and 1980s was substantial, economists claimed that the natural rate at that time might be as high as 6 or 7 percent. Today, however, economists, for the most part, have come back to accept a current range somewhere between 5.0 and 5.5 percent. The natural rate of unemployment may change over time as technological, demographic, institutional, and other conditions vary, ranging somewhere from 4.5 to 6 percent. In any case, for some economists, the operational definition of full employment is the elimination of cyclical unemployment.

G L O B A L   W A T C H

UNEMPLOYMENT AROUND THE GLOBE, 1996

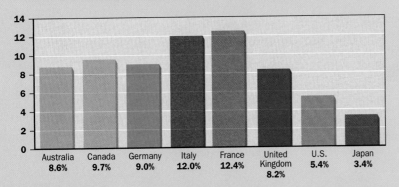

| Australia 8.6% | Canada 9.7% | Germany 9.0% | Italy 12.0% | France 12.4% | United Kingdom 8.2% | U.S. 5.4% | Japan 3.4% |

SOURCE: Organization for Economic Cooperation and Development, *Quarterly Labor Force Statistics.*

CONSIDER THIS:
Many developed countries had higher unemployment rates than the United States in 1996. Generous unemployment benefits and sluggish economic growth in European countries have helped cause higher unemployment rates than in the United States.

A LIGHT THAT NEVER GOES OUT

(CNN)—Lighthouses have been called the most altruistic structures ever built. After almost 300 years of guiding ships along the U.S. coasts and Great Lakes, their usefulness is waning. But they have never lost their power to ignite poetry in those who visit them.

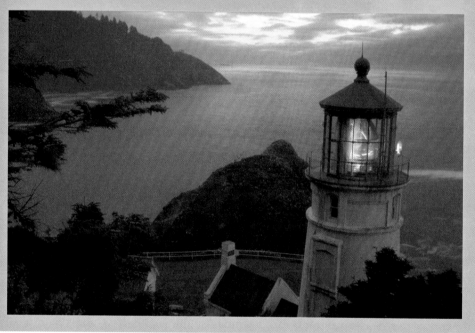

"Lighthouses are to America what castles are to Europe. They're among the oldest standing structures in (the U.S.)," says Tim Harrison, editor of the Maine-based *Lighthouse Digest*.

When the United States became a country, 12 lighthouses kept vigil over settled shores, according to Wayne Wheeler, founder of the U.S. Lighthouse Society. Over the years, he says more than 2,000 light stations were built. Today, the National Park Service estimates about 634 lighthouses remain, 405 of which are in service.

Automation has virtually eliminated the romantic tradition of lighthouse keepers—salty, solitary souls guiding ships safely through treacherous storms. And electronic pings are replacing the mournful drone of the foghorn calling sailors home.

SOURCE: CNN Interactive, Destinations, April 19, 1997. http:// cnn.com/TRAVEL/DESTINATIONS/9704/light houses.usa

CONSIDER THIS:
Just like elevator operators and service station attendants, now lighthouse keepers have given way to automation. In a world of scarcity, lighthouse keepers can now be employed producing something that is more valuable from society's perspective.

CONCEPT CHECK

1. The four types of unemployment are frictional unemployment, structural unemployment, cyclical unemployment, and seasonal unemployment.
2. Frictional unemployment results from the movement of persons from one job to another.
3. Structural unemployment results when people who are looking for jobs lack the required skills for the jobs that are available.
4. Cyclical unemployment is caused by an inadequate level of aggregate demand.
5. Imperfections in the labor market and institutional factors result in higher rates of unemployment.
6. When cyclical unemployment is almost completely eliminated, our economy is said to be operating at full employment.

---

1. Why do we want some frictional unemployment?
2. Why might a job retraining program be a more useful policy to address structural unemployment than to address frictional unemployment?
3. What is the traditional government policy "cure" for cyclical unemployment?
4. Does new technology increase unemployment?
5. What types of unemployment are present at full employment (at the natural rate of unemployment)?
6. Why might frictional unemployment be higher in a period of plentiful jobs (low unemployment)?
7. If the widespread introduction of the automobile caused a very productive maker of horse-drawn carriages to lose his job, would he be structurally or frictionally unemployed?
8. If a fall in demand for domestic cars causes auto workers to lose their jobs in Michigan, while there are plenty of jobs for lumberjacks in Montana, what kind of unemployment results?

D Inflation

- Why is the overall price level important?
- How has the price level behaved this century?
- Who are the winners and losers during inflation?
- Can wage earners avoid the consequences of inflation?
- Why is it important to anticipate inflation correctly?

WHY IS PRICE LEVEL STABILITY A DESIRABLE GOAL?

Just as full employment brings about economic security of one kind, an overall stable price level increases another form of security. The **price level** is the average level of all prices in the economy. When the price level is rising, we have **inflation,** and when the price level is falling, we have **deflation.** In both inflation and deflation, a country's currency unit changes in purchasing power. Without price level stability, consumers and producers will experience more difficulty in coordinating their plans and decisions.

WHAT HAS HAPPENED TO THE PRICE LEVEL OVER THE YEARS?

Unanticipated and sharp changes in the price level are almost universally considered to be a "bad" thing that needs

to be remedied by some policy. What is the historical record of changes in the overall price level in the United States? Exhibit 1 shows changes in the **Consumer Price Index,** the standard measure of inflation, from 1914 to 1996. For the typical college-age reader of this book, the average price level has more than doubled in his or her lifetime. Moreover, the same statement could have been made to readers of 20 years ago. Over the past 40 years, the average price level has roughly quintupled (risen five-fold). Can you believe that in 1940 stamps were three cents per letter, postcards were a penny, the median price of a house was $2,900, and the price of a new car was $650?

Compare, however, the price level in 1940 with that in 1800. Both consumer and wholesale prices in 1940 were actually lower than in 1800. Before 1940, inflation rates rose a great deal in wartime but tended to fall in peacetime, remaining roughly stable over long time periods. Since 1940, however, inflation rates have risen in peacetime as well as wartime.

| EXHIBIT 1 | THE PRICE LEVEL IN THE UNITED STATES, 1914–1996 |

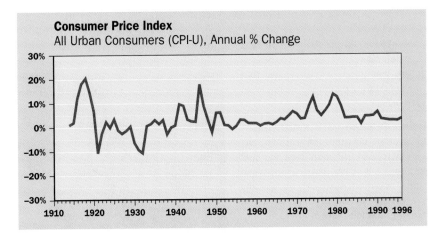

SOURCE: U.S. Bureau of Labor Statistics.

WHO LOSES WITH INFLATION?

Suppose you retire on a fixed pension of $2,000 per month. Over time, the $2,000 will buy less and less if prices generally rise. Your real income—your income adjusted to reflect changes in purchasing power—falls. Inflation lowers income in real terms for persons on fixed-dollar incomes. Creditors likewise can be hurt by inflation. If you loaned someone $1,000 in 1985 and were paid back $1,000 plus interest in 1995, the $1,000 in principal that was paid back actually is worth less in 1995 than it was in 1985 because inflation has eroded the purchasing power of the dollar. Thus, the real wealth of the creditor is eroded because of inflation. Another group that sometimes loses at least temporarily from inflation includes people whose incomes are tied to long-term contracts. If inflation begins shortly after a labor union signs a three-year wage agreement, it may completely eat up the wage gains provided by the contract. The same applies to businesses who agree to sell a quantity of something, say, coal, for a fixed price for a given number of years.

If some people lose because of changing prices, others must gain. The debtor pays back dollars worth less in purchasing power than those he borrowed. Corporations who can quickly raise the prices on their goods may have revenue gains greater than their increase in costs, providing additional profits. Wage earners sometimes lose from inflation.

If you borrowed money from a bank at 5 percent for 20 years and inflation averaged 10 percent over that period, who got the better end of the deal, you or the bank?

THE REDISTRIBUTION IMPACT OF INFLATION

A key point in our discussion of inflation is that it brings about changes in real incomes of persons, and these changes may be either desirable or undesirable. The redis-

TUNE UP

INFLATION

Q: Di Gress, in her presentation to her Economics 101 class, stated that inflation meant that people have less money to spend, that there are less goods available, and that one must pay more money for goods they purchase. So far, what kind of a grade would you give Di?

A: Of the three statements Di made about inflation, only one is correct: With inflation, we must, on average, pay more money for the goods we purchase. Inflation does not necessarily mean we have fewer goods but rather that, on net, these goods have higher price tags. Inflation does not necessarily mean that people have less money to spend. Employees and unions will bargain for higher wages when there is inflation.

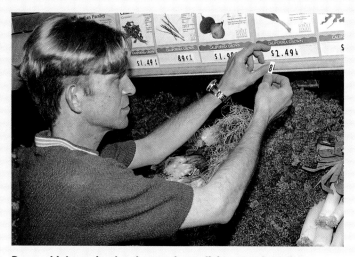

Does a higher price level mean lower living standards?

tributional impact of inflation is not the result of conscious public policy; it just happens. Moreover, inflation can raise one nation's price level relative to price levels in other countries, which can lead to difficulties in financing the purchase of foreign goods or to a decline in the value of the national currency relative to that of other countries. In its extreme form, inflation can lead to a complete erosion in faith in the value of the pieces of paper we commonly call money. In Germany after both World Wars, prices rose so fast that people in some cases finally refused to take paper money, insisting instead on payment in goods or metals whose prices tend to move predictably with inflation.

THE MENU AND SHOE LEATHER COSTS OF INFLATION

One cost of inflation is the cost that firms incur as a result of being forced to change their prices more frequently. For example, a restaurant may have to print new menus, or a department or mail-order store may have to print new catalogs to reflect changing prices. These costs are called **menu costs,** and they are the costs of changing posted prices. In some South American economies in the 1980s, inflation increased at over 300 percent per year, with prices changing on a daily, or even hourly, basis in some cases. Imagine how large the menu costs could be in an economy such as this!

Another cost of inflation is **shoe leather cost.** Shoe leather cost is the cost of going to and from the bank (and thus wearing out the leather on your shoes) to check on your assets. For example, higher inflation rates lead to higher nominal interest rates. The higher interest rate may induce more individuals to put money in the bank rather than allowing it to depreciate in their pockets.

NOMINAL VERSUS REAL INTEREST RATES

The interest rate is usually reported as the **nominal interest rate.** We determine the actual **real interest rate** by taking the nominal rate of interest and subtracting the inflation rate.

Real interest rate = Nominal interest rate – Inflation rate

For example, if the nominal interest rate was 5 percent and the inflation rate was 3 percent, then the real interest rate would be 2 percent.

WHAT IS ANTICIPATED INFLATION?

Most of the possible evils of inflation may not occur in periods of rising price levels. If people correctly anticipate inflation, they will behave in a manner that will largely protect them against loss. Consider the creditor who believes that it is likely that the price level will rise 6 percent a year, based on the immediate past experience. Would

that creditor lend money to someone at a 5 percent rate of interest? No. A 5 percent rate of interest means that a person borrowing $1,000 now will pay back $1,050 ($1,000 plus 5 percent of $1,000) one year from now. But if prices go up 6 percent, it will take $1,060 to buy what $1,000 does today ($1,060 is 6 percent more than $1,000). Thus, the person who lends at 5 percent will get paid back an amount ($1,050) that is less than the purchasing power of the original loan ($1,000) at the time it was made. The real interest rate, then, would actually be negative. Hence, to protect themselves, lenders will demand a rate of interest that is large enough to compensate for the deteriorating value of the dollar.

HOW DOES ANTICIPATED INFLATION AFFECT THE INTEREST RATE?

The economic theory behind the behavioral responses of creditors and debtors to anticipated inflation is straightforward and can be expressed in a simple diagram (Exhibit 2). An interest rate is, in effect, the price that one pays for the use of funds. Like other prices, interest rates are determined by the interaction of demand and supply forces. The lower the interest rate (price), the greater the quantity of funds people will demand, *ceteris paribus;* the higher the interest rate (price), the greater the quantity of loanable funds supplied by individuals and institutions like banks, *ceteris paribus.* Suppose that in an environment where prices are in general expected to remain stable in the near future, the demand for loanable funds is depicted by D_0 and the supply of such funds is indicated by S_0. In this

| EXHIBIT 2 | NOMINAL INTEREST RATES |

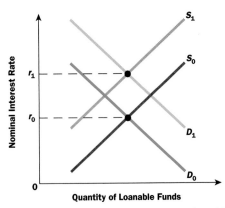

Nominal interest rates are determined by the intersection of the demand and supply curves for loanable funds. The lower the interest rate (price), the greater the quantity of loanable funds demanded, *ceteris paribus;* the higher the interest rate, the greater the quantity of loanable funds supplied by individuals and institutions like banks, *ceteris paribus.* Expected inflation shifts the supply curve left and the demand curve right, both of which tend to increase nominal (money) interest rates.

scenario, the equilibrium price, or interest rate, will be r_0, where the quantity demanded equals the quantity supplied.

When people start expecting future inflation, creditors such as banks will become less willing to lend funds at any given interest rate, because they fear they will be repaid in dollars of lesser value than those they loaned. This is depicted by a leftward shift in the supply curve of loanable funds (a decrease in supply) to S_1. Likewise, demanders of funds (borrowers) are more anxious to borrow, because they think they will pay their loans back in dollars of lesser purchasing power than the dollars they borrowed. Thus, the demand for funds increases from D_0 to D_1. Both the decrease in supply and the increase in demand push up the interest rate to a new equilibrium, r_1. Whether the equilibrium quantity of loanable funds will increase or decrease depends on the relative sizes of the shifts in the respective curves.

TUNE UP

ANTICIPATED INFLATION AND INTEREST RATES

Q: Carrie A. Loan has a 30-year, fixed-interest mortgage on her home, which she purchased six years ago. In the meantime, the inflation rate has fallen considerably and probably will not reach that higher level again. Is Carrie happy?

A: No. Carrie guessed incorrectly. If she stays with the initial loan, Carrie will be paying a higher interest rate to borrow money than others who have borrowed money more recently. Now, of course, Carrie could refinance to get a lower interest rate, but she would need to calculate how much she would save on her loan and compare it to the cost of refinancing to determine whether that would be worth doing.

DO CREDITORS ALWAYS LOSE DURING INFLATION?

Very often lenders are able to anticipate inflation with reasonable accuracy. For example, in the early 1960s, when prices were rising only about 1 percent a year, nominal rates of interest on a 90-day treasury bill ran a bit over 4 percent. Today, with prices rising around 2 percent a year,

the nominal interest rate is around 5.5 percent. The real interest rate received by the lender in both periods was between 3 and 4 percent (early 1960s: 4 percent nominal interest rate – 1 percent inflation = 3.0 percent real interest rate; 1998: 5.5 – 2 = 3.5). With inflation anticipated, new creditors did not lose, nor did debtors gain, from inflation. However, nominal interest rates and real interest rates do not always run together. For example, in periods of high unexpected inflation, the nominal interest rates can be very high while the real interest rates are low or even negative.

DO WAGE EARNERS ADJUST THEIR DEMANDS TO ACCOUNT FOR EXPECTED INFLATION?

Like creditors, wage earners, especially when organized by strong labor unions, adjust their wage demands to reflect the impact of inflation. In the mid-1990s, wage increases of slightly more than 4 percent a year were common. After allowing for inflation of slightly more than 3 percent a year, real wages rose about 1 percent. However, if expected inflation grew to 7 or 8 percent, wage demands would grow in response to the growing inflation rate; that is, money wages would rise to around 8 or 9 percent per year, again implying real wage increases of around 1 percent a year.

HOW CAN WE PROTECT OURSELVES FROM INFLATION?

Increasingly, groups try to protect themselves from inflation by using cost-of-living clauses in contracts. With these clauses, laborers automatically get wage increases that reflect rising prices. The same is true of many pensioners, including those on Social Security. Personal income taxes are also now indexed for inflation. Some economists have argued that we should go one step further and index everything, meaning that all contractual arrangements would be adjusted frequently to take account of changing prices. Such an arrangement might reduce the impact of inflation, but it would also entail additional contracting costs (and not every good—notably currency—can be indexed). An alternative approach has been to try to stop inflation through various policies relating to the amount of government spending, tax rates, or the amount of money created. **Wage and price controls**—legislation limiting wage and price increases—offer still another approach to the inflation problem. We will discuss this topic in greater detail later in the text.

AVERAGE ANNUAL INFLATION RATES, SELECTED COUNTRIES, 1996

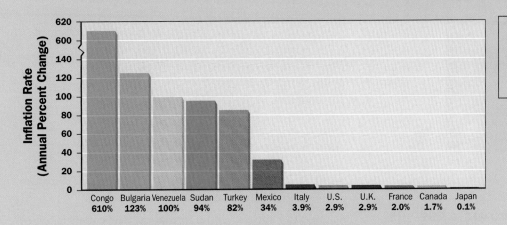

CONSIDER THIS:
Many countries around the world had a serious problem with inflation in 1996.

Country	Congo	Bulgaria	Venezuela	Sudan	Turkey	Mexico	Italy	U.S.	U.K.	France	Canada	Japan
Rate	610%	123%	100%	94%	82%	34%	3.9%	2.9%	2.9%	2.0%	1.7%	0.1%

SOURCE: International Monetary Fund, 1997.

CONCEPT CHECK

1. Price stability provides security in the marketplace by ensuring constant purchasing power of a nation's currency.
2. Prior to 1940, prices tended to fall during peacetime, but since that time, they have been rising consistently each year, regardless of external factors.
3. Inflation generally hurts creditors and those on fixed incomes and pensions; debtors generally benefit from inflation.
4. The nominal interest rate is the actual amount of interest you pay. The real interest rate is the nominal rate minus the inflation rate.
5. Wage earners attempt to keep pace with inflation by demanding higher wages each year or by indexing their annual wage to inflation.

1. How does price level instability increase the difficulties buyers and sellers have in coordinating their plans?
2. What will happen to the nominal interest rate if the real interest rate rises, *ceteris paribus?* What if expected inflation increases, *ceteris paribus?*
3. Say you owe money to the River Bank. Will you gain or lose from an unanticipated decrease in inflation?
4. How does a variable interest rate loan "insure" the lender against unanticipated increases in inflation?
5. Why will neither creditors nor debtors lose from inflation if it is correctly anticipated?
6. How can inflation make people turn to exchange by barter?
7. What would happen in the loanable funds market if suppliers of loanable funds expect a substantial fall in inflation, while demanders of funds expect a substantial rise in inflation?

Economic Growth

- What benefits does economic growth provide?
- How can a nation achieve economic growth?
- Is the economy of the United States growing?

WHY DO NATIONS WANT ECONOMIC GROWTH?

The desire to bring about long-term economic growth—an increase in the output of goods and services—has been expressed in nearly every economy. To be sure, there is not unanimous agreement that economic growth is desirable, as some writers have been outspoken about negative impacts of growth, such as increased environmental problems, growing inequalities, higher crime, a decline in moral standards, and so on. Still, economic growth is considered a "good" thing by most people, and in some countries it has been the primary concern of public policy. Economic growth, of course, enhances the potential amount of individual consumption; the greater the economic growth, the more goods we and our descendants have to consume in the future. In addition, economic growth increases a nation's potential military and political power, enhancing prestige and security.

WHICH COUNTRIES CAN ACHIEVE ECONOMIC GROWTH?

Economic growth is not something reserved exclusively for prosperous nations. Some relatively poor nations, like Chile and China, had growth rates during the 1990s that exceeded those of most European countries and the United States. Even India, with a per capita income level among the lowest in the world, achieved substantial annual growth during the 1990s. Economic growth varies widely between nations, even between these that presently have similar levels of per capita output.

HOW CAN A NATION IMPROVE ITS GROWTH RATE?

Nations engage in a variety of policies designed to increase their output over time. Some of these policies are designed to increase capital formation. The construction of tools and machinery today increases output in future time periods. Thus, it is not an accident that the nations with high investment and capital formation as a percent of gross domestic product (GDP) have had higher average annual growth rates. Nor is it an accident that the nations devoting the smallest proportion of their output to capital formation have had lower growth rates. Nations can encourage capital formation through such policies as favorable tax treatment of investment spending, using tax revenues to form capital, and through subsidies for capital-intensive forms of production. In centrally planned economies like Cuba or North Korea, the government simply emphasizes the production of capital goods at the expense of consumer goods.

Nations also attempt to increase their rate of per capita economic growth by increasing the output of the labor force by education, training programs, and improved health standards, or by using tariffs to protect native industries from foreign competition.

IS THE UNITED STATES ECONOMY STRUGGLING?

Despite faster growth rates in many other countries, the per capita GDP in the United States is still higher than that in any other nation. Exhibit 1 shows per capita U.S. output compared to other industrialized countries in 1995, using **purchasing power parity.** The use of purchasing power parity allows us to estimate the number of units of currency that are needed in one country to buy the same amount of goods and services that one unit of currency will buy in another country. We see from Exhibit 1 that the United States has the highest per capita GDP, followed by Switzerland, Luxembourg, Germany, Canada, Japan, and France. Exhibit 2 shows the growth rates for selected advanced economies from 1979 to 1998.

EXHIBIT 1	1995 PER CAPITA GDP IN SELECTED COUNTRIES USING PURCHASING POWER PARITY[1]

Country	Per Capita GDP (dollars)
Canada	$21,031
France	19,939
Germany	20,497
Italy	19,465
Japan	21,795
Norway	22,672
Sweden	18,673
Switzerland	24,809
United Kingdom	17,776
United States	26,438

[1]PPP shows how many units of currency are needed in one country to buy the same amount of goods and services that one unit of currency will buy in the other country.

SOURCE: Organization for Economic Cooperation and Development, Paris, France, *National Accounts, Main Aggregates*, vol. 1, annual; and "OECD Statistics GDP," published January 1997; http://www.oecd.org/std/gdp.htm

EXHIBIT 2	GROWTH IN REAL PER CAPITA GDP, SELECTED INDUSTRIAL COUNTRIES

	10-Year Averages	
	1980–1989	1990–1999
United States	1.8%	1.2%
Japan	3.1	1.5
Germany[1]	1.7	2.0
France	1.8	1.4
Italy	2.3	1.5
United Kingdom	2.2	1.4
Canada	1.7	0.7

[1]Data through 1991 apply to West Germany only.

SOURCE: International Monetary Fund, *World Economic Outlook*, May 1998.

CONCEPT CHECK

1. Economic growth increases the potential amount of individual consumption and enhances a nation's potential military and political power.
2. Nations can achieve economic growth by encouraging increases in investment, which increases capital formation, as well as through other, more controversial, methods.
3. While the United States economy has lagged behind many other nations in its per capita growth rate, it has the highest per capita GDP in the world.

1. In what way does the desire for economic growth arise from scarcity?
2. How does encouraging capital investment or educational training enhance economic growth?
3. Why do we use purchasing power parity to compare per capita GDP across countries?
4. If a country increased its rate of capital formation, what would happen to its current consumption possibilities? What would happen to its consumption possibilities 15 years from now?

Economic Fluctuations

MODULE 7

- What are short-term economic fluctuations?
- What are the four stages of a business cycle?
- Is there a difference between a recession and a depression?
- Can an economy be in a recession while still growing?

ARE THERE SHORT-TERM FLUCTUATIONS IN ECONOMIC GROWTH?

The aggregate amount of economic activity in the United States and most other nations has increased markedly, even on a per capita basis, over time; there has been economic growth. There are short-term fluctuations in the level of economic activity, however. We sometimes call these short-term fluctuations **business cycles.** The distinction between long-term economic growth and short-term economic fluctuations is illustrated in Exhibit 1. Over a long period of time, the line representing economic activity slopes upwards, indicating increasing real output. Over short time periods, however, there are downward, as well as upward, output changes. Business cycles refer to the short-term ups and downs in economic activity, not to the long-term trend in output, which in modern times has been upward.

WHAT ARE THE PHASES OF A BUSINESS CYCLE?

A business cycle has four phases—expansion, peak, contraction, and trough—as illustrated in Exhibit 2. The period of expansion is when output is rising significantly. Usually during the expansion phase, unemployment is falling and both consumer and business confidence is high. Thus, investment is rising, as well as expenditures for expensive durable consumer goods, such as automobiles and household appliances. The peak is the point in time when the expansion comes to an end, when output is at the highest point in the cycle. The contraction is a period of falling real output, and is usually accompanied by rising unemployment and declining business and consumer confidence. Investment spending and expenditures on consumer durable goods fall sharply in a typical contraction.

EXHIBIT 1	BUSINESS CYCLES AND ECONOMIC GROWTH

In a growing economy, business downturns are temporary reversals from a long-term trend of economic growth.

EXHIBIT 2	FOUR PHASES OF A BUSINESS CYCLE

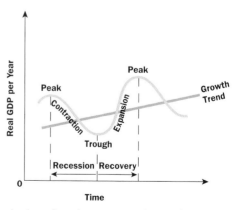

Business cycles have four phases: expansion, peak, contraction, and trough. The expansion phase usually is longer than the contraction, and in a growing economy, output (real GDP) will rise from one business cycle peak to the next.

The trough is the point in time when output stops declining; it is the moment when business activity is at its lowest point in the cycle. Unemployment is relatively high at the trough, although the actual maximum amount of unemployment may not occur exactly at the trough. Often, unemployment remains fairly high well into the expansion phase.

HOW LONG DOES A BUSINESS CYCLE LAST?

There is no uniformity to a business cycle's length. In both the 1980s and 1990s, one cycle lasted eight years—an unusually long period by historical standards. By contrast, two years would be a very short cycle. The contraction phase is one of recession, a decline in business activity. Severe recessions are called **depressions**. Likewise, a prolonged expansion in economic activity is sometimes called a **boom**. Exhibit 3 shows the record of American business cycles over recent times, in terms of deviations from its long-term trend in economic activity. Note in Exhibit 3 that contractions seem to be getting shorter over time.

CAN SEASONAL FLUCTUATIONS AFFECT ECONOMIC ACTIVITY?

While the determinants of cyclical fluctuations in the economy are the major thrust of the next several Modules, it should be mentioned that some fluctuation in economic activity reflects seasonal patterns. Business activity, whether measured by production or by the sale of goods, tends to be high in the two months before the winter holidays, and somewhat lower in summertime, when many families are on vacation. Within individual industries, of course, seasonal fluctuations in output often are extremely

Is there a correlation between the strength of the economy and an incumbent being reelected?

pronounced, agriculture being the best example. Often, key economic statistics, like unemployment rates, are seasonally adjusted, meaning the numbers are modified

---

| **EXHIBIT 3** | **A HISTORICAL RECORD OF U.S. BUSINESS CYCLES, 1928–1998** |

Since 1928, real GDP has increased, on average, 3 percent per year. However, we do see alternating swings from the average.

SOURCE: *Economic Report of the President*, 1998.

IS THE BUSINESS CYCLE GONE?

Boom times never last forever. A recession is inevitable. But experts say it will be short and mild—nothing like the Great Depression of the 1930s. "The old-fashioned business cycle, in its virulence, should be as gone as the old-fashioned diphtheria and pre-penicillin diseases are gone," maintains MIT economist Paul Samuelson.

Why? Because America has learned how to keep the economy growing with a balanced budget, low interest rates, and efficient companies—all making Main Street a prosperous place.

And what about Wall Street? It's been an incredible run by the bulls with three years in a row of huge gains averaging 27 percent a year. The question is, How long can it last? And will it all come crashing down?

Experts predict a big fall, of 20 percent to 25 percent, within the next two to three years, but then stocks will start up again, partly because of all the money being pumped in by young people like Brian O'Neal.

"Basically, everything I have saved up is riding on this market," says O'Neal. He's 26, and he's a new breed of investor—he trades on the Internet. O'Neal says he absolutely will not dump out when the markets take a tumble. "I feel like at this point, if I'm going to lose anything, I can take the losses," he says.

It is truly a Goldilocks economy: not too hot, not too cold, but just right, and it shows no sign of faltering.

SOURCE: http://www.msnbc.com/NEWS/150339.asp

CONSIDER THIS:

Many believe that the stability of the economy is shaped by government and its ability to counteract economic fluctuations—stimulating the economy with tax cuts, spending, easy money, and low interest rates when the economy is weak, and restraining it when it overheats. However, this is a difficult task. The first assumption is that economists know exactly where the economy is headed and, secondly, that will they apply the right amount of stimulus or impediment with their economic policies to promote long-term stable economic growth. Information about the economy will always be less than perfect. In fact, a standard joke in economics is that the purpose of economic forecasting is to make astrologers look respectable.

to take account of normal seasonal fluctuations. Thus, seasonally adjusted unemployment rates in summer months are below actual unemployment rates, because unemployment is normally high in summertime as a result of the inflow of school-age workers into the labor force.

HOW CAN POLITICS AFFECT THE ECONOMY?

Studies have shown there is a strong correlation between the performance of the economy and the fate of an incumbent's bid for reelection. In fact, the 1992 presidential election sheds light on this hypothesis. President Bush had lost his reelection bid shortly after the economy had struggled through the 1990–1991 recession. Some scholars have speculated that if the election had taken place a few months later when the economic data looked a lot stronger, President Bush would have been reelected.

If this correlation between the strength of the economy and a successful reelection bid does exist, then it would be in the best interest of the incumbent to do everything in his power to stimulate the economy in the period leading up to the election. This might take the form of trying to pressure the Federal Reserve System into lowering the interest rate or pressing Congress to cut taxes or increase government spending—anything that might generate more spending and thus greater employment. Of course, the negative side to all of this is that although the incumbent may get reelected, the economy may have been overstimulated, causing inflationary problems.

JAPANESE GOVERNMENT EXPECTS SLOW RECOVERY

TOKYO (AP)—The Japanese government now expects the troubled economy could take up to three years to recover instead of the two years it previously projected, a top official says.

In another burst of bad news, a research agency reported today that Japanese bankruptcies rose in September, pushing the debt left over from failed businesses for the month to more than $25 billion, a post-war high.

The comments by Chief Cabinet Secretary Hiromu Nonaka, reported today by Kyodo News agency, was the second time in recent days that a Japanese official has played down hopes for a quick end to Japan's deepest recession since World War II.

Last week, the government revised downward its economic forecast for the fiscal year ending March 31, predicting shrinkage of 1.8 percent instead of the previously forecast growth of 1.9 percent.

"We think the economy will recover in two or three years," Nonaka was quoted as saying to reporters. Until now, the government has said the recovery would take one or two years.

> **CONSIDER THIS:**
> For years the Japanese economy seemed as if it was immune to recession—but it finally hit and hit hard. It has been over 50 years since Japan has gone through a recession.

CONCEPT CHECK

1. Business cycles are short-term fluctuations in the amount of economic activity, relative to the long-term trend in output.
2. The four phases of a business cycle are expansion, peak, contraction, and trough.
3. Recessions occur during the contraction phase of a business cycle. Severe, long-term recessions are called depressions.
4. The economy often goes through short-term contractions even during a long-term growth trend.

1. Why would you expect unemployment to tend to fall during an economy's expansionary phase and to rise during a contractionary phase?
2. Why might a politician want to stimulate the economy prior to his or her reelection bid?
3. Why is the output of investment goods and durable consumer goods more sensitive to the business cycle than that of most goods?
4. Why might the unemployment rate fall after output starts recovering during the expansion phase of the business cycle?

Application: Economic Freedom and Economic Growth

What is economic freedom? Does economic freedom lead to greater economic growth?

ECONOMIC FREEDOM AND THE GROWTH OF EMERGING MARKETS

DOES ECONOMIC THEORY PROVIDE A PRECISE RECIPE FOR GROWTH? Probably not. But according to economists James Gwartney and Robert Lawson, it does reveal several of the important ingredients. Other things being constant, their research suggests that countries investing a larger share of their GDP (gross domestic product) will tend to grow more rapidly. Until the troubles hit Southeast Asia in early 1998, high investment rates had contributed to high levels of growth in several Asian countries, including Singapore, Malaysia, and South Korea. However, if investment is going to exert a strong impact on growth, it must be channeled into productive projects. As the experience of Eastern European countries and the former Soviet Union illustrates, high investment rates do not guarantee rapid growth and prosperity.

WHAT IS ECONOMIC FREEDOM? According to Gwartney and Lawson, a country's institutional arrangements and policies will also influence growth and the efficiency of resource use. The two researchers created a rating system based on economic freedom. Specifically, a country has a high level of economic freedom if it has the following characteristics: private ownership, a stable monetary environment, low taxes, and freedom of exchange. They used a rating system of economic freedom to determine the countries that improved the most as well as those that regressed the most during the 1975–1994 period.

WHAT HAPPENED TO THE COUNTRIES WHOSE ECONOMIC FREEDOM EXPANDED? The 12 countries with the largest increases in economic freedom achieved impressive growth rates during 1985–1994 (Exhibit 1). On average, the real per capita GDP of the nations in the most improved category grew at an annual rate of 4 percent between 1985 and 1994. At this rate, their real per capita income would double every 18 years.

WHAT HAPPENED TO THE COUNTRIES WHOSE ECONOMIC FREEDOM CONTRACTED? In the 11 countries for which the index of economic freedom fell the most, the level of real per capita GDP declined, on average, at an annual rate of 1.2 percent during 1985–1994 (Exhibit 2).

SOURCE: James Gwartney and Robert Lawson, *Economic Freedom of the World: 1975–1995*, Cato Institute, 1996. http://www.cipe.org/e20/gwa_E20.html

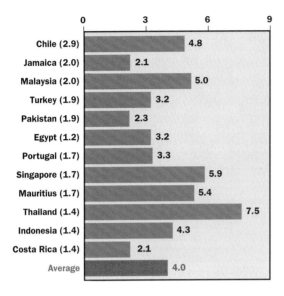

	0	3	6	9
Chile (2.9)			4.8	
Jamaica (2.0)	2.1			
Malaysia (2.0)			5.0	
Turkey (1.9)		3.2		
Pakistan (1.9)	2.3			
Egypt (1.2)		3.2		
Portugal (1.7)		3.3		
Singapore (1.7)			5.9	
Mauritius (1.7)			5.4	
Thailand (1.4)				7.5
Indonesia (1.4)			4.3	
Costa Rica (1.4)	2.1			
Average			4.0	

Note: Changes in ratings, 1975–1990, are in parentheses.

SOURCE: James Gwartney and Robert Lawson, *Economic Freedom of the World 1975–1995*, Cato Institute, 1996.

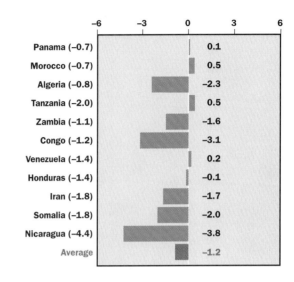

	-6	-3	0	3	6
Panama (–0.7)			0.1		
Morocco (–0.7)			0.5		
Algeria (–0.8)		–2.3			
Tanzania (–2.0)			0.5		
Zambia (–1.1)		–1.6			
Congo (–1.2)		–3.1			
Venezuela (–1.4)			0.2		
Honduras (–1.4)			–0.1		
Iran (–1.8)		–1.7			
Somalia (–1.8)		–2.0			
Nicaragua (–4.4)		–3.8			
Average		–1.2			

Note: Changes in ratings, 1975–1990, are in parentheses.

SOURCE: James Gwartney and Robert Larson, *Economic Freedom of the World 1975–1995*, Cato Institute, 1996.

Along with high investment, Gwartney and Lawson have argued that countries need a high degree of economic freedom. Recall from Module 1 our discussion of the 10 powerful ideas in economics. Many of these ideas are scattered throughout the success stories of developed and developing countries. Specifically, most economists believe that greater growth can be achieved when government is enforcing property rights, supporting freer trade, and ensuring a stable monetary environment. Of course, all economies, developed and developing, have to deal with the issues of scarcity and choice. As individuals and nations seek to make themselves better off, they will choose to specialize and produce those goods and services they produce best or most efficiently. This, coupled with trade and a legal system that protects property rights, has historically led to greater economic growth and higher standards of living.

Changes in economic freedom between 1985 and 1994 resulted in an increase in the per capita GDP of Malaysia and a decrease in Nicaragua's per capita GDP during that same time period.

If you are a full-time student, are you part of the labor force? Are you unemployed? Not sure? Use the problems and questions in your Workbook to solidify your grasp on the three primary macroeconomic goals, and then click on the World Wide Web links on your EconActive CD-ROM to connect to current data and statistics on unemployment in the United States.

Economic Growth

A. Economic Growth
What is economic growth?

B. The Impact of Economic Growth
How does economic growth impact other variables?

C. Determinants of Economic Growth
What changes lead to economic growth?

D. Population Growth and Economic Growth
How can an increasing population affect economic growth?

E. Desirability of Economic Growth
Why wouldn't economic growth be desirable?

F. Application: Economic Growth and Relative Happiness
Is economic growth the key to greater happiness?

Economic Growth

■ What is economic growth?
■ How dramatic are the differences in economic growth between countries?

SHORT RUN VERSUS LONG RUN

John Maynard Keynes, one of the most influential economic thinkers of all times, once said that "in the long run we are all dead." The reason Keynes said this is that he was primarily concerned with explaining and reducing short-term fluctuations in the level of business activity. He wanted to smooth out the business cycle, largely because of the implications that cyclical fluctuations had for buyers and sellers in terms of unemployment and price instability. No one would deny that Keynes' concerns were important and legitimate.

At the same time, however, Keynes' flippant remark about the long run ignores the fact that human welfare is greatly influenced by long-term changes in a nation's capacity to produce goods and services. Emphasis on short-run economic fluctuations ignores the longer-term dynamic changes that affect output, leisure, real incomes, and life styles.

Putting it differently, it is unlikely that a nation that has cyclical stability (little troughs and peaks) but little long-term growth in output will be better off than a nation with greater instability but more long-term growth. Consider Exhibit 1. Is nation A (with much economic stability but little economic growth) better off than nation B (with much growth but little stability)? While this question probably cannot be definitively answered, many would argue that in the long run, economic growth is a crucial determinant of people's well-being. Therefore, we now turn to study the forces that permit long-term growth in output and production.

What are the determinants of long-run economic change in our ability to produce goods and services? What are some of the consequences of rapid economic change? Why are some nations rich while others are poor? Does growth in output improve our economic welfare? These are a few questions that we wish to explore.

HOW IS ECONOMIC GROWTH DEFINED?

Economic growth is usually measured by the annual percent change in real output of goods and services per capita (real GDP per capita). In Module 3, we introduced

the production possibilities curve. Along the production possibilities curve, the economy is producing at its potential output. How much the economy will produce at its potential output, sometimes called its natural level of output, depends on the quantity and quality of an economy's resources, including labor, capital (like factories, machinery, and tools), and natural resources (land, coal, timber, oil, iron, and so on). In addition, technology can increase

| EXHIBIT 1 | GROWTH VERSUS STABILITY |

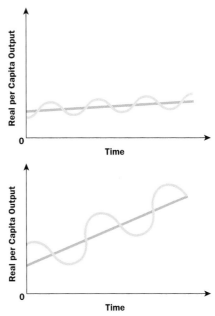

Nation A has little short-term economic instability and thus does not continually face great economic changes, and the uncertainties they cause; at the same time, however, output per capita grows little in the long term. Nation B, by contrast, has great instability, resulting in sharp variations in unemployment rates, and other economic circumstances, but is growing rapidly over long time horizons. We would typically like both growth and stability, so nations often attempt to implement stabilization policies in ways they hope will not retard long-term growth rates.

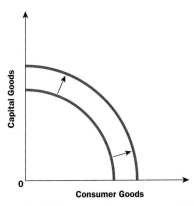

Increases in capital, land, labor, and entrepreneurial activity can expand the production possibilities curve.

the economy's production capabilities. As shown in Exhibit 2, improvements in and greater stocks of land, labor, capital, and entrepreneurial activity will shift out the production possibilities curve. Another way of saying that economic growth has shifted the production possibilities curve out is to say that it has increased potential output.

HOW MUCH VARIATION IN GDP IS THERE IN THE WORLD?

The "richest" or "most-developed" countries today have many times the market output of the "poorest" or "least-developed" countries (see Exhibit 3). Put differently, the most-developed countries produce and market more output in a day than the least-developed countries do in a year. The international differences in income, output, and wealth are indeed striking and have caused a great deal of friction between developed and less-developed countries. The United States and the nations of the European Union have had sizeable increases in real output over the past two centuries, but even in 1800 most of these nations were better off in terms of market output than such contemporary impoverished countries as Ethiopia, India, or Nepal.

EXHIBIT 3 | SELECTED ECONOMIES BY SIZE OF GDP

Country	GDP (billions of dollars)
United States	$7,100
Japan	4,964
Germany	2,252
France	1,451
United Kingdom	1,095
Italy	1,088
China	745
Brazil	580
Canada	574
Russia	332
India	320
Mexico	305
Hong Kong	142
Chile	59
Egypt	46
Cuba	14
Costa Rica	9
Kenya	8
Iceland	7

SOURCE: *World in Figures, 1998 edition* (New York: John Wiley & Sons, Inc., 1998), p. 22.

CONCEPT CHECK

1. Economic growth is usually measured by the annual percent change in real output of goods and services per capita.

2. Improvements in and greater stocks of land, labor, capital, and entrepreneurial activity will shift out the production possibilities curve.

1. Why does the production possibilities curve shift out with economic growth?
2. Even if "in the long run we are all dead," are you glad that earlier generations of Americans worked and invested for economic growth?

3. If long-run consequences were not important, would many students go to college or participate in internship programs without pay? Why or why not?
4. When the Dutch "created" new land with their system of dikes, what did it do to their production possibilities curve? Why?

The Impact of Economic Growth

■ What is the relationship between economic growth and other economic and social factors?

■ How is urbanization affected by economic growth?

■ How has industrialization been affected by economic growth?

■ Why is the saving rate so important in economic growth?

WHAT IS THE IMPACT OF ECONOMIC GROWTH?

Economic growth means more than an increase in the real income (output) of the population. Changes in output are accompanied by a number of other important changes. The most comprehensive investigation of the relationship between economic growth and other economic and social factors was done by the late Nobel laureate Simon Kuznets, although others have made important contributions in Kuznets' tradition.

Before listing some of the observed relationships between economic growth and other variables, it is important to distinguish between cause and effect. Several things that increase in abundance with economic growth may be by-products or effects of growth, while other things may be causes. Wine consumption may be higher in developed than in less-developed countries. Does this mean that wine consumption causes growth by making people more productive, or that wine consumption is a result of that growth (with growth people have higher disposable incomes)? Showing that a statistical relationship exists, then, does not say anything about the direction of causation—that is, correlation does not prove causation.

Generally speaking, the greater the level of per capita real output (which reflects past economic growth),

1. the greater the proportion of the population living in urban areas;

2. the smaller the proportion of the labor force engaged in agricultural pursuits;

3. the greater the amount of specialization, trade, and economic interdependence, and the smaller the amount of self-sufficiency;

4. the greater the average educational attainment of the population and the lower the amount of illiteracy;

5. the lower the birth rate;

6. the lower the death rate;

7. the greater the amount of capital available per capita;

8. the greater the mobility of human and physical resources.

Note that the preceding list reflects relationships that generally, but do not always, hold. For example, New Zealand has a greater proportion of its population engaged in agriculture than many countries with lower per capita incomes. In other words, the correlation between the eight factors above and economic growth is not perfect.

This list does not include many other variables that are related to growth, but perhaps less conclusively. For example, does work effort rise or fall with economic growth? We might think that it falls, because rising incomes in many developed countries have resulted in shorter work weeks and longer vacations. On the other

Urbanization tends to rise with the level of per capita output.

hand, labor force participation by women typically rises with per capita incomes. Moreover, the move from farm to non-farm activities sometimes means an increase in hours worked given the seasonal nature of farm activity.

Some have also claimed that economic growth stimulates political freedom or democracy, but the correlation here is far from conclusive. While there are rich democratic societies and poor authoritarian ones, the opposite also holds. That is, some features of democracy, such as majority voting and special interest groups, may actually be growth retarding. For example, if the majority decides to vote in large land reforms and wealth transfers, this will lead to higher taxes and market distortions that will reduce incentives for work, investment, and ultimately economic growth. A decline in religious influences often accompanies economic growth, but again the correlation is not a perfect one.

HOW IS URBANIZATION AFFECTED BY ECONOMIC GROWTH?

Elaborating on the eight relationships suggested above, the majority of the population of most highly developed nations lives in urban areas. In 1790, when per capita income was only $400 or $500, only 5 percent of the American population lived in urban areas; now, three-fourths of the population is urbanized. Closely related to that, in 1790 some 80 percent of American workers were farmers, while less than 3 percent are today. Why? On the supply side, agricultural productivity has risen dramatically, meaning that a given farmer today is producing far more than his counterpart of two centuries ago. On the demand side, incomes have risen, but the population has chosen to spend a smaller proportion of its income on food. That is, as incomes rise, people increase their consumption of luxury goods (often manufactured in cities) relatively faster than their consumption of essential items like food.

HOW HAS INDUSTRIALIZATION BEEN AFFECTED BY ECONOMIC GROWTH?

The corollary to the decline in the relative importance of agriculture has been an increase in the relative importance of non-agricultural pursuits, especially manufacturing but also transportation, construction, and service industries (professional services, education, health care, recreation and tourism, etc.). As an illustration, in 1820 the United States had at least 10 times as many farmers as workers in manufacturing; a century later the number in manufacturing exceeded the number of farmers.

How did New Zealand and Denmark, which are primarily agricultural countries, experience high rates of economic growth?

Could an increase in manufacturing occur without improvement in agricultural productivity?

WHAT IS THE RELATIONSHIP BETWEEN ECONOMIC GROWTH AND LITERACY?

With economic growth, illiteracy falls and formal education grows. This is demonstrated in Exhibit 1, which shows the adult literacy rates and per capita output levels for various nations. The correlation between per capita output and the proportion of the population that is unable to read or write is striking. Improvements in literacy stimulate economic growth by reducing barriers to the flow of information; when information costs are high, out of ignorance many resources flow to or remain in uses that are rather unproductive. Moreover, education imparts skills that are directly useful in raising labor productivity, whether it is mathematics taught to a sales clerk, engineering techniques taught to a college graduate, or just good ideas that facilitate production and design.

Education may also, however, be a consequence of economic growth, because as incomes rise, people's tendency to consume education increases. People increasingly look to education for more than the acquisition of immediately applicable skills. Education becomes a consumption good as well as a means of investing in human capital.

EXHIBIT 1	LITERACY AND ECONOMIC DEVELOPMENT	
Country	**Output Per Capita**	**Adult Literacy Rates**
United States	$27,500	97%
Japan	21,300	99
Italy	18,700	97
Brazil	6,100	83
India	1,500	52
Haiti	1,000	45
Ethiopia	400	35

NOTE: The literacy rates are based on the ability to read and write at an elementary school level.

SOURCE: *The Wall Street Journal Almanac, 1998.*

HOW ARE BIRTH RATES AFFECTED BY ECONOMIC GROWTH?

The assertion that economic growth results in lower birth and death rates is supported by Exhibit 2. The poorer a nation, the higher the birth rate is likely to be. Thus, Ethiopia has nearly 45 babies born every year for every 1,000 persons, while the United States has one-third that number, 15. Why? To be sure, the answer is complex, and numerous cultural factors are involved (e.g., religious attitudes or traditional extended families). Still, the primary reason that birth rates in richer nations like the United States have fallen dramatically in the past two centuries is economic.

Countries with low incomes tend to be primarily agricultural; in these societies, children fairly quickly reach an age where they can "earn their own keep" (even though their "keep" may be relatively primitive by standards of developed nations). At the age of 8 or 10, a child in a rural area may be contributing more to the output of a farm than his maintenance costs; in a financial sense, then, this child is "profitable." By contrast, children living in developed countries are usually a substantial financial liability to their parents until the age of 18 or even 21 or 22 (or even longer), particularly given the tendency to attend school for longer periods of time. Moreover, in less-developed countries, the children usually care for their parents when they get old; having children is a means of getting the equivalent of social security and a pension. Children, in short, serve both as investment goods and consumer goods in poorer countries, while in more economically advanced nations, children are primarily consumer goods.

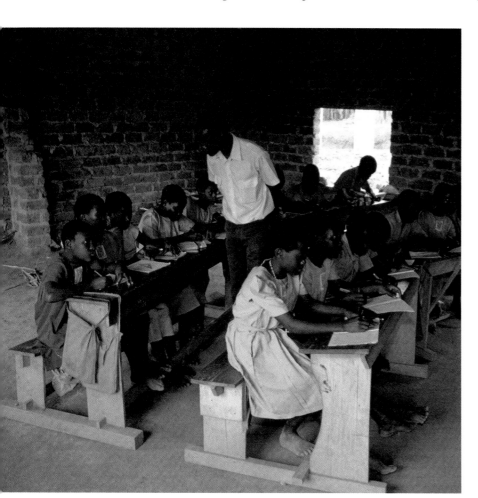

Is this one possible answer to economic growth in poorer countries?

EXHIBIT 2	BIRTHS, DEATHS, AND ECONOMIC GROWTH

Nation	Output Per Capita	Birth Rate*	Death Rate*	Natural Population Increase*
United States	$27,500	15	9	6
Japan	21,300	10	8	2
Italy	18,700	10	10	0
Brazil	6,100	21	9	12
India	1,500	26	10	16
Haiti	1,000	39	16	23
Ethiopia	400	46	18	28

*Per 1,000 inhabitants living at the beginning of the year.

SOURCE: *The Wall Street Journal Almanac*, 1998.

HOW ARE DEATH RATES RELATED TO DIFFERENT LEVELS OF ECONOMIC DEVELOPMENT?

As you can see in Exhibit 2, death rates often fall fairly sharply early in the development process, as per capita output rises from, say, the $100 to $500 level to the $3,000 level. Nations place a high priority on using sufficient quantities of their increased resources to the task of reducing death rates. Health and sanitation get major attention after the elemental needs of nourishment and clothing are attended to in an adequate fashion. Therefore, in the early stages of development, the natural rate of population increase (births minus deaths) actually grows, as death rates fall faster than birth rates. As nations get still more developed (to perhaps $10,000 output per capita), natural population growth begins to fall, because death rates fall more slowly, while birth rates begin to decline dramatically.

SAVINGS RATES, INVESTMENT, CAPITAL STOCK, AND ECONOMIC GROWTH

One of the most important determinants of economic growth is the savings rate. In order to consume more in the future, we must save more now. Generally speaking, higher levels of savings will lead to higher rates of investment and capital formation and, therefore, to greater economic growth. Individuals can either consume or save their income. If individuals choose to consume all of their income, there will be nothing left for savings, which businesses could use for investment purposes to build new plants or replace worn-out or obsolete equipment. With little investment in capital stock, there will be lit-

tle economic growth. Capital can also increase as a result of capital injections from abroad (foreign direct investments), but the role of national saving rates in economic growth is of particular importance.

Exhibit 3 clearly shows that sustained rapid economic growth is associated with high rates of saving and investment around the world. However, investment alone does not guarantee economic growth. Economic growth hinges importantly on the quality and the type of investment as well as on investments in human capital and improvements in technology.

WHY DO RESOURCES BECOME MORE MOBILE WITH ECONOMIC DEVELOPMENT?

Mobility of resources—human and physical capital—tends to speed up somewhat with economic development, partly because movement and search costs decline. As transportation and communications improve in the course of economic growth, people become more aware of economic opportunities and can better afford to respond to them (given the decline in transport costs). Indeed, in the United States the extent of human migration has not increased too much over time, but the responsiveness of migrants to economic opportunities has grown significantly. The United States has received millions of immigrants, has had a massive internal geographic redistribution of the population as

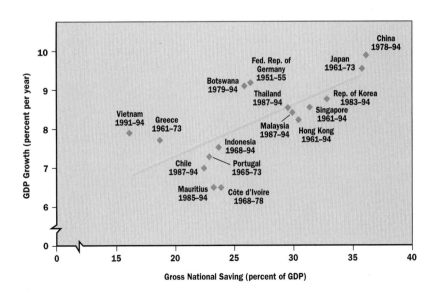

NOTE: Data are annual averages for the periods indicated.

SOURCE: World Bank, *World Development Report, 1996*, Oxford University Press, 1996.

a consequence of the Westward Movement, and has through migration also become a nation of urban dwellers rather than farmers. In a dynamic, growing economy, then, resources are constantly moving to opportunities that are perceived to be better.

WHAT IS THE RELATIONSHIP BETWEEN ECONOMIC GROWTH AND SELF-SUFFICIENCY?

The notion that with economic development people tend to work increasingly for other people rather than being self-employed is closely related to the growth in urbaniza-tion and the accompanying decline in the relative impor-tance of agriculture. Farmers tend to be self-employed; non-farmers usually are not. Even within manufacturing, however, the scale of operations tends to grow with devel-opment, meaning that workers are not only working for others, but they are less likely to even know who their boss really is. In 1860, the average American manufacturing firm employed fewer than 10 workers and only a handful of firms employed more than 1,000. By the 1990s however, almost half of the manufacturing firms employed 500 or more employees.

CONCEPT CHECK

1. Economic growth is usually defined as increases in the real income of the population. Economic devel-opment includes increasing affluence and other fun-damental changes in lifestyles and the social environment.

2. With economic growth tends to come urbanization, industrialization, greater specialization, rising liter-acy, falling birth and death rates, greater capital for-mation, and increased mobility.

3. Higher savings rates generally lead to greater in-vestment and capital formation, which lead to eco-nomic growth.

1. Why does knowing what factors are correlated with economic growth not tell us what causes economic growth?

2. How does increasing the capital stock lead to eco-nomic growth?

3. How do increases in savings affect long-run eco-nomic growth?

4. Why would you expect an inverse relationship be-tween self-sufficiency and real GDP per capita?

5. If a couple was concerned about their retirement, why could that lead to them having more children if they lived in an agricultural society but fewer chil-dren if they were in an urban society?

Determinants of Economic Growth

- What quantifiable factors contribute to economic growth?
- What qualitative factors add to economic growth?
- How can prices of exports affect economic development?

WHAT DO ECONOMISTS BELIEVE LEADS TO ECONOMIC GROWTH?

Many of the great pioneering economists of the eighteenth and nineteenth centuries had theories on the process of economic growth. For example, Adam Smith, in 1776, argued that the wealth of nations derived from the accumulation of capital, which, in turn, resulted from thrift and savings. Capital formation was the key ingredient in Smith's model of economic growth. He also thought that specialization and the division of labor were important, and he criticized the then-accepted ideas of mercantilism, with its emphasis on the need for barriers to trade between people and countries, the accumulation of gold and silver, and various types of governmental regulation.

Other economists emphasized other factors. Karl Marx, for example, argued that all value ultimately derives from labor and that economic growth, therefore, depends on increasing contributions by labor. Some economists, notably the great twentieth century economist Joseph Schumpeter, argued that growth depended to a considerable extent on innovation and technological change, for which the role of managerial or entrepreneurial skills was particularly vital. Schumpeter believed that rewards (temporary monopoly) should go to the innovators, or there would be little incentive to carry out costly and often unsuccessful research projects. A few economists, most notably the Rev. Thomas Robert Malthus, argued that in the long run, per capita economic growth will not occur at all! Still others, including the French philosopher Montesquieu, argued that economic growth and development was a function of climate. Output levels are lower in tropical zones, partly because, or so Montesquieu argued, the work effort is less intense in the heat of the tropics.

WHAT FACTORS ARE BELIEVED TO CONTRIBUTE TO ECONOMIC GROWTH?

In short, many separate explanations of the process of economic growth have been proposed. Which is correct? None of them, by themselves, can completely explain economic growth. However, each of the explanations may be part of a more complicated reality. Economic growth is a complex process involving many important factors, no one of which completely dominates. We can list at least eight factors that nearly everyone would agree have contributed to economic growth in some or all countries:

1. Growth in the quantity and quality of labor resources used;
2. Increase in the use of inputs provided by the land (natural resources);
3. Growth in physical capital inputs (machines, tools, buildings, inventories);
4. Technological advances (new ways of combining given quantities of labor, natural resources, and capital inputs) allowing greater output than previously possible;
5. Economies of scale—efficiencies gained by producing on a larger scale than before (lower input use per unit of output);
6. Greater division of labor (specialization) and trade;
7. Migration of resources from areas of low productivity to areas of high productivity;
8. Government protection of property rights.

HOW CAN CHANGES IN LABOR AFFECT ECONOMIC GROWTH?

We know that labor is needed in all forms of productive activity. But other things being equal, an increase in labor input does not necessarily increase output per capita. If the increase in labor input results from an increase in population, per capita growth might not occur, because the increase in output could be offset by the increase in population. However, if a greater proportion of the population works (that is, the labor force participation rate rises) or if workers put in longer hours, output per capita will increase—assuming that the additional work activity adds something to output. Qualitative improvements in workers (learning new skills, for example) can also enhance output. Indeed, it has become popular to view labor as "human capital" that can be augmented or improved by education and on-the-job training.

WHY ARE NATURAL RESOURCES AN IMPORTANT PART OF ECONOMIC GROWTH?

Greater use of natural resources also can enhance output. The more natural resources (such as more land or better soil) a farmer has to work with, for example, the more he will be able to produce, other things being equal. The abundance of natural resources in the United States has been cited by many observers as a major contributor to U.S. economic growth. Land is obviously an important factor of production in agriculture, and natural resources are also vital as inputs in the manufacture of industrial goods. Resources are, however, not the whole story, as is clear with reference to Japan or especially Hong Kong, both of which have relatively few natural resources.

HOW IMPORTANT IS PHYSICAL CAPITAL TO ECONOMIC GROWTH?

Even in primitive economies, workers usually have some rudimentary tools to further their productive activity. Take the farmer who needs to dig a ditch to improve drainage in his fields. If he used just his bare hands, it might take a lifetime to complete the job. If he used a shovel, he could dig the ditch in hours or days. But with a big earth-moving machine, he could do it in minutes. There is nearly universal agreement that capital formation has played a significant role in the economic development of nations. Perhaps one-third of the economic growth of the United States during its period of great growth from 1840 to 1920 is directly attributable to the growth in per capita capital over time. However, because much technological advance gets "embodied" into new capital, some of the previous estimate may well overstate the critical importance of capital relative to technological advances.

HOW DO TECHNOLOGICAL ADVANCES LEAD TO GROWTH?

Technological advances stem from man's ingenuity and creativity in developing new ways of combining the factors of production to enhance the amount of output from a given quantity of resources. The process of technological advance involves invention and innovation. Innovation is the adoption of the product or process. For example, in the United States, the invention and innovation of the cotton gin, the Bessemer steel-making process, and the railroad were important stimuli to economic growth. New technology, however, must be introduced into productive use by managers or entrepreneurs who must weigh the perceived estimates of benefits of the new technology against estimates of costs.

The wealth of natural resources enhances growth.

The invention and innovation of the elevator was a major contributor to the growth of cities. As a result of the elevator, buildings could be built up as well as out.

Thus, the entrepreneur is an important economic factor in the growth process.

Technological advance permits us to economize on one or more inputs used in the production process. It can permit savings of labor, as occurs when a new machine is invented that does the work of many workers. When this happens, technology is said to be embodied in capital and to be labor saving. Technology, however, can also be land (natural resource) saving or even capital saving. For example, nuclear fission has permitted us to build power plants that economize on the use of coal, a natural resource. The reduction in transportation time that accompanied the invention of the railroad allowed businesses to reduce the capital they needed in the form of inventories. Because goods could be obtained more quickly, businesses could reduce the stock kept on their shelves.

Some scholars believe that the importance of research and development (R & D) is understated. The concept of R & D is broad indeed—it can include new products, management improvements, production innovations, or simply learning-by-doing. However, it is clear that investments in R & D and rewarding innovators with patents have paid big dividends in the past 50 to 60 years. Some would argue that even larger rewards for research and development would spur even more rapid economic growth. In addition, there is an important link between research and development and capital investment. As already noted, when capital depreciates over time, it is replaced with new equipment that embodies the latest technology. Consequently, R & D may work hand-in-hand with investment to improve growth and productivity. In Exhibit 1, we see R & D expenditures as a percentage of GDP in a selected group of industrialized countries.

EXHIBIT 1	RESEARCH AND DEVELOPMENT EXPENDITURES AS A PERCENTAGE OF GDP, 1981–1994	
Country	Non-Defense	Total
United States	2.00	2.49
Japan	2.66	2.69
Germany*	2.26	2.33
France	NA	2.38
United Kingdom	1.88	2.19
Italy	1.14	1.19
Canada	1.53	1.57

*Germany's data for 1981–1990 are for West Germany.

SOURCES: NSF, Division of Science Resources Studies; Organization for Economic Cooperation and Development.

IN THE NEWS

THE NEW ECONOMY?

Microsoft's rise is a testimony to the power of ideas in the new economy. Working with information is very different from working with the steel and glass from which our grandparents built their wealth. Information is easier to produce and harder to control than stuff you can drop on your foot. For a start, computers can copy it and ship it anywhere, almost instantly and almost for free. Production and distribution, the basis of industrial power, can increasingly be taken for granted. Innovation and marketing are all.

So an information economy is more open—it doesn't take a production line to compete, just a good idea. But it's also more competitive. Information is easy not just to duplicate, but to replicate. Successful firms have to keep innovating to keep ahead of copycats nipping at their heels. The average size of companies shrinks. New products and knockoffs alike emerge in months rather than years, and market power is increasingly based on making sense of an overabundance of ideas rather than rationing scarce material goods. Each added connection to a network's pool of knowledge multiplies the value of the whole—one reason for Microsoft's astonishing growth. The result: new rules of competition, new sorts of organization, new challenges for management.

Some zealots talk about a New Economy, capital N, capital E, all too easily caricatured as "there won't be inflation anymore, because of technological change." Alas, as Stanford economist Paul Romer has reminded us, "If a majority of the Fed's board of governors decided to have 20 percent inflation, they could have it in a year, possibly in months." Then there's the idea that recessions are things of the past. This comes up at the end of every expansion.

CONSIDER THIS:
The move to the information economy is shaping the way we think about the future. However, it is difficult to accurately measure the gains computers and telecoms are generating. Almost 75 percent of all computers are used in the service sector, like finance and health. In these areas, productivity gains have been difficult to measure. In addition, many of the benefits come in the form of quality or convenience, like 24-hour-a-day automated bank tellers. Some of these quality-of-life improvements are not accurately measured in macroeconomic data.

SOURCE: John Browning and Spencer Reiss, *Wired Magazine* ONLINE http://www.hotwired.com/special/ene/index.html?word=intro_two

HOW ARE ECONOMIES OF SCALE MOST BENEFICIAL IN ECONOMIC GROWTH?

Sheer size of productive organization might also enhance economic growth. If a firm increases the use of each input by 1.0 percent, but output rises by 1.1 percent, economies of scale are said to exist. This is sometimes referred to as economies of mass production. To the extent that economies of scale exist, they are more likely to be utilized if there are extensive trade and specialization.

HOW IS COMPARATIVE ADVANTAGE USED TO PROMOTE ECONOMIC GROWTH?

Trade can also lead to greater output because of the principle of comparative advantage. Essentially, the principle of comparative advantage suggests that if two nations or individuals with different resource endowments and production capabilities specialize in producing a smaller number of goods and services they are relatively better at and engage in trade, both parties will benefit. Total output will rise. This will be discussed in greater detail in the Module on international trade.

HOW DOES MOBILITY OF RESOURCES ADD TO ECONOMIC GROWTH?

The migration of the factors of production can involve physical movement (geographical mobility) or merely occupational change within a given geographic area. If a man can produce 15 loaves of bread in area A but can increase his output to 25 loaves merely by moving to area B

(with its better availability of natural resources needed to make bread), total output in the economy can rise.

HOW DOES THE PROTECTION OF PROPERTY RIGHTS IMPACT ECONOMIC GROWTH?

Economic growth rates tend to be higher in countries where the government enforces property rights. As we discussed in Module 6, property rights give owners the legal right to keep or sell their property—land, labor, or capital. Without property rights, life would be a huge "free-for-all," where people could take whatever they wanted; in this scenario, protection for property, such as alarm systems and private security services, would have to be purchased.

In most developed countries, property rights are effectively protected by the government. However, in developing countries, this is not usually the case. And if the government is not enforcing these rights, the private sector must respond in costly ways that stifle economic growth. For example, an unreliable judiciary system means that entrepreneurs are more often forced to rely on informal agreements that are difficult to enforce. As a result, they may have to pay bribes to get things done, and even then, they may not get the promised services. Individuals will have to buy private security or pay "organized crime" for protection against crime and corruption. In addition, landowners and business owners might be fearful of coups or takeovers from a new government, which might confiscate their property all together. In short, if government is not adequately protecting property rights, the incentive to invest will be hindered, and political instability, corruption, and lower rates of economic growth will be likely.

CONCEPT CHECK

1. The factors that contribute to economic growth are increased quantity of labor, natural resources, physical capital, technological advances, economies of scale, comparative advantage, mobility of resources, and government protection of property rights.

1. Why is no single factor capable of completely explaining economic growth patterns?
2. Why might countries with relatively scarce labor be leaders in labor-saving innovations? In what area would countries with relatively scarce land likely be innovative leaders?
3. Why could an increase in the price of oil increase real GDP growth in oil-exporting countries like Saudi Arabia and Mexico, while decreasing growth in oil-importing countries like the United States and Japan?

4. How is Hong Kong a dramatic example of why abundant natural resources are not necessary to rapid economic growth?
5. Why is the effective use of land, labor, capital, and entrepreneurial activities dependent on the protection of property rights?

Population Growth and Economic Growth

MODULE 8

■ When is population growth beneficial to per capita economic growth?

■ When is population growth detrimental to per capita economic growth?

HOW DOES POPULATION GROWTH AFFECT ECONOMIC GROWTH?

The world's population at the beginning of the English Industrial Revolution around 1750 was perhaps 700 million. It took 150 years, to 1900, for that population to slightly more than double to 1.6 billion. In just 64 years (1964), it had doubled again, to 3.2 billion. By another 40 years, 2004, it is very possible that the population will have doubled again, to 6.4 billion (the world population was 5.8 billion in 1997). We have had economic development amidst all this growth in population, but what role did population play in the economic growth?

The impact of population growth on per capita economic growth is far from obvious. If population were to expand faster than output, per capita output would fall; population growth would be growth-inhibiting. With a greater population, however, comes a greater labor force. Also, economies of large-scale production may exist in some forms of production, so larger markets associated with greater populations lead to more efficient-sized production units. Certainly very rapid population growth—over 3 percent a year—did not seem to impede American economic growth in the mid-nineteenth century. America's economic growth until at least World War I was accompanied by population growth that was among the highest in the world for the time.

There is a general feeling, however, that in many of the less-developed countries today, rapid population growth threatens the possibility of attaining sustained economic

What impact does a large population have on economic growth?

growth. These countries are predominantly agricultural with very modest natural resources, especially land. The land–labor ratio is very low. Why is population growth a threat in these countries? One answer was provided nearly two centuries ago by the English economist, the Rev. Thomas Malthus.

WHAT IS THE MALTHUSIAN PREDICTION?

Malthus formulated a theoretical model that predicted that per capita economic growth would eventually become negative and that wages would ultimately reach an equilibrium at a subsistence level, or just large enough to provide enough income to stay alive. Malthus assumed an agricultural society where goods were produced by two inputs, land and labor. He further assumed that the supply of land was fixed in quantity. Further, he assumed that the sexual desires of humans would work to increase population.

WHAT IS THE LAW OF DIMINISHING RETURNS?

As population increased, the number of workers would increase. Thus with greater labor inputs available, output would also go up. At some point, however, output would increase by diminishing amounts because of the law of diminishing returns, which states that if you add variable amounts of one input (in this case, labor) to fixed quantities of another input (in this case, land), output would rise but by diminishing amounts (as the land–labor ratio falls, there is less land per worker).

HOW CAN AN ECONOMY AVOID MALTHUS' PREDICTION?

Fortunately, Malthus's theory proved spectacularly wrong for much of the world. While the law of diminishing returns is a valid concept, Malthus's other assumptions were unrealistic. Agricultural land is not completely fixed in quantity or quality. Irrigation, fertilizer, and conservation techniques have effectively increased arable land. More important, Malthus implicitly assumed there would be no technological advance, and ignored the real possibility that improved technology, often embodied in capital, could overcome the impact of the law of diminishing returns. Moreover, the Malthusian assumption that sexual desire would necessarily lead to population increase is not even accurate. True, sexual desire may always be with us, but births can be reduced by birth-control techniques.

ARE THERE SOME COUNTRIES THAT FIT MALTHUS' PREDICTION TODAY?

Unfortunately, the Malthusian assumptions are not too widely at variance from reality for several less-developed countries today. Some nations of the world are having substantial population increases, with a virtually fixed supply of land and little technological advance. Population growth has a negative impact on per capita output in this case, since the added output derived from having more workers on the land is very small. In short, for some places in the modern world, the Malthusian model may be relevant.

In this situation, it is scarcely surprising that population control is considered to be of critical importance, not only in India but in many other less-developed countries. The implementation of birth control has been far from routine, however. While greater population, other things equal, may lower per capita output, from the perspective of an individual family, the production of children may mean greater security in old age, more labor for the farm now, and so forth. Governments have sometimes absorbed most or all of the cost of birth control, and even given financial incentives to persons opting for surgical procedures designed to control births. Still, in most countries, efforts to date have been only modestly successful. Population control remains a key factor in the growth patterns in countries with high populations in relation to natural resources and capital equipment.

CONCEPT CHECK

1. Population growth may increase per capita output in resource-rich countries like the United States, Australia, and Saudi Arabia, because they have more resources for each laborer to produce with. They are more likely to be able to exploit economies of large-scale production, and they are more likely to have rapidly expanding technology.

2. In some countries, the Malthusian dilemma posed by population growth and diminishing returns is a problem, and they may suffer as a result of population growth.

1. What happens to per capita real output if population grows faster than output? If population grows more slowly than output?
2. How can economies of large-scale production allow per capita output to rise as population rises?

3. How did Malthus' prediction on population growth follow from the law of diminishing returns?
4. Why is population control a particularly important issue in countries with very low levels of per capita income?

Desirability of Economic Growth

■ Why are rising expectations detrimental to the desirability of economic growth?

■ How do environmental concerns affect the desirability of economic growth?

IS ECONOMIC GROWTH DESIRABLE?

Our discussions thus far have certainly implied that economic growth is a good thing, something that nations should seek to enhance or maximize. Actually, that contention is debatable. At least two lines of arguments can be used to support the position that economic growth is not necessarily good and indeed may even be harmful.

WHAT ARGUMENTS SUGGEST THAT ECONOMIC GROWTH IS NOT DESIRABLE?

The first argument, which we developed earlier in the text, is that economic growth brings with it increased expectations. Indeed, sometimes it has been said that there is a revolution of rising expectations in newly developing countries. Happiness, or utility, may depend not only on the level of real consumption of goods and services but also on expectations of what you think you want or what you expect to have.

Second, many environmentalists have argued that economic growth is potentially life threatening in the long run, because with economic growth comes not only more goods but also more bads in the form of pollution. Per capita pollution would be expected to rise with per capita output, perhaps to the point where life is seriously threatened. This "pessimistic" view of the world might be a modern equivalent of Malthus's. Economic growth also involves the greater use of physical inputs, including natural resources. The stock of natural resources, however, is relatively fixed. Economic growth may increase the rate of depletion of these resources, again potentially sentencing future generations to death or a life of misery at the subsistence level.

WHAT DO THE CRITICS SAY ABOUT THESE ARGUMENTS?

These arguments are susceptible to criticism. Because utility is difficult to measure, the validity of the first argument can be questioned, although there is at least some crude evidence to support it.[1] At the same time, however, if a nation were unilaterally to decide to endorse policies leading to little or no economic growth, the country would soon be surpassed in income by other nations. In this day of advanced communications, the nation with zero growth might well develop new frustrations as it sees people in other countries with new gadgets, more services, better health, more leisure, and all of the other by-products of economic growth. Moreover, economic growth is important to national security. A nation that declines relative to other nations in its productive capacity is also falling behind in its potential military strength, because output can be converted to military rather than civilian purposes fairly readily (e.g., we can turn auto assembly lines into tank assembly lines, and can make bombers instead of commercial jet aircraft).

The environmental-resource arguments are also debatable. It is not clear, for example, that pollution necessarily rises as output increases. Some of the increasing output can and is used for pollution abatement; air pollution levels in the United States today are far below levels prevailing 40 years ago for nearly all types of pollution. For example, Environmental Protection Agency data suggests that the volume of particulate matter in the air has declined well over 50 percent since 1940. During the same period, however, there has been considerable economic growth. Production techniques can be altered to reduce the level of environmental damage from air, water, noise, or even visual pollution.

The natural resource limitation considered so crucial by some "doomsday" social scientists sounds very similar to the assumption that Malthus made, namely that land is fixed in quantity. In fact, technological advances, changes in relative prices, and new discoveries have led us to

---

[1] Richard A. Easterlin, "Does Economic Growth Improve the Human Lot? Some Empirical Evidence," in Paul David and Melvin Reder, *Nations and Households in Economic Growth* (New York: Academic Press, 1974).

harness new resources, as well as to find more of traditional resources. Thus, nuclear power comes from minerals that had no energy uses just 50 years ago. Solar energy depends upon the sun, a resource that went virtually untapped for millennia. Hence, while it is true that the process of economic growth tends to lead to increased resource use, it does not necessarily follow that a depletion of resources poses any immediate or even longer-term threat. For example, the reserves-to-consumption ratio for oil and other resources has increased despite growth in consumption. The pessimistic arguments may have some validity, but they largely proceed from the same unrealistic assumptions that made Malthus's predictions so spectacularly untrue in the Western world.

CONCEPT CHECK

1. Happiness, or utility, may not depend solely on the amount of real income but also on the increased expectations resulting from economic growth.

2. The desirability of economic growth may be diminished because of the fact that usually with economic growth come economic "bads," such as pollution.

---

1. Is it possible that utility, or happiness, could fall as income rises? Why or why not?
2. Why does economic growth not necessarily lead to environmental damage? How can it lead to environmental improvements?

3. Economic growth leads to increased resource use. Does this mean that economic growth will necessarily lead to a depletion of natural resources in the long run? Why or why not?

Application: Economic Growth and Relative Happiness

Can expectations affect our welfare? Do our expectations change over time?

THE RELATIVE DEPRIVATION PRINCIPLE: HAPPINESS IS RELATIVE TO OTHERS' ATTAINMENTS

Happiness is relative not only to our past experience, but also to our comparisons with others. We are always comparing ourselves to others. And whether we feel good or bad depends on who those others are. . . .

An example: To explain the frustration expressed by U.S. Air Corps soldiers during World War II, researchers formulated the concept of relative deprivation—the sense that we are worse off than others with whom we compare ourselves. Despite a relatively rapid promotion rate for the group, many soldiers were frustrated about their own promotion rates (Merton & Kitt, 1950). Apparently, seeing so many others being promoted inflated the soldiers' expectations. And when expectations soar above attainments, the result is frustration. When the Oakland Athletics signed outfielder José Canseco to a $4.7 million annual salary, his fellow outfielder Rickey Henderson became openly dissatisfied with his $3 million salary and refused to show up on time for spring training (King, 1991).

Such comparisons help us understand why the middle- and upper-income people in a given country tend to be slightly more satisfied with life than the relatively poor, with whom the better-off can compare themselves (Diener, 1984). Nevertheless, once a person reaches a moderate income level, further increases do little to increase happiness. Why? Because as people climb the ladder of success they mostly compare themselves with those who are at or above their current level (Gruder, 1977; Suls & Tesch, 1978). For Rickey Henderson, José Canseco was the standard of comparison. For many American physicians earning an average $170,000, the higher salaries of professional athletes and corporate CEOs become a point of comparison (Associated Press,

1993). As Bertrand Russell (1930, pp. 68–69) observed, "Napoleon envied Caesar, Caesar envied Alexander, and Alexander, I daresay, envied Hercules, who never existed. You cannot, therefore, get away from envy by means of success alone, for there will always be in history or legend some person even more successful than you are."

By "counting our blessings" when we compare ourselves with those less fortunate, we can, however, increase our satisfaction. As comparing ourselves with those better off creates envy, so comparing ourselves with those less well off boosts contentment. Marshall Dermer and his colleagues (1979) demonstrated this by asking University of Wisconsin-Milwaukee women to study others' deprivation and suffering. After viewing vivid depictions of how grim life was in Milwaukee in 1900, or after imagining and then writing about various personal tragedies, such as being burned and disfigured, the women expressed greater satisfaction with their own lives. Similarly, when mildly depressed people read about someone who is even more depressed, they feel somewhat better (Gibbons, 1986).

The effect of comparison with others helps us understand why students of a given level of academic ability tend to have a higher academic self-concept if they attend a school where most other students are not exceptionally able (Marsh & Parker, 1984). If you were near the top of your class in high school, you might feel inferior upon entering a college where everyone was near the top of their class.

SOURCE: David G. Myers, *Exploring Psychology,* Third Edition (Worth Publishers, 1996), pp. 346–350.

"I've got the bowl, the bone, the big yard. I know I should be happy."

As we see in this article, material welfare probably depends not only on the amount people consume in a given period but also on the relationship of their consumption to their expectations as to what they want to consume. If my neighbor buys a new car, puts in a swimming pool, or hires a landscaper, I may have an increased desire to have the same consumer goods and services. "Keeping up with the Joneses" is a reality that confronts many of us. Karl Marx put it well when he said

> A house may be large or small; as long as the surrounding houses are equally small it satisfies all social demand for a dwelling. But if a palace rises besides the little house, the little house shrinks into a hut.[1]

With rising incomes over time, our expectations also rise. That is, a rise in real per capita income or output may not mean an increase in happiness if expected consumption rises as fast or faster than actual consumption expenditures. As incomes rise, a given amount of income may mean less than before. For example, a person in 1949 may have derived more happiness than the same person in 1999 with the same real income per capita. And this unhappiness may be a result of rising expectations. For example, in 1949, our mythical person may have had a new small black-and-white TV, one radio, a small record player, and one car. Today, the same person would expect to have two color TVs, two or three radios, a stereo with both a CD player and a tape deck, a VCR, and two automobiles.

Studies have shown that, at any moment of time, the higher the income of a person, the happier he or she tends

to be—that is, there is a movement along the utility curve. On the other hand, similar studies show that *over time*, the level of happiness has not tended to increase in spite of rising incomes—a downward shift in the total utility curve. This phenomenon is graphically illustrated in Exhibit 1, which looks at the relationship between utility, or happiness, and income, or GDP per capita. Looking at the hypothetical curve for 1949, note that the person's utility rose as income rose. But over time, as a result of higher expectations and "bads" like air and water pollution, crime, and traffic congestion, the utility curve might shift down. The result could hypothetically be a situation in which higher per capita income might lead to lower utility.

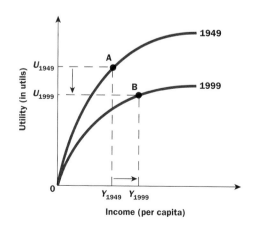

EXHIBIT 1 **THE HYPOTHETICAL UTILITY-INCOME RELATIONSHIP**

---

[1] Karl Marx, as quoted in S. M. Lipset, *Political Man: The Social Bases of Politics* (Garden City, NY: Doubleday, 1960), p. 63.

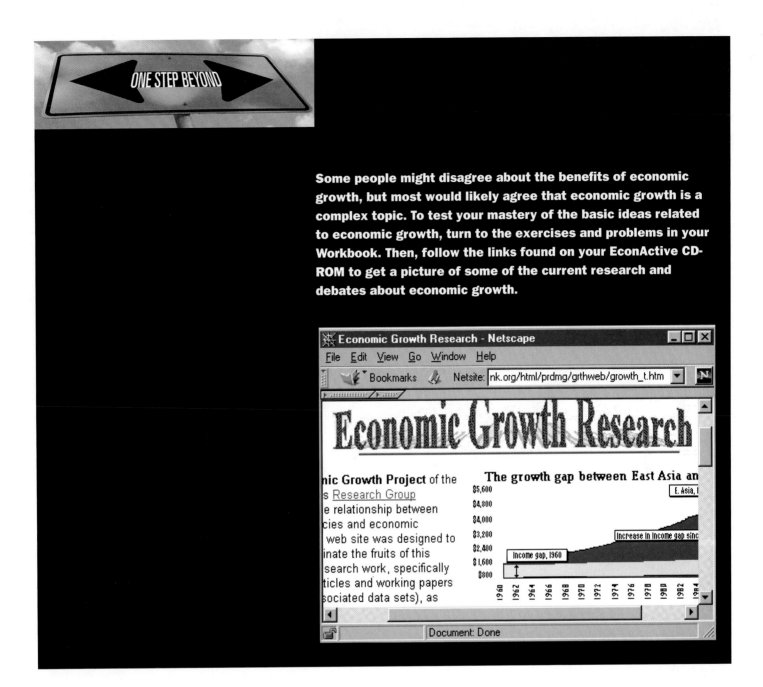

ONE STEP BEYOND

Some people might disagree about the benefits of economic growth, but most would likely agree that economic growth is a complex topic. To test your mastery of the basic ideas related to economic growth, turn to the exercises and problems in your Workbook. Then, follow the links found on your EconActive CD-ROM to get a picture of some of the current research and debates about economic growth.

Measuring Economic Performance

A. The Circular Flow Model
Why does total spending equal
total income?

B. National Income Accounting: Measuring Economic Performance
How can we measure our nation's economic performance?

C. The Expenditure Approach to Measuring GDP
What are the four categories of purchases in the expenditure approach?

D. The Income Approach to Measuring GDP
How do we compute GDP using the income approach?

E. Problems in Calculating an Accurate GDP
What factors make it difficult to accurately calculate GDP?

F. Problems with GDP as a Measure of Economic Welfare
How does GDP fail to accurately measure economic welfare?

G. Application: The Declining *Real* Cost of Living
What are the shortcomings of using money prices
to calculate the cost of living?

The Circular Flow Model

■ What are product and factor markets?
■ What is the circular flow model?

WHAT WERE EARLY ECONOMIES LIKE?

In a very primitive society, where there is virtually no trade and persons are almost totally self-sufficient, the analysis of the entire economy—macroeconomics—is very simple. Every household is, in effect, a self-contained economy. The concept of the "domestic" product of an economy is not terribly meaningful because economic activity occurs on a localized basis with no trade.

Human interdependence, of course, does exist, because people have found it mutually beneficial to engage in trade. The institution of money has arisen to meet the needs of trade, as have modern corporate business enterprises and banks and other financial institutions. A whole framework of economic institutions has grown up both in response to the growth in economic interrelationships, and to facilitate their further growth.

WHAT ARE PRODUCT MARKETS?

An **exchange economy,** which uses money as the basis for settling debts incurred in the process of trade, results in a constant flow of goods and services and monetary payments between the various economic institutions in society. The output of goods and services produced by some institutions in society provides income for others in society, namely the persons who provide the labor, capital, and raw material inputs used to produce those goods. Likewise, the producers of goods—business enterprises—receive income payments when they sell the goods they produce to households. Payments flow to businesses at the same time as goods flow to households. These transactions are carried out in what economists call **product markets.**

WHAT ARE FACTOR MARKETS?

Where do the households get the funds to pay businesses for the goods they buy? They get the money from the businesses themselves, as payment for the labor, land, capital,

and entrepreneurship needed to produce goods and services. These payments take the form of wages (salaries), rent, interest payments, and profits. These transactions between businesses and households are carried out in what economists call **factor (or input) markets.**

WHAT IS THE CIRCULAR FLOW MODEL?

There is a continuous flow of goods and payments between the producers of goods and services, which we call businesses, and individuals, who typically live in family units called households. The nature and direction of these

The macroeconomy is relatively simple in an economy with self-sufficiency and little trade.

exchanges are presented in the **circular flow model of income and output.** This model is illustrated in Exhibit 1.

Income and output are flow concepts; that is, they are measured over a span of time. The flow of incomes from businesses to households and vice versa will continue unabated at a stable, or equilibrium, magnitude if income received is utilized or spent at the same rate, and if there is no siphoning of funds (resources) out of the flow. For example, a teacher's supply of services brings in income that can be used to buy automobiles, vacations, food, and other goods. In sum, the total spending is the total amount that households spend and that equals the total amount that buyers of factors had to pay. In other words, total spending equals total income.

EXHIBIT 1   THE CIRCULAR FLOW MODEL OF INCOME AND OUTPUT

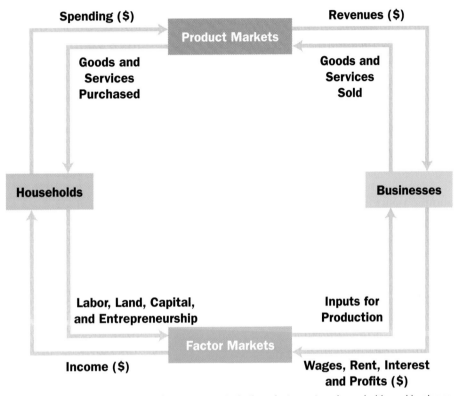

The two major institutional economic arrangements in the private sector—households and business enterprises—continuously trade goods and services and payments between each other. To a considerable extent, households receive income from firms in exchange for working and providing other inputs. Households then recycle that income to the firms in exchange for goods and services.

CONCEPT CHECK

1. Wages, rent, interest, and profits are the payments for the land, labor, capital, and entrepreneurship needed to produce goods and services. These transactions are carried out in factor, or input, markets.

2. The circular flow model illustrates the flow of goods, services, and payments among businesses and households.

1. Why does the circular flow of money move in the opposite direction from the flow of goods and services?

2. Why would an increase in your income in factor markets likely increase your demand in product markets?

3. Why would a decrease in demand for what you produce in product markets decrease your income in factor markets?

National Income Accounting: Measuring Economic Performance

■ What reasons are there for measuring our economy's performance?

■ What is gross domestic product?

■ What are the different methods of measuring GDP?

WHY DO WE MEASURE OUR ECONOMY'S PERFORMANCE?

There is a great desire to measure the success, or performance, of our economy. Are we getting "bigger" (and hopefully better) or "smaller" (and worse) over time? Aside from reasons of intellectual curiosity, the need to evaluate the magnitude of our economic performance is important to macroeconomic policymakers, who want to know how well the economy is performing so that they can set goals and develop policy recommendations.

Measurement of the economy's performance is also important to private business because inaccurate measurement can lead to bad decision making. Traders in stocks and bonds are continually checking economic statistics—buying and selling in response to the latest economic data.

WHAT IS NATIONAL INCOME ACCOUNTING?

To fulfill the desire for a reliable method of measuring economic performance, **national income accounting** was

born early in the twentieth century. The establishment of a uniform means of accounting for economic performance was such an important accomplishment that one of the first Nobel Prizes in economics was given to the late Simon Kuznets, a pioneer of national income accounting in the United States.

Several measures of aggregate national income and output have been developed, the most important of which is gross domestic product (GDP). We will examine GDP and other indicators of national economic performance in detail later in this Module.

WHAT IS GROSS DOMESTIC PRODUCT?

The measure of aggregate economic performance that gets the most attention in the popular media is **gross domestic product (GDP),** which is defined as the value of all final goods and services produced within a country during a given period of time. By convention, that period of time is almost always one year. But let's examine the rest of this definition. What is meant by "final good or service" and "value"?

HOW DO WE MEASURE THE VALUE OF GOODS AND SERVICES?

How is the value of a good or service determined? Value is determined by the market prices at which goods and services sell. Underlying the calculations, then, are the various equilibrium prices and quantities for the multitude of goods and services produced.

WHAT IS A FINAL GOOD OR SERVICE?

The word "final" means that the good is ready for its designated ultimate use. Many goods and services that are produced are intermediate goods or services, goods that are used in the production of other goods. For example, suppose United States Steel Corporation produces some steel that it sells to General Motors Corporation for use in

We have always had a preoccupation with measurement, whether it is a fastball or the growth in the economy.

making an automobile. If we counted the value of steel used in making the car as well as the full value of the finished auto in the GDP, we would be engaging in **double counting**—adding the value of the steel in twice, first in its raw form and second in its final form, the automobile. Another example is the paper used in this book. The paper is an intermediate good; it is the book, the final good, that is included in the GDP.

MEASURING GROSS DOMESTIC PRODUCT

There are two primary ways of calculating economic output: the expenditure approach and the income approach. Although these methods differ, their result, GDP, is the same, apart from minor "statistical discrepancies." In the following two Concepts, we will examine each of these approaches in turn.

TUNE UP

DEFINING GDP

Q: Jay Loppy just bought a 10-year-old used car. Will Jay's car be included in this year's GDP figures?

A: No. Only goods and services produced in the current period are included in this year's GDP. Jay's car was included in GDP 10 years ago when it was produced. That is, even though they are still being used this year, houses, cars, CD players, and so forth produced last year are only included in last year's GDP figures. If, however, Jay bought the car from a used car dealer, the value of the service provided would be counted, but that would be quite small relative to the price of the car.

If we count the steel that goes into a car as well as the finished car, are we guilty of double counting?

CONCEPT CHECK

1. We measure our economy's status in order to see how its performance has changed over time. These economic measurements are important to government officials, private businesses, and investors.
2. National income accounting, pioneered by Simon Kuznets, is a uniform means of measuring national economic performance.
3. Gross domestic product (GDP) is the value of all final goods and services produced within a country during a given time period.
4. Two different ways to measure GDP are the expenditure approach and the income approach.

1. Why does GDP measure only *final* goods and services produced, rather than all goods and services produced?
2. Why aren't all of the expenditures on used goods in an economy included in the current GDP?
3. Why do GDP statistics include real estate agents' commissions from selling existing homes and used car dealers' profits from selling used cars but not the value of existing homes and used cars when they are sold?
4. Why are sales of previously existing inventories of hula hoops not included in the current year's GDP?

The Expenditure Approach to Measuring GDP

- What are the four categories of purchases included in the expenditure approach?
- What are durable and nondurable goods?
- What are fixed investments?
- What types of government purchases are included in the expenditure approach?
- How are net exports calculated?

WHAT IS THE EXPENDITURE APPROACH TO MEASURING GDP?

One approach to measuring GDP is the **expenditure approach.** With this method, GDP is calculated by adding up the expenditures of market participants on final goods and services over a period of time. For convenience and for analytical purposes, economists usually categorize spending into four categories: consumption, identified symbolically by the letter C; investment, I; government spending, G; and net exports (which equals exports (X) minus imports (M), or $X - M$). Following the expenditure method, then

$$GDP = C + I + G + (X - M)$$

WHAT IS CONSUMPTION (C)?

Consumption refers to the purchase of consumer goods and services by households. For most of us, a large percentage of our income in a given year goes for consumer goods and services. The consumption category does not include purchases by business or government. As Exhibit 1 indicates, in 1997, consumption expenditures totaled well over $5 trillion ($5,486 billion). This figure was 68 percent of GDP. In that respect, the 1997 data were fairly typical. In every year since 1929, when GDP accounts began to be calculated annually, consumption has been more than half of total expenditures on goods and services (even during World War II).

Consumption spending, in turn, is usually broken down into three subcategories, nondurable goods, durable consumer goods, and services.

What Are Nondurable and Durable Goods?

Nondurable goods include tangible consumer items that are typically consumed or used up in a relatively short period of time. Food and clothing are examples, as are such quickly consumable items as drugs, toys, magazines, soap, razor blades, light bulbs, and so on. Nearly everything purchased in a supermarket or drug store is a nondurable good.

Durable goods include longer-lived consumer goods, the most important single category of which is automobiles and other consumer vehicles. Appliances, stereos, and furniture are also included in the durable goods category. On occasion, it is difficult to decide whether a good is durable or nondurable, and the definitions are, therefore, somewhat arbitrary.

The distinction between durables and nondurables is important because consumer buying behavior is somewhat different for each of these categories of goods. In boom periods, when GDP is rising rapidly, expenditures on durables often increase dramatically, while in years of stagnant or falling GDP, sales of durable goods often plummet. By contrast, sales of nondurables like food tend to be more stable over time because purchases of such goods are more difficult to shift from one time period to another. You can "make do" with your car for another year, but not your lettuce.

What Are Services?

Services are intangible items of value, as opposed to physical goods. Education, health care, domestic housekeeping, professional football, legal help, automobile repair, haircuts, airplane transportation—all of these are

EXHIBIT 1	U.S. GDP BY TYPE OF SPENDING, 1997	
Category	**Amount (billions of current dollars)**	**Percent of GDP**
Gross domestic product	$8,080	
Consumption (C)	5,486	68%
Investment (I)	1,243	15
Government purchases (G)	1,453	18
Net exports of goods and services (X – M)	–101.1	–1.2

SOURCE: U.S. Bureau of Economic Analysis, *Survey of Current Business*, May 1998.

services. In recent years, service expenditures have been growing faster than spending on goods; the share of total consumption going for services increased from 35 percent in 1950 to almost 60 percent by 1997. As incomes have risen, Americans have devoted an increasing amount of their resources to services, and accordingly, service industries such as health, education, and tourism have grown dramatically.

WHAT IS INVESTMENT (*I*)?

Investment, as used by economists, refers to the creation of capital goods—inputs like machines and tools whose purpose is to produce other goods. This definition of investment deviates from the popular use of that term. It is common for someone to say that he invested in a stock, meaning that he has traded money for a piece of paper, called a stock certificate, that says he owns a share in some company. That transaction was not an investment as defined by economists (i.e., an increase in capital goods), even though that action could provide resources for the business enterprise selling the stock (assuming they were newly issued shares) to finance or pay for new capital goods, which would be counted as investment by economists.

There are two categories of investment purchases measured in the expenditures approach: fixed investment and inventory investment.

What Are Fixed Investments?

Fixed investments include all spending on capital goods—sometimes called **producer goods**—such as machinery, tools, and factory buildings. All of these goods increase our future production capabilities. Residential construction is also included as an investment expenditure in GDP calculations. The construction of a house allows for a valuable consumer service—shelter—to be provided, and is thus considered to be an investment. Residential construction is the only part of investment that is directly tied to household expenditure decisions.

Why are inventories considered a form of investment?

Durable goods include longer-lasting goods, such as major household appliances.

What Is Inventory Investment?

Inventory investment includes all purchases by businesses that add to their inventories—stocks of goods kept on hand by businesses to meet customer demands. Every business needs inventory and, other things equal, the greater the inventory, the greater the amount of goods and services that can be sold to a consumer in the future. Thus, inventories are considered a form of investment. Consider a grocery store. If the store expands and increases the quantity and variety of goods on its shelves, future sales can rise. An increase in inventories, then, is presumed to increase the firm's future sales, and this is why we say it is an investment.

How Stable Are Investment Expenditures?

In recent years, investment expenditures have generally been around 15 percent of gross domestic product. Investment spending is the most volatile category of GDP, however, and tends to fluctuate considerably with changing business conditions. When the economy is booming, investment purchases tend to increase dramatically. In downturns, the reverse happens. In the first year of the Great Depression, investment purchases declined by 37 percent. U.S. expenditures on capital goods have been a smaller proportion of GDP in most recent years than in many other developed nations, a fact that worries some people who are concerned about U.S. GDP growth compared to other countries, because investment in capital goods is directly tied to a nation's future production capabilities.

WHAT PART OF GOVERNMENT SPENDING IS INCLUDED IN GDP (*G*)?

The part of government spending that is included in GDP is expenditures on goods and services. For example, the government must pay the salaries of its employees, and it must also make payments to the private firms with which it contracts to provide

various goods and services, such as highway construction companies and weapons manufacturers. All of these payments would be included in GDP. However, transfer payments are not included in government purchases, because that spending does not go to purchase newly produced goods or services, but is merely a transfer of income among that country's citizens (which is why such expenditures are called transfer payments). The government purchase proportion of GDP has grown rapidly over the last 30 years.

HOW DO EXPORTS AFFECT GDP (*X* – *M*)?

Some of the goods and services that are produced in the United States are exported for use in other countries. The fact that these goods and services were made in the United States means that they should be included in a measure of U.S. production. Thus, we include the value of exports when calculating GDP. At the same time, however, some of our expenditures in other categories (consumption and investment in particular) were for foreign-produced goods and services. These imports must be excluded from GDP in order to obtain an accurate measure of American production. Thus, GDP calculations measure net exports, which equals total exports (*X*) minus total imports (*M*). Net exports are a small proportion of GDP and are often negative for the United States.

Highway construction is part of government spending.

1. The expenditure approach to measuring GDP involves adding up the purchases of final goods and services by market participants.
2. Four categories of spending are used in the GDP calculation: consumption (C), investment (I), government spending (G), and net exports ($X - M$).
3. Consumption spending includes spending on nondurable consumer goods, tangible items that are usually consumed in a short period of time; durable consumer goods, longer-lived consumer goods; and services, intangible items of value that do not involve physical production.

4. Fixed investment includes all spending on capital goods, such as machinery, tools, and buildings. Inventory investment includes the net expenditures by businesses to increase their inventories.
5. The part of government spending that is included in GDP includes purchases of goods and services only. Transfer payments are not included in these calculations, because that spending is not a payment for a newly produced good or service.
6. Net exports are calculated by subtracting total imports from total exports.

---

1. What would happen to GDP if consumption purchases (C) and net exports ($X - M$) both rose, holding other things equal?
2. Why do you think economic forecasters focus so much on consumption purchases and their determinants?
3. Why are purchases of durable goods more unstable than purchases of nondurable goods?

4. Why does the investment component of GDP include purchases of new capital goods but not purchases of corporate stock?
5. If Mary received a welfare check this year, would that transfer payment be included in this year's GDP? Why or why not?
6. Could inventory investment or net exports ever be negative?

The Income Approach to Measuring GDP

- How is national income calculated?
- What are factor payments?
- What does personal income measure?

WHAT IS THE INCOME APPROACH TO MEASURING GDP?

In the last Concept, we outlined the expenditure approach to GDP calculation. There is, however, also an alternative method, which is called the **income approach.** This approach involves summing the incomes received by producers of goods and services.

When someone makes an expenditure for a good or service, that spending creates income for someone else. For example, if you buy $10 in groceries at the local supermarket, your $10 in spending creates $10 in income for the grocery store owner. The owner, then, must buy more goods to stock her shelves as a consequence of your consumer purchases; in addition, she must pay her employees, her electricity bill, and so on. Consequently, much of the $10 spent by you will eventually end up in the hands of someone other than the grocer. The basic point, however, is that someone (one person or many) receives the $10 you spent, and that receipt of funds is called income. Therefore, by adding up all of the incomes received by producers of goods and services, we can also calculate the gross domestic product, because output creates income of equal value.

WHAT ARE FACTOR PAYMENTS?

As we stated earlier in this Module in our discussion of the circular flow model, incomes received by persons providing goods and services are actually payments to the owners of productive resources. These payments are sometimes called **factor payments.** Factor payments include wages for the use of labor services, rent for land, payments for the use of capital goods in the form of interest, and profits for entrepreneurs who put labor, land, and capital together.

WHAT ARE NON-INCOME EXPENSE ITEMS?

Although we can identify and sum the various factor payments, the total will not exactly equal GDP. In order to find an accurate GDP, two additional factors must be considered: indirect business taxes and depreciation. Together, these factors are called **non-income expense items.**

Indirect Business Taxes

Sales taxes that are sent by businesses to the government are **indirect business taxes.** The best example of an indirect business tax is a sales tax. For example, a compact disc may cost $14.95 plus a tax of $1.20, for a total of $16.15. The retail distributor (record store), record producer, and others will share $14.95 in proceeds, even though the actual equilibrium price is $16.15. In other words, the output (compact disc) is valued at $16.15, even though recipients only get $14.95 in income. Besides sales taxes, other important indirect business taxes include excise taxes (e.g., taxes on cigarettes, automobiles, and liquor) and gasoline taxes.

Depreciation

Depreciation payments are annual allowances set aside for the replacement of worn-out plant and equipment. The depreciation factor is also known as the **capital consumption allowance.**

Are gasoline taxes an example of an indirect business tax?

ADDING IT UP: THE STATISTICAL DISCREPANCY FIGURE

As you can see in Exhibit 1, when added together, all of these components in the income approach equal GDP—just as the factors in the expenditure approach equal GDP. However, the sum calculated using the income approach is always slightly different than that found with the spending approach because of errors in collecting data. To make the two GDP calculations identical, a statistical discrepancy figure is added. As shown in Exhibit 1, this figure was $41 billion in 1997.

WHAT ARE NATIONAL INCOME AND PERSONAL INCOME?

National income and personal income are two additional measurements that economists often use.

National Income

National income (NI) is a measure of the income earned by owners of resources used in making final goods and services—factor payments. Accordingly, national income includes payments for labor services (wages, salaries, and fringe benefits), for use of land and buildings (rent), money lent to finance economic activity (interest), and payments for use of capital resources (profits). However, it excludes income earned to pay indirect business taxes, depreciation, and income earned by foreigners in the United States.

Personal Income

Very often, we are interested in the income *received* by persons rather than the income *earned*, because the income received reflects the amount available for spending. **Personal income (PI)** measures the amount of income received by individuals.

Some owners of productive resources do not receive all of the income that they earn. For example, some of the profits earned by stockholders of corporations are retained by the corporations to help finance business expansion. In recent years, only about one-third of before-tax corporate profits have been distributed to the owners of corporations. In addition, workers do not receive that part of their paycheck earmarked as their Social Security contributions. Social Security payroll taxes have been growing steadily in recent years.

EXHIBIT 1	AGGREGATE INCOME, BY TYPE OF INCOME, 1997	
	Amount (billions of current dollars)	**Percent of Total**
Aggregate income		
Wages	$4,704	58%
Profits	1,350	17
Interest	448	6
Rent	148	2
Indirect business taxes (e.g., Sales taxes)	542.5	7
Depreciation	868	10
Net income of foreigners*	−20	−.3
Statistical discrepancy**	41	0.5
equals GDP	$8,080	

*Net income of foreigners is the income earned abroad by U.S. firms or residents minus income earned by foreign firms or residents in the United States.

**The statistical discrepancy is relatively small at $41 billion; it is added to the components of national income to equal domestic income, which equals GDP.

1. The income approach to measuring GDP involves summing the incomes received by the producers of goods and services. These payments to the owners of productive resources are also known as factor payments.

2. The income approach also takes two non-income expense items into consideration: (1) indirect business taxes, such as sales taxes; and (2) depreciation, payments set aside for the replacement of worn-out capital.

3. National income (NI) is measured by adding together the payments to the factors of production—wages, rent, interest, and profit.

4. Personal income (PI) measures the amount of income received by individuals rather than the amount earned.

---

1. Why should we expect the total expenditures that go into GDP to equal total income in an economy?

2. What two non-income expense items does the income approach take into consideration?

3. How is personal income different from national income?

Problems in Calculating an Accurate GDP

MODULE 9

- What are the problems with GDP in measuring output?
- What is the purpose of a price level index?
- What inherent problems exist with a price level index?
- What is per capita GDP?

WHAT PROBLEMS ARE THERE IN CALCULATING AN ACCURATE GDP?

The primary problem in calculating accurate GDP statistics becomes evident when attempts are made to compare the GDP over time. Between 1970 and 1978, a period of relatively high inflation, GDP in the United States rose over 100 percent. What great progress! Unfortunately, however, the "yardstick" used in adding together the values of different products, the U.S. dollar, also changed in value over this period of time. A dollar in 1979, for example, would certainly not buy as much as a dollar in 1970, because the *overall* price level for goods and services increased.

HOW DO WE SOLVE THIS PROBLEM?

One solution to this problem would be to use physical units of output—which, unlike the dollar, don't change in value from year to year—as our measure of total economic activity. The major problem with this approach is that different products have different units of measurement. How do you add together tons of steel, bushels of wheat, kilowatts of electricity, gallons of paint, cubic feet of natural gas, miles of air passenger travel, number of games of bowling, and number of magazines sold? In order to compare GDP values over time, a common or standardized unit of measure, which only money can provide, must be used in the calculations.

HOW CAN A PRICE LEVEL INDEX HELP?

The dollar, then, is the yardstick of value that we can use to correct the inflation-induced distortion of the GDP. We must adjust for the changing purchasing power of the dollar by constructing a **price index.** Essentially, a price index attempts to provide a measure of the trend in prices paid for a certain bundle of goods and services over time. The price index can be used to deflate the nominal or current dollar GDP values to a real GDP expressed in dollars of constant purchasing power.

WHAT ARE THE CONSUMER PRICE INDEX (CPI) AND THE GDP DEFLATOR?

There are many different types of price indices. The most well known index, the **consumer price index (CPI),** provides a measure of the trend in the prices of certain goods and services purchased for consumption purposes. The CPI is the price index that may be most relevant to households trying to evaluate their changing financial position over time.

The price index used to correct GDP statistics for changing prices is an even broader index called the **GDP deflator.** The GDP deflator measures the average level of prices of all consumer goods and services produced in the economy.

HOW IS A PRICE INDEX CREATED?

Constructing a price index is complicated. To begin with, there are literally thousands of goods and services in our economy; attempting to include all of them in an index would be cumbersome, make the index expensive to compute, and would take a long period of time (to gather necessary price data). Therefore, a "bundle" or "basket" of representative goods and services is selected by the index calculators (the Bureau of Labor Statistics of the U.S. Department of Labor for consumer and wholesale price indices; the Office of Business Economics of the Department of Commerce for the GDP deflator).

Unfortunately for our ability to calculate inflation, not all prices move by the same amount or in the same direction, so an average of the many price changes must be calculated. This is complicated by several factors. First, goods and services change in quality over time, so the observed price change may, in reality, reflect a quality change in the product rather than the purchasing power of the dollar. A $500 television set today is dramatically better than a television set in 1950 that cost many times more. Second, new products come on the market and occasionally old products disappear. For example, color TV sets did not exist in 1950 but are a major consumer item now. How do

THE BOX-OFFICE LEADERS

Everyone knows that *Titanic* is one of the biggest box-office hits of all time. But where would it rank if the grosses of old-time releases were adjusted for inflation?

How does *Gone with the Wind* rank when box office receipts are adjusted for inflation?

ALL-TIME LEADERS AS OF AUGUST 3, 1998

Rank	Title (distributor)	Release date	Total domestic gross	Adjusted domestic gross*
1	Gone with the Wind (MGM)**	1939	$196,636,563	$866,326,760
2	Star Wars (Fox)**	5/25/77	460,935,665	774,992,216
3	E.T. (Universal)**	6/11/82	399,804,539	594,267,291
4	Titanic (Paramount)	12/19/97	590,489,873	590,489,873
5	The Ten Commandments (Paramount)	1956	65,500,000	572,470,000
6	The Sound of Music (Fox)	1965	163,214,286	570,597,144
7	Jaws (Universal)	6/20/75	260,000,000	559,704,433
8	Doctor Zhivago (MGM)	1965	111,721,910	542,471,941
9	The Jungle Book (Buena Vista)**	1967	135,475,556	485,269,000
10	Snow White and the Seven Dwarfs (RKO/Buena Vista)**	1937	184,925,486	476,330,000
11	Ben-Hur (MGM)	1959	70,000,000	470,615,385
12	101 Dalmatians (Buena Vista)**	1961	152,551,111	459,757,486
13	The Empire Strikes Back (Fox)**	5/21/80	290,158,751	431,710,050
14	Return of the Jedi (Fox)**	5/25/83	309,125,409	413,782,013
15	The Exorcist (Warner Brothers)	12/26/73	165,000,000	412,028,571

**Gross totals include reissues.

SOURCE: http://www.MrShowbiz.com/reviews/moviereviews/NUMBERS/top100adjusted.html

---

CONSIDER THIS:

In this article, we see the importance of adjusting for prices when ranking the great movies of all time. The left-hand column indicates total box office gross receipts. The problem is that films move up on this list if they were released later in the era of higher-priced tickets. In the right-hand column, Exhibitor Relations, a company that tracks box office receipts, used 1996 dollars to compute inflation-adjusted gross receipts. The central point of this article is that ignoring price changes leads to vastly different rankings of the all-time greatest revenue earning movies. As we have seen in this Module, adjusting for prices is very important when trying to measure the growth of the economy. Imagine if we failed to index for prices when we computed GDP. Because the price level has been rising steadily over the last 30 years, if we failed to index for price level changes, we would certainly overstate the value of goods and services being produced in the economy. And grossly inaccurate GDP figures would make it even more difficult for policy makers to manage the economy, an already difficult task.

you calculate changes in prices over time when some products did not even exist in the earlier period?

Clearly, calculating a price index is not a simple, direct process. As you can see from the *In the News* article, there are many factors that could potentially distort the CPI.

HOW DO WE CALCULATE REAL GDP?

Once the price index has been calculated, the actual procedure for adjusting nominal, or current dollar, GDP to get real GDP figure is not complicated. For convenience, an index number of 100 is assigned to some base year. The base year is arbitrarily chosen—it can be any year.

The formula for converting any year's nominal GDP into real GDP (in base year dollars) is as follows:

$$\text{Real GDP} = \frac{\text{Nominal GDP}}{\text{Price level index}} \times 100$$

Say the GDP deflator (price index) was expressed in terms of 1992 prices (1992 = 100), and the index figure for 1996

was 109.9. This means that prices were 9.9 percent higher in 1996 than they were in 1992. Now, in order to correct the 1996 nominal GDP, we take the nominal GDP figure, $7,576 billion, and divide it by the price level index, 109.9, which results in a quotient of $68.94 billion. We then multiply this number by 100, giving us $6,894 billion, which is the 1996 GDP in 1992 dollars (that is, 1996 real GDP, in terms of a 1992 base year).

IS REAL GDP ALWAYS LESS THAN NOMINAL GDP?

In modern times, inflation has been prevalent. For most readers of this book, the price level (as measured by the consumer price index) has risen in every single year of their lifetime, because the last year of a declining price level was 1955. Therefore, the adjustment of nominal (money) GDP to real GDP will tend to reduce the growth in GDP suggested by nominal GDP figures. Given the distortions introduced by inflation, most news reports about GDP today speak of real GDP changes, although this is not always made explicit.

Which one is more expensive, adjusting for quality and inflation?

HOW ACCURATE IS THE CPI INDEX?

Bill Clinton, Bob Dole, Pat Moynihan, and Newt Gingrich have each hinted they'd like to "correct" the CPI downward. Revamping the CPI is a politician's dream: Seemingly painless tax increases and spending cuts result. The Congressional Budget Office says lowering the CPI by one percentage point would increase the IRS's annual take by $45 billion a decade from now (because tax brackets are adjusted for inflation each year). At the same time, it would reduce the growth of Social Security payments, military pensions, and interest payments by $90 billion. Much of this could even be done in the name of "fairness," since too-high cost-of-living adjustments cause inequitable transfers of wealth from the young (taxpayers) to the old (pensioners). . . .

The basic problem with the CPI is rooted in the way the Bureau of Labor Statistics (BLS) collects and adds up the data. Every day, some 400 government price collectors fan out across the country to note the price of everything from green beans to rent on a house. The BLS weights each product category according to the basket of goods and services a typical American bought in, roughly, 1983.

But the BLS often collects the prices companies charge rather than the prices people actually pay. If you stock up on lower-priced Wal-Mart film instead of the name brand at your local store, the BLS doesn't necessarily count your saving as a reduction in price. Nor does it subtract most coupons. These and similar biases make the CPI overstate the inflation rate by about 0.2, says Michael Boskin, a Stanford professor who heads a panel of economists studying the CPI's upward bias. But even these obvious and comparatively small fixes are controversial. BLS officials say the effect of discount shopping and coupons is so small it's not worth fixing.

A bigger fight is likely to arise over the panel's contention that the whole idea of the CPI—tracking the price of a fixed bas-

ket of goods over many years—gives a poor picture of the cost of living. If the price of a favorite cookie, for example, shoots up, some consumers switch to lower-priced substitutes, changing their basket and saving money. And the BLS's fixed basket doesn't fully capture quality improvements and price drops in new products like computers. Sub-

stitution and quality improvements probably account for 0.7 of the CPI rate, the panel believes, and all its biases together most likely overstate the rate by between one and 1.5 points.

SOURCE: Kim Clark, "How Best to Measure Inflation? The Glamorous World of Economic Indicators," *Fortune*, November 11, 1996.

If people prefer buying in bulk at discount stores, will the CPI accurately measure inflation?

CONSIDER THIS:
The consumer price index (CPI), the current measure of inflation, may have serious problems. Some economists believe that it might overstate the inflation rate by as much as 1.5 points. That is, an officially measured inflation rate of 5 percent might only really represent 3.5 percent inflation. This has important implications for welfare and Social Security recipients because these programs are adjusted for inflation using the CPI. In other words, we may be overpaying these recipients because the CPI overstates the real rate of inflation.

The problems with the CPI are numerous. It does not adjust accurately for quality changes or new products and services like cellular phones (which may be included in 1998 or 1999). In addition, it does not take into consideration the use of coupons or discount stores. However, most importantly, it does not accurately reveal how consumers will substitute away from higher-priced goods in favor of goods that fall in price. That is, the appropriate "basket" of goods and services is constantly changing, while the CPI continues to use a constant basket.

WHAT IS PER CAPITA GDP?

The measure of economic welfare most often cited is real **per capita gross domestic product.** We use a measure of real GDP for reasons already cited. To calculate per capita GDP, we divide the real GDP by the total population to get the value of real output of final goods and services per person. *Ceteris paribus,* people prefer more goods to fewer, so a higher GDP would seemingly make people better off. Economic growth, then, is usually considered to have occurred anytime the real GDP per capita has risen.

WHY IS THE MEASURE OF PER CAPITA GDP SO IMPORTANT?

Because one purpose of using GDP as a crude welfare measure is to relate output to human desires, we need to adjust for population change. If we do not take population growth into account, we can be misled by changes in real GDP values. For example, in some less-developed countries in some time periods, real GDP has risen perhaps 2 percent a year but the population has grown just as fast. In these cases, the real output of goods and services per person has remained virtually unchanged, but this would not be apparent in an examination of real GDP trends alone.

CONCEPT CHECK

1. It is difficult to compare real GDP over time because of the changing value of money over time.
2. A price index allows us to compare prices paid for goods and services over time by creating a measure of how many dollars it would take to maintain a constant purchasing power over time. The consumer price index (CPI) is the most well-known index.
3. The GDP deflator is a price index that measures the average level of prices of all consumer goods and services produced in the economy.

4. The problems with the consumer price index are that it fails to account for an increase in the quality of goods, new goods introduced, or changes in the relative quantities of goods purchased.
5. Per capita GDP is real output of goods and services per person. In some cases, real GDP may increase, but per capita GDP may actually drop, as a result of population growth.

1. If we overestimated inflation over time, would our calculations of real GDP growth likely be over- or underestimated?
2. Why does the consumer price index tend to overstate inflation if the quality of goods and services is rising over time?

3. Why would the growth in real GDP overstate the growth of output per person in a country with a growing population?
4. Why doesn't the consumer price index accurately adjust for the cost-of-living effects of a tripling in the price of bananas relative to the prices of other fruits?

Problems with GDP as a Measure of Economic Welfare

- What are some of the deficiencies of GDP as a measure of economic welfare?
- What are nonmarket transactions?
- What is the underground economy?
- Does GDP reflect the value of externalities?

As we have noted throughout this Module, real GDP is often used as a measure of the economic welfare of a nation. The accuracy of this measure for that purpose is, however, questionable, because several important factors are excluded from its calculations. These factors include nonmarket transactions, the underground economy, leisure, externalities, the types of goods purchased, the distribution of income, and expectations.

WHAT IS THE IMPACT OF NONMARKET TRANSACTIONS ON OUR ECONOMY?

Nonmarket transactions include the provision of goods and services outside of traditional markets for which no money is exchanged. We simply do not have information on this output that is reliable enough to include it in the GDP. The most important single nonmarket transaction omitted from the GDP is the services of housewives or househusbands. These services are not sold in any market, so they are not entered into the GDP, but they are nonetheless performed. For example, if a single woman hires a male housekeeper to

Are her efforts included in the GDP?

clean house for her, those payments enter into the calculation of GDP. Suppose, though, that the woman marries the housekeeper. Now the woman no longer pays her husband for his housekeeping services. Reported GDP falls after the marriage, although output does not change.

In less-developed countries, where a significant amount of food and clothing output is produced in the home, the failure to include nonmarket economic activity in GDP is a serious deficiency. Even in the United States, homemade meals, housework, and the vegetables and flowers produced in home gardens are excluded, even though they clearly represent an output of goods and services.

HOW LARGE IS THE UNDERGROUND ECONOMY?

It is impossible to know for sure the magnitude of the underground economy, which includes unreported income from both legal and illegal sources. For example, illegal gambling and prostitution are not included in the GDP, leading to underreporting of an unknown dimension. The reason these activities are excluded, however, has nothing to do with the morality of the services performed, but rather results from the fact that most payments made for these services are neither reported to governmental authorities nor go through normal credit channels. Likewise, cash payments made to employees "under the table" slip through the GDP net. The estimates of the size of the underground economy vary from less than 4 percent to more than 20 percent of GDP. It also appears that a good portion of this unreported income comes from legal sources, such as self-employment.

CAN WE MEASURE THE VALUE OF LEISURE?

The value that individuals place on leisure is omitted in calculating GDP. Most of us could probably get a part-time job if we wanted to, earning some additional money by working in the evening or on weekends. Yet we choose not

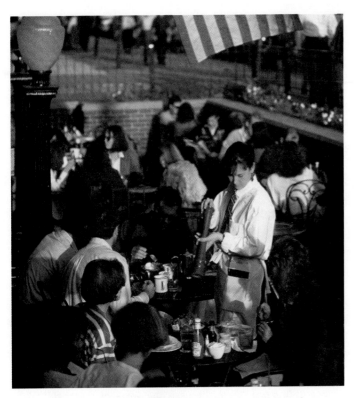

Do you think all restaurant tips are declared as income?

DOES GDP MEASURE EXTERNALITIES?

As we discussed in earlier Modules, positive and negative externalities can result from the production of some goods and services. As a result of these externalities, the equilibrium prices of these goods and services—the figure used in GDP calculations—does not reflect their true values to society (unless, of course, the externality has been internalized). For example, if a steel mill produces 100,000 more tons of steel, GDP increases; GDP does not, however, decrease to reflect damages from the air pollution that resulted from the production of that additional steel. Likewise, additional production of a vaccine would be reflected in the GDP, but the positive benefit to others in society than the purchaser would not be included in the calculation. In other words, while GDP measures the goods and services that are produced, it does not adequately measure the "goods" and "bads" that result from the production processes.

DOES GDP ACCOUNT FOR INCOME DISTRIBUTION?

Another problem with real per capita GDP as a welfare measure is that it ignores the distribution of output, or of incomes generated from that output, among members of society. While the welfare implications of income distribution are explored in greater detail in the microeconomic portion of this text, it can be demonstrated that under certain assumptions, a redistribution of income from the very rich to the very poor might raise the welfare of the poorer persons more than it reduces the welfare of the rich, so that, on balance, the redistribution increases overall economic welfare. Redistribution of income from rich to poor

to do so. Why? The opportunity cost is too high—we would have to forego some leisure. If you work on Saturday nights, you cannot see your friends, go to parties, see concerts, watch television, or go to the movies. The opportunity cost of the leisure is the income foregone by not working. Leisure, then, has a positive value that does not show up in the GDP accounts. To put leisure in the proper perspective, ask yourself if you would rather live in Country A, which has a per capita GDP of $20,000 a year and a 30-hour work week, or Country B, with a $20,000 per capita GDP and a 50-hour work week. Non-workaholics might well choose the former. The problem that this omission in GDP poses can be fairly significant in international comparisons, or when one looks at one nation over time, because the amount of leisure varies considerably, usually falling with rising GDP (suggesting an understatement of economic growth).

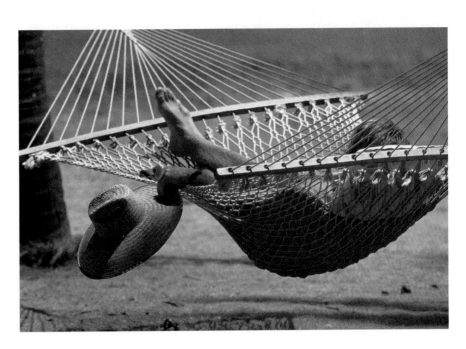

Is leisure time measured in GDP?

AN INVALUABLE ENVIRONMENT

Environmentalists have long felt cross with the way governments measure national incomes and wealth. These figures for GDP, they point out, fail to value a country's environmental assets, such as fine public parks. They treat the use of natural capital differently from that of man-made capital: a country that depletes its stock of production equipment grows poorer, while one that chops down its forests appears to grow richer. And they treat the costs of cleaning up environmental damage as an addition to national income without subtracting the environmental loss caused by the damage in the first place.

The answer might seem obvious: adjust national accounts to take account of changes in the environment. Statisticians have laboured for more than a decade to find ways to do this. The difficulties of creating environmental statistics that are comparable to national income and wealth statistics are serious. GDP is measured in money, but putting monetary values on environmental assets is a black art. Some assets, such as timber, may have a market value, but that value does not encompass the trees' role in harbouring rare beetles, say, or their sheer beauty. Methods for valuing such benefits are controversial. To get round these problems, the U.N. guidelines suggest measuring the cost of repairing environmental damage. But some kinds of damage, such as extinction, are beyond costing, and others are hard to estimate.

For economists, the average value of a good or service is usually less important than the marginal value—the cost or benefit of one more unit. Marginal value, how-

ever, is a tricky concept to bring into environmental analysis. It may be clear that the cost of wiping out an entire species of beetle would be high, but what value should be attached to the extermination of a few hundred bugs?

Putting environmental concepts into economic terms raises other difficulties as well. Geography weighs differently: a ton of sulphur dioxide emitted in a big city may cause more harm than the same ton emitted in a rural area, while a dollar's worth of output counts the same wherever it is produced. And the exploitation of natural resources may not always have a cost. Is a country depleting resources if it mines a ton of coal? All other things equal, the mining of that ton might raise the value of the coal that remains in the ground, leaving the value of coal assets unchanged.

SOURCE: *The Economist*, April 18, 1998, p. 75.

CONSIDER THIS:
GDP doesn't measure everything that contributes or detracts from our well-being, because it is very difficult to measure the value of those effects. Environmentalists believe that national income accounts should adjust for changes in the environment. However, this leads to many conceptual problems, such as measuring the marginal values of goods and services that are not sold in markets, and adjusting for geographical differences in environmental damage. The critical issue is whether there are important trends in "uncounted" goods and services that result in questionable conclusions about whether we are getting better or worse off.

---

does not always enhance welfare, however, because redistribution schemes reduce work incentives for productive members of society. Still, the distribution of income does have some bearing on welfare, and the per capita GDP statistics give no indication of what that distribution is.

WHAT IS THE MEASURE OF ECONOMIC WELFARE (MEW)?

Conceptually, we would like a measure of economic activity that adds the value of positive externalities and subtracts the value of negative externalities to GDP. Two

distinguished economists have developed such an indicator, called a **measure of economic welfare,** or MEW. They (and others) have developed broader-based welfare measures that attempt to correct for the deficiencies in GDP, such as the failure to account for the spillover effects of pollution or the value of leisure. Work in the direction of developing a "quality of life" indicator may ultimately reduce reliance on GDP as a measure of performance. One difficulty is that construction of such indicators involves many subjective judgments (e.g., what is the value of leisure?). Given the deficiencies with GDP as a welfare measure, however, the work will no doubt continue.

PROBLEMS WITH MEASURING GDP

Q: Sally Mander, a biologist, often works in the streams near the automobile plant. Sally claims that every day the company dumps tons of waste into the river. Is the waste included in GDP accounts?

A: The negative effects of environmental externalities are not currently accounted for in GDP measurements. While it may be difficult to accurately assess the damages, many think that if GDP is going to accurately attempt to gauge standard of living, then at least some attempt needs to be made to incorporate economic bads, like pollution and crime.

SHOULD GDP BE USED AS A MEASURE OF OUR WELFARE?

There are severe defects with real GDP as a welfare measure. Nonetheless, at the present time, there is no alternative measure that is generally accepted as better, although it is possible that, in time, a broader-based "quality of life" measure (such as MEW) will be devised that wins wide acceptance. The GDP indicator is, however, useful in making comparisons of the market values over time and across countries, even if we cannot be completely sure of the welfare implications of the comparisons. We can probably even sometimes be fairly confident about the welfare implications of changing GDP. An unexpectedly fast increase in GDP probably will lead to an increase in consumption relative to expectations, almost certainly increasing welfare. Likewise, a sharp fall in GDP leads to reduced consumption—a decline in the ratio of what people have to what they want—and therefore almost certainly a decline in human welfare.

CONCEPT CHECK

1. There are several factors that make it difficult to use GDP as a welfare indicator, including nonmarket transactions, the underground economy, leisure, and externalities.
2. Nonmarket transactions are the exchange of goods and services that do not occur in traditional markets, and so no money is exchanged.
3. The underground economy is the unreported production and income that come from legal and illegal activities.
4. The presence of positive and negative externalities makes it difficult to measure GDP accurately.

1. Why do GDP measures omit nonmarket transactions?
2. How would real GDP comparisons between two countries be impacted by the existence of a high level of nonmarket activities in one of the countries?
3. If we choose to decrease our hours worked because we value the additional leisure more, would the resulting change in real GDP accurately reflect the change in our well-being? Why or why not?
4. How do pollution and crime affect GDP? How do pollution- and crime-control expenditures impact GDP?

Application: The Declining *Real* Cost of Living in America

Why is time at work used as a measure of the cost of goods and services? What are the shortcomings of using money prices?

TIME WELL SPENT

As America exits the twentieth century, we'd be hard-pressed to find a five and dime store. Penny candy now goes for a nickel or more. Five cents no longer buys a good cigar. Dime novels can't be found. Even a 3¢ stamp costs 32¢. Over the century, prices have gone up. The buying power of a dollar is down. We know this from statistical measures of inflation. We know it also from Grandpa's stories about paying 15¢ for a ticket to *Gone with the Wind* or 19¢ for a gallon of gasoline. Even a casual observer of the U.S. economy can see that the prices of milk, bread, houses, clothes, cars, and many other goods and services rise from year to year.

The cost of living is indeed going up—in money terms. What really matters, though, isn't what something costs in money; it's what it costs in time. Making money takes time, so when we shop, we're really spending time. The real cost of living isn't measured in dollars and cents but in the hours and minutes we must work to live. American essayist Henry David Thoreau (1817–62) noted this in his famous book, *Walden*: "The cost of a thing is the amount of . . . life which is required to be exchanged for it, immediately or in the long run."

The shortcoming of money prices is that they mean little apart from money wages. A pair of stockings cost just 25¢ a century ago. This sounds wonderful until we learn that a worker of the era earned only 14.8¢ an hour. So paying for the stockings took 1 hour 41 minutes of work. Today a better pair requires only about 18 minutes of work. Put another way, stockings cost an 1897 worker today's equivalent of $22, whereas now a worker pays only about $4. If modern Americans had to work as hard as their forebears did for everyday products, they'd be in a continual state of sticker shock—$67 scissors, $913 baby carriages, $2,222 bicycles, $1,202 telephones.

The best way to measure the cost of goods and services is in terms of a standard that doesn't change—time

at work, or real prices. There's a regular pattern to real prices in our dynamic economy.

Americans come in all shapes and sizes. We differ in height and weight, gender, race, and age. We vary in talents, skills, education, experience, determination, and luck. Quite naturally, our paychecks differ, too. Some of us scrape by at minimum wage, while movie stars, corporate chieftains, and athletes sometimes make millions of dollars a year.

Calculations of the work time needed to buy goods and services use the average hourly wage for production and nonsupervisory workers in manufacturing. A century ago this figure was less than 15¢ an hour. By 1997 it had hit a record $13.18, a livable wage, but nothing worthy of *Lifestyles of the Rich and Famous*. What's most important about this wage is that it roughly represents what's earned by the great bulk of American society.

In calculating our cost of living, a good place to start is with the basics—food, shelter, and clothing. In terms of time on the job, the cost of a half-gallon of milk fell from 39 minutes in 1919 to 16 minutes in 1950, 10 minutes in 1975 and 7 minutes in 1997. A pound of ground beef steadily declined from 30 minutes in 1919 to 23 minutes in 1950, 11 minutes in 1975 and 6 minutes in 1997. Paying for a dozen oranges required 1 hour 8 minutes of work in 1919. Now it takes less than 10 minutes, half what it did in 1950. The money price of a 3-pound fryer chicken rose from $1.23 in 1919 to $3.15 in 1997, but its cost in work time fell from 2 hours 37 minutes to just 14 minutes. A sample of a dozen food staples—a market basket broad enough to provide three squares a day—shows that what required 9.5 hours to buy in 1919 and 3.5 hours in 1950 now takes only 1.6 hours.

SOURCE: W. Michael Cox and Richard Alm. *1997 Annual Report: Time Well Spent*, Federal Reserve Bank of Dallas.

EXHIBIT 1 — DOMESTIC SERVANTS

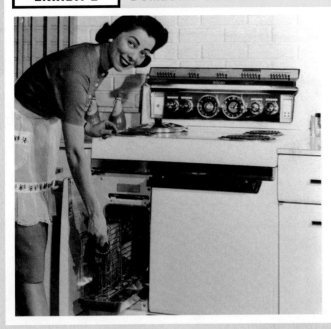

Electric Range

1910	1950	1970	1997
$67	$420	$380	$288
345 hr.	292 hr.	113 hr.	22 hr.

Hughes Electric's three-burner stove listed for $40 in 1910 (a separate oven cost $27), the equivalent of about 5 weeks' wages for middle-income Americans. General Electric's midline models today sell for around $288, less than one-tenth the work-time cost of comparable models offered in the 1950s.

EXHIBIT 2 — FOOD ON THE GO

Big Mac

1940	1997
$0.30	$1.89
27 min.	9 min.

In the currency of work time, today's 1/5-pound Big Mac costs a third of the McDonald brothers' 1/8-pound burgers in 1940.

Large Pepperoni Pizza

1958	1970	1980	1997
$1.99	$3.99	$7.99	$10.99
57 min.	71 min.	66 min.	50 min.

Compared with the huge initial investment required to start say, long-distance phone service, the outlay for setting up a pizza shop is relatively small. Even with mostly recurring costs—ingredients, labor, rent and so on—Pizza Hut has managed to cut the work-time tab for its large pepperoni pizza from 57 minutes in 1958 to just 50 today.

EXHIBIT 3 — FALLING FASTER AT FIRST

VCR

1972	1978	1984	1990	1997
$1,395	$985	$499	$329	$199
365 hr.	160 hr.	54 hr.	30 hr.	15 hr.

Video recorders that used cassettes and would both play and record crept into the market in 1972 at prices ranging from $1,395 to $1,850. Better models today sell for just 4 percent of the 1972 work-time price.

Cellular Phone

1984	1997
$4,195	$120
456 hr.	9 hr.

Motorola introduced the DynaTAC 8000X cellular phone in late 1984 with a suggested retail price range of $3,995–$4,395. Better equipped Motorola models today sell for $120 or less, and monthly service fees are half what they were 13 years ago. The number of cellular subscribers has grown from only one—on the streets of downtown Chicago—to nearly 55 million as the work-time cost of a phone has fallen to under 2 percent of what it was in 1984.

SOURCE: W. Michael Cox and Richard Alm. *1997 Annual Report: Time Well Spent*, Federal Reserve Bank of Dallas.

According to Michael Cox and Richard Alm, the real cost of living measured in the hours and minutes we must work to live is surely falling. That is, what does it cost to buy a particular good or service in terms of time on the job? Many goods like microwaves, cellular phones, and camcorders have fallen in money prices. This, coupled with higher wages and better quality, has been a real boon to the consumer.

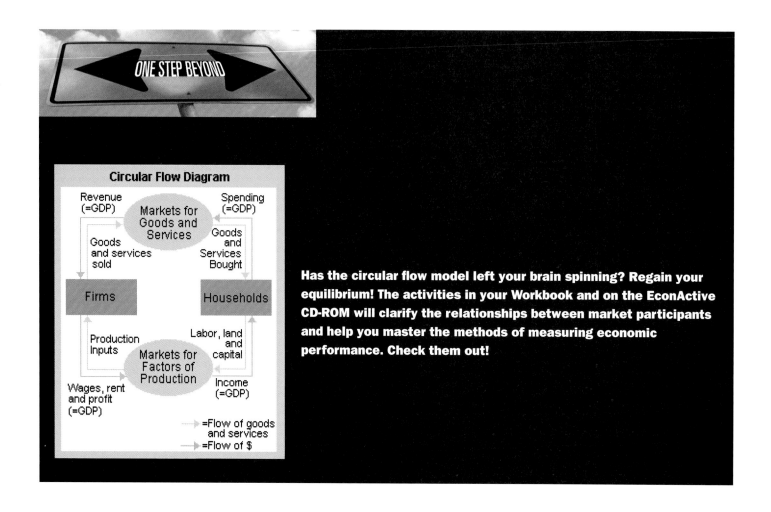

ONE STEP BEYOND

Circular Flow Diagram

Has the circular flow model left your brain spinning? Regain your equilibrium! The activities in your Workbook and on the EconActive CD-ROM will clarify the relationships between market participants and help you master the methods of measuring economic performance. Check them out!

MODULE 10

Aggregate Demand

**A. Consumption: The Primary
Determinant of Aggregate Demand**
What happens to consumption
as income rises?

B. Investment, Government Spending, and Net Exports
How do investment, government spending, and
net exports impact aggregate demand?

C. The Aggregate Demand Curve
What is the aggregate demand curve?

D. Shifts in the Aggregate Demand Curve
What causes the aggregate demand curve to shift?

E. Application: The Consumer Confidence Index
How are changes in consumer confidence
reflected in aggregate demand?

Consumption: The Primary Determinant of Aggregate Demand

- What is aggregate demand?
- What is the permanent income hypothesis?
- What is the average propensity to consume?
- What is the marginal propensity to consume?

WHAT IS AGGREGATE DEMAND?

Aggregate demand (AD) is the sum of the demand for all goods and services in the economy. It can also be seen as the quantity of real GDP demanded at different price levels. Specifically, aggregate demand reflects the summation of expenditures by household consumers, business investors, government, and foreign buyers on newly produced goods and services. The four major components of aggregate demand are consumption (C), investment (I), government spending (G), and net exports $(X - M)$. Aggregate demand, then, is equal to $C + I + G + (X - M)$.

In this Concept, we will examine the first of these four components—consumption. Investment, government spending, and net exports are covered in detail in Concept B.

HOW IMPORTANT IS CONSUMPTION (C) TO AGGREGATE DEMAND?

Consumption is by far the largest component in aggregate demand. Expenditures for consumer goods and services typically absorb almost 70 percent of total economic activity, as measured by GDP. Understanding the determinants of consumption, then, is critical to an understanding of the forces leading to changes in aggregate demand, which in turn, change total output and income.

DOES HIGHER INCOME MEAN GREATER CONSUMPTION?

The notion that the higher a nation's income, the more it spends on consumer items, has been validated empirically. At the level of individuals, most of us spend more money when we have higher incomes. But what matters most to us is not our total income but our after-tax, or **disposable income.** Moreover, there are other factors that might explain consumption. Some consumer goods are "lumpy"; that is, the expenditures for these goods must come in big amounts rather than in small dribbles. Thus, in years in which a consumer buys a new car, takes the family on a European trip, or has major surgery, consumption may be much greater in relation to income than in years in which

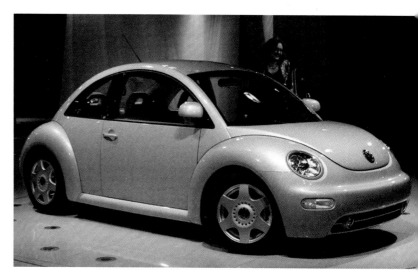

What impact might the purchase of a new car have on consumption in relation to income?

the consumer does not buy such high-cost consumer goods or services. Interest rates also affect consumption because they affect savings. At higher real interest rates, people save more and consume less. At lower real interest rates, people save less and consume more.

WHAT IS THE PERMANENT INCOME HYPOTHESIS?

Milton Friedman, a Nobel laureate in economics who taught for many years at the University of Chicago, observed that consumption is related to permanent income rather than to current income levels. This is called the **permanent income hypothesis.** Studies show, for example, that college students often consume more than their total income; the same is true of very old persons. These groups **dissave.** On the other hand, people in their 30s and 40s tend to save quite a bit and consume relatively less of their income (even so, though, a higher-income person of 40 is likely to consume more than a low-income person of 20 or 70). Why? College-age persons expect to earn more income later, and gauge their consumption in part by their

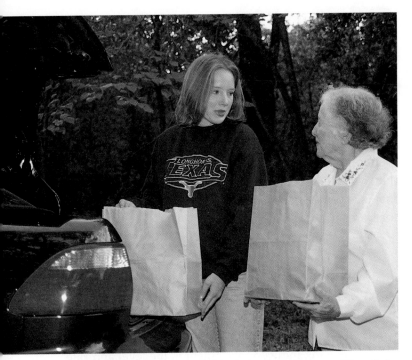

College-age and elderly individuals tend to dissave, although for different reasons.

years to maintain consumption in the bad years. People, then, consume on the basis of lifetime income expectations, which are only partly determined by current income. Looking at the economy as a whole, however, we have many groups of people with many different expectations. So, for the economy as a whole, consumption has been shown to be closely related to current income.

WHAT IS THE AVERAGE AND MARGINAL PROPENSITY TO CONSUME?

Households typically spend a large portion of their total income—the rest they save. The fraction of their total income that households spend on consumption is called the **average propensity to consume (APC)**. For example, a household that consumes $450 out of $500 total income has an APC of 0.9 ($450/$500). However, households tend to behave differently with additional income than with their income as a whole. How much increased consumption results from an increase in income? That depends upon the **marginal propensity to consume (MPC)**, which is the additional consumption that results from an additional dollar of disposable income. If consumption goes from $450 to $600 when disposable income goes from $500 to $700, what is the marginal propensity to consume out of disposable income? First, we calculate the change in consumption: $600 − $450 = $150. Next, we calculate the change in income: $700 − $500 = $200. The marginal propensity to consume, then, equals change in consumption divided by change in disposable income. In this example,

$$MPC = Consumption/Disposable\ income = \$150/\$200 = 3/4 = 0.75$$

For each additional dollar in after-tax income over this range, this household consumes three-fourths of the addition, or 75 cents.

expectations of future (lifetime) income. Likewise, middle-age persons expect to retire at some future date on a lower income and save for that eventuality. Older, retired persons expect to die and, accordingly, feel justified in drawing down their savings. A highly paid 35-year-old baseball player may consume less than a 35-year-old lawyer with the same income, because the baseball player expects his income to fall soon, while the lawyer does not. Farmers have "good" years and "bad" years and save more in good

---

CONCEPT CHECK

1. Aggregate demand is the sum of the demand for all goods and services in the economy. It can also be seen as the quantity of real GDP demanded at different price levels.
2. The four major components of aggregate demand are consumption *(C)*, investment *(I)*, government spending *(G)*, and net exports *(X − M)*. Aggregate demand, then, is equal to *C + I + G + (X − M)*.

3. Empirical evidence suggests that consumption increases directly with any increase in income.
4. According to the permanent income hypothesis, consumption is more closely related to permanent income than current income.
5. The additional consumption spending stemming from an additional dollar of disposable income is called the marginal propensity to consume (MPC).

---

1. What are the major components of aggregate demand?
2. If consumption is a direct function of disposable income, how would an increase in personal taxes or a decrease in transfer payments affect consumption?

3. What does the permanent income hypothesis imply about consumption as a fraction of income for young and old consumers versus middle-aged consumers?
4. Would you spend more or less on additional consumption if your marginal propensity to consume increased?

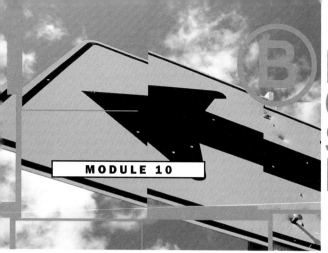

Investment, Government Spending, and Net Exports

- What are induced and autonomous investment?
- What five factors determine investment behavior?
- What is government spending?
- What are net exports?

INVESTMENT (*I*)

Because investment expenditures (purchases of investment goods) are an important component of aggregate demand, which in turn is a determinant of the level of GDP, changes in investment spending are often responsible for changes in the level of economic activity. If consumption is determined largely by the level of disposable income, what determines the level of investment expenditures? As you may recall, investment expenditures is the most unstable category of GDP; it is sensitive to changes in economic, social, and political variables.

Many factors are important in determining the level of investment expenditures. In order to better understand the impact of these factors, it is helpful to distinguish between two types of investment: induced investment and autonomous investment. When businesses decide to proceed with an investment on the basis of increases in income or output, we call this **induced investment.** Good business conditions "induce" firms to invest, because a healthy growth in demand for products in the future seems likely based on current experience. Investment that is not determined by the level of income is called **autonomous (or independent) investment.** Consider some of the key variables that impact these two types of investments.

Factors Impacting Induced Investment

Optimism Because investment depends so much on expectations as to the future, the mood of the businessperson at the time of the investment decision is crucial. Is he or she optimistic or pessimistic about the future? The more optimistic the person is, the greater the investment. Optimism, in turn, seems to be highly correlated with the rate of economic growth, both in the period in which the investment decisions are being made and in the immediate past. The more rapid the rate of growth in the level of economic activity (GDP) in a period, the greater the investment begun in that period and completed in the next time period. There are some inevitable time lags from the time

decisions are made until the investment is actually completed; it takes time to get machines that have been ordered, to construct buildings, and so on.

Level of and Rate of Change in Profits A second factor impacting induced investment is the level and rate of change in profits in the present and immediate past. Investment spending is largely carried out by businesses, whose primary motive is to maximize their profits, investing where the expected rate of return on capital assets exceeds the opportunity cost of capital. Generally, when economic growth is high, profits are high and rising. The higher the profits, the greater the expected rate of return on future ventures. Present-day success breeds optimism about the future. This is significant, because capital goods are typically used over a long period, so investment decisions depend largely on expectations of the long-term profit potential of capital expenditures.

Moreover, the existence of large profits eases the problem of obtaining funds to pay for capital expenditures, allowing firms to internally finance investment rather than having to obtain funds from outsiders. Because profits, the difference between total revenue and total cost, are income to the firm, investment is partly a function of firm income, much as consumption is a function of household income. For example, if total revenue rises more rapidly than total cost, the resulting profit enables firms to invest more.

Factors Impacting Autonomous Investment

Interest Rates One factor affecting autonomous investment is the real interest rate. The higher the interest rate, the higher the opportunity cost of investments in capital; fewer investments will now have benefits greater than the new higher costs. If an investment is expected to return 10 cents in income annually for every dollar invested (a 10 percent rate of return), the project is expected to be profitable if the firm can borrow the money at 6 percent interest, meaning it pays six cents a year for the use of each dollar. Even after paying the lender six cents on every

Are businesses as likely to invest when interest rates are high?

If inventories are excessive, will firms increase their investment in inventories in the next period?

dollar borrowed, the business expects to be four cents ahead. If the interest rate were higher, the business decision maker might decide against the investment, because the expected profit would be lower, or even negative, and there is the possibility that results won't live up to profit expectations. If the interest rate is 12 percent, the potential investor will definitely not proceed, as the investment appears to be unprofitable. Many forms of investment spending are highly sensitive to changing interest rates.

Rate of Capital Utilization A second determinant that impacts autonomous investment is the size of the capital stock of firms, relative to the current demand for goods. When output is low relative to the ability of business capital to produce goods, capital utilization rates are also low, and new investment will be lower than if firms are functioning at or near their productive capacities. The overall magnitude of the capital stock of firms is important in another respect. A large proportion of gross investment is to offset depreciation—replacing old, worn-out, or obsolete capital equipment and structures. The greater the stock of existing capital, the greater the magnitude of investment necessary to replace a depreciating capital stock, just to keep the amount of available productive capital from declining. Depreciation rates tend to be fairly independent of income, and in recent years, over half of gross investment has been accounted for by depreciation, although the relative importance of replacement investment varies considerably from year to year.

Inventories The last determinant of investment spending relates to inventories. When sales are at a level that is different from what was expected for a particular time period, firms' inventories change in unintended ways. If sales were lower in the previous period than intended, for example, inventories will have accumulated above their desired levels and inventory investment will have been greater than intended. What will businesses do now, as a result? Worried about excessive inventories, they may reduce planned investment in the current time period (they may also cut output). Very small inventories in relation to sales can lead to shortages and some foregone sales; very high inventories in relation to sales mean that too much of a firm's capital is tied up in relatively unprofitable excess inventories. Thus, firms try to achieve what they perceive to be an optimal inventory–sales ratio from the standpoint of profit maximization.

GOVERNMENT SPENDING (*G*)

Government spending varies over time for many reasons, some of them relatively noneconomic or quasi-economic in character. In 1996, the federal government accounted for slightly more than 18 percent of total spending. While volatile shifts in government spending are less frequent than volatile shifts in investment spending, they do occasionally occur, often at the beginning or end of wars. In any case, government spending tends to fall with rising income, because higher income means lower welfare payments, less unemployment compensation, and so on. Government tax receipts clearly increase with income. So when income rises over a business cycle, budget deficits automatically get smaller.

NET EXPORTS (*X* − *M*)

The interaction of the U.S. economy with the rest of the world is becoming increasingly important. Up to this

"*This should jump-start the economy.*"

point, for simplicity, we have not included the foreign sector. However, international trade must be incorporated into the framework. Models that include international trade effects are called **open economy** models.

Exports are those goods and services that we sell to foreign customers, like movies, wheat, or Mustangs. Imports are those goods and services that we buy from foreign customers, like BMWs, French wine, or Sony TVs.

Exports and imports can alter aggregate demand. It makes no difference to sellers if the buyers that purchase their goods and services are in this country or in some other country. A buyer is a buyer, foreign or domestic. That is, exports (X) must be added to the demand side of our equation. But what about goods and services that are consumed here but not produced by the domestic economy? When U.S. consumers buy foreign goods and services, it has no direct impact on the total demand for U.S. goods and services. In other words, imports (M) have to be subtracted from our equation.

Exports minus imports is what we call **net exports,** and it represents the balance of trade. When the economy is running a trade surplus, we have positive net exports ($X > M$); exports are greater than imports. And when the economy is running a trade deficit, net exports are negative ($X < M$); imports are greater than exports.

The impact that net exports ($X - M$) have on aggregate demand is similar to the impact that government spending has on aggregate demand. Suppose a country has a balanced trade, with no trade surplus and no trade deficit— zero net exports. Now say that foreign consumers start buying more American goods and services while American consumers continue to buy imports at roughly the same rate. This will lead to positive net exports ($X > M$), and as a result of a greater demand for U.S. goods and services, a higher level of aggregate demand. From a policy standpoint, this might explain why countries that are currently in a recession might like to run a trade surplus by increasing exports.

Of course, it is also very possible that a country could run a trade deficit. Again let us assume that the economy was initially in a position with zero net exports. A trade deficit, or negative net exports ($X < M$), other things equal, would lower aggregate demand in the United States.

CONCEPT CHECK

1. When businesses invest because of positive changes in income or output, it is called induced investment.
2. Investment that is not determined by the level of income is called autonomous investment.
3. The five major factors that determine investment behavior are optimism, profits, interest rates, capital stock, and inventories.
4. Government spending is generally independent of income levels.
5. Trade deficits lower aggregate demand, other things equal; trade surpluses increase aggregate demand, other things equal.

1. Why does increased business optimism lead to increased investment?
2. Why do decisions to invest depend largely on the expected rate of return on investments compared to the opportunity cost of borrowed money (the market interest rate)?
3. Why might a larger existing capital stock tend to increase the rate of new capital goods investment?
4. If inventories have risen above the desired level for a firm, what does that tell it about the demand for its product relative to what it expected demand to be?
5. What would an increase in exports do to aggregate demand, other things equal? An increase in imports? An increase in both imports and exports, where the change in exports was greater in magnitude?

The Aggregate Demand Curve

- How is the aggregate demand curve different from the demand curve for a particular good?
- Why is the aggregate demand curve downward sloping?

WHAT IS THE AGGREGATE DEMAND CURVE?

The **aggregate demand curve** reflects the total amounts of real goods and services that all groups together want to purchase in a given time period. In other words, it indicates the quantities of real gross domestic product demanded at different price levels. Note that this is different from the demand curve for a particular good presented in Module 4, which looked at the relationship between the relative price of a good and the quantity demanded.

HOW IS THE QUANTITY OF REAL GDP DEMANDED AFFECTED BY THE PRICE LEVEL?

The aggregate demand curve slopes downward, which means that there is an inverse (or opposite) relationship between the price level and real gross domestic product (RGDP) demanded. This relationship is illustrated in Exhibit 1, where the quantity of RGDP demanded is measured on the horizontal axis and the overall price level is measured on the vertical axis. As we move from point A to point B on the aggregate demand curve, we see that an increase in the price level causes RGDP demanded to fall. Conversely, if there is a reduction in the price level, a movement from B to A, quantity demanded of RGDP increases. Why do purchasers in the economy demand less real output when the price level rises, and more real output when the price level falls?

WHY IS THE AGGREGATE DEMAND CURVE NEGATIVELY SLOPED?

There are three complementary explanations for the negative slope of the aggregate demand curve: the real wealth effect, the interest rate effect, and the open economy effect.

What Is the Real Wealth Effect?

Imagine that you are living in a period of high inflation on a fixed pension that is not indexed for the changing price

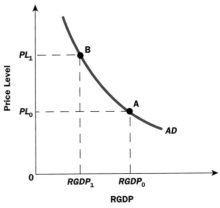

| EXHIBIT 1 | THE AGGREGATE DEMAND CURVE |

The aggregate demand curve slopes downward, reflecting an inverse relationship between the overall price level and the quantity of real GDP demanded. When the price level increases, the quantity of RGDP demanded decreases; when the price level decreases, the quantity of RGDP demanded increases.

level. As the cost of goods and services you buy rises by leaps and bounds, your monthly pension check remains the same. Therefore, the purchasing power of your pension will continue to decline as long as inflation is occurring. The same would be true of any asset of fixed dollar value, like cash. If you had $1,000 in cash stashed under your bed while the economy suffered a serious bout of inflation, the purchasing power of your cash would be eroded by the extent of the inflation. That is, an increase in the price level reduces real wealth and would consequently decrease your planned purchases of goods and services, lowering the quantity of RGDP demanded.

In the event that the price level falls, the reverse would hold true. A falling price level would increase the real value of your cash assets, increasing your purchasing power and increasing RGDP. The connection can be summarized as follows:

If you keep your savings in a cookie jar, what will happen to your real wealth as a result of a price level increase? A price level decrease?

$$\uparrow \text{Price level} \Rightarrow \downarrow \text{Real wealth} \Rightarrow \downarrow \text{Purchasing power} \Rightarrow \downarrow \text{RGDP demanded}$$

and

$$\downarrow \text{Price level} \Rightarrow \uparrow \text{Real wealth} \Rightarrow \uparrow \text{Purchasing power} \Rightarrow \uparrow \text{RGDP demanded}$$

What Is the Interest Rate Effect?

The effect of the price level on interest rates can also cause the aggregate demand curve to have a negative slope. Suppose the price level increases. As a result, most goods and services will now have a higher price tag. Consequently, consumers will wish to hold more dollars in order to purchase those items that they want to buy. That will increase the demand for money. If the demand for money increases and the Federal Reserve System, the controller of the money supply, does not alter the money supply, then interest rates will rise. In other words, if the demand for money increases relative to the supply, then the demanders of dollars will bid up the price of those dollars—the interest rate.

At higher interest rates, the opportunity cost of borrowing rises, and fewer interest-sensitive investments will be profitable, reducing the quantity of investment goods demanded. Businesses contemplating replacing worn-out equipment or planning to expand capacity may cancel or delay their investment decisions unless interest rates decline again. Also, at the higher interest rate, many consumers may give up plans to buy new cars, boats, or houses. The net effect of the higher interest rate, then, is that it will result in fewer investment goods demanded and, consequently, a lower RGDP demanded.

On the other hand, if the price level fell, and people demanded less money as a result, then interest rates would fall. Lower interest rates would trigger greater investment spending, and a larger real GDP demanded would result. We can summarize this process as follows:

$$\uparrow \text{Price level} \Rightarrow \uparrow \text{Money demand (Money supply unchanged)} \Rightarrow \uparrow \text{Interest rate} \Rightarrow \downarrow \text{Investments} \Rightarrow \downarrow \text{RGDP demanded}$$

and

$$\downarrow \text{Price level} \Rightarrow \downarrow \text{Money demand (Money supply unchanged)} \Rightarrow \downarrow \text{Interest rate} \Rightarrow \uparrow \text{Investments} \Rightarrow \uparrow \text{RGDP demanded}$$

What Is the Open Economy Effect of Changes in the Price Level?

Many goods and services are bought and sold in global markets. If the prices of goods and services in the domestic market rise relative to those in global markets due to a

If the domestic price level rises, will domestic consumers buy more foreign goods?

higher domestic price level, consumers and businesses will buy more from foreign producers and less from domestic producers. Because real GDP is a measure of domestic output, the reduction in the willingness of consumers to buy from domestic producers leads to a lower real GDP demanded at the higher domestic price level. And if domestic prices of goods and services fall relative to foreign prices, more domestic products will be bought, increasing real GDP demanded. This relationship can be shown as follows:

$$\uparrow \text{Price level} \Rightarrow \downarrow \text{Demand for domestic goods} \Rightarrow \downarrow \text{RGDP demanded}$$

and

$$\downarrow \text{Price level} \Rightarrow \uparrow \text{Demand for domestic goods} \Rightarrow \uparrow \text{RGDP demanded}$$

CONCEPT CHECK

1. A microeconomic demand curve shows the relationship between the relative price of a good and how much of that good is demanded, while an aggregate demand curve relates the amounts of real goods and services willingly purchased in an economy to the general price level for these goods and services.

2. The aggregate demand curve is downward sloping because of the real wealth effect, the interest rate effect, and the open economy effect.

1. How is the aggregate demand curve different from the microeconomic demand curve?
2. How does an increased price level reduce the quantities of investment goods and consumer durables demanded?
3. What is the real wealth effect, and how does it imply a downward-sloping aggregate demand curve?
4. What is the interest rate effect, and how does it imply a downward-sloping aggregate demand curve?
5. What is the open economy effect, and how does it imply a downward-sloping aggregate demand curve?

Shifts in the Aggregate Demand Curve

- What variables shift the aggregate demand curve to the right?
- What variables shift the aggregate demand curve to the left?
- What is the difference between a movement along and a shift in the aggregate demand curve?

DOES A CHANGE IN THE PRICE LEVEL SHIFT THE AGGREGATE DEMAND CURVE?

As for the supply and demand curves of Module 4, there can be both shifts in and movements along the aggregate demand curve. In the previous section, we discussed three factors—the real wealth effect, the interest rate effect, and the foreign market effect—that result in the downward slope of the aggregate demand curve. Each of these factors, then, generates a movement *along* the aggregate demand curve, because the general price level changed. In this section, we will discuss some of the many factors that can cause the aggregate demand curve to shift to the right or left.

The whole aggregate demand curve can shift to the right or left, as seen in Exhibit 1. Put simply, if some non-

price level determinant causes total spending to increase, then the aggregate demand curve will shift to the right. If a non-price level determinant causes the level of total spending to decline, then the aggregate demand curve will shift to the left. Now let's look at some specific factors that could cause the aggregate demand curve to shift.

AGGREGATE DEMAND CURVE SHIFTERS

Anything that changes the amount of total spending in the economy (holding price levels constant) will impact the aggregate demand curve. An increase in any component of GDP (C, I, G, and $X - M$) can cause the aggregate demand curve to shift rightward. Conversely, decreases in C, I, G, or ($X - M$) will shift aggregate demand leftward.

Changing Consumption (C) Demand

A whole host of changes could alter consumption patterns. For example, an increase in consumer confidence, an increase in wealth, or a tax cut, each can increase consumption and shift the aggregate demand curve to the right. An increase in population would also increase the aggregate demand, as there are now more consumers spending more money on goods and services.

Of course, the aggregate demand curve could shift to the left due to decreases in consumption demand. For example, if consumers sensed that the economy was headed for a recession or if the government imposed a tax increase, this would result in a leftward shift of the aggregate demand curve. Because consuming less is saving more, an increase in savings, *ceteris paribus*, will shift aggregate demand to the left. Consumer debt may also be a reason that some consumers might put off additional spending. In fact, some economists believe that part of the 1990–1992 recession was due to consumer debt that had built up during the 1980s. Aside from maxing out their credit cards, some individuals also lost equity in their homes and, consequently, had a reduction in their wealth

EXHIBIT 1	SHIFTS IN THE AGGREGATE DEMAND CURVE

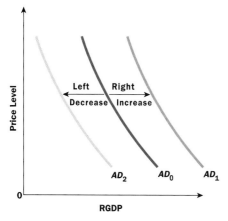

An increase in aggregate demand shifts the curve to the right (from AD_0 to AD_1). A decrease in aggregate demand shifts the curve to the left (from AD_0 to AD_2).

and purchasing power—again shifting aggregate demand to the left.

Changing Investment (*I*)

Investment is also an important determinant of aggregate demand. Increases in the demand for investment goods occur for a variety of reasons. For example, if business confidence increases or real interest rates fall, business investment will increase and aggregate demand will shift to the right. A reduction in business taxes would also shift the aggregate demand curve to the right, because businesses would now retain more of their profits to invest. However, if interest rates or business taxes rise, then we would expect to see a leftward shift in aggregate demand.

Changing Government Spending (*G*)

Government spending is also part of total spending and therefore must impact aggregate demand. An increase in

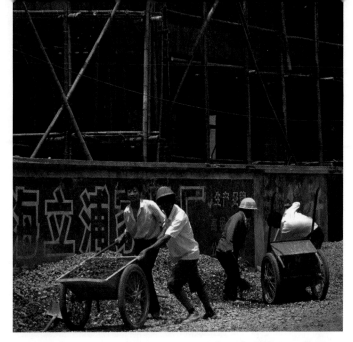

How would a boom in China's economy impact U.S. aggregate demand?

TUNE UP

CHANGES IN AGGREGATE DEMAND

Q: Any aggregate demand category that has the ability to change total purchases in the economy will shift the aggregate demand curve. That is, changes in consumption purchases, investment purchases, government purchases, or net export purchases shift the aggregate demand curve. For each component of aggregate demand (*C, I, G,* and *X − M*), list some changes that can increase aggregate demand. Then, list some changes that can decrease aggregate demand.

A: In Exhibit 1, we list some aggregate demand curve shifters.

INCREASES IN AGGREGATE DEMAND (RIGHTWARD SHIFT)

Consumption Spending (*C*)
—lower income taxes
—a rise in consumer confidence
—greater stock market wealth

Investment (*I*)
—lower real interest rates
—optimistic business forecasts

Government Spending (*G*)
—an increase in government defense outlays
—an increase in social security benefits or welfare payments

Net Exports (*X − M*)
—income increases abroad, which will likely increase the sale of domestic goods (exports)

DECREASES IN AGGREGATE DEMAND (LEFTWARD SHIFT)

Consumption Spending (*C*)
—higher income taxes
—a fall in consumer confidence
—reduced stock market wealth

Investment (*I*)
—higher real interest rates
—a pessimistic economic outlook

Government Spending (*G*)
—a cutback in government defense outlays
—a reduction in social security benefits or welfare payments

Net Exports (*X − M*)
—income falls abroad, which will lead to a reduction in the sales of domestic goods (exports)

government spending, other things equal, shifts the aggregate demand curve to the right, while a reduction shifts aggregate demand to the left.

Changing Net Exports ($X - M$)

Global markets are also very important in a domestic economy. For example, if major trading partners are experiencing economic slowdowns (such as is occurring in the Asian market in the late 1990s), then they will demand fewer U.S. imports. This causes U.S. net exports ($X - M$) to fall, shifting aggregate demand to the left. Alternatively, an economic boom in the economies of major trading partners may lead to an increase in our exports to them, causing net exports ($X - M$) to rise and aggregate demand to increase.

CONCEPT CHECK

1. A change in the price level causes a movement along the aggregate demand curve, not a shift in the aggregate demand curve.

2. Aggregate demand is made up of total spending, or $C + I + G + (X - M)$. Any change in these factors will cause the aggregate demand curve to shift.

1. How is the distinction between a change in demand and a change in quantity demanded the same for aggregate demand as for the demand for a particular good?
2. What happens to aggregate demand if the demand for consumption goods increases, *ceteris paribus?*
3. What happens to aggregate demand if the demand for investment goods falls, *ceteris paribus?*
4. Why would an increase in the money supply tend to increase expenditures on consumption and investment, *ceteris paribus?*

Application: The Consumer Confidence Index

How does consumer confidence impact aggregate demand? How would stock market wealth, joblessness, and inflation alter the aggregate demand curve?

A BRIEF DESCRIPTION OF THE CONSUMER CONFIDENCE SURVEY

The Consumer Confidence Survey measures the level of confidence individual households have in the performance of the economy. Survey questionnaires are mailed to a representative nationwide sample of 5,000 households, of which approximately 3,500 respond. Households are asked five questions that include (1) a rating of current business conditions in the household's area, (2) a rating of expected business conditions in six months, (3) current job availability in the area, (4) expected job availability in six months, and (5) expected family income in six months. The responses are seasonally adjusted. An index is constructed for each response and then a composite index is fashioned based on the responses. Two other indexes, one for an assessment of the present situation and one for expectations about the future, are also constructed. Expectations account for 60 percent of the index, while the current situation is responsible for the remaining 40 percent. In addition, indexes for the present and expected future economic situations

are calculated for each of the nine census divisions. In the base year, 1985, the value of the index was 100.

The Conference Board also tracks consumer buying plans over the next six months. Among the items tracked are automobiles, homes, vacations, and major appliances. If the economy experiences a long-term expansion, buying intentions may eventually decline even if the jobless rate stays low, because of the satisfaction of pent-up demand. Conversely, if inflation begins to accelerate, spending plans may increase for the short-term as consumers buy now to avoid having to pay higher prices later.

Consumer confidence correlates closely with joblessness, inflation, and real incomes. The growth of help wanted advertising (a measure of job prospects) is also correlated with strong consumer confidence. Rising stock market prices also boost consumer confidence.

Dismal Sciences (http://www.dismal.com/toolbox/dict_consumer.stml), 1998.

JUMP IN EXPECTATIONS SPURS NEW GAINS, THE CONFERENCE BOARD REPORTS TODAY

Consumers' expectations for the economy over the next six months climbed sharply. More than 18 percent of all consumers look for business conditions to improve during the next six months, up from 17 percent in March. Nearly 18 percent also expect jobs to become more plentiful, up from about 15 percent in March.

The latest Conference Board probe also reports that nearly 28 percent say their family's income will rise by next fall, up from 25 percent in March.

But there was a modest decline in consumers' assessments of current conditions. The proportion of consumers rating present business conditions as "good" was unchanged, but nearly 10 percent now label business conditions as "bad," up about one point from March. Slightly more consumers (nearly 15 percent vs. 14 percent) say jobs are difficult to find.

The Conference Board (http://www.conference-board.org/search/dpress.cfm?pressid=cciapril98), April 28, 1998.

The consumer confidence index has the potential to reflect important aggregate demand shifters. For example, if inflation is expected, consumers may increase their spending now. This would shift the aggregate demand curve to the right. Also, if the consumer confidence survey shows that consumer and business confidence in the economy is rising, we would also expect to see an increase in aggregate demand. Stock market wealth would increase consumption and shift the aggregate demand curve to the right. Of course, if the consumer confidence survey showed pessimism and signs of a downturn, we would expect the aggregate demand curve to shift to the left. In short, consumers and business perceptions of the economy are often important aggregate demand shifters and can have significant impact on price level, real output, and employment as a result.

Fall is the time of year, when the aspens are bursting with colorful autumn leaves and the excitement of the upcoming ski season at one of the nation's finest ski resorts fills the crisp, clean mountain air. Come to Breckenridge. Mountain setting. Historic past. Colorful present. Special events, activities, and festivals for the whole family. CIRCLE 20 ON REPLY CARD.

Airfare and lodging 888-533-9879 • www.gobreck.com

Planning a trip in the next six months? What might this say about your confidence in the economy?

Are you finding the concepts of aggregate demand to be too demanding? Never fear! The explanations on your EconActive CD-ROM can help you solidify your grasp of the four determinants of aggregate demand, and you can check your understanding of the aggregate demand curve and its shifters using the graphs and problems found in your Workbook!

Aggregate Supply and Macroeconomic Equilibrium

A. The Aggregate Supply Curve
What do the short-run and long-run aggregate supply curves represent?

B. Shifts in the Aggregate Supply Curve
What causes the aggregate supply curves to shift?

C. Macroeconomic Equilibrium
What are demand-pull and cost-push inflation?

D. Application: El Niño and the AD/AS Model
How did El Niño impact aggregate supply?

The Aggregate Supply Curve

■ What do the aggregate supply curves represent?

■ Why do producers supply more as the price level increases in the short run?

■ Why do the short-run and the long-run aggregate supply curves differ?

WHAT IS THE AGGREGATE SUPPLY CURVE?

Aggregate supply (AS) is the relationship between the total quantity of final goods and services that suppliers are *willing* and *able* to produce and the overall price level. The aggregate supply curve represents how much RGDP suppliers will be willing to produce at different price levels. In fact, there are two aggregate supply curves—a **short-run aggregate supply curve** and a **long-run aggregate supply curve.** The short-run relationship refers to a period when output can change in response to supply and demand, but input prices have not yet been able to adjust. For example, nominal wages are assumed to adjust slowly in the short run. The long-run relationship refers to a period long enough for the prices of outputs and all inputs to fully adjust to changes in the economy.

WHY IS THE SHORT-RUN AGGREGATE SUPPLY CURVE POSITIVELY SLOPED?

In the short run, the aggregate supply curve is upward sloping, as shown in Exhibit 1. This means that at a higher price level, producers are willing to supply more real output, and at lower price levels, they are willing to supply less real output. Why would producers be willing to supply more output just because the price level increases? There are two possible explanations: the profit effect and the misperception effect.

The Profit Effect

To many firms, input costs—like wages and rents—are relatively constant in the short run. The slow adjustments of input prices are due to the longer-term input contracts that do not adjust quickly to price changes. So when the

| EXHIBIT 1 | THE SHORT-RUN AGGREGATE SUPPLY CURVE |

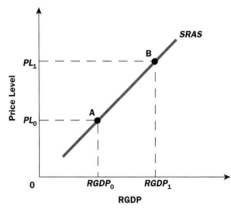

The short-run aggregate supply *(SRAS)* curve is upward sloping. Suppliers are willing to supply more RGDP at higher price levels and less at lower price levels, other things equal.

price level rises, output prices rise relative to input prices (costs), raising producers' short-run profit margins. These increased profit margins make it in the producers' self-interest to expand their production and sales at higher price levels.

If the price level falls, output prices fall and producers' profits tend to fall. Again, this is because many input costs, such as wages and other contracted costs, are relatively constant in the short run. When output prices fall, producers will find it more difficult to cover their input costs and, consequently, will reduce their level of output.

The Misperception Effect

The second explanation of the upward-sloping short-run aggregate supply curve is that producers can be fooled by price changes in the short run. For example, say a cotton rancher sees the price of his cotton rising. If he thinks that the relative price of his cotton is rising (i.e., that cotton is becoming more valuable in real terms), he will supply more. In actuality, however, it might be that it was not just cotton prices that were rising; the prices of many other goods and services could also be rising at the same time as a result of an increase in the price level. The relative price of cotton, then, was not actually rising, although it appeared so in the short run. In this case, the producer was fooled into supplying more based on his short-run misperception of relative prices.

WHY IS THE LONG-RUN AGGREGATE SUPPLY CURVE VERTICAL?

Along the short-run aggregate supply curve, we assume that wages and other input prices are constant. This is not the case in the long run, which is a period long enough for the price of all inputs to fully adjust to changes in the economy. When we move along the long-run supply curve, then we are looking at the relationship between RGDP produced and the

If the price of cotton rises, along with the average of all other prices, cotton ranchers may be fooled into supplying more cotton to the market.

price level, once input prices have been able to respond to changes in output prices. Along the long-run aggregate supply *(LRAS)* curve, two sets of prices are changing—the prices of outputs and the price of inputs. That is, along the *LRAS* curve, a 10 percent increase in the price of goods

T U N E   U P

THE SHORT-RUN AGGREGATE SUPPLY CURVE

Q: Why would a firm be willing to supply more if output prices (the price level) are rising?

A: It is critical to remember that along the short-run aggregate supply curve, many input prices are constant even though the output prices are changing. This means two things to producers. One, greater short-run profits can be made if you expand production because the price of the output you are selling is rising faster than what you have to pay for your inputs. Two, in the short run, you can be fooled into producing more because you think the relative price of the good you are selling is rising. Only later do you find out that it's not just your prices that are rising but that the price level (the average of all prices) is rising.

and services is matched by a 10 percent increase in the price of inputs. The long-run aggregate supply curve, then, is insensitive to the price level. As you can see in Exhibit 2, the *LRAS* curve is drawn as perfectly vertical, reflecting the fact that the level of RGDP producers are willing to supply is not affected by changes in the price level. Note that the vertical long-run aggregate supply curve will always be positioned at the natural rate of output, where all resources are fully employed ($RGDP_{FE}$). That is, in the long run, firms will always produce at the maximum level allowed by their capital, labor, and technological inputs, regardless of the price level.

The long-run equilibrium level is where the economy will settle when undisturbed and when all resources are fully employed. Remember that the economy will always be at the intersection of aggregate supply and aggregate demand but that will *not* always be at the natural rate of output, $RGDP_{FE}$. Long-run equilibrium will only occur where the aggregate supply and aggregate demand curves intersect along the long-run aggregate supply curve at the natural, or potential, rate of output.

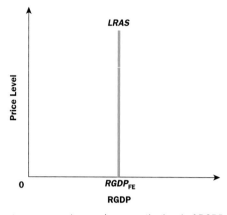

| EXHIBIT 2 | THE LONG-RUN AGGREGATE SUPPLY CURVE |

Along the long-run aggregate supply curve, the level of RGDP does not change with the price level. The position of the LRAS curve is determined by the natural rate of output, $RGDP_{FE}$, which reflects the levels of capital, land, labor, and technology in the economy.

CONCEPT CHECK

1. The short-run aggregate supply curve measures how much RGDP suppliers will be willing to produce at different price levels.
2. In the short run, producers supply more as the price level increases because wages and other input prices tend to be slower to change than output prices. For this reason, they can make a profit by expanding production when the price level rises. They also may be fooled into thinking that the relative price of the item they are producing is rising, so they increase production.

3. In the long run, the aggregate supply curve is vertical. In the long run, input prices change proportionally with output prices. The position of the *LRAS* curve is determined by the level of capital, land, labor, and technology at the natural rate of output, $RGDP_{FE}$.

1. What relationship does the short-run aggregate supply curve represent?
2. What relationship does the long-run aggregate supply curve represent?
3. Why is focusing on producers' profit margins helpful in understanding the logic of the short-run aggregate supply curve?
4. Why is the short-run aggregate supply curve upward sloping, while the long-run aggregate supply curve is vertical at the natural rate of output?

5. What would the short-run aggregate supply curve look like if input prices always changed instantaneously as soon as output prices changed? Why?
6. If the price of cotton increased 10 percent when cotton producers thought other prices were rising 5 percent over the same period, what would happen to the quantity of real GDP supplied in the cotton industry? What if cotton producers thought other prices were rising 20 percent over the same period?

Shifts in the Aggregate Supply Curve

MODULE 11

■ What is the main cause of shifts in aggregate supply?

■ Which factors of production affect aggregate supply?

■ What nonmarket forces affect aggregate supply?

WHAT CAUSES BOTH LONG-RUN AND SHORT-RUN SUPPLY CURVES TO SHIFT?

We will now examine the determinants that can shift the whole aggregate supply curve to the right or left, as shown in Exhibit 1. The underlying determinant of shifts in short-run aggregate supply is production costs. *Ceteris paribus*, lower production costs will motivate producers to produce more at any given price level, shifting the aggregate supply curve rightward. Likewise, higher production costs will motivate producers to produce less at any given price level, shifting the aggregate supply curve leftward.

Any change in the quantity of any factor of production available—capital, entrepreneurship, land, or labor—can cause a shift in both the long-run and short-run aggregate supply curves. In the following paragraphs, we will see how these factors can change the position of the aggregate supply curve.

EXHIBIT 1	SHIFTS IN BOTH LONG-RUN AND SHORT-RUN AGGREGATE SUPPLY

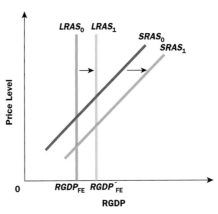

Increases in any of the factors of production—capital, land, labor, or technology—can shift both the *LRAS* and *SRAS* curves to the right.

Exploring and finding new oil supplies can shift the SRAS and LRAS curves.

How Do Changes in Capital Affect Aggregate Supply?

As we learned in the previous module, changes in the stock of capital will alter the amount of goods and services the economy can produce. Investing in capital improves the quantity and quality of the capital stock. And more and better quality capital will lower the costs of production in the short run, shifting the short-run aggregate supply curve rightward, and allow output to be permanently greater than before, shifting the long-run aggregate supply curve rightward, *ceteris paribus*.

Changes in human capital can also alter the aggregate supply curve. Investments in human capital may include educational or vocational programs or on-the-job training. All of these investments in human capital would cause productivity to rise. As a result, the short-run aggregate supply curve would shift to the right, because a more skilled work

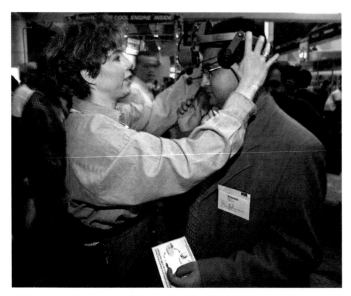

Will new technology shift the *LRAS* and *SRAS* curves?

force will lower the costs of production, and the *LRAS* curve would shift to the right because greater output is achievable on a permanent, or sustainable, basis, *ceteris paribus*.

How Do Technology and Entrepreneurship Affect Aggregate Supply?

Bill Gates of Microsoft and Steve Jobs, the founding father of Apple Computer, are just a couple of examples of entrepreneurs who, through inventive activity, can increase both the short-run and long-run aggregate supply curves by lowering costs and expanding real output possibilities. As another example, a few years ago, two scientists claimed that they had found a way to create energy out of cold fusion. Attempts to duplicate their results were futile, but one can only imagine the huge impact that an inexpensive source of energy would have had on production costs and potential output. If entrepreneurial activities lower the costs of production and expand what can be produced with the resources available to the economy, then the aggregate supply curves both shift to the right.

How Do Changes in Land (Natural Resources) Affect Aggregate Supply?

Remember that land is an all-encompassing definition that includes all natural resources. An increase in natural resources, such as successful oil exploration, would presumably lower the costs of production and expand the economy's sustainable rate of output shifting both the

short-run and long-run aggregate supply curves to the right. Likewise, a decrease in the amount of natural resources available would result in a leftward shift of both the short-run and long-run aggregate supply curves. For example, in the 1970s and early 1980s when the OPEC cartel was strong and effective at raising world oil prices, the *AS* curve shifted to the left, as the members of the cartel deliberately controlled the production of oil.

How Do Changes in the Quantity and Quality of the Labor Force Affect Aggregate Supply?

The addition of workers to the labor force, *ceteris paribus*, can increase aggregate supply. For example, during the 1960s, women and baby boomers entered the labor force in large numbers. This increase tended to depress wages and increase short-run aggregate supply, *ceteris paribus*. The expanded labor force also increased the economy's potential output, increasing long-run aggregate supply. Increases or decreases in labor productivity will also affect the aggregate supply curve. Lower output per worker causes production costs to rise and potential real output to fall, resulting in a leftward shift in both the short-run and long-run aggregate supply curves.

How Can Government Regulations Affect Aggregate Supply?

Increases in government regulations can make it more costly for producers. This increase in production costs results in a leftward shift of the short-run aggregate supply curve, and the reduction in society's potential output would shift the long-run aggregate supply curve to the left as well. Likewise, a reduction in government regulations on businesses would lower the costs of production and expand potential real output, causing both the *SRAS* and *LRAS* curves to shift to the right.

WHAT FACTORS SHIFT SHORT-RUN AGGREGATE SUPPLY ONLY?

Some factors shift the short-run aggregate supply curve but do not impact the long-run aggregate supply curve. The most important of these factors are changes in input prices and natural disasters. The impact of these factors on short-run aggregate supply is illustrated in Exhibit 2.

How Do Input Prices Affect Short-Run Aggregate Supply?

The price of factors, or inputs, that go into producing outputs will affect only the short-run aggregate supply curve if they don't reflect permanent changes in the suppliers of some factors of production. For example, if wages increase without a corresponding increase in labor productivity, then it will become more costly for suppliers to produce goods and services at every price level, causing the *SRAS* curve to shift to the left. Long-run aggregate supply will not shift, however, because with the same supply of labor as before, potential output does not change. For example, if the price of steel rises, automobile producers will find it more expensive to do business, because their production costs will rise, again resulting in a leftward shift in the short-run aggregate supply curve. The *LRAS* curve will not shift, however, as long as the capacity to make steel has not been reduced.

It is supply and demand in factor markets (like capital, land, and labor) that cause input prices to change. The reason that changes in input prices only affect short-run aggregate supply and not long-run aggregate supply, unless they reflect permanent changes in the supplies of those inputs lies in our definition of long-run aggregate supply. Recall that the long-run aggregate supply curve is vertical at the natural level of real output, determined by the supplies of the various factors of production. A fall in input prices, which shifts the short-run aggregate supply curve to the right, only shifts long-run aggregate supply to the right if potential output has risen, and that only occurs if the supply of those inputs is increased.

How Do Natural Disasters Affect Aggregate Supply?

Major widespread flooding, earthquakes, droughts, and other natural disasters can increase the costs of production. Any of these disasters could cause the short-run aggregate supply curve to shift to the left, *ceteris paribus*. However, once the temporary effects of these disasters have been felt, no appreciable change in the economy's productive capacity has occurred, so the long-run aggregate supply doesn't shift as a result.

EXHIBIT 2

SHIFTS IN SHORT-RUN AGGREGATE SUPPLY BUT NOT LONG-RUN AGGREGATE SUPPLY

A change in input prices that does not reflect a permanent change in the supply of those inputs will shift the *SRAS* curve but not the *LRAS* curve. Likewise, adverse supply shocks, such as those caused by natural disasters, may cause a temporary change that will only impact short-run aggregate supply.

Temporary natural disasters like droughts can destroy crops and leave land parched like in the picture above. This may shift the *SRAS* curve but not the *LRAS* curve.

TUNE UP

SHIFTS IN THE SHORT-RUN AGGREGATE SUPPLY CURVE

Q: Bill M. Later works in the auditing department of a big company. He wants to know why wage increases (and other input prices) impact the short-run aggregate supply but *not* the long-run aggregate supply. Can you help Bill out?

A: Remember, in the short run, wages and other input prices are assumed to be constant along the *SRAS* curve. If the firm has to pay more for its workers or any other input, its costs will rise. That is, the *SRAS* curve will shift to the left. This is shown in Exhibit 3 in the shift from $SRAS_0$ to $SRAS_1$. The reason the *LRAS* curve will *not* shift is that unless these input prices reflect permanent changes in input supply, those changes will only be temporary, and output will not be permanently or sustainably different as a result. Other things equal, if an input price is to be permanently higher relative to other goods, its supply must have decreased, but that would mean that potential real output, and hence long-run aggregate supply, would also shift left.

EXHIBIT 3

(Along LRAS, price level and input prices rise by the same percentage.)

LRAS

$SRAS_1$ (An increase in input prices shifts the SRAS.)

$SRAS_0$ (Along SRAS, price level changes but input prices do not.)

Price Level

$RGDP_{FE}$

RGDP

0

CONCEPT CHECK

1. Any increase in the quantity of any of the factors of production—capital, land, labor, or technology—available will cause both the long-run and short-run aggregate supply curves to shift to the right. A decrease in any of these factors will shift both of the aggregate supply curves to the left.

2. Changes in input price and temporary supply shocks shift the short-run aggregate supply curve but do not affect the long-run aggregate supply curve.

---

1. Which of the aggregate supply curves will shift in response to a change in the price level? Why?

2. Why do lower input costs increase the level of real GDP supplied at any given price level?

3. What would discovering huge new supplies of oil and natural gas do to the short-run and long-run aggregate supply curves?

4. What would happen to the short-run and long-run aggregate supply curves if the government required every firm to file explanatory paperwork each time a decision was made?

5. What would happen to the short-run and long-run aggregate supply curves if the capital stock grew and available supplies of natural resources expanded over the same period of time?

6. How can a change in input prices change the short-run aggregate supply curve but not the long-run aggregate supply curve? How could it change both long-run and short-run aggregate supply?

7. What would happen to short- and long-run aggregate supply if unusually good weather led to bumper crops of most agricultural products?

8. If OPEC temporarily restricted the world output of oil, what would happen to short- and long-run aggregate supply? What would happen if the output restriction was permanent?

Macroeconomic Equilibrium

MODULE 11

- What is short-run macroeconomic equilibrium?
- What is long-run macroeconomic equilibrium?
- What is demand-pull inflation?
- What is cost-push inflation?
- Can both aggregate supply and aggregate demand shift?

HOW IS MACROECONOMIC EQUILIBRIUM DETERMINED?

The short-run equilibrium level of real output and the price level are determined by the intersection of the aggregate demand curve and the short-run aggregate supply curve. When this equilibrium occurs at the potential output level, on the long-run aggregate supply curve the economy is operating at full employment, as seen in Exhibit 1. Only a short-run equilibrium that is at potential output is also a long-run equilibrium. Short-run equilibrium can change when the aggregate demand curve or the short-run aggregate supply curve shifts rightward or leftward, but the long-run equilibrium level of RGDP only changes when the LRAS curve shifts. Sometimes, these supply or demand changes are anticipated; at other times, however, the shifts occur unexpectedly. Economists call these unexpected shifts, **shocks**.

EXHIBIT 1 — **LONG-RUN MACROECONOMIC EQUILIBRIUM**

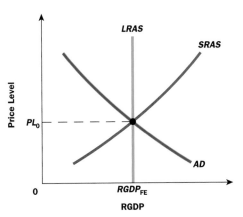

Long-run macroeconomic equilibrium occurs at the level where short-run aggregate supply and aggregate demand intersect at a point on the long-run aggregate supply curve. At this level, real GDP will equal potential GDP at full employment ($RGDP_{FE}$).

WHAT IS DEMAND-PULL INFLATION?

Demand-pull inflation occurs when the price level rises as a result of an increase in aggregate demand. Consider the case in which there is an increase in consumer optimism that results in a corresponding increase in aggregate demand. As shown in Exhibit 2, this increase in aggregate demand causes an increase in the price level and an increase in real output. This is demonstrated in Exhibit 2 in the movement along $SRAS_0$ from point A to point B. Recall that the increase in output as a result of the increase in price level is a result of its effect on their profits; firms have an incentive to increase real output when the prices of the goods they are selling are rising faster than the costs of the inputs they use in production.

Note that point B in Exhibit 2 is positioned beyond $RGDP_{FE}$. It seems peculiar that the economy can operate beyond its potential, but this is possible, temporarily, as firms encourage workers to work overtime, extend the hours of part-time workers, hire recently retired employees, reduce frictional unemployment through more extensive searches for employees, and so on. However, this level of output and employment cannot be sustained in the long run. Because the price level is now higher, workers become disgruntled with wages that have not yet adjusted to the new price level (if prices have risen, but wages have not risen as much, real wages have fallen). Recall that along the SRAS curve, wages and other input prices are assumed to be constant. Therefore, workers' and input suppliers' purchasing power falls as output prices rise. Real (adjusted for inflation) wages have fallen. Consequently, workers and other suppliers demand higher prices to be willing to supply their inputs. As input prices respond to the higher level of output prices, the short-run aggregate supply curve shifts to the left, from $SRAS_0$ to $SRAS_1$. Suppliers will continually seek higher prices for their inputs until they reach the new long-run equilibrium, point C in Exhibit 2. At point C, input suppliers' purchasing power is now restored at full employment equilibrium. The only difference from point A is the new, higher price level.

Concept C | **279** | **Macroeconomic Equilibrium**

EXHIBIT 2	DEMAND-PULL INFLATION

EXHIBIT 3	COST-PUSH INFLATION

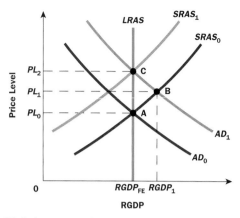

Demand-pull inflation occurs when the aggregate demand curve shifts to the right along the short-run aggregate supply curve. This leads, however, to rising input prices, which raises costs and shifts the SRAS curve to the left, until AD and SRAS once again intersect on the LRAS curve.

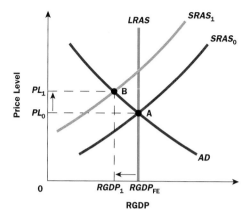

Cost-push inflation is caused by a leftward shift in the aggregate supply curve, from $SRAS_0$ to $SRAS_1$.

WHAT IS COST-PUSH INFLATION?

The 1970s and early 1980s witnessed a phenomenon known as **stagflation,** where lower growth and higher prices occurred together. Some economists believe that this was caused by a leftward shift in the aggregate supply curve, as seen in Exhibit 3. If the aggregate demand curve did not change significantly and the price level increased, then the inflation was caused by supply-side forces, not demand. This is what is called **cost-push inflation.**

The primary culprits responsible for the leftward shift in the aggregate supply curve were OPEC and the price of

oil, as oil barrel prices reached record high levels during that period ($40 dollars a barrel as compared to less than $15 today). As we discussed in the last Concept, an increase in input prices can cause the short-run aggregate supply curve to shift to the left, and this spelled big trouble for the U.S. economy—higher price levels, lower output, and higher rates of unemployment. The impact of cost-push inflation is illustrated in Exhibit 3.

In Exhibit 3, we see that the economy is initially at full employment equilibrium at point A. Now suppose there is a sudden increase in input prices, such as the increase in the price of oil. This increase would shift the SRAS curve to the left—from $SRAS_0$ to $SRAS_1$. As a result of the shift in short-run aggregate supply, the price level rises to PL_1 and real output falls to $RGDP_1$ from $RGDP_{FE}$ (point B). Now firms may demand fewer workers as a result of the higher input costs that cannot be passed on to the consumers. The result is higher prices, lower real output, and more unemployment.

WHAT HELPED THE UNITED STATES RECOVER?

As far as energy prices are concerned, the 1980s witnessed falling oil prices as OPEC lost some of its clout due to internal problems. In addition, many non-OPEC oil producers increased production. The net result was a rightward shift in the aggregate supply curve. Holding aggregate demand constant, this rightward shift in the aggregate supply curve would lead to lower prices, greater output, and lower rates of unemployment.

"GO BACK TO SLEEP, ALAN... IF THERE IS A MONSTER IN YOUR CLOSET, IT'S ONLY A LITTLE ONE!"

Could too much money chasing too few goods cause demand-pull inflation?

ANOTHER CAUSE OF RECESSION

Just as cost-push inflation can cause a recession, so can a decrease in aggregate demand. For example, consider the case in which consumer confidence plunges and the stock market "tanks." As a result, aggregate demand would fall, shown in Exhibit 4 as the shift from AD_0 to AD_1. Now, at every price level, households, firms, and governments are buying fewer goods and services. In response to this drop in demand, output would fall from $RGDP_{FE}$ to $RGDP_1$, and the price level would fall from PL_0 to PL_1. So, in the short run, this fall in aggregate demand causes higher unemployment and a reduction in output.

HOW PRECISE IS THE AGGREGATE SUPPLY AND DEMAND MODEL?

In this Module, we have been shifting the aggregate supply and aggregate demand curves around as if we knew exactly what we were doing. But it is very important to mention that the AD/AS model is a crude tool.

In the supply and demand curves covered in Modules 4 and 5, we saw how this simple tool is very rich in explanatory power. But even supply and demand analysis does not always provide precise estimates of the shifts or of the exact price and output changes that accompany those shifts. However, while supply and demand analysis is not perfect, it does provide a framework to predict the direction that certain important variables will change under different circumstances.

The same is true in the AD/AS model, but it is less precise because of the complexities and interrelationships that exist in the macroeconomy. The slopes of the aggregate de-

EXHIBIT 4 — SHORT-RUN DECREASE IN AGGREGATE DEMAND

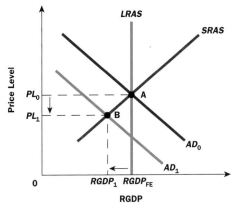

A fall in aggregate demand from a drop in consumer confidence can cause a short-run change in the economy. The decrease in aggregate demand (shown in the movement from point A to point B) causes lower output and higher unemployment in the short run.

mand and aggregate supply curves, the magnitudes of the shifts, and the interrelationship of the variables are to some extent a mystery. For example, if a reduction in aggregate demand leads to lower real GDP and, as a result, there are fewer workers that are willing to look for work, it impacts the aggregate supply curve. There are other examples of the interdependence of the aggregate demand and aggregate supply curves that make this analysis not completely satisfactory. Nevertheless, the framework still provides important insights into the workings of the macroeconomy.

CONCEPT CHECK

1. Short-run macroeconomic equilibrium is determined by the intersection of the aggregate demand curve and the short-run aggregate supply curve. A short-run equilibrium is also a long-run equilibrium only if it is at potential output on the long-run aggregate supply curve.
2. Demand-pull inflation occurs when the price level rises as a result of an increase in aggregate demand.

3. Firms have an incentive to increase real output if the price of the goods they are selling is rising faster than the cost of their inputs. As this happens, though, suppliers and workers experience diminished purchasing power. In the long run, input suppliers will demand higher wages or other input prices, and the end result will be a higher price level—inflation.
4. Cost-push inflation is caused by a leftward shift in the short-run aggregate supply curve.

1. What is demand-pull inflation?
2. What is cost-push inflation?
3. Starting from long-run equilibrium on the long-run aggregate supply curve, what happens to the price level, real output, and unemployment as a result of cost-push inflation?

4. How would a drop in consumer confidence impact the short-run macroeconomy?
5. What would happen to the price level, real output, and unemployment in the short run if world oil prices fell sharply?

Application: El Niño and the AD/AS Model

How will a supply shock like El Niño-induced flooding impact short-run aggregate supply? How about long-run aggregate supply?

EFFECTS OF EL NIÑO FELT IN LETTUCE HARVEST, PRICES

SALINAS, California (AP)— The heavy rains have stopped but the effects of El Niño storms on supermarket produce have only begun. Growers in California, the nation's top farm state, say incessant rains earlier this year sharply reduced the supply of lettuce and the shortage will be a problem until at least the middle of May. "El Niño weather conditions out here have created a little havoc with the supply situation," grower-shipper Frank Pinney said last week. "We expect a roller-coaster effect for the next four to five weeks with supply."

California's planting season, December through spring, was interrupted by storms that drenched the region in January and February. "Guys couldn't get the tractors in the field to do proper fertilization, aeration and cultivation," Pinney said. In some instances, farmers couldn't plant for about three weeks.

Shortages will be felt especially among loose leaf lettuce, growers said. "Romaine, red leaf, and green leaf are in very short supply," said Steve Adlesh, sales director at Apio, a grower and lettuce shipper in northern Santa Barbara County. "This is only going to maintain itself for the next two weeks. By the beginning of May, it should improve, but it will be fragmented as far as the supply goes for the next month." Just how short the supply will be remains in question, but Adlesh said it could be as low as 50 percent of normal during some weeks.

The price already has doubled. A box of 24 heads of lettuce, which usually costs $8 to $10, ranged from $16 to $25

Friday, Adlesh said. Although it's difficult to translate the increases into supermarket prices, Adlesh said he thinks lettuce that typically costs 60 to 70 cents a head would be $1 or more.

There are problems other than missing planting season. "Yields will be off due to fungus and other moisture-related diseases," Pinney said. "Plants in general will be weaker with more defects, and they will have shorter shelf life." Growers said they hope the supply will begin leveling out as the peak summer season begins in Salinas Valley. But the effects of earlier losses won't be forgotten quickly. "I have never seen a year like this before and I think it goes across the board for other farmers," said Pinney, who's been in the lettuce business for 25 years.

SOURCE: http://cnn.com/US/9804/21/lettuce.prices.ap/index.html.

In Exhibit 1, we see the impact of bad weather on the aggregate supply curve. These unanticipated adverse effects are called supply shocks. In 1997–1998, the shock was El Niño; in other years, it was major flooding in the Midwest that destroyed a considerable portion of the wheat crop. Unexpected bad weather causes production costs in input markets to rise. As a result of this increase, the aggregate supply curve shifts to the left.

Supply shocks are not always bad news. Unusually good weather can cause production costs to fall, resulting in a rightward shift of the aggregate supply curve. It is also possible that a major oil discovery would have the same effect—lowering production costs and shifting the aggregate supply curve to the right. Unless these shocks permanently alter an economy's productive capacity, however, they will not affect long-run aggregate supply. For example, a bad crop due to unusual weather one year does not imply a reduced output of that crop next year, and the falling of oil prices one year does not guarantee that oil prices will stay down the next year.

EXHIBIT 1   **THE EL NIÑO EFFECT**

ONE STEP BEYOND

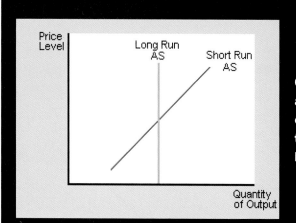

Can you supply all of the answers when it comes to long- and short-term aggregate supply and macroeconomic equilibrium? Test your mastery of these concepts using the exercises in your Workbook and the self-tests on the EconActive CD-ROM!

Fiscal Policy

A. Fiscal Policy
What is fiscal policy?

B. The Multiplier Effect
How can the total impact of an initial increase
in purchases be calculated?

C. Fiscal Policy and the AD/AS Model
How can government stimulus or contraction of aggregate
demand change inflation or unemployment?

D. Possible Obstacles to Effective Fiscal Policy
What factors can reduce the effectiveness of a fiscal policy?

E. Automatic Stabilizers
How do automatic stabilizers affect the economy?

F. Supply-Side Economics
Does fiscal policy have a supply side?

G. Fiscal Policy in its Prime—the 1960s
Why were the early 1960s a model for effective fiscal policy?

H. Financing the Deficit
How does the government finance its budget deficit?

I. Application: The Balanced Budget Amendment
Do we want a balanced budget amendment?

Fiscal Policy

- What is fiscal policy?
- How does expansionary fiscal policy affect the government's budget?
- How does contractionary fiscal policy affect the government's budget?

WHAT IS FISCAL POLICY?

It is possible that short-run equilibrium real GDP can be accompanied by undesirably high levels of unemployment and/or high price levels. The government can use fiscal policy to change such results. **Fiscal policy** is the use of government purchases, taxes, and transfer payments to alter real GDP and price levels.

When government spending (for purchases of goods and services and transfer payments) exceeds tax revenues, there is a **budget deficit.** When tax revenues are greater than government spending, a **budget surplus** ex-

ists. A balanced budget, where government expenditures equal tax revenues, may seldom occur unless efforts are made to deliberately balance the budget as a matter of public policy.

Deficits and Expansionary Fiscal Policy

In the United States, the federal government has followed a typical practice of running at least a modest deficit, with large deficits in recession years, such as in the early 1980s and early 1990s (see Exhibit 1). From 1970 to 1997, the federal budget was in a deficit in every year. In many of those years, particularly since the 1970s, the deficit was fairly

---

EXHIBIT 1 | **THE U.S. FEDERAL BUDGET DEFICIT AS A PERCENT OF GDP**

The budget is projected to be in balance in fiscal 1999 for the first time since 1969.

SOURCES: Department of Commerce (Bureau of Economic Analysis) and Office of Management and Budget.

---

substantial, often exceeding 2 percent of GDP. Thus, federal government policy, until very recently, seems to have gotten away from the notion accepted by many economic policymakers in earlier years that the budget ought to be roughly balanced over the business cycle, running surpluses in good times and offsetting deficits in bad times. While the growing U.S. economy is forecast to generate a federal budget surplus in 1999, and possibly beyond, the size of government has been rising steadily, with increased government spending in this country and other industrial countries as well, as seen in Exhibit 2, financed by a combination of increased taxes and larger budget deficits.

HOW IS THE BUDGET AFFECTED BY FISCAL STIMULUS?

When the government wishes to stimulate the economy by increasing aggregate demand, it will increase government purchases of goods and services, increase transfer payments, lower taxes, or use some combination of these approaches. Any of those options will increase the budget deficit (or reduce the budget surplus). Thus, **expansionary fiscal policy** is associated with increased government budget deficits. Likewise, if the government wishes to dampen a boom in the economy by reducing aggregate demand, it will reduce its purchases of goods and services, increase

taxes, reduce transfer payments, or use some combination of these approaches. Thus, **contractionary fiscal policy,** will tend to create or expand a budget surplus, or reduce a budget deficit, if one exists.

"In a compromise move to cut the budget, Congress and the president agreed to move the decimal one point to the left."

GLOBAL WATCH

GOVERNMENT SPENDING AS A PERCENT OF GDP

EXHIBIT 2								
Country	1870	1913	1920	1937	1960	1980	1990	1996
Canada	—	—	13.3	18.6	28.6	38.8	46.0	44.7
France	12.6	17.0	27.6	29.0	34.6	46.1	49.8	54.5
Germany	10.0	14.8	25.0	42.4	32.4	47.9	45.1	49.0
Italy	11.9	11.1	22.5	24.5	30.1	41.9	53.2	52.9
Japan	8.8	8.3	14.8	25.4	17.5	32.0	31.7	36.2
Norway	3.7	8.3	13.7	—	29.9	37.5	53.8	45.5
Sweden	5.7	6.3	8.1	10.4	31.0	60.1	59.1	64.7
Britain	9.4	12.7	26.2	30.0	32.2	43.0	39.9	41.9
United States	3.9	1.8	7.0	8.6	27.0	31.8	33.3	33.3

The United States government spending is a smaller percentage of GDP than that in most other industrial countries. However, there is a clear trend towards bigger government.

SOURCE: IMF.

1. Fiscal policy is the use of government purchases of goods and services, taxes, and transfer payments to affect aggregate demand and alter GDP and price levels.
2. Expansionary fiscal policies will increase the budget deficit (or reduce a budget surplus) through greater government spending, lower taxes, or both.

3. Contractionary fiscal policies will create a budget surplus (or reduce a budget deficit) through reduced government spending, higher taxes, or both.

1. If, as part of its fiscal policy, the federal government increased its purchases of goods and services, would that be an expansionary or contractionary tactic?
2. If the federal government decreased its purchases of goods and services, would the budget deficit increase or decrease?
3. If the federal government increased taxes or decreased transfer payments, would that be an expansionary or contractionary fiscal policy?

4. If the federal government increased taxes or decreased transfer payments, would the budget deficit increase or decrease?
5. If the federal government increased government purchases and lowered taxes at the same time, would the budget deficit increase or decrease?

The Multiplier Effect

- What is the multiplier effect?
- How does the marginal propensity to consume affect the multiplier effect?
- How does investment interact with the multiplier effect?

WHAT CAN CAUSE A DECREASE IN TOTAL PURCHASES?

The GDP will change anytime the amount of any one of the four forms of purchases—consumption, investment, government purchases, and net exports—changes. If, for any reason, people generally decide to purchase more in any of these categories out of given income, aggregate demand will shift rightward.

WHAT CAN CAUSE A CHANGE IN TOTAL OUTPUT?

Any one of the components of purchases of goods and services (C, I, G, or $X - M$) can initiate changes in aggregate demand, and thus a new short-run equilibrium. Changes in total output are often brought about by alterations in investment plans, because investment purchases are a relatively volatile category of expenditures. However, if policymakers are unhappy with the present short-run equilibrium GDP, perhaps because they consider unemployment too high, they can deliberately manipulate the level of government purchases in order to obtain a new short-run equilibrium value. Similarly, by changing taxes or transfer payments, they can alter the amount of disposable income of households and thus bring about changes in consumption purchases.

WHAT IS THE MULTIPLIER EFFECT?

Usually when an initial increase in purchases of goods or services occurs, the ultimate increase in total purchases will tend to be greater than the initial increase. This is called the **multiplier effect.** But how does this effect work? Suppose the government increases its defense budget by $10 billion to buy aircraft carriers. When the government purchases the aircraft carriers, not only does it add to the total demand for goods and services directly, it also provides $10 billion in added income to the companies that actually construct the aircraft carriers. Those companies will then hire more workers and buy more capital equipment and other inputs in order to produce the new output. The owners of these inputs therefore receive more income because of the increase in government purchases. And what will they do with this additional income? While behavior will vary somewhat among individuals, collectively they will probably spend a substantial part of the additional income on additional consumption purchases, pay some additional taxes incurred because of the income, and save a bit of it as well. The additional consumption purchases made as a portion of the additional income is measured by the **marginal propensity to consume (MPC).**

HOW DOES THE MULTIPLIER EFFECT WORK?

Suppose that out of every dollar in *added* income generated by increased investment purchases, individuals collectively spend two-thirds, or 67 cents on consumption purchases. In other words, the MPC is 2/3. The initial $10 billion increase in government purchases causes both a $10 billion increase in aggregate demand and an income increase of $10 billion to suppliers of the inputs used to produce aircraft carriers; the owners of those inputs, in turn, will spend an additional $6.67 billion (two-thirds of $10 billion) on additional consumption purchases. A chain reaction has been started. The added $6.67 billion in consumption purchases by those deriving income from the initial investment brings a $6.67 billion increase in aggregate demand and in new income to suppliers of the inputs that produced the goods and services. These persons, in turn, will spend some two-thirds of their additional $6.67 billion in income, or $4.44 billion on consumption purchases. This means a $4.44 billion more in aggregate demand and income to still another group of persons, who will then proceed to spend two-thirds of that amount, or $2.96 billion on consumption purchases.

The chain reaction continues, with each new round of purchases providing income to a new group of persons who, in turn, increase their purchases. At each round, the added income generated and the number of resulting

EXHIBIT 1   THE MULTIPLIER PROCESS

Round	Increase in Income Generated (billions of dollars)	Increase in Purchases (billions of dollars)
1	$10.00	$10.00—direct effect on AD
2	6.67	6.67
3	4.44	4.44
4	2.96	2.96
5	1.98	1.98
6	1.32	1.32
7	.88	.88
8	.59	.59
9	.39	.39
Total all Rounds	$30.00	$30.00 = Total effect on purchases (AD)

The sum of the indirect effect on AD, through induced additional consumption purchases is equal to $20 billion

consumer purchases get smaller, because some of each round's increase in income goes to savings and tax payments that do not immediately flow into greater investment or government expenditure. As Exhibit 1 indicates, by the eighth or ninth round of purchases, the magnitude of further rounds of the process are much smaller than the initial round. What is the total impact of the initial increase in purchases, after all the rounds of additional purchases and income have occurred? The multiplier is calculated as follows:

$$\text{Multiplier} = 1/(1 - MPC)$$

In this case,

$$\text{Multiplier} = 1/(1 - 2/3) = 1/(1/3) = 3$$

An initial increase in purchases of goods or services of $10 billion, then, will increase total purchases by $30 billion ($10 billion × 3), as the $10 billion in investment purchases also generates an additional $20 billion in consumption purchases.

HOW DO CHANGES IN THE MPC AFFECT THE MULTIPLIER PROCESS?

Note that the larger the marginal propensity to consume, the larger the multiplier effect, because relatively more additional consumption purchases out of any given income increase generates relatively larger secondary and tertiary income effects in successive rounds of the process. For example, if the MPC is 3/4, the multiplier is 4:

$$\text{Multiplier} = 1/(1 - 3/4) = 1/(1/4) = 4$$

If the MPC is only one-half, however, the multiplier is 2:

$$\text{Multiplier} = 1/(1 - 1/2) = 1/(1/2) = 2$$

THE MULTIPLIER AND THE AGGREGATE DEMAND CURVE

As we discussed earlier, when the Defense Department decides to buy additional aircraft carriers, it affects aggregate demand. It increases the incomes of owners of inputs used to make the aircraft carriers, including profits that go to owners of the firms involved. That is the initial effect. The secondary effect, the greater income that results, will lead to increased consumer purchases. In addition, the higher profits for the firms involved in carrier construction may lead them to increase their investment purchases. So the initial effect of the government's purchases will tend to have a multiplied effect on the economy. In Exhibit 2, we see that the initial impact of a $10 billion additional purchase by the government directly shifts the aggregate demand curve from AD_0 to AD_1. The multiplier effect then causes the aggregate demand to shift out $20 billion further, to AD_2. The total effect on aggregate demand of a $10 billion increase in government purchases is therefore $30 billion, if the marginal propensity to consume equals two-thirds.

EXHIBIT 2   **THE MULTIPLIER AND AGGREGATE DEMAND**

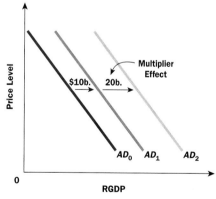

In this hypothetical example, an increase in government purchases of $10 billion for new aircraft carriers will shift the aggregate demand curve to the right by more than the $10 billion initial purchase, other things equal. It will shift aggregate demand by a total of $30 billion, to AD_2. (The shifts are shown larger than they would really be, for visual ease—$30 billion is a small shift in an $8,000 billion economy.)

HOW DO TIME LAGS, TAXES, AND IMPORTS AFFECT THE MULTIPLIER?

The multiplier process is not instantaneous. If I get an additional $100 in income today, I may spend two-thirds of that on consumption purchases eventually, but I may wait six months or even longer to do it. Such time lags mean that the ultimate increase in purchases resulting from an initial increase in purchases may not be achieved for a year or more. The extent of the multiplier effect visible within a

STEALTH BOMBERS AND MULTIPLIERS

DAVE BERRY

So far the B-2 project has cost us taxpayers $45 billion, which has purchased us 21 bombers, which works out to around $2 billion per bomber, making it the most expensive airplane ever built (bear in mind, however, that it comes with floor mats).

Now here's the problem: The General Accounting Office did a big study of the B-2 bomber, concluding that—I will try to put this in layperson's terms—flying is bad for it. Yes. It turns out that the secret stealthy materials are sensitive to moisture, which as luck would have it (Who could have predicted this?) is plentiful in the atmosphere, so according to the GAO, after the B-2 flies, it tends to need lots of costly repairs.

SOURCE: Dave Barry, "At Least the Stealth Bomber Has the Sense to Get Out of the Rain," *The Sacramento Bee,* http://www.sacbee.com/voices/national/barry/barry_oct26.html October 26, 1997

CONSIDER THIS:

In the real world, the multiplier process is important because it may help explain why small changes in consumption, investment, and government purchases can cause larger, multiplied changes in total purchases. These increased purchases, in turn, could lead to increased real output and reduced unemployment when the economy is not already fully employed.

In this application, when the government purchased the stealth bombers, we are assuming that it would not have purchased other goods and services with those same dollars instead. This is important because the purchase of B-2s has the potential to lead to a net increase in demand only so far as it increases total government purchases, which, if the economy is less than fully employed, will increase real output and employment. That is, the increase in demand for stealth bombers, other things equal, will lead to an increase in output for General Dynamics (which builds the B-2). As a result, General Dynamics will hire more employees, who will take their paychecks and spend some of it on clothes, restaurant meals, and other goods and services. Those purchases will result in further growth in those industries, many of which are located far from the B-2 plant. In other words, a government purchase has the potential to have an impact on the economy that is greater than the magnitude of that original purchase. This is the multiplier process at work.

However, if the stealth bomber purchases just replace other government purchases, the multiplied expansion in defense-related industries is offset by a multiplied contraction in industries where government purchases have fallen.

Contrast this example with government purchases of food for a school lunch program. Government purchases of school lunches rise, but private consumption falls as parents now purchase less food—perhaps by the same amount—for their children's lunches. Overall, we would expect only a small change in demand, if any, as government demand replaces private demand. In some real sense, the suppliers of apples, milk, cookies, and chips have just had the names of their customers change.

short time period will be less than the total effect indicated by the multiplier formula. In addition, savings, taxes, and money spent on import goods (which are not part of aggregate demand for domestically produced goods and services) will reduce the size of the multiplier, because each of them reduces the fraction of a given increase in income that will go to additional purchases of domestically produced consumption goods.

CONCEPT CHECK

1. The multiplier effect is a chain reaction of additional income and purchases that results in a final increase in total purchases that is greater than the initial increase in purchases.
2. An increase in the marginal propensity to consume leads to an increase in the multiplier effect.
3. Because of a time lag, the full impact of the multiplier effect on GDP may not be felt until a year or more after the initial investment.
4. An increase in government purchases will also cause an increase in aggregate income and stimulate additional consumer purchases, which will result in a magnified (or multiplying) effect on aggregate demand.

1. How does the multiplier effect work?
2. What is the marginal propensity to consume?
3. Why is the marginal propensity to consume always less than one?
4. Why does the multiplier effect get larger as the marginal propensity to consume gets larger?
5. If an increase in government purchases leads to a reduction in private-sector purchases, why could the effect on the economy be less than indicated by the multiplier?

Fiscal Policy and the AD/AS Model

- How can government stimulus of aggregate demand reduce unemployment?
- How can government reduction of aggregate demand reduce inflation?

FISCAL POLICY AND THE AD/AS MODEL

The primary tools of fiscal policy, government purchases, taxes, and transfer payments, can be presented in the context of the aggregate supply and demand model. In Exhibit 1, we have used the AD/AS model to show how the government can use fiscal policy as either an expansionary or contractionary tool to help control the economy.

BUDGET DEFICITS AND FISCAL POLICY

As we discussed earlier, when the government purchases more, taxes less, and increases transfer payments, the size of the government's budget deficit will grow. While budget deficits are often thought to be bad, a case can be made for using budget deficits to stimulate the economy when it is operating at less than full capacity. Such expansionary fiscal policy may have the potential to move an economy out of a recession and closer to full employment.

Expansionary Fiscal Policy at Less Than Full Employment

If the government decides to purchase more, cut taxes, and/or increase transfer payments, other things constant, total purchases will rise. That is, increased government purchases, tax cuts, or transfer payment increases can increase consumption, investment, and government purchases, shifting the aggregate demand curve to the right. The effect of this increase in aggregate demand depends on the position of the macroeconomic equilibrium prior to the government stimulus. For example, in Exhibit 1(a), the initial equilibrium is at E_0, a recession scenario, with real output below potential RGDP. Starting at this point and moving along the short-run aggregate supply curve, an increase in government purchases, a tax cut, and/or increase in transfer payments would increase the size of the budget deficit and lead to an increase in aggregate demand, ideally from AD_0 to AD_1. The result of such a change would be an increase in the price level, from PL_{100} to PL_{115}—an increase of 15 percent—and an increase in real GDP, from $RGDP_0$ to $RGDP_{FE}$. We must remember, of course, that some of this increase in aggregate demand is caused by the multiplier process, so the magnitude of the change in aggregate demand will be larger than the magnitude of the stimulus package of tax cuts, increases in transfer payments, and/or government purchases. If the policy change is of the right magnitude and timed appropriately, the expansionary fiscal policy might stimulate the economy, pulling it out of recession, resulting in full employment at $RGDP_{FE}$.

Expansionary Fiscal Policy at Full Employment

Now suppose that the economy is currently operating at full employment—$RGDP_{FE}$. This is seen as point E_0 in Exhibit 1(b). An increase in government spending, an increase in transfer payments, and/or a tax cut causes an increase in aggregate demand from AD_0 to AD_1. Moving along short-run aggregate supply curve $SRAS_0$, the price level rises and real output rises to $RGDP_1$ as we reach a short-run equilibrium at E_1. This is not a long-run, or sustainable, equilibrium, however, because at this point, the high level of aggregate demand at beyond full capacity will put pressure on input markets, sending wages and other input prices higher. The higher costs that result from these input price increases will shift the short-run aggregate supply curve leftward from $SRAS_0$ to $SRAS_1$. This, in turn, shifts the short-run equilibrium point from E_1 to E_2, which, because it is on the long-run aggregate supply curve, is a sustainable long-run equilibrium. So we see that real output returns to the full employment level, and the long-term effect is a 20 percent increase in the price level, from PL_{100} to PL_{120}.

BUDGET SURPLUSES AND FISCAL POLICY

When the government purchases less, taxes more, or decreases transfer payments, the size of the government's

| EXHIBIT 1 | **EXPANSIONARY FISCAL POLICY** |

a. At Less Than Full Employment

b. At Full Employment

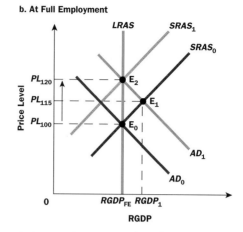

An increase in government purchases, an increase in transfer payments, and/or a tax cut at less than full employment

An increase in government purchases, an increase in transfer payments, and/or a tax cut at full employment

In Exhibit 1(a), the increase in government purchases, a tax cut, and/or an increase in transfer payments leads to a rightward shift in aggregate demand. This results in a change in equilibrium from E_0 to E_1, reflecting a higher price level and a higher RGDP. Because this result is on the LRAS curve, it is a long-run, sustainable equilibrium. In Exhibit 1(b), we see that the same policy change will only lead to a short-run increase in RGDP. Once input owners realize that the price level has changed, they will require higher input prices, raising costs and shifting the SRAS curve to the left. The final long-run equilibrium will only reflect the new higher price level (PL_{120}).

budget deficit will fall or the size of the budget surplus will rise, other things equal. Sometimes such a change in fiscal policy may help "cool off" the economy when it has overheated and inflation has become a serious problem. Then, contractionary fiscal policy has the potential to offset an overheated, inflationary boom.

Contractionary Fiscal Policy beyond Full Employment

Suppose that the price level is at PL_{130} and that short-run equilibrium is at E_0, as shown in Exhibit 2(a). Say that the government decides to reduce its purchases, increase taxes, or reduce transfer payments. A government purchase change may directly affect aggregate demand. A tax increase on consumers or a decrease in transfer payments will reduce households' disposable incomes, reducing purchases of consumption goods and services, and higher business taxes will reduce investment purchases. The reductions in consumption, investment, and/or government purchases will shift the aggregate demand curve leftward, ideally from AD_0 to AD_1. This lowers the price level from PL_{130} to PL_{100} and brings RGDP back to the full employ-

ment level at $RGDP_{FE}$, resulting in a new short- and long-run equilibrium at E_1.

A Contractionary Fiscal Policy at Full Employment

Now consider the case of an initial short- and long-run equilibrium at full employment, as indicated by point E_0, with a price level of PL_{130}, where AD_0 intersects both the SRAS curve and the LRAS curve. This situation is depicted in Exhibit 2(b). A decrease in aggregate demand from AD_0 to AD_1 that results from a reduction in government purchases, higher taxes, or lower transfer payments leads to a short-run equilibrium at E_1, with lower prices and real output reduced below its full employment level at $RGDP_1$. As prices fall, input suppliers then revise their price level expectations downward. That is, laborers and other input suppliers are now willing to take less for the use of their resources, and the resulting reduction in production costs shifts the short-run supply curve from $SRAS_0$ to $SRAS_1$. The resulting eventual long-run equilibrium is a reduction in the price level, with real output returning to its full employment.

EXHIBIT 2   **CONTRACTIONARY FISCAL POLICY**

a. Beyond Full Employment

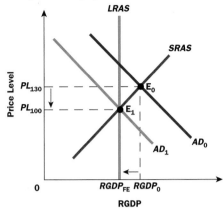

A reduction in government purchases, a decrease in transfer payments, and/or higher taxes beyond full employment

b. At Full Employment

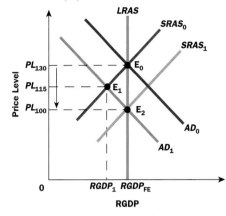

A reduction in government purchases, a decrease in transfer payments, and/or higher taxes at full employment

In Exhibit 2(a), the reduction in government purchases, tax increase, or transfer payment decrease leads to a leftward shift in aggregate demand and a change in the short-run equilibrium from E_0 to E_1, reflecting a lower price level and a return to full employment RGDP ($RGDP_{FE}$). In Exhibit 2(b), the reduction in aggregate demand leads to a short-run equilibrium at E_1, reflecting a lower price level and real output below its full employment level. At this point, input owners change their price level expectations and are now willing to accept lower compensation. This reduces production costs and shifts short-run aggregate supply to the right, from $SRAS_0$ to $SRAS_1$. The final long-run effect is a new lower price level and real output that has returned to $RGDP_{FE}$.

IN THE NEWS

JAPAN'S LEADER FAVORS PERMANENT TAX CUTS

TOKYO—Isolated by growing pressure for quick action to fix its anemic economy, Japan's prime minister on Friday said for the first time that he would support a permanent tax cut to stimulate consumer spending.

"I hope we will have not temporary tax cuts, but so-called permanent tax reforms. I think we'll move in that direction," Ryutaro Hashimoto said. Until now, he had favored one-time tax breaks instead of longer-term tax relief.

Temporary tax cuts failed to stimulate the economy in the past because the Japanese—

known for their high savings rate—simply squirreled away the extra money. Officials contend that a permanent tax break will bolster consumer confidence, lead to greater spending and help Japan out of its worst recession since World War II.

Hashimoto had previously resisted going beyond temporary tax relief measures for fear of ballooning the deficit, which he has pledged to shrink.

SOURCE: "Japan's Leader Favors Permanent Tax Cuts," *Los Angeles Times*, July 4, 1998, p. D1.

CONSIDER THIS:
Japan's former prime minster realized the importance of expansionary fiscal policy—permanent tax cuts to stimulate aggregate demand. However, the Japanese voted Hashimoto and his ruling party out of office as a result of his disastrous decision to *raise* consumption taxes and his tardiness on prescribing permanent tax cuts.

1. If the government decided to purchase more, cut taxes, and/or increase transfer payments, that would increase total purchases and shift out the aggregate demand curve.
2. If the correct magnitude of expansionary fiscal policy is used in a recession, it could potentially bring the economy to full employment.

3. Expansionary fiscal policy at full employment may lead to short-run increases in output and employment, but in the long run, the expansionary effect will only lead to higher price levels.
4. Contractionary fiscal policy has the potential to offset an overheated inflationary boom.

---

1. If the economy is in recession, what sorts of fiscal policy changes would tend to bring it out of recession?
2. If the economy is at a short-run equilibrium at greater than full employment, what sorts of fiscal policy changes would tend to bring the economy back to a full employment equilibrium?

3. What effects would an expansionary fiscal policy have on the price level and real GDP, starting from a full employment equilibrium?
4. What effects would a contractionary fiscal policy have on the price level and real GDP, starting from a full employment equilibrium?

Possible Obstacles to Effective Fiscal Policy

- How does the crowding out effect limit the economic impact of increased government purchases or reduced taxes?
- What is the Ricardian equivalence theorem?
- How do time lags in policy implementation affect policy effectiveness?

WHAT IS THE CROWDING OUT EFFECT?

The multiplier effect of an increase in government purchases implies that the increase in aggregate demand will tend to be greater than the initial fiscal stimulus, other things equal. However, this may not be true, because all other things will not tend to stay equal in this case. In particular, when the government borrows money to finance the deficit, it increases the overall demand for loanable funds, driving interest rates up. The increase in the demand for loanable funds sends the interest rate up (from r_0 to r_1), as seen in Exhibit 1(a). The higher interest rate means that

the opportunity cost of borrowing funds has risen. As a result of the higher interest rate, consumers may decide against buying a car, a home, or other interest-sensitive good, and businesses may cancel or scale back plans to expand or buy new capital equipment. In short, the higher interest rate will choke off private spending on goods and services, and as a result, the impact of the increase in government purchases may be smaller than we first assumed. Economists call this the **crowding out effect.** For example, in Exhibit 1(b), say the federal government borrows to finance a deficit created by expansionary fiscal policy. The increase in government spending and the multiplier shifts

---

EXHIBIT 1	THE CROWDING OUT EFFECT

a. Loanable Funds Market

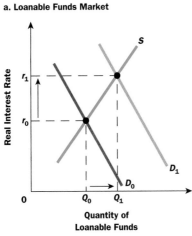

b. Changes in Aggregate Demand

In Exhibit 1(a), we see that if the government's demand for loans is added to the private sector demand for loans, demand increases, shifting from D_0 to D_1. This leads to a higher real interest rate and lower levels of investment and consumption. The lower levels of investment can either partially or completely offset the fiscal policy effect, shifting aggregate demand to the left from AD_1 to AD_2, or all the way back to AD_0.

---

the aggregate demand curve to the right, from AD_0 to AD_1. However, as this process takes place, interest rates are bid up, as seen in Exhibit 1(a). The higher real interest rate leads to a reduction in private-sector spending, because borrowing is now more expensive. This reduction in private spending shifts the aggregate demand curve from AD_1 to AD_2. If every dollar of government purchases crowded out a dollar of private purchases (100 percent crowding out), fiscal policy would have no *net* effect on aggregate demand, shifting the aggregate demand curve all the way back to AD_0.

In Exhibit 1(a), we see that when the government increases its borrowing to pay for increases in government purchases, the demand for loanable funds shifts the curve to the right (from D_0 to D_1), causing the equilibrium interest rate to rise. In Exhibit 1(b), we see that an initial $10 billion increase in government purchases, by itself, would shift aggregate demand right by $10 billion times the multiplier, from AD_0 to AD_1. However, because of the higher interest rates resulting from the additional government borrowing, interest-sensitive investments for consumers and businesses are choked off (seen in Exhibit 1(a)), which, by itself, would cause the aggregate demand curve to shift left by the purchases crowded out times the multiplier, from AD_1 to AD_2. Because both these processes are taking place at the same time, the net effect is an increase in aggregate demand equal to the difference between the added government purchases and the private purchases crowded out by higher interest rates, times the multiplier, or from AD_0 to AD_2.

The Crowding Out Effect in the Open Economy

Another form of crowding out can take place in international markets. For example, say the government cut taxes and is now running a larger budget deficit. To finance the deficit the United States government borrows more money—increasing the demand for loanable funds and driving up the interest rate. This is the basic crowding out effect. However, the higher U.S. interest rate will attract funds from abroad. In order to invest in the U.S. economy, foreigners will have to first convert their currencies into dollars. The increase in the demand for dollars relative to other currencies, will cause the dollar to appreciate in value, making foreign imports relatively cheaper in the U.S. and U.S. exports relatively more expensive in other countries. This will cause net exports $(X - M)$ to fall for two reasons. One, because of the higher relative price of the dollar, foreign imports become cheaper for those in the U.S., and imports will increase. Two, because of the higher relative price of the dollar, U.S.-made goods become more expensive to foreigners, so exports fall. The increase in imports and the decrease in exports causes a reduction in net exports and a fall in aggregate demand. The net effect, is that to the extent net exports are crowded out, fiscal policy

has a smaller effect on aggregate demand than it would otherwise.

WHAT IS THE RICARDIAN EQUIVALENCE THEOREM?

Another related problem undermining the power of fiscal policy to change aggregate demand is expressed in what is called the **Ricardian equivalence theorem.** This theory is named for the famous economist David Ricardo, who first presented this argument in the 1800s. The argument is that an increase in aggregate demand that would be expected as a result of an increase in government purchases will be partially or fully offset by an increase in savings (which is the same as a reduction in consumption purchases). If people realize that the increase in government purchases will lead to higher taxes in the future, they may increase their savings now to pay for those higher future taxes. Thus, the expected increase in aggregate demand as a result of an increase in government spending is offset by the reduction in current consumption as individuals save for the future tax increase. Just as with the crowding out effect, this implies that fiscal policy will have a smaller effect on aggregate demand than otherwise predicted. The more current consumption falls in response to the fiscal policy stimulus, the less effective that stimulus is in raising income. If savings changes exactly offset the fiscal stimulus, there will be no net effect on aggregate demand.

Graphically, this short-run effect looks much the same as the results of the crowding out effect shown in Exhibit 1(b). As a result of the government purchases alone, aggregate demand would shift rightward by the increase in government purchases, times the multiplier, from AD_0 to AD_1. To the extent individuals respond by saving more to pay the greater future tax burden and consuming less, the effect of this on aggregate demand would be to shift it left by the reduction in consumption purchases times the multiplier, or AD_1 to AD_2. The net effect is to increase aggregate demand from AD_0 to AD_2. If consumers fully anticipate the future tax liability, there will be no net effect on aggregate demand. It should be noted, however, that the empirical evidence of the 1980s does not fully support the theory, as large budget deficits were not accompanied with increases in the savings rate. In fact, since the early 1980s decreases in private savings have accompanied the large and growing budget deficits.

WHY ARE THERE TIME LAGS IN POLICY IMPLEMENTATION?

It is important to recognize that in a democratic country, fiscal policy is implemented through the political process, and that process takes time. Often, the lag between the time that a fiscal response is desired and the time an appropriate policy is implemented and its effects felt is considerable. Sometimes a fiscal policy designed to deal with a contracting economy may actually take effect during a period of economic expansion, or vice versa, resulting in a stabilization policy that actually destabilizes the economy.

HOW DOES THE POLICY MAKING PROCESS WORK?

Government tax or spending changes require both congressional and presidential approval. Suppose the economy is beginning a downturn. It may take two or three months before enough data are gathered to indicate the actual presence of a downturn. Sometimes a future downturn can be forecast through econometric models or by looking at the index of leading indicators, but usually decision makers are hesitant to plan policy on the basis of forecasts that are not always accurate.

At some point, however, policymakers may decide that some policy change is necessary. At this point, experts are consulted, and congressional committees have hearings about and listen to testimony on possible policy approaches. During the consultation phase, many decisions have to be made. If, for example, a tax cut is recommended, what form should the cut take and how large should it be? Across-the-board income tax reductions? Reductions in corporate taxes? More generous exemptions and deductions from the income tax (e.g., for child care, casualty losses, education of children)? In other words, who should get the benefits of lower taxes? Likewise, if the decision is made to increase government expenditures, which programs should be expanded or initiated and by how much? These are questions with profound political consequences, so reaching a decision is not always easy and usually involves much compromise and a great deal of time.

Finally, once the House and Senate have completed their separate deliberations and have arrived at a final version of the bill, it is presented to Congress for approval. After congressional approval is secured, the bill then goes to the president for approval or veto.

HOW LONG DOES IT TAKE FOR APPROVED POLICY TO TAKE EFFECT?

Even after legislation is signed into law, it takes time to bring about the actual fiscal stimulus desired. If the legislation provides for a reduction in withholding taxes, for example, it might take a few months before the changes actually show up in workers' paychecks. With respect to changes in government purchases, the delay is usually much longer. If the government increases spending for public works projects like sewer systems, new highways,

or urban renewal, it takes time to draw up plans and get permissions, to advertise for bids from contractors, to get contracts, and then to begin work. And there may be further delays because of government regulations. For example, an environmental impact statement must be completed before most public works projects can begin, a process that often takes many months or even years.

WHY IS TIMING SO IMPORTANT?

The timing of fiscal policy is crucial. Because of the significant lags before the fiscal policy has its impact, the increase in aggregate demand may occur at the wrong time. For example, imagine that we are initially at AD_0 in Exhibit 2. The economy is currently suffering from low levels of output and high rates of unemployment. In response, policymakers decide to increase government purchases and implement a tax cut. But during the period from the time when the policymakers recognized the problem to the time when the policies had a chance to work themselves through the economy, there was a large increase in business and consumer confidence, shifting the aggregate demand curve rightward from AD_0 to AD_1—increasing real GDP and employment. Now when the fiscal policy takes effect, the policies will have the undesired effect of causing inflation, with little permanent effect on output and employment. This is seen in Exhibit 2, as the aggregate demand curve shifts from AD_1 to AD_2.

EXHIBIT 2	TIMING EXPANSIONARY FISCAL POLICY

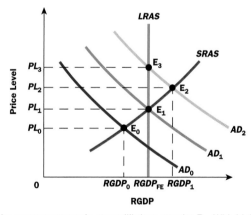

Initially, the macroeconomy is at equilibrium at point E_0. With high unemployment (at $RGDP_0$), the government decides to increase government purchases and cut taxes to stimulate the economy. This shifts aggregate demand from AD_0 to AD_1 over time—perhaps 12 to 16 months. In the meantime, if consumer confidence increases, the aggregate demand curve might shift to AD_2, leading to much higher prices (PL_3) in the long run, rather than at the target level, E_1, at price level PL_1.

TAXATION, GOVERNMENT ACTIVITY, AND ECONOMIC GROWTH

TALKING TAXES

- In terms of the size of its tax burden, the United States is a relatively low-tax nation: It is 21st of the 24 industrialized countries in the Organization for Economic Cooperation and Development.
- In terms of growth in taxes from 1965 to 1993, America was 23rd in the OECD.
- Various economic studies have shown that government taxation produces a drag on the economy that can amount to as much as 50 cents per dollar of tax revenues collected.
- Tax increases are usually accompanied by declines in per capita growth in GDP.

Why does government activity seem to impede economic growth? The reasons include the following:

Few economic incentives for efficiency in the public sector: Managers of government activities seldom receive rewards for initiating cost-reducing or output-enhancing measures. Indeed, in some cases, increases in productivity may mean the manager in question has a smaller budget and also must incur the wrath of fellow employees who suffer from the changes that generate an increase in output per worker.

Government monopolies: For many government services, there is a single provider that does not feel pressure to cut costs to meet competition from other providers of goods and services. The lack of competition may explain why, by most measures, productivity has not risen rapidly in the provision of, for example, education and postal services.

Special-interest groups: As government grows, efforts to use the political process to redistribute income from the general taxpaying public to specific individuals or groups intensify. Highway contractors promote "infrastructure investment," public employees seek large salary increases, businesses lobby for subsidies, and still others favor public assistance of one form or another.

Government regulation: In a world of limited government, private entrepreneurs have incentives to raise productivity—to use fewer resources to produce a given quantity of output. Government regulation, if it is heavy, interferes with this activity, leading to lower productivity. While some regulation may be needed, it can easily become excessive and generate more costs than benefits.

The political process: In the public sector, legislators, in particular, think primarily in terms of the immediate future. They are attuned to the rhythm of electoral cycles. In response to these cycles, they will often take actions that they perceive to be in their electoral interest but which have adverse long-term effects on economic activity.

This is not to say that all government activity is counterproductive. There are valuable things government does to enhance the functioning of an economy, such as providing for the common defense, establishing a legal framework for resolving disputes, constructing a basic infrastructure, and supervising a social safety net. These are the positive works of government.

But there are diminishing returns to government activity. And, as government expands—and so increases the level of taxation to finance its activities—the inefficiencies just described become more and more pronounced.

SOURCE: Lowell Gallaway, "Taxes around the World," *The World & I*, July 1996, pp. 100–105.

> **CONSIDER THIS:**
> While taxes may not be high in the United States relative to other countries, there may be other reasons why Americans find taxation and increased government activity burdensome.

CONCEPT CHECK

1. The crowding out effect states that as the government borrows to pay for the deficit, it drives up the interest rates and crowds out private spending and investment.
2. According to the Ricardian equivalence theorem, an increase in government spending will lead to higher taxes in the future, other things equal. If people save for the predictable future tax increase, there will be a reduction in current consumption. This would reduce, and could even completely offset, the effect of a fiscal stimulus.

3. The lag time between when a fiscal policy may be needed and when it is actually implemented is considerable.

---

1. Why does a larger government budget deficit increase the magnitude of the crowding out effect?
2. Why does fiscal policy have a smaller effect on aggregate demand, the greater the crowding out effect?
3. Why does the Ricardian equivalence theorem imply that if people correctly recognize the future tax liability represented by a current budget deficit, and save enough to pay for those future taxes as a result, then fiscal policy may have no effect on aggregate demand?

4. How do time lags impact the effectiveness of fiscal policy?

Automatic Stabilizers

MODULE 12

■ What are automatic stabilizers?

■ Which automatic stabilizers are the most important?

WHAT ARE AUTOMATIC STABILIZERS?

Some changes in government transfer payments and taxes take place automatically as business cycle conditions change, without deliberations in Congress or the executive branch of the government. Changes in government transfer payments or tax collections that automatically tend to counter business cycle fluctuations are called **automatic stabilizers.**

HOW DOES THE TAX SYSTEM STABILIZE THE ECONOMY?

The most important automatic stabilizer is the tax system. For example, with the personal income tax, as incomes rise, tax liabilities also increase automatically. Personal income taxes vary directly in amount with income, and in fact rise or fall by greater percentage terms than income itself rises or falls. Big increases and big decreases in GDP are both lessened by automatic changes in income tax receipts. For example, GDP declines, tax liabilities decline, increasing disposable incomes and stimulating consumption spending, partly offsetting the initial decline in aggregate demand.

There are, of course, other income-related payroll taxes, notably Social Security taxes. In addition, there is the corporate profit tax. Because incomes, earnings, and profits all fall during a recession, the government collects less in taxes. This reduced tax burden partially offsets the magnitude of the recession. Beyond this, the unemployment compensation program is another example of an automatic stabilizer. During recessions, unemployment is usually high

and unemployment compensation payments increase, providing income that will be consumed by recipients. During boom periods, such payments will fall as the number of the unemployed declines. The system of public assistance (welfare) payments tends to be another important automatic stabilizer, as the number of low-income persons eligible for some forms of assistance grows during recessions (stimulating aggregate demand) and declines during booms (reducing aggregate demand).

Automatic stabilizers work without legislative action.

ENTITLEMENT FRAUD GIVES "PRISON SECURITY" NEW MEANING

E.V. KONTOROVICH

William Bonin, California's infamous "freeway killer," spent 14 years on death row—about as long as the entire lives of the 21 boys he confessed to murdering. During his stretch in San Quentin, Bonin was getting monthly checks from the U.S. Treasury, some as high as $589. By the time his sentence was finally carried out in 1996, he had collected about $80,000 in Social Security payments while in prison.

Prisoners are ineligible for Social Security and most other benefit programs. Since the taxpayer already pays for their room, board, medical benefits and sometimes legal counsel, sending them benefit checks would amount to giving the perps pocket money. The Social Security Administration has always said it was vigilant about such fraud,

but its Bonin blunder was spotted only when his death papers were being shuffled.

Embarrassed by the error and hounded by the parents of Bonin's victims, the agency conducted an internal investigation, which concluded that Bonin's benefits were a fluke. Well, not quite. Congress began looking into the matter, and last March—two years after the Bonin mess—the SSA's inspector general, David Williams, admitted that some 60,000 inmates were taking the taxpayer to the tune of $500 million a year in fraudulent benefits.

Social Security isn't the only program from which prisoners profit: A GAO study of four states last year found that roughly 12,000 inmates were receiving illegal food stamp benefits because of the program's

"reliance on client-provided information"—the same obvious error as the SSA's.

SOURCE: E.V. Kontorovich, "Entitlement Fraud Gives 'Prison Security' New Meaning," *Wall Street Journal,* June 15, 1998.

> **CONSIDER THIS:**
> Although Social Security taxes are an automatic stabilizer that can help the economy, some people take advantage of them. Democrats and Republicans both want to get tough on government fraud on transfer programs.

CONCEPT CHECK

1. Automatic stabilizers are changes in government transfer payments or tax collections that happen automatically and whose effects vary inversely with business cycles.

2. The tax system is the most important automatic stabilizer; it has the greatest ability to smooth out swings in GDP during business cycles. Other automatic stabilizers are unemployment compensation and welfare payments.

1. How does the tax system act as an automatic stabilizer?
2. Are automatic stabilizers impacted by a time lag? Why or why not?

3. Why are transfer payments, such as unemployment compensation, effective automatic stabilizers?

Supply-Side Fiscal Policy

- What is supply-side fiscal policy?
- How do supply-side policies affect long-run aggregate supply?
- What do its critics say about supply-side ideas?

WHAT IS SUPPLY-SIDE FISCAL POLICY?

The debate over short-run stabilization policies has been going on for some time, and there is no sign that it is close to being settled. When policymakers discuss methods to stabilize the economy, the focus since the 1930s has been on managing the economy through demand-side policies. But there is a group of economists who believe that we should be focusing on the supply side of the economy as well, especially in the long run, rather than just on the demand side. In particular, they believe that individuals will save less, work less, and provide less capital when taxes, government transfer payments (like welfare), and regulations are too burdensome on productive activities. In other words, they believe that fiscal policy can work on the supply side of the economy as well as the demand side.

HOW WOULD SUPPLY-SIDE POLICIES IMPACT THE ECONOMY?

Supply-siders would encourage government to reduce individual and business taxes, deregulate, and increase spending on research and development. Supply-siders believe that these types of government policies could cause greater long-term economic growth by stimulating personal income, savings, and capital formation.

DO LOWER TAX RATES AFFECT THE SUPPLY SIDE OF THE ECONOMY?

"Supply-siders" believe that savings and investment could be improved through lowering taxes. Imagine that your family had $100,000 in a savings account with an interest rate of 10 percent per year. At the end of the year, the account would have accrued $10,000 in interest—but the interest is taxable, say at 30 percent. So instead of receiving $10,000, your family would receive only $7,000 in interest after taxes. According to supply-siders, this reduced after-tax return to saving discourages people from saving, and

that has wide-ranging implications, because greater savings encourages greater investment and capital formation.

WHY IS INVESTMENT IMPORTANT?

Workers without capital cannot be very productive. For example, a fisherman with only his hands will not do as well as those with capital such as nets, boats, and sonar equipment. That is, worker productivity (output per worker) depends to a large extent on the capital that is available to the worker. So taxing savings and investment heavily will reduce new capital investment, which will reduce the growth of worker productivity.

Businesses might also get similar relief in the form of **investment tax credits.** These allow businesses to accelerate the speed that businesses can write off some of their new investments for tax purposes, raising after-tax rates of return on investment. This tax break would also encourage firms to invest in new capital, raising worker productivity.

HOW DOES GOVERNMENT REGULATION AFFECT THE SUPPLY CURVE?

As we discussed in Module 6, it is important that government provide certain regulations for the environment, workers' safety, consumer protection, and so on. However, the costs imposed on producers as a result of these regulations have an effect similar to taxes, and as a result, make goods and services more expensive. As a result, these regulations reduce the economy's potential production, reflected in a leftward shift of the aggregate supply curve.

For example, in its attempt to provide health benefits to consumers, the Food and Drug Administration (FDA) often takes years to approve new drugs. These procedures are very costly and increase the price of new drugs. Higher minimum wages, designed to ensure workers a "livable" wage, also increase the cost of doing business and the unemployment rate in the unskilled labor market. This is also true of the Family Leave Act, which allows workers to be absent from work for up to 12 weeks without losing their fringe benefits, such as health care. All of these government regulations shift the short- and long-run aggregate supply curves to the left, because they increase the cost of producing these goods, which drives up prices for consumers, and they reduce the economy's potential real output. For this reason, supply-siders support reductions in government regulations where the benefits don't justify the costs.

WHAT EFFECT DO HIGHER MARGINAL TAX RATES HAVE ON WORKERS?

Some economists emphasize the idea that higher marginal tax rates will discourage people from working as much as they otherwise would. Recall that the *marginal* tax rate is the tax rate on the last, or marginal, dollar earned from additional work, and that workers are concerned with their after-tax earnings. A lower marginal tax rate will raise after tax earnings, improving productive incentives—it may entice more people to seek work, it may encourage workers to postpone their retirement, it may mean that more workers will work longer hours, and it could lead to more two-income families in the labor force. It is also possible that the high tax rates reduce work efforts in the market sector and encourage work efforts in the underground economy instead, where cash and barter transactions are very difficult to observe and tax.

WHAT EFFECT DO HIGHER TAX RATES HAVE ON INVESTORS?

Higher tax rates also discourage investment. In pursuit of higher after-tax returns on investment, both foreign and domestic investors will tend to seek areas where taxes are lower, *ceteris paribus*. Higher marginal tax rates will also lead investors to spend more scarce resources looking for tax shelters, which harms the economy, as high-return but highly taxed investments give way to lower-return tax shelters. For example, tax-free municipal bonds may be substituted for higher-return investments that are taxable.

HOW DOES RESEARCH AND DEVELOPMENT IMPACT THE SUPPLY-SIDE OF THE ECONOMY?

Some economists believe that investment in research and development will have long-run benefits for the economy. In particular, greater research and development will lead to new technology and knowledge, which will permanently shift the short- and long-run aggregate supply curves to the right. The government could encourage investments in research and development by giving tax breaks or subsidies to firms.

HOW DO SUPPLY-SIDE POLICIES AFFECT LONG-RUN AGGREGATE SUPPLY?

We see in Exhibit 1 that rather than being primarily concerned with short-run economic stabilization, supply-side policies are aimed at increasing both the short-run and long-run aggregate supply curves. If these policies are successful and maintained, output and employment will increase in the long run, as seen in the shift from $RGDP_{FE}$ to $RGDP'_{FE}$. Both short- and long-run aggregate supply will increase over time, as the effects of deregulation and major structural changes in plant and equipment work their way through the economy. It takes workers some time to fully respond to improved work incentives.

DO THESE POLICIES ALSO AFFECT THE AGGREGATE DEMAND?

You can see in Exhibit 1 that in addition to the aggregate supply curves, the aggregate demand curve is also shifting to the right. For example, if supply-siders call for a reduction in tax rates, it is quite possible that the demand-side stimulus from the increased disposable income (income after taxes) that results may be equal to, or even greater than may the supply-side effects. This causes higher price levels, and even greater short-run real output levels, although the long-run real output level increases with the long-run aggregate supply curve.

ANDY CAPP By Reggie Smythe

Reprinted by permission of North American Syndicate

Is this an example of fiscal policy operating on the supply side?

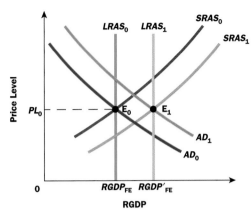

The impact of a reduction in tax rates and regulations and investments in research and development could create long-term effects on income, savings, and capital formation, shifting both the SRAS curve and the LRAS curve rightward. As income rises, it is spent, shifting the aggregate demand curve to the right.

WHAT DO THE CRITICS SAY ABOUT SUPPLY-SIDE ECONOMICS?

Of course, those that believe in the supply-side effects of fiscal policy have their critics. The critics are skeptical of the magnitude of the impact of lower taxes on work effort and the impact of deregulation on productivity. Critics claim that the tax cuts of the 1980s led to moderate real output growth but only through a reduction in real tax revenues, inflation, and large budget deficits.

While real economic growth followed the tax cuts, the critics say that it came as a result of a large budget deficit. And the critics question whether people will save and invest much more if capital gains taxes are reduced (capital gains are increases in the value of an asset). How much more work effort will we see if marginal tax rates are lowered? Will the new production that occurs from deregulation be enough to offset the benefits thought by many to come from regulation?

WHAT IS THE RESPONSE TO THE SUPPLY-SIDE CRITICS?

Defenders of the supply-side approach argue that the real tax revenues of those in the highest marginal tax brackets actually increased as their tax rates fell in the 1980s (as they also had for earlier reductions in tax rates on the most heavily taxed high income groups) and that, compared to other developed countries in the world, the United States had very prosperous growth from 1982 to 1989. In addition, many supply-siders argue that most of their policy prescriptions were never really even tried, for at least three reasons. First, many of supply-siders' proposals for improving productive incentives were ignored, and in some cases, productive incentives were made worse rather than better. Second, the real output effects of the initial tax cuts were minimized by the restrictive, inflation fighting policies of the Federal Reserve in the early 1980s. Third, Congress did not reduce federal expenditures, which was at least partially responsible for the growing deficit.

CONCEPT CHECK

1. Supply-side fiscal policy advocates believe that people will save less, work less, and provide less capital when taxes, government transfer, and regulations are too burdensome.
2. Supply-side policies are designed to increase output and employment in the long run, causing the long-run and short-run aggregate supply curves to shift to the right.

3. Critics of supply-siders question the magnitude of impact of lower taxes on work effort, saving, and investment and the impact of deregulation on productivity.

1. Is supply-side economics more concerned with short-run economic stabilization or long-run economic growth?
2. Why could you say that supply-side economics is really more about after-tax wages and after-tax returns on investment than it is about tax rates?

3. Why do government regulations have the same sorts of effects on businesses as taxes?
4. Why aren't the full effects of supply-side policies seen quickly?
5. If taxes increase, what would you expect to happen to employment in the underground economy? Why?

Fiscal Policy in Its Prime—The 1960s

- How did Kennedy's fiscal stimulus affect our economy?
- Can a tax cut lead to larger tax revenues?

HOW DID KENNEDY'S EXPANSIONARY POLICY AFFECT OUR ECONOMY?

Real GDP rose only very slowly in 1960 and 1961 and unemployment increased; by 1961, the unemployment rate of 6.7 percent approached the highest rate since the Depression. The new President, John F. Kennedy, was lectured on the need for counter-cyclical fiscal policy by his chairman of the Council of Economic Advisers, Walter Heller, and two future Nobel laureates in economics, James Tobin and Robert Solow. Kennedy accepted the view that a more expansionary policy was needed, and he advocated both some increase in government spending and a tax cut. In short, he wanted to use both fiscal policy mechanisms to

How did President Kennedy fine-tune the economy of the early 1960s?

shift the aggregate demand curve to the right. (Supply-siders believe that the tax cut stimulated work effort—it is sometimes hard to tell "what causes what"!) In fiscal 1962, federal government spending rose by $9 billion, or more than 9 percent, while revenues rose by only $5 billion. The doubling of the federal deficit (from $3 to $7 billion) provided added stimulus to the economy. The 1962 unemployment rate fell to 5.5 percent, a major drop from the previous year, and real GDP surged by more than 6 percent. Given the substantial slack in the economy, the increase in output and employment was not accompanied by massive inflation. The GDP deflator rose by only a bit over 1 percent a year in both 1961 and 1962.

In addition, President Kennedy proposed an investment tax credit plan that lowered taxes for firms that invested in new capital equipment. The impact of this move was to shift out the aggregate supply curve. The impact of these policies on the two curves is shown in Exhibit 1.

| EXHIBIT 1 | THE 1961 KENNEDY TAX CUT |

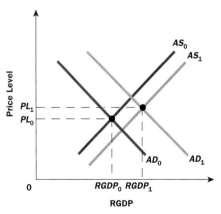

The Kennedy tax cut, increase in government spending, and investment tax credit in the early 1960s led to greater output and employment and only slightly higher price levels (shifting from PL_0 to PL_1).

Module 12 | **308** | Fiscal Policy

DID JOHNSON CONTINUE TO FOLLOW TRADITIONAL FISCAL POLICY?

President Lyndon B. Johnson, Kennedy's successor, defied tradition and conventional fiscal policy response by announcing plans in his 1965 inaugural address for a great expansion in governmental social welfare programs in the tradition of Franklin D. Roosevelt's New Deal of three decades earlier. Between fiscal year 1965 and fiscal year 1968, government spending increased by more than $60 billion—over 50 percent. While tax revenues rose as personal income increased, tax rates were not increased, and the increase in tax revenues was much smaller than the growth in expenditures. In fiscal year 1968, the federal government's deficit exceeded $25 billion, roughly 3 percent of GDP. The fiscal stimulus when the economy was at full employment came at a considerable cost, as the inflation rate more than doubled to over 4 percent a year with little effect on real output or unemployment, as seen in Exhibit 2.

WHAT ARE THE DANGERS OF FISCAL POLICY?

The success of the fiscal policy of the early 1960s in reducing unemployment in a largely non-inflationary manner is often cited as an example of how fiscal policy can work. The factual evidence seemed undeniable at the time. It is

| EXHIBIT 2 | JOHNSON'S "GREAT SOCIETY" |

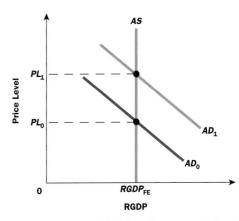

In the late 1960s, the Johnson Administration pursued a large increase in government spending programs. With tax revenues rising at a slower rate than spending, a large deficit caused the aggregate demand curve to shift to the right, from AD_0 to AD_1. Because the economy was already at full employment, the stimulus program resulted in higher prices with little increases in output and employment.

true, however, that when politicians saw the *political* gains from economic stimulus, it led to excesses, such as the post-1965 stimulus that brought about increasing inflation.

CONCEPT CHECK

1. Kennedy's stimulus (an increase in government spending and a tax cut) led to a large increase in GDP, decreases in unemployment, and only a very small increase in inflation.

2. Johnson's increase in government spending and large budget deficits during full employment led to an increase in the price level with little effect on real output or unemployment.

1. When President Kennedy cut tax rates and instituted an investment tax credit, was he using a demand-side or a supply-side strategy?
2. If Kennedy's policy had been adopted during a period of full employment, would it have worked as well? Why or why not?

3. What effect did President Johnson's economic policies have on the economy?

Financing the Deficit

■ Is the national debt a problem for our economy?

■ Who are the three major types of buyers of federal debt?

■ How do the effects of selling Treasury bonds to these three groups vary?

HOW CAN A GOVERNMENT FINANCE A BUDGET DEFICIT?

How has the government run continuous budget deficits for such a long period of time? After all, it has to have some means of paying out the funds necessary to support government expenditures that are in excess of the funds derived from tax payments. One thing the government could do is simply print money—dollar bills. This approach was used to finance much of the Civil War budget deficit, both in the North and in the Confederate States. However, printing money to finance activities is highly inflationary and also undermines confidence in the government. The more respectable and conservative method of financing deficits is by issuing debt. The federal government in effect borrows an amount necessary to cover the deficit by issuing bonds, or IOUs, payable typically at some maturity date. The sum total of the values of all bonds outstanding constitutes the federal debt. As Exhibit 1 indicates, the ten-

dency of the federal government to engage in budget deficits has led to increasing federal debt over time.

The increase in federal government debt since 1945 has actually been much less than the growth in GDP, so the total debt today equals the value of only 5 or 6 months of total U.S. GDP, compared with nearly 15 months of output in 1945.

HOW DOES THE DEBT AFFECT OUR ECONOMY?

Is a national debt of $5 trillion life-threatening to the economy? The answer is surprisingly "no." However, it does have an impact on the economy. To begin, the debt is primarily an obligation of the United States government to its citizens; relatively little of the debt is typically owned by foreigners (10 to 15 percent), although that amount has grown in recent years—foreigners currently own about 17 percent of the debt. Since 1980, the national debt has

Is the national debt a problem?

	PUBLIC DEBT, FEDERAL
EXHIBIT 1	**GOVERNMENT, SELECTED YEARS**

Fiscal Year	Public Debt (billions of dollars)	Public Debt as a Percentage of GDP
1929	$16.9	18%
1940	43.0	45
1945	260.2	120
1950	256.8	94
1955	274.4	69
1960	290.5	56
1965	322.3	47
1970	380.9	38
1975	541.9	35
1980	909.1	33
1985	1,817.5	44
1990	3,206.6	56
1996	5,207.3	71

SOURCES: Office of Management and Budget, 1997.

grown from over 30 percent to roughly 70 percent of GDP, and as a result of large deficits and reduced national savings, both public and private savings fell. When the government borrows to finance the debt, it causes the interest rate to rise. The higher interest rate will crowd out private investment by households and firms. To make interest payments on the debt, the government must use existing tax revenues. Currently, such debt service absorbs only a bit more than 3 percent of GDP. Thus, resources equal to about one week's GDP per year must be taken from the taxpaying public and transferred to the owners of debt. It is when the interest on the debt is very large that the redistribution of income to bondholders by way of higher taxes on productive workers may have damaging disincentive and morale effects.

IS THE NATIONAL DEBT A HUGE PROBLEM?

The public debt does not pose a serious problem for two other reasons. First, a large proportion of the debt (about 30 percent in recent years) is actually "owned" by the government itself, in trust funds supporting such activities as Social Security or federal deposit insurance. The Federal Reserve System, a quasi-governmental agency, owns another 10 percent of the debt. The remaining 60 or 65 percent of the debt is held outside the federal government by state and local governments (roughly 30 percent), financial institutions (10 to 15 percent), foreign investors (10 to 15 percent), and U.S. individuals (5 to 10 percent). Second, the government does not have to repay the debt in the sense that it must reduce its debt obligations to zero. When a bond matures (comes due), the government can issue a new bond to obtain funds to pay off the owner of the maturing bond. The government is constantly refunding its debt just as private corporations often refund theirs. To be sure, the

ability of the government to refund depends on the willingness of people to buy its bonds. As long as the federal government retains control over resources with its taxing powers and continues to honor its debt obligations, however, refunding the debt should not be a major problem.

WHO BEARS THE BURDEN OF PUBLIC DEBT?

The "burden" of the debt is a topic that has long interested economists, particularly whether it falls on present or future generations. Arguments can be made that the generation of taxpayers living at the time that the debt is issued shoulders the true cost of the debt, because the debt permits the government to take command of resources that might be available for other, private uses. In a sense, the resources its takes to purchase government bonds might take away from private activities, such as private investment financed by private debt. There is no denying, however, that the issuance of debt does involve some intergenerational transfer of incomes. Long after federal debt is issued, a new generation of taxpayers is making interest payments to persons of the generation that bought the bonds issued to finance that debt. If public debt is created intelligently, however, the "burden" of the debt should be less than the benefits derived from the resources acquired as a result; this is particularly true when the debt allows for an expansion in real economic activity or for the development of vital infrastructure for the future. The opportunity cost of expanded public activity may be very small in terms of private activity that must be foregone to finance the public activity, if unemployed resources are put to work. The real issue of importance is whether the government's activities have benefits that are greater than costs; whether taxes are raised, money is printed, or deficits are run are for the most part "financing issues."

CONCEPT CHECK

1. Our national debt is not a serious problem for our economy. Much of the debt is owned by the government itself; only 10 to 15 percent is owned by foreigners. Also, the benefits of debt in terms of economic expansion may be greater than the opportunity cost of lost private investment activity.
2. The government finances a budget deficit primarily by issuing debt to government agencies, private institutions, and private individuals.

3. Selling new debt issues to public agencies, such as the Federal Reserve System or to private institutions, tends to have a more expansionary impact than selling debt to private individuals because the purchase of government debt by individuals tends to result in reduced consumption.

1. Why can't the federal government finance its debt by printing more money?
2. How can the federal government finance the national debt?

3. Should we worry about the national debt?
4. What must be true for Americans to be better off as a result of an increase in the federal debt?

Application: The Balanced Budget Amendment

What are the arguments for and against balancing the budget? If we had a balanced budget, how could we allow the government to run deficits during emergencies?

THE BALANCED BUDGET AMENDMENT

BACKGROUND: The United States has not had a balanced budget since 1969. Over the last quarter of a century, Congress has consistently demonstrated its inability to devise a federal spending plan in which outlays do not exceed revenues. Thus, today, we are faced with a national debt which exceeds $5.32 trillion.

The balanced budget amendment was a significant component of the Republican party's 1994 "Contract with America." The amendment would generally prohibit the federal government from spending more than it receives in revenue in any given year. Such legislation would eliminate the budget deficit and would allow us to begin to work to reduce the nation's long-term debt. The proposal includes an exception to permit Congress to run a deficit during times of war or national emergency if both chambers vote to do so by a three-fifths supermajority. In order for a Constitutional amendment to be ratified, it must receive a two-thirds vote in each chamber of Congress and must be ratified by three-quarters of the states.

STATUS: During the 104th Congress, the House passed the balanced budget amendment by a vote of 300 to 132. However, the Amendment received only 65 votes in the Senate, 1 vote less than the two-thirds required for passage.

In January 1997, Senator Orrin Hatch (R-UT) and 62 co-sponsors introduced the balanced budget amendment in the Senate as S J Res 1. With the election of so many fiscally conservative Democrats to the Senate in 1996, passage there seemed imminent. However, in the weeks prior to the vote, some of the Democrats who promised to vote for the bill defected, arguing that the amendment did not sufficiently protect Social Security. As a result, the balanced budget amendment was defeated in the Senate on March 4, 1997 by a vote of 66 to 34.

Although supporters of the amendment pledged that the fight is not over, the fact that the federal budgets for the next several years are expected to be in surplus has made near-term passage of a balanced budget amendment less likely.

SOURCE: AED Issue Summary, March 27, 1998: The Balanced Budget Amendment http://www.aednet.org/govt/legissue/balbud.htm

From 1960 to 1998, the federal budget has been in deficit every year except one, when the government ran a small balanced surplus in 1969. However, some economists believe the real problem is not the deficit but rather that federal spending is out of control. Some individuals believe that we must control the deficits through responsible fiscal restraint—a belief that has prompted a drive to add a balanced budget amendment to the U.S. Constitution.

But the possibility that the spending activities of the federal government may be constitutionally restricted is terrifying to some. Opponents' arguments can be summarized as follows:

By the powers vested, we declare ourselves joined at the wallet

So long as we both shall prosper

BALANCED BUDGET

First, at best, a balanced budget amendment would be ineffective because there is no way to guarantee that revenues and expenditures will always match up on an annual basis. Second, at worst, a balanced budget amendment would reduce the fiscal flexibility of the federal government, thereby making it more difficult to respond appropriately to changing economic circumstances. Furthermore, if the public really wants the government to balance its budget, our elected representatives already have the power to respond to this desire.

It is certainly true that no amendment to the Constitution can ensure that the budget will ever be perfectly balanced. It is impossible to predict either revenues or expenditures over a specified interval. And there are circumstances in which budget flexibility can be justified. Finally, it is true that Congress has the control over taxing and spending needed to eliminate the chronic deficits if it chooses to do so. Given that this is the case, why should we clutter up the Constitution with a balanced budget amendment?

Proponents of a balanced budget amendment argue that, in the absence of fiscal restraints, excessive government spending will occur because the private advantages that each of us realizes from spending on our government programs are paid for almost entirely by other taxpayers. Of course, each of us suffers from having to pay for the programs of others, and most of us would be willing to reduce our special-interest demands if others would do the same. But we all recognize that as long as we continue to pay for the programs of others, there is no advantage in reducing our individual demands on the government treasury. In this uncontrolled setting, we are in a spending free-for-all, with penalties for the fiscally responsible and rewards for the fiscally irresponsible.

Of course, if all it took to balance the federal budget was for the American public to want it balanced, it would have been balanced a long time ago. According to public opinion polls, the vast majority of the American public wants the federal government to balance its budget. In an ideal world in which broad public preferences were transmitted effectively through political institutions, there would be no need for a balanced budget amendment to control spending. However, political institutions, even democratic political institutions, can be exploited by the organized few to gain special-interest benefits at the expense of the unorganized many.

Of course, a balanced budget amendment could be written that would allow the government to run deficits in time of special emergencies like military involvement, earthquakes, fires, or floods. In addition, the voters might adopt a plan that would allow for a two-thirds vote to increase the deficit or that would opt for a running average balanced budget instead of balancing the budget every year. Any of these proposals could work towards controlling runaway federal spending to some degree.

The most important issue of all might be at what *level* the budget should be balanced. Many would prefer deficits in a small budget to a much larger, but balanced, budget. However, the real issue, as always, is: Are we getting government goods and services with benefits that are greater than costs?

ONE STEP BEYOND

Is there a deficit in your understanding of how the government impacts the economy through its fiscal policies? Don't worry—there is a surplus of information on expansionary and contractionary fiscal policies, the multiplier effect (shown here), the crowding out effect, and supply-side policies in your Workbook and on the EconActive CD-ROM!

Money and the Banking System

A. What Is Money?
What are the different forms of
money?

B. The Functions of Money
What is the purpose of money?

C. The Demand for Money
Why do people choose to hold money?

D. How Banks Create Money
What is the process for increasing the supply of money?

E. The Money Multiplier
How does a new loan lead to multiple expansions in the money supply?

F. The Collapse of America's Banking System, 1920–1933
What led to the collapse of the banking system
between 1920 and 1933?

G. Application: Internet Banking
Are Internet banks the banks of the future?

(A) What Is Money?

■ What is money?
■ In what forms is money held?
■ What is included in the money supply?
■ Why have demand deposits become less popular?

WHAT IS MONEY?

Money is anything that is generally accepted in exchange for goods or services; it is a medium of exchange. In colonial times, commodities such as tobacco and wampum (Native American trinkets) were sometimes used as money. At some times and in some places, even cigarettes and whiskey have been used as money. But commodities have several disadvantages when used as money, the most important of which is that many commodities deteriorate easily after a few trades. Precious metal coins have been used for money for millennia, partly because of their durability.

WHAT IS CURRENCY?

Currency consists of coins and / or paper that some institution or government has created to be used in the trading of goods and services and the payment of debts. Currency in the form of metal coins is still used as money throughout the world today. But metal currency has a disadvantage: It is bulky. Also, certain types of metals traditionally used in coins, like gold and silver, are not available in sufficient quantities to meet our demands for a monetary instrument. For these reasons, metal coins have for centuries been supplemented by paper currency, often in the form of bank notes. In the United States, the Federal Reserve System issues Federal Reserve Notes in various denominations, and this paper currency, along with coins, provides the basis for most transactions of relatively modest size in the United States today.

Is this money?

What is currency? What makes this paper and metal valuable?

HOW DOES CURRENCY BECOME LEGAL TENDER?

In the United States and in most other nations of the world, metallic coins and paper currency are the only forms of **legal tender.** In other words, coins and paper money have been officially declared to be money—to be acceptable for the settlement of debts incurred in financial transactions. In effect, the government says, "We declare these instruments to be money, and citizens are expected to accept them as a medium of exchange." Legal tender is **fiat money**—a means of exchange that has been established not by custom and tradition, or because of the value of the metal in a coin, but by government fiat, or declaration.

WHAT ARE CHECKABLE DEPOSITS?

Most of the money that we use for day-to-day transactions, however, is not official legal tender. Rather, it is a monetary instrument that has become "generally accepted" in exchange over the years and has now, by custom and tradition, become money. What is this instrument? It is assets in checking accounts in banks, more formally called **demand deposits.**

Demand deposits are defined as deposits in banks that can be withdrawn on demand, by simply writing a check. Some other forms of accounts in financial institutions also have virtually all of the attributes of demand deposits. For example, there are also other checkable deposits that earn interest but have some restrictions, such as higher monthly fees or minimum balance requirements. These interest-earning checking accounts effectively permit the depositors to write "orders" similar to checks and assign the

rights to deposit to other persons, just as we write checks to other parties. Practically speaking, funds in these accounts are the equivalent of demand deposits and have become an important component in the supply of money. Both of these types of accounts are forms of **transaction deposits,** because they can be easily converted into currency or used to buy goods and services directly. **Travelers checks,** like currency and demand deposits, are also easily converted into currency or used directly as a means of payment.

WHY IS THE USE OF DEMAND DEPOSITS AND OTHER CHECKABLE DEPOSITS SO POPULAR?

Why have demand deposits and other checkable deposits replaced paper and metallic currency as the major source of money used for larger transactions in the United States and in most other relatively well-developed nations? There are several reasons, including ease and safety of transactions, lower transaction costs, and transaction records.

Ease and Safety of Transactions

Paying for goods and services with a check is easier (meaning cheaper) and less risky than paying with paper money. Paper money is readily transferable: If someone takes a $20 bill from you, it is gone, and the thief can use it to buy goods with no difficulty. If, however, someone steals a check that you have written to the telephone company to pay a monthly bill, that person probably will have great difficulty using it to buy goods and services, because the individual has to be able to identify himself as a representative of the telephone company. If your checkbook is stolen, a person can use your check as money only if he or

SHOULD WE GET RID OF THE PENNY?

Americans know where to find pennies—in jars and fountains and on the countertops of convenience stores. What's not known is just what ought to be done about the nation's lowliest coin. At a House hearing last week, lobbyists for the penny—Americans for Common Cents—reported a poll showing that 73 percent of the American public wants the government to keep circulating pennies. The Treasury wants to do that, although the government's General Accounting Office reported that penny production costs taxpayers over $8

million a year. The U.S. Mint disputed this, saying penny production nets the U.S. government between $17.9 and $26.6 million.

The GAO found that only about a third of existing pennies are in circulation. And a poll commissioned by the GAO showed that most Americans (52 percent) would prefer that prices be rounded to the nearest nickel. Penny backers responded with an estimate by Penn State economist Raymond Lombra, who said that rounding prices would result in overcharges costing consumers at least $600 million extra a year.

SOURCE: "Whither the Penny?" *U.S. News & World Report*, July 29, 1996, p. 8.

> **CONSIDER THIS:**
> While a penny doesn't seem like much, rounding up could cost U.S. consumers approximately $600 million a year.

IN THE NEWS

she can successfully forge your signature and provide some identification. Hence, transacting business by check is much less risky than using legal tender; there is, then, an element of insurance or safety in the use of transaction deposits instead of currency.

Lower Transaction Costs

Suppose that you decide that you want to buy a compact disc player from the current J.C. Penney's mail-order catalogue that costs $81.28. It is much cheaper, easier, and safer for you to send a check for $81.28 rather than four $20 bills, a $1 bill, a quarter, and three pennies. Transaction deposits are a popular monetary instrument precisely because they lower transaction costs compared with the use of metal or paper currency. In very small transactions, the gains in safety and convenience of checks are outweighed by the time and cost required to write and process them; in these cases, transaction costs are lower with paper and metallic currency. For this reason, it is unlikely that the use of paper or metallic currency will disappear entirely.

Transaction Records

Another useful feature of transaction deposits is that they provide a record of financial transactions. Each month, the bank sends the depositor canceled checks and/or a statement recording the deposit and withdrawal of funds. In an age where detailed records are often necessary for tax purposes, this is a useful feature. Of course, it can work both ways. Paper currency transactions are also popular, in part, probably because a substantial amount of business activity is going on with cash payments so that no record will be available for the tax collectors to review.

ARE CREDIT CARDS A FORM OF MONEY?

Credit cards are "generally acceptable in exchange for goods and services." At the same time, however, credit card payments are actually guaranteed loans available on demand to users, which merely defers customer payment for transactions using a demand deposit. Ultimately, things purchased with a credit card must be paid for with

T U N E   U P

DEMAND DEPOSITS

Q: In recent years, we have moved increasingly towards a "checkless" society. Do you think that this means that demand deposits will eventually be abolished?

A: No. Increasingly, deposits and withdrawals are handled electronically, through electronic impulses sent from store cash registers to bank computers, for example. Thus, the physical effort of writing and processing checks, an expensive and labor-intensive task, has been largely eliminated, and people are actually paying for many of their goods with bank credit cards and automated teller machine (ATM) cards.

Calvin and Hobbes   by Bill Watterson

USING CREDIT CARDS ON THE INTERNET

KURT DAHL

Enough is enough. The public is being badly served by the hysterical reporting about credit-card security on the Internet. The reality is far different from the picture painted in the press. The reality is this. Using your credit card in a secured browser on the Internet is hundreds, if not thousands, of times more secure than any other way you use it. A secured Internet transaction goes from your computer to the commercial Web site without any human intervention. This is true of virtually no other credit-card transactions. We all give our credit cards willingly to waiters, cashiers, bank tellers, gas station attendants and phone operators at catalog companies. Every day, somewhere around 10 million people handle close to 100 million credit cards in the course of their jobs. Talk about a security risk!

But do we see headlines like: "Two Berkeley graduate students discover they can steal credit-card numbers by going to work for Wal-Mart." I suppose the press is interested in security on the Internet because of the intriguing and somewhat scary idea that remote hackers can magically steal your card number as it zooms past on the phone network. But if a hacker had a mind to steal credit-card numbers from the phone network, there are significantly more fertile grounds than the Internet. How do you suppose the credit card that you give to the cashier at Wal-Mart or any other retailer gets authorized and transferred to the bank? In most cases it is over the same kind of phone network as the Internet.

Here is another one. What percentage of credit-card fraud is a result of lost or stolen cards? I'm sure it is quite high, but it is virtually impossible to lose your credit card while doing business in your home or at work. Once again, Internet commerce is far more secure. How about this headline: "Police recommend leaving your purse at home; you might lose it." The press coverage about commerce on the Internet has made the public think it is not safe to use your credit card on the Internet. That's just plain wrong. If you want to use your credit card in the most secure way possible, by far, use a secure browser on the Internet.

SOURCE: Kurt Dahl, "Internet Is Safest Way to Use Your Credit Card," *Seattle Times*, September 24, 1995.

CONSIDER THIS:
Credit cards have certainly become a convenient way of purchasing goods. Over 30 percent of large purchases ($100 or more) are done with credit cards. The ease and safety of using the credit card will inevitably lead to even greater use in the future.

---

a check; monthly payments on credit card accounts are required in order to have continued use of the card. Credit cards, then, are not money, but rather a convenient means to carry out transactions that minimizes the physical transfer of checks and currency. In that sense, they are substitutes for the use of money in exchange; they also allow any given amount of money to facilitate more exchanges.

ARE SAVINGS ACCOUNTS "MONEY"?

Economists are not completely in agreement on what constitutes money for all purposes. Coins, paper currency, demand and other checkable deposits, and travelers checks are certainly forms of money, because all are accepted as direct means of payment for goods and services. There is nearly universal agreement on this point. Some economists, however, argue that for some purposes "money" should be more broadly defined to include **nontransaction deposits.** Nontransaction deposits are fund accounts against which the depositor *cannot* directly write checks—hence the name. If these funds cannot be used directly as a means of payment, but must first be converted into money, then why do people hold such accounts? People use these accounts primarily because they generally pay higher interest rates than transaction deposits.

Two primary types of nontransaction deposits exist—savings accounts and time deposits (sometimes referred to as certificates of deposit, or CDs). Most purists would argue that nontransaction deposits are **near money** assets but not money itself. Why? Savings accounts and time deposits cannot be used directly to purchase a good or service. They are not a direct medium of exchange. For example, you cannot go into a supermarket, pick out groceries, and give the clerk the passbook to your savings account. You must convert funds from your savings account into currency or demand deposits before you can buy goods and services. So, strictly speaking, nontransaction deposits do not meet the formal definition of money. At the same time, however, savings accounts are assets that can be quickly converted into money at the face value of the account. In the jargon of finance, savings accounts are highly liquid assets. True, under federal law, commercial banks legally can require depositors to request withdrawal of funds in writing, and then can defer making payment for several weeks. But in practice, no bank prohibits instant withdrawal, although early withdrawal from some time deposits, especially certificates of deposit, may require the depositor to forgo some interest income as a penalty.

WHY ARE MONEY MARKET MUTUAL FUNDS CONSIDERED NEAR MONEY?

Money market mutual funds are interest-earning accounts provided by brokers who pool funds into investments like Treasury bills. These funds are invested in short-term securities, and the depositor is allowed to write checks against his or her account subject to certain limits. This type of fund has experienced tremendous growth over the last 20 years. Money market mutual funds are highly liquid assets. They are considered to be near money because they are relatively easy to convert into money for the purchases of goods and services.

ARE NONMONETARY ASSETS SUCH AS STOCKS AND BONDS CONSIDERED MONEY?

There are many other forms of financial assets that virtually everyone agrees are not "money." Stocks and bonds are good examples. Suppose you buy 100 shares of Gen-

Is this money?

eral Motors common stock at $70 per share, for a total of $7,000. The stock is traded daily on the New York Stock Exchange and elsewhere; you can readily sell the stock and get paid in legal tender or a demand deposit. Why, then, is this stock not considered money? First, it takes a few days to receive payment for the sale of stock; the asset cannot be turned into cash as quickly as a savings deposit in a financial institution. Second and more important, the value of the stock fluctuates over time, and there is no guarantee that the owner of the asset can obtain its original nominal value at any moment in time. Thus, stocks and bonds are not sufficiently liquid assets to be considered "money."

WHAT IS THE MONEY SUPPLY?

Because a good case can be made both for including and for excluding savings accounts, certificates of deposits (CDs), and money market mutual funds from our operational definition of the money supply for different purposes, we will compromise and do both. Economists call the narrow definition of money—currency, checkable deposits, and travelers checks—**M1.** The broader definition of money, encompassing M1, plus saving accounts, time deposits (except for some large-denomination certificates of deposits), and money market mutual funds, is called **M2.**

The difference between M1 and M2 is striking, as evidenced by the varying size of the total stock of money using different definitions as seen in Exhibit 1. M2 is more than three times the magnitude of M1. This means that people prefer to keep the bulk of their liquid assets in the form of savings accounts of various kinds, rather than as currency or in transactions accounts.

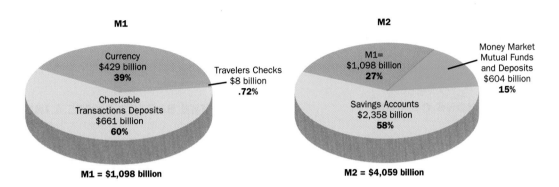

| EXHIBIT 1 | TWO DEFINITIONS OF THE MONEY SUPPLY: M1 AND M2 |

M1

Currency
$429 billion
39%

Travelers Checks
$8 billion
.72%

Checkable
Transactions Deposits
$661 billion
60%

M1 = $1,098 billion

M2

M1=
$1,098 billion
27%

Money Market
Mutual Funds
and Deposits
$604 billion
15%

Savings Accounts
$2,358 billion
58%

M2 = $4,059 billion

SOURCE: Board of Governors, Federal Reserve System, *Federal Reserve Bulletin*, May 1998.

CONCEPT CHECK

1. Money is anything used as a medium of exchange for goods or services.
2. Coins, paper currency, demand and other checkable deposits, and travelers checks are all forms of money.
3. M1 is made up of currency, checkable deposits, and travelers checks. M2 is made up of M1, plus savings accounts, time deposits, and money market mutual funds.

1. If everyone in an economy accepted poker chips as payment in exchange for goods and services, would poker chips be money?
2. If you were buying a pack of gum, would using currency or a demand deposit have lower transactions costs? What if you were buying a house?
3. What is the main advantage of a transaction deposit for tax purposes? What is its main disadvantage for tax purposes?
4. Are credit cards money?
5. What are M1 and M2?
6. How have interest-earning checking accounts and overdraft protection led to the relative decline in demand deposits?

The Functions of Money

■ Is using money better than barter?

■ How does money lower the costs of making transactions?

■ Why can money be an efficient way to store value?

■ Is it less risky to make loans of money or of goods?

WHAT ARE THE FUNCTIONS OF MONEY?

We have already indicated that the primary function of money is to serve as a medium of exchange, to facilitate transactions, and to lower transactions costs. However, money is not the only medium of exchange; rather, it is the only medium that is generally accepted for most transactions. How would people trade with one another in the absence of money? They would **barter** for goods and services they desire.

THE FAR SIDE   By GARY LARSON

To begin, I'd like to show you this!.. Isn't it a beaut'?

New York 1626: Chief of the Manhattan Indians addresses his tribe for the last time.

WHY IS THE BARTER SYSTEM INEFFICIENT?

Under a barter system, individuals pay for goods or services by offering other goods and services in exchange. Suppose I am a farmer who needs some salt. I go to the merchant selling salt and offer her 30 pounds of wheat for 2 pounds of salt. The wheat that I use to buy the salt is not money, because the salt merchant may not want wheat and therefore may not accept it as payment. That is one of the major disadvantages of barter: The buyer may not have appropriate items of value to the seller. The salt merchant may reluctantly take the wheat that she does not want, later bartering it away to another customer for something that she does want. In any case, barter is inefficient because several trades may be necessary in order to receive the desired goods.

Moreover, barter is extremely expensive over long distances. What would it cost me, living in California, to send wheat to Maine in return for an item in the L.L. Bean catalogue? It is much cheaper to mail a check. Finally, barter is time consuming, because of difficulties in evaluating the value of the product that is being offered for barter. For example, the person that is selling the salt may wish to inspect the wheat first to make sure that it is pure and not filled with dirt or other unwanted items. Barter, in short, is expensive and inefficient and generally prevails only where limited trade is carried out over short distances, which generally means in relatively primitive economies. The more complex the economy (e.g., the higher the real per capita GDP), the greater the economic interactions between people, and consequently, the greater the need for one or more universally accepted assets serving as money. Only in a Robinson Crusoe economy, where people live in isolated settlements and are generally self-sufficient, is the use of money unnecessary.

T U N E   U P

THE BARTER SYSTEM

Q: Ann Chovie owns a pizza parlor in a college town. She has decided that she is no longer going to take cash for the sale of pizzas; instead, she is going to work on a barter system. Is Ann making a time-consuming, costly mistake?

A: Imagine this: Last week, after 15 minutes of haggling, you traded Ann a pair of slightly used hiking boots for a deep dish supreme pizza. What will your next pizza cost you, and how long will it take the two of you to figure it out? Bartering can be a costly and tedious process, and for those reasons, Ann is undoubtedly going to regret her decision.

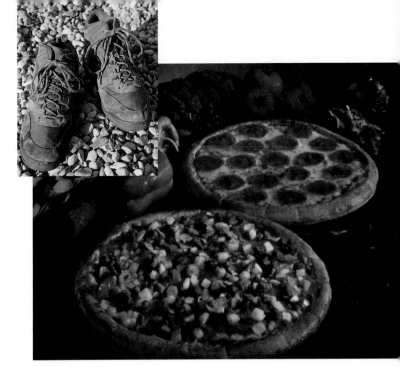

Bartering lacks a standard measure of value.

HOW IS MONEY A STANDARD OF VALUE?

Besides serving as a medium of exchange, money is also a standard of value. With a barter system, one does not know precisely what 30 pounds of wheat are worth relative to 2 pounds of salt. With money, a common "yardstick" exists so that the values of diverse goods and services can be very precisely compared. Thus, if wheat cost 50 cents a pound and salt costs $1 a pound, we can say that a pound of salt is valued precisely two times as much as a pound of wheat ($1 divided by 50 cents = 2). By providing a universally understood measure of value, money serves to lower the information costs involved in making transactions. Without money, a person might not know what a good price for salt is, because so many different commodities can be bartered for it. With money, there is but one price of salt, and that price is readily available as information to the potential consumer.

HOW IS MONEY A STORE OF VALUE?

Money also serves as a store of value. It can provide a means of saving or "storing" things of value in an efficient manner. The farmer in a barter society who wants to save for retirement might accumulate enormous inventories of wheat, which he would then gradually trade away for other goods in his old age. This is a terribly inefficient way to save. Storage buildings would have to be constructed to hold all of the wheat, and the interest payments that the farmer would earn on the wheat would actually be negative, as rats will eat part of it or it will otherwise deteriorate. Most important, physical goods of value would be tied up in unproductive use for many years. With money, the farmer saves pieces of paper that can be used to purchase goods and services in old age. It is both cheaper and safer to store paper rather than wheat.

HOW IS MONEY A MEANS OF DEFERRED PAYMENT?

Finally, money is a **means of deferred payment.** Money makes it much easier to borrow and to repay loans. With barter, lending is cumbersome and subject to an added problem. If a wheat farmer borrows some wheat and agrees to pay it back in wheat next year, what if the value of wheat soars because of a poor crop resulting from drought? The debt will be paid back in wheat that is far more valuable than that borrowed, causing a problem for the borrower. Of course, fluctuations in the value of money can also occur, and indeed, inflation has been a major problem in our recent past and continues to be a problem in many countries. But the value of money fluctuates far less than the value of many individual commodities, so lending in money imposes fewer risks on buyers and sellers than lending in commodities.

1. Barter is inefficient compared to money because a person may have to make several trades before receiving something that is truly wanted.
2. By providing a universally understood measure of value, money serves to lower the information costs involved in making transactions.
3. Money is both cheaper and easier to store than other goods.
4. Because the value of money fluctuates less than specific commodities, it imposes fewer risks on borrowers and lenders.

---

1. Why does the advantage of monetary exchange over barter increase as an economy becomes more complex?
2. How can uncertain and rapid rates of inflation erode money's ability to perform its functions efficiently?
3. In a world of barter, would useful financial statements, like balance sheets, be possible? Would stock markets be possible? Would it be possible to build cars?
4. Why do you think virtually all societies create something to function as money?

The Demand for Money

MODULE 13

■ Why do people choose to hold money?
■ How is money "backed"?

WHY DO PEOPLE HOLD MONEY?

Money has several functions, but what stimulates persons to hold money as opposed to other financial assets? There are at least three motives: transaction purposes, precautionary reasons, and asset purposes.

Transaction Purposes

First, money is demanded for transactions purposes, to facilitate exchange. The higher one's income, the more transactions a person will make (because consumption is income related), the greater will be GDP and the greater the demand for money for transactions purposes, other things equal.

Precautionary Reasons

Second, people like to have money on hand for precautionary reasons. If unexpected medical or other expenses

require an unusual outlay of cash, people like to be prepared. The extent to which people demand cash for precautionary reasons depends partly on an individual's income and partly on the opportunity cost of holding money, which is determined by market rates of interest. The higher market interest rates are, the higher the opportunity cost of holding money instead, and people will hold less of their financial wealth as money.

Asset Purposes

Third, money has a trait (liquidity) that makes it a desirable asset. Other things equal, people desire more-liquid assets in preference to less-liquid assets. That is, they would like to easily convert some of their money into goods and services. For this reason, most people wish to have some of their portfolio in money form. At higher interest rates on other assets, the amount of money desired for this purpose will be smaller because the opportunity cost of holding money desired for this purpose will be smaller. Why? Because the opportunity cost of holding money will have risen.

HOW IS MONEY "BACKED"?

Until fairly recent times, coins in most nations were largely made from precious metals, usually gold or silver. These metals had a considerable intrinsic worth: If the coins were melted down, the metal would be valuable for use in jewelry, industrial applications, dentistry, and so forth. Until 1933, the United States was on an internal **gold standard,** meaning that the dollar was defined as equivalent in value to a certain amount of gold, and paper currency or demand deposits could be freely converted to gold coin. The U.S. left the gold standard, however, eventually phasing out gold currency. Some silver coins and paper money convertible into silver remained, but by the end of the 1960s, even this tie of the monetary system to precious metals ended, in part because the price of silver soared so high that the metal in coins had an intrinsic worth greater

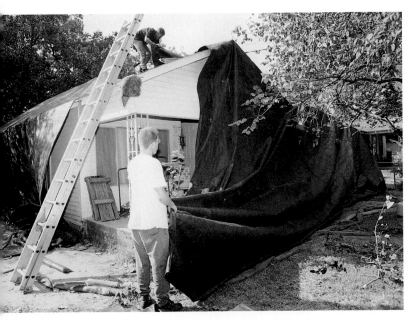

People might keep money around for unexpected expenses.

At one time, cash was backed by gold. What backs our money now?

than its face value, leading people to hoard coins or even melt them down. When there are two forms of money available, people prefer to spend the form of money that is less valuable. This is a manifestation of **Gresham's Law:** "Cheap money drives out dear money."

WHAT REALLY BACKS OUR MONEY?

Consequently, today, there is no meaningful precious metal "backing" to give our money value. Why, then, do people accept dollar bills, for example, in exchange for goods? After all, a dollar bill is a piece of generally wrinkled paper about 6 inches by 2.5 inches in size, with virtually no inherent utility or worth. Do we accept these bills because it states on the front of the bills, "This note is legal tender for all debts, public and private"? Perhaps, but we accept some forms of currency and money in the form of demand deposits without that statement, which says, in effect, that by fiat the U.S. government has declared the instrument to be money.

The true backing behind our money is our faith in the government's ability to provide an instrument people will take in exchange for goods and services. We accept with great eagerness these small pieces of green paper with pictures of long deceased individuals with funny looking hair simply because we believe that they will be exchangeable for goods and services with an intrinsic value. If you were to drop two pieces of paper of equal size on the floor in front of 100 students, one a blank piece of paper and the other a $100 dollar bill, and then leave the room, the group would probably start fighting for the $100 dollar bill while the blank piece of paper would be ignored. Such is our faith in the green paper's practical value that some will even fight for it. As long as people have confidence in something's convertibility into goods and services, "money" will exist and no further backing is necessary.

Because governments represent the collective will of all the people, they are the institutional force that traditionally defines money in the legal sense. People are willing to accept pieces of paper as money only because of their faith in the government. When people lose faith in the exchangeability of pieces of paper that the government decrees as money, even legal tender loses its status as meaningful money. Something is money only if people will generally accept it. While governments play a key, vital role in defining money, much of it is actually created by private businesses in the pursuit of profit. A majority of our money, whether M1 or M2, is in the form of deposits at privately owned financial institutions.

People who hold money, then, must not only have faith in their government, but also in banks and other financial institutions as well. If I accept a check drawn on a regional bank, I believe that bank or, for that manner, any bank will be willing to convert that check into legal tender (currency) enabling me to buy goods or services that I want to have. Thus I have faith in the bank as well. One Nobel laureate in economics, the late Friedrich von Hayek, has even gone so far as to suggest that all money could be created by privately owned businesses and that governmental participation is unnecessary and possibly undesirable. While few economists would go that far, the fact remains that our "money" is money because of confidence that we have in private financial institutions as well as our government.

How do these institutions create (and destroy) the money that we use? That is the major question addressed in the next Concept.

1. Three motives exist for demanding money: transaction purposes, precautionary reasons, and asset purposes.

2. Money is no longer backed by gold. The true backing is our faith that others will accept it from us in exchange for goods and services.

---

1. If the earnings available on other financial assets rose, would you want to hold more or less money? Why?

2. For the economy as a whole, why would individuals want to hold more money as GDP rises?

3. If in an era of very rapid inflation, many people stopped accepting a country's currency for payment, would that currency still be money?

4. Why might people who expect a major market "correction" (a fall in the value of stock holdings) wish to increase their holdings of money?

How Banks Create Money

- How is money created?
- What is a reserve requirement?
- How do reserve requirements affect how much money can be created?

WHO ARE THE PLAYERS IN THE BANKING INDUSTRY?

The biggest players in the banking industry are **commercial banks.** Commercial banks are distinct from most other financial institutions in that they can create demand deposits. The right to create money by increasing demand deposits is a valuable right, and persons wanting to engage in commercial banking practices must seek a charter from the state or federal government. Commercial banks account for more than two-thirds of all of the deposits in the banking industry; they maintain almost all of the demand deposits and close to half of the savings accounts.

There are nearly 1,000 commercial banks in the United States. This number is in marked contrast to most other nations, where the leading banks operate throughout the country and where a large proportion of total bank assets are held in a handful of banks. Until recently, banks were restricted by federal law from operating in more than one state. This has now changed, and the structure of banking as we now know it will inevitably change with the emergence of interstate banking, mergers, and "hostile" takeovers.

Aside from commercial banks, the banking system includes two other important financial institutions: **Savings and Loan Associations** and **Credit Unions.** Savings and loan associations provide many of the same services as commercial banks, including checkable deposits, a variety of time deposits, and money market deposit accounts. The almost 2,000 members of savings and loan associations have typically invested most of their savings deposits into home mortgages. Credit unions are cooperatives, made up of depositors with some common affiliation, like the same employer or union.

WHAT ARE THE FUNCTIONS OF FINANCIAL INSTITUTIONS?

Financial institutions offer a large number of financial functions. For example, they often will pay an individual's monthly bills by automatic withdrawals, administer es-tates, rent safe deposit boxes, and so on. Most important, though, they are depositories for savings and liquid assets that are used by individuals and firms for transaction purposes. They can create money by making loans. In making loans, financial institutions act as intermediaries (middlemen) between savers, who supply funds, and borrowers seeking funds to invest.

HOW DO BANKS CREATE MONEY?

As we have already learned, most money, narrowly defined, is in the form of transaction deposits, assets that can be directly used to buy goods and services. But how did the assets in, say, a checking account get there in the first place? Perhaps it was through a loan made by a commercial bank. When a bank lends to a person, it does not typically give the borrower cash (paper and metallic currency). Rather, it gives the person the funds by a check or by adding funds to an existing checking account of the borrower. If you go into a bank and borrow $1,000, the bank probably will simply add $1,000 to your checking account at the bank. In doing so, a new checkable deposit—money—is created.

HOW DO BANKS MAKE PROFITS?

Banks make loans and create checkable deposits in order to make a profit. How do they make their profit? By collecting higher interest payments on the loans they make than they pay their depositors for those funds. If I borrow $1,000 from Loans R Us National Bank, the interest payment I make, less the expenses the bank incurs in making the loan, including their costs of acquiring the funds, represents profit to the bank.

WHAT ARE RESERVE REQUIREMENTS?

Because the way to make more profit is to make more loans, banks want to make a large volume of loans. Stockholders of banks want the largest profits possible, so what keeps banks from making nearly infinite quantities of loans? Primarily, government regulatory authorities limit the loan issuance of banks by imposing **reserve requirements.** Reserve requirements require banks to keep on hand a quantity of cash or reserve accounts with the Federal Reserve equal to a prescribed proportion of their checkable deposits.

WHAT IS A FRACTIONAL RESERVE SYSTEM?

Even in the absence of regulations restricting the creation of checkable deposits, a prudent bank would put some limit on their loan (and therefore deposit) volume. Why? For people to accept checkable deposits as money, the checks written must be generally accepted in exchange for goods and services. People will accept checks only if they know that they are quickly convertible at par (face value) into legal tender. For this reason, banks must have adequate cash reserves on hand (including reserves at the Fed that can be almost immediately converted to currency, if necessary) to meet the needs of customers who wish to convert their checkable deposits into currency or spend them on goods or services.

Our banking system is sometimes called a **fractional reserve system,** because banks, by law as well as by choice, find it necessary to keep cash on hand and reserves at the Federal Reserve equal to some fraction of their checkable deposits. If a bank were to create $100 in demand deposits for every $1 in cash reserves that it had, the bank might well find itself in difficulty before too long. Why? Consider a bank with $10,000,000 in demand and time deposits and $100,000 in cash reserves. Suppose a couple of large companies with big accounts decide to withdraw $120,000 in cash on the same day. The bank would be unable to convert into legal tender all of the funds requested. The word would then spread that the bank's checks are not convertible into lawful money. This would cause a so-called "run on the bank." The bank would have to quickly convert some of its other assets into currency, or it would be unable to meet its obligations to convert its deposits into currency, and it would have to close.

Therefore, even in the absence of reserve regulations, few banks would risk maintaining fewer reserves on hand than they thought prudent for their amount of deposits (particularly demand deposits). Reserve requirements exist primarily to control the amount of demand and time deposits, and thus the size of the money supply; they do not exist simply to prevent bank failures.

While banks must meet their reserve requirements, they do not want to keep any more of their funds as additional reserves than necessary for safety, because cash assets do not earn any interest. In order to protect themselves but also earn some interest income, banks usually keep some of their assets in highly liquid investments such as United States government bonds. These types of highly liquid, interest-paying assets are often called **secondary reserves.**

WHAT IS A BALANCE SHEET?

Earlier in this Module, we learned that money is created when banks make loans. We will now look more closely at the process of bank lending and its impact on the stock of money. In doing so, we will take a closer look at the structure and behavior of our hypothetical bank, the Loans R Us National Bank. To get a good picture of the size of the bank, what it owns, and what it owes, we look at its **balance sheet,** which is sort of a financial "photograph" of the bank at a single moment in time. Exhibit 1 presents a balance sheet for the Loans R Us Bank.

WHAT ARE A BANK'S ASSETS?

The assets of a bank are those things of value that the bank owns (e.g., cash, reserves at the Federal Reserve, bonds, and its buildings), including contractual obligations of individuals and firms to pay funds to the bank (loans). The largest asset item for most banks is loans. Banks maintain most of their assets in the form of loans because interest payments on loans are the primary means by which they earn revenue. Some assets are kept in the form of non-interest-bearing cash and reserve accounts at the Federal Reserve, in order to meet legal reserve requirements (and secondly, to meet the cash demands of customers). Typically, relatively little of a bank's reserves, or cash assets, is physically kept in the form of paper currency in the bank's vault or at tellers' windows. Most banks keep a majority of their reserves as reserve accounts at the Federal Reserve. As previously indicated, banks usually also keep some assets in the form of bonds that are quickly convertible into cash if necessary (secondary reserves).

WHAT ARE A BANK'S LIABILITIES?

All banks have substantial liabilities, which are financial obligations that the bank has to other people. The predominant liability of virtually all banks is deposits. If you have money in a demand deposit account, you have the right to demand cash for that deposit at any time. Basically, the bank owes you the amount in your checking account. Time deposits similarly constitute a liability of banks.

WHAT IS A BANK'S CAPITAL?

For a bank to be healthy and solvent, its assets, or what it owns, must exceed its liabilities, or what it owes others. In other words, if the bank were liquidated and all the assets converted into cash and all the obligations to others (liabilities) paid off, there would still be some cash left to distribute to the owners of the bank, its stockholders. This difference between a bank's assets and its liabilities constitutes the bank's capital. Note that this definition of capital differs from the earlier definition, which described capital as goods used to further production of other goods (machines, structures, tools, etc.). As you can see in Exhibit 1, capital is included on the right side of the balance sheet so that both sides (assets and liabilities plus capital) are equal in amount. Any time the aggregate amount of bank assets changes, the aggregate amount of liabilities and capital also must change by the same amount, by definition.

WHAT IS A REQUIRED RESERVE RATIO?

Suppose for simplicity that the Loans R Us National Bank faces a reserve requirement of 10 percent on all deposits. That percentage is often called the **required reserve ratio.** But what does a required reserve ratio of 10 percent mean? This means that the bank *must* keep cash on hand or at the Federal Reserve Bank equal to one-tenth (10 percent) of its deposits. For example, if the required reserve ratio was 10 percent, banks would be required to hold $100,000 in required reserves for every $1 million in deposits. The remaining 90 percent of cash is called **excess reserves.**

Reserves in the form of cash and reserves at the Federal Reserve earn no revenue for the bank; there is no profit to be made from holding cash. Whenever excess reserves appear, banks will invest the excess reserves in interest-earning assets, sometimes bonds but usually loans.

WHAT HAPPENS WHEN A BANK LOANS ITS EXCESS RESERVES?

To see what happens to new demand deposits of $100,000, let's return to the Loan R Us Bank. We will continue to assume that the required reserve ratio is 10 percent. That is, the bank is required to hold $10,000 in required reserves for this new deposit of $100,000. The remaining 90 percent, or $90,000, becomes excess reserves, and most of this will likely become available for loans for individuals and businesses.

However, this is not the end of the story. Let us say that the bank loans out all of its new excess reserves of $90,000 to an individual who is remodeling her home. At the time that the loan is made, the money supply will increase by $90,000. Specifically, no one has less money—the original depositor still has $100,000 and the bank now adds $90,000 to the borrower's checking account (demand deposit). A

EXHIBIT 1   **BALANCE SHEET, LOANS R US NATIONAL BANK**

Assets		Liabilities and Capital	
Cash (reserves)	$2,000,000	Transaction deposits (Checking deposits)	$5,000,000
		Savings and time deposits	4,000,000
Loans	6,100,000	Total Liabilities	9,000,000
Bonds (U.S. govt. and municipal)	1,500,000		
		Capital	1,000,000
Bank building, equipment, fixtures	400,000		
		Total Liabilities	
Total Assets	**$10,000,000**	**and Capital**	**$10,000,000**

new demand deposit, or checking acount, of $90,000 has been created. Since demand deposits are money, the issuers of the new loan have created money.

Furthermore, borrowers are not likely to keep the money in their checking accounts for long, since you usually take out a loan to buy something. Say that the loan is used for remodeling; then the borrower pays the construction company and the owner will likely deposit the money into his account at another bank to add even more funds to additional money expansion. This whole process is summarized in Exhibit 2.

In short, banks create money when they increase demand deposits through the process of creating loans. In the next Concept, we will see how the process of loans and deposits has a multiplying effect throughout the banking industry.

EXHIBIT 2 | **FRACTIONAL RESERVE BANKING SYSTEM**

When a new deposit enters the banking system, much of that money will be used for loans. Banks create money when they increase demand deposits through the process of creating loans.

---

1. Money is created when banks make loans. Borrowers receive newly created demand deposits.
2. Required reserves are the amount of cash or reserves—equal to a prescribed proportion of their deposits—that banks are required to keep on hand or in reserve accounts with the Federal Reserve.
3. A balance sheet is a financial record that indicates the balance between a bank's assets and its liabilities plus capital.
4. Banks create money by increasing demand deposits through the process of making loans.

1. How did laws against interstate banking lead to a large number of U.S. banks? What is happening to the number of banks now that interstate banking is allowed?
2. In what way is it true that "banks make money by making money"?
3. How do legal reserve deposit regulations lower bank profits?
4. Is a demand deposit an asset or a liability?
5. If the Bonnie and Clyde National Bank's only deposits were demand deposits of $20 million, and it faced a 10 percent reserve requirement, how much money would it be required to hold in reserves?
6. How would a new deposit into your demand deposit account create a situation of excess reserves at your bank?

The Money Multiplier

MODULE 13

■ How does the multiple expansion of the money supply process work?

■ What is the money multiplier?

WHAT IS THE MULTIPLE EXPANSION EFFECT?

You learned in Concept D that banks can create money (demand deposits) by making loans and that the monetary expansion of an individual bank is limited to its excess reserves. While this is true, it ignores the further effects of a new loan and the accompanying expansion in the stock of money. New loans create new money directly, but they also create excess reserves in other banks, which leads to still further increases in both loans and the stock of money. There is a multiple expansion effect, where a given volume of bank reserves creates a multiplied amount of money.

HOW DO BANK DEPOSITS LEAD TO MULTIPLE EXPANSIONS?

To see how the process of multiple expansion works, let us extend our earlier example. Say Loans R Us Bank receives a new cash deposit of $100,000. (In the next Module we will discuss in detail how this deposit happens to arrive at the bank.) For convenience, say the bank was only required to keep new cash reserves equal to one-tenth (10 percent) of new deposits. With that, Loans R Us is only required to hold $10,000 of the $100,000 deposit for required reserves. Thus, Loans R Us Bank now has $90,000 in excess reserves as a consequence of the new cash deposit.

Loans R Us Bank, being a profit maximizer, will probably put its newly acquired excess reserves to work in some fashion earning income in the form of interest. Most likely, it will make one or more new loans totaling $90,000.

WHEN DOES THE MULTIPLE EXPANSION PROCESS STOP?

The process does not stop there. When the borrowers from Loans R Us Bank get their loans, the borrowed money will almost certainly be spent on something—such as new machinery, a new house, a new car, or greater store inventories. The new money will lead to new spending.

The $90,000 spent by persons borrowing from Loans R Us Bank likely will end up in bank accounts in still other banks, such as Bank A shown in Exhibit 1. Bank A now has a new deposit of $90,000 with which to make more loans and create still more money. This process continues with Bank B, Bank C, Bank D, and others. Loans R Us Bank's initial cash deposit, then, has a chain reaction impact that ultimately involves many banks and a total monetary impact that is far greater than suggested by the size of the original deposit of $100,000. That is, every new loan gives rise to excess reserves, which lead to still further lending and deposit creation. Each round of lending is smaller than the preceding one, because some (we are assuming 10 percent) of the new money created must be kept as required reserves.

WHAT IS THE MONEY MULTIPLIER?

The following formula can be used to measure the total maximum potential impact on the supply of money:

$$\text{Potential money creation} = \text{Initial deposit} \times \text{Money multiplier}$$

The **money multiplier** is simply 1 divided by the reserve requirement. The larger the reserve requirement, the smaller the money multiplier. Thus, a reserve requirement of 25 percent, or one-fourth, means a money multiplier of four. Likewise, a reserve requirement of 10 percent, or one-tenth, means a money multiplier of 10.

In the example in Exhibit 1, where Loans R Us Bank (facing a 10 percent reserve requirement) receives a new $100,000 cash deposit, initial deposit equals $100,000. Potential money creation, then, equals $100,000 (initial deposit) multiplied by 10 (the money multiplier), or $1,000,000. Using the money multiplier, we can calculate that the total potential impact of the initial $100,000 deposit is some $1,000,000 in money being created. In other words, the final monetary impact is 10 times as great as the initial deposit. Most of this increase, $900,000, has been created by the increase in demand deposits generated

| EXHIBIT 1 | THE MULTIPLE EXPANSION PROCESS |

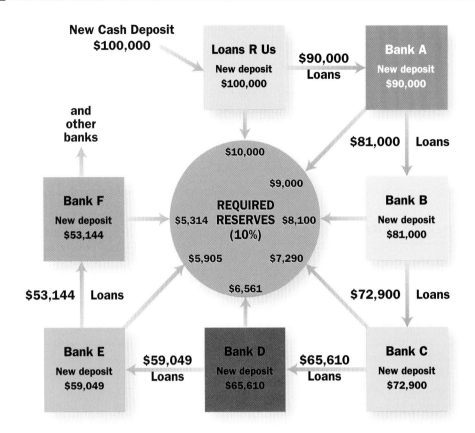

New Cash Deposit
$100,000

Loans R Us
New deposit
$100,000

$90,000
Loans

Bank A
New deposit
$90,000

$81,000 Loans

and other banks

$10,000

$9,000

REQUIRED RESERVES (10%)
$5,314 $8,100

Bank F
New deposit
$53,144

Bank B
New deposit
$81,000

$5,905 $7,290

$6,561

$53,144 Loans

$72,900 Loans

Bank E
New deposit
$59,049

$59,049
Loans

Bank D
New deposit
$65,610

$65,610
Loans

Bank C
New deposit
$72,900

A $100,000 new cash deposit in Loans R Us Bank has the potential to create $1,000,000 in a chain reaction that involves many banks. The process repeats itself, as the money lent from one bank becomes a new deposit in another bank.

when banks make loans; the remaining $100,000 is from the initial deposit.

WHY IS IT ONLY "POTENTIAL" MONEY CREATION?

Note that the expression "potential money creation" was used in describing the impact of creating loans and deposits out of excess reserves. Why "potential"? Because it is possible that some banks will choose not to lend all of their excess reserves. Some banks may simply be extremely conservative and keep some extra newly acquired cash assets in that form. When that happens, the chain reaction effect is reduced by the amount of excess reserves not loaned out.

Moreover, some borrowers may not spend all of their newly acquired bank deposits, or they may wait a considerable period of time before doing so. Others may put their borrowed funds into time deposits rather than checkable deposits, which would reduce the M1 expansion process

but not the M2 money expansion process. Still others may choose to keep some of their loans as currency in their pockets. Such leakages and time lags in the bank money

TUNE UP

THE MULTIPLE EXPANSION PROCESS

Q: Holden Reserves is a banker. If someone borrows money from Holden's bank and doesn't spend it, will the money supply increase through the banking multiplier?

A: No. If the borrower keeps the money, a new account does not get created and the multiple expansion process will not work.

expansion process usually mean that the actual monetary impact of an initial deposit created out of excess reserves within a short time period is less than indicated by the money multiplier. Still, the multiplier principle does work, and a multiple expansion of deposits will generally occur in a banking system that is characterized by fractional reserve requirements.

HOW IS MONEY DESTROYED?

The process of money creation can be reversed, and in the process, money is destroyed. When a person pays a loan back to a bank, she usually does so by writing a check to the bank for the amount due. As a result, demand deposits decline, directly reducing the money stock.

IN THE NEWS

CHANGES IN THE BANKING INDUSTRY

More competition or bigger is better? It looks like the financial industry is going for the bigger is better idea.

Two more bank mega-mergers have been announced. The largest is the nearly $60 billion deal with BankAmerica Corp., and NationsBank Corp. At the same time Banc One is joining with First Chicago in a nearly $30 billion deal.

As usual they promise better service and more products for consumers. It usually comes at a cost.

NationsBank Corp., Chairman Hugh McColl and BankAmerica Corp., Chairman David Coulter shook hands on a deal that will create the nation's biggest bank, in yet another banking merger that will affect millions of banking customers and thousands of employees. The merger will include some 29 million households and two million business accounts in 22 states.

They'll keep the BankAmerica name and will operate in 22 states, with 4,800 branches and 15,000 automated teller machines. The banks have 180,000 employees

and the merger could eliminate 5,000 to 8,000 positions.

BankAmerica has been a California fixture and San Francisco based institution for 94 years. The two banks say it will be good for their customers but there's always a downside to mergers.

The cost consumers often pay when banks merge are:

■ The costs of checking accounts often go up.

■ There may be branch closings.

■ Account terms often change.

■ There are often higher banking fees.

■ There are sometimes new fees in larger banks.

■ Sometimes accounts have to be restructured.

■ And mergers cause account computer confusion.

Yet during the news conference to announce the merger there were no hints of

the potential confusion from the leaders of the two banks. Hugh McColl of NationsBank said, "The resources that such a bank can put together for customers and shareholders alike is a good one. We're here because in the words of Victor Hugo an invasion of armies can be resisted but not an idea whose time has come."

Whether it's good for the consumer or not the makeover of the nation's banking industry is moving very quickly and it is a fact of life, a fact of life that will affect all of us.

SOURCE: J. D. Kohn, ed., "How Will the Latest Bank Merger Affect Consumers?" http://www.abcnews.com/local/kabc/news/7200_4131998.html

---

CONSIDER THIS:
Are there economies of scale in the banking industry? That is, can the merger of two banks bring about lower costs? The banks claim the mergers will lead to better service and more products.

1. New loans mean new money (demand deposits), which can increase spending as well as the stock of money.

2. The banking system as a whole can potentially create money equal to several times the amount of total reserves or new money equal to several times the amount of excess reserves, the exact amount determined by the money multiplier, which is equal to one divided by the reserve requirement.

1. Why do the stock of money and the volume of bank loans both increase or decrease at the same time?

2. Why would each bank in the money supply multiple expansion process lend out a larger fraction of any new deposit it receives, the lower the reserve requirement?

3. If a particular bank with a reserve requirement of 10 percent has $30,000 in a new cash deposit, how much money could it create through making new loans?

4. Why do banks choosing to hold excess reserves or borrowers choosing to hold some of their loans in the form of currency reduce the actual impact of the money multiplier to a level below that indicated by the multiplier formula?

The Collapse of America's Banking System, 1920–1933

■ What caused the collapse of the banking system between 1920 and 1933?

■ How are bank failures avoided today?

WHAT LED TO THE COLLAPSE OF THE BANKING SYSTEM BETWEEN 1920 AND 1933?

Perhaps the most famous utterance from Franklin D. Roosevelt, the President of the United States from 1933 to 1945, was made on the day he assumed office, when he declared, "The only thing we have to fear is fear itself." Those 10 words succinctly summarize the problems that led the world's leading economic power to a near total collapse in its system of commercial banking and, with that, to an abrupt and unprecedented decline in the stock of money. The decline in the money stock, in turn, contributed to an economic downturn that had dire consequences for many, especially for the one-fourth of the labor force unemployed at the time of Roosevelt's first inaugural address.

WHAT HAPPENED TO THE BANKING INDUSTRY?

In 1920, there were 30,000 banks in the United States; by 1933, the number had declined to about 15,000. What happened? During the prosperous 1920s, nearly 6,000 banks closed their doors. In some cases, bank failure reflected imprudent management or even criminal activity on the part of bank officers (stealing from the bank). A few banks had a sufficient amount of resources stolen by others to make them insolvent (the Bonnie and Clyde effect). More often, though, banks in rural areas closed as a consequence of having large sums of assets tied up in loans to farmers who, because of low farm prices, were not in a position to pay off the loans when they came due. Rumors spread that a bank was in trouble, and these rumors, even if false, became self-fulfilling prophecies. Bank "runs" developed and even conservatively run banks with cash equal to 15 or 20 percent of their deposit liabilities found themselves with insufficient cash reserves to meet the withdrawal requests of panicky depositors.

The bank failures of the 1920s, while numerous, were generally scattered around small towns in the country. Confidence in banks actually generally increased in that decade, and by the fall of 1929, there were $11 in bank deposits for every $1 in currency in circulation.

The first year following the stock market crash of 1929 saw little dramatic happen to the banking system, but in late 1930, a bank with the unfortunately awesome sounding name of the Bank of the United States failed, the largest bank failure in the country to that time. This failure had a ripple effect. More bank "runs" occurred as depositors began to get jittery. Banks, fearing runs, began to not lend their excess reserves, thereby aggravating a fall in the money stock and reducing business investment.

As depositors converted their deposits to currency, bank reserves fell, and with that the ability of banks to support deposits. The situation improved a bit in 1932, when a newly created government agency, the Reconstruction Finance Corporation (RFC), helped banks in distress with loans. By early 1933, however, the depositor confidence decline had reached such a point that the entire banking system was in jeopardy. On March 4, newly inaugurated President Roosevelt declared a national bank holiday, closing every bank in the country for nearly two weeks. Then, only the "good" banks were allowed to reopen, an action that increased confidence. By this time the deposit–currency ratio had fallen from 11 to 1 (in 1929) to 4 to 1. Passage of federal deposit insurance in mid-1933 greatly strengthened depositor confidence and led to money reentering the banks. The recovery process began.

WHAT CAUSED THE COLLAPSE?

The collapse occurred for several reasons. First, the nation had thousands of relatively small banks. Customers believed that depositor withdrawals could force a bank to close, and the mere fear of bank runs made them a reality. Canada, with relatively few banks that were mostly very large with many branches, had no bank runs. Second, governmental attempts to stem the growing distress were weak and too late. Financial aid to banks was nonexistent; the Federal Reserve System and other governmental efforts began only in 1932—well into the decline. Third, deposit insurance, which would have bolstered customer confidence, did not exist. The financial consequences of bank failures were correctly perceived by the public to be great. Fourth, growing depositor fear was enhanced by the fact that the economy was in a continuous downward spiral—there was no basis for any optimism that bank loans would be safely repaid.

WHY DON'T WE HAVE BANK FAILURES TODAY?

The combination of the Federal Deposit Insurance Corporation (FDIC) and the government's greater willingness to assist distressed banks has largely eliminated bank runs and failures in recent times. Now, when a bank runs into financial difficulty, the FDIC may assist another bank in taking over the assets and liabilities of the troubled bank so that no depositor loses a cent. Thus, changes in the money supply resulting from a loss of deposits from failed banks are no longer a big problem. Better bank stability means a greater stability in the money supply, which means, as will be more explicitly demonstrated in the next Module, a greater level of economic stability.

What changes have been made to prevent this from happening today?

CONCEPT CHECK

1. The entire banking system was in jeopardy by 1933.
2. The banking collapse occurred because of customers' fears and the government's weak attempt to correct the problem.

3. The creation of the Federal Deposit Insurance Corporation has largely eliminated bank runs in recent times.

---

1. How did the combination of increased holding of excess reserves by banks and currency by the public lead to bank failures in the 1930s?

2. What are the four reasons cited in the text for the collapse of the U.S. banking system in this period?
3. What is the FDIC, and how did its establishment increase bank stability and reassure depositors?

Application: Internet Banking

What are the cost-saving advantages of Internet banking? How can smaller banks compete with multi-billion-dollar banks?

INTERNET BANKING

AMY OLMSTEAD

NEW YORK, August 14—Internet banks have started to chip away at their concrete and steel competitors' business.

Net.Bank, Security First Network Bank (which has one walk-in customer service center), *TeleBank* and Principal Bank have more than 64,000 accounts combined. At least one—Net.Bank—is turning a profit.

They're winning customers largely because of their lower cost structures. Physical branches are expensive to staff and operate. Without those costs, Internet banks can offer higher interest rates on accounts and lower fees.

It's often enough to entice customers to open an account. But cyberbanking's inconveniences mean many consumers are reluctant to completely convert to branchless banking.

Internet banks push their cost advantages. Net.Bank CEO D. R. Grimes says his bank can offer 95 percent of the services traditional banks offer at almost half the cost. (Net.Bank is changing its name from Atlanta Internet Bank.)

"In the most recent quarter, our expenses—everything except interest—were about 40 percent less than a traditional bank of our size," says Grimes. "That's a very significant advantage."

Better interest rates on accounts and CDs are the top selling point. Net.Bank offers interest checking accounts with annual interest rates from 3.0 to 3.93 percent on a deposit of at least $100. TeleBank offers rates starting at 3.10 percent on interest checking accounts of $2,500.

In comparison, interest checking accounts at two East Coast *Citibank* branches offer rates of 1.0 to 1.14 percent, with no minimum balance. Interest checking accounts at two *Bank of America* branches in the West offered rates of 1.0 percent on accounts with $2,000 or more. The difference in fees is substantial, too.

"It costs pennies for any bank to do transactions over the Internet," says Aileen Lopez Pugh, CFO of TeleBank, "but you don't see large banks offering any benefits to their customers. We pass on our cost savings."

There are other obstacles for Internet banks. They can't offer some bank services, like safety deposit boxes, without a physical location.

The paper trail can be even more burdensome. Checks that are traditionally slipped into an ATM have to be mailed. Wire transfers replace cash deposits. Funds not withdrawn at an ATM are sent as cashiers checks or wire transfers.

. . . Despite the uncertainties, Internet banks believe there's at least one market that will be a cinch to convert—expatriates. Many Americans living abroad still have bills to pay back home. With an Internet bank, they can do their banking from their laptop at a cafe.

SOURCE: ABCNEWS.com fromTheStreet.com. Copyright 1998 ABCNEWS and Starwave Corporation.

The financial industry is looking at some new very large bank mergers. Why would one bank merge with another? The obvious reason is that there are sometimes economies of scale in mergers. That is, two companies may be able to lower their production costs by joining forces. However, consolidation is not the only way to cut costs in an increasingly competitive financial world. Internet banking looks like it is here to stay and it can cut costs with low overhead—no tellers, expensive buildings, or security guards. Many experts believe that we are not far from a cashless society in which one debit credit card will be used to take care of all transactions.

How does Internet banking allow small banks to compete with large banks?

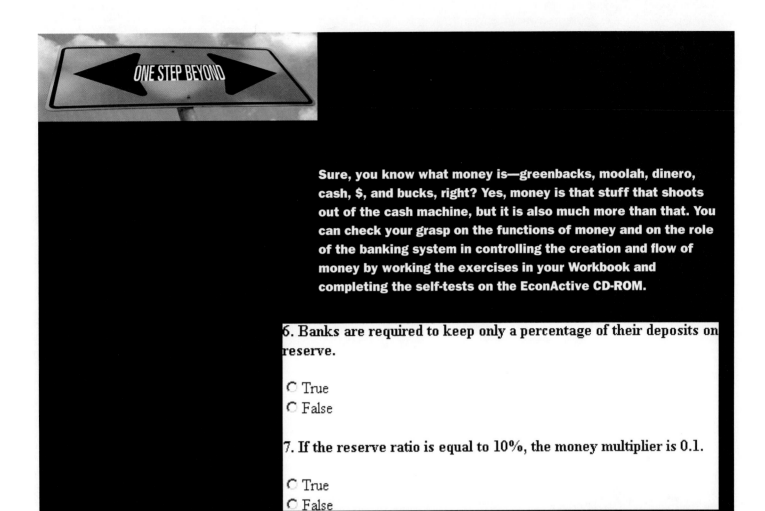

ONE STEP BEYOND

Sure, you know what money is—greenbacks, moolah, dinero, cash, $, and bucks, right? Yes, money is that stuff that shoots out of the cash machine, but it is also much more than that. You can check your grasp on the functions of money and on the role of the banking system in controlling the creation and flow of money by working the exercises in your Workbook and completing the self-tests on the EconActive CD-ROM.

6. Banks are required to keep only a percentage of their deposits on reserve.

○ True
○ False

7. If the reserve ratio is equal to 10%, the money multiplier is 0.1.

○ True
○ False

The Federal Reserve System and Monetary Policy

A. The Federal Reserve System
What is the role of a central bank?

B. The Equation of Exchange
How does the equation of exchange help our understanding
of the role of money in the economy?

C. Implementing Monetary Policy: Tools of the Fed
What are the three major tools of the Fed?

D. Money, Interest Rates, and Aggregate Demand
How do changes in money supply and money demand
affect interest rates in the money market?

E. Problems in Implementing Monetary Policy
What factors can limit the effectiveness of monetary policy?

F. Application: The Independence of the Fed
Should the Fed be independent from the administration and Congress?

The Federal Reserve System

MODULE 14

- What are the functions of a central bank?
- Who controls the Federal Reserve System?
- How is the Fed tied to Congress and the executive branch?

WHAT ARE THE FUNCTIONS OF A CENTRAL BANK?

In most countries of the world, the job of manipulating the supply of money belongs to the central bank. A central bank has many functions. First, a central bank is a "banker's bank." It serves as a bank where commercial banks maintain their own cash deposits—their reserves. Second, a central bank performs a number of service functions for commercial banks, such as transferring funds and checks between various commercial banks in the banking system. Third, the central bank typically serves as the major bank for the central government, handling, for example, its payroll accounts. Fourth, the central bank buys and sells foreign currencies and generally assists in the completion of financial transactions with other countries. Fifth, it serves as a "lender of last resort" that helps banking institutions in financial distress. Sixth, the central bank is concerned with the stability of the banking system and the supply of money, which as you have already learned, results from the loan decisions of banks. The central bank can and does impose regulations on private commercial banks; it thereby regulates the size of the money supply and influences the level of economic activity. The central bank also implements monetary policy, which along with fiscal policy, forms the basis of efforts to direct the economy to perform in accordance with macroeconomic goals.

WHERE IS THE FEDERAL RESERVE SYSTEM LOCATED?

In most countries, the central bank is a single bank; for example, the central bank of Great Britain, the Bank of England, is a single institution located in London. In the United States, however, the central bank is 12 institutions, closely tied together and collectively called the Federal Reserve System. The Federal Reserve System, or Fed, as it is nicknamed, has separate banks in Boston, New York, Philadelphia, Richmond, Atlanta, Dallas, Cleveland, Chicago, St. Louis, Minneapolis-St. Paul, Kansas City, and

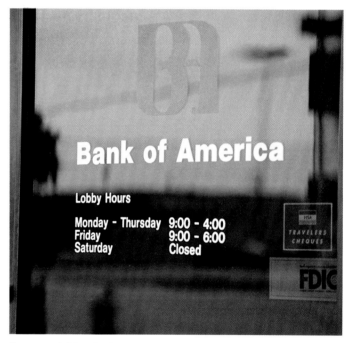

Commercial banks keep reserves with the Central Bank.

San Francisco. As Exhibit 1 shows, these banks and their branches are spread all over the country, but they are most heavily concentrated in the Eastern states.

Each of the 12 banks has branches in key cities in its district. For example, the Federal Reserve Bank of Cleveland serves the fourth Federal Reserve district and has branches in Pittsburgh and Cincinnati. Each Federal Reserve bank has its own board of directors and, to some limited extent, can set its own policies. Effectively, however, the 12 banks act largely in unison on major policy issues, with effective control of major policy decisions resting with the Board of Governors and the Federal Open Market Committee of the Federal Reserve System, headquartered in Washington, D.C. The Chairman of the Federal Reserve Board of Governors (currently Alan Greenspan) is generally regarded as

The letter indicates which of the Fed banks issued the $20 bill. A "B" and the number 2 indicate that the bill was issued in New York, the second Federal Reserve District.

one of the most important and powerful economic policy-makers in the country.

WHAT IS THE FED'S RELATIONSHIP TO THE FEDERAL GOVERNMENT?

The Federal Reserve was created in 1913 because the U.S. banking system had so little stability and no central direction. Technically, the Fed is privately owned by the banks that "belong" to it. All banks are not required to belong to the Fed; however, since the passage of new legislation in 1980, virtually no difference exists between the requirements of member and nonmember banks.

The private ownership of the Fed is essentially meaningless, because the Board of Governors of the Federal Reserve, which controls major policy decisions, is appointed by the president of the United States, not by the stockholders. The owners of the Fed have relatively little control over its operations and receive only small fixed dividends on their modest financial stake in the system. Again, the private ownership but public control feature was a compromise made to appease commercial banks opposed to direct public (government) regulation.

WHAT ARE THE FED'S TIES TO THE EXECUTIVE BRANCH?

An important aspect of the Fed's operation is that, historically, it has had a considerable amount of independence from both the executive and legislative branches of government. True, the president appoints the seven members of the Board of Governors, subject to Senate approval, but the term of appointment is 14 years. This means that no member of the Federal Reserve Board will face reappointment from the president who initially made the appointment, because presidential tenure is limited to two four-year terms. Moreover, the terms of board members are staggered, so a new appointment is made only every two years. It is practically impossible for a single president to appoint a majority of the members of the board, and

| EXHIBIT 1 | BOUNDARIES OF FEDERAL RESERVE DISTRICTS AND THEIR BRANCH TERRITORIES |

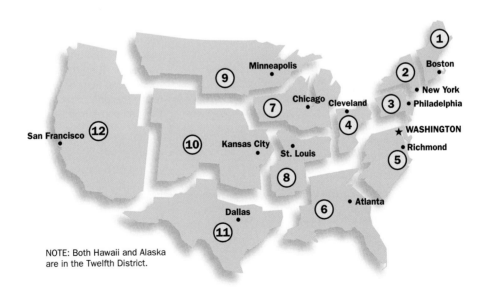

NOTE: Both Hawaii and Alaska are in the Twelfth District.

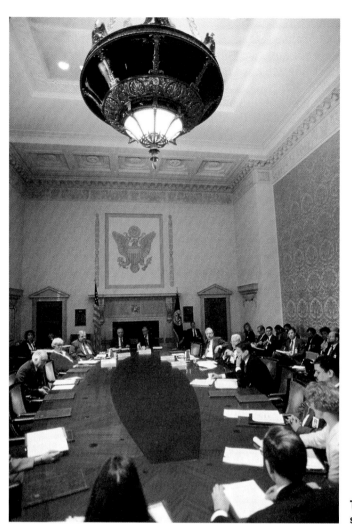

even if it were possible, members have little fear of losing their jobs as a result of presidential wrath. The Chair of the Federal Reserve Board is a member of the Board of Governors and serves a four-year term. The Chair is truly the chief executive officer of the system, and he effectively runs it with considerable help from the presidents of the 12 regional banks.

HOW DOES THE FED OPERATE?

Many of the key policy decisions of the Federal Reserve are actually made by its Federal Open Market Committee (FOMC), which consists of the seven members of the Board of Governors; the President of the New York Federal Reserve Bank, and four other presidents of Federal Reserve Banks, who serve on the committee on a rotating basis. The FOMC makes most of the key decisions influencing the direction and size of changes in the money stock, and their regular, secret meetings are accordingly considered very important by the business community and government.

The chair of the Fed is truly the chief executive officer of the system.

1. What are the six primary functions of a central bank?
2. What is the FOMC and what does it do?

3. How is the Fed tied to the executive branch? How is it insulated from executive branch pressure to influence monetary policy?

(B) The Equation of Exchange

■ What is the equation of exchange?
■ What is the velocity of money?
■ How is the equation of exchange useful?

As we discussed in the previous Concept, perhaps the most important function of the Federal Reserve is its ability to regulate the money supply. In order to fully understand the significant role that the Federal Reserve plays in the economy, we will first examine the role of money in the national economy.

WHAT IS THE EQUATION OF EXCHANGE?

The role that money plays in determining equilibrium GDP, the level of prices, and real output of goods and services has attracted the attention of economists for generations. In the early part of this century, economists noted a useful relationship that helps our understanding of the role of money in the national economy, called the **equation of exchange**. The equation of exchange can be presented as follows:

$$MV = PQ$$

where M is the money supply, however defined (usually M1 or M2), V is the income velocity of money, P is the average level of prices of final goods and services, and Q is the physical quantity of final goods and services produced in a given period (usually one year).

We have previously defined M. V, the velocity of money, refers to the "turnover" rate, or the intensity with which money is used. Specifically, V represents the average number of times that a dollar is used in purchasing final goods or services in a one-year period. Thus, if individuals are hoarding their money, velocity will be low; if individuals are writing lots of checks on their checking accounts and spending currency as fast as they receive it, velocity will tend to be high.

The expression PQ represents the dollar value of all final goods and services sold in a country in a given year. Does that sound familiar? It should, because that is the definition of nominal gross domestic product (GDP). Thus, for our purposes, we may consider the average level of prices (P) times the physical quantity of final goods and

services (Q) to be equal to nominal GDP. We could say then, that

$$MV = \text{Nominal GDP}$$

or,

$$V = \text{Nominal GDP}/M$$

That, in fact, is the definition of velocity: The total output of goods in a year divided by the amount of money is the same thing as the average number of times a dollar is used in final goods transactions in a year.

The actual magnitude of V will depend on the definition of money that is used. For example, using M1, the velocity of money in 1993 equaled

$$V = \text{Nominal GDP}/\text{M1} = \$6,374 \text{ billion } /\$1,128 \text{ billion} = 5.65$$

Using the broader definition of money, M2, the velocity of money in 1993 equaled

$$V = \text{Nominal GDP}/\text{M2} = \$6,374 \text{ billion}/\$3,566 \text{ billion} = 1.79$$

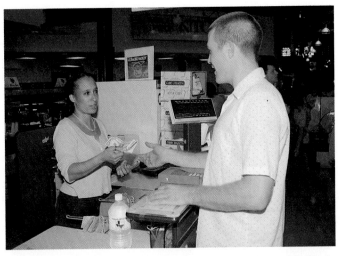

Velocity is the average number of times a dollar is used in final goods transactions in a year.

The average dollar of money, then, turns over a few times in the course of a year, with the precise number depending on the definition of money.

HOW IS THE EQUATION OF EXCHANGE USEFUL?

The equation of exchange is a useful tool when we try to assess the impact in a change in the stock of money (M) on the aggregate economy. If M increases, then one of the following must happen:

1. V must decline by the same magnitude, so that MV remains constant, leaving PQ unchanged.
2. P must rise.
3. Q must rise.
4. P and Q must each rise some, so that the product of P and Q remains equal to MV.

In other words, if the money stock increases and the velocity of money does not change, there will be either higher prices (inflation), greater output of final goods and services, or a combination of both. If one considers a macroeconomic policy to be successful if output is increased but unsuccessful if the only effect of the policy is inflation, then an increase in M is a good policy if Q increases but a bad policy if P increases.

Likewise, dampening the rate of increase in M or even causing it to decline will cause nominal GDP to fall, unless the change in M is counteracted by a rising velocity of money. Intentionally decreasing M can also either be good or bad, depending on whether the declining money GDP is reflected mainly in falling prices (P) or in falling output (Q).

Therefore, expanding the money supply, unless counteracted by increased hoarding of currency (leading to a decline in V), will have the same type of impact on aggregate demand as an expansionary fiscal policy—increasing government purchases, reducing taxes, or increases in transfer payments. Likewise, policies designed to reduce the money supply will have a contractionary impact (unless offset by a rising velocity of money) on aggregate demand, similar to the impact obtained from increasing taxes, decreasing transfer payments, or decreasing government purchases.

In sum, what these relationships illustrate is that monetary policy can be used to obtain the same objectives as fiscal policy. Some economists, often called monetarists, believe that monetary policy is the most powerful determinant of macroeconomic results.

HOW VOLATILE IS THE VELOCITY OF MONEY?

Economists once considered the velocity of money a given. We now know that it is not constant, but often moves in a fairly predictable pattern. Thus, the connection between money supply and GDP is still fairly predictable. Historically, the velocity of money has been quite stable over a long period of time, and it has been particularly stable using the M2 definition. However, velocity is less stable when measured using the M1 definition and over shorter periods of time. For example, an increase in velocity can occur with anticipated inflation. When individuals expect inflation, they will spend their money more quickly. They don't want to be caught holding money that is going to be worth less in the future. Also, an increase in the interest rates will cause people to hold less money. That is, people want to hold less money when the opportunity cost of holding money increases. This, in turn, means that the velocity of money increases.

CONCEPT CHECK

1. The equation of exchange is $MV = PQ$, where M is the money supply, V is the velocity of money, P is the average level of prices of final goods and services, and Q is the physical quantity of final goods and services produced in an economy in a given year.

2. The velocity of money (V) represents the average number of times that a dollar is used in purchasing final goods or services in a one-year period.
3. The equation of exchange is a useful tool when analyzing the effects of a change in the stock of money on the aggregate economy.

1. If the money stock is $10 billion and velocity is 4, what is the product of the price level and output? If the price level is 2, what does output equal?
2. If nominal GDP is $200 billion and the money stock is $50 billion, what must velocity be?

3. If the money stock increases and velocity does not change, what will happen to nominal GDP?
4. If velocity is unstable, does stabilizing the money stock help stabilize the economy? Why or why not?

Implementing Monetary Policy: Tools of the Fed

- What are the three major tools of the Fed?
- What is the purpose of the Fed's tools?
- What other powers does the Fed have?

HOW DOES THE FED MANIPULATE THE SUPPLY OF MONEY?

As noted previously, the Board of Governors of the Fed and the Federal Open Market Committee are the prime decision makers for monetary policy in the United States. They decide whether to expand the stock of money and, hopefully, the real level of economic activity, or to contract the money stock, hoping to cool inflationary pressures. How does the Fed control the stock of money, particularly when, as we discussed in the previous Module, it is the privately owned commercial banks that actually create and destroy money by making loans?

The Fed has three major methods that it can use to control the supply of money: It can engage in open market operations, change reserve requirements, or change its discount rate. Of these three tools, the Fed uses open market operations the most. It is by far the most important device used by the Fed to influence the money supply.

WHAT ARE OPEN MARKET OPERATIONS?

Open market operations involve the purchase and sale of government securities by the Federal Reserve System. Decisions regarding whether to buy or sell government bonds are made by the Federal Open Market Committee at its regular meetings. For several reasons, open market operations are the most important method the Fed uses to change the stock of money. To begin, it is a device that can be implemented quickly and cheaply—the Fed merely calls an agent who buys or sells bonds. It can be done quietly, without a lot of political debate or a public announcement. It is a rather powerful tool, as any given purchase or sale of securities has an ultimate impact several times the amount of the initial transaction.

When the Fed buys bonds, it pays the seller of the bonds by a check written on one of the 12 Federal Reserve banks. The person receiving the check will likely deposit it in his or her bank account, increasing the money stock in the form of added transactions deposits. More importantly, the commercial bank, in return for crediting the account of the bond seller with a new deposit, gets cash reserves or a higher balance in their reserve account at the Federal Reserve Bank in its district.

For example, suppose the Loans R Us National Bank has no excess reserves and that one of its customers sells a bond for $10,000 through a broker to the Federal Reserve System. The customer deposits the check from the Fed for $10,000 in his or her account, and the Fed credits the Loans R Us Bank with $10,000 in reserves. Suppose the reserve requirement is 10 percent. The Loans R Us Bank, then, only needs new reserves of $1,000 ($10,000 × .10) to support its $10,000, meaning that it has acquired $9,000 in new excess reserves ($10,000 new actual reserves minus $1,000 in new required reserves). Loans R Us can, and probably will, lend out its excess reserves of $9,000, creating $9,000 in new deposits in the process. The recipients of the loans, in turn, will likely spend the money, leading to still more new deposits and excess reserves in other banks, as discussed in the previous Module.

In other words, the Fed's purchase of the bond directly creates $10,000 in money in the form of bank deposits, and indirectly permits up to $90,000 in additional money to be created through the multiple expansion in bank deposits. (The money multiplier is the reciprocal of 1/10, or 10. 10 × $9,000 = $90,000.) Thus, if the reserve requirement is 10 percent, a total of up to $100,000 in new money is potentially created by the purchase of one $10,000 bond by the Fed.

The process works in reverse when the Fed sells a bond. The individual purchasing the bond will pay the Fed by check, lowering demand deposits in the banking system. Reserves of the bank where the bond purchaser has a bank account will likewise fall. If the bank had zero excess reserves at the beginning of the process, it will now have a reserve deficiency that must be met by selling secondary reserves or by reducing loan volume, either of which will lead to further destruction of deposits. A multiple contraction of deposits will begin.

TUNE UP

OPEN MARKET OPERATIONS

Q: Cass Sheer is a worker at a branch of the Federal Reserve. She is trying to explain to her mother, who owns several government bonds, how the money supply can increase as result of open market operations. Can you help Cass?

A: Cass explains that in order for people to want to put more money in banks and less in government bonds, the Fed must offer bond holders an attractive price. If the Fed's price is high enough, it will tempt some investors to sell their government bonds. When those individuals place the proceeds from the sale in the bank, new deposits are created, increasing reserves in the banking system. The excess reserves can then be loaned by the banks, creating more new deposits and increasing the excess reserves in still other banks.

Years	M_2	Inflation*
1960–69	7.0	2.5
1970–79	9.6	7.6
1980–89	7.7	3.5
1990–96	2.9	3.2
1960–96	7.4	4.5

Inflation and the growth in money supply (M_2) tend to move together.

*Inflation based on GDP deflector.

SOURCE: DRI/McGraw-Hill Macroeconomic Database.

HOW DO THE FED'S OPEN MARKET ACTIVITIES AFFECT THE EQUATION OF EXCHANGE?

Generally, in a growing economy where the real value of goods and services is increasing over time, an increase in the supply of money is needed even to maintain stable prices. If the velocity of money (V) in the equation of exchange is fairly constant and real GDP (denoted by Q in the equation of exchange) is rising between 3 and 4 percent a year (as it has over the period since 1840), then a 3 or 4 percent increase in M is consistent with stable prices. We would expect, then, that over long time expanses, the Fed's open market operations would more often lead to monetary expansion than monetary contraction. In other words, the Fed would more often purchase bonds than sell them. Moreover, in periods of rising prices, if V is fairly constant, the growth of M likely will exceed the 3 to 4 percent annual growth that appears to be consistent with long-term price stability.

WHAT IS THE RELATIONSHIP BETWEEN INFLATION AND THE GROWTH IN THE MONEY SUPPLY?

From 1970 to 1979, the United States experienced considerable inflation, reflecting in part a sizeable increase in the growth in the money supply (M2). This is documented in Exhibit 1. Note that inflation tended to rise more in periods of rapid monetary expansion (reflecting, to a considerable extent, open market operations) than in periods of slower growth in the money supply. The positive correlation between money growth (M2) and inflation is not perfect, however; inflation during the early 1960s rose slowly despite a fairly large growth in the money supply. This reflected the fact that real output (measured by Q in the equation of exchange) rose quite substantially; also V declined somewhat to offset increases in the money supply.

There is also international support for the relationship between higher money growth and higher inflation. This data is presented in Exhibit 2.

EXHIBIT 2 | MONEY SUPPLY GROWTH AND INFLATION RATES, 1985–1994

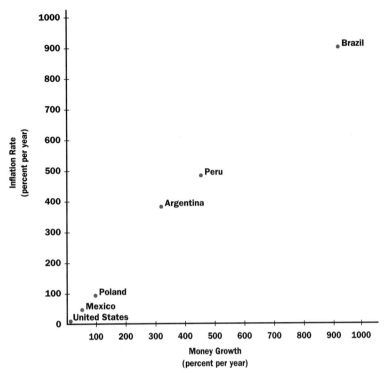

There is often a strong positive correlation between a country's average annual inflation rate and its annual growth in money supply.

SOURCE: Data from World Bank, *World Development Report 1996.*

HOW DOES CHANGING THE RESERVE REQUIREMENTS IMPACT A BANK'S ABILITY TO CREATE MONEY?

While open market operations are the most important and widely utilized tool that the Fed has to achieve its mone-tary objectives, it is not its potentially most powerful tool. The Fed possesses the power to change the reserve requirements of member banks by altering the reserve ratio. This can have an immediate, significant impact on the ability of member banks to create money. Suppose the banking system as a whole has $500 billion in deposits and $60 billion in reserves, with a reserve ratio of 12 percent. Because $60 billion is 12 percent of $500 billion, the system has no excess reserves. Suppose now that the Fed lowers reserve requirements by changing the reserve ratio to 10 percent. Now, banks are required to keep only $50 billion in reserves ($500 billion $\times$ .10), but they still have $60 billion. Thus, the lowering of the reserve requirement gives banks $10 billion in excess reserves. The banking system as a whole can expand deposits and the money stock by a multiple of this amount, in this case 10 (10 percent equals 1/10; the banking multiplier is the reciprocal of this, or 10). The lowering of the reserve requirement in this case, then, would permit an expansion in deposits of $100 billion, which represents a 20 percent increase in the stock of money, from $500 to $600 billion.

WHEN DOES THE FED USE THIS TOOL?

Relatively small reserve requirement changes, then, can have a big impact on the potential supply of money. The tool is so potent, in fact, that it is used relatively seldom. Carpenters don't use sledge hammers to hammer small nails or tacks; the tool is too big and powerful to use effectively. Similarly, the Fed changes reserve requirements rather infrequently for the same reason, and when it does make changes, it is by very small amounts. For example, between 1970 and 1980, the Fed changed the reserve requirement twice, and less than 1 percent on each occasion. The Fed did make an out-of-the-ordinary move in 1992 when it lowered the reserve requirement from 12 to 10 percent.

Frank and Ernest

© 1988 Thaves/Reprinted with permission.

TOOLS OF THE FED

Q: Chase Manhattan, a New York banker, argued that required reserve ratios are a potentially more powerful tool for the Fed than open market operations. Do you agree? If so, why isn't this tool used as often as open market operations?

A: The advantage of the reserve requirement is that it is a very powerful tool. However, this is also its disadvantage because a very small reduction in the reserve requirement, for example, can make a huge change in the number of dollars that are in excess reserves in banks all over the country. Such huge changes in required reserves and excess reserves have the potential to be disruptive to the economy.

WHAT IS THE DISCOUNT RATE AND HOW DOES IT AFFECT BANKS?

Banks having trouble meeting their reserve requirement can borrow funds directly from the Fed. The interest rate the Fed charges on these borrowed reserves is called the **discount rate.** If the Fed raises the discount rate, it makes it more costly for banks to borrow funds from it to meet their reserve requirements. The higher the interest rate banks have to pay on the borrowed funds, the lower the potential profits from any new loans made from borrowed reserves, and fewer new loans will be made and less money created. If the Fed wants to contract the money stock, it will raise the discount rate, making it more costly for banks to borrow reserves; if the Fed is promoting an expansion of money and credit, it will lower the discount rate, making it cheaper for banks to borrow reserves.

The discount rate changes fairly frequently, often several times a year. Sometimes the rate will be moved several times in the same direction within a single year, which has a substantial cumulative effect.

WHAT IS THE SIGNIFICANCE OF THE DISCOUNT RATE?

The discount rate is a relatively unimportant tool, mainly because member banks do not rely heavily on the Fed for borrowed funds in any case. There seems to be some stigma among bankers about borrowing from the Fed; borrowing from the Fed is something most bankers believe should be reserved for real emergencies. When banks have short-term needs for cash to meet reserve requirements, they are more likely to take a very short-term (often overnight) loan from other banks in the **federal funds market.** For that reason, many people pay a lot of attention to the interest rate on federal funds.

The discount rate's main significance is that changes in the rate are commonly viewed as a signal of the Fed's intentions with respect to monetary policy. Unlike open market operations, which are carried out in secret, with the operations being announced in the minutes of the FOMC published only several weeks after the decisions have been made, discount rate changes are widely publicized. People look to these changes for clues as to the type of monetary policy the Fed is pursuing, although increasingly in recent years, the Fed has announced publicly its "target" rates of growth for the stock of money (although actual monetary growth sometimes is outside the "target" range).

HOW DOES THE FED REDUCE THE MONEY STOCK?

Summarizing the previous discussion, the Fed can do three things if it wants to reduce the money stock. It can: (1) sell bonds ("buy" money from the economy), (2) raise reserve requirements, or (3) raise the discount rate. Of course, the Fed could also opt to use some combination of these three tools in its approach.

These moves would tend to reduce nominal GDP, hopefully through a decrease in P rather than Q. These actions would be the monetary policy equivalent of a fiscal policy of raising taxes, lowering transfer payments, and/or lowering government purchases.

THE WALL STREET JOURNAL

MIKE SHAPIRO

"You want to know what Alan Greenspan is thinking? Hey. I'm good, but I'm not that good."

TUNE UP

THE DISCOUNT RATE

Q: Rhonda has just finished a report on banking, and she says that the discount rate is more of a signal than it is an opportunity to borrow from the Fed. Why might this be the case?

A: Banks do not want to reveal any weaknesses or signs of reckless behavior to the Fed because they fear the dreaded audit. This is why banks tend to borrow from other banks in the federal funds market rather than borrowing from the Fed. However, the discount rate is an important signal to banks. If the Fed lowers the discount rate, it is essentially telling banks to be more expansionary. If you get in trouble, I will bail you out with cheap loans. On the other hand, if the Fed raises the discount rate, then the message it is sending banks is to be more cautious in their lending practices—and if banks heed this message, then the money supply will tend to contract.

TUNE UP

TOOLS OF THE FED

Q: It is 11:00 P.M. and Stella D. Knight is cramming for her macro final tomorrow morning. She is almost sure that her economics teacher is going to ask about the three possible methods the Fed can use to reduce the money supply (or its rate of growth) and the three ways it can increase the money supply. Can you help Stella?

A: In the case of persistent, high inflation, the Fed would pursue a contractionary policy. To decrease the money supply, it would sell bonds, raise the discount rate, and/or raise the reserve requirement. If the Fed wanted to pursue an expansionary policy, because of a severe recession, it would increase the money supply by buying bonds, lowering the reserve requirement, and/or lowering the discount rate.

HOW DOES THE FED INCREASE THE SUPPLY OF MONEY?

If the Fed is concerned about underutilization of resources (e.g., unemployment), it would engage in precisely the opposite policies: (1) buy bonds, (2) lower reserve requirements, or (3) lower the discount rate. The government could use some combination of these three approaches.

These moves would tend to raise nominal GDP, hopefully through an increase in Q (in the context of the equation of exchange) rather than P. Equivalent expansionary fiscal policy actions would be to lowering taxes, increasing transfer payments, and/or increasing government purchases.

HOW ELSE CAN THE FED INFLUENCE ECONOMIC ACTIVITY?

The Fed's control of the money supply is largely exercised through the three methods outlined above, but it can influence the level and direction of economic activity in numerous less important ways as well. First, the Fed can attempt to influence banks to follow a particular course of action by the use of **moral suasion.** For example, if the Fed thinks the money supply and credit are growing too fast, it might write a letter to bank presidents urging them to be more selective in making loans, and suggesting that good banking practices mandate that banks maintain some excess reserves. During business contractions, the Fed may urge bankers to lend more freely, hoping to promote an increase in the stock of money.

The Federal Reserve also has at its command some selective controls, meaning regulatory authority over specific types of economic activity. For example, the Federal Reserve Board of Governors establishes margin requirements for the purchase of common stock. This means that the Fed specifies the proportion of the purchase price of stock that a purchaser must pay in cash. By allowing the Fed to control limits on borrowing for stock purchases, Congress believes that the Fed can limit speculative market dealings in securities and reduce instability in securities markets (although whether the margin requirement rule has in fact helped achieve such stability is open to question).

In the last few decades or so, the Federal Reserve regulatory authority has been extended to new areas. Beginning in 1969, the Fed began enforcing provisions of the Truth in Lending Act, which requires lenders to state actual interest rate charges when making loans. Similarly, in the mid-1970s, the Fed assumed the authority of enforcing provisions of the Equal Lending Opportunity Act, designed to eliminate discrimination against loan applicants.

THE FED AND THE MEDIA

May 19—The Federal Reserve met again this week to decide whether or not to alter interest rates. But just how did the world's most powerful central bank let everyone from Wall Street to Main Street know its decision?

. . . Just how is this information, which can change the economic landscape and impact everything from the rate on new car loans to the interest on credit cards, disseminated to the public at large?

WAITING FOR THE CALL

. . . shortly before 2 P.M. ET Wednesday, members of the financial press squeeze into a small, poorly lit, dingy room at the Treasury Department across town and wait for a phone call from the influential Fed. Indeed, the room is so small that some of the 25 or so reporters who turn up have to wait in a back room.

At 2, the doors to the pressroom are closed. Then, sometime between 2 and 2:15 P.M., a phone rings in the room—and what happens next has to be seen to be believed.

On the phone is Joseph Coyne, assistant to the Board of Governors of the Federal Reserve. Coyne tells the one reporter who takes the call in the Treasury pressroom that either a fax is en route or that the Federal Open Market Committee meeting ended at a certain time and there will be no further announcement. (By the way, the reporter that takes the call is nearly always the Dow Jones reporter since Dow Jones is regarded as the leading disseminator of financial news in the United States.)

If Coyne tells the reporter that the FOMC meeting ended and there'll be no further announcement, this means the central bank is leaving interest rates right where they are, although Coyne doesn't specifically say that.

AT THE SOUND OF THE BELL

After thanking Coyne, the reporter will then tell the others in the pressroom and they'll all hurriedly fine-tune their stories to say, "Fed leaves interest rates unchanged," or words to that effect. Then, when they're all ready—yes, when the press are all ready, not when the Fed says the news can be released—one of the reporters rings a bell, and all the news stories are electronically filed to thousands of information news screens around the world.

Bizarre eh? Well . . . it gets stranger.

Let's say Coyne calls over to the Treasury pressroom and tells the reporter who takes the call that a fax is en route. Knowing that a fax is coming means the Fed has decided to change interest rates, since the Fed only issues a press release if it has opted to raise or lower rates. But that's all the press knows at this point—which way rates are going is unknown.

The reporters wait for the fax. But sometimes the fax machine jams and the vital information they're all waiting for has to be re-sent to another fax machine down the hall. Finally, the fax arrives. One reporter then makes copies and hands them out to the reporters present. The pre-written stories are adjusted to reflect either an increase or decrease in rates, and then the one reporter on "bell" duty asks if everyone is ready. Once all the reporters give the thumbs up, the bell is rung and the news goes out to the world.

SOURCE: Colin Hurlock, "How Does the Fed Spread the Word?" *MSNBC*, May 19, 1998 from http://www.msnbc.com/news/104317.asp

---

CONSIDER THIS:

Decisions made by the Federal Reserve affect just about everyone. They influence car loans, mortgage rates, and stock markets, just to mention a few. It is no surprise, then, that journalists hover over the phone in a tiny little room in the Treasury Department awaiting the call from the assistant to the Board of Governors of the Federal Reserve. As you have read in this Module, changes in the money supply can drastically alter the course of the economy, so those in the financial markets are particularly interested in any actions or inactions taken by the Fed. Many consider the chair of the Federal Reserve System to be the second most important leader (and perhaps the most powerful single economic policymaker) in the country because of the importance of the money supply.

1. The three major tools of the Fed are open market operations, changing reserve requirements, and changing the discount rate.
2. If the Fed wants to stimulate the economy, it will increase the money supply by buying government bonds, lowering the reserve ratio, and/or lowering the discount rate.
3. If the Fed wants to restrain the economy, it will lower the money supply by selling bonds, increasing the reserve ratio, and/or raising the discount rate.

4. The Fed has some lesser tools that can influence specific sectors of the economy, such as the authority to establish and change margin requirements on the purchase of common stock (thus hopefully controlling excess speculation).

1. What three main tactics could the Fed use in pursuing a contractionary monetary policy?
2. What three main tactics could the Fed use in pursuing an expansionary monetary policy?
3. Would the money stock rise or fall if the Fed made an open market purchase of government bonds, *ceteris paribus?*

4. If the Fed raised the discount rate from 12 to 15 percent, what impact would that have on the money supply?
5. What is moral suasion, and why would the Fed use this tactic?

Money, Interest Rates, and Aggregate Demand

MODULE 14

- What causes the demand for money to change?
- What is the banking system's role in money market equilibrium?
- How do changes in income change the money market equilibrium?

WHAT IS THE MONEY MARKET?

The Federal Reserve's policies with respect to the supply of money has a direct impact on short-run real interest rates, and accordingly, on the components of aggregate demand. The **money market** is the market where money demand and money supply determine the equilibrium interest rate. When the Fed acts to change the money supply by changing one of its policy variables, it alters the money market equilibrium.

WHAT AFFECTS THE DEMAND FOR MONEY?

In an earlier Module, we learned that people have three basic motives for holding money instead of other assets: for the purpose of carrying out transactions, for precautionary reasons, and for asset reasons. The quantity of money demanded varies inversely with the rate of interest. When interest rates are higher, the opportunity cost—in terms of the interest income on alternative assets foregone—of holding monetary assets is higher, and persons will want to hold less money for each of these reasons. At the same time, the demand for money, particularly for transactions purposes, is highly dependent on income levels, because the transactions volume varies directly with income.

The previous discussion is summarized graphically in Exhibit 1. At lower interest rates, the quantity of money demanded is greater, a movement from A to B in Exhibit 1. An increase in income will lead to an increase in the demand for money, depicted by a rightward shift in the money demand curve, a movement from A to C in Exhibit 1.

WHY IS THE SUPPLY OF MONEY RELATIVELY INELASTIC?

The supply of money is largely governed by the regulatory policies of the central bank. Whether interest rates are 4 percent or 14 percent, banks seeking to maximize profits will increase lending as long as they have reserves above their desired level, because even a 4 percent return on

loans provides more profit than maintaining those assets in non-interest-bearing cash or reserve accounts at the Fed. Given this fact, the supply of money is effectively almost perfectly inelastic with respect to interest rates over their plausible range, controlled by Federal Reserve policies that determine the level of bank reserves (through open market purchases or sales of government bonds and changes in the discount rate) and the money multiplier (through changes in reserve requirements). Therefore, we draw the money supply curve as vertical, other things equal, in Exhibit 2, with changes in Federal Reserve policies acting to shift the money supply curve.

WHAT IS MONEY MARKET EQUILIBRIUM?

Combining the money demand and money supply curves (Exhibit 2), money market equilibrium occurs at that inter-

EXHIBIT 1	MONEY DEMAND, INTEREST RATES, AND INCOME

An increase in the level of income will increase the amount of money that people want to hold for transactions purposes at any given interest rate; therefore it shifts the demand for money to the right, from MD_0 to MD_1. The demand for money curve is downward sloping because at lower interest rates, the opportunity cost of holding money is lower.

EXHIBIT 2

MONEY MARKET EQUILIBRIUM

An increase in income will shift the money demand curve to the right, from MD_0 to MD_1, raising interest rates from r_0 to r_1. This results in a new equilibrium at point B. An increase in the money supply resulting from expansionary monetary policies (e.g., the Fed buying bonds or lowering the discount rate or required reserves) will shift the money supply curve to the right (from MS_0 to MS_1), lowering the rate of interest (from r_1 to r_2) and shifting the equilibrium to point C.

est rate (r_0) where the quantity of money demanded equals the quantity of money supplied, at point A. At a below-equilibrium interest rate, people try to hold more money than is available from the banking system, given the level of bank reserves and reserve requirements. The result is that the quantity of money demanded at that interest rate exceeds the quantity supplied—a shortage. Competition for funds will then lead financial institutions to raise interest rates in response making it more costly to hold or bor-

row money. At an above-equilibrium interest rate, the quantity of money banks would like to supply by making loans at that interest rate, given their level of reserves and reserve requirements, exceeds the quantity of money demanded at that interest rate—a surplus. Competition to make loans will then lead to lower interest rates, until people are willing to hold the amount of money banks are able to create by making loans to borrowers.

HOW DO INCOME CHANGES AFFECT THE EQUILIBRIUM POSITION?

Rising national income increases the demand for money, shifting the money demand curve to the right from MD_0 to MD_1, and leading to a new higher equilibrium interest rate.

HOW WOULD AN INCREASE IN THE STOCK OF MONEY AFFECT EQUILIBRIUM INTEREST RATES AND AGGREGATE DEMAND?

A Federal Reserve policy change that increased the money supply would be depicted by a shift in the money supply curve to the right. As a result of this shift, the equilibrium quantity of money demanded increases and equilibrium interest rates fall. The immediate impact of expansionary monetary policy is to decrease real interest rates. The lower interest rate, or the fall in the cost of borrowing money, then leads to an increase in aggregate demand for goods and services at the current price level. The lower interest rate will increase home sales, car sales, business investments, and so on. That is, an increase in the money supply will lead to lower interest rates and an increase in aggregate demand, as seen in Exhibit 3. In contrast, a

EXHIBIT 3

THE IMPACT OF AN INCREASE IN THE STOCK OF MONEY

a. Impact on the Money Market

b. Impact on Aggregate Demand

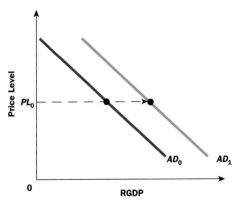

The increase in the money stock in the money market causes the real interest rate to fall in the short run, as seen in Exhibit 3(a). At lower interest rates, households and businesses invest more and buy more goods and services, shifting the aggregate demand curve to the right, as shown in Exhibit 3(b).

fiscal policy or other change that increases aggregate demand, and therefore income, will have the immediate effect of increasing interest rates (unless offset by monetary policy).

EXPANSIONARY MONETARY POLICY AT LESS THAN FULL EMPLOYMENT

An increase in aggregate demand through monetary policy can lead to an increase in real GDP if the economy is currently operating at less than full employment, the output level to the left of $RGDP_{FE}$ in Exhibit 5. The initial equilibrium is E_0, the point at which AD_1 intersects the short-run aggregate supply curve. At this point, output is equal to $RGDP_0$ and the price level is PL_0. If the Fed engages in an expansionary monetary policy, it can shift the aggregate demand curve from AD_0 to AD_1, expanding output to $RGDP_{FE}$ and increasing the price level to PL_1.

EXPANSIONARY MONETARY POLICY AT FULL EMPLOYMENT

Suppose that the Fed increases the money supply via open market operations. As a result, there is an increase in the money supply. This increase in the money supply will increase aggregate demand, shifting it from AD_0 to AD_1 as shown in Exhibit 6. However, if the economy is initially at full employment, $RGDP_{FE}$, the increase in aggregate demand moves the economy to a temporary short-run equilibrium at E_1, where the price level is PL_1 and real output is $RGDP_1$. This equilibrium at E_1 is *not* sustainable, because the economy is beyond full capacity. This puts pressure on input markets, sending wages and other input prices higher. The higher input costs shift the short-run aggregate supply curve leftward, from $SRAS_0$ to $SRAS_1$. As a result of this shift in aggregate supply, a new equilibrium, E_2, is reached. Because this new equilibrium is on the long-run aggregate supply curve, it is a sustainable long-run equilibrium. So we see that real output returns to the full employment output level, but at a higher price level, PL_2 rather than PL_0.

TUNE UP

MONEY AND THE AD/AS MODEL

Q: During the Great Depression in the United States, the price level fell, real GDP fell, and unemployment reached 25 percent. Investment fell, and as banks failed, the money supply fell dramatically. Can you show the effect of these changes from a vibrant 1929 economy to a battered 1932 economy using the AD/AS model?

A: The 1929 economy was at PL_{1929} and $RGDP_{1929}$ in Exhibit 4. The lack of consumer confidence coupled with the large reduction in the money supply and falling investment sent the aggregate demand curve reeling. As a result, the aggregate demand curve fell from AD_{1929} to AD_{1932}, real GDP fell to $RGDP_{1932}$, and the price level fell to PL_{1932}—deflation.

EXHIBIT 4

<table>
<tr><td>

EXHIBIT 5	**EXPANSIONARY MONETARY POLICY AT LESS THAN FULL EMPLOYMENT**

</td><td>

EXHIBIT 6	**EXPANSIONARY MONETARY POLICY AT FULL EMPLOYMENT**

</td></tr>
</table>

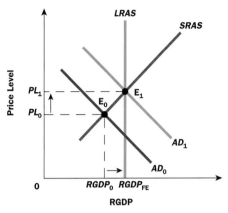

Expansionary monetary policy can shift the aggregate demand curve to the right, from AD_0 to AD_1, causing an increase in output and in the price level.

Expansionary monetary policy shifts the aggregate demand curve from AD_0 to AD_1. At the short-run equilibrium, E_1, the economy is operating beyond full capacity, which puts pressure on input markets. The higher cost in input markets causes the short-run aggregate supply curve to shift from $SRAS_0$ to $SRAS_1$. The resulting new long-run equilibrium, E_2, is at a higher price level, PL_2.

IN THE NEWS

FED LEAVES INTEREST RATES ALONE

. . . The much-advertised slowdown in U.S. economic growth has arrived. Employment rose a moderate 205,000 in June, while wages advanced just a penny, the slowest rate in more than two years. The National Association of Purchasing Management's index fell below 50%, indicating factory activity slowed for the first time in 22 months. Inventories are high. Exports are slowing. New orders for durable goods are off. All of this spells one thing: Steady Fed policy. "After months of hoping and waiting, the Fed is getting some very comforting news," says Anthony Karydakis, senior economist at First Chicago.

It's not that the Fed isn't concerned about the outlook for growth and inflation. A summary of the May 19 FOMC meeting released Thursday shows that two district Fed presidents—hard-line monetarists Jerry Jordan of Cleveland and William Poole of St. Louis—wanted higher short-term rates to slow money-supply growth. The Fed is still biased toward higher rates and there's pressure on Fed Chairman Alan Greenspan to discard his growing faith in the New Economy.

Still, the Fed held its fire last week. Clearly, Greenspan isn't about to okay a tightening with Asia still in the throes of crisis and growth softening at home.

Another sign the Fed is not about to add liquidity to the economy came last week. The central bank took the unusual step of warning banks against lowering lending standards on business loans. Greenspan has cautioned in recent months that loans ex-

tended in the latter years of an expansion—for instance, right now—are the ones banks usually wind up regretting. So, the Fed told bankers to avoid any assumption that "unusually favorable economic environment of the last few years will continue indefinitely."

SOURCE: William Pesek Jr., "Fed Holds Rates Steady Amid Signs of Slowing; Will the Second Half Bring Continued Stability?" *Barron's* Online, July 6, 1998.

CONSIDER THIS:

The Board of Governors is not always in agreement. There are several key terms in this box that are important. For example, the Fed finds the slowdown in economic growth to be "comforting news," because it may help eliminate the fears of unsustainable real output growth that can lead to increasing inflation. In addition, the "Fed is biased towards higher rates" implies that Fed policymakers are leaning towards higher interest rates to safeguard against inflationary pressures. "Greenspan is not about to okay a tightening with Asia" means that he does not want to follow a restrictive policy—that is, why increase interest rates if it may not be necessary. Finally, liquidity means adding money to banking reserves; the Fed doesn't want banks to be too aggressive in their lending practices.

1. The quantity of money demanded varies inversely with interest rates (a movement along the money demand curve) and directly with income (a shift of the money demand curve). Monetary policies that increase the supply of money will lower interest rates in the short run, other things equal. Fiscal policy or other changes that increase aggregate demand and incomes will increase the demand for money and raise interest rates, other things equal.

2. The competition to make or acquire additional loans when interest rates are not at their equilibrium level in the money market causes interest rates to move toward their equilibrium levels.

3. Rising incomes increase the demand for money. This will lead to a new higher equilibrium interest rate, other things equal.

4. An expansionary monetary policy at less than full employment can cause an increase in real GDP and price level.

5. An expansionary monetary policy at full employment can *temporarily* increase real GDP, but in the long run, only the price level will rise.

---

1. Who controls the supply of money in the money market?

2. How does an increase in income or a decrease in the interest rate increase the demand for money?

3. What Federal Reserve policies would shift the money supply curve to the left?

4. Will an increase in the money stock increase or decrease the short-run equilibrium real interest rate, other things equal?

5. Will an increase in national income increase or decrease the short-run equilibrium real interest rate, other things equal?

6. What is the relationship between interest rates and aggregate demand in monetary policy?

7. How will an expansionary monetary policy impact real GDP and the price level at less than full employment?

8. How will an expansionary monetary policy impact real GDP and the price level at full employment?

Problems in Implementing Monetary Policy

■ What problems exist in implementing monetary policy?
■ What problems exist in coordinating monetary and fiscal policies?

WHAT PROBLEMS EXIST IN CONDUCTING MONETARY POLICY?

The lag problem inherent in adopting fiscal policy changes is much less acute for monetary policy, largely because the decisions are not slowed by the same budgetary process. The FOMC of the Federal Reserve, for example, can act quickly (in emergencies, almost instantly, by conference call) and even secretly to buy or sell government bonds, the key day-to-day operating tool of monetary policy. However, the length and variability of the impact lag before its effects on output and employment are felt are still significant—roughly 12 to 20 months in most cases—and the time before the full price level effects are felt is even longer and more variable.

HOW DO COMMERCIAL BANKS IMPLEMENT THE FED'S MONETARY POLICIES?

One limitation of monetary policy is that it ultimately must be carried out through the commercial banking system. The Central Bank (Federal Reserve System in the United States) can change the environment in which banks act, but the banks themselves must take the steps necessary to increase or decrease the stock of money. Usually, when the Fed is trying to constrain monetary expansion, there is no difficulty in getting banks to make appropriate responses. Banks must meet their reserve requirements, and if the Fed raises bank reserve requirements, sells bonds, and/or raises the discount rate, banks must obtain the necessary cash or reserve deposits at the Fed to meet their reserve requirements. In response, they will call in loans that are due for collection, sell secondary reserves, and so on, to obtain the necessary reserves, and in the process of contracting loans, they lower the stock of money.

When the Federal Reserve wants to induce monetary expansion, however, it can provide banks with excess reserves (e.g., by lowering reserve requirements or buying government bonds), but it cannot force the banks to make

loans, thereby creating new money. Ordinarily, of course, banks want to convert their excess reserves to work earning interest income by making loans. But in a deep recession or depression, banks might be hesitant to make enough loans to put all those reserves to work, fearing that they will not be repaid. Their pessimism might lead them to perceive that the risks of making loans to many normally credit-worthy borrowers outweigh any potential interest earnings (particularly at the low real interest rates that are characteristic of depressed times). Some have argued that banks maintaining excess reserves rather than loaning them out was, in fact, one of the monetary policy problems that arose in the Great Depression.

HOW CAN BANKS THAT ARE NOT PART OF THE FEDERAL RESERVE SYSTEM AFFECT ITS POLICY IMPLEMENTATION?

A second problem with monetary policy relates to the fact that the Fed can control deposit expansion at member banks, but it has no control over global and nonbank institutions that also issue credit (loan money) but are not subject to reserve requirement limitations, like pension funds and insurance companies. Therefore, while the Fed may be able to predict the impact of its monetary policies on member bank loans, the actions of global and nonbanking institutions can serve to alter the impact of monetary policies adapted by the Fed on the money market or equivalently, the loanable funds market. Hence, there is a real question of how precisely the Fed can control the short-run real interest rates through its monetary policy instruments.

WHY ARE THERE FISCAL AND MONETARY COORDINATION PROBLEMS?

Another possible problem that arises out of existing institutional policy making arrangements is the coordination of fiscal and monetary policy. Decision making with respect to fiscal policy is made by Congress and the president, while monetary policy decision making is in the hands of the Federal Reserve System. A macroeconomic problem arises if the federal government's fiscal decision makers differ on policy objectives or targets with the Fed's monetary decision makers. For example, the Fed may be more concerned about keeping inflation low, while fiscal policymakers may be more concerned about keeping unemployment low.

HOW ARE THE COORDINATION PROBLEMS ALLEVIATED?

In recognition of potential macroeconomic policy coordination problems, the Chairman of the Federal Reserve Board has participated for several years in meetings with top economic advisers of the president. An attempt is made in those meetings to reach a consensus on the appropriate policy responses, both monetary and fiscal. Still, there is often some disagreement, and the Fed occasionally works to partly offset or even neutralize the effects of fiscal policies that it views as inappropriate. Some people believe that monetary policy should be more directly controlled by the president and Congress, so that all macroeconomic policy will be determined more directly by the political process. Also, it is argued that such a move would enhance coordination considerably. Others, however, argue that it is dangerous to turn over control of the nation's money stock to politicians, rather than allowing decisions to be made by technically competent administrators who are focused more on price stability and more insulated from political pressures from the public and from special interest groups.

OVERALL PROBLEMS WITH MONETARY AND FISCAL POLICY

Much of macroeconomic policy in this country is driven by the idea that the federal government can counteract economic fluctuations: stimulating the economy (with increased government purchases, tax cuts, transfer payment increases, and easy money) when it is weak, and restraining it when it is overheating. But policymakers must adopt the right policies in the right amounts at the right time for such "stabilization" to do more good than harm. And for this, government policymakers need far more accurate and timely information than experts can give them.

First, economists must know not only which way the economy is heading, but also how rapidly. And the unvarnished truth is that in our incredibly complicated world, no one knows exactly what the economy will do, no matter how sophisticated the econometric models used. It has often been said, and not completely in jest, that the purpose of economic forecasting is to make astrology look respectable.

But let's assume that economists can outperform astrologers at forecasting. Indeed, let's be completely unrealistic and assume that economists can provide completely accurate economic forecasts of what will happen if macroeconomic policies are unchanged. Even then, they could not be certain of how to best promote stable economic growth.

If economists knew, for example, that the economy was going to dip into another recession in six months, they would then need to know exactly how much each possible policy would spur activity in order to keep the economy stable. But such precision is unattainable, given the complex forecasting problems faced. Furthermore, despite assurances to the contrary, economists aren't always sure what effect a policy will have on the economy. Will an increase in government purchases quicken economic growth? It is widely assumed so. But how much? And increasing government purchases increases the budget deficit, which could send a frightening signal to the bond markets. The result can be to drive up interest rates and choke off economic activity. So even when policymakers know which direction to nudge the economy, they can't be sure which policy levers to pull, or how hard to pull them, to fine-tune the economy to stable economic growth.

But let's further assume that policymakers know when the economy will need a boost, and also which policy will provide the right boost. A third crucial consideration is how long it will take a policy before it has its effect on the economy. The trouble is that, even when increased government purchases or expansionary monetary policy does give the economy a boost, no one knows precisely how

Some economists believe that fine-tuning the economy is like driving a car with an unpredictable steering lag on a winding road.

long it will take to do so. The boost may come very quickly, or many months (or even years) in the future, when it may add inflationary pressures to an economy that is already overheating, rather than helping the economy recover from a recession.

In this way, macroeconomic policy making is like driving down a twisting road in a car with an unpredictable lag and degree of response in the steering mechanism. If you turn the wheel to the right, the car will eventually veer to the right, but you don't know exactly when or how much. In short, there are severe practical difficulties in trying to fine-tune the economy. Even the best forecasting models and methods are far from perfect. Economists are not exactly sure where the economy is or where or how fast it is going, making it very difficult to prescribe an effective policy. Even if we do know where the economy is headed, we cannot be sure how large a policy's effect will be or when it will take effect.

CONCEPT CHECK

1. Monetary policy faces somewhat different implementation problems than fiscal policy. Both face difficult forecasting and lag problems. But the Fed can take action much more quickly. But its effectiveness depends largely on the reaction of the private banking system to its policy changes, and those effects can be offset by global and nonbank financial institutions, over which the Fed lacks jurisdiction.

2. In the United States, monetary and fiscal policy are carried out by different decision makers, thus requiring cooperation and coordination for effective policy implementation.

1. Why is the lag time for adopting policy changes shorter for monetary policy than for fiscal policy?
2. Why would a banking system that wanted to keep some excess reserves rather than lending them all out hinder the Fed's ability to increase the money stock?
3. How can the activities of global and nonbank institutions weaken the Fed's influence on the money market?

4. If fiscal policy was expansionary, but the Fed wanted to counteract the fiscal policy effect on aggregate demand, what could it do?
5. What are the arguments for and against having monetary policy be more directly controlled by the political process?
6. How is fine-tuning the economy like driving a car with an unpredictable steering lag on a winding road?

Application: The Independence of the Fed

Should the Fed be independent from Congress and the Administration? Is there any evidence that the Fed does act independently?

FEDERAL RESERVE CHIEF SHOWS HIS POLICY INDEPENDENCE

When Federal Reserve Board chairman Alan Greenspan raised short-term interest rates earlier this month, he did so, he said, to head off inflation.

Many Fed-watchers also believe he was asserting independence from the Clinton administration, which has implored the central banker to maintain a monetary policy loose enough to stimulate the consumer purchases and business investments that help the economy grow and generate jobs.

. . . Fed chairmen are used to pressure. "All the way back to the beginning, the head of the Federal Reserve Board who served during the same term as the president who appointed him was the tool of the White House," recalls a monetary official, offering a historical review of Federal Reserve Board-Executive Branch dynamics.

Perhaps the most obvious example in relatively recent history, he says, was President Nixon's appointment of Arthur Burns to the top Fed position in 1970. Mr. Burns then "helped set wage and price controls and served as chairman of the wage and price-control review panel, carrying out essentially a Cabinet-level duty." He was "widely believed to have pumped up the money supply during 1972 to help reelect Nixon."

Paul Volcker, appointed by President Carter in 1979, "essentially asked for a mandate from Carter to be as independent as he needed to combat inflation," recounts the monetary official. But President Reagan, who inherited Mr. Volcker as Fed chairman, "feared Volcker's tight monetary policy during a time when he wanted a stimulative policy," he says. Volcker's conduct under Mr. Carter, and Mr. Reagan's distrust of him "did much to build up the idea of an independent Fed," the official says.

Mr. Greenspan, he adds, "is not close to the White House at all, notwithstanding the 1993 State of the Union address," when the Fed chairman occupied the symbolically important seat next to Hillary Rodham Clinton—a placement many observers said was designed to show a close working relationship between Greenspan and the president. . . .

SOURCE: Amy Kaslow, "Federal Reserve Chief Shows His Policy Independence," *The Christian Science Monitor*, February 24, 1994.

While the Fed is an independent agency, it is hard to imagine that it is not subject to, and potentially responsive to, pressure from the Administration and Congress. However, because the Fed is responsible for maintaining price stability, it is important that it is not manipulated to generate gains for a political party.

The Fed is not very dependent on Congress, either. For example, while federal agencies must ask Congress for an annual appropriation, the Fed does not, as it owns a large portfolio of government securities (whose purchases and sales are used to alter bank reserves) that provides enough interest income to make the Fed entirely self-supporting. Hence, the Fed is somewhat insulated from political pressures, such as threats of withholding budget appropriations, from both the president and from Congress, although the mere threat of legislation that would curb its independence usually keeps the Fed from following a policy too much at variance from the wishes of the executive and/or legislative branches of government. Still, it is true that monetary policy is implemented by a privately owned, quasi-public institution that has a considerable amount of political independence from the federal government.

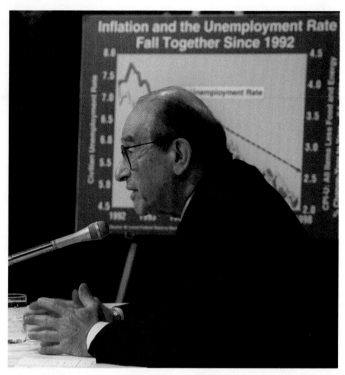

What relationship exists between the Fed and Congress?

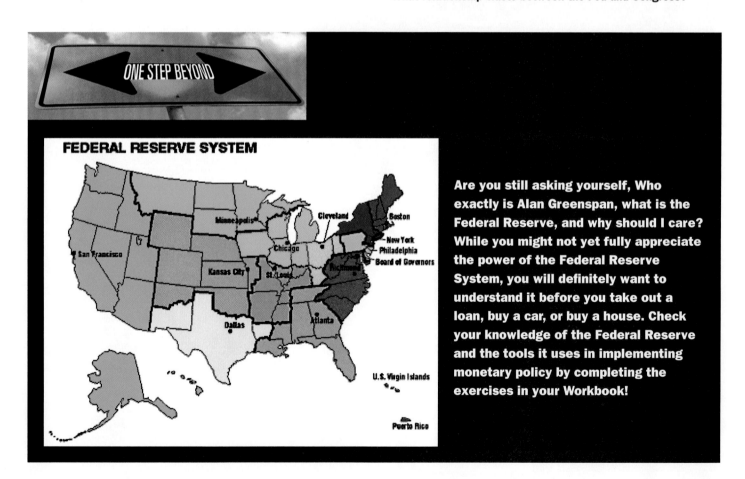

FEDERAL RESERVE SYSTEM

Are you still asking yourself, Who exactly is Alan Greenspan, what is the Federal Reserve, and why should I care? While you might not yet fully appreciate the power of the Federal Reserve System, you will definitely want to understand it before you take out a loan, buy a car, or buy a house. Check your knowledge of the Federal Reserve and the tools it uses in implementing monetary policy by completing the exercises in your Workbook!

Inflation, Unemployment, and Expectations

A. The Phillips Curve
Is there a relationship between
unemployment and inflation?

B. The Phillips Curve Over Time
Why does the Phillips curve shift?

C. Rational Expectations
What is the rational expectations theory?

D. Wage and Price Controls and Indexing
What purpose do wage and price controls and indexing serve?

E. Application: The Role of Expectations in Macroeconomics
Are rational expectations the same as perfect information?

The Phillips Curve

- What is the Phillips curve?
- How does the Phillips curve relate to the aggregate supply and demand model?

WHAT IS THE HISTORY OF UNEMPLOYMENT AND INFLATION?

Despite legislation committing the federal government to the goal of full employment and the development of macroeconomic theory arguing that full employment can be achieved by manipulating aggregate demand, periods of high unemployment still occur.

Similarly, price stability, which had been achieved for long periods before the 1930s, has not been consistently observed since that time. In every year in the lifetimes of most readers of this book, the general level of prices has risen.

HOW DO INFLATION AND UNEMPLOYMENT INTERACT?

We usually think of inflation as an evil—higher prices mean lower real incomes for persons on fixed incomes, while those with the power to raise the prices charged for goods or services they provide may actually benefit. Some economists believe that inflation could actually help eliminate unemployment. For example, if output prices rise but money wages do not go up as quickly or as much, real wages fall. At the lower real wage, unemployment is less because the lower wage makes it profitable to hire more, now cheaper, employees than before. The result is real wages that are closer to the full employment equilibrium wage that clears the labor market. Hence, with increased inflation, one might expect lower unemployment.

WHAT IS A PHILLIPS CURVE?

In fact, an inverse relationship between the rate of unemployment and the changing level of prices has been observed to have in fact occurred in many periods and places in history. Credit for identifying this relationship generally goes to British economist A.H. Phillips, who in the late 1950s published a paper setting forth what has since been called the Phillips curve. Phillips, and many others since, have suggested that at higher rates of inflation, the rate of unemployment is lower, while during periods of relatively stable or falling prices, there is substantial unemployment. In short, the cost of lower unemployment appears to be greater inflation, and the cost of greater price stability appears to be higher unemployment.

The actual inflation–unemployment relationship for the United States for the 1960s is shown in Exhibit 1. The points in this graph represent the combination of the inflation rate and the rate of unemployment in each of the 10 years of the decade. The curved line—the Phillips curve—is the smooth line that best "fits" the data points.

WHY IS THE SLOPE OF THE PHILLIPS CURVE NOT CONSTANT?

In examining Exhibit 1, it is evident that the slope of the Phillips curve is not the same throughout its length. The curve is steeper at higher rates of inflation and lower levels of unemployment. This suggests that once the economy has relatively low unemployment rates, further reductions in the unemployment rate can occur only by accepting larger increases in the inflation rate. Once unemployment is low, it takes larger and larger doses of inflation to eliminate a given quantity of unemployment. Presumably, at lower unemployment rates, an increased part of the economy is already operating at or near full capacity, and further fiscal or monetary stimulus primarily triggers inflationary pressures in sectors already at capacity, while eliminating decreasing amounts of unemployment in those sectors where some excess capacity and unemployment still exist.

EXHIBIT 1 | THE PHILLIPS CURVE RELATIONSHIP, UNITED STATES, 1960s

THE PHILLIPS CURVE AND AGGREGATE SUPPLY AND DEMAND

In Exhibit 2, we see the relationship between aggregate supply and demand analysis and the Phillips curve. Imagine that the economy has moved from a 2 percent annual inflation rate to a 4 percent inflation rate and that the unemployment rate has simultaneously fallen from 5 percent to 4 percent. In the Phillips rate curve we see this as a move up the curve from point A to point B in Exhibit 2(a). We can see the same relationship in the AD/AS model in Exhibit 2(b). Imagine that there is an increase in aggregate demand. Consequently, the price level increases from PL_{102} to PL_{104} and output increases from $RGDP_0$ to $RGDP_1$. To increase output, firms employ more workers, so employment increases and unemployment falls from 5 percent to 4 percent. This drop in unemployment is shown in the movement from point A to point B in Exhibit 2(b).

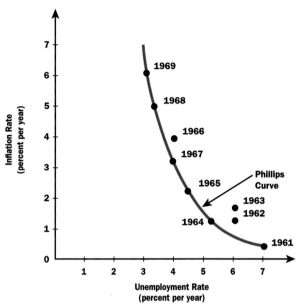

The Phillips curve illustrates an inverse relationship between the rate of unemployment and the rate of inflation. The slope of the Phillips curve becomes more steep as the unemployment rate drops, indicating that at very low unemployment rates, further decreases in unemployment can occur by accepting much larger increases in inflation rates.

EXHIBIT 2 | **THE PHILLIPS CURVE AND THE AD/AS CURVES**

As shown in Exhibit 2(b), if the aggregate supply curve is positively sloped, an increase in aggregate demand will cause higher prices and higher output (lower unemployment); a decrease in aggregate demand will cause lower prices and lower output (higher unemployment). This same trade-off is illustrated in the Phillips curve in Exhibit 2(a) in the shift from point A to point B.

TIGHT LABOR MARKET MAKING IT HARD FOR FAIR TO FIND TEMPORARY WORKERS

CARY STEMLE

The Kentucky State Fair doesn't have a musical theme, but if it did, this year's might be "Help!" With Louisville-area unemployment at 4.0 percent in June, and with stiff competition among employers, finding enough workers for the 11-day run is an increasing challenge, organizers say. Geralyn Clements, personnel director for the Kentucky State Fair Board, said about 500 temporary workers are needed to work gates, handle cleanup and setup, drive trams and serve as tour guides for the event, which begins August 14 at the Kentucky Fair and Exposition Center.

"We do experience difficulty," Clements said. "The low unemployment rate is definitely a factor. We do a lot of recruiting, and we work with temporary services and other organizations, like schools or softball teams. But usually, by the end of the fair, we're short-staffed."

One result of the tight labor market is pressure on wages. This year's salary is generally $5.50 an hour, up 25 cents an hour from last year. . . . Turnover is always a problem, he said. It can run as high as 150 percent. . . .

SOURCE: http://www.amcity.com/louisville/stories/081197/story4.html August 11, 1997

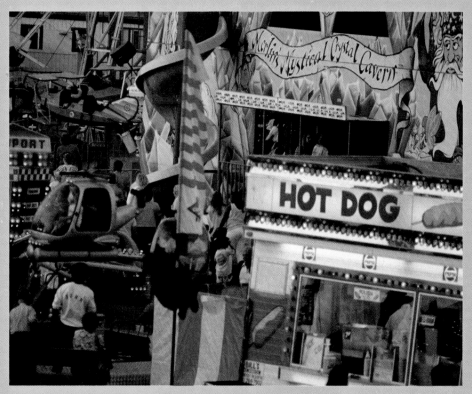

In tight labor markets, even temporary workers can bargain for higher wages.

> **CONSIDER THIS:**
> When unemployment falls to very low levels, competition for workers will tend to drive wages up.

CONCEPT CHECK

1. The inverse relationship between the rate of unemployment and the rate of inflation is called the Phillips curve.

2. The Phillips curve relationship can also be seen indirectly from the AD/AS model.

---

1. How does the rate of inflation affect real wage rates, if nominal wages rise less or more slowly than output prices?
2. How does the change in real wage rates (relative to output prices) as inflation increases affect the unemployment rate?
3. What is the argument for why the Phillips curve is relatively steeper at lower rates of unemployment and higher rates of inflation?
4. For a given upward-sloping short-run aggregate supply curve, how does an increase in aggregate demand correspond to a movement up and to the left along a Phillips curve?

The Phillips Curve Over Time

- How reliable is the Phillips curve?
- Is the Phillips curve stable over time?
- What is the difference between the long-run and short-run Phillips curves?

WAS THE PHILLIPS CURVE WELL ACCEPTED IN THE 1960S?

It became widely accepted in the 1960s that policy makers merely had to decide on the combination of unemployment and inflation they wanted from the Phillips curve, and then simply pursue the appropriate economic policies. To be sure, a reduction in the rate of unemployment came at a cost (more inflation), as did a reduction in the amount of inflation (more unemployment). Nonetheless, policy makers believed they could influence economic activity so that some goals could be met, though with a trade-off in terms of other macroeconomic goals. The empirical evidence on prices and unemployment seemed to fit the Phillips curve approach so beautifully at first that it is not surprising that it was embraced so rapidly and completely. Economists like Milton Friedman and Edmund Phelps who questioned the long-term validity of the Phillips curve were largely ignored in the 1960s. These economists believed there might be a short-term trade-off between unemployment and inflation but not a permanent trade-off. According to Friedman, the short-run trade-off comes from *unanticipated* inflation.

IS THE PHILLIPS CURVE STABLE?

Unfortunately, in the 1970s (and 1980s and 1990s also) economists recognized that macroeconomic decision-making was not as simple as picking a point on a stable Phillips curve. As shown in Exhibit 1, the data from the 1970s indicates that the Phillips curve starts to break down.

In fact, since 1969, every data point has been to the right of the 1960s Phillips curve, meaning a worsening trade-off between inflation and unemployment. In 1975, for example, the unemployment rate was 8.5 percent, the worst for any full year since the Great Depression. Moreover, in that year, prices rose 9.1 percent. In short, the 1970s experienced more of both inflation and unemployment than existed in the 1960s.

EXHIBIT 1	THE PHILLIPS CURVE, 1960–1979

The Phillips curve relationship breaks down in the 1970s; it no longer neatly fits the observations, and it does not have a consistent, pronounced negative slope, calling into question the notion that one can continue to "buy" full employment with inflation.

THE SHORT-RUN AND LONG-RUN PHILLIPS CURVE

The **long-run Phillips curve** shows the relationship between the inflation rate and the unemployment rate when the actual and expected inflation rates are the same. In Exhibit 2, we see that the long-run Phillips curve is vertical at the natural rate of unemployment. This is equivalent to the vertical long-run aggregate supply curve introduced in an earlier Module. Along the long-run Phillips curve we see that the natural rate of unemployment can occur at any rate of inflation. That is, regardless of fiscal and monetary stimulus output and employment will be at the natural rate in the long run.

| EXHIBIT 2 | THE LONG-RUN PHILLIPS CURVE |

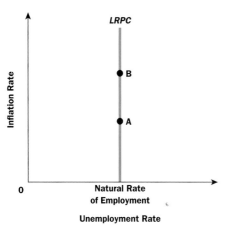

The long-run Phillips curve shows the relationship between the inflation rate and the unemployment rate when the actual and expected inflation rates are the same. Along the long-run Phillips curve we see that the natural rate of unemployment can occur at any rate of inflation.

HOW IS THE SHORT-RUN PHILLIPS CURVE RELATED TO THE LONG-RUN PHILLIPS CURVE?

Suppose the economy is at point A in Exhibit 3(a). At that point, the inflation rate is 3 percent and the unemployment rate is at the natural rate, 5 percent. Now suppose the growth rate of the money supply increases. The increase in the growth rate of money supply will stimulate aggregate demand. In the short run, the increase in aggregate demand will increase output and decrease unemployment, as the economy moves up along the short-run Phillips curve, from point A to point B, where the actual inflation rate has increased from 3 percent to 6 percent and the unemployment rate has fallen below the natural rate to 3 percent.

Because the increase in inflation was unanticipated, real wages fall. Firms are now receiving higher prices relative to their input costs, so they expand output. Consequently, unemployment rates fall, seen in Exhibit 3(a) as a movement along the short-run Phillips curve from A to B. Eventually, workers (and other input owners) realize that their real wage has fallen because of the increase in the inflation rate that was not initially anticipated. Workers now vigorously negotiate for higher wages. This increases costs to

producers, and as a result, they reduce output and unemployment rises—rightward shift in the short-run Phillips curve from point B to point C in Exhibit 3(a).

In short, the higher expected inflation rate shifts the short-run Phillips curve up. If the 6 percent inflation rate continues, the adjustment of expectations will move the economy to point C, where the expected and actual inflation rates are equal at the natural level of output and the natural rate of unemployment.

In the long run, the economy moves from A to C as inflation increases from 3 percent to 6 percent. This reveals that there is no trade-off between the inflation rate and the unemployment rate in the long run. The policy implication is that the use of fiscal or monetary policy to alter real output from the natural level of real output or unemployment from the natural rate of unemployment is ineffective in the long run.

Alternatively, say there was a decrease in the rate of growth in the money supply as a result of the Federal Reserve System's inflationary concerns. The decrease in the rate of growth in the money supply would reduce aggregate demand. In the short run, the decrease in aggregate demand moves the economy down along the short-run Phillips curve from point C to point D, where the actual inflation rate has decreased from 6 percent to 3 percent and the unemployment rate has risen above the natural rate, to 7 percent. The decrease in aggregate demand has led to lower production and a higher unemployment rate.

Initially, the reduction in the inflation rate is not anticipated and real wages rise; firms are now receiving lower prices relative to their input costs, so they reduce their output. This leads to a higher unemployment rate, as seen in the movement from point C to point D in Exhibit 3(b). If this new inflation rate remains steady at 3 percent, the actual and expected inflation rates will eventually become the same. The growth in wages will slow, lowering the cost of production, increasing output, and lowering the unemployment rate as the short-run Phillips curve shifts leftward from point D to point E in Exhibit 3(b).

In short, when people recognize that prices are not rising as rapidly as before, at only 3 percent rather than 6 percent, they adjust their expectations to reflect that fact, and the short-run Phillips curve shifts leftward, moving from point D to point E in Exhibit 3(b). The inflation rate is now lower, and unemployment and output have returned to their natural rates. In this scenario, the economy's road to lower inflation rates has come at the expense of higher unemployment in the short run, until people's expectations adapt to the new lower inflation rate in the long run.

| EXHIBIT 3 | THE SHORT-RUN AND LONG-RUN PHILLIPS CURVES |

a. An Increase in the Growth of the Money Supply

b. A Reduction in the Growth of the Money Supply

The economy initially moves along the short-run Phillips curve as actual inflation deviates from expected inflation. When expected inflation rates then adapt to take into account actual inflation rates, the short-run Phillips curve shifts back to the natural level of real output and to the natural rate of unemployment at that inflation rate on the long-run Phillips curve.

CONCEPT CHECK

1. The Phillips curve depicting the period of high inflation and unemployment in the 1970s no longer suggests the strong inverse relationship between the two variables that was evident in the 1960s.

2. The short-run Phillips curve relationship is seen as unstable and not a permanent relationship between unemployment and inflation rates.

3. The long-run Phillips curve shows the relationship between the inflation rate and the unemployment rate when the actual and expected inflation rates are the same.

4. Along the long-run Phillips curve, the natural rate of unemployment can occur at any rate of inflation.

---

1. Is the Phillips curve stable over time?
2. Why would you expect there to be no relationship between inflation and unemployment in the long run?
3. Why is the economy being on the long-run Phillips curve equivalent to its being on the long-run aggregate supply curve?

4. Why would inflation have to accelerate over time to keep unemployment below its natural rate (and real output above its natural level) for a sustained period of time?
5. What does the long-run Phillips curve say about the relationship between macroeconomic policy stimulus and unemployment in the long run?

Rational Expectations

■ What is the rational expectations theory?

■ What do critics say about the rational expectations theory?

CAN HUMAN BEHAVIOR COUNTERACT GOVERNMENT POLICY?

Is it possible that people can anticipate the plans of policy makers and alter their behavior quickly, to neutralize the intended impact of government action? For example, if workers see that the government is allowing the money supply to expand rapidly, they may quickly demand higher money wages in order to offset the anticipated inflation. In the extreme form, if people could instantly recognize and respond to government policy changes, it might be impossible to alter real output or unemployment levels through policy actions, because government policy-makers could no longer surprise consumers and businesses. An increasing number of economists believe that there is at least some truth to this point of view. At a minimum, most economists accept the notion that real output and the unemployment rate cannot be altered with the ease that was earlier believed; some believe that the unemployment rate can seldom be influenced by fiscal and monetary policies.

WHAT IS RATIONAL EXPECTATIONS THEORY?

The relatively new extension of economic theory that leads to this rather pessimistic conclusion regarding macroeconomic policy's ability to achieve our economic goals is called the **theory of rational expectations.** The notion that expectations or anticipations of future events are relevant to economic theory is not new; for decades, economists have incorporated expectations into models analyzing many forms of economic behavior. Only in the recent past, however, has a theory evolved that tries to incorporate expectations as a central factor in the analysis of the entire economy.

The interest in rational expectations has grown rapidly in the last decade. Acknowledged pioneers in the develop-

ment of the theory include Professor Robert Lucas of the University of Chicago and Professor Thomas Sargent of the University of Minnesota. In 1995, Professor Lucas won the Nobel Prize for his work in rational expectations.

Rational expectation economists believe that wages and prices are flexible, and that workers and consumers incorporate the likely consequences of government policy changes quickly into their expectations. In addition, rational expectation economists believe that the economy is inherently stable after macroeconomic shocks, and that tinkering with fiscal and monetary policy cannot have the desired effect unless consumers and workers are caught "off guard" (and catching them off guard gets harder the more you try to do it).

HOW DO RATIONAL EXPECTATIONS AFFECT THE CONSEQUENCES OF GOVERNMENT MACROECONOMIC POLICIES?

Rational expectations theory, then, suggests that government economic policies designed to alter aggregate demand to meet macroeconomic goals are of very limited effectiveness. When policy targets become public, it is argued, people will alter their own behavior from what it would otherwise have been, in order to maximize their own utility, and in so doing, they largely negate the intended impact of policy changes. If government policy seems tilted towards permitting more inflation in order to try to reduce unemployment, people start spending their money faster than before, become more adamant in their wage and other input price demands, and so on. In the process of quickly altering their behavior to reflect the likely consequences of policy changes, they make it more difficult (costly) for government authorities to meet their macroeconomic objectives. Rather than fooling people into changing real wages, and therefore unemployment, with inflation "surprises," changes in inflation are quickly reflected into expectations with little or no effect on unemployment or real output even in the short run. As a consequence, policies intended to reduce unemployment through stimulating aggregate demand will often fail to have the intended effect. Fiscal and monetary policy, according to this view, will work only if the people are caught off guard or fooled by policies so that they do not modify their behavior in a way that reduces policy effectiveness.

HOW DOES ANTICIPATION OF AN EXPANSIONARY MONETARY POLICY AFFECT THE AD/AS MODEL?

Consider the case in which there is an increase in aggregate demand as a result of an expansionary monetary policy. This increase is reflected in Exhibit 1 in the shift from AD_0 to AD_1. As a result of anticipating the predictable inflationary consequences of that expansionary policy, the price level will immediately adjust to a new price level at PL_1. Consumers, producers, workers, and lenders who have anticipated the effects of the expansionary policy simply built the higher inflation rates into their product prices, wages, and interest rates. That is, consumers, producers, and workers realize that expansionary monetary policy can cause inflation if the economy is working close to capacity. Consequently, in an effort to protect themselves from the higher anticipated inflation, workers ask for higher wages, suppliers increase input prices, and producers raise their product prices. Because wages, prices, and interest rates are assumed to be flexible, the adjustments take place immediately. This increase in input costs for wages, interest, and raw materials causes the aggregate supply curve to shift up or leftward, shown as the movement from AS_0 to AS_1 in Exhibit 1. So the desired policy effect of greater real output and reduced unemployment from a shift in the aggregate demand curve is offset by an upward or leftward shift in the aggregate supply curve caused by an increase in input costs.

WHAT HAPPENS IF A DECLINE IN AGGREGATE DEMAND IS ANTICIPATED?

A decline in the aggregate demand curve would have the opposite effect. Consider the case in which the Fed wants to fight inflation with a reduction in the money supply. If consumers and producers anticipate the reduced inflation that will accompany a reduction in the money supply, wages and input prices will quickly fall to reflect the new lower price levels. As a result of the lower input prices, the

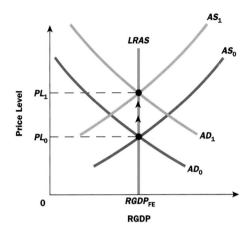

| EXHIBIT 1 | RATIONAL EXPECTATIONS AND THE AD/AS MODEL |

aggregate supply curve shifts down or rightward, shown in Exhibit 1 as the shift from AS_0 to AS_1. The price level quickly falls back to PL_0 without a change in real output or unemployment. Of course, the same would be true if we used fiscal policy rather than monetary policy in an expansionary or contractionary effort. The upshot of this discussion is that changed policy prescriptions that one expected cannot alter real output and unemployment. That is, stimulus policies proposed by the government are ineffective because consumers and producers anticipate the consequences of those changes and rapidly adjust their expectations, neutralizing the desired policy effects.

WHAT DO CRITICS SAY ABOUT RATIONAL EXPECTATIONS THEORY?

Of course, rational expectations theory does have its critics. Critics want to know if consumers and producers are completely informed about the impact that say, an increase in money supply will have on the economy. In general, all citizens will not be completely informed, but key players like corporations, financial institutions, and labor organizations may well be informed about the impact of these policy changes. But there are other problems, too. For example, are wages and other input prices really that flexible? That is, even if decision makers could anticipate the eventual effect of policy changes on prices, those prices may still be slow to adapt (e.g., what if you had just signed a three-year labor or supply contract when the new policy is implemented?).

1. Rational expectation economists believe that wages and prices are flexible and thus should be left alone. They also believe that workers and consumers form rational expectations that essentially negate the desired effect of a policy change.

2. Critics of rational expectations theory believe that most people are truly not informed about the effects of a policy change and therefore do not adjust their behavior. Additionally, they question whether prices and wages are really that flexible.

1. What is the rational expectations theory?
2. Why could an unexpected change in inflation change real wages and unemployment, while an expected change in inflation could not?
3. Why can the results of rational expectations be described as generating the long-run results of a policy change in the short run?
4. In a world of rational expectations, why is it harder to reduce unemployment below its natural rate but potentially easier to reduce inflation rates?

5. Even if people could quickly anticipate the consequences of government policy changes, how could long-term contracts (e.g., 3-year labor agreements and 30-year fixed-rate mortgages) and the costs of changing price lists and catalogs result in unemployment still being affected by those policy changes?
6. Why do expected rainstorms have different effects on people than unexpected rainstorms?

Wage and Price Controls and Indexing

- How are wage and price controls imposed and what purpose do they serve?
- What are some problems associated with wage and price controls?
- What is indexing and how can it be used?

WHAT PURPOSE DO WAGE AND PRICE CONTROLS SERVE?

If monetary and fiscal policy are ineffective or counterproductive, what policies are left to control inflation? It is possible that the federal government could set up a comprehensive program over nominal wages and prices—this is often called **incomes policy.** One method to deal with existing inflationary pressures is to impose controls on wages and/or prices. We have imposed such controls three times in modern American history, during World War II, during the Korean War, and in 1971 near the end of the Viet Nam War. Wage and price controls involve either a complete freeze on wages and prices at pre-control levels or some rigid limits as to the increases in wages and prices that will be permitted. One or more government agencies are created to monitor the program.

HOW CAN PRICE CONTROLS BE IMPLEMENTED WITHOUT GOVERNMENT REGULATION?

Sometimes it is felt that it is more desirable to establish voluntary guidelines or guideposts than to force companies and unions to limit their price and wage levels. This approach avoids the expense and political acrimony associated with establishing a control bureaucracy. Sometimes the "jawboning," the verbal pressuring or persuasion, gets pretty intense. The one memorable instance of jawboning in modern history came in the early 1960s, when President Kennedy became angered when major steel producers announced price increases. All sorts of pressures were placed on steelmakers, who were summoned to Washington, pleaded with, and even threatened with possible legal action under the antitrust laws. Finally, one company decided not to go along with the price increases, and then other companies quickly fell in line. In 1978, voluntary wage and price guidelines were imposed by the Carter administration. Those guidelines explicitly stated that pressure would be used by the government to insure compliance, making them virtually mandatory controls.

WHAT ARE THE JUSTIFICATIONS FOR WAGE AND PRICE CONTROLS?

There are two justifications given for wage and price controls. First, by limiting price increases by law, the government directly reduces the rate of inflation legally allowed. In this connection, it is interesting to note that during the four years of direct U.S. involvement in World War II, when price controls were in effect, consumer prices rose only a bit more than 20 percent, despite a huge increase in aggregate demand. Second, especially with respect to wage controls, it is argued that wage and price controls lower the inflationary expectations of workers and their unions, reducing the "inflation psychology" that contributes to cost-push inflation.

IF WAGE AND PRICE CONTROLS HAVE THESE ADVANTAGES, WHY ARE THEY NOT USED MORE OFTEN?

Wage and price controls also have several major disadvantages, which are very likely to be viewed as being greater than the advantages, except possibly during wartime situations when aggregate demand is growing very rapidly. The problem of enforcing the controls has already been mentioned. With millions of businesses, products, and workers in our economy, the administrative problem of monitoring wages and prices is immense, and any effective enforcement is likely to be costly. Black markets (illegal sales) often develop. These problems are often very hard to solve.

To give one example, suppose the price administrators say that next year's models of automobiles can be priced 4 percent higher than this year's. Suppose now that an automaker brings out a new model selling for only 3 percent more than the old model. At the same time, however, suppose that the new model is slightly smaller than the old one, has less "frills" than the previous model, has a slightly smaller engine, and so forth. Is the automaker in violation of the price control? The company would say no, because the price is up only 3 percent. Others might say yes, because the new product is inferior to the old one in several ways.

Another even more fundamental problem with wage and price controls is that they lead to shortages of goods, services, and workers. With these controls, inflationary pressures are not eradicated but rather disguised, manifesting themselves not as price increases but as a lack of desired goods or human resources. As a result, severe and prolonged controls can lead to a very serious misallocation of resources.

HOW DO PRICE CONTROLS LEAD TO A MISALLOCATION OF RESOURCES?

Straightforward supply and demand analysis indicates the misallocation of resources due to wage and price controls, as illustrated in Exhibit 1. Suppose the demand and supply for refrigerators are indicated by D_0 and S in Exhibit 1. The equilibrium price of refrigerators, P_0, is determined by the intersection of the demand and supply curves. Suppose that recent stock market wealth has led to higher income and an increase in demand for refrigerators to D_1. If the market is allowed to work without intervention, the price of refrigerators would increase to the new equilibrium price of P_1, where D_1 intersects S. But suppose wage and price controls are imposed and the price controllers consider an increase in price from P_0 to P_1 to be unacceptably large, declaring instead that the price can only rise to the government ceiling price, $P_{CEILING}$. At the price ceiling, however, the quantity demanded exceeds the quantity supplied and shortages arise.

EXHIBIT 1	THE IMPACT OF PRICE CONTROLS

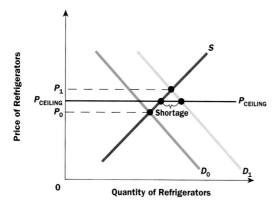

Suppose that price controls exist and the ceiling price on refrigerators is set at $P_{CEILING}$. Suppose for some reason the demand for refrigerators rises from D_0 to D_1. Without controls, price would be P_1. Price controls lead to a quantity demanded that is greater than quantity supplied, resulting in a shortage.

WHAT ARE SOME EXAMPLES OF PROBLEMS WITH PRICE CONTROLS?

During the 1973 Arab oil boycott, the federal government imposed price ceilings on gasoline that prevented gas prices from rising as they normally would have in response to reduced supply. At the ceiling price, quantity demanded exceeded quantity supplied; gas stations ran out of gas, were often closed, or placed a limit on the amount of gas they would sell. When drivers were able to buy gas, they often not only filled their tanks but also several containers they carried along to reduce the risk of being unable to buy gas when they needed it. In the former Soviet Union, where price-control-related shortages were commonplace, citizens typically carried briefcases or even suitcases and large quantities of cash, in case they were able to purchase a normally unavailable good. Rather than just buy the product for themselves, they would buy several items for their friends and relatives as well, to keep them from having to stand in line for hours, often in vain, trying to buy it. Winston Churchill once aptly termed a society with rigid price controls as a "queuetopia." (The British commonly used the term "queue" to refer to long lines.)

WHAT ARE EXAMPLES OF PROBLEMS CREATED BY WAGE CONTROLS?

In the case of prolonged wage controls, shortages of personnel can occur. Wages serve as market signals. Rising wages in an occupation increase an occupation's attractiveness, leading to new entrants of workers. In the early 1970s, for example, newly trained accountants were earning much more than other new college graduates. Predictably, there was a supply response, as accounting majors became much more numerous in colleges. By the late 1970s, the salary (or price) of accountants started to fall a bit relative to other occupations. If, however, the government had decreed that the salaries of new accountants in the five years after 1972 could not rise above, say, $12,000 a year, the increase in the quantity of new accountants supplied would not have occurred and an accountant shortage would have developed, causing all sorts of problems for businesses needing an accurate evaluation of their financial performance, individuals needing their tax returns prepared, and so forth.

Whether the gains from wage and price controls in the form of reduced inflation outweigh the costs in the form of shortages and inefficient resource allocation is debatable. This is a normative issue where honest, informed persons can differ in their perceptions of costs and benefits. The classic illustration of this was the monumental, prolonged debate in the U.S. Congress in 1977 over the removal of price controls on natural gas, with one side arguing that controls should be removed to end shortages and enhance long-term supply, while the other side argued that removing controls would lead to inflated prices for gas and inflated profits for gas producers, while causing hardships to lower-income users of gas. Eventually the issue was resolved by easing, but not completely removing, the controls until 1993.

HOW CAN PRICES BE KEPT DOWN WITHOUT THE USE OF PRICE CONTROLS?

The attempt to control prices politically can take another form. The presence of monopolistic elements in an industry can lead to higher prices for that industry's products than would be the case for a more competitive industry. By stimulating price competition among private firms, the government may be able to help in reducing inflationary pressures. In recent years, the possibility of using the antitrust laws to attack alleged monopoly influences in certain industries with rapidly increasing prices—such as the prescription drug industry—has been considered. However, despite much talk, there has been relatively little actual use of antitrust laws to try to reduce inflation pressures. Moreover, monopoly power can also be artificially created by government regulations; such has been the case in transportation. The relaxation of price regulation of airlines, for example, led to lower air fares in the late 1970s.

HOW COULD INDEXING REDUCE THE COSTS OF INFLATION?

Another approach to some of the problems posed by inflation is **indexing.** As you recall, inflation poses substantial equity and distributional problems only when it is unanticipated or unexpected. One means of protecting parties against unanticipated price increases is to write contracts that automatically change prices of goods or services whenever the overall price level changes, effectively rewriting agreements in terms of dollars of constant purchasing power. Wages, loans, and mortgage payments—everything possible—would be changed every month or so by an amount equal to the percent change in some broad-based price index. Thus, if prices rise by 1.2 percent this month and my last month's wage was $1,000, my wage this month will be $1,012 ($1,000 × 1.012). By making as many contracts as possible payable in dollars of constant purchasing power, those involved can protect themselves against unanticipated changes in inflation.

WHY ISN'T INDEXING MORE EXTENSIVELY USED?

Indexing seems to eliminate most of the wealth transfers associated with unexpected inflation. Why then is it not more commonly used? One main argument against indexing is that it could well worsen inflation. As prices go up, wages and certain other contractual obligations (e.g., rents) would also automatically increase. This immediate and comprehensive reaction to price increases will lead to greater inflationary pressures. One price increase likely might lead to a second, which in turn will lead to a third, and so on.

WHAT OTHER PROBLEMS EXIST WITH INDEXING?

One might say, so what? If prices are rising rapidly but wages, rents, and so forth are also moving up with prices, real wages and rents are remaining constant. Yet if the inflation gets bad enough, it may become almost impossible administratively to maintain the indexing scheme. The index, to be effective, might have to be changed every few days, but the information to make such changes is not currently readily available. To get such quick information, then, might be quite expensive, involving a small army of price-checking bureaucrats and a massive electronic communications system. There are other inefficiencies as well. During the German hyperinflation of the early 1920s, prices at one point rose so rapidly that workers demanded to be paid twice a day, at noon and at the end of work. During their lunch hour, workers would rush money to their wives, who would then run out and buy real goods before prices increased further.

Other big problems include the fact that indexing reduces the ability for relative price changes to allocate resources where they are more valuable. Not everything can be indexed, so indexing would cause wealth redistribution. In addition, costs would necessarily be incurred as a result of renegotiating cost-of-living (COLA) clauses.

Excessive inflation, then, leads to great inefficiency, as well as to a loss of confidence in the issuer of money—namely, the government. Furthermore, inflation influences world trade patterns. Limited indexing, in fact, has already been adopted, as some wage and pension payments are changed with changes in the cost-of-living index. Whether on balance those escalator clauses are "good" or "bad" is a debatable topic, a normative judgment that we will leave to the reader to make.

1. Wage and price controls can be imposed by government regulation or "voluntarily" with the use of moral suasion. The purpose of such controls is to reduce inflation and lower future inflation expectations.
2. Besides the problems of enforcing wage and price controls, these policies lead to shortages of goods and personnel as well as misallocations of goods.

3. Indexing is a process of adjusting payment contracts to automatically adjust for changes in inflation. Indexing reduces the impact of inflation on the distribution of income but may also intensify the inflationary effects of expansionary monetary policy by increasing inflationary pressures.

1. In what ways might "voluntary" government inflation guidelines not be completely voluntary?
2. If holding down legal price increases through price controls reduces official inflation rates, why are black markets likely to arise?
3. How might wage and price controls lead to shortages of goods and services (a "queuetopia")?

4. How might wage and price controls lead to the production of inferior products over time?
5. If every possible good was indexed to changes in the general price level, would it be very easy for relative price changes to signal changing relative scarcities? Why or why not?

Application:
The Role of
Expectations in
Macroeconomics

Policy makers agree that the art of economic forecasting is a different one. One important aspect of policy making is how consumers, producers, and investors form their expectations. Do consumers, producers, and investors have rational expectations about the future of the economy? If so, do those expectations impact the economy? In this article, we see the contribution that Professor Lucas has made in the area of expectations.

GETTING IT RIGHT

ROBERT BARROW

. . . Bob Lucas's contributions to macroeconomics in the 1970s permanently changed the very center of the discipline. Moreover, his influence has been as great on critics, primarily Keynesians, as on supporters, who tend to represent market-clearing or equilibrium-style approaches.

In some key articles published from 1972 to 1975, Bob applied John Muth's insights on rational expectations to monetary theories of the business cycle. Previous analyses had relied on simplistic Phillips curve models in which increased inflation led mechanically to lower unemployment and higher output. But these theories assumed that workers and firms did not exploit available information and thereby would commit the same mistakes time after time. For instance, higher inflation was assumed to raise the willingness to work because workers were continually fooled into thinking that their real wage was higher than it was.

In Bob's theory, where expectations are formed rationally, people can be confused temporarily by monetary surprises. (Rational expectations are not the same as complete information or perfect foresight.) In particular, an unanticipated expansion of money and the general price level may temporarily fool workers into thinking that their real wage had risen and producers into believing that the relative price of their product had gone up. Through these channels, a monetary stimulus may cause a temporary boom, but one that must end soon after the errors in expectations are recognized.

In the older style theory, the permanent trade-off between inflation and unemployment meant that monetary policy had a key role in fine-tuning the economy. The revised theory has dramatically different implications because the monetary authority has its main influence when it does something surprising. Thus, it is not enough to print more money when the economy is contracting and to print less when the economy is expanding. The expectations of this policy pretty much neutralize the real effects. . . .

Unfortunately, the easiest way for the monetary authority to create surprises is to behave erratically, an approach that has effects that are real but harmful. Therefore, an important policy influence from Lucas's theory is that the central bank ought to relinquish the idea of fine-tuning and instead concentrate on long-run objectives such as price stability. . . .

The role of expectations is not limited to monetary policy but is crucial in many areas of economics, as Bob showed in his later research on investment, unemployment, taxation, public debt management, and asset pricing. In all of these situations, the appropriate evaluation of policy must take account of the way that expectations would be rationally formed; the older analyses, which failed to consider this exceptional adjustment, are now described as failing the "Lucas critique. . . ."

SOURCE: Robert Barrow, *Getting It Right*, MIT Press, 1996, pp. 168–170.

The rational expectations hypothesis is that consumers, producers, and investors can forecast the future as well as economic forecasters and that people are continuously updating their information and revising their expectations so that they will not be continuously surprised. The real point is that people are influenced by expectations and policy makers must anticipate the impact of changing expectations on a policy proposal like a tax cut. The implications are important, because if Lucas and his supporters are correct, then the macroeconomic policy that is anticipated will be offset by workers and businesses who anticipate these changes.

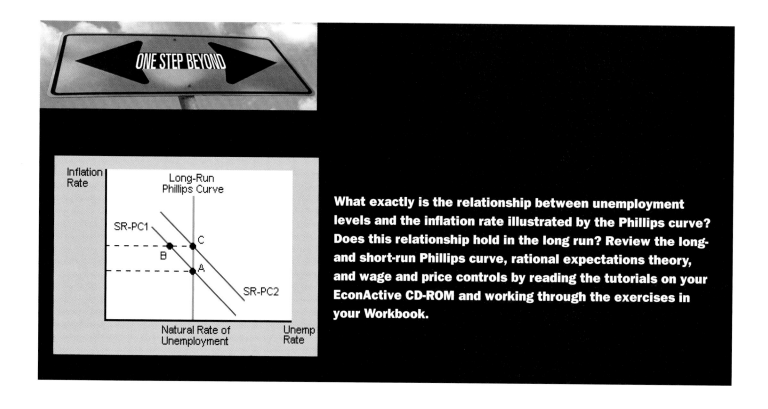

ONE STEP BEYOND

What exactly is the relationship between unemployment levels and the inflation rate illustrated by the Phillips curve? Does this relationship hold in the long run? Review the long- and short-run Phillips curve, rational expectations theory, and wage and price controls by reading the tutorials on your EconActive CD-ROM and working through the exercises in your Workbook.

Page **372:** © Nik Wheeler/Corbis Images.

International Trade

A. The Growth in World Trade
How important is international trade?

B. Comparative Advantage and Gains from Trade
What is the difference between comparative advantage and absolute advantage?

C. Supply and Demand in International Trade
Who gains and who loses from exports and imports?

D. Tariffs, Import Quotas, and Subsidies
How do tariffs, import quotas, and subsidies impact the domestic economy?

E. Application: Common Misperceptions on Trade
Are the welfare gains associated with trade overstated?

The Growth in World Trade

MODULE 16

- What has happened to the volume of international trade over time?
- Who trades with the United States?

HOW IMPORTANT IS INTERNATIONAL TRADE?

In a typical year, about 15 percent of the world's output is traded in international markets. Of course, the importance of the international sector varies enormously from place to place on the planet. Some nations are almost closed economies, with foreign trade equaling only a very small proportion (perhaps 5 percent) of total output. In the United States, in the mid-1990s, exports were over 11 percent of gross domestic product (GDP), while imports were a little higher, at almost 13 percent of GDP. In Germany, by contrast, nearly 33 percent of all output produced was exported, while in Belgium exports accounted for over 70 percent of GDP.

The volume of international trade has increased substantially in the United States over the last 50 years, in which time exports and imports have gone from less than 5 percent of GDP to over 10 percent of GDP. There has also been an explosion of trade in world markets since the 1950s. From 1950 to 1990, world output rose over 400 percent and world exports rose over 1,000 percent. Exports of one nation are imports to another, so world exports are conceptually equal in magnitude to world imports. During this 40-year period, the world exhibited remarkable rates of economic growth (in part because of trade), but the growth in world trade was faster than output growth generally, so trade as a proportion of gross world product more than doubled.

WITH WHOM DOES THE U.S. TRADE?

In its early history, U.S. international trade was largely directed towards Europe and to Great Britain in particular. In recent years, however, trade has become highly multidirectional, with no one nation or small geographic area being of dominant importance. This is indicated in Exhibit 1, which suggests that our most important single trading partner, Canada, accounts only for around one-fifth of our imports and exports. Trade with Japan, Germany, China, Taiwan, and Italy are also particularly important.

Canada is the United States' most important trading partner.

EXHIBIT 1   MAJOR U.S. TRADING PARTNERS

Top Five Trading Partners—Exports of Goods in 1996

Rank	Country	Value of Goods (billions of dollars)	Percent of Total
1	Canada	$133.7	21.4
2	Japan	67.5	10.8
3	Mexico	56.8	9.1
4	United Kingdom	30.9	4.9
5	Korea	26.6	4.3

Top Five Trading Partners—Imports of Goods in 1996

Rank	Country	Value of Goods (billions of dollars)	Percent of Total
1	Canada	$156.5	19.8
2	Japan	115.2	14.6
3	Mexico	73.0	9.2
4	China	51.5	6.5
5	Germany	38.9	4.9

SOURCE: U.S. Census Bureau, *Wall Street Almanac,* 1998, p. 183.

IN THE NEWS

BAYWATCH IS WORLD WATCHED

In the world of entertainment exports, the syndicated series *Baywatch* is like the Boeing 747. You can see *Baywatch* in Bangladesh, Barbados, Bolivia, Brunei, and 140 other countries. Produced by a small, independent Los Angeles production company, the weekly dose of sun, sand, sea, and skin, with muscled lifeguards rescuing drowning damsels (and vice versa), earns about $100 million per year, 67 percent of which is currently from foreign distribution.

Baywatch is currently riding the crest of a wave being surfed by all of the Hollywood studios and production companies. At the Walt Disney Company in Burbank, Calif., CFO Richard Nanula says that while the Magic Kingdom has had a presence in some foreign markets for up to 50 years, the international demand for Disney products is now growing at an accelerated pace. This is especially true in film and television where international business now accounts for about 40 percent of revenue, but growth is twice that of domestic.

"The international markets really help the performance of a movie in its profit statement—substantially more than they used to," Nanula says. Overseas box office receipts used to add perhaps 20 percent to a film's gross. Now some movies, particularly animation and action-adventure, that make $100 million at home might eventually make twice as much internationally.

SOURCE: Steve Barth, "Exporting Fantasy," *World Trade,* March 1998, pp. 41–42.

CONSIDER THIS:
The international marketplace has become very important in the television and movie industry.

---

1. The volume of international trade has increased substantially in the United States over the last 50 years. During that time, exports and imports have grown from less than 5 percent to over 10 percent of GDP.

2. Our most important single trading partner, Canada, accounts only for around one-fifth of our imports and exports. Trade with Japan, Germany, China, Taiwan, and Italy is also particularly important to the United States.

1. Why is it important to understand the effects of international trade?

2. Why would producers and consumers in the United States be more concerned about Canadian trade restrictions than Swedish trade restrictions?

Comparative Advantage and Gains from Trade

- Does economic growth result from greater specialization?
- What is the principle of comparative advantage?
- What benefits are derived from specialization?

DOES ECONOMIC GROWTH LEAD TO A DECLINE IN SELF-SUFFICIENCY?

One of the most striking characteristics of any relatively poor nation undergoing a substantial amount of economic growth is the decline in self-sufficiency and the rise in specialization. Before growth begins, a large proportion of output produced in traditional agricultural societies is produced by family units, who also consume those goods and services. A relatively small proportion of goods are traded to others. Families are "Jacks and Jills of all trades," economic units that, in addition to producing a wide variety of foodstuffs, also engage in the manufacture of clothing items, the construction of buildings, and so on. The family's workers are, in addition to being farmers, part-time carpenters, plumbers, shoemakers, seamstresses, candle makers, soap makers, bakers, and even physicians. Household manufacturing tends to die out to a considerable extent, however, with economic growth, and even in their agricultural functions, farmers tend to specialize more and more in a few individual crops or forms of livestock, exporting surplus output from the farm in exchange for other goods that the farmer no longer produces. Why does this decline in self-sufficiency occur?

Using simple logic, we conclude that the very existence of trade suggests that trade is economically beneficial. This is true if one assumes that people are utility maximizers and are rational, intelligent, and engage in trade on a voluntary basis. Because almost all trade is voluntary, it would seem that trade occurs because the participants feel that they are better off because of the trade. Both participants of an exchange of goods and services anticipate an improvement in their economic welfare. Sometimes, of course, anticipations are not realized (because the world is uncertain), but the motive behind trade remains an expectation of some enhancement in utility or satisfaction by both parties.

Going beyond this rather simplistic explanation that "trade must be good because people do it," the classical economist David Ricardo is usually given most of the credit for developing the economic theory that more precisely explains how trade can be mutually beneficial to both parties, raising output and income levels in the entire trading area.

THE PRINCIPLE OF COMPARATIVE ADVANTAGE

Ricardo's theory of international trade centers on the concept of comparative advantage. A nation, geographic area, or even a person can gain from trade if it (the area or the person) produces a good or service relatively cheaper than other areas or persons can produce it. Put slightly differently, an area should specialize in producing and selling those items that it can produce at a lower opportunity cost than can other countries.

Comparative advantage analysis does not mean that nations or areas that export goods will necessarily be able to produce those goods or services more cheaply than other nations in an absolute sense. What is important is comparative advantage, not absolute advantage. For example, the United States may be able to produce more cotton cloth per worker than India, but that does not mean the United States should necessarily sell cotton cloth to India. Indeed, the United States has an absolute advantage or productive superiority over India in nearly every good, given the higher levels of output per person in the United States. Yet India's inferiority in producing some goods is much less than for others. In goods where India's productivity is only slightly less than that of the United States, such as perhaps in cotton cloth, it probably has a comparative advantage over the United States. How? For a highly productive nation to produce goods in which it is only marginally more productive than other nations, the nation must take resources from the production of other goods in which its productive abilities are markedly superior. As a result, the opportunity costs in India of making cotton cloth may be less than in the United States. With that, both can gain from trade, despite potential absolute advantages for every good in the United States.

If the U.S. can produce more shirts per year than India, should it necessarily do so?

COMPARATIVE ADVANTAGE AND THE PRODUCTION POSSIBILITIES CURVE

In Exhibit 1, we show the production possibilities curves for two individuals, Wendy and Calvin. Wendy and Calvin can produce either food or clothing. In Exhibit 1, we see that if Wendy devotes all of her resources to producing food, she can produce 30 pounds of food; if she devotes all of her resources to producing clothes, she can produce 10 yards of clothing. In Exhibit 1, we see that when Calvin uses all of his resources to produce food, he only produces 10 pounds; but when he uses all of his resources to produce clothing, he can produce 30 yards. In this example, Wendy actually has an absolute advantage in food, while Calvin has an absolute advantage in clothing, but as we shall see, it would not affect the result if Calvin could only produce 2 pounds of food and 6 yards of clothing.

For simplicity, we will assume each producer operates on a straight line production possibilities curve (*PPC*) and each initially chooses to produce 7.5 pounds of food and 7.5 yards of clothing, although any amount of each good could have been produced.

Wendy can produce food at a lower opportunity cost than Calvin. When Wendy produces 30 pounds of food, it costs only 10 yards of clothing. However, when Calvin produces only 10 pounds of food, it costs 30 yards of clothing. Wendy, then, is the lowest-cost producer of food. However, Calvin can produce clothing at a lower opportunity cost than Wendy. When Calvin produces 30 yards of clothing, it costs him 10 pounds of food. And when Wendy

produces 10 yards of clothing, it costs 30 pounds of food. Calvin, then, is the lowest-cost producer of clothing.

To demonstrate our point about comparative advantage, we have overlapped the two production possibility curves in Exhibit 1. At point A, we see that Wendy produces 7.5 pounds of food and 7.5 yards of clothing and Calvin produces 7.5 yards of clothing and 7.5 pounds of food. Together they would produce 15 pounds of food and 15 yards of clothing, point B. However, if each specialized and pursued his or her comparative advantage, the goods each can produce at the lowest opportunity cost, then Wendy could produce 30 pounds of food and Calvin could produce 30 yards of clothing, point C. That is, by specializing, Wendy and Calvin have produced 30 units of each good rather than 15 units. Now if Wendy does not want all food and Calvin does not want all clothing, they can trade with each other. In fact, if Wendy trades half of her food for half of the clothing Calvin has produced, then each will have 15 units of food and clothing. This is 7.5 more pounds of food and 7.5 more yards of clothing than they had before specialization and trade. Exhibit 1 also shows that as a result of specialization and trade, Wendy gains D to B in additional clothing and Calvin gains E to B in additional

| **EXHIBIT 1** | **SPECIALIZATION AND TRADE** |

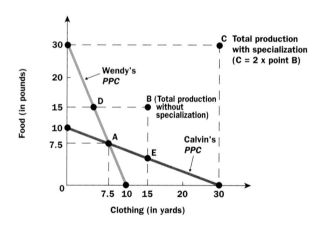

Before Trade
Point A—Without specialization, say that Wendy and Calvin each choose to produce 7.5 pounds of food and 7.5 yards of clothing.
Point B—Wendy and Calvin's total production if they do not specialize: Collectively they produce 15 pounds of food and 15 yards of clothing.
Point C—Wendy and Calvin's total production if they specialize: Wendy produces 30 pounds of food and Calvin produces 30 yards of clothing.

Specialization and Trade
Point B—If Wendy and Calvin split their total production after specialization equally, they will each have 15 pounds of food and 15 yards of clothing.
Point D—As a result of specialization and trade, Wendy gains D to B in additional clothing.
Point E—As a result of specialization and trade, Calvin gains E to B in additional food.

COMPARATIVE ADVANTAGE

Q: Surrey A. List, a famous artist, can complete one painting in each 40-hour workweek. Each painting sells for $2,000. As a result of his enormous success, however, Surrey is swamped in paperwork. To solve the problem, Surrey hires Dave to handle all of the bookkeeping and typing associated with buying supplies, answering inquiries from prospective buyers and dealers, writing art galleries, and so forth. Surrey pays Dave $300 per week for his work. After a couple of weeks in this arrangement, Surrey realizes that he handled the secretarial chores more quickly than Dave does. In fact, he estimates that he is twice as fast as Dave, completing in 20 hours what it takes Dave 40 hours to complete. Should Surrey fire Dave?

A: Clearly Surrey has an absolute advantage over Dave in both painting and paperwork because he can do twice as much paperwork in 40 hours as Dave can, and Dave can't paint well at all. Still, it would be foolish for Surrey to do his own secretarial work. If Surrey did his own secretarial work, 20 hours per week would be involved in secretarial chores, leaving him only 20 hours to paint. Because each watercolor takes 40 hours to paint, Surrey's output would fall from one painting per week to one painting per two weeks. Instead of getting $2,000 a week, he would only earn $1,000 a week.

When he had his own secretary, Surrey's net income was $1,700 ($2,000 minus $300 in secretarial wages); now it is only $1,000. While Surrey is both a better painter and a better secretary than Dave, it pays for him to specialize in painting, in which he has a comparative advantage, and allow Dave to do the typing. The opportunity cost to Surrey of secretarial work is high. For Dave, who lacks skills as a painter, the opportunity costs of being a secretary are much less.

---

food. The point is the differences in opportunity costs provided an incentive to gain from specialization and trade.

REGIONAL COMPARATIVE ADVANTAGE

In the last section, using a production possibilities curve, we saw how Wendy and Calvin could benefit from specialization and trade. The principle of comparative advantage can be applied to regional markets as well. In fact, trade has evolved in large part because different geographic areas have different resource endowments, and therefore different production possibilities. The impact of trade between two areas with differing factor endowments is shown in Exhibit 2. To keep the analysis simple, suppose two trading areas exist that can produce just two commodities, grain and computers. A "trading area" may be a locality, a region, or even a nation, but for our example, suppose we think in terms of two hypothetical regions, Grainsville and Techland.

Grainsville and Techland have various potential combinations of grain and computers that they can produce. For each region, the cost of producing more grain is the output of computers that must be foregone, and vice versa. Observe in this table that Techland has the capability of producing more of both grain (40 bushels) and computers (100 units) than Grainsville can (30 bushels; 30 units), reflecting perhaps superior resources (more or better labor, more land, and so on); this means that Techland has an absolute advantage in both products.

EXHIBIT 2	PRODUCTION POSSIBILITIES, TECHLAND AND GRAINSVILLE

Region	Grain (bushels per day)	Computers (units per day)
Techland	0	100
	10	75
	20	50
	30	25
	40	0
Grainsville	0	30
	6	24
	12	18
	18	12
	24	6
	30	0
Before Specialization		
Techland	10	75
Grainsville	18	12
Total	28	87
After Specialization		
Techland	0	100
Grainsville	30	0
Total	30	100

Suppose that, before specialization Techland chooses to produce 75 computers and 10 bushels of grain per day. Similarly, suppose Grainsville decides to produce 12 computers and 18 bushels of grain. Collectively, then the two areas are producing 87 computers (75 + 12) and 28 bushels of grain (10 + 18) per day before specialization.

Now, suppose the two nations specialize. Techland decides to specialize in computers and devotes all of its resources to making that product. As a result, computer output in Techland rises to 100 units per day, some of which is sold to Grainsville. Grainsville, in turn, devotes all of its resources to grain, producing 30 bushels of grain per day and selling some of it to Techland. Together, the two areas are producing more of both grain and computers than before—100 instead of 87 computers and 30 instead of 28 bushels of grain. Both areas could, as a result, have more of both products than before they began specializing and trading.

How can that happen? In Techland, the opportunity cost of producing grain is very high—25 computers must be foregone to get 10 more bushels of grain. The cost of one bushel of grain, then, is 2.5 computers (25 divided by 10). In Grainsville, by contrast, the opportunity cost of producing six more units of grain is six units of computers that must be foregone, so the cost of one unit of grain is one unit of computers. In Techland, a unit of grain costs 2.5 computers, while in Grainsville the same amount of grain

costs only one computer. Grain is more costly in Techland in terms of the computers foregone than in Grainsville, so Grainsville has the comparative advantage in the production of grain, even though Techland has an absolute advantage in grain.

With respect to computers, an increase in output by 25 units, say from 25 to 50 units, costs 10 bushels of grain foregone in Techland. The cost of one more computer is .4 bushels of grain (10 divided by 25). In Grainsville, an increase in computer output of six units, say from 12 to 18, is accompanied by a decrease in grain production by six bushels as resources are converted from grain to computer manufacturing. The cost of one computer is one bushel of grain. Computers are more costly (in terms of opportunity cost) in Grainsville and cheaper in Techland, so Techland should specialize in the production of computers.

Thus, by specializing in products in which it has a comparative advantage, an area has the potential of having more goods and services, assuming it trades the additional output for other desirable goods and services others can produce at a lower opportunity cost. In the scenario presented here, the people in Techland would specialize in computers, and the people in Grainsville would specialize in farming (grain). As you can see from this example, specialization increases the division of labor and increases the interdependence of one group of people on others.

THE MIRACLE OF TRADE

It is mere common sense that if one country is very good at making hats, and another is very good at making shoes, then total output can be increased by arranging for the first country to concentrate on making hats and the second on making shoes. Then, through trade in both goods, more of each can be consumed in both places.

That is a tale of absolute advantage. . . . Each country is better than the other at making a certain good, and so profits from specialization and trade. Comparative advantage is different: a country will have it despite being bad at the activity concerned. Indeed, it can have a comparative advantage in making a certain good even if it is worse at making that good than any other country.

This is not economic theory, but a straightforward matter of definition: a country has a comparative advantage where its margin of superiority is greater, or its margin of inferiority smaller.

. . . [W]hen people say of Africa, or Britain, or wherever, that it has no comparative advantage in anything, they are simply confusing absolute advantage (for which their claim may or may not be true) with comparative advantage (for which it is certainly false).

Why does this confusion over terms matter? Because the case for free trade is often thought to depend on the existence of absolute advantage and is therefore thought to collapse whenever absolute advantage is absent. But economics shows that gains from trade follow, in fact, from comparative advantage. Since comparative advantage is never absent, this gives the theory far broader scope than more popular critics suppose.

In particular, it shows that even countries which are desperately bad at making everything can expect to gain from international competition. If countries specialize according to their comparative advantage, they can prosper through trade regardless of how inefficient, in absolute terms, they may be in their chosen specialty.

SOURCE: *The Economist*, January 27, 1996, pp. 61, 62.

> **CONSIDER THIS:**
> Even countries that are not very good at producing anything can prosper from free trade.

1. As economic growth occurs, regions and countries tend to specialize in what they produce best.
2. A nation, geographic area, or even a person can gain from trade if the area produces for sale a good or service relatively cheaper than other areas or persons can produce it; that is, an area should specialize in producing and selling those items that it can produce at a lower opportunity cost than others.

3. Through trade and specialization in products in which it has a comparative advantage, a country can enjoy a greater array of goods and services at a lower cost.

1. Why do people voluntarily choose to specialize and trade?
2. How could a country have an absolute advantage in producing one good or service without also having a comparative advantage in its production?

3. Why do you think the introduction of the railroad reduced self-sufficiency in the United States?
4. If you can do the dishes in two-thirds the time it takes your younger sister, do you have a comparative advantage in doing the dishes compared to her?

Supply and Demand in International Trade

- What is consumer surplus?
- What is producer surplus?
- Who benefits and who loses when a country becomes an exporter?
- Who benefits and who loses when a country becomes an importer?

THE IMPORTANCE OF TRADE: PRODUCER AND CONSUMER SURPLUS

The difference between the most a consumer would be willing to pay for a quantity of a good and what a consumer actually has to pay is called **consumer surplus.** The difference between the least a supplier is willing to supply a quantity of a good or service for and the revenues a supplier actually receives for selling it is called **producer surplus.** With the tools of consumer and producer surplus, we can better analyze the impact of trade. Who gains? Who loses? What happens to net welfare?

The demand curve represents a collection of maximum prices that consumers are willing and able to pay for different quantities of a good or service while the supply curve represents a collection of minimum prices that suppliers require to be willing to supply different quantities of that good or service, as seen in Exhibit 1. For example, for the first unit of output, the consumer is willing to pay up to $7 and the producer would demand at least $1 for producing that unit. However, the equilibrium price is $4, as indicated by the intersection of the supply and demand curves. It is clear that the two would gain from getting together and trading that unit because the consumer would receive $3 of consumer surplus ($7 – $4) and the producer would receive $3 of producer surplus ($4 – $1). Both would also benefit from trading the second and third unit of output—in fact, from every unit up to the equilibrium output. Once the equilibrium output is reached at the equilibrium price, all of the mutually beneficial opportunities from trade between suppliers and demanders will have taken place; the sum of consumer surplus and producer surplus is maximized.

It is important to recognize that the total gains to the economy from trade is the sum of consumer and producer surplus. That is, consumers benefit from additional amounts of consumer surplus and producers benefit from additional amounts of producer surplus.

EXHIBIT 1	CONSUMER AND PRODUCER SURPLUS

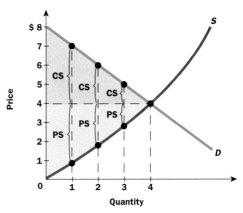

Consumer surplus is the difference between what a consumer has to pay ($4) and what the consumer is willing to pay. For unit 1, consumer surplus is $3 ($7 – $4). Producer surplus is the difference between what a seller receives for selling a good or service ($4) and the price at which he is willing to supply that good or service. For unit 1, producer surplus is $3 ($4 – $1).

FREE TRADE AND EXPORTS—DOMESTIC PRODUCERS GAIN MORE THAN DOMESTIC CONSUMERS LOSE

Using the concepts of consumer and producer surplus, we can graphically show the net benefits of free trade. Imagine an economy with no trade, where the equilibrium price, P_{BT}, and the equilibrium quantity, Q_{BT}, of wheat are determined exclusively in the domestic economy, as seen in Exhibit 2. Say that this imaginary economy decides to engage in free trade. You can see that the world price, P_W, is higher than the domestic price before trade, P_{BT}. In other words, the domestic economy has a comparative advan-

| EXHIBIT 2 | FREE TRADE AND EXPORTS |

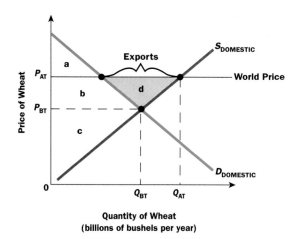

Domestic Gains and Losses from Free Trade (exports)

	Area
Domestic producers gain	+ b + d
Domestic consumers lose	− b
Net domestic gain from trade	+ d

Domestic producers gain more than domestic consumers lose from exports when there is free trade. On net, domestic wealth rises by area d.

tage in wheat, because it can produce wheat at a lower relative price than the rest of the world. So this wheat-producing country sells some wheat to the domestic market and some wheat to the world market, all at the going world price.

The price after trade (P_{AT}) is higher than the price before trade (P_{BT}). Because the world market is huge, the demand from the rest of the world at the world price (P_W) is assumed to be perfectly elastic. That is, domestic wheat farmers can sell all the wheat they want at the world price. If you were a wheat farmer in Nebraska, would you rather sell all of your bushels of wheat at the higher world price or the lower domestic price? As a wheat farmer, you would surely prefer the higher world price. But this is not good news for domestic cereal and bread eaters, who now have to pay more for products made with wheat, because P_{AT} is greater than P_{BT}.

Graphically, we can see how free trade and exports affect both domestic consumers and domestic producers. At the higher world price, P_{AT}, domestic wheat producers are receiving larger amounts of producer surplus. Before trade, they received a surplus equal to area c; after trade, they received surplus c + b + d, for a net gain of area b + d. However, part of the domestic producer's gain comes at domestic consumer's expense. Specifically, consumers had a consumer surplus equal to a + b before the trade (at P_{BT}), but they now only have area a (at P_{AT})—a loss of area b.

Area b reflects a redistribution of income, because producers are gaining exactly what consumers are losing. Is that good or bad? We can't say objectively whether consumers or producers are more deserving. However, the net benefits from allowing free trade and exports are clearly visible in area d. Without free trade, no one gets area d. That is, on net, members of the domestic society gain when domestic wheat producers are able to sell their wheat at the higher world price. While domestic wheat consumers lose from the free trade, those negative effects are more than offset by the positive gains captured by producers. On net, export trade increases domestic wealth.

"You like protectionism as a 'working man.' How about as a consumer?"

FREE TRADE AND IMPORTS

Now suppose that our economy does not produce shirts relatively as well as other countries of the world. In other words, other countries have a comparative advantage in producing shirts. This means that the domestic price for shirts is above the world price. This scenario is illustrated in Exhibit 3. At the new, lower, world price, the domestic producer will supply quantity Q_S. However, at the lower world price, the domestic producers will not produce the entire amount demanded by domestic consumers, Q_D. At the world price, reflecting the world supply and demand for shirts, the difference between what is domestically supplied and what is domestically demanded is supplied by imports.

At the world price, we assume the world supply curve to the domestic market is perfectly elastic—that the producers of the world can supply all that domestic consumers are willing to buy at the going price. At the world price, Q_S is supplied by domestic producers and the difference between Q_D and Q_S is imported from other countries.

Who wins and who loses from free trade and imports? Domestic consumers benefit from paying a lower price for shirts. In Exhibit 3, before trade, consumers only received area a in consumer surplus. But after trade, the price fell and quantity purchased increased, causing the area of consumer surplus to increase from area a to area a + b + d, a gain of b + d. Domestic producers lose because they are now selling their shirts at the lower world price, P_{AT}. The producer surplus before trade was b + c. After trade, the producer surplus falls to area c, reducing producer surplus by area b. Area b, then, represents a redistribution from producers to consumers, but area d is the net increase in domestic wealth from free trade and imports.

| EXHIBIT 3 | FREE TRADE AND IMPORTS |

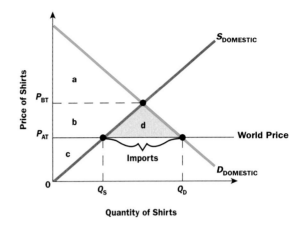

Domestic Gains and Losses from Free Trade (imports)

	Area
Domestic producers lose	– b
Domestic consumers gain	+ b + d
Net domestic gain from trade	+ d

Domestic consumers gain more than domestic producers lose from imports when there is free trade. On net, domestic wealth rises by area d.

CONCEPT CHECK

1. The difference between what a consumer is willing to pay and what a consumer actually has to pay is called consumer surplus.
2. The difference between what a supplier is willing to supply and the price a supplier receives for selling a good or service is called producer surplus.
3. With free trade and exports, domestic producers gain more than domestic consumers lose.
4. With free trade and imports, domestic consumers gain more than domestic producers lose.

---

1. How does voluntary trade generate both producer and consumer surplus?
2. If the world price of a good is greater than the domestic price prior to trade, why does that imply that the domestic economy has a comparative advantage in producing that good?
3. If the world price of a good is less than the domestic price prior to trade, why does that imply that the domestic economy has a comparative disadvantage in producing that good?
4. When a country has a comparative advantage in the production of a good, why do domestic producers gain more than domestic consumers lose from free international trade?
5. When a country has a comparative disadvantage in the production of a good, why do domestic consumers gain more than domestic producers lose from free international trade?
6. Why do U.S. exporters, such as farmers, favor free trade more than U.S. producers of domestic products who face competition from foreign imports, such as the automobile industry?

Tariffs, Import Quotas, and Subsidies

MODULE 16

- What are tariffs?
- What are the effects of a tariff?
- What is an import quota?
- What is the economic impact of subsidies?

WHAT ARE TARIFFS?

A tariff is a tax on imported goods. Tariffs are usually relatively small revenue producers that retard the expansion of trade. They bring about higher prices and revenues to domestic producers, and lower sales and revenues to foreign producers. Moreover, tariffs lead to higher prices to domestic consumers. In fact, the gains to producers are more than offset by the loss to consumers.

WHAT PURPOSE DO TARIFFS SERVE?

One factor in the growth in international trade has been the reduction in tariffs over time, lowering transaction costs of cross border trade. Because tariffs restrict trade and thus reduce the gains attributable to specialization and comparative advantage, why do nations levy them in the first place? One reason, of course, is to obtain revenue to run the government. In relatively underdeveloped countries, custom duties often provide a major part of the revenue of the central government. Custom duties are collected on trade passing through a generally small number of ports and are, therefore, relatively easy to collect. Taxes on income, sales, or property may be much harder to administer efficiently and equitably in such countries, particularly when much economic activity occurs outside markets and thus is not objectively and openly valued.

In the United States, up to the Civil War of the 1860s, nearly all federal government revenue came from custom duties. Even on the eve of World War I, nearly half of all the revenue of the federal government was derived from tariffs, although custom duties accounted for only 10 to 15 percent of the revenues of all governments (because state and local governments could not levy tariffs). Today, in most developed countries, custom duties are relatively unimportant as a revenue producer. In the United States, for example, duties account for less than 2 percent of all federal revenues, and less than 1 percent of all government revenue. Today, in most countries, tariffs exist mainly as a means of protecting domestic industry from foreign competition. Even in earlier years, duties were considered to be an effective means of helping domestic industry and the employees in domestic industry withstand the adverse economic effects of foreign competition.

WHAT IS THE DOMESTIC ECONOMIC IMPACT OF TARIFFS?

The domestic economic impact of tariffs is presented in Exhibit 1, which illustrates the supply and demand curves for domestic consumers and producers of shoes. In a typical international supply and demand illustration, the intersection of the world supply and demand curves would determine the domestic market price. However, with import tariffs, the domestic price of shoes is greater than the world price, as in Exhibit 1(a). We consider the world supply curve (S_{WORLD}) to domestic consumers to be perfectly elastic; that is, we can buy all we want at the world price (P_W). At the world price, domestic producers are only willing to provide quantity Q_S, but domestic consumers are willing to buy quantity Q_D—more than domestic producers are willing to supply. The difference is made up with imports.

As you can see in Exhibit 1, the imposition of the tariff shifts up the perfectly elastic supply curve from foreigners to domestic consumers from S_{WORLD} to $S_{WORLD + TARIFF}$, but it does not alter the domestic supply or demand curve. At the resulting higher domestic price ($P_{W + T}$), domestic suppliers are willing to supply more, Q_S, but domestic consumers are willing to buy less, Q_D. At the new equilibrium, the domestic price ($P_{W + T}$) is higher and the quantity of shoes demanded (Q'_D) is smaller. But at the new price, the domestic quantity demanded is lower and the quantity supplied domestically is greater, reducing the quantity of imported shoes. Overall, then, tariffs lead to (1) a smaller total quantity sold, (2) a higher price for shoes for domestic consumers, (3) greater sales of shoes at higher prices for domestic producers, and (4) lower sales of foreign shoes.

While domestic producers do gain more sales and higher earnings, consumers lose much more. The increase in price from the tariff results in a loss in consumer surplus, as shown in Exhibit 1. After the tariff, shoe prices rise to P_{W+T}, and, consequently, consumer surplus falls by area a + b + c + d, representing the welfare loss to consumers resulting from the tariff. Area A in Exhibit 1 shows the gain to domestic producers as a result of the tariff. That is, at the higher price, domestic producers are willing to supply more shoes, representing a welfare gain to producers resulting from the tariff. As a result of the tariff, government gains area c. This is the import tariff—the revenue government collects from foreign countries on imports. However, we see from Exhibit 1 that consumers lose more than producers and government gain from the tariff.

ARGUMENTS FOR TARIFFS

Despite the preceding arguments against tariffs, tariffs continue to be levied. Some rationale for their existence is necessary. Four common arguments for the use of tariffs deserve our critical examination.

Tariffs Help Infant Industries Grow

The most enduring argument for tariffs is that tariff protection will allow a new industry to more quickly reach a scale

EXHIBIT 1	THE IMPACT OF TARIFFS

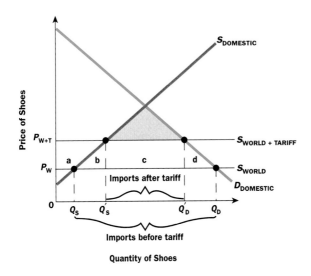

Gains and Losses from Tariffs

	Area
Domestic consumers lose	−(a + b + d + d)
Domestic producers gain	+ a
Government gains (Imports × Tariff)	+ c
Net domestic loss from tariffs	−(b + d)

In the case of a tariff, we see that consumers lose more than producers and government gain.

of operation at which economies of scale and production efficiencies can be realized. It is presumed that without this protection, the industry could never get on its feet. At first hearing, the argument sounds valid, but there are many problems with it. How do you identify "infant industries" that genuinely have potential economies of scale and will quickly become efficient with protection? We do not know the long-run average total cost curves of industries, a necessary piece of information. Moreover, if firms and governments are truly convinced of the advantages of allowing an industry to reach a large scale, would it not be wise to make massive loans to the industry, allowing it to instantly begin large-scale production rather than slowly and at the expense of consumers? In other words, the goal of allowing the industry to reach its efficient size can be reached without a protective tariff. Finally, the history of infant industry tariffs suggests that the tariffs often linger long after the industry is mature and no longer in "need" of protection.

Tariffs Can Reduce Domestic Unemployment

Exhibit 1 showed how tariffs increase output by domestic producers, thus leading to increased employment and reduced unemployment in industries where tariffs were imposed. Yet the overall employment effects of a tariff imposition are not likely to be positive; the argument is incorrect. Why? First, the imposition of a tariff by the United States on, say, foreign steel, is going to be noticed in the countries adversely affected by the tariff. If a new tariff on steel lowers Japanese steel sales to the United States, the Japanese very likely will retaliate by imposing tariffs on American exports to Japan, say, on machinery exports. The retaliatory tariff will lower American sales of machinery and thus employment in the U.S. machinery industries. As a result, the gain in employment in the steel industry will be offset by a loss of employment elsewhere.

Even if the other countries did not retaliate, U.S. employment would likely suffer outside the industry gaining the tariff protection. The way that other countries pay for U.S. goods is by getting dollars from sales to the United States—imports to us. If new tariffs lead to restrictions on imports, fewer dollars will be flowing overseas in payment for imports, which means that foreigners will have fewer dollars available to buy our exports. Other things equal, this will tend to reduce our exports, thus creating unemployment in the export industries.

Tariffs Are Necessary for National Security Reasons

Sometimes it is argued that tariffs are a means of preventing a nation from becoming too dependent on foreign suppliers of goods vital to national security. For example, if oil is vital to running planes and tanks, a cutoff of foreign supplies of oil during wartime could cripple a nation's defenses.

The national security argument is usually not valid. If a nation's own resources are depletable, tariff-imposed reliance on domestic supplies will hasten depletion of domestic reserves, making the country even *more* dependent in the future. If we impose a very high tariff on foreign oil to protect domestic producers, we will increase domestic output of oil in the short run, but in the process, we will deplete the stockpile of available reserves. Thus, the defense argument is often of questionable validity. From a defense standpoint, it makes more sense to use foreign oil in peacetime and perhaps stockpile "insurance" supplies so that larger domestic supplies would be available during wars.

THE POLITICAL ECONOMY OF TARIFFS

Except in rather unusual circumstances, then, the arguments for tariffs are rather suspect. Tariffs lower total world output and real income and involve income redistribution from domestic consumers, who are forced to pay higher prices, and foreign producers, who sell fewer goods they have a comparative advantage in, to domestic producers, who benefit from protection. Why, if tariffs are typically harmful to the whole economy, are they so widespread?

Tariff legislation, like other forms of legislation, is enacted largely in response to the actions of pressure groups. In the case of tariffs, a larger group of voters, consumers, have on the whole more to lose from the new tariffs than the gains received by domestic producers and workers in protected industries. Yet the producer lobbying efforts are often more effective than the consumer efforts. Why?

Suppose an industry has five producers who will equally share $100 million in gains from a new tariff, while 200 million consumers will equally share losses of $400 million from the tariff. On balance, the losses exceed the gains and, on net, society loses ($300 million). Yet each single producer stands to gain $20 million ($100 million divided by five). For each one, the potential gains if the law is adopted are enormous. Moreover, each producer knows it is a significant proportion of the total group lobbying for the tariff, and each is therefore likely to cooperate in the effort, perhaps through an industry association.

For consumers, though, the situation is often quite different. The losses from tariffs, while a considerable aggregate sum, average only $2 per consumer ($400 million divided by 200 million). The cost of fighting a tariff—even writing letters to a few members of Congress—is far greater to the average consumer than the expected benefits. Moreover, each individual consumer is such a small proportion of the total consuming population that he or she might doubt whether any lobbying effort on his or her part will have any real impact. Given the existence of spillover effects in lobbying, the consumer's attitude often is "let someone else do the lobbying." As a consequence, there are not too many who complain effectively on the consumer side. Using a cost–benefit approach, it pays the producer to lobby for tariffs, but it does not pay the consumer to lobby against them. Thus, many tariffs may be enacted that are not truly in the overall public interest but are rather due to the power of special interests.

WHAT IS AN IMPORT QUOTA?

Despite the fact that the politics of tariffs work in their favor, the benefits of free trade have been sufficiently recognized by citizens and politicians that tariff barriers have been significantly reduced in recent years. The protectionist forces have other weapons to attempt to restrict entry of foreign goods. While tariffs have generally fallen over time, various nontariff barriers have actually increased in use. Chief among these is the **import quota.** An import quota gives producers from another country a maximum number of units of the good in question that can be imported within any given time span. For example, the U.S. government might tell Japanese steel-makers that they can sell no more than 11 million tons of steel a year to the United States, or television-set manufacturers that they can sell no more than 3 million sets. Sometimes these quotas are "voluntary" in that they are negotiated with foreign governments.

The case for quotas is probably even weaker than the case for tariffs. Like tariffs, quotas directly restrict imports, leading to reductions in trade and thus preventing nations from fully realizing their comparative advantage. But tariffs at least use the price system as the basis of restricting trade, while quotas do not. Suppose that the Japanese have been sending 4 million TV sets annually to the United States but now are told that, because of quota restrictions, they can only send 3 million sets. If the Japanese manufacturers are allowed to determine how the quantity reduction is to occur, they will likely collude, leading to higher prices. Suppose that each producer is simply told to reduce sales by 25 percent. They will substantially raise the price of the sets to Americans above what the 4 million original buyers would have paid for them.

DOES THE GOVERNMENT COLLECT REVENUES FROM IMPORT QUOTAS?

Unlike what occurs with a tariff, the U.S. government does not collect any revenue as a result of the import quota. Despite the higher prices, the loss in consumer surplus, and the loss in government revenue, quotas come about because people often view them as being less "protectionist" than tariffs—the traditional, most maligned form of protection.

Besides the rather blunt means of curtailing imports by using tariffs and quotas, nations have devised still other, more subtle means to restrict international trade. For example, nations sometimes impose product standards ostensibly designed to protect consumers against inferior merchandise, but which in effect are sometimes a means to restrict foreign competition. For example, France might keep certain kinds of wine out of the country on the grounds that they were made with allegedly inferior grapes or had an inappropriate alcoholic content. Likewise, the United States might prohibit automobile imports that do not meet certain standards in terms of pollutants, safety, and gasoline mileage. Even if these standards are not intended to restrict foreign competition, the regulations may nonetheless have that impact, restricting consumer choice in the process.

WHAT IS THE ECONOMIC IMPACT OF SUBSIDIES?

Working in the opposite direction, governments sometimes try to encourage exports by subsidizing producers. With a subsidy, revenue is given to producers for each exported unit of output. This stimulates exports. While not a barrier to trade like tariffs and quotas, subsidies can be objected to on the ground that they distort trade patterns and lead to ones that are inefficient. How does this happen? With subsidies, producers will export goods not because their costs are lower than that of a foreign competitor, but because their costs have been artificially reduced by government action transferring income from taxpayers to the exporter. The actual labor, raw material, and capital costs of production are not reduced by the subsidy—society has the same opportunity costs as before. A nation's taxpayers end up subsidizing the output of producers who, relative to producers in other countries, are inefficient. The nation, then, exports products in which it does not have a comparative advantage. Gains from trade in terms of world output are eliminated or reduced by such subsidies. Thus, subsidies, usually defended as a means of increasing exports and improving a nation's international financial position, are usually of dubious worth to the world economy and even to the economy doing the subsidizing.

CONCEPT CHECK

1. A tariff is a tax on imported goods.
2. Tariffs bring about higher prices and revenues to domestic producers, and lower sales and revenues to foreign producers. Tariffs lead to higher prices and reduce consumer surplus for domestic consumers.
3. Arguments for the use of tariffs include: tariffs help infant industries grow, tariffs can reduce domestic unemployment, new tariffs can help finance our international trade, and tariffs are necessary for national security reasons.

4. Like tariffs, import quotas restrict imports, lowering consumer surplus and preventing countries from fully realizing their comparative advantage.
5. Sometimes government tries to encourage production of a certain good by subsidizing its production with taxpayer dollars. Because subsidies stimulate exports, they are not a barrier to trade like tariffs and import quotas. However, they do distort trade patterns and cause overall inefficiencies.

1. Why do tariffs increase domestic producer surplus but decrease domestic consumer surplus?
2. How do import tariffs increase employment in "protected" industries, but at the expense of a likely decrease in employment overall?
3. Why is the national security argument for tariffs questionable?

4. Why is the domestic argument for import quotas weaker than the case for tariffs?
5. Why would foreign producers prefer import quotas to tariffs, even if they resulted in the same reduced level of imports?
6. Why does subsidizing exports by industries that lack a comparative advantage tend to harm the domestic economy, on net?

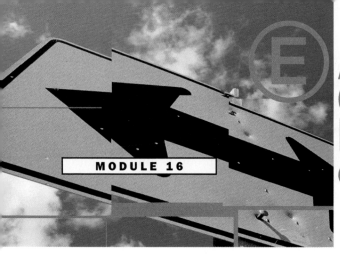

Application: Common Misperceptions on Trade

In this Module, we have stressed the economic gains associated with trade. However, there are still many skeptics who believe that there is a difference between theory and reality. In particular, they argue that freer trade will lead to problems because of national differences in factor endowments (like cheaper labor) and environmental standards. Professor Jagdish Bhagwati, an expert in international economics, addresses these issues. However, before reading this article, think of the following questions: If labor costs were the sole determining production factor, then why aren't all of the world's products produced in countries like Haiti and Portugal? Why are BMWs and Mercedes Benzs produced in Germany? Why are intricate computer parts produced in the United States?

FAST TRACK: NOT SO FAST

JAGDISH BHAGWATI

- *Trade is "unfair" if trading nations have different pollution and labor standards.* The truth, however, is that a diversity of standards is perfectly legitimate. The reason is simple: Different nations have different conditions and preferences. Thus, if Chile already has cleaner air and worse water than the U.S. does, it would only be sensible for it to have stiffer penalties for polluting water than the U.S., and smaller penalties for polluting air. Different regulatory burdens for an industry in different countries are therefore to be expected.

- *In competing to attract multinationals, countries will lower their standards.* This "race to the bottom" argument says the U.S. must seek harmonized international regulations in order to safeguard our own standards. The empirical evidence for this claim, however, is negligible. In fact, the economist Arik Levinson has shown that multinationals mostly use the most environmentally friendly technology. There are excellent economic reasons, including harm to their reputations, for companies not to exploit weaker standards. In addition, most poor countries are now democratic and have elements of an articulate civil society. It is hard to imagine their elected leaders trying to attract multinationals by inviting them to pollute their nations.

- *Products made with lower labor standards are morally unacceptable.* At first blush, it seems reasonable that we should want to exclude products made, for instance, in sweatshops. Shouldn't we then be able to say we will not trade with countries that fail to conform to our labor standards? Such "values"-based denials of access to the U.S.

market can surely open a Pandora's box, seriously disrupting trade. Because we think only of our values being imposed on others, we fail to see that the single worst aspect of some of our industries would be cited in efforts to curtail their international trade. For instance, many Americans strenuously object to the use of purse seine nets in tuna fishing because they kill dolphins. But what about the crowded U.S. hog farms? Or what if other nations want to suspend U.S. agricultural imports because of abuses against migrant workers in this country? Protectionist interests in other countries would quickly seize on such arguments, causing ever more economic damage.

- *Trade with poor countries is driving down U.S. workers' wages.* By now it has become commonplace to assert that up to 20 percent of the decline in real U.S. wages since the 1970s is due to international trade. Yet nearly all trade economists who have examined the issue conclude the adverse impact is negligible. The conventional view is that U.S. wages must move in tandem with the prices of labor-intensive goods, which are increasingly produced in low-wage countries. Yet my latest research shows that real U.S. wages rose in the 1970s even though the prices of labor-intensive goods produced abroad fell, and U.S. wages fell in the 1980s while these prices rose. Indeed, I conclude that trade with poor countries has likely benefited U.S. workers.

SOURCE: Jagdish Bhagwati, "Fast Track: Not So Fast," *The Wall Street Journal*, September 10, 1997.

The Clinton Administration has garnered some impressive victories in the name of free trade: the North American Free Trade Agreement (NAFTA) and the Uruguay Round of General Agreement on Tariffs and Trade (GATT). However, despite these impressive gains, there are still some important steps that most economists believe should be made. For example, sanctions have been imposed on both Mexico and Canada to protect domestic agricultural interests. In addition, U.S. citrus and sugar producers are among several domestic industries that have the political clout to maintain their tariff protection.

With public sentiment behind the president on NAFTA, this was an excellent opportunity to reduce protectionism in global markets. Individuals are finally realizing that the argument for trade protection based on the notion that world trade has cost us jobs does not sit well with the facts. Furthermore, protection against imports will have the undesirable effect of protecting less productive jobs at the expense of more productive jobs. A typical job that is "saved" costs Americans thousands of dollars.

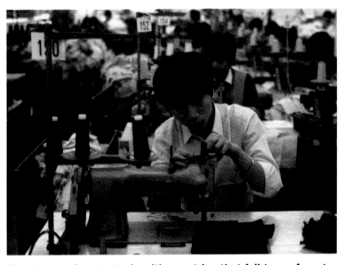

Should we refuse to trade with countries that fail to conform to U.S. labor standards?

International trade increases our wealth by allowing us to specialize in those products we produce best and trade for those products that others produce best. As Professor Bhagwati points out, some argue that without import restrictions we cannot compete with foreign producers because their costs are too low and because they are government-subsidized. Some products can be produced more cheaply in foreign countries than here. The United States cannot be the most efficient producer of everything. But neither are we the least efficient producer of everything. Indeed, the reason why wages are so low in many foreign countries is that workers are not as productive, lacking capital infrastructure and training.

It is true that foreign producers often receive government subsidies to ship goods to the United States. That is an unfortunate practice because it encourages inefficient production, but it is certainly no reason to fear that we are unable to compete successfully against other countries. It is impossible for a government to subsidize all goods. Subsidizing some goods requires imposing taxes on other goods, and our consumers benefit from lower prices on the subsidized goods.

But won't some people lose their jobs if we take full advantage of international trade? In the short run, yes. Consider, however, that we are a rich country because businesses have been forced to compete for the consumer's dollar by providing better products at lower prices. Every time some firms become more successful in this competition, other firms lose sales and are forced to reduce their work forces. The result is unemployment in the short run but the movement of capital and labor into more valuable employment in the long run.

In short, free trade should facilitate a more efficient economy, faster growth, more high-paying jobs, and higher standards of living. In addition, trade can lower inflationary pressure by increasing the supply of goods and services competing for consumers' dollars. In the case of the automobile, we have seen that free trade and international competition have led to higher quality vehicles.

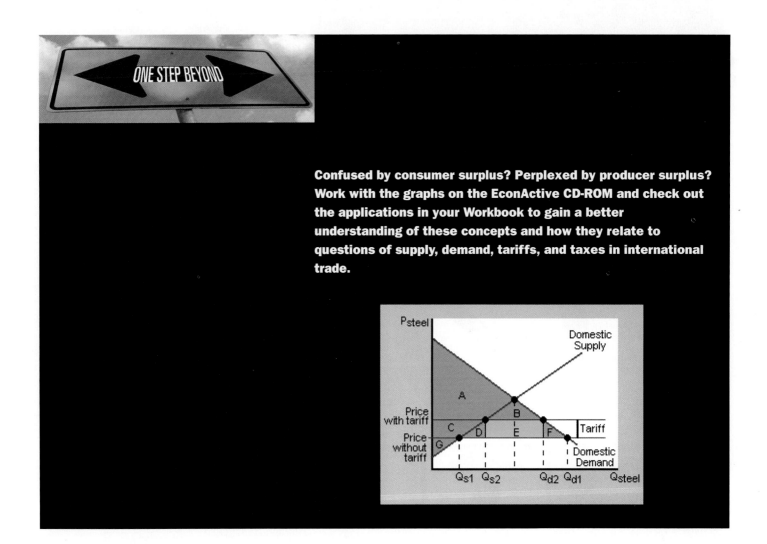

ONE STEP BEYOND

Confused by consumer surplus? Perplexed by producer surplus? Work with the graphs on the EconActive CD-ROM and check out the applications in your Workbook to gain a better understanding of these concepts and how they relate to questions of supply, demand, tariffs, and taxes in international trade.

International Finance

A. The Balance of Payments
What is the difference between the balance of payments and the balance of trade?

B. Exchange Rates
How do exchange rates affect the demand for foreign goods?

C. Equilibrium Changes and the Foreign Exchange Market
What forces cause the supply and demand for currencies to shift?

D. Flexible Exchange Rates
How are exchange rate changes different with flexible rates than with a fixed-rate system?

E. Application: The United States Intervenes to Boost the Yen
Why did the United States buy yen in the currency market?

The Balance of Payments

MODULE 17

- What is the balance of payments?
- What are the three main components of the balance of payments?
- What is the balance of trade?
- What are the four types of official reserve assets?

WHAT IS THE BALANCE OF PAYMENTS?

The record of all of the international financial transactions of a nation over a year is called the **balance of payments**. The balance of payments is a statement that records all the exchanges those in a nation engaged in that required an outflow of funds to foreign nations or an inflow of funds from other nations. Just as an examination of gross domestic product accounts gives us some idea of the economic health and vitality of a nation, the balance of payments provides information about a nation's world trade position. The balance of payments is divided into three main sections: the current account, the capital account, and the official reserve assets. It also includes an "error term" called the statistical discrepancy.

WHAT IS THE CURRENT ACCOUNT?

The current account is made up of current imports and exports of goods and services. Any time a foreign buyer buys a good from a U.S. producer, the foreign buyer must pay the U.S. producer for the good. Usually, the foreigner must pay for the good in U.S. dollars, because the seller wants to pay for his workers and other inputs with dollars. This requires the foreign buyer to exchange units of his currency at a foreign exchange dealer for U.S. dollars. Because the United States gains claims over foreign buyers by obtaining foreign currency in exchange for the dollars needed to buy exports, all exports of U.S. goods abroad are considered a credit or plus (+) item in the U.S. balance of payments. Those foreign currencies are later exchangeable for goods and services made in the country that purchased the U.S. exports.

HOW DO IMPORTS AFFECT THE CURRENT ACCOUNT?

When a U.S. consumer buys an imported good, however, the reverse is true: The U.S. importer must pay the foreign producer, usually in that nation's currency. Typically, the

U.S. buyer will go to a foreign exchange dealer and exchange dollars for units of that foreign currency. Imports are thus a debit (–) item in the balance of payments, because the dollars sold to buy the foreign currency add to foreign claims against U.S. buyers, which are later exchangeable for goods and services made in the U.S. Our imports, then, provide the means by which foreigners can buy our exports.

HOW DO SERVICES AFFECT THE CURRENT ACCOUNT?

While imports and exports of merchandise (goods) are the largest components of the balance of payments, they are not the only ones. Nations import and export services as well. A particularly important service is tourism. When a tourist from the U.S. goes abroad, he or she is buying foreign-produced services in addition to those purchased by citizens there. Those services include the use of hotels, sightseeing tours, restaurants, and so forth. In the current account, these services are included in imports. On the other hand, foreign tourism in the United States provides us with foreign currencies and claims against foreigners, so they are included in exports. Airline and shipping services also affect the balance of payments. When someone from Italy flies American Airlines, that person is making a payment to a U.S. company. Because the flow of international financial claims is the same, this payment is treated just like a U.S. merchandise export in the balance of payments. If an American flies on Alitalia, however, Italians acquire claims against the U.S., and so it is included as a debit (import) item in the U.S. balance of payments accounts.

WHAT ELSE AFFECTS THE CURRENT ACCOUNT?

Another major type of import or export expenditure is income from financial investments. These payments can be viewed as compensation for the use of capital services. In the past, the United States has made huge financial

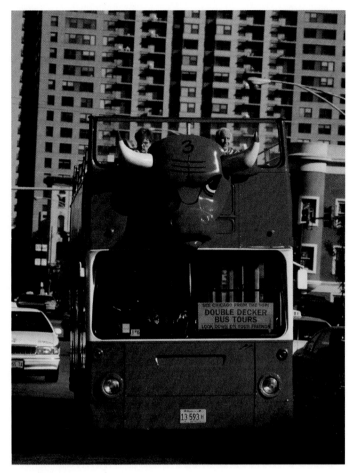

How is the current account affected when a foreign tourist rides a sightseeing bus in the United States?

porting capital services. Similarly, when a foreign company, such as Royal Dutch Shell or Mercedes Benz makes profits in the United States, they obtain their profits in dollars. This creates claims against the United States and is recorded as a debit item in the U.S. balance of payments, similar to the import of merchandise.

HOW DOES THE GOVERNMENT AFFECT THE CURRENT ACCOUNT?

One other item that affects the current account is government grants to other countries. When the U.S. gives foreign aid to another country, this creates a debit in the U.S. balance of payments because it gives foreigners added claims against the United States in the form of dollars. Private donations, such as individuals sending money to relatives or friends in foreign countries, shows up in the current account as debit items as well.

WHAT IS THE BALANCE ON CURRENT ACCOUNT?

The balance on current account is the net amount of credits or debits after adding up all transactions of goods (merchandise imports and exports), services (including investment income), and fund transfers (e.g., foreign aid). If the sum of credits exceeds the sum of debits, the nation is said to run a balance of payments surplus on current account. If debits exceed credits, however, the nation is running a balance of payment deficit on current account.

investments abroad, both through the establishment of U.S. corporations overseas and by purchasing securities of foreign business enterprises or governments. By doing this, the U.S. obtains claims on foreign countries just as it does when it exports goods, only in this case, we are ex-

HOW IS THE BALANCE OF TRADE RELATED TO THE BALANCE ON CURRENT ACCOUNT?

The balance of payments of the United States for 1996 is presented in Exhibit 1. Note that exports and imports of

EXHIBIT 1	U.S. BALANCE OF PAYMENTS, 1996 (BILLIONS OF DOLLARS)

Type of Transaction

Current Account		Capital Account	
1. Merchandise exports	$612	7. U.S. capital inflow	$547
2. Merchandise imports	−803	8. U.S. capital outflow	−351
Balance of Trade (lines 1–2)	−191	Capital Account Balance (lines 7–8)	194
3. Service exports	237	9. Statistical discrepancy	−46
4. Service imports	−157	Net Balance (lines 1–9)	0
5. Investment income (net)	3		
6. Unilateral transfers (net)	−40		
Current Account Balance (lines 1–6)	−148		

SOURCE: *Survey of Current Business*, May 1998, Table F.3, p. D-53.

goods and services are by far the largest credits and debits. Note also that the U.S. merchandise exports were $191 billion less than merchandise imports. The merchandise import/export relationship is often called the balance of trade. The U.S. therefore experienced a balance of trade deficit that year of $191 billion. A historical balance on current account table is presented in Exhibit 2. How could the U.S. buy more goods abroad than it sold? Note that total imports were only $108 billion more than total exports, because a good deal of the $191 billion trade deficit was offset by credits from an $80 billion surplus in service exports and $3 billion in net investment income. Then, when $40 billion of net unilateral transfers from the U.S. is included, the total deficit on current account was $148 billion.

WHAT IS THE CAPITAL ACCOUNT?

How was this deficit on current account financed? Remember that U.S. credits give us the financial means to buy foreign goods, and that our credits were $194 billion less than our debits from our imports and net unilateral transfers to foreign countries. This deficit on current account balance is settled by movements of financial, or capital, assets. These transactions are recorded in the capital account, so that a current account deficit is financed by a capital account surplus.

WHAT DOES THE CAPITAL ACCOUNT RECORD?

These capital account transactions include items such as international bank loans, purchases of corporate securities, government bond purchases, and direct investments in

foreign subsidiary companies. In 1996, the U.S. made new foreign financial investments of nearly $351 billion, which was a further debit because it provided foreigners with U.S. dollars. On the other hand, foreign investments in the U.S. were over $547 billion, most of which were purchases of U.S. government securities. On net, then, foreigners made about $194 billion more new financial investments in the U.S. than Americans did abroad. On balance, then, there was a surplus (positive credit) in the Capital account from capital movements of $194 billion, offsetting the $148 billion deficit on current account.

WHAT IS THE STATISTICAL DISCREPANCY?

In the final analysis, it is true that the balance of payments account must balance so that credits and debits are equal. Why is this so? Due to the reciprocal aspect of trade, every credit eventually creates a debit of equal magnitude. But, in 1996, the measured $194 net capital inflow didn't match the measured $148 deficit on current account. If debits and credits do not come out equal, as in 1996, it is because of some errors and/or omissions of accounting. These errors are often rather large ($46 billion, or $194 billion minus $148 billion, in 1996), and are entered into the balance of payments as the statistical discrepancy. Including the errors and omissions recorded as the statistical discrepancy, the balance of payments do balance.

HOW DO NATIONS MEET THEIR BALANCE OF PAYMENTS DEFICITS?

Transactions are used to equalize a nation's balance of payments account and provide debits equal to credits. For example, if the U.S. lacks adequate foreign currency to meet its international financial requirements, it can seek to borrow funds from other countries or from an international financial institution. In this manner, nations with balance of payments difficulties have often gone to nations with balance of payments surpluses and borrowed from them to meet their deficit.

Balance of Payments:
A Useful Analogy

The international balance of payments is very similar conceptually to the personal financial transactions of individuals. Each individual has his own "balance of payments," reflecting his trading with other economic units: other individuals, corporations, or governments. People earn income or credits by "exporting" their labor service to other economic units, or by receiving investment income (a return on capital services). Against that, they "import" goods from other economic units; we call these imports "consumption." This debit

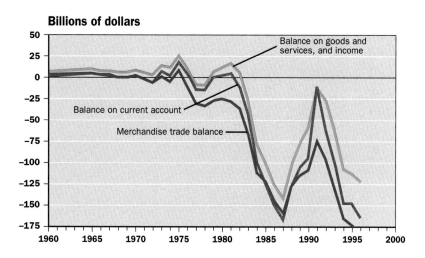

| EXHIBIT 2 | U.S. BALANCE OF TRADE, 1960–1996 |

Billions of dollars

Balance on goods and services, and income

Balance on current account

Merchandise trade balance

SOURCE: Chart prepared by the U.S. Bureau of the Census.

item is sometimes augmented by payments made to out-siders (e.g., banks) on loans, and so forth. Fund transfers, such as gifts to children or charities, are other debit items (or credit items if persons are recipients of this assistance).

As individuals, if our spending on our consumption exceeds our income from our exports of our labor and capital services, we have a "deficit" that must be financed by borrowing or selling assets. If we "export" more than we "import," however, we can make new investments and/or increase our "reserves" (savings and investment holdings). Like nations, individuals who run a deficit in daily transactions must make up for it through accommodating transactions (e.g., borrowing or reducing one's savings or investment holdings) to bring about an ultimate balance of credits and debits to their personal account.

CONCEPT CHECK

1. The balance of payments is the record of all the international financial transactions of a nation for any given year.
2. The balance of payments is made up of the current account, the capital account, as well as an "error term" called the statistical discrepancy.
3. The balance of trade refers strictly to the imports and exports of merchandise (goods) with other nations. If our imports of foreign goods are greater than our exports, we are said to have a balance of trade deficit.

1. What is the balance of payments?
2. Why would a British purchaser of U.S. goods or services have to first exchange pounds for dollars?
3. How is it true that U.S. imports provide the means by which foreigners can buy U.S. exports?
4. What would have to be true in order for the U.S. to have a balance of trade deficit and a balance of payments surplus?
5. What would have to be true in order for the U.S. to have a balance of trade surplus and a current account deficit?
6. If there are no errors or omissions in the recorded balance of payments accounts, what should the statistical discrepancy equal?
7. A Nigerian family visiting Chicago enjoys a Chicago Cubs baseball game at Wrigley Field. How would that expense be recorded in the balance of payments accounts? Why?

Exchange Rates

- What are exchange rates?
- How are exchange rates determined?
- How do exchange rates affect the demand for foreign goods?

WHY DO WE NEED FOREIGN CURRENCIES?

When U.S. consumers buy goods from persons in other countries, the sellers of those goods want to be paid in their own domestic currencies. The U.S. consumers, then, must first exchange U.S. dollars for the seller's currency in order to pay for those goods. American importers must therefore constantly buy yen, Euros, pesos, and other currencies in order to finance their purchases. Similarly, persons in other countries buying goods made in the United States must sell their currencies to obtain U.S. dollars in order to pay for those goods.

WHAT ARE EXCHANGE RATES?

The price of a unit of one foreign currency in terms of another is called the **exchange rate.** If an importer in the U.S. has agreed to pay Euros (the new currency of the European Union) to buy a cuckoo clock made in the Black Forest in Germany, he or she would then have to exchange U.S. dollars for Euros. If it takes $1.00 to buy one Euro, then the exchange rate is $1.00 per Euro. From the German perspective, the exchange rate is one Euro per U.S. dollar.

HOW DO CHANGES IN EXCHANGE RATES AFFECT THE DOMESTIC DEMAND FOR FOREIGN GOODS?

Prices of goods in their currencies combine with exchange rates to determine the domestic price of foreign goods. Suppose the cuckoo clock sells for 100 Euros in Germany. What is the price to U.S. consumers? Let us assume that tariffs and other transactions costs are zero. If the exchange rate is $1 = 1 Euro, then the equivalent U.S. dollar price of the cuckoo clock is 100 Euros times $1 per Euro, or $100. If the exchange rate were to change to $2 = 1 Euro, fewer clocks would be demanded in the United States. This is be-

cause the effective U.S. dollar price of the clocks would rise to $200 (100 Euros times $2 per Euro). The new higher relative value of a Euro compared to the dollar (or equiva-

If the Euro becomes relatively more expensive in terms of dollars (it costs more dollars to buy a Euro), what will happen to the domestic demand for European goods?

lently, the lower the relative value of a dollar compared to the Euro) would lead to a reduction in U.S. demand for German-made clocks.

HOW DO CHANGES IN THE DEMAND FOR GOODS AFFECT EXCHANGE RATES?

The demand for foreign currencies is what economists call a derived demand. This is because the demand for a foreign currency derives directly from the demand for foreign goods and services or for foreign capital. The more foreign goods are demanded, the more of that foreign currency that will be needed to pay for those goods. Such an increased demand for the currency will push up the exchange value of that currency relative to other currencies.

WHAT DETERMINES THE SUPPLY OF A FOREIGN CURRENCY?

Similarly, the supply of foreign currency is provided by foreigners who want to buy the exports of a particular nation. For example, the more that foreigners demand U.S. products, the more of their currencies they will supply in exchange for U.S. dollars, which they use to buy our products.

HOW ARE EXCHANGE RATES DETERMINED?

We know that the demand for foreign currencies is derived from the demand for foreign goods, but how does that af-

How is the equilibrium price of the Euro determined?

fect the exchange rate? Just as in the product market, the answer lies with the forces of supply and demand. In this case, it is the supply of and demand for a foreign currency that determine the equilibrium price (exchange rate) of that currency.

WHY DOES THE DEMAND CURVE FOR A FOREIGN CURRENCY SLOPE DOWNWARD?

As Exhibit 1 shows, the demand curve for a foreign currency—Euros, for example—is downward sloping, just as it is in product markets. In this case, however, the demand curve has a negative slope because as the price of the Euro falls relative to the dollar, European products become relatively more inexpensive to U.S. consumers, who therefore buy more European goods. To do so, the quantity of Euros demanded by U.S. consumers will increase to buy more European goods as the price of the Euro falls. This is why the demand for foreign currencies is considered to be a derived demand.

WHY DOES THE SUPPLY CURVE FOR FOREIGN CURRENCY SLOPE UPWARD?

The supply curve for a foreign currency is upward sloping, also just as it is in product markets. In this case, as the price, or value, of the Euro increases relative to the dollar, American products will become relatively more inexpensive to European buyers and increase the quantity of dollars they demand. Europeans will, therefore, increase the quantity of Euros supplied to the U.S. by buying more U.S. products. Hence, the supply curve is upward sloping. (Note: The supply curve here is upward sloping because we have assumed that the European demand for U.S. goods is price elastic.)

WHERE IS EQUILIBRIUM IN THE FOREIGN EXCHANGE MARKET?

Equilibrium is reached where the demand and supply curves for a given currency intersect. In Exhibit 1, equilibrium price of a Euro is $1.20. As in the product market, if the dollar price of Euros is higher than the equilibrium price, there will be an excess quantity of Euros supplied at that price, or a surplus of Euros, and competition among Euro sellers will push the price of Euros down toward equilibrium. Likewise, if the dollar price of Euros is lower than the equilibrium price, there will be an excess quantity of Euros demanded at that price, or a shortage of Euros. Competition among Euro buyers will push the price of Euros up toward equilibrium.

EXHIBIT 1 **EQUILIBRIUM IN THE FOREIGN EXCHANGE MARKET**

The foreign exchange market is in equilibrium at 1 Euro = $1.20. At any price higher than $1.20, there will be a surplus of Euros. At any price lower than $1.20, there will be a shortage of Euros.

TUNE UP

EXCHANGE RATES

Q: Why is a strong dollar a mixed blessing?

A: A strong dollar will lower the price of imports and make trips to foreign countries less expensive. However, it makes U.S. exports more expensive. Consequently, foreigners will buy fewer U.S. goods and services. The net effect is a fall in exports and a rise in imports—net exports fall. Note that some Americans are helped (vacationers going to foreign countries and those preferring foreign goods), while others are harmed (producers of U.S. exports, operators of hotels dependent on foreign visitors in the U.S.).

CONCEPT CHECK

1. The exchange rate is the price in one country's currency of one unit of another country's currency.
2. The exchange rate for a currency is determined by the supply of and demand for that currency in the foreign exchange market.
3. If the dollar appreciates in value relative to foreign currencies, foreign goods become more inexpensive to U.S. consumers, increasing U.S. demand for foreign goods.

1. What is an exchange rate?
2. When a U.S. dollar buys relatively more French francs, why does the cost of imports from France fall in the U.S.?
3. When a U.S. dollar buys relatively fewer Austrian shillings, why does the cost of U.S. exports fall in Austria?
4. How does an increase in domestic demand for foreign goods and services increase the demand for those foreign currencies?
5. As Euros get cheaper relative to U.S. dollars, why does the quantity of Euros demanded by Americans increase? Why doesn't the demand for Euros increase as a result?
6. Who competes exchange rates down when they are above their equilibrium value? Who competes exchange rates up when they are below their equilibrium value?

Equilibrium Changes in the Foreign Exchange Market

■ What factors cause the demand curve for a currency to shift?

■ What factors cause the supply curve for a currency to shift?

WHAT FACTORS SHIFT THE DEMAND FOR AND SUPPLY OF A CURRENCY?

The equilibrium exchange rate of a currency changes many times daily. Sometimes, these changes can be quite significant. Any force that shifts either the demand for or supply of a currency will shift the equilibrium in the foreign exchange market, leading to a new exchange rate. These factors include changes in tastes for goods, changes in income, changes in relative real interest rates, and changes in relative inflation rates.

HOW DO TASTE CHANGES AFFECT THE EQUILIBRIUM EXCHANGE RATE?

Because the demand for foreign currencies is derived from the demand for foreign goods, any change in the demand for foreign goods will shift the demand schedule for foreign currency in the same direction. For example, if a cuckoo clock revolution sweeps through the U.S., German producers would have reason to celebrate, knowing that many U.S. buyers will turn to Germany for their cuckoo clocks. The Germans, however, will only accept payment in the form of Euros, and so U.S. consumers and retailers must convert their dollars into Euros before they can purchase their clocks. The increased tastes for European goods in the U.S. would, therefore, lead to an increased demand for Euros. As shown in Exhibit 1, this increased demand for Euros shifts the demand curve to the right, resulting in a new, higher equilibrium price for Euros.

HOW DO CHANGES IN INCOME OR REDUCTIONS IN U.S. TARIFFS AFFECT THE EQUILIBRIUM EXCHANGE RATE?

Any change in the average income of U.S. consumers will also change the equilibrium exchange rate, *ceteris paribus*.

If on the whole, incomes increased in the U.S., Americans would buy more goods, including imported goods, so more European goods would be bought. This increased demand for European goods would lead to an increased demand for Euros, resulting in a higher exchange rate for Euros. A decrease in U.S. tariffs on European goods would tend to have the same affect as an increase in incomes by making European goods more affordable. As Exhibit 1 shows, this would again lead to an increased demand for European goods and a higher short-run equilibrium exchange rate for Euros.

EXHIBIT 1	IMPACT OF U.S. TASTE OR INCOME INCREASE, OR TARIFF DECREASE, ON THE FOREIGN EXCHANGE MARKET

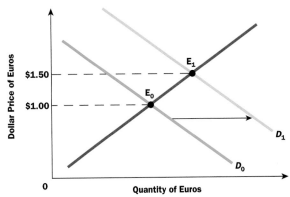

An increase in taste for European goods, an increase in U.S. income, and a decrease in U.S. tariffs all have the potential to cause an increase in demand for Euros, shifting the demand for Euros to the right and leading to a higher equilibrium exchange rate.

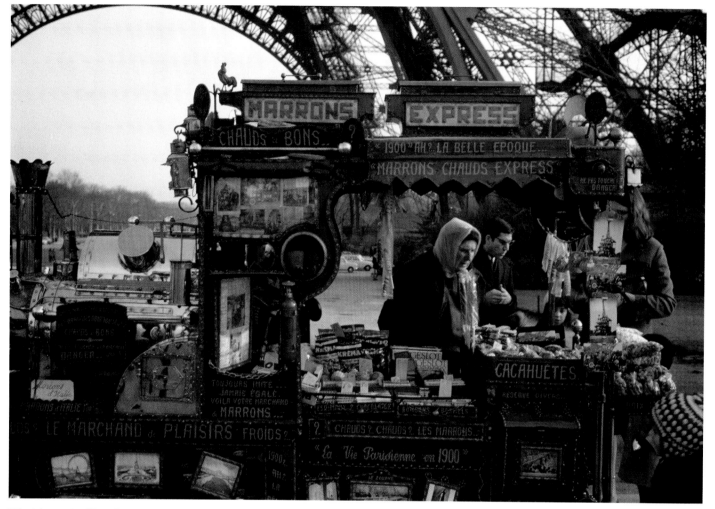

What impact will an increase in travel to Paris by U.S. consumers have on the Euro?

WHAT IF EUROPEAN TASTES, TARIFFS, OR INCOME CHANGED?

If European incomes rose, European tariffs on U.S. goods fell, or their tastes for American goods increased, the supply of Euros in the Euro foreign exchange market would increase. Any of these changes would cause Europeans to demand more U.S. goods, and therefore more U.S. dollars in order to purchase those goods. To obtain those added dollars, Europeans must exchange more of their Euros, increasing the supply of Euros on the Euro foreign exchange market. As Exhibit 2 demonstrates, the effect of this would be a rightward shift in the Euro supply curve, leading to a new equilibrium at a lower exchange rate for Euros.

HOW DO CHANGES IN INTEREST RATES AFFECT EXCHANGE RATES?

If interest rates in the United States were to increase relative to say European interest rates, other things equal, the rate of return on U.S. investments would increase relative to that on European investments. European investors would thus increase their demand for U.S. investments, and therefore offer Euros for sale to buy dollars to buy U.S. investments, shifting the supply curve for Euros to the right, from S_0 to S_1 in Exhibit 3.

In this scenario, U.S. investors would also shift their investments away from Europe by decreasing their demand for Euros relative to their demand for dollars, from D_0 to D_1 in Exhibit 3. Exhibit 3 shows the subsequent lower equilibrium price ($1.50) that would result for the Euro due to an increase in the U.S. interest rate. That is, there will be a depreciation of the Euro because Euros can now buy fewer units of dollars than before. In short, the higher interest rate in the United States attracted more capital to the U.S. and led to a relative appreciation of the dollar and a relative depreciation of the Euro.

HOW DO CHANGES IN THE RELATIVE INFLATION RATES AFFECT THE EQUILIBRIUM EXCHANGE RATE?

If Europe experienced an inflation rate greater than that experienced in the United States, other things equal, what would happen to the exchange rate? In this case, European products would become more expensive to U.S. consumers. Americans would decrease the quantity of European goods demanded and, therefore, decrease their demand for Euros. The result would be a leftward shift of the demand curve for Euros.

On the other side of the Atlantic, U.S. goods would become relatively cheaper to Europeans, leading Europeans to increase the quantity of U.S. goods demanded, and therefore, to demand more U.S. dollars. This increased demand for dollars translates into an increased supply of Euros, shifting the supply curve for Euros outward. Exhibit 4 shows the shifts of the supply and demand curves and the new lower equilibrium price for the Euro resulting from the higher European rate.

| EXHIBIT 2 | IMPACT OF EUROPEAN TASTE OR INCOME INCREASE, OR TARIFF DECREASE, ON THE FOREIGN EXCHANGE MARKET |

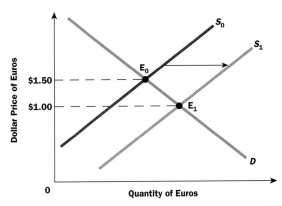

If European incomes increased, European tariffs on U.S. goods fell, or European tastes for American goods increased, the supply of Euros would increase. The increase in demand for dollars would cause an increase in the supply of Euros, shifting it to the right, from S_0 to S_1.

| EXHIBIT 3 | IMPACT OF U.S. INTEREST RATE INCREASE ON THE FOREIGN EXCHANGE MARKET |

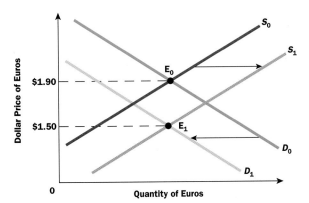

When interest rates increase in the United States, European investors will increase their supply of Euros to buy dollars—the supply curve of Euros increases from S_0 to S_1. In addition, U.S. investors will also shift their investments away from Europe, decreasing their demand for Euros and shifting the demand curve from D_0 to D_1. This will lead to a depreciation of the Euro; that is, Euros can now buy fewer units of dollars.

| EXHIBIT 4 | IMPACT OF EUROPEAN INFLATION RATE INCREASE ON THE FOREIGN EXCHANGE MARKET |

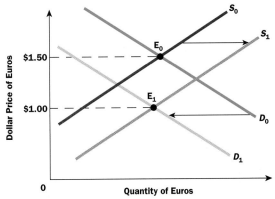

If Europe experienced a higher inflation rate than the U.S., European products would become more expensive to U.S. consumers. As a result, those consumers would demand fewer Euros, shifting the demand for Euros to the left, from D_0 to D_1. At the same time, U.S. goods would become relatively cheaper to Europeans, who would then buy more dollars by supplying Euros, shifting the Euro supply curve to the right, from S_0 to S_1. The result: a new lower equilibrium price for the Euro.

BIG MACCURRENCIES

As the yen plunges and sterling soars, economists are being forced to revise their currency forecasts. To help them get their teeth into the subject, The Economist has updated its Big Mac index, which seeks to make exchange-rate theory a bit more digestible.

The Big Mac index is based upon the theory of purchasing-power parity (PPP), the notion that a dollar should buy the same amount in all countries. That is, the exchange rate between any two currencies reflects the differences in the price level. In the long run, purchasing power parity theory states that the exchange rate between two currencies should move towards the rate that would equalize the prices of an identical basket of goods and services in each country. Many economists believe that there are many factors that are more important than the price level in exchange rate determination in the short run. However, in the long run, purchasing power parity is very important in exchange rate determination.

Our "basket" is a McDonald's Big Mac, produced in 110 countries. The Big Mac PPP is the exchange rate that would leave hamburgers costing the same in America as abroad. Comparing actual rates with PPPs signals whether a currency is under- or overvalued.

The first column of the table shows local-currency prices of a Big Mac; the second converts the prices into dollars. The cheapest Big Macs are now in Indonesia and Malaysia, where they cost $1.16. At the other extreme, Big Mac fans in Switzerland have to pay $3.87. Given that Americans in four cities pay an average of $2.56, the rupiah and the ringgit look massively undervalued, the Swiss franc massively overvalued.

The third column calculates Big Mac PPPs. For example, dividing the Japanese price by the American price gives a dollar PPP of ¥109. On April 6th, the exchange rate was ¥135, implying that the yen is 19% undervalued against the dollar. Three years ago the index suggested that the yen was 100% overvalued against the dollar. Likewise, the D-mark is now only 5% overvalued, against 50% in April 1995.

Thanks to the dollar's rise—long predicted by burgernomics—it is now closer to its PPP against other big currencies than for many years. Indeed, only five currencies in the table are now significantly overvalued against the greenback, among them Britain's, Sweden's, and Denmark's. All three countries have decided not to adopt Europe's single currency, the Euro, next year. The pound is 19% overvalued against the dollar, which implies it is 14% overvalued against the D-mark. In contrast, the currencies of the Euro-block countries are close to Mcparity against the D-mark.

The most dramatic changes in the index over the past year are in East Asia, where devaluations have left currencies significantly undervalued. This competitive advantage, however, is being eroded by inflation. In Indonesia, the price of a Big Mac has more than doubled over the past year. East European currencies also look cheap, with the Hungarian forint 52% undervalued against the dollar.

The Big Mac index is not a perfect measure of PPP. Price differences may be distorted by trade barriers on beef, sales taxes, local competition and changes in the cost of non-traded inputs such as rents. But despite its flaws, the Big Mac index produces PPP estimates close to those derived by more sophisticated methods. A currency can deviate from PPP for long periods, but several studies have found that the Big Mac PPP is a useful predictor of future movements—enabling the hungry investor to get rich by putting his money where his mouth is.

SOURCE: http://www.economist.com/editorial/just-foryou/11-4-98/fn7226.html

---

CONSIDER THIS:

Since 1989, *The Economist* magazine has been tracking the values of different currencies around the world with their "Big Mac index." This index is based on the theory of purchasing power parity (PPP). This theory suggests that one unit of currency (a dollar) would buy the same amount of a traded good anywhere in the world. PPP therefore suggests that a Big Mac, for example, should cost the same amount of dollars all around the world. The index shows, however, that this is not the case.

EXHIBIT 5   **BIG MAC INDEX**

The hamburger standard

	Big Mac prices		Implied PPP* of the dollar	Actual $ exchange rate 6/4/98	Under (-)/over(+) valuation against dollar, %
	in local currency	in dollars			
United States[†]	$2.56	2.56	–	–	–
Argentina	Peso2.50	2.50	0.98	1.00	-2
Australia	A$2.65	1.75	1.04	1.51	-32
Austria	Sch34.0	2.62	13.28	12.96	+2
Belgium	BFr109	2.87	42.58	38.00	+12
Brazil	Real3.10	2.72	1.21	1.14	+6
Britain	£1.84	3.05	1.39[‡]	1.66[‡]	+19
Canada	C$2.79	1.97	1.09	1.42	-23
Chile	Peso1,250	2.75	488	455	+7
China	Yuan9.90	1.20	3.87	8.28	-53
Czech Republic	CKr54.0	1.57	21.1	34.4	-39
Denmark	DKr23.8	3.39	9.28	7.02	+32
France	FFr17.5	2.84	6.84	6.17	+11
Germany	DM4.95	2.69	1.93	1.84	+5
Hong Kong	HK$10.2	1.32	3.98	7.75	-49
Hungary	Forint259	1.22	101	213	-52
Indonesia	Rupiah9,900	1.16	3,867	8,500	-55
Israel	Shekel12.50	3.38	4.88	3.70	+32
Italy	Lire4,500	2.47	1,758	1,818	-3
Japan	¥280	2.08	109	135	-19
Malaysia	M$4.30	1.16	1.68	3.72	-55
Mexico	Peso17.9	2.10	6.99	8.54	-18
Netherlands	Fl5.45	2.63	2.13	2.07	+3
New Zealand	NZ$3.45	1.90	1.35	1.82	-26
Poland	Zloty5.30	1.53	2.07	3.46	-40
Russia	Rouble12,000	2.00	4,688	5,999	-22
Singapore	S$3.00	1.85	1.17	1.62	-28
South Africa	Rand8.00	1.59	3.13	5.04	-38
South Korea	Won2,600	1.76	1,016	1,474	-31
Spain	Pta375	2.40	146	156	-6
Sweden	SKr24.0	3.00	9.38	8.00	+17
Switzerland	SFr5.90	3.87	2.30	1.52	+51
Taiwan	NT$68.0	2.06	26.6	33.0	-20
Thailand	Baht52.0	1.30	20.3	40.0	-49

*Purchasing-power parity: local price divided by price in United States
†Average of New York, Chicago, San Francisco and Atlanta   ‡Dollars per pound
Source: McDonald's

TUNE UP

DETERMINANTS OF EXCHANGE RATES

Q: How will the following events impact the foreign exchange market?

A. American travel to Europe increases.

B. Japanese investors' money flows into U.S. stock market.

C. U.S. real interest rates abruptly increase relative to world interest rates.

D. Other countries become less political and economically stable than the United States.

A:
A. Demand for Euro increases (demand shifts right in the Euro market), the dollar will depreciate and the Euro will appreciate, *ceteris paribus*.

B. Demand for dollars increases (demand shifts right in the dollar market), the dollar will appreciate and the Yen will depreciate, *ceteris paribus*. Alternatively, you could think of this as an increase in supply in the yen market.

C. International investors will increase their demand for dollars in the dollar market to take advantage of the higher interest rate. The dollar would appreciate relative to other foreign currencies, *ceteris paribus*.

D. More foreign investors will want to buy U.S. assets, causing an increase in demand for dollars.

CONCEPT CHECK

1. Any force that shifts either the demand or supply curves for a foreign currency will shift the equilibrium in the foreign exchange market and lead to a new exchange rate.

2. Any changes in tastes, income levels, relative real interest rates, or relative inflation rates will cause the demand for and supply of a currency to shift.

1. Why will the exchange value of a foreign currency relative to U.S. dollars decline when U.S. domestic tastes change, reducing the demand for foreign-produced goods?

2. Why does the demand for foreign currencies shift in the same direction as domestic income? What happens to the exchange value of those foreign currencies in terms of dollars?

3. How would increased U.S. tariffs on imported European goods affect the exchange value of Euros in terms of dollars?

4. Why do changes in tastes, incomes, or tariffs in the U.S. change the demand for Euros, while similar changes in Europe change the supply of Euros?

5. What would happen to the exchange value of Euros in terms of U.S. dollars if incomes rose in both Europe and the U.S.?

6. Why does an increase in interest rates in Germany relative to U.S. interest rates increase the demand for Euros but decrease their supply?

7. What would an increase in U.S. inflation relative to Europe do to the supply and demand for Euros and to the equilibrium exchange value (price) of Euros in terms of U.S. dollars?

Flexible Exchange Rates

MODULE 17

- How are exchange rates determined today?
- How are exchange rate changes different under a flexible-rate system than in a fixed system?
- What major problems exist in a fixed-rate system?
- What are the major arguments against flexible rates?

HOW WAS THE FLEXIBLE EXCHANGE RATE SYSTEM DEVELOPED?

Since 1973, the world has essentially operated on a system of flexible exchange rates. Flexible exchange rates mean that currency prices are allowed to fluctuate with changes in supply and demand, without governments stepping in to prevent those changes. Before that, governments operated under what was called the Bretton Woods fixed exchange rate system, in which they would maintain a stable exchange rate by buying or selling currencies or reserves to bring demand and supply for their currencies together at the fixed exchange rate. The present system evolved out of the Bretton Woods fixed-rate system, and occurred by accident, not design. Governments were unable to agree on an alternative fixed-rate approach when the Bretton Woods system collapsed, so nations simply let market forces determine currency values.

ARE EXCHANGE RATES MANAGED AT ALL?

To be sure, governments sensitive to sharp changes in the exchange value of their currencies do still intervene from time to time to prop up their currency's exchange rate was if it considered to be too low or falling too rapidly, or to depress its exchange rate if it was considered to be too high or rising too rapidly. Such was the case as the U.S. dollar declined in value in the late 1970s, but the U.S. government intervention appeared to have little if any effect in preventing the dollar's decline. However, present-day fluctuations in exchange rates are not determined solely by market forces. Economists sometimes say that the current exchange rate system is a "dirty float" system, meaning that fluctuations in currency values are partly determined by market forces and partly influenced by government intervention. Over the years, however, such governmental support attempts have been insufficient to dramatically alter exchange rates for long, and currency exchange rates have changed dramatically. These rather drastic fluctuations in exchange rates are indicated in Exhibit 1, which shows how exchange rates for the U.S. dollar have changed over the years.

HOW DO THESE CHANGES AFFECT TRADE?

When exchange rates change, they affect not only the currency market but the product markets as well. For example, if U.S. consumers were to receive fewer and fewer British pounds and Japanese yen per U.S. dollar, the effect would be an increasing price of foreign imports, *ceteris paribus*, because it would now take a greater number of dollars to buy a given number of yen or pounds, which U.S. consumers use to purchase those foreign products. It would, however, lower the cost of U.S. exports to foreigners. And if the dollar increased in value relative to other currencies, then this would lower the relative price of foreign goods, *ceteris paribus*. However, foreigners would find that U.S. goods were more expensive in terms of their own currency prices, and, as a result, would import fewer U.S. products.

WHAT ARE THE ADVANTAGES OF FLEXIBLE RATES?

As mentioned earlier, the present system of flexible exchange rates was not planned. Indeed, most central bankers thought that a system where rates were not fixed would lead to chaos. What in fact has happened? Since the advent of flexible exchange rates, world trade has not only continued, but expanded. Over a one-year time period, the world economy adjusted to the shock of a four-fold increase in the price of its most important internationally traded commodity, oil. Although the OPEC oil cartel's price increase certainly had adverse economic impacts, it did so without paralyzing the economy of any one nation.

The most important advantage of the flexible-rate system is that the recurrent crises that led to speculative rampages and major currency revaluations under the fixed Bretton Woods system have significantly diminished. Under the fixed-rate system, price changes in currencies

Japanese Yen per U.S. Dollar

German Marks per U.S. Dollar

British Pound in U.S. Dollars

SOURCE: *The Wall Street Journal Almanac*, 1998, p. 361.

came infrequently, but when they came, they were of a large magnitude: 20 or 30 percent changes overnight were fairly common. Today, price changes occur daily or even hourly, but each change is much smaller in magnitude, with major changes in exchange rates typically occurring only over periods of months or years.

HOW CAN FIXED EXCHANGE RATES LEAD TO CURRENCY SHORTAGES?

Perhaps the most significant problem with the fixed-rate system is that it can result in currency shortages, just as

domestic price and wage controls lead to shortages. Suppose we had a fixed-rate system with the price of one Euro set at $1.00, as shown in Exhibit 2. In this example, the original quantity of Euros demanded and supplied is indicated by curves D_0 and S, so that $1.00 is the equilibrium price. That is, at a price of $1.00, the quantity of Euros demanded (by U.S. importers of European products and others wanting Euros) equals the quantity supplied (by European importers of U.S. products and others).

Suppose that some event happens to increase U.S. demand for Dutch goods. For this example, let us assume that Royal Dutch Shell discovers new oil reserves in the North Sea and thus has a new product to export. As U.S.

Under a flexible-rate system, small changes in exchange rates occur daily or even hourly.

consumers begin to demand Royal Dutch Shell oil, the demand for Euros increases. That is, at any given dollar price of Euros, U.S. consumers want more Euros, shifting the demand curve to the right, to D_1. Under a fixed exchange rate system, the dollar price of Euros must remain at \$1, where the quantity of Euros demanded (Q_0) now exceeds the quantity supplied, Q_1. The result is a shortage of Euros—a shortage that must be corrected in some way. As a solution to the shortage, the U.S. may borrow Euros from the Netherlands, or perhaps ship the Netherlands some of its reserves of gold. The ability to continually make up the shortage (deficit) in this manner, however, is limited, particularly if the deficit persists for a substantial period of time.

HOW DO FLEXIBLE RATES SOLVE THE CURRENCY SHORTAGE?

Under flexible exchange rates, a change in the supply or demand for Euros does not pose a problem. Because rates are allowed to change, the rising U.S. demand for Euro-

pean goods (and thus for Euros) would lead to a new equilibrium price for Euros, say at \$1.50. At this higher price, European goods are more costly to buyers in the U.S. Some of the increase in demand for European imports, then, is offset by a decrease in quantity demanded resulting from higher import prices. Similarly, the change in the exchange rate will make U.S. goods cheaper to Europeans, thus increasing U.S. exports and, with that, the quantity of Euros supplied. For example, a \$40 software program that cost Europeans 40 Euros when the exchange rate was \$1 per Euro, costs less than 27 Euros when the exchange rate increases to \$1.50 per Euro (\$40 divided by 1.50).

HOW DO FLEXIBLE RATES AFFECT MACROECONOMIC POLICIES?

With flexible exchange rates, the imbalance between debits and credits arising from shifts in currency demand and/or supply is accommodated by changes in currency prices, rather than through the special financial borrowings or reserve movements necessary with fixed rates. In a pure

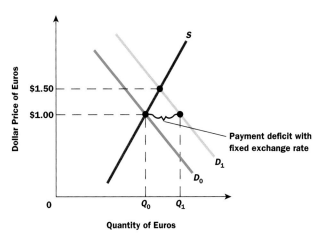

EXHIBIT 2 | HOW FLEXIBLE EXCHANGE RATES WORK

As increase in demand for Euros shifts the demand curve to the right, from D_0 to D_1. Under a fixed-rate system, this increase in demand results in a shortage of Euros at the equilibrium price of $1, because the quantity demanded at this price (Q_1) is greater than the quantity supplied (Q_0). If the exchange rate is flexible, however, no shortage develops. Instead, the increase in demand forces the exchange rate higher, to $1.50. At this higher exchange rate, the quantity of Euros demanded doesn't increase as much, and the quantity of Euros supplied increases as a result of the now relatively lower cost of imports from the United States.

flexible exchange rate system, balance of payments deficits and surpluses tend to disappear automatically. The market mechanism itself is able to address world trade imbalances, dispensing with the need for bureaucrats attempting to achieve some administratively determined price. Moreover, the need to use restrictive monetary and/or fiscal policy to end such an imbalance while maintaining a fixed exchange rate is alleviated. Nations are thus able to feel less constraint in carrying out internal macroeconomic policies under flexible exchange rates. For these reasons, many economists welcomed the collapse of the Bretton Woods system and the failure to arrive at a new system of fixed or quasi-fixed exchange rates.

WHAT ARE THE DISADVANTAGES OF FLEXIBLE RATES?

Despite the fact that world trade has grown and dealing with balance of payments problems has become less difficult, flexible exchange rates have not been universally endorsed by everyone. Several disadvantages of this system have been cited.

Have flexible rates hurt world trade?

Traditionally, the major objection to flexible rates was that they introduce considerable uncertainty into international trade. For example, if you order some perfume from France with a commitment to pay 1,000 Euros in three months, you are not certain what the dollar price of Euros, and therefore, of the perfume, will be three months from now, because the exchange rate is constantly fluctuating. Because people prefer certainty to uncertainty and are generally risk averse, this uncertainty raises the costs of international transactions. As a result, flexible exchange rates can reduce the volume of trade, thus reducing the potential gains from international specialization.

Proponents of flexible rates have three answers to this argument. First, the empirical evidence shows that international trade has, in fact, grown in volume faster since the introduction of flexible rates. The exchange rate risk of trade has not had any major adverse impact. Second, it is possible to, in effect, buy insurance against the proposed adverse impact of currency fluctuations. Rather than buying currencies for immediate use in what is called the "spot" market for foreign currencies, one can contract today to buy foreign currencies in the future at a set exchange rate in the "forward" or "futures" market. By using this market, a perfume importer can buy Euros now for delivery to her in three months; in doing so, she can be certain of the dollar price she is paying for the perfume. Since floating exchange rates began, booming futures markets in foreign currencies have opened in Chicago, New York, and in foreign financial centers. The third argument is that the alleged certainty of currency prices under the old Bretton Woods system was fictitious, because the possibility existed that nations might, at their whim, drastically revalue their currencies to deal with their own fundamental balance of payments problems. Proponents of flexible rates, then, argue that they are therefore no less disruptive to trade than fixed rates.

Do flexible rates lead to inflation?

A second, more valid criticism of flexible exchange rates is that they can contribute to inflationary pressures. Under fixed rates, domestic monetary and fiscal authorities have an incentive to constrain their domestic prices, because lower domestic prices increase the attractiveness of exported goods. This discipline is not present to the same extent with flexible rates. The consequence of a sharp monetary or fiscal expansion under flexible rates would be a decline in the value of one's currency relative to those of other countries. Yet even that may not seem to be as serious a political consequence as the Bretton Woods solution of an abrupt devaluation of the currency in the face of a severe balance of payments problem.

Advocates of flexible rates would argue that inflation need not occur under flexible rates. Flexible rates do not cause inflation; rather it is caused by the expansionary macroeconomic policies of governments and central banks.

Actually, flexible rates give government decision makers greater freedom of action than fixed rates; whether they act responsibly is determined by exchange rates, but rather by domestic policies.

CONCEPT CHECK

1. While rates are free today to fluctuate based on market transactions, governments occasionally intervene to increase or depress the price of their currencies.
2. Changes in exchange rates occur more often under a flexible-rate system, but the changes are much smaller than the drastic, overnight revaluations of currencies that occurred under the fixed-rate system.

3. Under a fixed rate system, as the supply and demand for currencies shift, currency prices are not allowed to shift to the new equilibrium, leading to surpluses and shortages of currencies.
4. The main arguments presented against flexible exchange rates are that international trade levels will be diminished due to the uncertainty of future currency prices and that the flexible rates would lead to inflation. Proponents of flexible exchange rates have strong counter-arguments to those views.

1. What are the arguments for and against flexible exchange rates?
2. When the U.S. dollar starts to exchange for fewer Japanese yen, other things equal, what happens to U.S. and Japanese imports and exports as a result?
3. Why is the system of flexible exchange rates sometimes called a "dirty float" system?

4. Were exchange rates under the Bretton Woods system really stable? How could you argue that exchange rates were more uncertain under the fixed rate system than with floating exchange rates?
5. What is the uncertainty argument against flexible exchange rates? What evidence do proponents of flexible exchange rates cite in response?
6. Do flexible exchange rates cause higher rates of inflation? Why or why not?

Application: The United States Intervenes to Boost the Yen

In this Module we have examined the interworkings of the exchange market. In this application, we see that the United States recently intervened in the foreign exchange market to bolster another country's currency—the Japanese yen. Why would the United States do this? How would a further fall in the value of the yen impact the global economy?

U.S. INTERVENES IN ASIAN CRISIS

WASHINGTON, June 17—In the latest sign of the seriousness of the Asian crisis, the United States intervened in currency markets Wednesday, selling dollars and buying yen in an effort to bolster the value of the sagging Japanese currency. The sales of dollars for yen marked the first time the Clinton administration has sold dollars to support another currency and underscored concerns about the deepening economic troubles of the world's second-largest economy.

The move was also the first time the administration had tried directly to influence exchange rates since August 1995.

The dollar immediately responded, tumbling against the yen. Dollar/yen screeched past several key support levels, falling rapidly from its 142.03 yen level in early New York trading to a session low of 136.18.

In early Tokyo trading on Thursday, the dollar continued to skid, falling to 135.72, more than 6 yen below its close Wednesday on Asian markets. The foreign exchange action was also having an uplifting effect on Asia's stock exchanges. In early morning trading, Japan's 225-share Nikkei average jumped 4.23 percent, or 621.83 points, to 15,337.21; South Korea's main index was up some 8 percent; and Hong Kong's 6 percent.

Dealers in New York said the United States likely spent up to $2 billion during the intervention on Wednesday. "We have been hearing the figure is around $2 billion," one market source said. Others said the total intervention, including that spent by the Bank of Japan, was likely in the $6 billion range. It was the first U.S. intervention on behalf of the yen in more than six years.

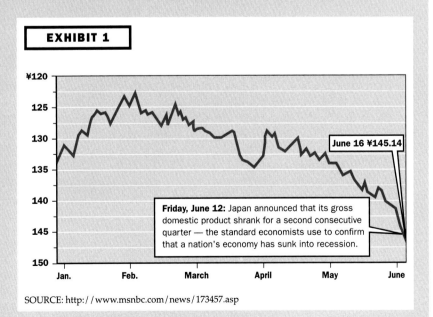

EXHIBIT 1

June 16 ¥145.14

Friday, June 12: Japan announced that its gross domestic product shrank for a second consecutive quarter — the standard economists use to confirm that a nation's economy has sunk into recession.

SOURCE: http://www.msnbc.com/news/173457.asp

The U.S. government is concerned with the weakening yen. The government is concerned that if the yen falls any more, it will have substantial implications in other East Asian countries and, ultimately, in the United States. The depreciating yen has broad implications for both consumers and producers. For example, a lower exchange rate will lead to lower prices for Japanese computer chips and the computers made with those chips, as well as other Japanese goods, like cars, camcorders, and car stereos. On the other hand, higher relative prices for U.S. goods means that Japanese buyers will look elsewhere. This may keep inflation from rising but could lead to a reduction in manufacturing job growth in the United States.

ONE STEP BEYOND

What would happen to the exchange rate for the Euro if pizzas made with special imported Italian cheeses, sausages, spices, and sauces suddenly became all of the rage on college campuses across the United States? Can you identify other factors that impact the foreign exchange market? Use the problems in your Workbook to gauge your understanding of these topics, and then check out recent data and information about U.S. exports by following the links provided on your EconActive CD-ROM.

Module 1: Economics: Ten Powerful Ideas
Concept A

1. What is the definition of economics?
Economics is the study of the allocation of our scarce resources to satisfy our unlimited wants for goods and services.

2. Why does scarcity force us to make choices?
Scarcity, the fact that our wants exceed what our resources can produce, means that we are forced to make choices on how best to use those limited resources.

3. Why are choices costly?
In a world of scarcity, whenever we choose one option, we also choose to do without something else that we also desire. This want that we choose not to satisfy is the opportunity cost of that choice.

4. Why do even "non-economic" issues have an economic dimension?
Even apparently non-economic issues have an economic dimension because economics concerns anything worthwhile to some human being (including love, friendship, charity, etc.) and the choices we make among those things we value.

5. If a genie gave you three wishes, would that solve the problem of scarcity for you?
No. You couldn't satisfy all of your wants with three wishes if we assume that none of your wishes could be used for more wishes. That is, wishes would still be scarce.

Concept B

1. What are resources?
Resources are the scarce inputs that are used to produce the goods and services we want. They include both man-made (e.g., machinery) and natural (e.g., land) inputs, labor, and the entrepreneurship that puts the other resources together.

2. How do finite resources impact our ability to produce goods and services?
The fact that resources are finite (limited) means that the things that can be produced from them—the goods and services we want—are also limited as a result.

3. What must be true for something to be an economic good?
An economic good, tangible or intangible, is any good or service that we value or desire. This definition includes the reduction of things we don't want, bads, as a good (e.g., trash is a bad, while trash clean-up is a good).

4. Does wanting more tangible and intangible goods and services make us selfish?
No. Among the goods many of us want more of is helping others (charity), so to say that we all want more goods does not imply that we are selfish, merely that we are "self-interested."

5. Why might sunshine be scarce in Seattle but not in Tucson?
For a good to be scarce, we must want more of it than we are able to have freely available from nature. Residents of Tucson typically have all of the sunshine they desire, while rain may be something that is very scarce relative to residents' desires. For residents of Seattle, where the sun shines much less and it rains much more, the opposite might well be true.

Concept C

1. Does everyone face scarcity?
Because no one can have all the goods and services that he or she desires, we all face scarcity as a fact of life.

2. Why does scarcity affect each of us differently?
Because our desires and the extent of the resources we have available to meet those desires vary, scarcity affects each of us differently.

3. Why can't a country become so technologically advanced that its citizens won't have to choose?
No matter how productive a country becomes, its citizens' desires will continue to outstrip their ability to satisfy them. As we get more productive and incomes grow, we discover new wants that we would like to satisfy, so our ability to produce never catches up with our wants.

4. If Penny Pincher became a billionaire after winning the largest lotto ever, would she still face scarcity?
Becoming a billionaire does make some goods more available to an individual, but it does not eliminate scarcity. Among other very scarce goods, it can't guarantee us as long a lifespan, as many friends, or as much happiness as we might like.

Concept D

1. Would we have to make choices if we had unlimited resources?
We would not have to make choices if we had unlimited resources, because we would then be able to produce all of the goods and services we wanted, and having more of one thing would not require having less of other goods or services. However, unlimited resources also means unlimited time—most of us would always desire more leisure time—meaning that labor is likely to remain scarce, regardless of what happens to other inputs.

2. What is given up when we make a choice?
When you make a choice, you give up the opportunity to pursue other valued alternatives with the same time or resources.

3. What do we mean by opportunity cost?
The opportunity cost of a choice is the highest valued foregone opportunity resulting from a decision. It can usefully be thought of as the value of the opportunity a person would have chosen if their most-preferred option was taken away.

4. Why is there no such thing as a free lunch?
There is no such thing as a free lunch because the production of any good uses up some of society's resources. As a result, those resources are then no longer available for use in the production of other goods and services we want.

5. How are prices and costs different?
A price reflects the monetary value of the good; it is an objective fact. Costs are personal and subjective, reflecting the relative values of foregone goods and services to individuals that result from choices made. Because individuals have different preferences and face different circumstances, the costs they incur from making a choice will be different.

6. Why was the opportunity cost of staying in college higher for Tiger Woods than for most undergraduates?
The alternative to Tiger Woods of staying in school—starting a very highly paid professional golf career sooner than he could

have otherwise—was far more lucrative than the alternatives facing most undergraduates. Because the alternative was more valuable for Tiger Woods, his opportunity cost of staying in school was higher than for most.

7. Why is the opportunity cost of time spent getting an MBA typically lower for a 22-year-old straight out of college than for a 45-year-old experienced manager?

The opportunity cost of time for a 45-year-old experienced manager—the earnings he would have to give up to spend a given period of time getting an MBA—is higher than that of a 22-year-old straight out of college, whose income-earning alternatives are far less.

Concept E

1. What are marginal choices? Why does economics focus on them?

Marginal choices are choices of how much of something to do, not choices of whether to do something or not. Economics focuses on marginal choices because those are the sort of choices we most frequently face: Should I do a little more of this or a little less of that?

2. What is the rule of rational choice?

The rule of rational choice is that in trying to make themselves better off, people alter their behavior if the expected marginal benefits from doing so outweigh the expected marginal costs they will bear as a result. If the expected marginal benefits of an action exceed the expected marginal costs, a person will do more of that action; if the expected marginal benefits of an action are less than the expected marginal costs, a person will do less of that action.

3. Why does rational choice involve expectations?

Because the world is uncertain in many important respects, we can seldom know for certain whether the marginal benefits of an action will in fact exceed the marginal costs. Therefore, the rule of rational choice deals with expectations that decision makers hold at the time they make their decisions, recognizing that mistakes can be made.

4. Why do students often stop taking lecture notes when a professor announces that the next few minutes of material will not be on any future test or assignment?

The benefit, in terms of grades, from taking notes in class falls when the material discussed will not be tested or "rewarded," and because the marginal benefits of note taking are now smaller in this situation relative to the unchanged marginal costs, students do less of it.

5. If you decide to speed to get to a doctor's appointment and then get into an accident as a result, does your decision to speed invalidate the rule of rational choice?

No. Remember, the rule of rational choice deals with expectations at the time decisions are made. If you thought you would get into an accident due to speeding in this situation, you would not have decided to speed. The fact that you got in an accident doesn't invalidate the rule of rational choice; it only means that your expectations at the time you decided to speed proved to be incorrect.

Concept F

1. What is the difference between positive incentives and negative incentives?

Positive incentives are those that either increase the benefits or decrease the costs of an action, thus encouraging the action.

Negative incentives are those that either decrease the benefits or increase the costs of an action, thus discouraging the action.

2. According to the rule of rational choice, would you do more or less of something if its expected marginal benefits increased?

If the expected marginal benefits of an activity increased, you would do more of that activity, because you would get a higher overall benefit level by doing so.

3. According to the rule of rational choice, would you do more or less of something if its expected marginal costs increased?

If the expected marginal costs of an activity increased, you would do less of that activity, because you would incur fewer costs (and therefore have a higher overall benefit level) by doing so.

4. How does the rule of rational choice imply that young children are typically more likely to misbehave at a supermarket checkout counter than at home?

When a young child is at a supermarket checkout counter, the benefit of misbehaving (the potential payoff to pestering Mom or Dad for candy) is greater. Also, because his parents are less likely to punish him, or to punish him as severely, in public as in private for his misbehavior, the costs are lower as well. Because the benefits of misbehavior are higher and the costs are lower at a supermarket checkout counter, more child misbehavior is to be expected there.

5. Why do many parents refuse to let their children have dessert before they eat the rest of their dinner?

Children often find that the costs of eating many foods at dinner exceed the benefits (e.g., "If it's green, it must be yucky"), but that is seldom true of dessert. If parents let their children eat dessert first, they would often not eat the food that was "good for them." But by adding the benefit of getting dessert to the choice of eating their other food, parents can get their children to eat the rest of their dinner also.

Concept G

1. Why do people specialize?

People specialize because by concentrating their energies on the activities to which they are best suited, individuals incur lower opportunity costs. That is, they specialize in doing those things that they can do at lower opportunity costs than others, and they let individuals who can do other things at lower opportunity costs than they can specialize in doing those activities.

2. What do we mean by comparative advantage?

A person, region, or country has a comparative advantage in producing a good or service when it can produce it at a lower opportunity cost than other persons, regions, or countries.

3. Why does the combination of specialization and trade make us better off?

Trade increases wealth by allowing a person, region, or a nation to specialize in those products that it produces relatively better than others and to trade for those products that others produce relatively better than it does. Exploiting our comparative advantages and then trading allows us to produce, and therefore consume, more than we could otherwise from our scarce resources.

4. If you can mow your lawn in half the time it takes your younger brother to do it, do you have a comparative advantage in mowing the lawn?

No, not necessarily. Your faster speed at mowing the lawn does not establish that you have a comparative advantage in mowing. That can only be established relative to other tasks. The person with a comparative advantage in mowing lawns is the one with the lowest opportunity cost, and that could be your younger brother in this case. For instance, if you could earn $12 an hour, mowing the lawn in half an hour implies an opportunity cost of $6 of foregone output elsewhere. If your brother could only earn $5 per hour (he was less than half as productive in doing other things compared to you), the opportunity cost of him mowing the lawn in an hour is $5. In this case, your younger brother has a comparative advantage in mowing the lawn.

5. If you became far more productive than before in completing yard chores, could that eliminate your current comparative advantage in doing the dishes?
The opportunity cost of you doing the dishes is the value of other chores you must give up to do the dishes. Therefore, an increase in your productivity in doing yard chores would increase the opportunity cost of doing the dishes, and could well eliminate your current comparative advantage in doing the dishes compared to other members of your family.

6. Could a student who gets a C in one class but a D or worse in everything else have a comparative advantage in that class over someone who gets a B in that class but an A in everything else?
A student who gets a C in a class is less good, in an absolute sense, at that class than a student who gets a B in it. But if the C student gets Ds in other classes, he is relatively, or comparatively, better at the C class, while if the B student gets As in other classes, he is relatively, or comparatively, worse at that class.

7. How can Michael Jordan help feed more poor people by playing basketball than by serving meals in a homeless shelter?
Michael Jordan could earn a great deal of money by playing two hours of basketball (his comparative advantage), which he could then donate to feed a large number of people in a homeless shelter. The result would be to feed far more people than if he spent those two hours serving meals at the shelter himself.

Concept H

1. Why must every society choose some manner by which to allocate its scarce resources?
Every society must choose some manner by which to allocate its scarce resources because the collective wants of its members always far outweighs what can be produced from those resources.

2. How does a market system allocate resources?
A market system allows individuals, both as producers and consumers, to indicate their wants and desires through their actions (how much they are willing to buy or sell at various prices). The market then acts to bring about that level of prices which coordinates the plans of the buyers and sellers.

3. What do market prices communicate to others in society?
The prices charged by suppliers communicate the relative availability of products to consumers; the prices consumers are willing to pay communicate the relative values consumers place on products to producers. That is, market prices provide a way for both consumers and suppliers to communicate about the relative value of goods, services, and resources.

4. How do price controls undermine the market as a communication device?
Price controls, price floors, price ceilings, and overall caps on all prices (as during war) prevent the market from communicating relevant (changing) information between consumers and suppliers.

A price floor set above the market price prevents suppliers from communicating their willingness to sell for less to consumers. A price ceiling set below the market price prevents consumers from indicating their willingness to pay more to suppliers. And price controls don't allow expressions of willingness-to-pay to operate throughout an economy.

5. Why can markets sometimes fail to allocate resources efficiently?
Markets can sometimes fail to allocate resources efficiently. Such situations, called market failures, represent situations such as externalities, where costs can be imposed on some individuals without their consent (e.g., from dumping "crud" in their air or water), where information in the market may not be communicated honestly and accurately, and where firms may have market power to distort prices in their favor (against consumers' interests).

Concept I

1. What justifications are there for government involvement in the economic decision-making process?
At least seven reasons have been used to justify government involvement in the economic decision-making process: (1) To provide a legal framework to enforce and protect property rights; (2) to provide goods and service that are inherently public in character, like national defense; (3) to overcome inefficiencies due to a lack of competition in some markets; (4) to provide information to help market participants make better choices; (5) to correct inappropriate market signals in cases of externalities, like pollution; (6) to change a market-determined income distribution considered unfair or undesirable; and (7) to improve the overall level of output, employment, or prices from what might result from the market mechanism alone. (Note: Not all of these justifications receive universal support nor are they of equal importance.)

2. What are property rights?
Property rights are the powers granted owners of property to use, sell, rent, dispose of, and enhance the value of those goods or resources.

3. How do different property rights alter incentives?
Different property rights alter incentives because they change the expected marginal benefits and the expected marginal costs of a wide range of actions. For example, private property serves as a powerful incentive for individuals to maintain and conserve their resources, because they will be able to benefit from any future increase in the value of those resources. Under public ownership, individuals cannot benefit from future increases in the value of those resources, and as a result, they have less incentive to maintain and conserve those goods and resources.

4. What is the law of unintended consequences?
The law of unintended consequences is the term used to remind us that the results of actions are not always as they appear, because the secondary effects of an action often include many consequences that were not part of what was intended. Indeed, the unintended consequences of an action often work counter to the original intent.

5. Why is the law of unintended consequences so important in making public policy?
It is impossible to change just one incentive to achieve a particular result through a government policy. A policy will change the incentives facing multiple individuals making multiple decisions,

and changes in all of those effected choices will result. Sometimes, the unintended consequences can be so substantial that they completely undermine the intended effects of a policy.

6. Why is the shared, common area of a dormitory often messier than the students' individual rooms?

When cleaning her own area, a student gets all of the benefits and bears all the costs of cleaning. But when cleaning the common area, she gets only a small part of the benefits, which are shared with others, while still bearing all of the costs of that cleaning. The result is less effort spent cleaning common areas.

Concept J

1. Why do we want economic growth to take place?

In a world of scarcity, we would rather have more goods and services to consume than less, and economic growth expands the amount of consumption possible in the future.

2. Can economic growth have negative side effects?

Economic growth in the amounts of goods and services available for consumption can potentially have negative side effects, including environmental damage, increased economic inequality, and so forth. However, it is important to realize that expanding economic opportunities do not necessarily result in these negative side effects. Indeed, properly measured, growth incorporates any negative side effects.

3. What sorts of policies can encourage economic growth?

Economic growth can be encouraged by policies that increase capital formation, encourage new technology development, and lead to the discovery of more efficient methods of doing things.

4. Is it possible for economic growth to increase the quality of the environment?

Yes. Economic growth indicates that more of many goods can be produced than before. One of those goods that we could produce more of with economic growth is environmental quality. That is, economic growth can produce more environmental quality, but it may not do so because environmental quality is usually supplied in a political setting where the proper amounts of many things may not always be forthcoming because political incentives differ from economic incentives.

5. If a country is building a bridge or road that nobody uses, will that kind of investment contribute to economic growth?

It is valuable investments, not just investments per se, that add to the future productive capacity of the economy. Investments in bridges and roads that nobody uses do not add to the economy's productivity and thus do not add to its economic growth. Indeed, the opportunity cost of using a country's resources in this particular way are very high.

Concept K

1. What is inflation?

Inflation describes the situation where overall prices are rising (even though some prices may be falling).

2. What is deflation?

Deflation describes the situation where overall prices are falling (even though some prices may be rising).

3. Why is price stability useful?

Price stability is useful because it enables producers and consumers to more accurately predict the general level of prices in the society and thus allows them to better coordinate their plans and decisions through the market.

4. How can inflation distort price signals?

With inflation, not all prices change at the same time and in the same amount. As a result, inflation distorts relative prices, undermining their ability to communicate accurately about relative scarcities in the economy.

5. Why is the mere *possibility* of inflation costly to society?

Just the possibility of inflation is costly to society because it increases the uncertainty, and the costs of that uncertainty, about what the general price level will be in the future. The less one can be sure about the future price level, the harder it is to determine the appropriate prices to charge or pay in market negotiations.

6. Why does writing a five-year supply agreement for coal become more difficult when the future price level becomes more uncertain?

Setting an agreed-upon price for a five-year supply agreement requires the parties involved to estimate today the price level over the next five years. The more uncertain the future price level, the riskier it becomes to lock in prices today and the more difficult it is to negotiate such a long-term agreement.

Module 2: The Role and Method of Economics

Concept A

1. What makes economics a social science?

Economics is a social science because it is concerned with reaching generalizations about human, or social, behavior.

2. What distinguishes macroeconomics from microeconomics?

Macroeconomics deals with the economy as a whole, analyzing issues such as inflation, unemployment, business cycles, and economic growth. Microeconomics deals with smaller units within the economy, such as the behavior of individuals, households, firms, and industries. Both, however, ultimately strive to understand people's behavior.

3. Why is it worth studying economics?

Perhaps the best reason to study economics is that so many of the things that concern us are at least partly economic in character. Economics helps us intelligently evaluate our options and determine the most appropriate choices in given situations; it helps develop a disciplined method of thinking about problems. Economics also helps us to understand how the many choices made by economic "actors" are coordinated in the market.

4. Why is the market for running shoes considered a microeconomic topic?

Because a single industry is small relative to the economy as a whole, the market for running shoes (or the running shoe industry) is a microeconomic topic.

5. Why is inflation considered a macroeconomic topic?

Because inflation—a change in the overall price level—has effects throughout the entire economy rather than just in certain small areas of the economy, it is a macroeconomic topic.

Concept B

1. What do economists mean by self-interest?

By self-interest, economists simply mean that people try to improve their own situation (as they see it, not necessarily as others see it).

2. What does rational behavior involve?

Economists consider individuals to be acting rationally if they are striving to do their best to achieve their goals with their limited income, time, and knowledge, given the prices they face and their expectations of the likely future consequences (both benefits and costs) of their behavior.

3. Why are observation and prediction more difficult in the social sciences?

Observation and prediction are more difficult in the social sciences than in physical sciences because social sciences are concerned with human behavior, which is more variable and often less readily predictable than the behavior of experiments observed in a laboratory. Social scientists can seldom run truly "controlled" experiments like those of the biological scientists.

4. Why do economic predictions refer to the behavior of groups of people rather than individuals?

Economists' predictions usually refer to the collective behavior of large groups rather than individuals because looking at the behaviors of a large group of individuals allows economists to discern general patterns of actions and therefore make more reliable generalizations.

5. Why is it typically rational for students to make some mistakes (get less than 100 percent) on a test?

Rational behavior reflects benefits and costs at the margin. A student who expects to get in the high 90 percent range on a test expects to get an A on the test. In that circumstance, the marginal benefit of continued studying to get closer to 100 percent is normally very small, so that the marginal costs of additional studying typically exceed the marginal benefits of added studying before 100 percent mastery is expected.

6. Can you sometimes get a high grade on a test without studying? Does that mean that additional studying does not lead to higher grades?

There may be some instances where a student can get a high grade on an exam without studying. However, because additional studying increases mastery of the material, additional studying will typically increase test performance and grades. That is, while there are some unusual situations (for example, an unusually intelligent person who can absorb most of the material from just going to class) where added studying will not raise grades, additional studying does, in general, lead to higher grades.

Concept C

1. What are economic theories?

A theory is an established explanation that accounts for known facts or phenomena. Economic theories are statements or propositions about patterns of human behavior that are expected to take place under certain circumstances.

2. What is the purpose of a theory?

The purpose of a theory is primarily to explain and predict well. They are necessary because the huge number of potential facts of a complex world do not organize themselves.

3. Why must economic theories be abstract?

Economic theories must be abstract because they could not possibly include every possible event, circumstance, or factor that might affect behavior. Like a road map, an economic theory abstracts from some issues to focus more clearly and precisely on the central questions it is designed to explain. It is actually unde-

sirable for a theory to be realistic, because if it were, it would be just as hard to understand as the world we are trying to understand (for example, a map showing the way from Los Angeles to San Francisco would be hundreds of miles long).

4. What is a hypothesis? How do we determine if it is tentatively accepted?

A hypothesis is a testable proposal that makes some type of predictions about behavior in response to certain changed conditions. An economic hypothesis is a testable proposal about how people will behave or react to a change in economic circumstances. It is tentatively acceptable if its predictions are consistent with what actually happens. In economics, empirical analysis is often used to see if the hypothesis is supported by the facts.

Concept D

1. Why do economists hold other things constant (*ceteris paribus*)?

The *ceteris paribus* assumption is used in economics because, in trying to assess the effect of one variable on another, we must isolate their relationship from other important events or variables that might also influence the situation the theory tries to explain or predict. This way of thinking is the analog of the controlled experiment in biology, where everything is held constant but the variable of interest.

2. What is the relationship between association and causation?

Association means that two things are related; causation means that one thing caused the other to occur. While causation implies association, association does not necessarily imply causation.

3. To what types of misinterpretations does confusing association and causation lead?

Mistaking association between variables as causation can lead to three types of misinterpretations: (1) It can lead a person to "see" causation between two variables or events where there is none; (2) it can lead a person to "see" causation between two variables or events when a third variable or event is actually responsible for causing both of them; and (3) it can lead a person to "see" one variable or event causing the other, when in fact the causation runs in the opposite direction.

4. What is the fallacy of composition?

The fallacy of composition is the sometimes incorrect idea that if something is true for an individual, it must also always be true for many individuals as a group.

5. If U.S. consumers bought more gasoline in 1998, when prices averaged $1.20 per gallon, than they did in 1970, when prices averaged $0.30 per gallon, does that mean that people buy more gas at higher prices? Why or why not?

No. Other things were far from constant between these two years. The overall price level changed dramatically, as did people's incomes, the safety and convenience of automobiles, distances between home and work, and so forth. Only if people bought more gas at a higher price, holding these and all other important determinants of gasoline purchases constant, could we conclude that higher gas prices lead people to buy more gas.

6. If rain dancing is correlated with rain, does that mean that rain dancing causes rain? Why or why not?

No. The causation is more likely that both rain dancing and rain are caused by the onset of an area's traditional rainy season. When rains come later than normal, this could lead to rain dancing to appease "the rain gods" who are not sending the rain on time. If those dances last long enough in the rainy season, it will rain, but because it is the rainy season rather than because of the rain dancing.

7. Why could getting up earlier to beat the other fishermen to the fish lead anglers to catch the same number of fish at 5 A.M. as they would at noon?

A fisherman gets up earlier hoping to beat the other fishermen to the fish. That would likely lead him to catch more fish, provided none of the other fishermen do the same thing. If they all get up earlier to beat the crowd, however, they may catch no more fish than before as a result. This is an example of the fallacy of composition.

Concept E

1. What is positive analysis? Must positive analysis be testable?

Positive analysis focuses on how people actually behave, rather than on how people should behave; it deals with how variable A impacts variable B. Positive analysis must be testable in order to determine whether its predictions are borne out by the evidence.

2. What is normative analysis? Is normative analysis testable?

Normative analysis focuses on what should be or what ought to happen; it involves opinions about the desirability of various actions or results. Normative analysis is not testable, because there is no scientific way to establish whether one value judgment is better than another value judgment.

3. Why is the positive–normative distinction important?

It is important to distinguish between positive and normative analysis because many controversies in economics revolve around policy considerations that contain both. Deciding whether a policy is good requires both positive (what will happen) and normative (is what happens good or bad) analysis.

4. Why are there policy disagreements among economists?

As with most disciplines, economists do disagree. However, the majority of those disagreements stem from differences in normative analysis, because the evidence cannot establish whether one set of value judgments is better or more appropriate than other sets of value judgments.

5. Is the statement, "UFOs land in my back yard at least twice a week," a positive statement? Why or why not?

A positive statement need not be true; it simply needs to be testable in order to determine whether it is borne out by the evidence. Assuming that the UFOs in question are visible or otherwise detectable, this statement is a positive one because it can be verified or proven false.

6. Is there any way to scientifically determine if the "rich" pay their "fair share" of taxes? Why or why not?

No. There is no scientific way to determine to who qualifies as "rich" or what would constitute their "fair share" of taxes. Such issues necessarily involve value judgements that cannot be proven right or wrong.

Module 3: Scarcity and the Economizing Problem
Concept A

1. What are factors of production?

Factors of production are the resources, or inputs, that are used to produce outputs of final goods and services. They include capital, land, labor, and entrepreneurship.

2. What do economists mean by land? Labor? Capital? Entrepreneurship?

Land refers to all natural resources. Labor refers to the physical and mental effort expended by people in the economy. Capital refers to human-made resources used to produce final goods. Entrepreneurship refers to the process of looking for new possibilities, new products, and new methods of production. The entrepreneur is the one who "puts it all together," hoping to make a profit.

3. What is the difference between capital goods and money capital?

Capital goods are produced goods that are used to produce further goods. Money capital is an instrument of exchange—a means by which other commodities are acquired.

4. Why do you think economists often refer to training that increases the quality of workers' skills as "adding to human capital"?

Training increases a worker's ability to produce goods, just as capital goods increase an economy's ability to produce goods. Because of this similarity in their effects on productive abilities, training is often referred to as adding to workers' human capital.

5. What are some of the ways that students act as entrepreneurs as they seek higher grades?

There are a wide variety of ways that students are entrepreneurs in seeking higher grades. They sometimes form study groups, often even assigning different material to different members. They often share notes. They study harder for those questions they believe will be more likely to be tested. Sometimes they try to get hold of old tests or to cheat. All of this and more is part of different students' efforts to discover the lowest-cost way to get higher grades.

Concept B

1. What does a production possibilities curve illustrate?

The production possibilities curve illustrates the potential output combinations of any two goods in an economy that is operating at full capacity, given the inputs and technology available to the economy.

2. What distinguishes consumption goods and investment goods?

Consumption goods are goods that give us immediate satisfaction. Investment goods do not give immediate satisfaction, but they increase our future ability to produce goods and services.

3. How are opportunity costs shown by the production possibilities curve?

Opportunity cost, the foregone output of one good necessary to increase output of another good, is illustrated by the slope between the two goods at a given point on the production possibilities curve.

4. Why do the opportunity costs of added production increase with output?

Opportunity costs of added production increase with output because some resources cannot be easily adapted from their current uses to alternative uses. At first, easily adaptable resources can be switched to producing more of a good. But once those easily adapted resources have been switched, producing further output requires the use of resources that are less well adapted to expanding that output, thus raising the opportunity cost of output.

5. How does the production possibilities curve illustrate increasing opportunity costs?

Increasing opportunity costs are illustrated by a bowed (concave from below) production possibilities curve. It shows that initial units of one good can be produced by giving up little of another good, but progressive increases in output will require greater and greater sacrifices of the other good.

6. If people reduced their saving (thus reducing the funds available for investment), what would that do to society's production possibilities curve over time?

Reduced savings reduces investment. Investment acts to shift labor's productivity over time, as each unit of labor has more capital with which to work, so reduced savings reduces the growth of the capital stock, which slows the growth of the production possibilities curve over time (and in extreme cases, it could cause the capital stock and the production possibilities curve to fall over time).

7. If Robin's son Crusoe could produce 20 fishing nets in a day or catch 60 fish in a day, while Robin could produce only 10 fishing nets a day or catch 20 fish in a day, who would you pick to begin making fishing nets first? Why?

You would choose the lower opportunity cost producer of fishing nets first, according to the principle of increasing cost. Robin is the lower opportunity cost producer of fishing nets, because he gives up catching two fish with the time and resources it takes him to produce one fishing net, while Crusoe gives up catching three fish with the time and resources it takes him to produce one fishing net.

Concept C

1. Why does scarcity force us to decide what to produce?

Because our wants exceed the amount of goods and services that can be produced from our limited resources, it must be decided which wants should have (marginal) priority over others.

2. How is a command economy different from a market economy?

A command economy makes decisions about what and how much to produce centrally by members of a planning board or organization. In a market economy, those decisions are the result of decentralized decision making by individual producers and consumers, coordinated by their offers to buy and sell on markets.

3. How does consumer sovereignty determine production decisions in a market economy?

Consumer sovereignty determines production decisions in a market economy because producers make those goods and services that they believe consumers will "vote" for by being willing to pay for them.

4. Do you think that what and how much an economy produces depends on who will get the goods and services produced in that economy? Why or why not?

Who will get the goods produced in an economy affects the incentives of the producers. The less a producer will benefit from increased production, the smaller are his incentives to increase his production, and the smaller will be total output in an economy.

5. Why do consumers have to "vote" for a product with their dollars for it to be a success?

Unlike in the political sector, where politicians typically need the votes of a majority to win, many products can be profitable even if they attract only a small number of possible dollar votes in the market sector. A wide variety of niche products exist in the market sector as a result.

Concept D

1. Why must we choose among multiple ways of producing the goods and services we want?

We must choose among multiple ways of producing the goods and services we want because goods can generally be produced in several ways, using different combinations of resources. That requires a decision to be made about how to produce the goods and services we want.

2. Why might production be labor intensive in one economy, but be capital intensive in another?

Production will tend to be labor intensive where labor is relatively plentiful, and therefore relatively less expensive; it will tend to be capital intensive where capital is relatively plentiful, and therefore relatively less expensive. Because the factors of production have different relative prices in different situations, different manners of production can be efficient in different situations (for example, a hand-sewn necktie made in Thailand versus a machine-made necktie made in the United States).

3. If a tourist from the United States notices on an overseas trip that other countries don't produce crops "like they do back home," would he be right to conclude that farmers in the other country produce crops less efficiently than U.S. farmers?

No. The different ways of farming in different areas reflect the different relative scarcities of land, labor, and capital faced by farmers in those areas. Those factors of production that are relatively scarce in an economy are also relatively costly there as a result. Producers will economize on the use of those more costly resources by using more of relatively less scarce, and less costly, resources instead. For example, where land is very scarce, it is very intensively cultivated with relatively cheaper (less scarce) labor and capital, but where capital is very scarce, relatively cheaper (less scarce) land and labor are substituted for capital.

4. Why are the golf tee areas on driving ranges in Japan often multileveled, while they are usually on a single level in the United States?

Because land is relatively more scarce, and thus relatively more costly, in Japan than in the United States, the tee areas on Japanese driving ranges are often multileveled to conserve on that relatively more scarce land.

Concept E

1. In a market economy, what determines "who gets what"?

In a market economy, "who gets what" depends on people's willingness to pay. This willingness to pay is limited by individuals' incomes, which are determined by the quantity, quality, and value of the scarce resources they supply to others.

2. In what way does scarcity determine income?

Relative scarcity determines the market values of the scarce resources people offer to others in exchange for income.

Concept F

1. Why are we concerned with unemployed or underemployed resources in a society?

We are concerned with unemployed or underemployed resources in a society because, if we could reduce the extent of unemployed or underemployed resources, people could have more scarce goods and services available for their use.

2. What do we mean by efficiency, and how is it related to underemployment of resources?

Efficiency means getting the most we can out of our scarce resources. Underemployment of resources means that a society is not getting the most it can out of its resources, either because they are not fully employed or because they are not matched to their best uses.

3. How are efficiency and inefficiency illustrated with a production possibilities curve?

Efficient combinations of outputs are illustrated by points on the production possibilities curve, along which more of one good can be produced if less of some other good is also produced. Inefficient combinations of outputs are illustrated by points inside the production possibilities curve, because more of both goods could then be produced with the resources available to the economy.

4. Will a country that makes being unemployed illegal be more productive than one that does not? Why or why not?

A more productive economy is one that makes the best use of those who wish to work. Making unemployment illegal (as was true in the old USSR) does not eliminate underemployment, nor does it guarantee that people and other resources are employed where they are most productive (especially because it is more difficult to search for a better job when you are working than when you are not working).

5. If a 68-year-old worker in the United States chooses not to work at all, does that mean that the United States is functioning inside its production possibilities curve? Why or why not?

A person who chooses retirement rather than work must consider himself better off not working, when all of the relevant considerations are taken into account. He is therefore as fully employed, given his circumstances, as he would like to be, and so there is no implication that the United States would be inside its production possibilities curve as a result. However, if such workers became more willing to work, that would shift the United States' production possibilities curve outward.

Concept G

1. What is the essential question behind issues of economic growth?

The essential question behind issues of economic growth is: How much are we willing to give up today to get more in the future?

2. What is the connection between sacrifices and economic growth?

The more current consumption is sacrificed in an economy, the larger the fraction of its current resources it can devote to producing investment goods, which will increase its rate of economic growth.

3. How is economic growth shown in terms of production possibilities curves?

Economic growth, the expansion of what an economy can produce, is shown as an outward shift in the production possibilities curve, with formerly unattainable output combinations now made possible.

4. Why doesn't economic growth eliminate scarcity?

Economic growth doesn't eliminate scarcity, because people's wants still exceed what they are capable of producing, so that trade-offs among scarce goods must still be made.

5. What would happen to the production possibilities curve in an economy where a new innovation greatly increased its ability to catch fish but did not change its ability to make fishing nets?

If fishing nets are on the vertical axis and fish are on the horizontal axis of the production possibilities curve, such a technological change would leave the vertical intercept unchanged, but make it less steep (reflecting the reduced opportunity cost of producing additional fish), shifting out the curve's intercept with the horizontal axis.

Module 4: Supply and Demand

Concept A

1. What are transaction costs?

Transactions costs are the costs of making exchanges. Markets and middlepersons arise to reduce transactions costs.

2. Why is it hard to precisely define a market?

Every market is different. There is an incredible variety of exchange arrangements, with different types of products, different degrees of organization, different geographical limits, and so forth.

3. Why do you get your produce at a supermarket rather than directly from farmers?

Supermarkets act as middlepersons between growers of produce and consumers of produce. You hire them to do this task for you when you buy produce from them, rather than directly from growers, because they conduct those transactions at lower costs than you could (if you could do this more cheaply than supermarkets, you would buy directly from farmers rather than from supermarkets).

4. Why do the prices people pay for similar items at garage sales vary more than the prices they pay for similar items in a department store?

Items for sale at department stores are more standardized, easier to compare, and more heavily advertised, which makes consumers more aware of the prices at which they could get a particular good elsewhere, reducing the differences in price that can persist among department stores. Garage sale items are non-standardized, costly to compare, and not advertised, which means that people are often quite unaware of how much a given item could be purchased for elsewhere, so that price differences for similar items at different garage sales can be substantial.

Concept B

1. How are money prices and relative prices different?

Money prices are what are paid in dollars and cents (or other currency); relative prices are the prices of goods relative to (or in terms of) the prices of other goods and services.

2. Why are economists so concerned about relative prices?

Relative prices—the prices of goods relative to other goods and services—reflect the tradeoffs people face in making choices among those goods and services in markets. Changing relative prices alter the opportunity costs of choices, changing the choices that are made.

3. The money price of most goods has risen over time. What does that mean?

Most prices have risen in money terms. However, the relative prices of all goods cannot rise, because if the price of good A rises relative to the price of good B, the price of good B must fall relative to the price of good A. The fact that most goods have risen in money price really means that the value of money has fallen relative to the value of goods.

4. If Motel 6 began by charging $6 per night for a room but now charges $36 per night, what would have to be true for the relative price of its motel rooms to have fallen in that period?
If Motel 6's room prices have gone up six times since it began, its relative price is lower than before only if other prices have gone up more than six times over the same period.

Concept C

1. What is an inverse, or negative, relationship?
An inverse, or negative, relationship is one where one variable changes in the opposite direction from the other. For example, if one variable increases, the other decreases.

2. How do lower prices change buyers' incentives?
A lower price for a good means that the opportunity cost to buyers of purchasing it is lower than before, and self-interest leads buyers to buy more of it as a result.

3. How do higher prices change buyers' incentives?
A higher price for a good means that the opportunity cost to buyers of purchasing it is higher than before, and self-interest leads buyers to buy less of it as a result.

4. How does demand represent willingness to pay?
Demand reflects the value of other things someone would be willing to give up for each unit of a good or service. Expressed in terms of dollars for convenience, this represents that person's willingness to pay for each unit of that good or service.

5. Why do economists prefer talking about wants and desires rather than needs?
By definition, needs are goods for which there are no substitutes. But there are usually many substitutes for a particular good or service. Therefore, to analyze choices in a world with large numbers of substitution possibilities, we must focus on wants and desires (reflected in willingness to pay) rather than needs.

6. If even a minor cheating infraction was punished by expulsion, what would happen to the extent of cheating on campus?
By raising the "price" of cheating on campus, this policy would decrease the amount of cheating.

7. Assume that we "need" water, food, clothing, and shelter to survive. Why is talking about these as needs not very helpful in analyzing choices that must be made among them?
We must often choose among quantities of different goods we need (in some amount) to survive. Talking in terms of need seems to imply that there could be no such choices, which doesn't help us to understand the tradeoffs among the goods that are involved or to analyze those choices.

Concept D

1. What is an individual demand schedule?
An individual demand schedule reveals the different amounts of a good or service a person would be willing to buy at various possible prices in a particular time interval.

2. What difference is there between an individual demand curve and a market demand curve?
The market demand curve shows the total amounts of a good or service that all of the buyers as a group are willing to buy at various

possible prices in a particular time interval. The market quantity demanded at a given price is just the sum of the quantities demanded by each individual buyer at that price.

3. Why does the amount of dating on campus tend to decline just before and during finals?
The opportunity cost of dating—in this case, the value to students of the studying time foregone—is higher just before and during finals than during most of the rest of an academic term. Because the cost is higher, students do less of it.

Concept E

1. What is the difference between a change in demand and a change in quantity demanded?
A change in demand shifts the entire demand curve, while a change in quantity demanded refers to a movement along a given demand curve.

2. If the price of zucchini increases and it causes the demand for yellow squash to rise, what do we call the relationship between zucchini and yellow squash?
Whenever an increased price of one good increases the demand for another, they are substitutes. This reflects the fact that some people consider zucchini as an alternative to yellow squash, so that as zucchini becomes more costly, some people substitute into buying now relatively cheaper yellow squash instead.

3. If income rises and, as a result, demand for jet skis increases, how do we describe that good?
If income rises and, as a result, demand for jet skis increases, we call jet skis a normal good, because for most (or normal) goods, we would rather have more of them than less, so an increase in income would lead to an increase in demand for such goods.

4. How do expectations about the future influence the demand curve?
Expectations about the future influence the demand curve because buying a good in the future is an alternative to buying it now. For example, if higher future prices for a good are expected, future purchases become less attractive. As a result, we would expect current demand for that good to increase, as people will buy more now when it is expected to be cheaper, rather than later, when it is expected to be more costly.

5. Would a change in the price of ice cream cause a change in the demand for ice cream? Why or why not?
No. The demand for ice cream represents the different quantities of ice cream that would be purchased at different prices. In other words, it represents the relationship between the price of ice cream and the quantity of ice cream demanded. Changing the price of ice cream does not change this relationship, so it does not change demand.

6. Would a change in the price of ice cream likely cause a change in the demand for frozen yogurt, a substitute?
Yes. Changing the price of ice cream, a substitute for frozen yogurt, would change the quantity of frozen yogurt demanded at every price.

7. If plane travel is a normal good and bus travel is an inferior good, what will happen to the demand curves for plane and bus travel if people's incomes increase?
The demand for plane travel and all other normal goods will increase if incomes increase, while the demand for bus travel and all other inferior goods will decrease if incomes increase.

Concept F

1. What is a direct, or positive, relationship?

A direct, or positive, relationship is one where both variables involved change in the same direction at the same time if one increases, the other increases.

2. What are the two reasons why a supply curve is positively sloped?

A supply curve is positively sloped because (1) the benefits to sellers from selling increase as the price they receive increases, and (2) the opportunity costs of supplying additional output rise with output (the law of increasing opportunity costs), so it takes a higher price to make increasing output in the self-interest of sellers.

3. What is the difference between an individual supply curve and a market supply curve?

The market supply curve shows the total amounts of a good that all of the sellers as a group are willing to sell at various prices in a particular time period. The market quantity supplied at a given price is just the sum of the quantities supplied by each individual seller at that price.

4. When we say that the supply curve for economics tutoring services is upward sloping, what relationship does that statement represent?

An upward-sloping supply curve for economics tutoring services simply means that there will be more hours of economics tutoring offered for sale—a higher quantity supplied—at a higher price than at a lower price, other things constant.

Concept G

1. What is the difference between a change in supply and a change in quantity supplied?

A change in supply shifts the entire supply curve, while a change in quantity supplied refers to a movement along a given supply curve.

2. What causes a movement along a supply curve?

A movement along a supply curve is caused by a change in the price of that good (called that good's own-price).

3. What causes a shift in the entire supply curve?

A shift in the supply curve is cause by anything that changes the quantity of that good supplied except a change in its own-price. These supply curve shifters are summarized by the term SPENT: (S) supplier input prices; (P) prices of related goods; (E) expectations of sellers; (N) the number of sellers; and (T) technology, taxes, tampering, and temperature.

4. If a seller expects the price of a good to rise in the near future, how will that affect his current supply curve?

Selling a good in the future is an alternative to selling it now. Therefore, the higher the expected future price relative to the current price, the more attractive future sales become and the less attractive current sales become. This will lead sellers to reduce (shift left) the current supply of that good, as they will want to sell later, when the good is expected to be more valuable, rather than now.

5. Would a change in the price of wheat change the supply of wheat? Would it change the supply of corn, if wheat and corn can be grown on the same type of land?

The supply of wheat represents the different quantities of wheat that would be offered for sale at different prices. In other words, it represents the relationship between the price of wheat and the quantity of wheat supplied. Changing the price of wheat does not change this relationship, so it does not change the supply of wheat. However, a change in the price of wheat changes the relative attractiveness of raising wheat instead of corn, which changes the supply of corn.

6. If a guitar manufacturer had to increase its wages in order to keep its workers, what would happen to the supply of guitars as a result?

An increase in wages (or any other input price) raises the opportunity cost of producing guitars. This would decrease (shift left) the supply of guitars, making fewer guitars available for sale at any given price.

7. What happens to the supply of baby-sitting services in an area when many teenagers get their driver's licenses at about the same time?

When teenagers get their drivers licenses, their increased mobility expands their alternatives to baby-sitting substantially, thus raising the opportunity cost of babysitting. This decreases (shifts left) the supply of baby-sitting services.

Module 5: Markets in Motion
Concept A

1. How does the intersection of supply and demand indicate the equilibrium price and quantity in a market?

The intersection of supply and demand indicates the equilibrium price and quantity in a market, because at higher prices, sellers would be frustrated by their inability to sell all they would like, leading sellers to compete by lowering the price they charge; at lower prices, buyers would be frustrated by their inability to buy all they would like, leading buyers to compete by increasing the price they offer to pay.

2. What can cause a change in the supply and demand equilibrium?

Changes in any of the PYNTE demand curve shifters or the SPENT supply curve shifters will change the supply and demand equilibrium.

3. What must be true about the price charged for there to be a shortage?

The price charged must be less than the equilibrium price, with the result that buyers would like to buy more at that price than sellers are willing to sell.

4. What must be true about the price charged for there to be a surplus?

The price charged must be greater than the equilibrium price, with the result that sellers would like to sell more at that price than buyers are willing to buy.

5. Why do market forces tend to eliminate both shortages and surpluses?

Market forces tend to eliminate both shortages and surpluses because of the self-interest of the market participants. A seller is better off successfully selling at a lower equilibrium price than not being able to sell at a higher price (the surplus situation), and a buyer is better off successfully buying at a higher equilibrium price than not being able to buy at a lower price (the shortage situation). Therefore, we expect market forces to eliminate both shortages and surpluses.

6. Why do economists refer to the "invisible hand" of the market?

Economists refer to the "invisible hand" of the market because no one person or group (a visible hand) determines the market outcome. Rather, the interaction of all of the demanders and suppliers is the invisible hand that determines the market outcome.

7. If tea prices were above their equilibrium level, what force would tend to push tea prices down? If tea prices were below their equilibrium level, what force would tend to push tea prices up?

If tea prices were above their equilibrium level, sellers, frustrated by their inability to sell as much tea as they would like at those prices, would compete the price of tea down, as they tried to make more attractive offers to tea buyers. If tea prices were below their equilibrium level, buyers, frustrated by their inability to buy as much tea as they would like at those prices, would compete the price of tea up, as they tried to make more attractive offers to tea sellers.

8. Why does the time you spend in supermarket checkout lines tend to be about the same, regardless of which line you are in?

If you knew that you could check out faster in one line than the others, you would choose that line. But the same is true of other shoppers. The result of self-interested shoppers all looking to save time is that the time spent checking out tends to be about the same for all the checkout lines.

Concept B

1. When demand increases, does that create a shortage or a surplus at the original price?

An increase in demand increases the quantity demanded at the original equilibrium price, but it does not change the quantity supplied at that price, meaning that it would create a shortage at the original equilibrium price.

2. What happens to equilibrium price and quantity as a result of a demand increase?

Frustrated buyers who are unable to buy all they would like at the original equilibrium price will compete the market price higher, and that higher price will induce suppliers to increase their quantity supplied. The result is a higher market price and a larger market output.

3. When supply increases, does that create a shortage or surplus at the original price?

An increase in supply increases the quantity supplied at the original equilibrium price, but it does not change the quantity demanded at that price, meaning that it would create a surplus at the original equilibrium price.

4. What happens to equilibrium price and quantity as a result of a supply increase?

Frustrated sellers who are unable to sell all they would like at the original equilibrium price will compete the market price lower, and that lower price will induce demanders to increase their quantity demanded. The result is a lower market price and a larger market output.

5. Why do heating-oil prices tend to be higher in the winter?

The demand for heating oil is higher in cold winter months. The result of this higher winter heating oil demand, for a given supply curve, is higher prices for heating oil in the winter.

6. Why are evening and weekend long-distance calls cheaper than weekday long-distance calls?

The demand for long-distance calls is greatest during weekday business hours, but far lower during other hours. Because the demand for "off-peak" long-distance calls is lower, for a given supply curve, prices during those hours are lower.

Concept C

1. What would have to be true for both supply and demand to shift in the same time period?

For both supply and demand to shift in the same time period, one or more of both the SPENT supply curve shifters and the PYNTE demand curve shifters would have to change in that same time period.

2. How do we "add up" the effects of simultaneous changes in both supply and demand on equilibrium prices and quantities?

Adding up simultaneous changes in both supply and demand considers the effects of each of the shifts on the market price and quantity separately, then "adds up" the directions of those changes to see the net change in each variable. If both shifts change a variable in the same direction, that will also be the net effect, but if they push a variable in opposite directions, the net effect will be indeterminate without knowing the relative magnitudes of the shifts.

3. When both supply and demand shift, what added information do we need to know in order to determine in which direction the indeterminate variable changes?

When both supply and demand shift, we need to know which of the shifts is of greater magnitude, so we can know which of the opposing effects in the indeterminate variable is larger; the larger effect will determine the direction of the net effect on the indeterminate variable.

4. If both buyers and sellers of coffee expect coffee prices to rise in the near future, what will happen to coffee prices and sales today?

If coffee buyers expect coffee prices to rise in the near future, it will increase their current demand to buy coffee, which would tend to increase current prices and increase the current quantity of coffee sold. If coffee sellers expect coffee prices to rise in the near future, it will decrease their current supply of coffee for sale, which would tend to increase current prices and decrease the current quantity of coffee sold. Because both of these effects tend to increase the current price of coffee, coffee prices will rise. However, the supply and demand curve shifts tend to change current sales in opposing directions, so without knowing which of these shifts was of a greater magnitude, we do not know what will happen to current coffee sales. They could go up, down, or even stay the same.

5. If demand for peanut butter increases and supply decreases, what will happen to equilibrium price and quantity?

An increase in the demand for peanut butter increases the equilibrium price and quantity of peanut butter sold. A decrease in the supply of peanut butter increases the equilibrium price and quantity of peanut butter sold. The result is an increase in peanut butter prices and an indeterminate effect on the quantity of peanut butter sold.

Concept D

1. What happens in a market when demand is greater than anticipated?

When demand is greater than anticipated, there is a temporary disequilibrium shortage, leading to competition among frustrated buyers bidding the price up, and those higher prices lead sellers to increase output. These responses drive the market to a new higher market equilibrium price and output.

2. How do market adjustments resolve the temporary disequilibrium that results when demand is incorrectly estimated?

Temporary shortages and surpluses set in motion competitive processes in which frustrated market participants compete the price toward the new equilibrium level, and the incentives caused by that change in price moves the market output to its new equilibrium level.

3. If the maker of Beanie Babies found that its inventories were plummeting, what kind of temporary disequilibrium would that indicate?

Plummeting Beanie Baby inventories would indicate that the quantity demanded at the current price is greater than sellers expected and had produced for sale at that price. In other words, it indicates a temporary shortage at the current price, which leads to Beanie Baby price and output increases until the temporary disequilibrium is eliminated.

Concept E

1. How is rent control an example of a price ceiling?

A price ceiling is a maximum price set below the equilibrium price by the government. Rent control is an example because the controlled rents are held below the market equilibrium rent level.

2. What predictable effects result from price ceilings like rent control?

The predictable effects resulting from price ceilings include shortages, reduced amounts of the controlled good being made available by suppliers, reductions in the quality of the controlled good, and increased discrimination by sellers among potential buyers of the good.

3. How is the minimum wage law an example of a price floor?

A price floor is a minimum price set above the equilibrium price by the government. The minimum wage is an example because the minimum wage is set above the market equilibrium wage level for some low-skill workers.

4. What predictable effects result from price floors like the minimum wage?

The predictable effects resulting from price floors include surpluses, reduced amounts of the controlled good being purchased by demanders, increases in the quality of the controlled good, and increased discrimination by demanders among potential suppliers of the good.

5. What may happen to the amount of discrimination against groups such as families with children, pet owners, smokers, or students when rent control is imposed?

Rent control laws prevent prospective renters from compensating landlords through higher rents for any characteristic landlords find less attractive, whether it is bothersome noise from children or pets, odors from smokers, increased numbers of renters per unit, or risks of non-payment by lower-income tenants such as students, and so forth. As a result, it lowers the cost of discriminating against anyone possessing what landlords consider unattractive characteristics, as there are other prospective renters without those characteristic who are willing to pay the same controlled rent.

6. Why does rent control often lead to condominium conversions?

Rent control applies to rental apartments but not to apartments owned by their occupants. Therefore, one way to get around rent control restrictions on apartment owners' ability to receive the market value of their apartments is to convert those apartments to condominiums by selling them to tenants instead. Then, what was once a controlled rent becomes part of an uncontrolled mortgage payment. This effect harms poor individuals the most, which is ironic, in that concern for the welfare of lower-income individuals motivates the politics of rent control.

Module 6: Government and the Economy
Concept A

1. What are the arguments for government intervention in the economy?

Seven arguments for government intervention are given in the text: (1) enforcement of property rights, (2) externalities, (3) provision of public goods, (4) information costs, (5) imperfect competition in markets, (6) macroeconomic goals, and (7) income redistribution.

2. How is government enforcement of property rights necessary to a market economy?

The definition and enforcement of property rights—the power to use, sell, rent, dispose of, or enhance the value of one's resources—is necessary to a market economy because such property rights act as incentives for owners to use their resources efficiently and because trade is far more costly to conduct without clear property rights.

3. How does the government right of eminent domain affect property rights?

Eminent domain gives the government the power to force you to sell your property, so citizens do not have the right to maintain ownership against the government. However, under eminent domain, government must compensate owners for that property, so citizens retain the right to be paid for their property. But only if that payment is equal to the market value of the property are property rights not damaged by eminent domain.

4. Would many bicycles be produced in a country where a person maintained his ownership of a bicycle only as long as he was sitting on it? Why?

Without clear, enforceable property rights in bicycles, a buyer would not be willing to pay very much to buy a bicycle (perhaps only the value placed on riding the bicycle once). With buyers willing to pay so little, bicycle sellers would not find it profitable to produce bicycles, and there would be few if any bicycles produced in that country.

5. How do laws against selling stolen property make private property rights more secure?

Laws against stolen property reduce the payoff to potential thieves from stealing (they get less money from their "fence," who must bear greater risks to sell the stolen goods), leading to less theft and making property rights more secure as a result.

Concept B

1. Why are externalities also called spillover effects?

An externality exists whenever the benefits or costs of an activity impact individuals outside the market mechanism. That is, some of the effects spill over to those who have not voluntarily agreed to bear them or compensate others for them, unlike the voluntary exchange of the market.

2. How are externalities related to property rights?

Externalities tend to involve goods for which there are not clearly defined property rights. For example, if you could demand, and receive, compensation for the costs that dirtier air imposes on you, you would have an effective property right to clean air, which you would give up voluntarily only if you were sufficiently compensated. But if your voluntary agreement is required, the effect is no longer an externality because it is internalized by the market mechanism.

3. How do external costs affect the price and output of a polluting activity?

Because the owner of a firm that pollutes does not have to bear the external costs of pollution, he can ignore those real costs of pollution to society. The result is that the private costs he must pay are less than the true social costs of production, so that the market output of the polluting activity is greater, and the resulting market price lower, than it would be if producers did have to bear the external costs of production.

4. How can the government intervene to force producers to internalize external costs?

If the government could impose on producers a tax or fee equal to the external costs imposed on people without their consent, producers would have to take into account those costs. The result would be that those costs would no longer be external costs because they would be internalized by producers.

5. How does internalizing the external costs improve efficiency?

Internalizing external costs eliminates those trades where the marginal benefits to society (measured by the willingness to pay along the market demand curve) exceeds the private marginal costs but are less than the social marginal costs (including the external costs). The resulting net gain in efficiency is that illustrated by the triangle in Exhibit 1 in this concept.

6. How do external benefits affect the output of an activity that causes them?

External benefits are benefits that spill over to others that are not involved in producing or consuming the good. That is, the total benefits of an activity are not fully reflected in the private demand curve; the private demand curve lies further to the left than it would if all spillover benefits were taken into consideration by the market. The result is that the market produces too little of the good—an underallocation from society's standpoint.

7. How can the government intervene to force external benefits to be internalized?

Just as taxes can be used to internalize external costs imposed on others, subsidies can be used to internalize external benefits generated for others. For example, education is subsidized by virtually all developed countries for this reason.

8. Why do most cities have more stringent noise laws for the early morning and late evening hours than for during the day?

The external costs to others from loud noises in residential areas are higher early in the morning and late in the evening (because residents are home and trying to sleep) than in the daytime (when many people are gone at work or are already awake). Given those higher potential external costs, most cities impose more restrictive noise laws for nighttime hours to reduce them.

Concept C

1. How are public goods different from private goods?

Private goods are rival in consumption (we cannot both consume the same unit of a good) and exclusive (non-payers can be prevented from consuming the good unless they pay for it). Public goods are nonrival in consumption (more than one person can consume the same good) and nonexclusive (non-payers can't be effectively kept from consuming the good, even if they don't voluntarily pay for it).

2. Why does the free rider problem arise in the case of public goods?

The free rider problem arises in the case of public goods because people cannot be prevented from enjoying the benefits of public goods once they are provided. Therefore, people have an incentive to not voluntarily pay for those benefits, because they know that their specific contribution will not be important in determining whether they get the good. Thus, it is very difficult or even impossible to finance the efficient quantity of public goods through voluntary market arrangements.

3. How does the free rider problem relate to property rights?

The free rider problem arises in cases where property rights to goods are not easy to prescribe and enforce, as with externalities and public goods.

4. In what way can government provision of public goods solve the free rider problem?

The government can overcome the free rider problem by forcing people to pay for the provision of a public good through taxes.

5. Why is it difficult for the government to determine the proper amount of a public good to produce?

Unlike the case for private goods, people do not reveal the values they place on public goods through the prices they are willing to pay in markets. As a result, there is no way for the government to accurately measure and take into account the magnitudes of the relevant benefits and costs of a public good to individuals.

6. How does a TV broadcast have characteristics of a public good?

An over-the-air broadcast can be watched by a viewer without reducing other viewers' ability to watch the same broadcast, and a viewer of such broadcasts cannot be excluded from watching if he refuses to pay for it. Note that cable broadcasts, in contrast, can exclude non-payers, so they don't have both characteristics of a public good.

7. Can lighthouse services be privately provided if all of the boats using the services of a lighthouse are heading for the port nearest that lighthouse? Why or why not?

If boats that used the port could be charged a docking fee to pay for the lighthouse services, that would create a mechanism to pay for the private provision of lighthouse services. (There must, of course, not be another port sufficiently close that the boats could use the lighthouse to navigate safely to the other port.)

Concept D

1. How long should you continue to seek more information before making a decision?

As with any other choice, one should seek more information before making a decision as long as the expected marginal benefits from having added information exceed the marginal expected costs of acquiring that information. This implies that it is often rational to be less than completely informed when making decisions.

2. What is the rationale for government provision of information?
In some cases, the government might be able to gather or communicate information at lower costs than citizens could otherwise. By lowering information costs, more information is acquired before choices are made, and citizens benefit by making better-informed choices (i.e., making fewer mistakes).

3. What are the objections to government provision of information?
Government-provided information may be more costly to acquire than through market channels, it may be inaccurate or misleading, and it can be manipulated by special interest groups for their own advantages rather than to benefit consumers.

4. Why do consumers spend more time researching a home purchase than an electric can opener purchase?
The likely benefits from an additional hour researching a home purchase is likely to be far larger, whether in terms of a better price or a better match for your preferences, than the likely benefits from spending that hour researching an electric can opener purchase.

5. If someone argues that we need occupational licensing of gardeners to guarantee that misinformed consumers don't get shoddy service, is that person more likely to be a (highly trained) gardener or a homeowner who uses a gardening service? Why?
Occupational licensing has very often been advocated by existing producers of the services involved as a way to reduce competition from potential new producers who would otherwise enter and reduce the profits of the existing producers. Most homeowners, on the other hand, feel sufficiently protected from serious problems with gardening services because of the market information conveyed by gardeners' reputations and the large number of alternative gardeners available.

Concept E

1. Why would the government want to prevent market conditions of insufficient competition?
When there is insufficient or restricted competition, outputs are lower and prices paid by consumers are higher than they would be with more effective competition. By encouraging competition and discouraging monopoly, then, consumers can benefit.

2. What are the macroeconomic goals of government intervention in the economy?
The primary macroeconomic goals of government intervention in the economy include full employment, price stability, and economic growth.

3. What government policy changes might be effective in increasing employment in recessions?
Government policies to stimulate the economy, such as decreasing taxes or increasing government purchases, could potentially increase employment in recessions.

4. What government policy changes might be effective in controlling inflation?
Government policies to control inflation can include increasing taxes, decreasing government purchases, and reducing the growth in the money supply through the banking system.

Concept F

1. What is the basic argument in favor of government redistribution of income?
The basic argument in favor of government redistribution of income is that some believe the market-determined distribution of income is unfair or inequitable. Therefore, the government could improve equity or fairness by redistributing income toward those who are needier.

2. What are the objections to government intervention intended to redistribute income?
The central objection to government intervention to redistribute income is that not everyone agrees about what is fair (e.g., helping someone get their "fair share" through the government means taking those resources from someone else, and they might not consider the result fair). Another objection is that there is no way to redistribute income without undermining incentives to work hard and be productive.

3. How does the government use taxes, subsidies, and transfer payments to redistribute income toward lower-income groups?
Taxes, particularly progressive ones such as the individual income tax, are borne more heavily by higher-income citizens than lower-income citizens, while most subsidy and transfer payment programs are primarily focused on lower-income citizens.

4. If a government wanted to make the distribution of income more equal, would it be more effective to impose a tax on luxury cars or on food?
To equalize the distribution of income, a tax would have to be borne more heavily by higher-income individuals than by lower income individuals. A tax on luxury cars achieves this result far better than a tax on food.

Concept G

1. What principles does the public choice analysis of government behavior share with the economic analysis of market behavior?
Public choice analysis of government behavior is based on the principle that the behavior of individuals in politics, just like that in the marketplace, is influenced by self-interest. That is, it applies basic economic theory to politics, looking for differences in incentives to explain people's behavior.

2. Why is it rational to be relatively less informed about most political choices than about your own market choices?
It is rational to be relatively less informed about most political choices than about your own market choices because the costs of becoming more informed about political choices tend to be higher and the benefits of becoming more informed about political choices tend to be lower than for your own market choices.

3. Why can't the majority of citizens effectively counter the political power of special-interest groups?
The majority of citizens can't effectively counter the political power of special interest groups because even if the special interest group is successful in getting everyone else to pay for a project that benefits it, the cost to each citizen will be small. In fact, this cost is very likely far smaller than the cost to a member of the majority of becoming informed and active to successfully oppose it.

4. According to public choice theorists, what is the primary advantage of government? What is the biggest threat from government?
The primary advantage of government is its ability to establish a legal and economic environment that provides general opportunity for people to benefit from their own efforts through productive cooperation with others. The biggest threat from government is the risk that its power can be captured by special interests and used to advance their objectives at the expense of the general public.

5. Why are college students better informed about their own teachers' and schools' policies than about national education issues?

The benefits from "local knowledge" of teachers and school policies to students can be large, say, in a higher GPA, and the costs of acquiring that information is typically low for those on campus. On the other hand, the benefits from being more informed on national educational issues are typically much lower, because your actions are very unlikely to change those policies, and the costs of acquiring that information can be very large for what are far more complex national educational issues. The result is that students are better informed about their own teachers and school policies than national educational issues.

6. How can you be forced to pay for something you do not want to "buy" in the political sector? Is this sometimes good?

The government can use its power to tax to force you to pay for services they provide, even if you do not want to pay for those services. This can be useful, such as in overcoming the free rider problem in financing public goods or solving externality problems, as well as bad, as in the case of special interest dominance.

7. Why do you think news reporters are more informed than average citizens about public policy issues?

The benefits news reporters receive from being more informed about public policy issues are greater than for most citizens, because being better informed allows reporters to do a better job, which they benefit from in higher wages, greater honors, and so forth. Because the benefits of being better informed are typically higher for news reporters, they are better informed than average citizens.

Concept H

1. What accounts for most of the growth of government spending as a share of total output since 1965?

Most of the growth of government spending as a share of total output since 1965 has come from an increase in transfer payments, for programs such as Social Security and welfare.

2. What options are available for a government to finance its spending?

A government can finance its spending through taxes, borrowing, or inflation.

3. What is the difference between a progressive tax and a regressive tax?

A progressive tax is one that takes a higher proportion of income from higher income individuals than from lower income individuals; a regressive tax is one that takes a smaller proportion of income from higher income individuals than from lower income individuals.

4. What are some advantages and disadvantages of a flat tax? Would it be progressive?

With a flat tax, everyone would be taxed the same percentage of their income above a stipulated income level. A flat tax would be simpler than the current tax system, and traditional exemptions, along with their abuses, would be eliminated. A flat tax would be progressive as long as there was some initial level of income exempt from the tax. Higher-income people would then pay the flat tax rate on a larger share of their incomes than lower-income people.

Module 7: Introduction to the Macroeconomy
Concept A

1. What are the three major macroeconomic goals of most societies?

The three major macroeconomic goals of most societies are full employment (so that jobs are relatively plentiful and financial suffering from lack of income is relatively uncommon), price stability (so consumers and producers can make better decisions), and economic growth (so output, and therefore income and consumption, increases over time).

2. What is the Employment Act of 1946? Why was it significant?

The Employment Act of 1946 was a law that committed the federal government to policies designed to reduce unemployment in a manner consistent with price stability. It was significant because it was the first formal acknowledgment of government's primary macroeconomic goals.

Concept B

1. What happens to the unemployment rate when the number of unemployed people increases, *ceteris paribus*? When the labor force grows, *ceteris paribus*?

The unemployment rate is defined as the number of people officially unemployed divided by the labor force. Therefore, the unemployment rate rises as the number of unemployed people increases, and it falls when the labor force grows, as long as the increase in the labor force takes the form of added employment. An increase in the labor force may increase both the unemployed and the employed, leaving the impact on the unemployment rate ambiguous.

2. How might the official unemployment rate understate the "true" degree of unemployment? How might it overstate it?

The official unemployment rate understates the "true" degree of unemployment by not including discouraged workers as unemployed, by counting part-time workers who cannot find full-time jobs as "fully" employed, and by counting those employed in jobs that underutilize worker skills as "fully" employed. It overstates the "true" degree of unemployment by not counting those working overtime or multiple jobs as "overemployed," by counting those employed in the underground economy as unemployed, and by including those just "going through the motions" of job search to maintain unemployment benefits or other government benefits as unemployed.

3. Why might the fraction of the unemployed who are job leavers be higher in a period of strong labor demand?

In a period of strong labor demand, people would be more confident of their ability to find other jobs, and therefore they would be more likely to leave (quit) their current jobs.

4. Suppose you live in a community of 100 people where no one was unwilling or unable to work. If 80 people are over 16 years old and 72 people are employed, what is the unemployment rate in that community?

The unemployment rate in this community is the number of unemployed (8) divided by the labor force (80), or 10 percent.

5. What would happen to the unemployment rate if a substantial group of unemployed people started going to school full time? What would happen to the size of the labor force?

Full-time students are not considered part of the labor force, so the labor force, the number officially unemployed, and the unemployment rate would all fall if unemployed people became full-time students.

6. What happens to the unemployment rate when unemployed people become discouraged workers? Does anything happen to employment in this case?

When unemployed workers become discouraged workers, they stop seeking jobs and are no longer counted as either part of the labor force or as unemployed, reducing the unemployment rate. However, because they do not find jobs, there is no effect on employment as a result.

Concept C

1. Why do we want some frictional unemployment?

We want some frictional unemployment because we want human resources employed in areas of higher productivity, and some period of job search (frictional unemployment), rather than taking the first job offered, can allow workers to find more productive employment through better matching of jobs with worker skills, which takes some time.

2. Why might a job retraining program be a more useful policy to address structural unemployment than to address frictional unemployment?

Structural unemployment reflects people who lack the necessary skills for the jobs available. A job retraining program to develop skills to match the jobs available addresses such structural unemployment, not frictional unemployment, which reflects a temporary period of search between jobs. This presumes, of course, that the job retraining programs are "effective" in that the training is relevant to potential job prospects.

3. What is the traditional government policy "cure" for cyclical unemployment?

The traditional government policy "cure" for cyclical unemployment is to adopt policies designed to increase aggregate demand for goods and services.

4. Does new technology increase unemployment?

New technology can increase unemployment among those whose skills are replaced by that technology. However, it also creates new jobs manufacturing, servicing, and repairing the new equipment, and by lowering costs, new technology frees up more income to demand other goods and services, creating jobs in those industries.

5. What types of unemployment are present at full employment (at the natural rate of unemployment)?

At full employment (at the natural rate of unemployment), both frictional and structural unemployment, but not cyclical unemployment, are present.

6. Why might frictional unemployment be higher in a period of plentiful jobs (low unemployment)?

In a period of plentiful jobs, frictional unemployment can be higher because job opportunities are plentiful, which stimulates mobility between jobs, thus increasing frictional unemployment.

7. If the widespread introduction of the automobile caused a very productive maker of horse-drawn carriages to lose his job, would he be structurally or frictionally unemployed?

If the carriage maker's skills were in demand in other industries, this would result in frictional unemployment, but if his skills were not in demand in other industries, this would result in structural unemployment.

8. If a fall in demand for domestic cars causes auto workers to lose their jobs in Michigan, while there are plenty of jobs for lumberjacks in Montana, what kind of unemployment results?

This would be an example of structural unemployment, resulting from skills mismatched to the jobs available.

Concept D

1. How does price level instability increase the difficulties buyers and sellers have in coordinating their plans?

Price level instability increases the difficulties buyers and sellers have in coordinating their plans by reducing their certainty about what price changes mean: Do they reflect changes in relative prices or changes in inflation? Eliminating this uncertainty makes the meaning of price changes clearer, allowing buyers and sellers to better coordinate their plans through the price system.

2. What will happen to the nominal interest rate if the real interest rate rises, *ceteris paribus*? What if expected inflation increases, *ceteris paribus*?

The nominal interest rate is the sum of the real interest rate and the expected inflation rate. If either the real interest rate or the expected rate of inflation increases, nominal interest rates will also increase.

3. Say you owe money to the River Bank. Will you gain or lose from an unanticipated decrease in inflation?

An unanticipated decrease in inflation will mean that the dollars you must pay back on your loan will be worth more than you expected, raising the real interest rate you must pay on that loan, which makes you worse off.

4. How does a variable interest rate loan "insure" the lender against unanticipated increases in inflation?

With a variable interest rate loan, an unanticipated increase in inflation does not reduce the real interest rate received by the lender, but instead increases the nominal interest rate on the loan to compensate for the increased inflation.

5. Why will neither creditors nor debtors lose from inflation if it is correctly anticipated?

Correctly anticipated, inflation will be accurately reflected in the terms to which creditors and debtors agree, so that neither will lose from inflation. Only unexpected inflation can redistribute wealth between debtors and creditors.

6. How can inflation make people turn to exchange by barter?

If inflation is very rapid, people lose faith in the value of their monetary unit, and this can lead to exchange by barter, because goods can then have a more predictable value than their country's money.

7. What would happen in the loanable funds market if suppliers of loanable funds expected a substantial fall in inflation, while demanders of funds expected a substantial rise in inflation?

If suppliers of loanable funds expected a substantial fall in inflation, they would demand a smaller "inflation premium" to loan money, increasing the supply of loanable funds. If demanders of funds expected a substantial rise in inflation, they would be willing to offer a greater "inflation premium" to borrow, increasing the demand for loanable funds. The increased supply of loanable funds would push down interest rates, while the increased demand for loanable funds would push up interest rates; the net effect on interest rates is unknown, without further information about the relative sizes of the shifts in the curves, but the quantity of loanable funds exchanged would definitely increase.

Concept E

1. In what way does the desire for economic growth arise from scarcity?

In a world of scarcity, we are unable to have or consume as many or as much of goods and services as we would like. This leads to the desire for economic growth, which increases the amounts of goods and services that are available for consumption.

2. How does encouraging capital investment or educational training enhance economic growth?

Both capital investment and educational training can enhance economic growth by increasing worker productivity.

3. Why do we use purchasing power parity to compare per capita GDP across countries?

Purchasing power parity allows us to estimate how much of one currency it would take in one country to buy what one unit of a different currency would buy in another country. This allows us to compare per capita GDP across countries in terms of a common unit of measurement.

4. If a country increased its rate of capital formation, what would happen to its current consumption possibilities? What would happen to its consumption possibilities 15 years from now?

At any point in time, increasing capital formation reduces current consumption possibilities, assuming that we are near full employment. But that current investment increases the future consumption possibilities of a country, as the production possibilities curve shifts outward due to the impact of more capital on worker productivity.

Concept F

1. Why would you expect unemployment to tend to fall during an economy's expansionary phase and to rise during a contractionary phase?

Output increases during an economy's expansion phase. To produce that increased output in the short term requires more workers, which increases employment and reduces the unemployment rate, other things equal.

2. Why might a politician want to stimulate the economy prior to his or her reelection bid?

A politician may want to stimulate the economy prior to his or her reelection bid because there is a strong correlation between the performance of the economy and the fate of an incumbent's bid for reelection.

3. Why is the output of investment goods and durable consumer goods more sensitive to the business cycle than that of most goods?

When output is growing and business confidence is high, investment rises sharply because it appears highly profitable; when incomes and consumer confidence are high, the demand for durable goods, purchases of which are often delayed in less prosperous times, rises sharply. In recessions, investment and consumer durables purchases fall sharply, as such projects no longer appear profitable, and plans are put on hold until better times.

4. Why might the unemployment rate fall after output starts recovering during the expansion phase of the business cycle?

Often unemployment remains fairly high well into the expansion phase, because it takes a period of recovery before businesses become convinced that the increasing demand for their output is going to continue, making it profitable to hire added workers.

Module 8: Economic Growth
Concept A

1. Why does the production possibilities curve shift out with economic growth?

Economic growth means the ability of an economy to produce more goods and services than before. An outward shift in a country's production possibilities curve simply illustrates that fact graphically.

2. Even if "in the long run we are all dead," are you glad that earlier generations of Americans worked and invested for economic growth?

The fact that earlier generations of Americans worked and invested for economic growth means that there is currently a greater stock of capital in the U.S. than there would have been otherwise. If you have more tools with which to work, you are more productive, resulting in a higher income and greater consumption possibilities.

3. If long-run consequences were not important, would many students go to college or participate in internship programs without pay? Why or why not?

No. These are two of many examples where people sacrifice in the short run in order to benefit in the long run. Saving and research and development are other obvious examples.

4. When the Dutch "created" new land with their system of dikes, what did it do to their production possibilities curve? Why?

Building dikes in Holland increased the quantity of usable land the Dutch had to work with, and an increase in the amount of usable natural resources shifts a country's production possibilities curve out.

Concept B

1. Why does knowing what factors are correlated with economic growth not tell us what causes economic growth?

Knowing what factors are correlated with economic growth does not tell us what causes economic growth because correlation does not prove causation. A factor may cause changes in economic growth, or economic growth could cause changes in it, or changes in both the factor and economic growth may be caused by yet another variable.

2. How does increasing the capital stock lead to economic growth?

Increasing the capital stock adds to the tools workers have to work with, increasing their productivity over time, which in turn increases output over time.

3. How do increases in savings affect long-run economic growth?

Increases in savings provide more funds for capital investment, and greater capital investment (which often also embodies advances in technology) increases productivity and output growth.

4. Why would you expect an inverse relationship between self-sufficiency and real GDP per capita?

Because of different endowments and abilities, both people and countries have different opportunity costs of production for large numbers of goods and services (different comparative advantages). Specialization and large-scale production, combined with domestic and international trade, allow an expansion of productive and consumption possibilities by taking advantage of lower-cost production, while self-sufficiency sacrifices those potential gains.

5. If a couple was concerned about their retirement, why could that lead to them having more children if they lived in an agricultural society, but fewer children if they were in an urban society?

In an agricultural society, children can typically "earn their own keep," making them financially "profitable" investments. In an urban society, however, children are a substantial financial liability to their parents.

Concept C

1. Why is no single factor capable of completely explaining economic growth patterns?

No single factor is capable of completely explaining economic growth patterns because economic growth is a complex process involving many important factors, no one of which completely dominates.

2. Why might countries with relatively scarce labor be leaders in labor-saving innovations? In what area would countries with relatively scarce land likely be innovative leaders?

Countries with relatively scarce, and therefore more costly, labor would benefit more from labor-saving innovations, and so would be likely to be leaders in such innovations. Similarly, countries with relatively scarce, and therefore more costly, land would likely be leaders in innovative ways to conserve on land.

3. Why could an increase in the price of oil increase real GDP growth in oil-exporting countries like Saudi Arabia and Mexico, while decreasing growth in oil-importing countries like the United States and Japan?

Because GDP measures the market value of goods and services produced, an increase in the price of a country's exports adds to its GDP. However, an increase in the price of oil will raise costs and reduce output in oil-importing countries, other things equal.

4. How is Hong Kong a dramatic example of why abundant natural resources are not necessary to rapid economic growth?

Although Hong Kong has virtually no natural resources, it has long been among the fastest growing economies in the world, proving that abundant natural resources are not necessary to rapid economic growth.

5. Why is the effective use of land, labor, capital, and entrepreneurial activities dependent on the protection of property rights?

Without protected property rights, both production and exchange become far more difficult, costly, and uncertain, undermining the ability of market incentives to induce the effective use of the factors of production. Similarly, without protected property rights, the rewards to investors and those who seek new and better ways of doing things are also more uncertain, reducing the incentives to make such investments and innovations.

Concept D

1. What happens to per capita real output if population grows faster than output? If population grows more slowly than output?

If population grows faster than real output, per capita real output falls; if population grows more slowly than real output, per capita real output rises.

2. How can economies of large-scale production allow per capita output to rise as population rises?

Economies of large-scale production mean that output can expand more than proportionately to an increase in inputs, so that the increasing labor force that accompanies a larger population may increase output enough through more efficient-sized production units that per capita real output rises as population rises.

3. How did Malthus' prediction on population growth follow from the law of diminishing returns?

Malthus' prediction that population growth results in a subsistence level of wages was based on the assumption of an agricultural society with land and labor as the only factors of production. Assuming that the amount of land was fixed, population and the labor force would grow to the point at which production exhibited the law of diminishing returns, with output growing more slowly than the geometrically increasing variable input, labor, which would reduce per capita incomes, eventually to the point of subsistence.

4. Why is population control a particularly important issue in countries with very low levels of per capita income?

In countries with a fixed supply of land and little if any technological advance, Malthus' assumptions are not far from the reality. Population control is one way to hold down the rate of population increase and thus to prevent the Malthusian subsistence wage result. It is, of course, a possibility that, even for very poor countries, the problem is not population growth but "something else" (e.g. bad government policies or other institutional problems).

Concept E

1. Is it possible that utility, or happiness, could fall as income rises? Why or why not?

Utility, or happiness, depends on both real income and expectations. Therefore, if real income increases faster than one's expectations, utility could rise, while if real income increases more slowly than one's expectations, utility could fall as a result.

2. Why does economic growth not necessarily lead to environmental damage? How can it lead to environmental improvements?

Economic growth can lead to increasing market output at the expense of environmental damage. But economic growth (illustrated by an outward shift in a production possibilities curve with market goods on one axis and environmental quality on the other axis) also makes it possible to have more of both market goods and environmental quality over time. People would become willing to spend more on environmental quality as economic growth raises their incomes, and devoting those added resources to the environment can improve it at the same time more market goods and services are being produced.

3. Economic growth leads to increased resource use. Does this mean that economic growth will necessarily lead to a depletion of natural resources in the long run? Why or why not?

Economic growth increases resource use, but it also increases the incentives to discover and develop new natural resource supplies, as well as to conserve and develop new substitutes for those natural resources. It also generates more and better resources for such discovery and development. The result need not be a depletion of usable natural resources in the long run.

Module 9: Measuring Economic Performance
Concept A

1. Why does the circular flow of money move in the opposite direction from the flows of goods and services?
The circular flow of money moves in the opposite direction from the flows of goods and services because the money flows are the payments made in exchange for the goods and services received by buyers.

2. Why would an increase in your income in factor markets likely increase your demand in product markets?
As your income rises, your demand for goods and services in product markets will also increase (remember that most goods are normal goods, for which demand increases as income increases). Also, saving tends to flow into investment demand.

3. Why would a decrease in demand for what you produce in product markets decrease your income in factor markets?
The value of an input's services is derived from the market value of the outputs produced by that input. When the demand for what you produce in product markets decreases, the price of what you produce decreases, and so does the market value of those services. Therefore, your income in factor markets also decreases.

Concept B

1. Why does GDP measure only *final* goods and services produced, rather than all goods and services produced?
If the market value of every good and service sold was included in GDP, the same output would be counted more than once in many circumstances (as when the sales price of, say bread, includes the value of the flour that was used in making the bread, and the flour, in turn, includes the value of the wheat that was used to make the flour). Only final goods and services are included in GDP to avoid such double counting.

2. Why aren't all of the expenditures on used goods in an economy included in the current GDP?
Current GDP does not include expenditures on used goods because GDP is intended to measure the value of currently produced goods and services in the economy. Used goods are not currently produced, and were already counted the year they were newly produced.

3. Why do GDP statistics include real estate agents' commissions from selling existing homes and used car dealers' profits from selling used cars but not the value of existing homes and used cars when they are sold?
Existing homes and used cars were both produced in the past and therefore aren't counted as part of current GDP. However, the services provided this year by real estate agents and used car lots are currently produced, so the market value of those services, measured by real estate agent commissions and the profits earned by used car lots, are included in GDP.

4. Why are sales of previously existing inventories of hula hoops not included in the current year's GDP?
Previously existing inventories of any product are not newly pro-

duced and are therefore not included in current year GDP. They were already produced and counted in an earlier period.

Concept C

1. What would happen to GDP if consumption purchases (*C*) and net exports (*X – M*) both rose, holding other things equal?
Because GDP is the sum of consumption purchases (*C*), investment purchases (*I*), government purchases (*G*), and net exports (*X – M*), an increase of any of those components of GDP will increase GDP, other things being equal. Because either an increase in consumption (*C*) or an increase in net exports (*X – M*) increases GDP, both changes in the same time period will also increase GDP, other things being equal.

2. Why do you think economic forecasters focus so much on consumption purchases and their determinants?
Economic forecasters focus so much on consumption purchases and their determinants because consumption purchases are by far the largest component (roughly two-thirds) of GDP, so that what happens to consumption purchases is crucial to what happens to GDP.

3. Why are purchases of durable goods more unstable than purchases of nondurable goods?
Purchases of durable goods are more unstable than purchases of nondurable goods because nondurable goods are used up in a relatively short period of time, so that their purchase is hard to shift from one time period to another. Durable goods, on the other hand, provide services for several periods, so that consumer durable purchases can be significantly delayed to "make do" during economic hard times and can be significantly accelerated during good times.

4. Why does the investment component of GDP include purchases of new capital goods but not purchases of corporate stock?
New capital goods are newly produced goods, by definition, so they are included in GDP. However, sales of company stock do not involve a newly produced good or service (although the services of the broker, measured by the transaction fee, are included as a newly produced service). When someone buys shares of stock from someone else, no goods are being newly produced. Instead, already existing ownership claims on the future income of the company are simply being transferred from one person to another.

5. If Mary received a welfare check this year, would that transfer payment be included in this year's GDP? Why or why not?
GDP includes only currently produced goods and services. But because transfer payments are not payments in exchange for newly produced goods and services, they are not included in GDP.

6. Could inventory investment or net exports ever be negative?
Yes. If year-end inventories are smaller than beginning of the year inventories, inventory investment is negative, and if the value of exports is smaller than the value of imports, net exports are negative.

Concept D

1. Why should we expect the total expenditures that go into GDP to equal total income in an economy?

Every dollar of purchases that goes into GDP must be paid out to the factors of production that produced it (categorized as wages, rents, interest, and profits). Therefore, total expenditures, properly measured, must equal total income, properly measured.

2. Which two non-income expense items does the income approach take into consideration?

The income approach takes indirect business taxes into consideration, because they are uses to which income is devoted, even though they are not payments for newly produced goods and services. It also takes depreciation, or the capital consumption allowance into consideration, because depreciation represents the amount of income that must be set aside to replace existing capital equipment as it wears out.

3. How is personal income different from national income?

Personal income, the amount of income available to consumers to spend, is not the same as national income, because owners of productive resources do not receive all of the income that they earn and because they receive "unearned" transfer payments. Undistributed corporate profits and social insurance taxes, which are not received by the factors of production, must be subtracted from, and transfer payments must be added to, national income to get personal income.

Concept E

1. If we overestimated inflation over time, would our calculations of real GDP growth likely be over- or underestimated?

Nominal GDP is deflated by the measure of inflation being used to calculate real GDP and real GDP growth. Therefore, for a given nominal GDP growth rate, overestimating inflation over time would result in underestimating real GDP growth over time.

2. Why does the consumer price index tend to overstate inflation if the quality of goods and services is rising over time?

The consumer price index does not adjust for most quality increases that take place in goods and services. Therefore, higher prices that actually reflect increased quality are counted as higher prices for a given quality, so that the consumer price index overstates increases in the cost of living.

3. Why would the growth in real GDP overstate the growth of output per person in a country with a growing population?

Real GDP growth measures what happens to output for the economy as a whole. But if the population is growing, real GDP is being split among an increasing number of people, and real GDP growth exceeds per capita real GDP growth.

4. Why doesn't the consumer price index accurately adjust for the cost-of-living effects of a tripling in the price of bananas relative to the prices of other fruits?

The consumer price index assumes that people continue to consume the same number of bananas as in the base year (survey period). Therefore, the cost of the banana component of the consumer price index triples when the price of bananas triples. However, in fact, consumers will substitute other fruits, which become relatively cheaper as a result of the banana price increase, for bananas so that this component of their cost of living has not actually increased as fast as banana prices.

Concept F

1. Why do GDP measures omit nonmarket transactions?

GDP measures omit nonmarket transactions because there is no accurate way to measure the values of those transactions, unlike the case for normal market transactions, where market prices can be used to measure the values involved.

2. How would real GDP comparisons between two countries be impacted by the existence of a high level of nonmarket activities in one of the countries?

Because nonmarket activities are not included in GDP, GDP would understate the true value of total output more for a country with a relatively high level of nonmarket activities than for a country with a smaller proportion of nonmarket activities, making countries with smaller shares of nonmarket activities look richer relative to countries with larger shares of nonmarket activities.

3. If we choose to decrease our hours worked because we value the additional leisure more, would the resulting change in real GDP accurately reflect the change in our well-being? Why or why not?

Decreasing hours worked would reduce real GDP, other things equal. But if we choose to do so voluntarily, that would mean we place a higher value on the leisure time (which is not counted in GDP) than on the market output (that is counted in GDP) foregone by reducing hours worked, so the change in real GDP would not accurately reflect the change in our well-being. That is, GDP would be going down, but well-being would be actually be going up!

4. How do pollution and crime affect GDP? How do pollution- and crime-control expenditures impact GDP?

Neither pollution nor crime are included (as "bads" to be subtracted) in GDP calculations. However, market expenditures for pollution and crime control are included in GDP, as currently produced goods and services.

Module 10: Aggregate Demand
Concept A

1. What are the major components of aggregate demand?

The major components of aggregate demand are consumption, planned investment, government purchases, and net exports.

2. If consumption is a direct function of disposable income, how would an increase in personal taxes or a decrease in transfer payments affect consumption?

Either an increase in taxes or a decrease in transfer payments decreases the disposable income of households, which would normally be expected to reduce their demands for consumption goods.

3. What does the permanent income hypothesis imply about consumption as a fraction of income for young and old consumers versus middle-aged consumers?

The young and the old earn less at those ages than their lifetime, or average, income, so they consume a higher percentage of their income at those ages; those in middle age earn more at those ages than their lifetime, or average, income, so they consume a lower fraction of their income during those years.

4. Would you spend more or less on additional consumption if your marginal propensity to consume increased?

Because the definition of the marginal propensity to consume is the fraction of an increase in disposable income one would spend on additional consumption purchases, you would spend more, the higher your marginal propensity to consume.

Concept B

1. Why does increased business optimism lead to increased investment?

Increased business optimism increases the expected rates of return on investment projects, increasing the number of such projects that are expected to be profitable, and therefore increasing purchases of investment goods for those projects.

2. Why do decisions to invest depend largely on the expected rate of return on investments compared to the opportunity cost of borrowed money (the market interest rate)?

If the expected rate of return on an investment project exceeds the opportunity cost of funds to finance it, pursuing it will generate economic profits; if the expected rate of return on an investment project is less than the opportunity cost of funds to finance it, pursuing it will generate economic losses.

3. Why might a larger existing capital stock tend to increase the rate of new capital goods investment?

The greater the capital stock for a given output, the lower is capacity utilization, and the smaller would be the rate of new capital goods investment. However, for a given capacity utilization rate, the greater the capital stock, the greater will be the amount of depreciation in any given time period, and the more investment is necessary just to offset depreciation.

4. If inventories have risen above the desired level for a firm, what does that tell it about the demand for its product relative to what it expected demand to be?

Inventories that are rising above desired levels mean that the demand for that firm's output is lower than anticipated.

5. What would an increase in exports do to aggregate demand, other things equal? An increase in imports? An increase in both imports and exports, where the change in exports was greater in magnitude?

An increase in exports would increase aggregate demand, other things equal, because net exports are part of aggregate demand. An increase in imports would decrease aggregate demand, other things equal, by reducing net exports (demand shifts from domestic producers to foreign producers). An increase in both imports and exports will increase aggregate demand if the increase in exports exceeds the increase in imports, other things equal, because the combination will increase net exports.

Concept C

1. How is the aggregate demand curve different from the microeconomic demand curve?

The microeconomic demand curve reflects what happens to the quantity of a particular good demanded as its price relative to other goods changes, with substitution among alternative goods the primary mechanism at work. Aggregate demand, on the other hand, reflects what happens to the total quantity of all real goods and services demanded in the economy as a whole as the overall price level changes, so substitution among goods is not the primary mechanism at work.

2. How does an increased price level reduce the quantities of investment goods and consumer durables demanded?

An increased price level increases the demand for money, which, in turn, increases interest rates. Higher interest rates increase the opportunity cost of financing both investment goods and consumer durables, reducing the quantities of investment goods and consumer durables demanded.

3. What is the real wealth effect, and how does it imply a downward-sloping aggregate demand curve?

A reduced price level increases the real value of people's currency holdings, and as their real wealth increases, so does the quantity of real goods and services demanded, particularly consumption goods. Therefore, the aggregate demand curve, which represents the relationship between the price level and the quantity of real goods and services demanded, slopes downward as a result.

4. What is the interest rate effect, and how does it imply a downward-sloping aggregate demand curve?

A reduced price level reduces the demand for money, which lowers interest rates and thus increases the quantity of investment goods and consumer durable goods people are willing to purchase. Therefore, the aggregate demand curve, which represents the relationship between the price level and the quantity of real goods and services demanded, slopes downward as a result.

5. What is the open economy effect, and how does it imply a downward-sloping aggregate demand curve?

The open economy effect occurs because a higher domestic price level raises the prices of domestically produced goods relative to the prices of imported goods. That reduces the quantity of domestically produced goods demanded (by both citizens and foreigners), as now relatively cheaper foreign-made goods are substituted for them. The result is again a downward-sloping aggregate demand curve, as a higher price level results in a lower quantity of domestic real GDP demanded, other things—in particular, exchange rates—held constant.

Concept D

1. How is the distinction between a change in demand and a change in quantity demanded the same for aggregate demand as for the demand for a particular good?

Just as a change in the price of a particular good changes its quantity demanded, but not its demand, a change in the price level changes the quantity of real GDP demanded, but not aggregate demand. Just as a change in any of the PYNTE demand curve shifters (other factors than the price of the good itself) changes the demand for a particular good, a change in any of the components of aggregate demand (C, I, G, and $X - M$) not caused by a change in the price level changes aggregate demand.

2. What happens to aggregate demand if the demand for consumption goods increases, *ceteris paribus*?

Because consumption purchases are part of aggregate demand, an increase in the demand for consumption goods increases aggregate demand, *ceteris paribus*.

3. What happens to aggregate demand if the demand for investment goods falls, *ceteris paribus*?

Because planned investment purchases are part of aggregate demand, a falling demand for investment goods makes aggregate demand fall, *ceteris paribus*.

4. Why would an increase in the money supply tend to increase expenditures on consumption and investment, *ceteris paribus*?

An increase in the money supply would lead to two effects. First, it would tend to lower interest rates, leading to more investment demand (and perhaps more consumption demand). Second, some individuals would directly spend excess money balances on goods, increasing consumption demand directly.

Module 11: Aggregate Supply and Macroeconomic Equilibrium
Concept A

1. What relationship does the short-run aggregate supply curve represent?

The short-run aggregate supply curve represents the relationship between the total quantity of final goods and services that suppliers are willing and able to produces (the quantity of real GDP supplied) and the overall price level, before all input prices have had time to completely adjust to the price level.

2. What relationship does the long-run aggregate supply curve represent?

The long-run aggregate supply curve represents the relationship between the total quantity of final goods and services that suppliers are willing and able to produce (the quantity of real GDP supplied) and the overall price level, once all input prices have had time to completely adjust to the price level (actually, it shows there is no relationship between these two variables, once input prices have had sufficient time to completely adjust to the price level).

3. Why is focusing on producers' profit margins helpful in understanding the logic of the short-run aggregate supply curve?

Profit incentives are important to understanding what happens to real output as the price level changes in the short run (before input prices completely adjust to the price level). When the prices of outputs rise relative to the prices of inputs (costs), as when aggregate demand increases in the short run, it increases profit margins, which increases the incentives to produce, leading to increased real output. When the prices of outputs fall relative to the prices of inputs (costs), as when aggregate demand decreases in the short run, it decreases profit margins, which decreases the incentives to produce, leading to decreased real output.

4. Why is the short-run aggregate supply curve upward sloping, while the long-run aggregate supply curve is vertical at the natural rate of output?

The short-run aggregate supply curve is upward sloping because in the short run, before input prices have completely adjusted to the price level, an increase in the price level increases profit margins by increasing output prices relative to input prices, which leads producers to increase real output. The long-run aggregate supply curve is vertical because in the long run, when input prices have completely adjusted to changes in the price level, input prices as well as output prices have adjusted to the price level, so that profit margins in real terms do not change as the price level changes; thus, there is no relationship between the price level and real output in the long run. The long-run aggregate supply curve is vertical at the natural rate of real output because that is the maximum output level allowed by capital, labor, and technological inputs at full employment (that is, given the determinants of the economy's production possibilities curve), which is therefore sustainable over time.

5. What would the short-run aggregate supply curve look like if input prices always changed instantaneously as soon as output prices changed? Why?

If input prices always changed instantaneously as soon as output prices changed, the short-run aggregate supply curve would look the same as the long-run aggregate supply curve—vertical at the natural rate of real output. That is because both input and output prices would then change proportionally, so that real profit mar-

gins (the incentives facing producers), and therefore real output, would not change as the price level changes.

6. If the price of cotton increased 10 percent when cotton producers thought other prices were rising 5 percent over the same period, what would happen to the quantity of real GDP supplied in the cotton industry? What if cotton producers thought other prices were rising 20 percent over the same period?

If the price of cotton increased 10 percent when cotton producers thought other prices were rising 5 percent over the same period, the quantity of real GDP supplied in the cotton industry would increase, because with other prices (including input prices) falling relative to cotton prices, the profitability of growing cotton would be rising. If the price of cotton increased 10 percent when cotton producers thought other prices were rising 20 percent over the same period, the quantity of real GDP supplied in the cotton industry would decrease, because with other prices (including input prices) rising relative to cotton prices, the profitability of growing cotton would be falling.

Concept B

1. Which of the aggregate supply curves will shift in response to a change in the price level? Why?

The short-run aggregate supply curve shifts in response to a change in the expected price level by changing the expected production costs, and therefore the expected profitability, of producing output at any given output price level. Remember that the long-run aggregate supply curve assumes that people have had enough time to completely adjust to a changing price level, so a change in the expected price level does not change expected profit margins along the long-run aggregate supply curve.

2. Why do lower input costs increase the level of real GDP supplied at any given price level?

Lower input costs increase the level of real GDP supplied at any given (output) price level by increasing the profit margin for any given level of output prices.

3. What would discovering huge new supplies of oil and natural gas do to the short-run and long-run aggregate supply curves?

Discovering huge new supplies of oil and natural gas would increase both the short-run and long-run aggregate supply curves, because those additional resources would allow more to be produced in the short-run, at any given output price level, as well as on a sustainable, long-run basis (because such a discovery would shift the economy's production possibilities curve outward).

4. What would happen to the short-run and long-run aggregate supply curves if the government required every firm to file explanatory paperwork each time a decision was made?

This would shift both the short-run and long-run aggregate supply curves to the left. It would permanently raise producers' costs of producing any level of output, which would reduce how much producers would produce in the short run at any given price level, as well as on a sustainable, long-run basis (because such a requirement would shift the economy's production possibilities curve inward).

5. What would happen to the short-run and long-run aggregate supply curves if the capital stock grew and available supplies of natural resources expanded over the same period of time?

Both an increase in the capital stock and increased available supplies of natural resources would shift both the short-run and long-run aggregate supply curves to the right (shifting the economy's production possibilities curve outward), increasing both short-run and sustainable levels of real output.

6. How can a change in input prices change the short-run aggregate supply curve but not the long-run aggregate supply curve? How could it change both long-run and short-run aggregate supply?

A temporary change in input prices can change the short-run aggregate supply curve by changing profit margins in the short run. However, when input prices return to their previous levels (reflecting a return to their previous relative scarcity) in the long run, the sustainable level of real output will be no different than before. If, on the other hand, input price changes reflect a permanently changed supply of inputs (lower input prices reflecting an increased supply), a change in input prices would increase both the short-run and long-run aggregate supply curves by increasing the real output producible both currently and on an ongoing basis (permanently shifting out the economy's production possibilities curve).

7. What would happen to short- and long-run aggregate supply if unusually good weather led to bumper crops of most agricultural products?

Because this reflects only a temporary change in output, it would increase the short-run aggregate supply curve but not the long-run aggregate supply curve.

8. If OPEC temporarily restricted the world output of oil, what would happen to short- and long-run aggregate supply? What would happen if the output restriction was permanent?

A temporary oil output restriction would temporarily increase oil (energy input) prices, reducing the short-run aggregate supply curve (shifting it left) but not the long-run aggregate supply curve. If the oil output restriction was permanent, the oil price increase would also reduce the level of real output producible on a sustainable basis, and so would shift both short-run aggregate supply and long-run aggregate supply to the left.

Concept C

1. What is demand-pull inflation?

Demand-pull inflation occurs when price levels increase as a result of an increase in aggregate demand.

2. What is cost-push inflation?

Cost-push inflation is output price inflation caused by an increase in input prices (that is, by supply-side forces, rather than demand-side forces). It is illustrated by a leftward, or upward, shift of the short-run aggregate supply curve, for given long-run aggregate supply and demand curves.

3. Starting from long-run equilibrium on the long-run aggregate supply curve, what happens to the price level, real output, and unemployment as a result of cost-push inflation?

Starting from long-run equilibrium on the long-run aggregate supply curve, cost-push inflation causes the price level to rise, real output to fall, and unemployment to rise in the short run.

4. How would a drop in consumer confidence impact the short-run macroeconomy?

A drop in consumer confidence would decrease the demand for consumer goods, other things equal, which would reduce (shift left) the aggregate demand curve, resulting in a lower price level, lower real output, and increased unemployment in the short run for a given short-run aggregate supply curve.

5. What would happen to the price level, real output, and unemployment in the short run if world oil prices fell sharply?

If world oil prices fell sharply, it would increase (shift right) the short-run aggregate supply curve, resulting in a lower price level, greater real output, and reduced unemployment in the short run, for a given aggregate demand curve.

Module 12: Fiscal Policy
Concept A

1. If, as part of its fiscal policy, the federal government increased its purchases of goods and services, would that be an expansionary or contractionary tactic?

An increase in government purchases of goods and services would be an expansionary tactic, increasing aggregate demand, other things equal.

2. If the federal government decreased its purchases of goods and services, would the budget deficit increase or decrease?

If the federal government decreased its purchases of goods and services, for a given level of tax revenue, a budget deficit (the difference between government spending and government revenues) would decrease.

3. If the federal government increased taxes or decreased transfer payments, would that be an expansionary or contractionary fiscal policy?

Either an increase in taxes or a decrease in transfer payment would be a contractionary tactic, decreasing aggregate demand by decreasing people's disposable incomes and therefore reducing the demand for consumption goods.

4. If the federal government increased taxes or decreased transfer payments, would the budget deficit increase or decrease?

If the federal government increased taxes or decreased transfer payments, for a given level of government purchases, a budget deficit (the difference between government spending and government revenues) would decrease.

5. If the federal government increased government purchases and lowered taxes at the same time, would the budget deficit increase or decrease?

Increased government purchases would increase a budget deficit, other things equal. Lowered taxes would also increase a budget deficit, other things equal. Therefore, both changes together would increase a budget deficit.

Concept B

1. How does the multiplier effect work?

The multiplier effect arises because the increased purchases during each "round" of the multiplier process generates increased incomes to the owners of the resources used to produce the goods purchased, which leads them to increase consumption purchases in the next "round" of the process. The result is a final increase in total purchases, including the induced consumption purchases, that is greater than the initial increase in purchases.

2. What is the marginal propensity to consume?

The marginal propensity to consume is the proportion of an additional dollar of income that would be spent on additional consumption purchases.

3. Why is the marginal propensity to consume always less than one?

This is true because all expenditures have to ultimately be

financed out of income, so that each dollar of added income cannot lead to more than a dollar of added purchases. In addition, taxes and savings also have to be financed out of income, and these do not directly increase aggregate demand.

4. Why does the multiplier effect get larger as the marginal propensity to consume gets larger?

The larger the marginal propensity to consume, the larger the fraction of increased income in each "round" of the multiplier process that will go to additional consumption purchases. Because each round of the multiplier process will therefore be larger the greater the marginal propensity to consume, the multiplier will also be larger, other things equal.

5. If an increase in government purchases leads to a reduction in private-sector purchases, why could the effect on the economy be less than indicated by the multiplier?

At the same time that the increased government purchases are leading to a multiple expansion of income and purchases for one set of citizens, the "crowded out" private sector purchases are causing a multiple contraction of income and purchases for other citizens. The net effect on the economy will therefore be less than the increase in government purchases times the multiplier.

Concept C

1. If the economy is in recession, what sorts of fiscal policy changes would tend to bring it out of recession?

If the economy is in recession, aggregate demand intersects short-run aggregate supply to the left of the long-run aggregate supply curve. Expansionary fiscal policy—increased government purchases, decreased taxes, and/or increased transfer payments—addresses a recession by shifting aggregate demand to the right.

2. If the economy is at a short-run equilibrium at greater than full employment, what sorts of fiscal policy changes would tend to bring the economy back to a full employment equilibrium?

If the economy is at a short-run equilibrium at greater than full employment, aggregate demand intersects short-run aggregate supply to the right of the long-run aggregate supply curve. Contractionary fiscal policy—decreased government purchases, increased taxes, and/or decreased transfer payments—addresses a short-run equilibrium at greater than full employment by shifting aggregate demand to the left.

3. What effects would an expansionary fiscal policy have on the price level and real GDP, starting from a full employment equilibrium?

Starting from a full employment equilibrium, an expansionary fiscal policy would increase aggregate demand, increasing the price level and real GDP in the short run. However, in the long run, real GDP will return to its full-employment long-run equilibrium level as input prices adjust (the short-run aggregate supply curve shifts up or left), and only the price level will end up higher.

4. What effects would a contractionary fiscal policy have on the price level and real GDP, starting from a full employment equilibrium?

Starting from a full employment equilibrium, a contractionary fiscal policy would decrease aggregate demand, decreasing the price level and real GDP in the short run. However, in the long run, real GDP will return to its full-employment long-run equilibrium level as input prices adjust (the short-run aggregate supply curve shifts down or right), and the price level will end up lower.

Concept D

1. Why does a larger government budget deficit increase the magnitude of the crowding out effect?

A larger government budget deficit increases the demand for loanable funds, increasing the magnitude of the increase in interest rates, crowding out more private sector investment as a result.

2. Why does fiscal policy have a smaller effect on aggregate demand, the greater the crowding out effect?

The greater the crowding out effect, the smaller the net effect (the increase in government purchases minus the private sector purchases crowded out) fiscal policy has on aggregate demand. For example, if each dollar of added government purchases crowds out 50 cents worth of private sector purchases, fiscal policy will have only half the effect on aggregate demand that it would if there was no crowding out effect.

3. Why does the Ricardian equivalence theorem imply that if people correctly recognize the future tax liability represented by a current budget deficit, and save enough to pay for those future taxes as a result, then fiscal policy may have no effect on aggregate demand?

The Ricardian equivalence theorem implies that if people correctly recognize the future tax liability represented by a current budget deficit, they will save enough today to pay for those added future taxes. But this increase in savings requires an equal reduction in consumption for a given income, and this reduction in consumption completely offsets the effect of expansionary fiscal policy (which increases the size of a budget deficit) on aggregate demand.

4. How do time lags impact the effectiveness of fiscal policy?

The time lag between when a policy change is desirable and when it is adopted and implemented (for data gathering, decisionmaking, etc.), as well as the time lag between when a policy is implemented and when it has its effects, make it difficult for fiscal policy to have the desired effect at the desired time, particularly given the difficulty in forecasting the future course of the economy.

Concept E

1. How does the tax system act as an automatic stabilizer?

Some taxes, such as progressive income taxes and corporate profits taxes, automatically increase as the economy grows, and this increase in taxes restrains disposable income and the growth of aggregate demand below what it would have been otherwise. Similarly, they automatically decrease in recessions, and this decrease in taxes increases disposable income and acts as a partial offset to the fall in aggregate demand. The result is reduced business cycle instability.

2. Are automatic stabilizers impacted by a time lag? Why or why not?

Because automatic stabilizers respond to business cycle changes without the need for legislative or executive action, there is no appreciable lag between when business cycle conditions justify a change in them and when they do change. However, there is still a lag between when those stabilizers change and when their full effects are felt.

3. Why are transfer payments, such as unemployment compensation, effective automatic stabilizers?

Some transfer payment programs, such as unemployment compensation, act as automatic stabilizers, because when business cycle conditions worsen, people can start receiving increased transfer payments as soon as they become eligible (lose their jobs, in the case of unemployment compensation). The same is true of some other welfare type programs, such as food stamps. As a consequence of these automatic stabilizers, aggregate demand does not fall as much as it otherwise would have, partially offsetting any recessionary tendencies.

Concept F

1. Is supply-side economics more concerned with short-run economic stabilization or long-run economic growth?
Supply-side economics is more concerned with long-run economic growth than short-run economic stabilization. It is focused primarily on adopting policies that will increase the long-run aggregate supply curve (society's production possibilities curve) over time, by improving incentives to work, save, and invest.

2. Why could you say that supply-side economics is really more about after-tax wages and after-tax returns on investment than it is about tax rates?
It is changes in after-tax wages and after-tax returns on investment that are the incentives that change people's behavior, not changes in the tax rates themselves.

3. Why do government regulations have the same sorts of effects on businesses as taxes?
To the extent that government regulations impose added costs on businesses, the effects of those added costs are the same as a decrease (leftward or upward shift) in supply—as if a tax of that amount was imposed on the business. (In important respects, the regulations are "worse" than taxes because they involve real resource usage (foregone other goods), while the tax revenue is merely a transfer to whomever benefits from the taxes raised.)

4. Why aren't the full effects of supply-side policies seen quickly?
It will often take a substantial period of time before improved productive incentives will have their complete effects. For instance, an increase in the after-tax return on investment will increase investment, but it will take many years before the capital stock has completed its adjustment. The same is true for human capital investments in education, research and development, and so forth; if a student or researcher learns more today, the full effect won't be observed immediately.

5. If taxes increase, what would you expect to happen to employment in the underground economy? Why?
The primary benefit of employment in the underground economy is the savings from not having to pay taxes (or bear some of the costs of regulations imposed on "legitimate" employment). The cost includes the risk of being caught, the difficulty of dealing on a cash-only or barter basis, and so forth. As tax rates increase, the benefits of working in the underground economy increase relative to the costs, and employment in the underground economy will tend to increase, other things equal.

Concept G

1. When President Kennedy cut tax rates and instituted an investment tax credit, was he using a demand-side or a supply-side strategy?
Both. Cutting tax rates and instituting an investment tax credit increased aggregate demand. But because those policies also im-

proved productive incentives to work harder, save and invest more, and so forth, they also increased aggregate supply, though perhaps over a longer time frame.

2. If Kennedy's policy had been adopted during a period of full employment, would it have worked as well? Why or why not?
Kennedy used expansionary fiscal policy to get out of a recession. However, if a similar expansionary policy had been used during a period of full employment, the resulting increase in real output and accompanying decrease in unemployment would have only been temporary, with the long-run effect being higher prices.

3. What effect did President Johnson's economic policies have on the economy?
President Johnson also used expansionary fiscal policy, but he did so with the economy already at full employment. The result was very little effect on real GDP or employment but a considerable increase in inflation.

Concept H

1. Why can't the federal government finance its debt by printing more money?
Printing money to finance a deficit or the debt is inflationary and undermines confidence in the government.

2. How can the federal government finance the national debt?
The federal government must ultimately finance the national debt by borrowing (which represents future taxes). Attempting to finance the debt through money creation will eventually break down.

3. Should we worry about the national debt?
The national debt is a potential source of worry, because as the interest on the debt becomes large relative to the economy, the crowding out and disincentive effects can be very substantial. However, the privately held federal debt is not now large enough relative to the size of the economy to be a serious concern.

4. What must be true for Americans to be better off as a result of an increase in the federal debt?
For Americans to be better off as a result of an increase in the federal debt, the value of the investments and other spending financed by the debt must be greater than the cost of financing it.

Module 13: Money and the Banking System
Concept A

1. If everyone in an economy accepted poker chips as payment in exchange for goods and services, would poker chips be money?
Because money is anything that is generally accepted in exchange for goods or services (a medium of exchange), if everyone in an economy accepted poker chips as payment in exchange for goods and services, poker chips would be money.

2. If you were buying a pack of gum, would using currency or a demand deposit have lower transactions costs? What if you were buying a house?
If you were buying a pack of gum, or making any other such small purchase, using currency would generally have lower transactions costs than a demand deposit (checking account). However, if you were buying a house, or making any other very large purchase, using a demand deposit would generally have lower transactions costs than paying with currency; it would be cheaper, easier, and safer, and it would generate a more reliable financial record.

3. What is the main advantage of a transaction deposit for tax purposes? What is its main disadvantage for tax purposes?

The main advantage of transactions deposits for tax purposes is that they provide more reliable financial records for complying with record-keeping requirements for tax purposes. The financial records that transaction deposits generate, on the other hand, are their main disadvantage for those who wish to hide their financial activities from tax authorities.

4. Are credit cards money?

Credit cards are not money. They are actually guaranteed loans available on demand to users, which can be triggered by consumers; they are convenient substitutes for making transactions directly with money. That is, they are substitutes for the use of money in exchange. Credit cards do, however, have an important impact on how much money is demanded by consumers and how rapidly that money "turns over" in transactions.

5. What are M1 and M2?

M1 is a narrow definition of money that focuses on money's use as a means of payment (for transactions purposes). M1 includes currency in circulation, checkable deposits, and travelers checks. M2 is a broader definition of money that focuses on money's use as a highly liquid store of purchasing power or savings. M2 equals M1 plus other "near moneys," including savings accounts, small denomination time deposits, and money market mutual funds.

6. How have interest-earning checking accounts and overdraft protection led to the relative decline in demand deposits?

Interest-earning checking accounts provide the same ability to make transactions as non-interest-earning demand deposit accounts, but they are more attractive to many consumers because they earn interest. Overdraft protection means that consumers do not have to keep as much money in demand deposit accounts "just in case," to protect against overdrawing their accounts.

Concept B

1. Why does the advantage of monetary exchange over barter increase as an economy becomes more complex?

As the economy becomes more complex, the number of exchanges between people in the economy grows very rapidly. This means that the transaction cost advantages of using money over barter for those exchanges also grows very rapidly as the economy becomes more complex.

2. How can uncertain and rapid rates of inflation erode money's ability to perform its functions efficiently?

Uncertain and rapid rates of inflation erode money's ability to perform its functions efficiently because money lowers transaction costs most effectively when its value is stable, and therefore more predictable. Uncertain and rapid rates of inflation reduce the stability and predictability of the value of money, reducing its usefulness as a universally understood store of value. It therefore reduces money's ability to reduce transaction costs.

3. In a world of barter, would useful financial statements, like balance sheets, be possible? Would stock markets be possible? Would it be possible to build cars?

In a world of barter, there is no common store of value to allow comparisons of all the "apples and oranges" that must be summarized in financial statements, making such statements virtually impossible. Without money to act as a common store of value, stock and other financial markets, as well as very complex (many transactions) production processes, would also be virtually impossible.

4. Why do you think virtually all societies create something to function as money?

Having some good function as money lowers transactions costs, allowing increasing specialization and exchange to create increasing wealth for a society. That increase in wealth made possible by using money is why virtually all societies create something to function as money.

Concept C

1. If the earnings available on other financial assets rose, would you want to hold more or less money? Why?

Because holding wealth in the form of other financial assets is the alternative to holding it in the form of money, non-money financial assets are substitutes for holding money. When the earnings (interest) available on alternative financial assets rise, the opportunity cost of holding money instead also rises, so that you would want to hold less money, other things equal.

2. For the economy as a whole, why would individuals want to hold more money as GDP rises?

Americans conduct a larger volume of transactions as GDP rises. Therefore, they would want to hold more money as GDP rises in order to keep the costs of those increasing transactions down.

3. If in an era of very rapid inflation, many people stopped accepting a country's currency for payment, would that currency still be money?

If in an era of very rapid inflation, many people stopped accepting a country's currency for payment, that currency could no longer function as meaningful money.

4. Why might people who expect a major market "correction" (a fall in the value of stock holdings) wish to increase their holdings of money?

When the value of alternative financial assets is expected to fall, holding money, which will not similarly fall in value, becomes more attractive. Therefore, in the case of an expected fall in the value of stocks, bonds, or other financial assets, people would want to increase their holdings of money as a precaution.

Concept D

1. How did laws against interstate banking lead to a large number of U.S. banks? What is happening to the number of banks now that interstate banking is allowed?

Laws against interstate banking prevented the formation of large, interstate banking organizations, resulting in a large number of banks in the United States. However, now that interstate banking is allowed, mergers are resulting in fewer, larger, interstate banks.

2. In what way is it true that "banks make money by making money"?

Banks make money (profits) by loaning out their deposits at a higher interest rate than they pay their depositors. However, it is the extension of new loans in search of profits that creates new demand deposits, increasing the stock of money.

3. How do legal reserve deposit regulations lower bank profits?

Unlike other bank assets, legal reserves do not earn interest. Therefore, requiring a larger portion of bank assets to be held in reserve than prudent banking practice would dictate reduces bank earnings and profits.

4. Is a demand deposit an asset or a liability?

A demand deposit is an asset for its owner but a liability of the bank at which the account is kept.

5. If the Bonnie and Clyde National Bank's only deposits were demand deposits of $20 million, and it faced a 10 percent reserve requirement, how much money would it be required to hold in reserves?

The Bonnie and Clyde National Bank would have to hold 10 percent of its $20 million in demand deposits, or $2 million, as reserves.

6. How would a new deposit into your demand deposit account create a situation of excess reserves at your bank?

A new deposit adds that amount to your demand deposit account and to the reserves of your bank. But only a fraction of the added reserves are required by the addition to your demand deposit account. The rest are excess reserves, which the bank will look to convert to interest-earning loans or other assets.

Concept E

1. Why do the stock of money and the volume of bank loans both increase or decrease at the same time?

The stock of money and the volume of bank loans both increase or both decrease at the same time because issuing new bank loans adds to the money stock, while calling in existing bank loans reduces the money stock, by reducing demand deposits.

2. Why would each bank in the money supply multiple expansion process lend out a larger fraction of any new deposit it receives, the lower the reserve requirement?

Each bank in the money supply multiple expansion process can lend up to the amount of its excess reserves. But the excess reserves created by each dollar deposited in a bank equals 1 minus the required reserve ratio. The lower this reserve requirement, the greater the excess reserves created by each new deposit, and therefore the greater the fraction of any new deposit that will be loaned out in this process.

3. If a particular bank with a reserve requirement of 10 percent has $30,000 in a new cash deposit, how much money could it create through making new loans?

Using the money multiplier formula, a $30,000 cash deposit could add $300,000 to the money supply ($30,000 × 10 = $300,000), with $30,000 coming from the initial deposit and $270,000 through the multiple expansion effect.

4. Why do banks choosing to hold excess reserves or borrowers choosing to hold some of their loans in the form of currency reduce the actual impact of the money multiplier to a level below that indicated by the multiplier formula?

If banks choose to hold excess reserves, each bank in the money supply expansion process will lend out less, and therefore create less new money, than if it loaned out all of its excess reserves. The result will be a smaller money supply than that indicated by the multiplier formula, because that formula assumes that banks lend out all of their excess reserves. If borrowers hold some of their loans as currency, that would reduce the amount of vault cash, which counts as a reserve, at banks. This would reduce the amount that could be loaned at each stage of the money supply creation process, and would therefore reduce the actual money multiplier below the level indicated by the multiplier formula.

Concept F

1. How did the combination of increased holding of excess reserves by banks and currency by the public lead to bank failures in the 1930s?

The desire by the public for increased currency holdings, caused largely by the fear of bank failures, also forced banks to sharply increase excess reserves and reduce lending, together causing a sharp fall in the money stock. Despite substantial excess reserves, however, bank runs led to the failure of even many conservatively run banks.

2. What are the four reasons cited in the text for the collapse of the U.S. banking system in this period?

The cited reasons include: 1) the large number of small banks, which were more at risk from bank runs; 2) governmental attempts to stem the distress in the banking industry that were both weak and too late; 3) the absence of deposit insurance, which would have bolstered consumer confidence; and 4) fear that the economy was in a continuous downward cycle, so that there was little basis for optimism that bank loans would be safely repaid.

3. What is the FDIC, and how did its establishment increase bank stability and reassure depositors?

The Federal Deposit Insurance Corporation insures bank deposits. That guarantee of deposits eliminated the risk to depositors if their bank failed, thus eliminating the bank runs that resulted from the fear of bank insolvency. No longer facing the risk of bank runs, banks were more stable. Note, however, that the elimination of that risk reduces depositor interest in how risky the bank's investments are—an important cause of many bank crises throughout the world today.

Module 14: The Federal Reserve System and Monetary Policy
Concept A

1. What are the six primary functions of a central bank?

A central bank: 1) is a "banker's bank," where commercial banks maintain their own deposits; 2) provides services, such as transferring funds and checks, for commercial banks; 3) serves as the major bank for the federal government; 4) buys and sells foreign currencies and assists in transactions with other countries; 5) serves as a "lender of last resort" for banking institutions in financial distress; and 6) regulates the size of the money supply.

2. What is the FOMC and what does it do?

The Federal Open Market Committee is a committee of the Federal Reserve System, made up of the seven members of the Board of Governors, the President of the New York Federal Reserve Bank, and four other presidents of Federal Reserve Banks. It makes most of the key decisions influencing the direction and size of changes in the money stock.

3. How is the Fed tied to the executive branch? How is it insulated from executive branch pressure to influence monetary policy?

The president selects the seven members of the Board of Governors, subject to Senate approval, one every two years, for 14-year terms. He also selects the Chair of the Board of Governors for a four-year term. However, because the president can only select one member every two years, he cannot appoint a majority of the Board of Governors for his term in office. Also, the president cannot use reappointment of his nominees or threats of firing members to pressure the Fed on monetary policy.

Concept B

1. If the money stock is $10 billion and velocity is 4, what is the product of the price level and output? If the price level is 2, what does output equal?

If the money stock is $10 billion and velocity is 4 (so that $MV = $40 billion), the product of the price level and real output (PQ, or nominal output), must also be $40 billion. If the price level was 2 in this case, real output would equal the $40 billion nominal output divided by the price level of 2, or $20 billion.

2. If nominal GDP is $200 billion and the money stock is $50 billion, what must velocity be?

Because $MV = PQ$, $V = PQ/M$. $V = $200 billion$/$50 billion, or 4, in this case.

3. If the money stock increases and velocity does not change, what will happen to nominal GDP?

If M increases and V does not change, MV must increase. Because $MV = PQ$, and PQ equals nominal GDP, nominal GDP must also increase as a result.

4. If velocity is unstable, does stabilizing the money stock help stabilize the economy? Why or why not?

If V is unstable, stabilizing M does not stabilize MV. Because MV will not be stabilized, PQ, or nominal GDP, will not be stabilized either.

Concept C

1. What three main tactics could the Fed use in pursuing a contractionary monetary policy?

The Fed could conduct an open market sale of government securities (bonds), increase reserve requirements, and/or increase the discount rate if it wanted to pursue a contractionary monetary policy.

2. What three main tactics could the Fed use in pursuing an expansionary monetary policy?

The Fed could conduct an open market purchase of government securities (bonds), decrease reserve requirements, and/or decrease the discount rate if it wanted to pursue an expansionary monetary policy.

3. Would the money stock rise or fall if the Fed made an open market purchase of government bonds, *ceteris paribus*?

An open market purchase of government bonds by the Fed would increase banking reserves, thereby increasing the money stock, *ceteris paribus*, in an amount dependent on the money multiplier.

4. If the Fed raised the discount rate from 12 to 15 percent, what impact would that have on the money supply?

Raising the discount rate makes it more costly for banks to borrow reserves directly from the Fed. To the extent that banks borrow fewer reserves directly from the Fed, this reduces total banking reserves, thereby decreasing the money stock, *ceteris paribus*.

5. What is moral suasion, and why would the Fed use this tactic?

Moral suasion is the term used to describe Federal Reserve attempts to persuade or influence banks to follow a particular course of action (e.g., be more selective in making loans) they might not otherwise take.

Concept D

1. Who controls the supply of money in the money market?

The banking system, through the loan expansion process, directly determines the supply of money in the money market. However, the Fed, through the policy variables it controls (primarily open market operations, reserve requirements, and the discount rate), indirectly controls the money supply by controlling the level of reserves and the money multiplier.

2. How does an increase in income or a decrease in the interest rate increase the demand for money?

An increase in income increases (shifts to the right) the demand for money, as people want to hold down the transactions costs on the increasing volume of transactions taking place. A decrease in interest rates, on the other hand, increases the quantity of money demanded (moving down along the money demand curve) but not the demand for money.

3. What Federal Reserve policies would shift the money supply curve to the left?

An open market sale of government securities (bonds), an increase in reserve requirements, and/or an increase in the discount rates would shift the money supply curve to the left.

4. Will an increase in the money stock increase or decrease the short-run equilibrium real interest rate, other things equal?

An increase in the money stock would decrease the short-run equilibrium real interest rate, other things equal, as the rightward shift of the money supply curve pushes the money market equilibrium down along the money demand curve.

5. Will an increase in national income increase or decrease the short-run equilibrium real interest rate, other things equal?

An increase in national income would shift the money demand curve to the right, which would increase the short-run equilibrium real interest rate, other things equal.

6. What is the relationship between interest rates and aggregate demand in monetary policy?

Lower interest rates will tend to stimulate aggregate demand for goods and services, other things equal.

7. How will an expansionary monetary policy impact real GDP and the price level at less than full employment?

An expansionary monetary policy shifts aggregate demand to the right. Starting from less than full employment, the result will be an increase in the price level, an increase in real output, and a decrease in unemployment, as the economy moves up along the short-run aggregate supply curve. This increased output would be sustainable if it did not exceed the natural level of real output.

8. How will an expansionary monetary policy impact real GDP and the price level at full employment?

An expansionary monetary policy shifts aggregate demand to the right. Starting from full employment, the result in the short run will be an increase in the price level, an increase in real output, and a decrease in unemployment. However, because the increase in real output is not sustainable, the long-run result will be real output returning to its natural level, but prices that have risen even more, where the new aggregate demand curve intersects the long-run aggregate supply curve.

Concept E

1. Why is the lag time for adopting policy changes shorter for monetary policy than for fiscal policy?

The lag time for adopting monetary policy changes is shorter than for fiscal policy because those decisions are not slowed by the budgetary process that fiscal tax and expenditure policy changes must go through.

2. Why would a banking system that wanted to keep some excess reserves rather than lending them all out hinder the Fed's ability to increase the money stock?

A desire by the banking system to keep some excess reserves would reduce the money stock, other things equal. Therefore, such a change would at least partly offset the effects of the Fed's expansionary policy changes, which would hinder the Fed's ability to successfully use expansionary monetary policy to increase the money stock.

3. How can the activities of global and nonbank institutions weaken the Fed's influence on the money market?

The Fed has no control over global and nonbank institutions that issue credit (loan money); these institutions are not subject to reserve requirement limitations. Thus, the Fed cannot control their behavior, nor the resulting effects of their activities on the economy, through its policies.

4. If fiscal policy was expansionary, but the Fed wanted to counteract the fiscal policy effect on aggregate demand, what could it do?

Expansionary fiscal policy would increase aggregate demand. To counteract that fiscal policy effect on aggregate demand, the Fed would want to adopt contractionary monetary policy (through an open market sale of government securities, an increase in reserve requirements, and/or an increase in the discount rate), which would tend to reduce aggregate demand, other things equal.

5. What are the arguments for and against having monetary policy be more directly controlled by the political process?

The argument for having monetary policy be more directly controlled by the political process is basically that because fiscal policy is already determined by the political process, and monetary policy (which is not determined by the same political process) can offset or even neutralize the macroeconomic effects of fiscal policy, it would be better for all macroeconomic policy to be directly controlled by the political process. The argument against having monetary policy be more directly controlled by the political process is that it would be dangerous to turn over control of the nation's money stock to politicians, rather than allowing monetary policy decisions made by technically competent administrators who are focused more on price stability and are more insulated from political pressures from the public and special interest groups.

6. How is fine-tuning the economy like driving a car with an unpredictable steering lag on a winding road?

Fine-tuning the economy is like driving a car with an unpredictable steering lag on a winding road, because to steer the economy successfully requires that policy makers have an accurate map of both which way and how rapidly the economy is headed; that they know exactly how much each possible policy would affect the economy, so that they "turn the policy wheels" just the right amount; and that they know how long it will take each possible policy before it actually "turns" the economy.

Module 15: Inflation, Unemployment, and Expectations
Concept A

1. How does the rate of inflation affect real wage rates, if nominal wages rise less or more slowly than output prices?

When nominal wages rise less or more slowly than output prices, real wages (adjusted for inflation) fall.

2. How does the change in real wage rates (relative to output prices) as inflation increases affect the unemployment rate?

The fall in real wage rates (relative to output prices) as inflation increases reduces the unemployment rate, because the lower real wage rates make it profitable to hire more, now relatively cheaper, employees than before. This presumes that workers are not fully aware that their wages have fallen in real terms, however.

3. What is the argument for why the Phillips curve is relatively steeper at lower rates of unemployment and higher rates of inflation?

The argument is that once capacity utilization is high and unemployment is low, an increased part of the economy is already operating at or near full capacity, and further fiscal or monetary policy stimulus primarily triggers inflationary pressures in sectors already at capacity, while eliminating decreasing amounts of unemployment in those fewer sectors where excess capacity and high unemployment still exist.

4. For a given upward-sloping short-run aggregate supply curve, how does an increase in aggregate demand correspond to a movement up and to the left along a Phillips curve?

For a given upward-sloping short-run aggregate supply curve, an increase in aggregate demand moves the economy up along the short-run aggregate supply curve to an increased price level and increased real GDP. The increase in the price level is an increase in inflation and the increase in real GDP is accompanied by a decrease in unemployment, so the same effects are shown by a move up (higher inflation) and to the left (lower unemployment) along a Phillips curve.

Concept B

1. Is the Phillips curve stable over time?

No. While the short-run Phillips curve was once considered to be stable, economists now recognize that it is unstable and that it does not represent a permanent relationship between unemployment and inflation rates.

2. Why would you expect there to be no relationship between inflation and unemployment in the long run?

You would expect there to be no relationship between inflation and unemployment in the long run because the long run represents what happens once people have completely adjusted to changed conditions. Therefore, in the long run, actual and expected rates of inflation are the same, and change rates of inflation do not change people's "real" behavior (reflected in unemployment and real GDP) because those changes are not unexpected.

3. Why is the economy being on the long-run Phillips curve equivalent to it being on the long-run aggregate supply curve?

Unemployment equals its natural rate along the long-run Phillips curve. Real GDP is equal to its natural level along the long-run aggregate supply curve. But the natural level of real GDP is the output level consistent with unemployment equal to its natural rate, so points on both curves illustrate the same results.

4. Why would inflation have to accelerate over time to keep unemployment below its natural rate (and real output above its natural level) for a sustained period of time?

Inflation would have to accelerate over time to keep unemployment below its natural rate (and real output above its natural level) for a sustained period of time, because over time, people would adapt to any given level of inflation. Therefore, at a given rate of inflation, unemployment would return to its natural rate over time. To keep people "fooled" into unemployment below its natural rate requires more inflation than people expected, and to maintain this requires accelerating inflation over time.

5. What does the long-run Phillips curve say about the relationship between macroeconomic policy stimulus and unemployment in the long run?

The vertical long-run Phillips curve indicates that there is no relationship between macroeconomic policy stimulus and unemployment in the long run, once people have had time to completely adapt to it. Unemployment will equal its natural rate in the long run, and macroeconomic policy will therefore only change the inflation rate in the long run.

Concept C

1. What is the rational expectations theory?

Rational expectations theory incorporated expectations as a central factor in the analysis of the entire economy. It is essentially the idea that people will rationally anticipate the predictable future consequences of present decisions, and change their behavior today to reflect those future consequences. For example, this would mean that people can anticipate the inflationary long-run consequences of macroeconomic policies adopted today, and that anticipation leads them to change their current behavior in a way that can quickly neutralize the intended impact of a government action.

2. Why could an unexpected change in inflation change real wages and unemployment, while an expected change in inflation could not?

An unexpected change in inflation could change real wages and unemployment precisely because it was unexpected, and people were "fooled" into changing their behavior (in the short run). An expected change in inflation would not change real wages and unemployment because no one is fooled, so no one changes their real behavior as a result.

3. Why can the results of rational expectations be described as generating the long-run results of a policy change in the short run?

The long run refers to the situation once people have had time to completely adjust their behavior to current circumstances. But under rational expectations, the long-run consequences will be anticipated and responded to today, so that people have completely adjusted their behavior to new policies in the short run. Therefore, the results of rational expectations can be described as generating the long-run results of a policy change in the short run.

4. In a world of rational expectations, why is it harder to reduce unemployment below its natural rate but potentially easier to reduce inflation rates?

Reducing unemployment below its natural rate requires that inflation is greater than expected. But under rational expectations, people are not fooled by inflationary policies (unless they are sur-

prises), so this is very hard to do. It is potentially easier to reduce inflation rates under rational expectations, though, because people will be more quickly convinced that inflation will fall when credible government policies are put in place, and it will not take an extended period of high unemployment before they adapt to the lower inflation rate that results.

5. Even if individuals could quickly anticipate the consequences of government policy changes, how could long-term contracts (e.g., 3-year labor agreements and 30-year fixed-rate mortgages) and the costs of changing price lists and catalogs result in unemployment still being affected by those policy changes?

Even if individuals could quickly anticipate the consequences of government policy changes, long-term contracts can't be instantly adjusted, so the real prices and wages subject to such contracts will be at least temporarily changed by inflation "surprises," at least until such contracts can be rewritten. Similarly, price lists and catalogs will not be changed instantly when new policies are adopted because of the cost of doing so, and those prices will not instantly adapt to new inflationary expectations. Because these prices will be "wrong" for a period after new policies are adopted, real wages and prices, and therefore unemployment, can still be affected by policy changes for a period of time.

6. Why do expected rainstorms have different effects on people than unexpected rainstorms?

Expected rainstorms don't catch you by surprise, so you prepare for them in a way that minimizes their effects (umbrellas, jackets, etc.). Unexpected rainstorms catch you by surprise and have much greater effects, because you haven't prepared for them.

Concept D

1. In what ways might "voluntary" government inflation guidelines not be completely voluntary?

"Voluntary" government inflation guidelines are not completely voluntary because such guidelines are backed up with threats of involuntary controls or other consequences for those that don't comply with them.

2. If holding down legal price increases through price controls reduces official inflation rates, why are black markets likely to arise?

Price controls hold official prices below their equilibrium levels, creating shortages at those prices. The shortages at official prices leads to black markets, where unofficial prices can move toward their equilibrium levels.

3. How might wage and price controls lead to shortages of goods and services (a "queuetopia")?

For wage and price controls to restrain price increases, they must be held below their equilibrium levels. But below-equilibrium prices will lead to shortages of those goods and services, which can result in queues.

4. How might wage and price controls lead to the production of inferior products over time?

Wage and price controls lead to shortages at official prices. Because prices for given quality goods are not allowed to rise, the same sort of adjustment to a higher price per "unit" of quality is accomplished by lowering quality instead.

5. If every possible good was indexed to changes in the general price level, would it be very easy for relative price changes to signal changing relative scarcities? Why or why not?

When all prices tend to change together (e.g., when one price goes up, the price level goes up, and so other indexed prices also go up as a result), it is harder for relative prices to change to reflect changing relative scarcity.

Module 16: International Trade
Concept A

1. Why is it important to understand the effects of international trade?

All countries are affected by international trade, although the magnitude of the international trade sector varies substantially by country. International connections mean that any of a large number of disturbances that originate elsewhere will have important consequences for the domestic economy.

2. Why would producers and consumers in the United States be more concerned about Canadian trade restrictions than Swedish trade restrictions?

The United States and Canada are the two largest trading partners in the world. That means the effects of trade restrictions into Canada would have a far larger magnitude effect on the United States than similar restrictions imposed by Sweden (although for certain items, we have a larger magnitude of trade with Sweden than with Canada, so Swedish restrictions would then be of more concern for such items).

Concept B

1. Why do people voluntarily choose to specialize and trade?

Voluntary specialization and trade among self-interested parties only takes place because all of the parties involved expect that their benefits from that specialization (according to comparative advantage) and exchange will exceed their costs.

2. How could a country have an absolute advantage in producing one good or service without also having a comparative advantage in its production?

If one country was absolutely more productive at everything than another country, but it wasn't equally more productive at everything, there would still be some things it had a comparative disadvantage in. For instance, if country A was three times as productive in making X and two times as productive in making Y as country B, it would have a comparative advantage in making X (it gives up less Y for each X produced) and a comparative disadvantage in making Y (it gives up more X for each Y produced), relative to country B.

3. Why do you think the introduction of the railroad reduced self-sufficiency in the United States?

Prior to the introduction of the railroad, the high cost of transportation overwhelmed the gains from specializing according to comparative advantage in much of the United States (production cost differences were smaller than the costs of transportation). The railroads reduced transportation costs enough that specialization and exchange became beneficial for more goods and services, and self-sufficiency caused by high transportation costs declined.

4. If you can do the dishes in two-thirds the time it takes your younger sister, do you have a comparative advantage in doing the dishes compared to her?

We can't know the answer to this question without more information. It is not the time taken to do the dishes that matters in determining comparative advantage, but the opportunity cost of the time in terms of foregone value elsewhere. If your younger sister is less than two-thirds as good at other chores than you, she is relatively better at doing the dishes, and so would have a comparative advantage in doing the dishes. If she is more than two-thirds as good at other chores, she is relatively better at those chores, and so would have a comparative disadvantage in doing the dishes.

Concept C

1. How does voluntary trade generate both producer and consumer surplus?

Voluntary trade generates consumer surplus because a rational consumer will not purchase a good if he does not value the benefits of that purchase at greater than its cost, and consumer surplus is the difference between that value and the cost consumers are forced to pay. Voluntary trade generates producer surplus because a rational producer will not sell additional units unless the price he receives is greater than his marginal cost, and producer surplus is the difference between the revenues received and the costs producers must bear to produce the goods that generate those revenues.

2. If the world price of a good is greater than the domestic price prior to trade, why does that imply that the domestic economy has a comparative advantage in producing that good?

If the world price of a good is greater than the domestic price prior to trade, that implies that the domestic marginal opportunity cost of production is less than the world marginal opportunity cost of production. This means that the domestic economy has a comparative advantage in that good.

3. If the world price of a good is less than the domestic price prior to trade, why does that imply that the domestic economy has a comparative disadvantage in producing that good?

If the world price of a good is less than the domestic price prior to trade, this implies that the domestic marginal opportunity cost of production is greater than the world marginal opportunity cost of production. This means that the domestic economy has a comparative disadvantage in that good.

4. When a country has a comparative advantage in the production of a good, why do domestic producers gain more than domestic consumers lose from free international trade?

When a country has a comparative advantage in the production of a good, the marginal benefit from exporting is the world price, which is greater than the foregone value domestically (along the domestic demand curve) for those units of domestic consumption "crowded out," and greater than the marginal cost of the expanded output. Therefore, there are net domestic gains to international trade (the gains to domestic producers exceeds the losses to domestic consumers).

5. When a country has a comparative disadvantage in the production of a good, why do domestic consumers gain more than domestic producers lose from free international trade?

When a country has a comparative disadvantage in producing a good, the marginal cost of importing is the world price, which is less than the additional value (along the domestic demand curve) for those units of expanded domestic consumption and less than the marginal cost of the domestic production "crowded out." Therefore, there are net domestic gains to international trade (the gains to domestic consumers exceeds the losses to domestic producers).

6. Why do U.S. exporters, such as farmers, favor free trade more than U.S. producers of domestic products who face competition from foreign imports, such as the automobile industry?

Exporters favor free trade over restrictions on what they sell in other countries because that increases the demand, and therefore the prices, for their products, which raises their profits. Those who must compete with importers want those imports restricted rather than freely traded, because that increases the demand, and therefore the prices, for their domestically produced products, raising their profits.

Concept D

1. Why do tariffs increase domestic producer surplus but decrease domestic consumer surplus?

Tariffs raise the price of imported goods to domestic consumers, which also results in higher prices received by domestic producers. The higher price reduces domestic consumer surplus but increases domestic producer surplus.

2. How do import tariffs increase employment in "protected" industries, but at the expense of a likely decrease in employment overall?

Import tariffs increase employment in "protected" industries because the barriers to lower-priced imports increase the demand faced by domestic producers, increasing their demand for workers. However, imports are the means by which foreigners get the dollars to buy our exports, so restricted imports will mean restricted exports (even more so if other countries retaliate with import restrictions of their own). In addition, by raising the prices domestic consumers pay for the protected products (remember that domestic consumers lose more than domestic producers gain from protectionism), consumers are made poorer in real terms, which will reduce demand for goods, and therefore the labor to make them, throughout the economy.

3. Why is the national security argument for tariffs questionable?

The national security argument for tariffs is questionable because tariffs increase current reliance on domestic supplies, which depletes the future stockpile of available reserves. With fewer domestic reserves, the country will be even more dependent on foreign supplies in the future. Buying foreign supplies and stockpiling them makes more sense as a way of reducing reliance on foreign supplies in wartime.

4. Why is the domestic argument for import quotas weaker than the case for tariffs?

Tariffs at least use the price system as the basis of trade. Tariff revenues end up in a country's treasury, where they can be used to produce benefits for country's citizens or to reduce the domestic tax burden. Import quotas, however, transfer most of those benefits to foreign producers as the higher prices they receive.

5. Why would foreign producers prefer import quotas to tariffs, even if they resulted in the same reduced level of imports?

Restricting imports reduces supply, which increases the price foreign producers receive on the units they sell, benefiting them. Tariffs, on the other hand reduce the after-tariff price foreign producers receive. If both reduce foreign sales the same amount, foreign producers would clearly prefer import restrictions over tariffs.

6. Why does subsidizing exports by industries that lack a comparative advantage tend to harm the domestic economy, on net?

Subsidizing industries where a country has a comparative disadvantage (higher costs) must, by definition, require shifting resources from where it has a comparative advantage (lower costs) to where it has a comparative disadvantage. The value of the out-

put produced from those resources (indirectly in the case of specialization and exchange) is lower as a result.

Module 17: International Finance
Concept A

1. What is the balance of payments?

The balance of payments is the record of all of the international financial transactions of a nation—both those involving inflows of funds and those involving outflows of funds—over a year.

2. Why would a British purchaser of U.S. goods or services have to first exchange pounds for dollars?

Because U.S. goods and services are priced in dollars, a British consumer who wanted to buy U.S. goods would have to first buy dollars in exchange for English pounds before he could buy the U.S. goods and services with dollars. Ultimately, this is because input suppliers want to be paid in dollars so they can buy goods in the U.S. with their incomes.

3. How is it true that U.S. imports provide the means by which foreigners can buy U.S. exports?

The domestic currency Americans supply in exchange for the foreign currencies to buy imports also supplies the dollars with which foreigners can buy U.S. exports.

4. What would have to be true in order for the U.S. to have a balance of trade deficit and a balance of payments surplus?

A balance of trade deficit means that we imported more merchandise (goods) than we exported. A balance of payments surplus means that the sum of our goods and services exports exceeded the sum of our goods and services imports, plus funds transfers from the U.S. For both to be true would require a larger surplus of services (including net investment income) and/or net fund transfer inflows than our trade deficit in merchandise (goods).

5. What would have to be true in order for the U.S. to have a balance of trade surplus and a current account deficit?

A balance of trade surplus means that we exported more merchandise (goods) than we imported. A current account deficit means that our exports of goods and services (including net investment income) were less than the sum of our imports of goods and services, plus net fund transfers. For both to happen would require that the sum of our deficit in services plus net transfers must be greater than our surplus in merchandise (goods) trading.

6. If there are no errors or omissions in the recorded balance of payments accounts, what should the statistical discrepancy equal?

If there were no errors and/or omissions in the recorded balance of payments accounts, the statistical discrepancy should equal zero, because properly recorded, credits and debits must be equal, because every credit creates a debit of equal value.

7. A Nigerian family visiting Chicago enjoys a Chicago Cubs baseball game at Wrigley Field. How would that expense be recorded in the balance of payments accounts? Why?

This would be counted as an export of services, because it would provide Americans with foreign currency (a claim against Nigeria) in exchange for those services.

Concept B

1. What is an exchange rate?

An exchange rate is the price in one country's currency of one unit of another country's currency.

2. When a U.S. dollar buys relatively more French francs, why does the cost of imports from France fall in the United States?

When a U.S. dollar buys relatively more French francs, the cost of imports from France falls in the United States because it takes fewer U.S. dollars to buy a given number of French francs in order to pay French producers. In other words, the price in U.S. dollars of French goods and services has fallen.

3. When a U.S. dollar buys relatively fewer Austrian schillings, why does the cost of U.S. exports fall in Austria?

When a U.S. dollar buys relatively fewer Austrian schillings, the cost of U. S. exports falls in Austria because it takes fewer Austrian schillings to buy a given number of U.S. dollars in order to pay U.S. producers. In other words, the price in Austrian schillings of U.S. goods and services has fallen.

4. How does an increase in domestic demand for foreign goods and services increase the demand for those foreign currencies?

An increase in domestic demand for foreign goods and services increases the demand for those foreign currencies because the demand for foreign currencies is derived from the demand for foreign goods and services and foreign capital. The more foreign goods and services are demanded, the more of that foreign currency will be needed to pay for those goods and services.

5. As Euros get cheaper relative to U.S. dollars, why does the quantity of Euros demanded by Americans increase? Why doesn't the demand for Euros increase as a result?

As Euros get cheaper relative to U.S. dollars, European products become relatively more inexpensive to Americans, who therefore buy more European goods and services. To do so, the quantity of Euros demanded by U.S. consumers will rise to buy them, as the price (exchange rate) for Euros falls. The demand (as opposed to quantity demanded) of Euros doesn't increase, because this represents a movement along the demand for Euros caused by a change in exchange rates, rather than a change in demand for Euros caused by some other factor.

6. Who competes exchange rates down when they are above their equilibrium value? Who competes exchange rates up when they are below their equilibrium value?

When exchange rates are greater than their equilibrium value, there will be a surplus of the currency and frustrated sellers of that currency will bid its price (exchange rate) down. When exchange rates are less than their equilibrium value, there will be a shortage of the currency and frustrated buyers of that currency will bid its price (exchange rate) up.

Concept C

1. Why will the exchange value of a foreign currency relative to U.S. dollars decline when U.S. domestic tastes change, reducing the demand for foreign-produced goods?

When U.S. domestic tastes change, reducing the demand for foreign-produced goods, the reduced demand for foreign-produced goods will also reduce the demand for the foreign currencies to buy them. This reduced demand for those foreign currencies will reduce their exchange rates, relative to U.S. dollars.

2. Why does the demand for foreign currencies shift in the same direction as domestic income? What happens to the exchange value of those foreign currencies in terms of U.S. dollars?

An increase in domestic income increases the demand for goods and services, including imported goods and services. This increases the demand for those foreign currencies to buy those additional imports, which increases their exchange rates (the exchange value of those currencies), relative to U.S. dollars.

3. How would increased U.S. tariffs on imported European goods affect the exchange value of Euros in terms of dollars?

Increased U.S. tariffs on imported European goods would make them less affordable in the U.S. This would lead to a reduced demand for European goods in the U.S., and therefore a reduced demand for Euros. This would reduce the exchange value of Euros in terms of dollars.

4. Why do changes in tastes, incomes, or tariffs in the United States change the demand for Euros, while similar changes in Europe change the supply of Euros?

Changes in U.S. tastes, incomes, or tariffs change the demand for Euros because it changes U.S. demand for European goods and services, which changes the demand for Euros to buy them. Similar changes in Europe change the supply of Euros because they change the European demand for U.S. goods and services, thus changing their demand for dollars with which to buy those goods and services. This requires them to change their supply of Euros in order to get those dollars.

5. What would happen to the exchange value of Euros in terms of U.S. dollars if incomes rose in both Europe and the United States?

These changes would increase both the demand (higher incomes in the U.S.) and supply (higher income in Europe) of Euros. The effect on the exchange value of Euros would be determined by whether the supply or demand for Euros shifted more (rising if demand shifted relatively more and falling if supply shifted relatively more).

6. Why does an increase in interest rates in Germany relative to U.S. interest rates increase the demand for Euros but decrease their supply?

An increase in interest rates in Germany relative to U.S. interest rates increases the rates of return on German investments relative to U.S. investments. U.S. investors therefore increase their demand for German investments, increasing the demand for Euros to make those investments. This would also reduce the demand by German investors for U.S. investments, decreasing the supply of Euros with which to buy the dollars to make the investments.

7. What would an increase in U.S. inflation relative to Europe do to the supply and demand for Euros and to the equilibrium exchange value (price) of Euros in terms of U.S. dollars?

An increase in U.S. inflation relative to Europe would make U.S. products relatively more expensive to European customers, decreasing the U.S. goods and services demanded by European customers, and therefore decreasing the supply of Euros to buy the dollars necessary for those purchases. It would also make European products relatively cheaper to U.S. consumers, increasing the European goods and services demanded by U.S. consumers, and therefore increasing the demand for Euros necessary for those purchases. The decreased supply of and increased demand for Euros results in an increasing exchange value of Euros in terms of U.S. dollars.

Concept D

1. What are the arguments for and against flexible exchange rates?

The arguments for flexible exchange rates include: the large expansion of world trade under flexible exchange rates; the fact that they allowed the economy to adjust to a quadrupling in the price of the world's most important internationally traded commodity—oil; and especially that it diminished the recurring crises that caused speculative rampages and currency revaluations, allowing the market mechanism to address currency shortages and world trade imbalances. The arguments against flexible exchange rates are that it increases exchange rate uncertainty in international trade and can contribute to inflationary pressures, due to the lack of the fixed-rate system's incentives to constrain domestic policies that would erode net exports.

2. When the U.S. dollar starts to exchange for fewer Japanese yen, other things equal, what happens to U.S. and Japanese imports and exports as a result?

When the U.S. dollar starts to exchange for fewer Japanese yen, other things equal, the U.S. cost of Japanese imports rises, decreasing the value of Japanese exports to the United States. It also decreases the cost to the Japanese of buying U.S. goods, increasing the value of U.S. exports to Japan.

3. Why is the system of flexible exchange rates sometimes called a "dirty float" system?

The system of flexible exchange rates is sometimes called a "dirty float" system because governments do intervene at times in foreign currency markets to alter their currencies' exchange rates, so that exchange rates are partly determined by market forces and partly by government intervention.

4. Were exchange rates under the Bretton Woods system really stable? How could you argue that exchange rates were more uncertain under the fixed-rate system than with floating exchange rates?

Exchange rates under the Bretton Woods system were not really stable. While exchange rate changes were infrequent, they were large, with large effects. It could be argued that the less frequent but larger exchange rate changes that were common under the Bretton Woods system generated more uncertainty than the more frequent but smaller exchange rate changes that occur with the floating exchange rate system.

5. What is the uncertainty argument against flexible exchange rates? What evidence do proponents of flexible exchange rates cite in response?

The uncertainty argument against flexible exchange rates is that flexible exchange rates add another source of uncertainty to world trade, which would increase the cost of international transactions, reducing the magnitude of international trade. Proponents of flexible exchange rates cite the faster growth of international trade since the introduction of flexible exchange rates, the fact that markets exist on which to hedge exchange rate risks (through forward, or futures, markets), and that the alleged exchange rate certainty was fictitious, because large changes could take place at a nations' whim.

6. Do flexible exchange rates cause higher rates of inflation? Why or why not?

Flexible exchange rates do not cause higher rates of inflation. However, they do reduce the incentives to constrain domestic inflation for fear of reducing net exports under the fixed exchange rate system. Inflation, though is ultimately caused by expansionary macroeconomic policies adopted by governments and their central banks.

aggregate demand (AD)   The sum of the demand for all goods and services in the economy. It reflects the total amounts of real goods and services that all groups together want to purchase in a given time period.

aggregate supply (AS)   The relationship between the total quantity of final goods and services that suppliers are willing and able to produce and the overall price level.

assets   Something of value held by a person or a firm.

asset demand   Money individuals hold as a store of value.

automatic stabilizers   Changes in government transfer payments or tax collections that automatically tend to counter business cycle fluctuations.

autonomous (independent) investment   Investment not determined by the level of income.

average propensity to consume (APC)   The fraction of total income that households spend on consumption.

bads   Items that we do not desire or want.

balance of payments   A statement that records all of the exchanges that those in a nation engaged in that required an outflow of funds to foreign nations or an inflow of funds from other nations.

balance sheet   A financial record that indicates the balance between a bank's assets and its liabilities plus capital.

barter   Trade in goods and services without the use of money.

boom   A prolonged expansion in economic activity.

budget deficit   What occurs when government spending exceeds tax revenue during a particular time period, usually a year.

budget surplus   When tax revenues are greater than government spending during a particular time period, usually a year.

business cycles   Short-term fluctuations in the level of economic activity, relative to the long-term trend in output.

capital consumption allowance   Another name for depreciation.

capital   Human-made resources used to produce final goods (e.g., office buildings, tools, machines, and factories).

capital intensive   A method of production using a relatively large amount of capital.

ceteris paribus   Let everything else be equal; holding everything else constant.

change in quantity demanded   The amount of a good that people are willing to buy at a given price.

change in quantity supplied   The amount of a good that producers are willing to sell at a given price.

circular flow model of income and output   A model that illustrates continuous flow of goods, services, and payments among businesses and households.

commercial banks   Banks organized chiefly to handle everyday financial transactions of businesses through demand deposit accounts and short-term commercial loans.

comparative advantage   A condition in which a person, a region, or a country can produce a good or service at a lower opportunity cost than others.

complementary goods   Things that go together and are often consumed and used simultaneously.

consumer price index (CPI)   The standard measure of inflation; it provides a measure of the trend in the prices of certain goods and services purchased for consumption.

consumer sovereignty   The consumer is "king" concept that individuals control the production decisions in mixed market economies by "voting" with their dollars.

consumer surplus   The difference between the maximum amount the consumer is willing to pay and what the consumer is required to pay.

consumption goods   Goods we consume that bring us immediate satisfaction, like food and clothing.

corporate income taxes   Income taxes levied on corporations.

cost-push inflation   Inflation caused by a leftward shift in the short-run aggregate supply curve.

crowding out effect   The theory that as the government borrows to pay for the deficit, it drives up the interest rates and crowds out private spending and investment.

currency   Coins and/or paper that some institution or government has created to be used in the trading of goods and services and the payment of debts.

cyclical unemployment   Unemployment due to a drop in the demand for labor caused by a recession.

deflation   A decrease in the overall price level of goods and services in the economy.

demand deposits   Non-interest earning in checking deposits.

demand-pull inflation   A price level increase resulting in an increase in aggregate demand.

dependent variable   A variable that depends on the independent variables.

depreciation   Annual allowance set aside for the replacement of wornout plant and equipment.

direct relationship   Variables move in the same direction. (See *positive relationship*.)

discount rate   The interest rate that the Fed charges commercial banks.

discouraged worker   Individuals who give up looking for a job because they believe they will not find a suitable one.

disposable income   Individual income available after personal taxes.

dissave   Persons consume more than their total income.

division of labor When production is broken down into specific tasks.

durable goods Longer-lived consumer goods, including automobiles, appliances, and furniture.

economic goods Scarce goods that are created from scarce resources.

economic growth An upward trend in the real output of goods and services.

economics The study of the allocation of our scarce resources to satisfy our unlimited wants for goods and services.

efficiency Getting the most from scarce resources.

eminent domain Right of the government to assume ownership of private property if compensation is made to the original owners.

Employment Act of 1946 Act passed that committed the United States to policies designed to reduce unemployment in a manner consistent with price stability.

entrepreneur Decision maker who decides how to combine land, labor, and capital together, which goods or services to produce, how many to produce, and so on.

entrepreneurship Decision-making input that is concerned with the application of resources and with identifying new possibilities, new products, and new methods of production.

equation of exchange M (money supply) times V (velocity of circulation) = P (average level of prices of final goods and services times Q (physical quantity of final goods and services produced in a given period).

equilibrium price The price at which quantity demanded equals the quantity supplied.

equilibrium quantity The quantity bought and sold at the equilibrium price.

excess reserves The actual reserves of a bank minus its required reserves.

exchange rate The price in one country's currency of one unit of another country's currency.

excludability The ability to exclude individuals from using a particular good.

expenditure approach A method of measuring GDP in which GDP is calculated by adding up the expenditures of market participants on final goods and services over a period of time.

externality Occurs whenever there are physical impacts (benefits or costs) of an activity on individuals not directly involved in the activity.

factor market A market where the factors of production (e.g., land, labor, and capital) are bought and sold.

factor payments Payments to the owners of productive resources.

fallacy of composition Even if something is true for an individual, it is not necessarily true for many individuals as a group.

federal funds market A market in which banks that provide cash to other banks who have short-term needs for cash to meet reserve requirements.

fiat money A means of exchange that has been established by government declaration, not by custom or tradition.

fiscal policy The use of government purchases, taxes, and transfer payments to alter equilibrium GDP and price levels.

fixed investments All new spending on capital goods by producers.

flat tax A tax designed so that everyone is charged the same percentage of income above some certain stipulated income level.

fractional reserve banking A system in which banks are required to keep reserves in the Federal Reserve equal to some fraction of their checkable deposits.

free rider A person who does not pay for the benefits received from a public good.

frictional unemployment Unemployment resulting from constant changes in the economy that make it difficult to match qualified unemployed workers with current job openings.

GDP deflator A price index that helps to measure the average level of prices of all consumer goods and services produced in the economy.

gold standard The dollar is defined as equivalent in value to a certain amount of gold, and paper currency or demand deposits could be freely converted to gold coin.

goods Objects that can be seen, held, heard, tasted, or smelled.

Gresham's Law "Cheap money drives out dear money." When there are two forms of money available, people prefer to spend the form of money that is less valuable.

gross domestic product (GDP) The value of all final goods and services produced within a country during a given period of time.

human capital People used as resources in production.

import quota The maximum number of units of a good that can be imported within any given time span.

income approach A method of measuring GDP in which GDP is calculated by summing the incomes received by producers of goods and services.

independent variable A variable that is not influenced by any other variable; it is determined outside the relationship in question.

indeterminate Change in price or quantity that cannot be determined without additional information about the size of the relative shift in supply and demand.

indexing The process of adjusting payment contracts to automatically adjust for changes in inflation.

indirect business taxes Taxes, like sales taxes, that are levied on goods that are sold.

individual-consumption-payment link In a private market, an individual selects what he or she wants and is willing to pay for it.

induced investment Investment that results when businesses decide to proceed with an investment on the basis of increases in income or output.

inelastic demand The percentage change in quantity demanded is less than the percentage change in price.

inferior goods Goods for which rising income leads to reduced demand.

inflation A situation in which the overall price level is rising, resulting in a fall of the purchasing power of money.

intangible goods Goods that are less overtly visible, such as friendship, knowledge, security, intelligence, and health.

interest rate The price of borrowed funds.

inventory investment Includes all purchases by businesses that add to their inventories.

investment Refers to the creation of capital goods.

investment goods Goods that help increase the output of goods and services in future time periods, thus providing us with satisfaction at a later date.

investment tax credits Allow businesses to accelerate the speed that they can write off some of their new investments for tax purposes, raising after-tax rates of return on investment.

job-entry discrimination A situation in which a worker is denied employment on the basis of some non-economic factor, such as race, religion, sex, or ethnic origin.

labor Resource that includes the total of physical and mental effort expended by people in the economy.

labor force The number of people over the age of 16 who are either employed or unemployed.

labor intensive Production that uses a relatively high level of labor input.

land Resource that includes all natural resources coming from the earth (e.g., trees, animals, water, and minerals), as well as physical space.

law of demand The quantity of a good or service demanded varies inversely with its price, *ceteris paribus*. Other things being equal, when the price of a good or service falls, the quantity demanded increases, and conversely, if the price of a good or service rises, the quantity demanded decreases.

law of supply The quantity supplied will vary directly with the price of the good, other things being equal.

law of unintended consequences The results of actions are not always as initially intended.

legal tender Instrument declared by the U.S. government to be acceptable for the settlement of debts incurred in financial transactions.

long-run aggregate supply Refers to a period long enough for the prices of outputs and all inputs to fully adjust to changes in the economy.

long-run Phillips curve Shows the relationship between the inflation rate and the unemployment rate when the actual and expected inflation rates are the same.

M1 Narrow definition of money that includes currency, checkable deposits, and travelers checks.

M2 Broader definition of money encompassing M1 plus savings accounts, time deposits, and money market mutual funds.

macroeconomics Branch of economics that deals with the total economy and looks at economic problems as they influence the whole of society.

marginal propensity to consume (MPC) The additional consumption that results from an additional dollar of income.

market A set of rules or an arrangement for the negotiation of exchange between buyers and sellers.

market demand curve The horizontal summing of the demand curves of many individuals.

market economy An economy that uses a decentralized decision-making process to determine what to produce.

market failure Situation in which the economy fails to allocate resources efficiently on its own.

market supply curve The horizontal summation of the supply curves for individual firms.

measure of economic welfare (MEW) A measure of economic activity that adds the value of positive externalities and subtracts the value of negative externalities to GDP.

Medicare A federal health insurance plan for the elderly and other qualified individuals.

menu costs A cost inflation that firms incur as a result of being forced to change posted prices.

microeconomics Branch of economics that deals with the smaller units within the economy, attempting to understand the decision-making behavior of firms and households and their interaction in markets for particular goods or services.

minimum-wage rate Standard wage set by the federal government.

mixed economies Economies in which some production decisions are made centrally by the government, while other decisions are made through the interaction of individual producers and purchasers.

money Anything that is generally accepted in exchange for goods or services.

money market The market where money demand and money supply determine the equilibrium interest rate.

money market mutual funds Interest-earning accounts provided by brokers who pool funds into investments like Treasury bills.

money multiplier The reciprocal of the reserve ratio. It is equal to 1 divided by the required reserve ratio.

money price The price that consumers would pay in dollars and cents.

moral suasion Federal Reserve's indirect influence upon banks to follow a particular course of action.

multiplier effect   Chain reaction of additional income and purchases that results in a final increase in total purchases that is greater than the initial increase in purchases.

national income (NI)   The total of factor payments to the owners of resources.

national income accounting   Uniform means of measuring national economic performance.

natural rate of unemployment   The sum of frictional unemployment and structural unemployment when they are at a maximum.

near money   Nontransaction deposits that are not money but that can be quickly converted into money.

negative externality   A cost that spills over to an outside party not involved in the production or consumption of the good or service.

negative incentives   Incentives that either reduce benefits or increase costs, resulting in a decrease in the level of the related activity or behavior.

negative relationship   Two variables move in different directions. (See *inverse relationship.*)

nominal interest rate   Interest rate not corrected for inflation.

nondurable goods   Tangible consumer items that are typically consumed or used up in a relatively short period of time.

non-income expense items   Indirect taxes and depreciation.

nonpecuniary   No outlay of money occurs.

normal good   A good that is in greater demand as a result of higher incomes.

normative statements   Opinions expressed about the desirability of various actions.

open market operations   The purchase and sale of government securities by the Federal Reserve system.

opportunity cost   The highest or best foregone opportunity resulting from a decision.

own-price   The price of a good or service.

payroll taxes   Taxes levied on payrolls (work-related income).

per capita gross domestic product   Real output of goods and services per person.

personal income (PI)   Measures the amount of income received by individuals before they pay personal income taxes.

permanent income hypothesis   Consumption is related to permanent income rather than to current income levels.

personal income taxes   Income taxes levied on individuals.

Phillips curve   A curve showing the relationship between the annual rate of increase in the price level and the unemployment rate.

pollution tax   Tax levied on a firm for polluting the environment.

positive analysis   Objective, value-free approach that uses the scientific method.

positive externality   A market activity that has a positive physical impact on an outside party.

positive incentives   Incentives that either increase benefits or reduce costs, resulting in an increase in the level of the related activity or behavior.

positive relationship   Variables move in the same direction. (See *direct relationship.*)

precautionary demand   An individual's inclination to hold money in case of emergency or other unexpected expenses.

price   The amount of money one has to pay for a good or service.

price ceiling   Government-imposed maximum prices set for goods deemed important.

price controls   Government policies forcing prices above or below what they would be in a market economy.

price floor   Government-imposed minimum prices set for goods.

price index   A measurement that attempts to provide a measure of the trend in prices paid for a certain bundle of goods and services over time.

price level   The average level of all prices in the economy.

producer surplus   The difference between the least a supplier is willing to supply a quantity of a good or service for and the revenues a supplier actually receives for selling it.

progressive tax   Tax designed so that those with higher incomes pay a greater proportion of their income in taxes.

property rights   The broad powers individuals have to use, sell, rent, dispose of, or enhance the value of their goods.

public choice theory   The theory that the behavior of individuals in politics is influenced by self-interest.

public good   Good with properties of being nonrival in consumption (one person's usage of it does not diminish another's ability to use it) and nonexclusive (no one can be excluded from using it), such as national defense.

purchasing power parity   Allows us to estimate the number of units of currency needed in one country to buy the same amount of goods and services that one unit of currency will buy in another country.

real interest rate   Interest rate corrected for inflation.

regressive taxes   Tax that takes a greater proportion of the income of lower-income groups than higher-income groups.

relative price   The price of one good relative to others.

required reserve ratio   Percentage of deposits that a bank must keep at the Federal Reserve Bank.

resources   Inputs, like land, labor, and capital, that are used to make goods and services

Ricardian equivalency theorem   Theory that an increase in government spending will lead to higher taxes in the future, other things equal.

rule of rational choice People alter their behavior if the expected marginal benefits to them from doing so outweigh the expected marginal costs they will bear.

savings and loan associations Cooperative associations organized to hold savings of members in the form of dividend-bearing shares and to invest chiefly in home mortgage loans.

scarcity The result that occurs when our wants exceed what our resources can produce.

seasonal unemployment Unemployment that occurs because certain types of jobs are seasonal in nature.

self-interest Motivation that causes people to improve their own situation.

services Intangible items of value, such as education and health care, as opposed to physical goods.

shocks Unexpected aggregate supply or aggregate demand changes.

shoe leather cost The inflation cost of going to and from the bank to check on your assets.

shortage A condition where the quantity demanded is greater than the quantity supplied, at the current price.

short-run aggregate supply Refers to a period when output can change in response to supply and demand, but input prices have not yet been able to adjust.

social costs The full resource cost of an activity including the external cost.

special-interest groups Political pressure groups formed by individuals with common political objectives to influence decision makers.

specialization Concentrating production in the hands of the most efficient producers.

stagflation Phenomenon caused when lower growth and higher prices occur together.

structural unemployment Reflects the existence of persons who lack the necessary skills for jobs that are available.

subsidy A payment to a producer from the government.

substitute good A good that can replace another good.

surplus A condition where the quantity supplied is greater than the quantity demanded at the current price.

tariff A tax on imports.

theory of rational expectations Belief that wages and prices are highly flexible and that workers and consumers quickly incorporate the likely consequences of government policy changes into their expectations.

time-series graph A graph that shows changes over time.

transaction costs The costs of making exchanges or transactions in a market.

transactions demand The tendency for individuals to keep cash on hand for the purposes of exchange.

travelers checks Transaction instruments that can be easily converted into currency.

underground economy Unreported cash and barter transactions.

unemployment rate Percent of the population over the age of 16 who are willing and able to work but are unable to obtain a job; calculated by dividing the number of people unemployed by the number in the labor force.

variable A quantity that can take on different numeric values.

wage and price controls Legislation limiting wage and price increases.

wage discrimination A situation in which workers are given employment at wages lower than those of other workers on some basis other than productivity differences, such as race or sex.

A

aggregate demand (AD)
 consumption and, **256**–257
 El Niño and, 282
 expansionary monetary policy and, 377
 fiscal policy and, 295
 money/interest rates and, 358–361
 Phillips curve and, 371
 supply-side policies and, 306–307
aggregate demand curve
 multiplier process and, 292
 overview of, **261**–263
 shifts in, 264–266
aggregate income (1997), 239
aggregate supply (AS)
 described, **272**
 El Niño and, 282
 natural disasters and, 277
 Phillips curve and, 371
aggregate supply curve
 overview of, 272–274
 shifts in, 275–278
 short-run, 272, 273, 275–277, 278
 long-run, 272–276, 306
agricultural price supports, 25
alcohol
 driving and use of, 20
 survey on high school students and, 19
Alm, Richard, 250, 251, 252
anticipated demand, 133–134
anticipated inflation, 195–196
anti-theft devices, 77
Arab oil boycott (1973), 380
assets
 bank's, 331–332
 considered to be money, 322
 money as, 327
association, 49
automatic stabilizers, 303–304
**autonomous (independent) investment,
 258**
average propensity to consume (APC), 257

B

bads, 8
balanced budget amendment, 312–313
balance of payments, 408–411
balance sheet, 331, 332–333
Banff (Canada), 84
Bank of America, 342
BankAmerica Corp., 337
banking industry, 337
banking system collapse (1930–1933),
 339–340
banks. *See* commercial banks
Barro, Robert, 383

barter system, **324**–325
Barth, Steve, 391
Baywatch (TV show), 391
Bergsten, Fred, 427
Bhagwati, Jagdish, 405, 406
Big Mac index, 418–419
Bok, Chip, 171
bowed production possibility curve, 70–71
box-office leaders, 242
Bretton Woods fixed exchange rate
 system, 421
Browning, John, 219
Buchanan, James M., 162
budget deficit
 described, **288**–289
 financing the, 310–311
budget surplus, 288, 295–297
Bureau of Labor Statistics (BLS), 184,
 185, 244
Burns, Arthur, 366
business cycles, 200–201, 202

C

Cabbage Patch Dolls, 133–134
Canseco, José, 225
capital
 aggregate supply and, 275–276
 bank's, 332
 described, **66**, 67
 economic growth and physical, 218
 human, 82
capital account, 410
capital consumption allowance, 238
capital goods, 67
capital intensive, 76
capital stock, 215
capital utilization rates, 259
Carter, Jimmy, 366
causation, 49–50
ceteris paribus **assumption**
 on aggregate demand curve, 264–265
 on aggregate supply curve, 275, 277
 on anticipated inflation/interest rates,
 195–196
 on complementary goods, 101–102
 described, **48**–49
 on higher tax rates, 306
 law of demand and, 92
 on per capita gross domestic product,
 245
 relative price and, 91
Champagne, Norm, 97
change in demand, 99
changes in quantity demanded, 99
changes in quantity supplied, 110
charity, 9

Chase Manhattan, 354
cheating behavior, 19
checkable deposits, 319
Checkpoint Systems' RF anti-theft system,
 77
Chicago Bulls, 23
Chicago Tribune, 23
choices
 opportunity costs and, 12–13
 as primarily marginal, 15
 rule of rational, 15
 scarcity and, 10, 12
Churchill, Winston, 380
**circular flow model of income and
 output, 230**–231
Citibank, 342
Clark, Kim, 244
Clinton, Bill, 9, 244, 427
Clinton, Hillary Rodham, 366
Coca-Cola, 100
coffee/cocoa prices, 126
Coleco, 133–134
command economies, 73
commercial banks
 balance sheets of, 331, 332–333
 Fed's monetary policies implemented
 by, 363
 impact of changing reserve requirements
 on, 353
 overview of, **330**–334
 See also Federal Reserve System
comparative advantage
 described, **21**
 economic growth and, 220, 391
 international trade and, 391–394
 production possibilities curve and,
 394–395
 regional, 395–396
comparative economic systems, 74
complementary goods, 101–102
Conference Board, 267–268
consequences, 43
consumer confidence index, 267–268
Consumer Confidence Survey, 267
consumer price index (CPI), 193, 241, 244
consumer protection, 153–154
consumer sovereignty, 74
consumer surplus, 398
consumption (c), 150, 234, 256–257,
 264–265
consumption goods, 70
"Contract with America" (Republican
 Party), 312
contractionary fiscal policy, 296, 297
Corbett, Sara, 97
corporate income taxes, 169
 See also taxation

cost-of-living (COLA) clauses, 381
cost-push inflation, 280, 281
costs
    considering opportunity, 12–13
    government and information, 153–155
    graphing external, 146–147
    human behavior and, 93
    needs and, 95
    prices vs., 13–14
    transaction, 88, 384
    See also opportunity costs
Coulter, David, 337
credit cards, 320–321
creditors, 196
crowding out effect, 299–300
currency
    described, **318**–319
    fixed exchange rates and shortages of,
        422–423
    shifting demand/supply of, 415
    supply of foreign, 413
current account, 408–410
cyclical fluctuations, 201–202
cyclical unemployment, 189

D

decision making
    economic, 27, 32, 53
    production, 73–75
    rational, 15–16, 43
deficit. *See* budget deficit
deflation, 32
demand
    anticipated, 133–134
    application of shift in, 116–117
    change in, 99–106
    change in quantity, 99, 105–106
    combinations of shifts in supply and,
        130
    equilibrium price/quantity and
        changes in, 124–125, 126
    hypothetical schedule for, 120
    income elasticity of, 201
    international trade and, 398–400
    law of, 92–95
    option, 166
    Super Bowl tickets and, 140–141
    See also aggregate demand (AD); supply
demand curve
    individual, 96
    market, 97–98
    market disequilibrium and, 133–134
    overview of, 60–62
    shifts in, 99–106
    See also supply curve
demand deposits, 319–320
demand-pull inflation, 279–280
dependent variable, 58
depreciation, 238
determinants of demand (PYNTE), 120

Diana, Princess, 9
diminishing return law, 222
direct relationship, 60
discount rate, 354, 354, 355
discouraged workers, 183–184
dissave, 256
distribution, 78
disutility, 8
Dole, Bob, 244
double counting, 233
downward sloping curves, 62
durable goods, 234

E

Easterlin, Richard A., 223
economic behavior, 43–44
economic decision-making
    freedom vs. fairness in, 53
    government policies and, 27, 168–169
    on production, 73–75
    stable monetary environment and, 32
economic fluctuations, 200–203
economic freedom, 204–206
economic goods, 8
    See also goods
economic growth
    birth rates/death rates and, 214–215
    comparative advantage and, 220, 391
    defining, **210**–211
    desirability of, 223–224
    determinants of, 217–220
    economic freedom and, 204–206
    government intervention regarding, 158
    impact of Fed on, 355
    impact of, 212–213
    industralization and, 213
    investments and, 215
    literacy and, 214
    mobility of resources and, 215–216
    population growth and, 221–222
    production and, 81–83
    relative happiness and, 225–227
    in selected countries, 199
    self-sufficiency and, 216, 391
    technology and, 218–219
    urbanization and, 212, 213
    ways to increase, 30–31, 198
    See also trade
economic performance measurement,
    232–233
economics
    defining, **4**
    disagreement in, 53
    exchange, 230
    politics and, 201, 202
    as a science, 40–42
    ten powerful ideas of, 5
    to analyze human behavior, 4
economic theories
    described, 45
    development of, 45–46

    on economic freedom, 205
    from hypothesis to, 46–47
    rational expectations, 376–377
    validity of, 53–54
economic welfare, 246–249
economies
    GDP of selected country, 211
    impact of Fed on, 355
    impact of public deficit on, 310–311
    impact of tariffs on domestic, 399–400
    mixed, 74
    primitive, 230
    production decisions by, 73–74
economies of scale, 220
economists
    agreement among, 54–55
    public choice, 166–167
ecosystems, 84–85
education
    economic growth and, 214
    unemployment and, 184
efficiency, 80
electric car subsidy, 18
El Niño, 126, 282–283
eminent domain, 145
empirical analysis, 45–46
employment
    full, 191, 295, 296
    labor market and temporary, 372
Employment Act of 1946, 157, 180–**181**
enforcement costs, 34–35
entrepreneur, 67–68
entrepreneurship, 66
environmental assets, 248
Environmental Protection Agency, 224
equation of exchange, 349–350, 352
equilibrium
    of foreign exchange market, 413–414
    foreign exchange market and changes
        in, 415–418
equilibrium price
    changes in, 124–127
    changing demand/supply and, 129
    defining, **120**
equilibrium quantity
    changes in, 124–127
    changing demand/supply and, 129
    defining, **120**
European taste/income, 416, 417
exchange economy, 230
exchange rates
    described, **412**–414
    flexible, 421–424
    foreign, 413–414, 415–418
excise tax, 169
excludability of consumption, 150
expansionary fiscal policy, 289, 295, 296,
    301, 377
expectations
    about future goods, 104–105
    shifting supply and, 112

expenditure approach, 234
exports
   domestic trade and, 398–399
   GDP and, 236
   government spending/investment and
     net, 258–260
external benefits graph, 148
externalities
   defining, **146**
   GDP measurement of, 247
   negative, 146–147, 372–375
   non-government solutions to, 149
   positive, 146, 147–149

F

factor (or input) markets, 230
factor payments, 238
fallacy of composition, 50
Family Leave Act, 305–306
Federal Deposit Insurance Corporation
   (FDIC), 340
Federal Open Market Committee
   (FOMC), 348
Federal Reserve Board of Governors, 346
Federal Reserve System
   interest rates and, 361
   media and the, 356
   monetary policy implemented by,
     351–356
   overview of, 311, 346–348
   policy independence of, 366–367
fiat money, 319
financial institutions, 330
fiscal policy
   AD/AS models and, 295–297
   contractionary, 296, 297
   coordinated monetary and, 363–365
   defining, **288**–289
   during the 1960s, 308–309
   expansionary, 289, 295, 296
   obstacles to effective, 299–301
   supply-side, 305–307
   timing of, 301
five richest/poorest nations, 81
fixed investments, 235
flat tax, 170, 172
flexible exchange rates, 421–424
Food and Drug Administration (FDA), 305
Ford, Henry, 67
foreign currency supply, 413
foreign exchange market
   equilibrium changes in, 415–417
   equilibrium of, 413–414
four Ts (technology, taxes, tampering,
   temperature), 112–114
fractional reserve system, 331
"free lunch," 13
free rider problem, 150–151
free trade. *See* trade
frictional unemployment, 188

Friedman, Milton, 256
full employment, 191, 295, 296, 360

G

gasoline prices, 90, 126
Gates, Bill, 5, 67, 68, 276
GDP deflator, 241
gender factor, 184–185
General Agreement on Tariffs and Trade
   (GATT), 405
Gingrich, Newt, 244
global warming, 56
gold standard, 327–328
Gone with the Wind, 242, 250
goods
   comparative advantage and, 21
   complementary, 101–102
   consumption and investment, 70
   defining, **7**–8
   distribution of, 78
   economic, 8
   exchange rates and demand for foreign,
     412–413
   expectations about future, 104–105
   intangible, 7
   measuring value of, 232
   nondurable and durable, 234
   normal and inferior, 103
   number of buyers for, 104
   price of closely related, 110–111
   producer, 235
   production of, 76
   public, 150–151
   substitute, 100–101
   taste changes and, 104
   utility/disutility of, 8
government
   changing role of, 168
   collecting revenues from import quotas,
     401–402
   current account and, 409
   externalities and, 146–149
   the Fed and Congress of, 367
   Federal Reserve relationship with,
     347–348
   financing budget deficit, 310
   full employment and, 185
   growing economic role of, 168–169
   income distribution and, 159–161
   information costs and, 153–155
   methods for controlling, 165–166
   property rights and, 144–145
   public goods and, 150–151
   revenue generated by, 169
   revenue of state/local, 170
   transportation bill passed by, 171
   See also United States
government intervention
   growing economic interests and,
     157–158

helmet law debate and, 174–175
government policies
   economic decision-making and, 27
   law of unintended consequences and, 28
   See also fiscal policy
government regulations
   aggregate supply and, 276
   positive externalities and, 149
   supply curve and, 305–306
   as supply shifters, 112
   to control negative externality, 147
   on wage and price controls, 196, 379–381
government spending
   aggregate demand curve and, 265–266
   changing role of, 168
   fiscal conservatives on, 171
   GDP and, 236, 289
   generating revenue for, 169–170
   government economic role and, 168–169
   investment/net exports and, 258–260
   sources for state/local, 170
government subsidies, 148, 160, 404
Great Depression, 168, 182–183, 339–340,
   360
Great Society programs, 309
Greenspan, Alan, 366
gross domestic product (GDP), 198, 211
   during the 1960s, 308–309
   economic performance measured
     by, **232**
   equation of exchange and, 349
   expenditure approach to, 234–236
   exports and, 236
   government spending portion of, 236,
     289
   income approach to, 238–239
   international trade portion of, 388
   as measure of economic welfare, 246–249
   as measure of welfare, 249
   measuring, 233
   problems in calculating accurate,
     241–245
   R&D and, 219
   real compared to nominal, 243
   U.S. federal budget deficit and, 288
gross national saving (percent of GDP),
   215
group behavior, 44
Gwartney, James, 204, 205

H

Happel, Stephen, 140–141
happiness, 225–227
Hashimoto Ryutaro, 427
Hatch, Orrin, 312
health care, 169
heavy metal music/teen suicide, 51
Heller, Walter, 308
helmet law debate, 174–175
Henderson, Rickey, 225

human behavior
  change in price/cost and, 93
  economics to analyze, 4
  incentives and, 17–18
  individual and group, 44
  rational, 43
  scientific study of, 43
human capital, 82
Hurlock, Colin, 356

I

import quota, 403–404
imports
  domestic trade and, 399–400
  multiplier effect and, 293–294
incentives
  positive and negative, 17
  responding to, 17
income
  aggregate (1997), 239
  consumption and, 256
  equilibrium exchange rate and, 415–416
  national, 239
  personal, 239
income approach, 238–239
income of the consumer (Y), 102–103
income distribution
  GDP and, 247
  government and, 159–161
income elasticity of demand, 201
income security programs, 169
incomes policy, 379
increasing opportunity cost, 71
independent variable, 58
indeterminate variable, 128
indexing, 381
  See also inflation
indirect business taxes, 238
individual behavior, 44
individual-consumption-payment link, 163
individual demand curve, 96
individual demand schedule, 96
individual supply curve, 108–109
induced investment, 258
industralization, 213
inferior goods, 103
inflation
  anticipated, 195–196
  Consumer Price Index and, 193
  cost-push, 280, 281
  costs of, 195
  creditors and, 196
  demand-pull, 279–280
  described, **32,** 193
  government intervention regarding, 158
  impact of, 194
  indexing and, 381
  money supply growth (1985–1994) and, 553
  protection from, 196

rates in selected countries (1996), 197
  redistribution impact of, 194–195
  unemployment and, 370
  in the U.S. (1965–1980), 352
information
  costs/benefits of political, 163–164
  provided by market prices, 24
information costs
  government and, 153–155
  in the political arena, 162–163
intangible goods, 7
interest rates
  aggregate demand curve and, 262
  anticipated inflation and, 195–196
  autonomous investment and, 258–259
  exchange rates and, 416–417
  the Fed and, 361
  money/aggregate demand and, 358–361
international trade
  balance of payments and, 408–411
  common misperceptions on, 403–405
  comparative advantage and, 391–394
  exchange rates and, 412–414
  flexible exchange rates and, 421, 424
  growth in, 388–389
  specialization and, 392
  supply and demand in, 396–398
  tariffs and, 399–402
Internet
  banking on, 341–342
  credit cards used on, 321
inventories, 259
inventory investment, 236, **237**
inverse relationship, 60, 92
investment goods, 70
investments, 31
  aggregate demand curve and, 265
  defining, **235**
  economic growth and, 215
  fixed, 235
  government spending/net exports and, 258–260
  impact of tax rates on, 306
  inventory, 236, 237
investment tax credits, 305
the invisible hand, 121

J

Japanese economic forecast, 203
jawboning, 379
J.C. Penny's, 320
Jennings, Marianne, 140–141
Jobs, Steve, 276
Johnson, Lyndon B., 309
Jordan, Michael, 23

K

Kaslow, Amy, 366
Kennedy, John F., 308, 379
Keynes, John Maynard, 41, 210
Kohn, J. D., 337

kidney transplants (China), 131
Korean War, 168
Kuznets, Simon, 212

L

labor, 66, 217–218
labor force
  aggregate supply and, 276
  defining, **182**
  during 1997, 183
  higher marginal tax rates and, 306
labor intensive, 76
labor market
  imperfections and unemployment in, 189
  temporary workers and, 372
  unemployment statistics and, 183–184
land, 66–67
Larson, Gary, 47
law of demand, 92–95
  See also demand
law of diminishing returns, 222
laws
  debate over helmet, 174–175
  enforcement costs and, 34–35
  occupational licensing, 153–154
Lawson, Robert, 204, 205
law of supply, 108–109
law of unintended consequences, 28
legal tender, 319
leisure value, 246–247
Levinson, Arik, 403
liabilities (bank), 332
linear curves, 62–63
Lipset, S. M., 226
literary, 214
L.L. Bean, 324
long-distance calls, 130
long-run aggregate supply curve, 272, 273–274, 275, 276, 306
long-run Phillips curve, 373–375
Lucas, Bob, 383, 384
"Lucas critique," 383
Lucas, Robert, 376

M

M1, 322–323, 328
M2, 323, 328
macroeconomics
  described, **40**
  equilibrium of, 279
  flexible rates and, 423–424
  goals of, 180–181
  role of expectations in, 383–384
Malthusian prediction, 222
Malthus, Rev. Thomas Robert, 217, 222
marginal propensity to consume (MPC), 257, 292
market demand curve, 97–98
market disequilibrium, 133–134
market economy, 73–74

market equilibrium price
  defining, 120
  shortages/surpluses and, 120–121, 122
  See also prices
market failures, 25–26, 75
market power, 25
market profits. *See* profits
markets
  compared to nonrush-hour traffic, 122
  defining, **88**–89
  economic freedom and emerging, 205
  factor (or input), 230
  income distribution by, 159
  monopoly of, 157
  See also labor market
market structures of monopolies, 157
market supply curve, 109
market supply (hypothetical), 120
market system
  failures of, 25–26
  price system and, 24–25
Marx, Karl, 217, 226
Matthews, Merrill, Jr., 155
means of deferred payment, 325
measure of economic welfare (MEW),
  248–249
media, 356
Medicaid, 160
Medicare, 160, **169**
menu costs, 195
microeconomics, 40
Microsoft, 5, 68
minimum wage rate, 25, **137**–138
mixed economies, 74
mobility of resources, 215–216, 220
monetary policy
  implemented by the Fed, 351–356
  problems in implementing, 363–365
money
  created by banks, 330–334
  creation of, 336–337
  demand for, 327–328
  destruction of, 337
  equation of exchange and, 349–350, 352
  Fed manipulation of, 351–356
  functions of, 324–325
  interest rates/aggregate demand and,
    358–361
  as means of deferred payment, 325
  overview of, **318**–323
  as standard of value, 325
  as store of value, 325
  velocity of, 350
money capital, 67
money market, 358
money market equilibrium, 358–360
money market mutual funds, 322
money multiplier, 335–337
money price, 90–91
money supply
  described, 322–323
  multiple expansion of, 335–337

monopolies, 157
Montesquieu, Baron de, 217
Moore, Steve, 35
movie ticket prices, 91
Moynihan, Pat, 244
multiplier effect, 291–294
Muth, John, 383
Myers, David G., 226

N

National Football League (NFL), 140–141
national income accounting, 232
national income (NI), 239
national security argument for tariffs,
  402–403
NationsBank Corp., 337
natural disasters, 277
natural rate of unemployment, 191
natural resources, 4, 218, 276
near money, 322
needs, 93–95
negative externalities, 146–147
negative incentives, 17
negative relationship, 60–61, 92
Net.Bank, 342
net exports
  aggregate demand curve and, 266
  described, **260**
  government spending/investment and,
    258–260
The New Yorker, 5
New York Yankees, 166
Nixon, Richard, 366
Noll, Roger G., 166
nominal interest rate, 195
nondurable goods, 234
non-income expense items, 238
nonlinear curve, 63
nonmarket transactions, 246
nontransaction deposits, 321–322
Nordhaus, William, 56
normal good, 103
normative statements, 52–53
North American Free Trade Agreement
  (NAFTA), 405

O

occupational licensing laws, 153–154
O'Connor, Anne-Marie, 116
oeconomicus, 4
oil industry supply shifters, 113
open economy model, 260, 262–263
open market operations, 351–352
opportunity costs
  considering, 12–13
  increasing, 71
  specialization and, 21
  See also costs
optimism, 258
option demand, 166

Oscar Mayer "Wienermobile," 100
own-price, 100, 105

P

payroll taxes, 169
  See also taxation
Peltzman, Sam, 154
penny circulation, 319
Pepsi, 100
per capital gross domestic product, 245
permanent income hypothesis, 256–257
personal income (PI), 239
personal income taxes, 169
  See also taxation
PETA (People for the Ethical Treatment of
  Animals), 100
Phillips, A. H., 370
Phillips curve, 370–371, 373–375
Pirsig, Robert, 46, 47
political information, 163–164
politics
  economic performance and, 201, 202
  tariffs and, 401
pollution tax, 147
population, 221–222
positive analysis, 52–53
positive externalities, 146, 147–149
positive incentives, 17
positive relationship, 60, 108
"potential money creation," 336–337
price ceiling, 136
price of closely related goods, 110–111
price controls, 24–25, 136–138
price floor, 136, 137–138
price index, 241, 243
price level, 193
prices
  costs and, 95
  costs vs. **13**–14
  El Niño and coffee/cocoa, 126
  equilibrium, 120, 124–127
  expectations of higher, 104
  human behavior and, 93
  market equilibrium, 120–121, 122
  market system and, 24–26
  money and (1889–1993), 352
  money, 90–91
  open economy effect and, 262–263
  real GDP demand and, 261
  relationship between quantity and, 108
  relative, 91, 98
  supplier input, 110, 111
  See also wage and price controls
Principal Bank, 342
producer goods, 235
producer surplus, 398
production
  costs of long-distance call, 130
  economic growth and, 81–83
  efficiency in, 79–80
  four factors of, 66

selecting method of, 76–77
substitutes in, 111
unemployed resources and, 80
production possibilities curve
on economic choices, 83
overview of, **69**–71
on tourism/ecosystems, 85
profits
investment and rate of, 258
made by banks, 330
progression taxes, 170
property rights
defining, **27**
economic growth and, 220
eminent domain and, 145
free rider problem and, 151
government and, 144–145
public assistance programs, 160
public choice, 162–167
public choice theory, 162
public debt, 311
See also budget deficit
public goods, 150–151
purchasing power parity, 198–199
PYNTE
changes in demand vs. quantity and, 105
changing price/quantity and, 124–125
defining, 99
shifting supply/demand and, 110, 116, 128

Q

quality of life, 248–249
quantity
change in demanded, 99
changes in equilibrium price and, 124–127
changes in supplied, 110
defining equilibrium, 120
"queuetopia," 380

R

race factor, 184–185
"race to the bottom" argument, 403
rational behavior, 43
rational decision-making, 15–16, 43
rational expectations theory, 376–377
rational ignorance, 164
Reagan, Ronald, 366
real gross domestic product (RGDP) demand, 261
real interest rate, 195
Reasons for Living Inventory (RFL), 51
recession, 280–281
Reconstruction Finance Corporation (RFC), 339
regional comparative advantage, 395–396
regressive tax, 170
Reiss, Spencer, 219
relative deprivation principles, 225–227

relative price, **91**, 98
rent controls, 28, 136–137
research and development (R&D), 219, 306
reserve requirement ratio, 332
reserve requirements, 331, 353
resources
defining, **4**, 7
economic development and mobile, 215–216, 220
economic growth and natural, 218
efficient use of, 79–80
inflation and wasting, 32
market system and allocation of, 24
matching, 79
natural, 4
price controls and misallocation of, 380
three kinds of, 66
unemployed/underemployed, 79
Ricardian equivalence theorem, 300
Ricardo, David, 391
Ripkin, Cal, 49
rivalrous consumption, 150
Roosevelt, Franklin D., 309, 339
Royal Dutch Shell, 422–423
the rule of rational choice, 15
Russell, Bertrand, 225

S

Sack, Steve, 56
Sargent, Thomas, 376
savings rates, 215
scarcity
choices and, 10, 12
creation of new, 10–11
defining, **4**
economic growth and, 82
in the public sector, 162
as universal condition, 10
Scheel, Karen R., 51
Schumpeter, Joseph, 217
seasonal unemployment, 190
secondary reserves, 331
Security First Network Bank, 342
self-interest, 43
self-sufficiency, 216, 391
services
comparative advantage and, 21
current account and, 408
defining, 7–8, 234–235
distribution of, 78
expectations about future, 104–105
measuring value of, 232–233
number of buyers for, 104
production of, 76
taste changes and, 104
utility/disutility of, 8
shoe leather cost, 195
shortage
of Cabbage Patch Dolls, 133–134
described, **121**, 122
due to rent controls, 136–137

short-run aggregate supply curve, 272, 273, 275, 276–277, 278
short-run decrease in aggregate demand, 281
short-run Phillips curve, 374–375
Smith, Adam, 121
Social Security
government spending on, 169
income distribution through, 160
taxation used to pay for, 169
Solow, Robert, 308
special interest groups, 163, 164–**165**
specialization, 21–22, 394
See also trade
SPENT, 110, 114, 120, 124, 128
stagflation, 280
standards of living, 30
statistical discrepancy, 410
See also balance of payments
Stigler, George, 153
structural unemployment, 188–189
subsidies, 148, 160, 402
substitute good, 100–101
substitutes in production, 111
substitution effect, 93
supplier input prices, 110, 111
supply
changes in quantity supplied vs., 115
combinations of shifts in demand and, 130
equilibrium price/quantity and change in, 125, 127
factors affecting shifts in, 110–115
hypothetical market, 120
international trade and, 398–400
law of, 108–109
shifting both demand and, 128–132
shifts in oil industry, 113
Super Bowl tickets and, 140–141
See also aggregate supply (AS); demand
supply curve
individual, 108–109
market, 109
shifts in the, 110–115
See also demand curve
supply-side fiscal policy, 305–307
surplus, 120–121, 122

T

tamagotchi, 106
tariffs, 401–403, 415–416
taxation
as automatic stabilizer, 303
global comparison of, 172
impact on workers/investors of, 306
income distribution by, 159
indirect business, 238
multiplier effect and, 293–294
personal income, 169
pollution, 147, 378–379

proposed flat, 170, 172
as supply shifters, 112
supply side of economy and, 305
types of, 169–170
technology
economic growth and, 218–219
LRAS and SRAS curves and, 276
unemployment and, 190–191
TeleBank, 342
Teresa, Mother, 9
theory of rational expectations, 376–377
Thoreau, Henry David, 250
ticket scalping, 140–141
time lags
in fiscal policy implementation, 300
multiplier process and, 293–294
Time magazine, 56
Tobin, James, 308
tourism, 84–85
Tower Records, 93
trade
exports/imports and domestic, 396–398
specialization and, 22
See also economic growth; international
trade
transaction costs, 88
transaction deposits, 319
transfer payments, 160
transportation bill, 171
travelers checks, 319
Trump, Donald, 10
Tullock, Gordon, 162

U

underemployed laborers, 79
underemployment, 185
underground economy, 246
unemployed laborers, 79
unemployment
consequences of, 182

demographics of, 184–185
duration of, 185–186
government intervention regarding, 157
inflation and, 370
labor market and, 183–184
minimum wage and, 137–138
natural rate of, 191
reasons for, 185
tariffs and, 402
technology and, 190–191
types of, 188–192
unemployment compensation, 190
unemployment rates
defining, **182**
during 1960–1997, 183
United States
balance of trade (1960–1996), 410
collapse of banking system (1920–1933)
in, 339–340
declining real cost of living in, 250–252
deficit practice in, 288–289
economic growth of, 198
efforts to boost the yen, 426–427
equilibrium exchange rate and tariffs
of, 415–416
GDP by type of spending (1997), 234
inflation (1965–1980) in, 352
international trade partners of, 388–389
labor force (1997) in, 183
Phillips curve relationship (1960s) in,
371
recovery from OPEC prices by, 280
unemployment demographics in, 185
worse case of unemployment in,
182–183
See also government
urbanization, 212, 213
Uruguay Round (GATT), 405
utility, 8
utility-income relationship, 226

V

value of leisure, 246–247
variables
causally related, 49
dependent and independent, 58
direct or positive relationships of, 60
graphs of three, 61–62
graphs to show relationship between,
60
indeterminate, 128
inverse or negative relationships of,
60–61
using graphs and charts to show, 59–60
velocity of money, 350
Vietnam War, 168
Volcker, Paul, 366
voter apathy, 163

W

wage and price controls, 196, 379–381
wages
inflation and, 196
minimum, 25, 137–138
Walden (Thoreau), 250
Walt Disney Company, 389
Woods, Tiger, 78

Y

yen (Japan), 422, 426–427

Z

Zen and the Art of Motorcycle Maintenance
(Pirsig), 46–47
zero pollution rational, 16